A History of Jeddah

Known as the 'Gate to Mecca' or 'Bride of the Red Sea', Jeddah has been a gateway for pilgrims travelling to Mecca and Medina and a station for international trade routes between the Indian Ocean and the Mediterranean for centuries. Seen from the perspective of its diverse population, this first biography of Jeddah traces the city's urban history and cosmopolitanism from the late Ottoman period to its present-day claim to multiculturalism, within the conservative environment of the Arabian Peninsula. Contextualizing Jeddah with developments in the wider Muslim world, Ulrike Freitag investigates how different groups of migrants interacted in a changing urban space and how their economic activities influenced the political framework of the city. Richly illustrated, this study reveals how the transformation of Jeddah's urban space, population, and politics has been indicative of changes in the wider Arab and Red Sea region, re-evaluating its place in the Middle East at a time when both its cosmopolitan practices and old city are changing dramatically against a backdrop of modernization and Saudi nation-building.

ULRIKE FREITAG is Director of Leibniz-Zentrum Moderner Orient (ZMO) and Professor of Islamic Studies at the Free University of Berlin (Freie Universität, Berlin). She is author of *Indian Ocean Migrants and State Formation in Hadhramaut* (2002) and co-editor of several volumes on urban history, including *Urban Violence in the Middle East* (2015).

A History of Jeddah

The Gate to Mecca in the Nineteenth and Twentieth Centuries

ULRIKE FREITAG
Leibniz-Zentrum Moderner Orient

CAMBRIDGE
UNIVERSITY PRESS

CAMBRIDGE
UNIVERSITY PRESS

Shaftesbury Road, Cambridge CB2 8EA, United Kingdom

One Liberty Plaza, 20th Floor, New York, NY 10006, USA

477 Williamstown Road, Port Melbourne, VIC 3207, Australia

314–321, 3rd Floor, Plot 3, Splendor Forum, Jasola District Centre, New Delhi – 110025, India

103 Penang Road, #05–06/07, Visioncrest Commercial, Singapore 238467

Cambridge University Press is part of Cambridge University Press & Assessment, a department of the University of Cambridge.

We share the University's mission to contribute to society through the pursuit of education, learning and research at the highest international levels of excellence.

www.cambridge.org
Information on this title: www.cambridge.org/9781108746205

DOI: 10.1017/9781108778831

First published 2020
First paperback edition 2022

A catalogue record for this publication is available from the British Library

Library of Congress Cataloging-in-Publication data
Names: Freitag, Ulrike, author.
Title: A history of Jeddah : the gate to Mecca in the nineteenth and twentieth centuries / Ulrike Freitag.
Description: Cambridge, United Kingdom ; New York, NY : Cambridge University Press, 2020. | Includes bibliographical references and index.
Identifiers: LCCN 2019038866 (print) | LCCN 2019038867 (ebook) | ISBN 9781108478793 (hardback) | ISBN 9781108746205 (paperback) | ISBN 9781108778831 (epub)
Subjects: LCSH: Sociology, Urban–Saudi Arabia–Jiddah. | Local government–Saudi Arabia–Jiddah. | Jiddah (Saudi Arabia)–History–19th century. | Jiddah (Saudi Arabia)–History–20th century. | Jiddah (Saudi Arabia)–Social conditions–19th century. | Jiddah (Saudi Arabia)–Social conditions–20th century. | Jiddah (Saudi Arabia)–Economic conditions–19th century. | Jiddah (Saudi Arabia)–Economic conditions–20th century. | Jiddah (Saudi Arabia)–Emigration and immigration.
Classification: LCC DS248.J5 F74 2020 (print) | LCC DS248.J5 (ebook) | DDC 953.8–dc23
LC record available at https://lccn.loc.gov/2019038866
LC ebook record available at https://lccn.loc.gov/2019038867

ISBN 978-1-108-47879-3 Hardback
ISBN 978-1-108-74620-5 Paperback

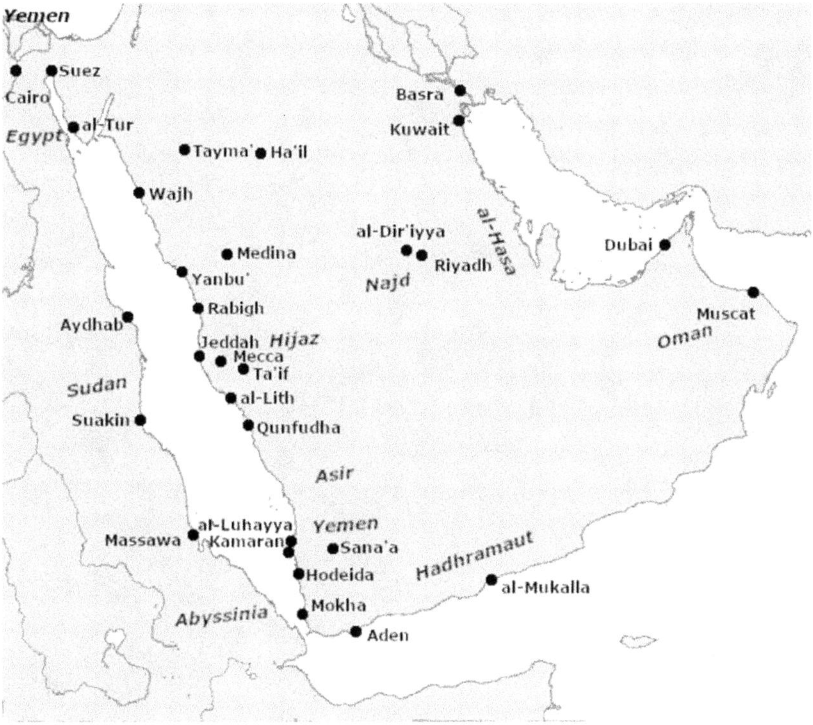

Map 1 Red Sea and surrounding areas.

Contents

List of Figures	*page* viii
List of Maps	x
List of Tables	xi
Acknowledgements	xii
Note on Transliteration and Terminology	xvi
1 Introduction: Why Jeddah	1
2 Between Sea and Land: Jeddah through the Ages	40
3 The Changing Faces of Jeddah	84
4 The Changing Urban Space of Jeddah	113
5 Solidarity and Competition: The Socio-Cultural Foundations of Life in Jeddah	159
6 The Economic Lifelines of Jeddah: Trade and Pilgrimage	218
7 Governing and Regulating Diversity: Urban Government in Jeddah	271
8 The Disappearance and Return of Old Jeddah: On the Temporality of Translocal Relations	328
Bibliography	345
Index	379

Figures

3.1	Ibn Saʿūd and Shaykh ʿAbdallāh ʿAlī Riḍā. Leiden University Libraries, Or. 12.288 J: 4, date 1925.	*page* 95
3.2	Hasan Efendi, Scribe of the Court. Leiden University Libraries, Or. 26.368: 19.	103
4.1	Engraving of Jeddah by G.W. Baurenfeind (1774). Carsten Niebuhr, Reisebeschreibung nach Arabien und anderen umliegenden Ländern, table LIII.	115
4.2	The port in 1895. Encl. in CADN, Const. Amb. Série D 6, Descoutures to Amb. Const. 30.4.1895.	125
4.3	Photograph of saltwater condenser 1926. Leiden University Libraries, Or. 12.288 B: 31.	130
4.4	Ribāṭ al-Khunjī al-Kabīr. Photographed by François Cristofoli, www.unesco.org/new/fileadmin/MULTIMEDIA/HQ/ERI/images/whc2014_saudi_arabia07.jpg.	139
4.5	Houses with wooden *rawashīn* and a *mirkāz*. Leiden University Libraries, Or. 12.288 J: 28, date unknown.	142
4.6	Storage halls in Bin Ḥimd house. Photograph by the author.	143
4.7	Outside of Bāb Makka. Photograph Wilfred Thesiger (Copyright Pitt Rivers Museum, Univ. of Oxford, 2004 130 31792 1-0).	147
4.8	Photograph of Nakutu. Van Voorthuysen 1926. Leiden University Libraries, Or. 12 288 B: 36.	149
4.9	Arial photograph of Jeddah and its surroundings in 1948.	150
4.10	Photograph of the Christian cemetery in Jeddah, March 1926. Van Voorthuysen. Leiden University Libraries Or. 12.288 B: 38.	157

5.1 Coffeeshop besides the Dutch consulate, 1926. Photographer Van Voorthuysen, Leiden University Libraries, Or. 12 288 B: 26. 174
5.2 Children celebrating *ʿĪd*. Leiden University Libraries, Or. 12.288 M: 36. 193
5.3 Arrival of the *maḥmal*. Leiden University Libraries, Or. 12.288 J: 10. 194
5.4 al-Falāh school. Photograph by the author, 2007. 206
6.1 Office in the Bin Ḥimd house. Photograph by the author, 2017. 227
6.2 Caravan to Mecca. Royal Geographical Society 091419. 228

Maps

4.1 Ground plan of Jeddah, drawn by Carsten Niebuhr (1774). Reisebeschreibung nach Arabien und andern umliegenden Ländern, table LV. *page* 115

4.2 Ottoman map of 1851. Drawn by Melody Mosaver on the basis of BOA PLK p. 45. 118

4.3 Map of Jeddah in 1880–1. Drawn by Melody Mosaver on the basis of an Ottoman map. 122

4.4 Map of the surroundings of Jeddah 1880–1. Drawn by Melody Mosaver on the basis of the Ottoman map of 1880–1. 145

5.1 Jeddah within the walls. Drawn by Dr. Muḥammad Bā Qādir. 172

Tables

Acknowledgements

The idea of writing a history of Jeddah was first suggested, jokingly, during my first visit to the city in 2000 with my husband and baby daughter, by Sultana al-Qu'aiṭi when introducing me to Sāmī Nawār, a long-time enthusiast and former mayor of Old Jeddah. At the time, I pursued a different research topic and the visit to Jeddah served to collect a final round of sources. I was surprised how many people were willing to help a foreign researcher and overwhelmed by the hospitality we experienced. I also discovered that Jeddah, which had seemed so inaccessible when the question of how to obtain a visa had haunted me, was a very lively and welcoming city. Being the end of the pilgrimage season, the bazaars and airport teemed with visitors from all parts of the Muslim world. This contradicted the stereotypical image of a closed Saudi society, and my curiosity as to how an urban society deals with such an annual influx, as well as a large number of resident foreigners, was aroused. When, in 2005, Yaḥyā al-Junayd of the King Faysal Centre for Research and Islamic Studies in Riyadh suggested that the Centre supported foreign researchers conducting research in the Kingdom of Saudi Arabia, I decided to try my luck and embark on this project.

A large number of persons and institutions have supported this project over the years. The King Faysal Centre in Riyadh, Effat and the King ʿAbd al-ʿAzīz Universities in Jeddah, as well as the German Consulate in Jeddah and ʿAbd al-Maqṣūd Khūja, invited me for visits and helped me to meet a large number of people knowledgeable about the city, from academics and business people to students and activists. I am particularly grateful to Yaḥyā al-Junayd, Saud al-Serhan and their staff, to Ḥaifāʾ Jamal al-Layl and Lisa Zuppé of Effat University for enabling me to teach in Jeddah for a few weeks, to German Consul-Generals Michael Zickerick and Annette Klein, as well as Hanāʾ al-Nuʿaym from King ʿAbd al-ʿAzīz University. I further thank Fahd al-Semari of the King ʿAbd al-ʿAzīz Foundation for Research and

Archives for access to the archives of the Foundation, as well as Jouharah Abalkhail for access to the archives of the Institute for Public Administration in Riyadh. ʿUsāma Shubukshī, long-standing Saudi ambassador to Germany, kindly facilitated many visa applications.

In Jeddah, more individuals were prepared to share their private collections and memories than I can possibly mention here. Yūsuf and Khālid ʿAlī Riḍā opened their archive, as well as that of the Falāḥ School, and kindly introduced me to their wider families. Māzin al-Saqqāf shared his wide knowledge of local endowments and property law, while Muḥammad Bin Ḥimd allowed me to consult his family archive. The late Talāl Bakkur discussed many of his images of old Jeddah with me, Muḥammad Ṭrābulsī, ʿAbdallāh Manāʿ, and the late Muḥammad Raqqām patiently explained their memories of old Jeddah. ʿAdnān al-Yāfī, ʿAbdallāh, ʿAbd al-Raḥmān, and Fāṭima Naṣīf helped me understand family histories and specific traditions, while colleagues from the university pointed me to local scholarship on Jeddah's history. ʿUmda Malak Bā ʿIsā and his colleague ʿAbd al-Ṣamad explained their office and its history. Hishām Murtaḍā organised a workshop on old Jeddah in 2010 providing the opportunity to meet with the owners of old houses and better understand local dynamics and relations between house owners, the old city, and its buildings.

My generous hosts and friends, Sultana and Sultan al-Qu'ayti, Mona Ba Ghour, Abu Khaled, and their family, as well as Dahlia al-Rahaimy, Andreas Haberbeck, and family, very generously hosted me during my fifteen visits to Jeddah over a period of more than ten years. They made me feel at home and part of their families, let me share their daily lives, introduced me to new people and provided a sounding board for new impressions, as well as the occasional frustration. Abū Bakr Bā Qādir and his family also count among the earliest friends I was able to make in Jeddah. My heartfelt thanks also extend to the many others who opened their doors for formal interviews, joint activities or visits. Our interactions certainly informed my understanding of *Jeddah ghayr* beyond strict historical research. I also thank Saad Sowayan, ʿAwaḍ al-Bādī, ʿAbd al-Raḥmān al-Shuqayr, and Hatoon al-Fasi in Riyadh for enhancing my understanding of wider Saudi society and introducing me to their city.

Nazan Maksudyan helped me find libraries and deal with archives during a brief research visit to Istanbul. She, as well as Leyla and Rana von Mende, Nora Lafi, Nicola Verderame, and Aysel Yıldız helped me find, copy, transcribe, and translate documents from the Ottoman Prime Minister's Archives. To them, as well as to the archivists and librarians in Riyadh, London, Nantes, Leiden, and Oxford, I extend my very warm thanks for their help in locating and providing material. Without a series of exceptional student assistants, the bibliography would look much poorer, not to speak of their invaluable assistance in many other fields. Leyla von Mende, Sarah Jurkiewicz, Larissa Schmid, and Nushin Atmaca became academic colleagues, while Philipp Dehne, Jannis Hagmann, Julia Clauß, and Christian Kübler pursued other careers. Constanze Fertig and Noel van den Heuvel were of particular help in the final phase of the project. I learnt more than I can individually acknowledge from my colleagues in the research group 'Cities as Laboratories of Change' at Leibniz-Zentrum Moderner Orient (ZMO), and I am grateful to them as well as other ZMO colleagues for their very helpful comments on an early version of the outline and the introduction.

Research for this book was financed in the context of Leibniz-Zentrum Moderner Orient by different bodies. The German Research Foundation (DFG), the German Ministry for Education and Research, and funding by the State of Berlin as well as a joint research promotion by the German Bund-Länder Commission have enabled me to carry out the research for this book by funding most of the research trips to Saudi Arabia, London and Istanbul. I gladly acknowledge this support.

This book could not have been written without a series of 'time-outs' from daily academic life. Research and writing time and space were provided by the Oxford Centre for Islamic Studies in 2006, by LUCIS in Leiden in 2015, and by the International Research Centre re:work in Berlin during the crucial writing time of 2017–8. Farhan Nizami, Léon Buskens, and Andreas Eckert are due special thanks for offering me these very precious spaces. I would also like to thank my generous Leiden host, Jan-Just Witkam, as well as Arnoud Vrolijk and Nico Kaptein in Leiden. At re:work, the fellow group was wonderfully supportive when discussing a draft section of the book, and I owe special thanks to On Barak and Benedetta Rossi for suggesting additional sources and commenting on sections of the text. Fe Hentschke's support was of particular importance. Without Sonja Hegasy's willingness to replace me for ten months, and her gracious way of protecting this precious time, this book would forever have remained a phantom. Abū Bakr Bā Qādir, Gerhard Dannemann, Nelida Fuccaro, Claudia Ghrawi, Birgit Meyer, Leyla von Mende, Philippe Pétriat, and Sultana al-Qu'aiṭi kindly read and commented upon sections of the text. Special thanks are also due to the two reviewers and their very helpful suggestions.

On a personal note, I would like to thank my family for enduring my long-lasting obsession with a topic quite far from their own interest, as well as tolerating long absences in the Middle East and at the computer. My parents patiently listened to accounts of the work, while Gerhard, Julia, and Philipp even visited Jeddah and Gerhard braved the traffic of Jeddah and took us all to Madāʿin Ṣāliḥ. Julia, I promised I would try to finish this by the time you finished school and, with your help in language editing, I almost managed to do so. I dedicate this book to my family, and to the people of Jeddah.

Note on Transliteration and Terminology

The transliteration for Arabic follows that of the *International Journal of Middle East Studies*, as does the transliteration of Ottoman titles in the bibliography. Ottoman terms and names in the text are rendered according to modern Turkish spelling. A certain arbitrariness as to terms of Arab origin but Ottoman administrative use cannot be avoided. Thus, terms which in this book occur predominantly in the local context, such as *muḥtasib*, or the various councils (*meclis, majlis*) are rendered in the transliteration from Arabic even though they denote an Ottoman administrative function to make the book more accessible for readers familiar with the local context. In some cases, both the Ottoman and Arabic term are indicated upon first use, notably if they differ considerably (*sancak* and *liwāʾ*).

Well-known names, such as Jeddah, Mecca, or Cairo, are not transliterated, whereas smaller towns like Yanbuʿ are. Arabic plurals are only used when the word occurs frequently (*wakīl, wukalāʾ*), otherwise, an unitalicised 's' is added to the italicised term (*nisba*s).

1 *Introduction: Why Jeddah*

Jeddah,
Enchantment of Babel,
Full of people,
All the people
Oh, Gate of Mecca.
Assuredly, Jeddah first
. . . and Jeddah last.[1]
(Ṭalāl Ḥamzah)

These words stem from a poem entitled 'Jeddah ghayr', 'Jeddah is different'. For the poet, bustling Jeddah with its more than four million inhabitants is superior to the famous Arab metropoles of Cairo, Beirut, and Casablanca. Although he hails from Tobuk in the Northwest of Saudi Arabia and has not lived in Jeddah, many of Jeddah's inhabitants, as well as many other Saudis, would agree with his characterization. They would, however, associate the city's 'difference' with quite dissimilar meanings. These range from the assertion of a relaxed lifestyle to the annual Jeddah summer festival, until recently called 'Jeddah ghair', marketed by the Saudi Tourism Agency[2], and might include a scathing indictment of the alleged lack of proper urban planning compared to other Saudi cities.[3]

[1] I would like to thank Abū Bakr Bā Qādir for his comments and discussions of this poem. I have benefitted greatly from his insights even if we continue to differ on a number of points. Poem by Ṭalāl Ḥamzah, 'Jidda Ghayr', www.alsh3r.com/poems/view/10246 (accessed October 16, 2019), for a short biography of the poet, see 'al-Adīb al-Shāʿir al-Sharīf Ṭalāl Bin Ḥamza Āl Badawī', *alsh3r*.com (accessed October 21, 2019).

[2] Fouzia Khan (June 7, 2014). 'Spectactular start to Jeddah Ghair', *Arab News*, www.arabnews.com/node/583047.

[3] Mushārī b. ʿAbdallāh al-Naʿīm (June, 2013). 'Lēh Jidda Ghayr?'. Article on *al-Riyādh*. www.alriyadh.com/847803.

It was a diffuse sense of an amazing diversity amongst the people of Jeddah, my own feeling of 'Jeddah ghayr', that struck me when first visiting the city in the year 2000. With its more than four million inhabitants (2017), Jeddah sprawls along the shores of the Red Sea, which also features later in the poem quoted above. It is situated in a region known as the Hijaz, which includes the holy cities of Mecca and Medina. My experience of Jeddah during this first visit differed significantly from the image of a country then known for fabulous wealth and inaccessibility to researchers. I was surprised and overwhelmed by the hospitality and support which I encountered for the research project I was pursuing at the time. This encouraged me to embark on a project about the city's history a few years later. With time I also came to recognise the differences between Jeddah and other regions, such as the capital of the Kingdom of Saudi Arabia, Riyadh, situated in the central Arabian Najd region, which has become politically and culturally dominant in many ways, some of which will be explored in this introduction. While the observation that there exists a difference between cities due to their specific histories and local identities is trivial, the sense of 'Jeddah ghayr', of a particular distinctiveness of this city, is a well-known trope in Saudi Arabia.

While the *Jiddawi* 'difference' might nowadays be mostly associated with the magnificent corniche which brims with life in the evenings, with a multitude of shopping malls, restaurants, and private beach resorts, all of which contrast with the image of most Saudi cities as rather austere, the distinctiveness is also evident in what is left of the formerly walled old city of Jeddah. Many old centres in Saudi Arabia have given way to modern structures. In Jeddah, the old town, or rather the old market streets (*sūq*) still serve as the city's centre in wholesale cloth trade. The beautiful coral stone buildings with their intricately carved wooden loggias give a sense of the former wealth of their owners. In the old city, as well as in the public spaces such as the corniche or malls, one sees people of many different origins, particularly, but not exclusively, during the season of the pilgrimage to nearby Mecca, the hajj.

In spite of the many changes to 'The Bride of the Red Sea', as some inhabitants proudly call their city, the poem composed in the twenty-first century would have resounded with the Swiss traveller John Lewis Burckhardt, who visited Jeddah in 1814. He noted with some astonishment that the inhabitants of Jeddah consisted mostly of 'foreigners or their descendants', with the exception of a few learned descendants of the prophet Muhammad.[4] While local Arabs had perished or emigrated, Burckhardt lists Hadhramis and Yemenis, Indians, Malays, Egyptians, Syrians, North Africans, as well as people from the European and Anatolian provinces of the Ottoman Empire, in addition to Abyssinian slaves. With the exception of the Indians, Burckhardt observes that these people 'are all mixed in one general mass, and live and dress in the same Arab manner'.[5] Similarly, a glance at the names of the old families of Jeddah, namely those who lived inside the city wall prior to its demolition in 1947, reveals that this plurality is no recent phenomenon. The names al-Baghdādī, al-Isfahānī, al-Bukhārī, al-Takrūnī, and al-Fattanī point to their forebearers' origins in present-day Iraq, Iran, Uzbekistan, the West African Sahel zone, and Pattani in Southern Thailand, respectively, while names like Bā Khashwayn point to the origin of that family in the Hadhramaut region of present-day Yemen.[6] Burckhardt declared this extraordinary diversity to be the result of the pilgrimage when, in the month of *muḥarram*, large crowds converged on Mecca, often via Jeddah. He also points out that most Jiddawis actually earned their living from trade. In the nineteenth century, labour migrants, merchants, and soldiers from Egypt and the Ottoman Empire at large swelled and diversified the ranks of strangers further. Indeed, Jeddah was not only a main node of pilgrim's journeys but, as will be shown in Chapter 2, a major trade entrepôt in the exchange between the Indian Ocean and the Mediterranean at various times.

How, I wondered, did people from these very different regions not only pass through the city when performing the pilgrimage but also become so much a part of its very fabric that they are now all recognised locally as its 'old families'? How and where did they find a place to stay and work? To what extent did immigrants form ethnic clusters in the city – something which is a frequent occurrence in present-day

4 John Burckhardt, *Travels in Arabia: Comprehending an Account of Those Territories in Hedjaz Which the Mohammedans Regard as Sacred*, vol. 1 (London: Colburn, 1829), p. 26. In the Hijaz, a sharif (*sharīf*) is understood to be the son of Ḥasan, whereas a *sayyid* is al-Ḥusayn's son.

5 Burckhardt, pp. 26–9, quote p. 27. The term 'Bride of the Red Sea' is also used for the Yemeni port of Hodeida, e.g. *nashwannews.com* (September 27, 2017). ' al-Ḥudayda. al-Ḥarb Taghtālu ʿArūs al-Baḥr al-Aḥmar'. https://nashwannews.com/83557.

6 Muḥammad Ṭrābulsī, *Jidda: Ḥikāyat madīna*, 2nd rev. edn. (1st edn. 2006) (Riyadh: Distributed by Kunūz al-Maʿrifa , 1429/2008), pp. 83–94.

Saudi Arabia due to the ways in which immigrants' lives are regulated? How did subsequent political regimes, Ottoman (1840–1916), Sharifian (1916–25), and Saudi (since 1925) attempt to govern and regulate the urban society and what did it take to become a 'subject' of these states? The Arabic root *gh-y-r* also denotes change, and one of the topics discussed throughout the book, though especially in Chapter 2, is in which ways Jeddah and its population changed throughout the period under investigation.

The aim of this study is hence to investigate the urban history of Jeddah in order to understand how people managed to live in a very diverse setting. 'Living with difference' is one of the ways in which the concept of conviviality has been defined, which makes this a central concept when trying to consider the particular history of Jeddah in a larger setting.[7] To do so, one needs to consider two related but analytically separate phenomena. The first is that this city of 10,000–20,000 permanent residents (in the nineteenth century) accommodated an annual influx of pilgrims which either doubled the number of inhabitants or multiplied them to up to ten times the normal number.[8] Until the 1870s and 1880s, when large numbers of pilgrims from the Indian Ocean rim travelled on steamers, shipping depended on the monsoon and often forced pilgrims to spend long periods in Jeddah, Mecca, or Medina either in order to perform the pilgrimage at the right time of the year, or before being able to return. Thus, it became difficult at times to distinguish pilgrims from the second group of people, those heading to Jeddah in search of work and commerce. In fact, it might be better to consider both groups as only partially distinct because some pilgrims, working while waiting for their return passage, eventually decided to settle, while not all of those who came in search of employment managed to establish themselves. Furthermore, some (but by no means all) trade was conducted during the pilgrimage, using the caravans and ships to transport pilgrims as well as goods. The pilgrimage also animated trade due to the large number of people in need of food and water, as well as other goods.

7 Magdalena Nowicka and Steven Vertovec, 'Comparing Convivialities: Dreams and Realities of Living-with-Difference', *European Journal of Cultural Studies*, 17 (2014), pp. 341–56.

8 For an overview, starting in 1858, see William Ochsenwald, *Religion, Society, and the State in Arabia: The Hijaz under Ottoman Control, 1840–1908* (Columbus: Ohio State University Press, 1984), p. 61.

This study deals with the past two centuries and zooms in on the 100 years between 1840 and 1947. Both dates refer to actual events and mark symbolic ruptures in the history of the city. In 1840, Mehmed Ali Pasha, the autonomous governor-general of Ottoman Egypt, had to return the administration of Jeddah to the central Ottoman authorities in Istanbul. This was, initially, a 'soft' break given that Egypt had always remained within the Ottoman fold, and that the Emir of Mecca, who had been appointed by Mehmed Ali in 1827 (although detained in Cairo from 1836–40), remained in power until 1851. However, Ottoman reforms, starting in 1838, began to impact Jeddah in different ways in the decades thereafter. Furthermore, 1840 almost coincides with the onset of steamshipping in the Red Sea, something which, together with other technological and geopolitical advances, was to change the economics of Jeddah considerably in the medium term (see Chapter 2).

The destruction of the city wall in 1947 allowed the streets to open to car traffic and for easy communication with the new quarters that had started development outside of the wall. Due to the conditions of World War II, which all but halted the early oil exports, Saudi Arabia's oil economy took off only in the early 1950s and allowed the country to enjoy an economic boom. In this context, the old urban population gradually moved to the newly established quarters, leaving the old city to new immigrants who often came from the very rural areas against which the wall had sheltered the old families only decades earlier. With time, this came to be understood locally as a fundamentally different phenomenon from the migratory trends which characterised the period under discussion, possibly due to both the different origin of the migrants and the scale of new settlement in the urban area.[9] It should be added that from the 1950s onwards, air traffic started to change the logistics of the pilgrimage, reducing the period of stay in Jeddah and, since the opening of the new airport in 1981, all but eliminating it through direct transfer from the airport to Mecca.[10]

The historical developments in Jeddah and the Red Sea, as well as themes from the urban history pertinent to the questions outlined above, form the bulk of this book. Before delving into the discussion

[9] This is stressed in most local histories, e.g. Muḥammad al-Nimr, *Ḥārat al-Baḥr: Mawṭin al-ābāʿ wa-l-ajdād* (Jeddah: Dār Manṣūr al-Zāmil, 1438/2016–17), p. 249.

[10] David Long, *The Hajj Today: A Survey of the Contemporary Pilgrimage to Makkah* (Albany: State University of New York Press, 1979), p. 48.

of these issues, however, it is worthwhile to briefly consider how the engagement with foreign visitors and residents was framed locally and how the local perspective can be brought into conversation with concepts commonly used to discuss such phenomena, namely cosmopolitanism and conviviality.

Conceptualising Diversity in Jeddah: Local Perspectives

For Jiddawis, the different origins of people settled in the city are a part of everyday life instead of a phenomenon which evokes the questions and reflections of the outsider. Because the annual pilgrimage was, and still is, a central element of life in Jeddah, albeit one which is not permanently present, there are local concepts which reflect practices of the pilgrimage and, at the same time, conceptualise the accommodation of strangers. These exist both locally and in conversations with the curious outsider, and recur in literature, proverbs, and oral history.

Hospitality for 'God's Guests' and Its Implications

From a local perspective, what is most commonly discussed and conceptualised both in historiography and in oral accounts is the reception of pilgrims. They are considered *ḍuyūf bayt Allāh al-ḥarām*, 'guests of God's sacred house'. To perform pilgrimage to the 'House of God', the Kaʿba in Mecca, at least once in one's life is a core duty for every Muslim who is physically and economically able to do so. The concept of 'God's guests' refers to the notion of a more or less global Muslim community (*umma*), united in faith and worship to the one God. The geographical location of Jeddah as the main port of Mecca put it upon the Jiddawis (as well as the Meccans) to fulfil the duty of hospitality, which obtained an almost sacred character and a moral obligation due to the religious context.

In the past as today, this service for 'God's guests' formed the basis of an entire infrastructure. While it was crucial to the Islamic legitimation of the state that security was guaranteed and sufficient supplies of foodstuffs reached the Hijaz in time, it was locals who provided housing and transport, in addition to selling food and drink to the pilgrims. This regularly entailed renting private accommodation to complete strangers. Nowadays, the organisation of the pilgrimage is a matter of pride and international recognition for the Saudi state. This is expressed perhaps most blatantly in the Saudi kings assuming the title 'Custodian of the Two Holy Places' in 1986.[11] Even if the Ottoman sultan, as well as the short-lived Sharifian government and the first Saudi king ʿAbd al-ʿAzīz Āl Saʿūd considered securing the pilgrimage as central to their local and international legitimacy, local actors and arrangements were far more central to the hajj in the pre-oil period than they have been since.

Hospitality is, of course, an important and almost proverbial component of Arab and Muslim culture. The early German writer Christian Hirschfeld published his treatise on hospitality in 1777 and assumes hospitality to be an almost universal virtue. However, he recognises Middle Eastern (in his case: Arab, Turkish, and Persian) culture as especially hospitable and devotes a very long passage to it.[12] Obviously, both concept and practice have undergone significant changes in meaning and application in recent years.[13] The traditional meaning of Arab hospitality encompasses aspects of 'security, protection, and respect', derived from the Bedouin culture of mutual dependence on such hospitality in the absence of government.[14] In the Arabian Peninsula, a number of sacred spaces, locally called *ḥaram, ḥawṭa*, or *hijra*, allowed for safe meetings of different tribespeople. Even before Islam, Mecca is said to have been such a space.[15] Outside

[11] The rhetoric of serving the 'guests of God' (nowadays frequently called *ḍuyūf al-raḥmān*), pervades Saudi official rhetoric, e.g. recent articles on various sections of Saudi society assisting pilgrims, *Tawāsul.info* (September 26, 2019). '15 Alf Ṭālib bi-Makka Yanfudhūn 7 Mashārīʿ Taṭawwuʿiyya li-Khidmat Ḍuyūf al-Raḥmān'. https://twasul.info/264129; and *al-Riyāḍ.com* (September 9, 2017). 'Khayr Ajnād al-Arḍ.. Khuddām Ḍuyūf Allāh'. www.alriyadh.com/1620985.

[12] Christian Hirschfeld, *Von der Gastfreundschaft: Eine Apologie für die Menschheit* (Leipzig: Weidmanns Erben und Reich, 1777), pp. 100–31. I owe this reference to Jürgen Osterhammel.

[13] Andrew Shryock, 'The New Jordanian Hospitality: House, Host, and Guest in the Culture of Public Display', *Comparative Studies in Society and History*, 46 (2004), pp. 35–62; Rana Sobh, Russel Belk and Jonathan Wilson, 'Islamic Arab Hospitality and Multiculturalism', *Marketing Theory*, 13 (2013), pp. 443–63; and Annegret Nippa, Peter Herbstreuth, and Hermann Burchardt, *Unterwegs am Golf: Von Basra nach Maskat, Photographien von Hermann Burchardt* (Berlin: Schiler, 2006).

[14] Shryock, *The New Jordanian Hospitality*, p. 36.

[15] Robert Serjeant, 'Ḥaram and Ḥawṭah, the Sacred Enclave in Arabia' in R. B. Serjeant (ed.), *Arabian History and Civilisation* (Aldershot, Burlington USA, Singapore, and Sydney: Ashgate Variorum Reprints, 1981); Archive Editions

of these sacred spaces, however, the traveller was at the mercy of his hosts, who housed and fed him (or, much more rarely, her). This made the stranger temporarily part of the 'house' of his host, removing the aspect of strangeness, placing him under the host's care and creating mutual bonds of obligation. This notion of hospitality hence differs somewhat from the one put forward, for example, by Kant, who promoted a basic right for strangers to sojourn without consideration for such rules.[16] After the onset of Islam, this traditional value was further enhanced by traditions of the Prophet Muhammad, who enjoined his followers to honour their guests in ways quite similar to the Jewish and Christian tradition.[17]

The combination of 'normal' hospitality and the special religious imperative resulting from the performance of a sacred duty seems to have created a bond different from that which normally developed between a host and an accidental guest. The temporary acceptance of strangers into local houses, described as 'voluntaristic cosmopolitanism' by Pollock, is a phenomenon which can also be observed in other religious contexts.[18] In terms of applied ethics, it might boil down to a wider humanistic attitude, even if rooted in scriptural sources, which Siddiqui aptly sums up as 'Hospitality in all its forms is what keeps the sacred alive in the ordinary.'[19] This is based on the belief that creation is a consequence of God's hospitable nature which requires humankind 'to act in ways that reflect the goodness of the creator'.[20] Given that the sojourn in Jeddah was already conducted in the garb of pilgrimage, the *iḥrām*, and that many of the hosts would also join the pilgrims in their journey to Mecca and the proper rites of the pilgrimage, this temporary community might almost be likened to the *communitas* of pilgrims

(Firm), India. Army General Staff Branch, Arab Bureau (Cairo, Egypt), and Great Britain Admiralty War Staff and Intelligence Division, *A Collection of First World War Military Handbooks of Arabia, 1913–1917* (Farnham Common, Buckinghamshire UK: Archive Editions, 1988), pp. 41–58; and T. Munt, *The Holy City of Medina: Sacred Space in Early Islamic Arabia*, Cambridge Studies in Islamic Civilization (New York: Cambridge University Press, 2014), p. 62.

16 Immanuel Kant, *Zum ewigen Frieden: Ein philosophischer Entwurf* (Königsberg: Friedrich Nicolovius, 1795), section 2.3.

17 Mona Siddiqui, *Hospitality and Islam: Welcoming in God's Name* (New Haven, CT and London: Yale University Press, 2015), pp. 20–72.

18 Sheldon Pollock, 'Cosmopolitan and Vernacular in History', *Public Culture*, 12 (2000), pp. 591–625, here p. 596.

19 Siddiqui, *Hospitality and Islam*, p. 219.

20 Ibid., p. 233.

discussed by Turner.[21] This does not preclude that the local population of Jeddah (as well as that of Mecca and Medina) derived considerable moral capital from their hospitable acts, which were seen as a special religious service.[22]

It might be this sense of proximity between the hosts and the visitors to God's house which conceptually allowed for an important variation of another central Arabian institution, namely marriage. Even though exogamous marriages were actually quite common in Central Arabian towns, among both people without as well as those with tribal lineages, the marriage with people from outside the tribal system remained suspicious and almost impossible, notably for women.[23] However, many histories of (male) migrants who settled in Jeddah mention marriage with local women.[24] Thus, Burckhardt's 'mixed in one general mass' does, indeed, not just describe the adoption of Arab language and dress, but also this phenomenon. A Jiddawi colleague expressed it differently: 'We became one with them, they are one of us'. 'They' refers here to all those who settled in Jeddah, irrespective of the distinction between pilgrims and other settled migrants who were quietly included.

The Hajj as a Necessity: Religious Tourism

While hospitality certainly comes first where the pilgrimage is concerned, both in Jeddah and the holy cities, as well as in Saudi Arabia at

[21] Victor Turner, 'The Center out There: Pilgrim's Goal', *History of Religions*, 12 (1973), pp. 191–230. I am using Turner's notion without wanting to enter his argument about the contrast between the 'counterstructure' of communitas versus (political) structure. On this, see Robert Bianchi, *Guests of God: Pilgrimage and Politics in the Islamic World* (Oxford: Oxford University Press, 2004), pp. 37–8.

[22] Marcel Mauss, *Die Gabe: Form und Funktion des Austauschs in archaischen Gesellschaften*, Suhrkamp-Taschenbuch Wissenschaft, 1st edn. (Frankfurt am Main: Suhrkamp, 1968), vol. 743, pp. 157–62; cf. Anne Meneley, *Tournaments of Value: Sociability and Hierarchy in a Yemeni Town*, Anthropological Horizons (Toronto and London: University of Toronto Press, 1996), vol. 9.

[23] Nadav Samin, 'Our Ancestors, Our Heroes: Saudi Tribal Campaigns to Suppress Historical Docudramas', *British Journal of Middle Eastern Studies*, 41 (2014), pp. 266–86; Nadav Samin, *Of Sand or Soil*, Princeton Studies in Muslim Politics (Princeton: Princeton University Press, 2015), pp. 117–20.

[24] For an example of a trader of Egyptian origin resident in Massawa (and for some time in Jeddah), see Jonathan Miran and Aharon Layish, 'The Testamentary *Waqf* as an Instrument of Elite Consolidation in Early Twentieth-Century Massawa (Eritrea)', *Islamic Law and Society*, 25 (2018), pp. 78–120, here p. 93.

large, the pilgrimage was also a business. This idea is also present in numerous proverbs, as well as in current Saudi projections of future economic development, such as the Vision 2030, which was developed in 2016. Historically, the Hijaz was an essentially poor area and hence it was important to make good use of the *mawsim*, the period of the hajj, in order to earn sufficient income to last for the remainder of the year. The saying *al-ḥajj ḥāja*, the hajj is a (pressing) need, reflects this double aspect of the hajj as a spiritual desire and a business.[25] Other proverbs are even more specific, for example 'they brought them in as believers, and made them leave her [Mecca, the Hijaz] plucked' (*adkhalūhum āminīn, wa-akhrajūhum mantūfīn*).[26] This economic approach is mirrored in laments found in many of the travelogues complaining about the local treatment of pilgrims and in particular of the irregular fees demanded from them, as well as the high prices for basic commodities.[27]

This view of the hajj is also reflected in modern studies. 'For all its dignity and nobility, sometimes the hajj seems like just another commodity or business venture, just another status symbol and pool of patronage,' observes Bianquis, author of an important study on the pilgrimage.[28] While such an attitude might seem an utter contradiction to 'the heart and soul of Islam', it is not at all perceived as such by the local population. 'How else', I was asked when enquiring about the phenomenon, 'could the pilgrimage be organised if the local economy did not benefit?'. In the present time, the Saudi state is adopting the same logic when trying to compensate for the

25 For this saying and its interpretation, I am indebted to Dr. ʿAdnān al-Yāfī, Jeddah, March 22, 2006.

26 Interview with ʿAbdallāh Muḥammad ʿAbdallāh ʿAlī Riḍā, Jeddah, March 4, 2010.

27 ʿAbdallāh Abkar, *Ṣuwar min turāth Makka al-Mukarrama fī 'l-qarn al-rābiʿ ʿashar al-hijrī* (Beirut: Muʾassasat ʿUlūm al-Qurʾān/Damaskus: Manār li-l-Nashr wa-l-Tawzīʿ, 1425/2004); Aḥmad Maḥmūd, *Riḥalāt al-ḥajj*, Jamharat al-Riḥalāt, 3 vols. (Jeddah: al-Maṭbaʿa al-Maḥmūdiyya, 1430/2009), vol. 1, p. 281 (voyage by Yaḥyā b. al-Muṭahhar b. Ismāʿīl b. Yaḥyā al-Ḥusayn al-Ḥusnā, visit 1797), p. 305 (Muḥammad Ṣādiq Bāshā, visit 1880), and p. 295 (visit of Muḥammad b. Muṣṭafā Bayram V., visit 1840). The entire report by the Nawab of Bhopal in 1863 is permeated by complaints, see Sikandar Begum (Nawab of Bhopal), *A Princess's Pilgrimage*, S. Lambert-Hurley (ed.) (Bloomington: Indiana University Press, 2008).

28 Bianchi, *Guests of God*, p. vii.

declining income from oil, in part by developing the sector of religious tourism further.[29]

Such a perspective tallies with recent literature on religious tourism. Even if there might be good reasons to distinguish between pilgrimage and tourism, especially when considering the historical perspective and the primary motives, a consideration of links between them also offers new perspectives on both. It is important to note that the hajj is only one case amongst many in this regard.[30] After all, hospitality is not necessarily free of all expectations of return. In its traditional understanding, outlined above, it is conceived as a practice creating bonds of mutual obligation, acting as 'an opening move in forging a long-term relationship of gift exchange and debt'.[31]

In the case of pilgrims in the cities of the Hijaz, this 'long-term relationship' can be thought of in a number of different ways. While quite a few pilgrims paid directly for services received, such as accommodation and food, it was also common for the entire journey to be arranged by pilgrims' guides, who also organised the financial exchanges. They were invested in the pilgrimage in the long term, maintaining relations with the countries of origin and introducing 'their' pilgrims to the same hosts year after year. Some hosts acted at the instigation of the local rulers (known as the emir or *sharif*) of Mecca, the Ottoman sultan or the Saudi king. In such cases, they could count on medium or long-term material rewards. Others had a vested interest in widening their mercantile or scholarly networks. Thus, the period before and after the hajj was (and to some extent still is) one of

[29] Ibid., p. vii. For the notion of religious tourism, see N. Collins-Kreiner, 'The Geography of Pilgrimage and Tourism: Transformations and Implications for Applied Geography', *Applied Geography*, 30 (2010), pp. 153–64; Kiran Shinde, 'Entrepreneurship and Indigenous Enterpreneurs in Religious Tourism in India', *International Journal of Tourism Research*, 12 (2010), pp. 523–35; and Saudi Gazette (August 15, 2016). 'Religious Tourism Plays Key Role in Bolstering Saudi, "Post Oil" Plan'. Article on *alarabiya.net*. http://english.alarabiya.net/en/business/economy/2016/08/15/Religious-tourism-plays-key-role-in-bolstering-Saudi-post-oil-plan.html.

[30] See Erik Cohen, 'Pilgrimage and Tourism: Convergence and Divergence' in A. Morinis (ed.), *Sacred Journeys: The Anthropology of Pilgrimage* (Westport, CA: Greenwood Press, 1992), pp. 47–61; cf. Michael Stausberg, 'Religion and Spirituality in Tourism' in A. A. Lew, C. M. Hall, and A. M. Williams (eds.), *The Wiley Blackwell Companion to Tourism* (Hoboken: Wiley-Blackwell, 2014). onlinelibrary.wiley.com/doi/full/10.1002/9781118474648.ch28, pp. 349–60.

[31] Mauss, *Die Gabe*, pp. 39–49.

intense socialising between different visitors and local hosts and scholars. Finally, the expectation of a heavenly reward might also have been an important additional motivation to offer hospitality.

The above considerations, from heavenly reward to material benefit, form part of the hospitality to the 'guests of God'. They also serve to complicate the wider notion of hospitality towards strangers and help to understand the different practices of and perspectives on hosting pilgrims in the specific case of the Muslim pilgrimage.

Jeddah: The Dihlīz (Entrance) of Mecca

The famous late eighteenth-century traveller Carsten Niebuhr, who visited Jeddah in 1762, begins his description of the city and its surroundings as follows:

> We entered this city under strong apprehensions of ill-treatment from its inhabitants. Recollecting with what contempt Christians are regarded at Cairo, and how our companions had been insulted by the Arab at Jambo; we feared, that we might experience still more of the inhospitable insolence of the Mussulmans, as we approached nearer to their holy cities. But we found ourselves agreeably disappointed. The inhabitants of Jidda, who are much accustomed to Christian merchants in the European dress, were not struck with any thing strange in our appearance, and did not seem to take much notice of us. We went freely to the coffee-houses and markets, without suffering any insults. But we understood, that none except Mussulmans, are permitted to pass through the gate that opens towards Mecca, or even to approach it; and kept therefore carefully at a distance from that gate, least we might be discovered.[32]

Niebuhr and his companions had donned local dress when visiting the Hijaz, which was considered quintessential Muslim territory. Mecca and Medina have long been considered spaces from which non-Muslims ought to be excluded. At different times in history, this notion was extended to other localities of the Hijaz, most notably Mecca's port: Jeddah.[33] Perhaps their dress, and the fact that Russian and European Muslims visited regularly, might have made them stand

[32] Carsten Niebuhr, *Travels through Arabia and Other Countries in the East* (Edinburgh: R. Morison and Son, 1792), p. 226.

[33] Sohail Hashmi, 'Political Boundaries and Moral Communities: Islamic Perspectives' in A. Buchanan and M. Moore (eds.), *States, Nations, and Borders: The Ethics of Making Boundaries* (Cambridge and New York: Cambridge

out less. However, even if people did not believe them to be Muslims, their local dress and respect of the recommendation to keep away from the Mecca Gate sufficed to mark them as less strange, conspicuous and potentially dangerous than European traders in Western dress. Nevertheless, they lived in the house of a Greek goldsmith, who, while probably an Ottoman, could be a Christian, Muslim or Jew. Thus, they were most likely recognised as Europeans.[34]

Niebuhr's description also contains an important spatial marker: the region of the eastern gate leading to Mecca as a place where non-Muslims were not tolerated. This links his description of the hospitality of the Jiddawis to the local image of Jeddah as the *dihlīz* of Mecca. A collection of local terms defines *dihlīz* as 'the entrance of a house, **or** its reception hall' (*madkhal al-dār aw bahūhu*) [my emphasis].[35] The most detailed depiction of the latter function is given by the architect Bokhari. In a Jeddah house, he tells us, this is usually a

> spacious entrance hall providing a reception area for guests. It was paved with larger flagstones. . .and furnished with long wooden benchens and other seating arrangements. During the hot days this entrance hall was normally sprinkled with water to keep it clean and cool. On both sides of the dahleez there were the office and business suite of the family patriarch, called al-maq'ad, as well as the servants' and aids quarters. A kitchenette for tea and coffee and bathrooms were also found on the ground level.[36]

University Press, 2003), pp. 181–227, here pp. 181–91, on the origins of the Meccan *ḥaram.*

34 Niebuhr, *Travels through Arabia*, p. 228.

35 Muḥammad Diyāb, *al-Mufradāt al-ʿāmmiyya fī madīnat Jidda* (n.p.: al-Maṭbaʿa al-Maḥmūdiyya, 1429/2008), p. 51. ʿAbdallāh al-Thaqafī, *al-ʿImāra bi-madīnat Jidda fī 'l-ʿaṣr al-ʿuthmānī 923–1334 h./1517–1916*, 2 vols. (Riyadh: Dārat al-Malik ʿAbd al-ʿAziz, 1436/2010), vol. 1, p. 327, discusses different types of *dihlīz* but does not include the side rooms in the definition.

36 Abdulla Bokhari, 'Jeddah: A Study in Urban Formation', PhD Thesis, University of Pennslyvania (1978), pp. 183–4; cf. Angelo Pesce, *Jiddah: Portrait of an Arabian City*, rev. edn. (London: Falcon Press, 1977), pp. 118–9; cf. Philippe Pétriat, *Le Négoce des Lieux Saints: Négociants Hadramis de Djedda, 1850–1950*, Bibliothèqe Historique des Pays d'Islam (Paris: Publications de la Sorbonne, 2016), vol. 9, p. 163; Stefan Maneval, 'The Architecture of Everyday Life in Twentieth Century Jiddah', PhD Thesis, Freie Universität Berlin (2015), pp. 68–9; and al-Thaqafī, *al-ʿImāra bi-madīnat Jidda*, p. 327. For the Red Sea context see Nancy Um, 'Reflections on the Red Sea Style: Beyond the Surface of Coastal Architecture', *Northeast African Studies*, 12 (2012), pp. 243–72, here pp. 243–71. For Suakin see also Muhammad Elfateh, 'Suakin (Sudan) and the Colonial Architecture of the Ottoman Empire in the Red Sea Region', PhD

While the exact layout was subject to some variations depending on the size of the house and the business of the family, the above description fits merchant houses not only in Jeddah but also other areas around the Red Sea. Situated just above ground level, the *dihlīz* and the rooms adjacent to it were also the coolest spaces of the house, which in the hot and humid climate of Jeddah added to its attractiveness. The *dihlīz* as the entrance hall is well described by the German traveller Eduard Rüppell, who visited Jeddah three times between 1826 and 1831. He mentions that Jiddawi merchants liked to hold their siesta in the entrance hall of the courtyard during the hot summer months.[37] They also received all their visitors in this space (or perhaps the adjacent *maqā'id* (pl. of *maq'ad*), which had the added advantage that they could oversee and direct everybody and everything coming in and out.[38] For Mecca, Abkar describes how servants and (male) children spent their time of rest and sometimes play in the *dihlīz* of the local houses.[39]

Thus, the *dihlīz*, both as the reception hall, as well as in its function as thoroughfare to other groundfloor quarters such as the offices and reception rooms, storage spaces, and the staircase, was more a semi-public than a private space. Women usually occupied quarters on the upper levels and received their visitors there. It needs to be noted that there were also small houses without such elaborate divisions and even huts, but the local memory refers to the merchant houses which were so central to the Jiddawi economy, serving both trade and pilgrimage.

Thesis, Brandenburgische Technische Universität Cottbus-Senftenberg (2015), pp. 115–35; and Paul Bonnenfant and Jeanne-Marie Gentilleau, 'Une Maison de Commerçant-armateur sur le mer Rouge: Bayt 'Abd al-Udūd à al-Luḥayya (Yemen)' in D. Panzac (ed.), *Les Villes dans l'Empire Ottoman: Activités et Sociétés 2*, Société Arabes et Musulmanes (Paris: Ed. du CNRS, 1994), pp. 125–88, here pp. 144–6.

37 Only some houses in Jeddah feature open courtyards which were common in Damascus.

38 Eduard Rüppell, *Reise in Abyssinien*, 2 vols + Atlas, vol. 1 (Frankfurt: Schmerber, 1838–40), vol. 1, p. 164; cf. al-Nimr, *Ḥārat al-Baḥr*, p. 325, who explicitly counts the *maqā'id* contained in the *dihlīz* in Ḥārat al-Baḥr as part of the latter; cf. Christiaan Snouck Hurgronje, *Mekka: Aus dem Heutigen Leben*, 2 vols. (Den Hague: Martinus Nijhoff, 1888–9), vol. 2, pp. 39–40. Philby also uses the term *dihlīz* when referring to a side room on the ground floor where a *majlis* was held, MECA, Philby Collection, GB 165–0229, 1/4/5/1, January 31, 1926.

39 Abkar, *Ṣuwar min Turāth Makka*, pp. 263–4.

If we now return to the analogy between the entrance hall and Jeddah, we can see that Jeddah can be conceived as a public or semi-public space as opposed to the private, or more sacred, space of Mecca and in particular the Holy Mosque. While hospitality can be offered both in the more public reception spaces and on the upper levels, depending on relationships, strangers usually did and do not venture beyond the reception spaces of houses. Pushing the analogy even further, we could argue that the bond of Islam, which allows Muslims from everywhere to proceed to Mecca, is comparable to the bond of familial relatedness which allows male relatives to enter the upper floors of the Jiddawi house. It thus makes perfect sense that Jeddah was less sheltered than Mecca in terms of who was received. Given the necessity to deal with people of different religious creed for trade purposes, something which greatly increased in the course of the nineteenth century as a result of changes in shipping and commerce, Jeddah fulfilled the role of the *dihlīz*. While the 'House of Islam' (*dār al-islām*) is commonly understood to encompass all regions ruled by Muslims, the architectural language locally employed suggests that Mecca and Jeddah formed a kind of quintessential 'House of Islam'.[40]

When introducing this understanding of Jeddah as the *dihlīz* of Mecca to scholars hailing from Mecca and Medina, they insisted on its meaning as a simple passageway leading into the house and rejected the inclusion of adjacent reception rooms in the notion.[41] Furthermore, they associated the term with a space to which servants of other households on an errand remained confined or, even worse, with a shady area of the house of rather dubious character. It is interesting that the first hint at this understanding of the *dihlīz* came from scholars hailing from Mecca and Medina. While they gave no indication that they personally associated Jeddah with shady activities, they clearly regarded their own cities of origin as more worthy of attention due to their sacred character.

The very function of Jeddah as the port of Mecca and the hajj has led many of my local interlocutors over the years to question whether it was important to write about a town which, in their eyes, owed its only raison d'être to the pilgrimage. For them, it was *only* a *dihlīz*, a point of

40 I thank Claudia Ghrawi for this suggestion.
41 This is how the term is used in a Syrian context; cf. Christian Saßmannshausen, 'Reform in Translation: Family, Distinction, and Social Mediation in Late Ottoman Tripoli', PhD Thesis, Freie Universität Berlin (2012), p. 168.

transition from the outside world to the holy spaces of Mecca and Medina. A recent historian of Jeddah turns this argument around: it is exactly the location of Jeddah next to Mecca which 'gave Jeddah as a place a singular specificity', while its people consist mostly of those coming from elsewhere (*al-wāfidīn*) who had merged with the original inhabitants through marriage, 'which makes the Jiddawi person stand out with a characteristic and singular personality', 'combining Eastern and Western cultures'.[42]

The sense of a moral distinction between Jeddah and Mecca is also present in the narrative about the history of one of the leading merchant families of Jeddah in the late nineteenth and first half of the twentieth centuries, the ʿAlī Riḍās. In an interview with one of the elders of the family, I was told that the family had originally intended to settle in Mecca. However, as a sin in Mecca on Judgment Day is said to weigh ten times as much as a sin committed elsewhere, they settled in Jeddah while maintaining a base in Mecca.[43] The rationality of such behaviour was confirmed to me by a number of other contacts. Irrespective of the fact that a merchant family in this period quite clearly had better prospects in Jeddah, the moral dimension was deemed important enough to be highlighted in this open conversation. My counterpart was presumably reflecting on sins committed in the world of business. Jeddah also seems to have offered other temptations. Consular sources, as well as travelogues, point to the existence of phenomena commonly associated with port cities such as alcohol and prostitution (see Chapter 7).

There existed a clear distinction between those who claimed Arab tribal background and are often called Bedouin (*badū*) irrespective of their mode of living, and the urban dwellers, or *ḥaḍar*. The unarmed, sedentary, and 'civilised' (*ḥadar*) urbanites considered the mobile and 'uncivilised' Bedouin a threat (in spite of a multitude of economic relations). The former looked down on the latter as a basically weak population that hid behind walls. In modern Saudi Arabia, this former antagonism has been somewhat transformed, reflecting a wider resurgence of tribal ideologies on the Peninsula in the wake of socio-economic changes. These ideologies have come to the foreground as

42 ʿAbdallāh b.ʿAbd al-ʿAzīz Bā Nāja, *Tārīkh Jidda min aqdam al-ʿuṣūr ḥattā nihāyat al-ʿahd al-ʿuthmānī* (Mecca, 2015), p. z.
43 Interview with ʿAbdallāh Muḥammad ʿAbdallāh ʿAlī Riḍā, March 4, 2010.

a notion of ethnic (Arab) purity, both in Saudi Arabia and elsewhere on the Arabian Peninsula. As a consequence, people who have intermarried with outsiders over generations, albeit by no means indiscriminately, are hardly considered respectable and, indeed, themselves stress an ethics of patrilineal parallel cousin marriage.[44]

When, in the remainder of this book, I refer to Jeddah as the *dihlīz* of Mecca, I choose to use it in the sense of a reception area in its own right. I fully recognise that, from a Makkāwī perspective, it resembled more a lowly passageway which only Muslims could traverse to reach the holy city, just like servants from other households on an errand had to remain on the threshold or in the hallway without being allowed to enter the sanctuary of a house. This does not, however, diminish the heuristic value of the image of the reception hall, which also distinguishes the types of cohabitation and interaction not only from the two holy cities but also from other Ottoman cities without a comparable sacred hinterland.

Conceptualising Diversity in Comparison: Cosmopolitanism and Conviviality

So far, this introduction has considered local perspectives on why and how Jeddah differs from other Saudi Arabian cities. 'God's guests' arrived mostly, although not exclusively, by sea, thus pointing to the need to understand Jeddah in a translocal Muslim context rather than in the exclusive context of an imperial (Ottoman) or national (Saudi Arabian) history. In the case at hand, we need to add to the decidedly Muslim – and hence almost global - context of the pilgrimage, the distinctly maritime one of the Red Sea, which transited to the Indian Ocean as well as to the Mediterranean worlds. Thus, one needs to combine a number of circulatory ambits which were decisive for Jeddah and its two lifelines, trade and pilgrimage. Certainly, the Red Sea deserves a special place in this context as Jeddah was deeply involved in the local trade, both along the coasts and across to the

44 For a discussion of this phenomenon in Saudi Arabia, see Samin, *Our Ancestors, Our Heroes*; for Oman, Mandana Limbert, 'Marriage, Status and the Politics of Nationality in Oman' in A. Alsharekh (ed.), *The Gulf Family: Kinship Policies and Modernity* (London: Saqi Books, 2007), pp. 167–79; cf. James Onley, 'Transnational Merchant Families in the Nineteenth- and Twentieth-Century Gulf' in M. al-Rasheed (ed.), *Transnational Connections and the Arab Gulf* (London: Routledge, 2005), pp. 59–89, here p. 62.

African shore. As will be shown throughout the book, there existed particularly close connections with such ports as Hodeida, Suakin, and Massawa, as well as with al-Wajh and, of course, with the trade metropoles of Aden and Cairo. The connections within the Red Sea have even given rise to the notion of a distinctive architectural style, even if this needs to be greatly nuanced.[45] The Red Sea ports also served as important relays to the adjacent maritime worlds of the Indian Ocean and the Mediterranean. Due to its location at the edge of the monsoon regime, as well as to the character of the Red Sea, Jeddah constituted an important centre connecting these two maritime worlds (cf. Chapter 2).[46]

The Braudelian notion of an interconnected 'archipelago of cities' has been adopted by Abu Lughod and turned into the notion of the Indian Ocean as a network of connected trade cities held together by seasonal trade networks whose participants shared a common culture.[47] According to Prange, *Monsoon Islam* thereby connected the Indian Ocean in spite of locally and temporally distinct negotiations of global and local influences.[48] These discussions have been adapted to the Red

[45] Um, *Reflections on the Red Sea Style*. Another prominent argument for Red Sea connectivity is made by Jonathan Miran, *Red Sea Citizens: Cosmopolitan Society and Cultural Change in Massawa* (Bloomington: Indiana University Press, 2009); Jonathan Miran, 'Red Sea Translocals: Hadrami Migration, Entrepreneurship, and Strategies of Integration in Eritrea, 1840s–1970s', *Northeast African Studies*, 12 (2012), pp. 129–67; for a concrete example of a Red Sea-centred merchant network from Jeddah in the twentieth century cf. Ulrike Freitag, 'A Twentieth-Century Merchant Network Centered on Jeddah: The Correspondence of Muḥammad b. Aḥmad Bin Ḥimd', *Journal of Northeast African Studies*, 17 (2017), pp. 101–29.

[46] For reservations against the historiography of the Red Sea as a primarily transitional space, cf. Jonathan Miran, 'The Red Sea' in D. Armitage, A. Bashford, and S. Sivasundaram (eds.), *Oceanic Histories*, Cambridge Oceanic Histories (Cambridge, New York, Melbourne, Delhi, and Singapore: Cambridge University Press, 2018), pp. 156–81, p. 158, see ibid. for a historiographical and conceptual survey.

[47] For a discussion of translocal, regional, or even global connections as quintessentially linked to oceanic studies, cf. Sujit Sivasundaram, Alison Bashford and David Armitage, 'Introduction' in D. Armitage, A. Bashford, and S. Sivasundaram (eds.), *Oceanic Histories*, Cambridge Oceanic Histories (Cambridge, United Kingdom: Cambridge University Press, 2018), pp. 1–28, 4–8.

[48] Janet Abu-Lughod, *Before European Hegemony: The World System A.D. 1250–1350* (New York: Oxford University Press, 1989) p. 32; Sebastian Prange, *Monsoon Islam: Trade and Faith on the Medieval Malabar Coast*, Cambridge

Sea, for example by Miran. They point to the need to also consider the connections to and resources of the hinterland as a crucial aspect of the emerging network of merchants and cities.[49] In the case of Jeddah, one must thus take into account the importance of the caravan routes linking the port with the interior – not only to the Holy cities of Mecca and Medina but also further beyond. Although both maritime and land-borne connections were subject to many variations over time, they have to be considered in conjunction, just as trade and pilgrimage are at times analytically inseparable. This net of connections over sea and land means that a holistic discussion of Jeddah cannot rely exclusively on approaches which privilege a particular maritime region (such as the Red Sea or Indian Ocean) or, indeed, sea-borne connections at the expense of land-borne ones (even if the latter have so far been less researched). Furthermore, the thallasocentric approach by Wick seems to sideline the important function of the Red Sea as a linking ocean.[50] This notwithstanding, the rich literature, notably on the Red Sea and the Western Indian Ocean, will be used extensively to contextualise, compare and at times contrast aspects of the history of Jeddah.

The question remains whether there are concepts which invite comparison, either with other cities in the wider Red Sea, or with those in the Ottoman, and the Mediterranean or Indian Ocean worlds. One such concept is the cosmopolitanism noted for many nodal points in global cultural and economic networks. Notably 'endpoints of migratory movements that produce cultural mosaics' have been thus conceptualised.[51] In this, Jeddah is comparable to other port cities the

Oceanic Histories (Cambridge: Cambridge University Press, 2018), pp. 27–32, 298–9.

49 Miran, *Red Sea Citizens*, pp. 7–11 and, more importantly, pp. 112–65 which discusses explicitly the sea-land connections.

50 For an 'oceanic' approach see Jerry Bentley, 'Sea and Ocean Basins as Frameworks of Historical Analysis', *Geographical Review*, 89 (1999), pp. 215–24. For a focus on the Red Sea, see Alexis Wick, *The Red Sea: In Search of Lost Space* (Oakland, CA: University of California Press, 2016), for the Red Sea as a space which links oceans, cf. Layla Fawaz and Chris Bayly (eds.), *Modernity and Culture: From the Mediterranean to the Indian Ocean* (New York: Columbia University Press, 2002); Valeska Huber, *Channelling Mobilities: Migration and Globalisation in the Suez Canal Region and Beyond, 1869–1914* (Cambridge and New York: Cambridge University Press, 2013).

51 Christina Horvath, 'The Cosmopolitan City' in M. Rovisco and M. Nowicka (eds.), *The Ashgate Research Companion for Cosmopolitism* (2011), p. 87, here p. 89.

world over and its cosmopolitan practices can, in many ways, be likened to those developed elsewhere. For example, Aljunied's study of mostly present-day Southeast Asian urban experiences – mainly situated in port cities - in many ways mirrors what this book discusses for Jeddah, from a historical perspective.[52]

Jeddah was closely linked to British India and in this way is comparable to Aden, even though the city remained outside of the formal British Empire, which absorbed Aden after 1839.[53] However, the diversity introduced through the hajj distinguishes the diversity of Jeddah from other ports in the Mediterranean, the Red Sea and the wider Indian Ocean.

Vernacular and Muslim Cosmopolitanism

To what extent, then, is the phenomenon locally discussed as the 'difference of Jeddah' a specifically Muslim variant of cosmopolitanism? In many ways, the religiously justified hospitality described above, which forms the basis for the Kantian minimal understanding of cosmopolitanism, could be a good starting point. Thus, Gaenszle has shown how a Nepali community could relatively easily integrate into the Indian city of Benares due to joint Hindu rituals, but also as a result of a common lifestyle.[54] Even if, one may argue, membership in specific global pious movements or the meeting in a particular space in the context of a pilgrimage are religiously specific, we would not hesitate to call them 'cosmopolitan' if the spaces in which they occur were Christian, such as the Jesuit order or the pilgrimage to Rome.

Werbner has argued that she uses 'vernacular cosmopolitanism' to refer to 'alternative, particularly non-Western, forms of cosmopolitan ethics, defined broadly as an openness to difference, whether to other ethnic groups, cultures, religions, or nations.'[55] She does so to 'escape

52 Khairudin Aljunied, *Muslim Cosmopolitanism: Southeast Asian Islam in Comparative Perspective* (Edinburgh: Edinburgh University Press, 2017), pp. xii–xxvi.

53 Scott Reese, *Imperial Muslims: Islam, Community and Authority in the Indian Ocean, 1839–1937* (Edinburgh: Edinburgh University Press, 2018), pp. 6–9.

54 Martin Gaenszle, '"Religiöser Kosmopolitismus": Der Nepali-Stadtteil in Benares, Indien', *Zeitschrift für Ethnologie*, 129 (2004), pp. 165–82.

55 Pnina Werbner, 'Vernacular Cosmopolitanism as an Ethical Disposition' in L. Baskins (ed.), *Islamic Studies in the Twenty-First Century: Transformations and Continuities* (Amsterdam: Amsterdam University Press, 2016), pp. 223–40, here p. 223.

the accusation of an imposed attribute implying the superiority and dominance of the West over a so-called cosmopolitan "other"'.[56] She thus responds to an earlier suggestion by Pollock, Bhabha, Breckenridge, and Chakrabarty to disentangle the concept of cosmopolitanism from a genealogy rooted in a specifically Western context.[57] This is necessary given the frequent accusation that 'cosmopolitanism' was a phenomenon of the elites and its spread is linked quite specifically to European imperialism.[58] However, it could be argued that an adjective like 'vernacular' re-introduces the very hierarchization and 'othering' vis-à-vis a norm which the authors rightly attempt to eliminate.

Should we then characterise the phenomenon observed in Jeddah not as 'vernacular' (Saudi/Hijazi/Jiddawi) but rather as 'Muslim' cosmopolitanism, a position to which Yamani, author of an ethnography of the Hijazi elite, would probably subscribe?[59] In many ways, one could see it as such, notably when investigating specifically Islamic networks, the hajj, etc. The exclusivity inherent in the hajj, and in access to the holy cities Mecca and Medina would support such a perspective. One can read texts by many Muslims in a similar way. For example, Abul Kalam Azad from India, writing in the interwar years, sees Mecca 'at the very center of world humanity as an alternative locus of ethical thought and action', and as refuge specifically for Muslims.[60] Although Jeddah was somewhat more tolerant of

[56] ibid., p. 239.

[57] Sheldon Pollock, Homi Bhaba, Carol Breckenridge, and Dipesh Chakrabarty, 'Cosmopolitanisms', *Public Culture*, 12 (2000), pp. 577–89. For further literature critical of the concept of cosmopolitanism, see Nowicka and Vertovec, *Comparing Convivialities*, p. 344; Ulrike Freitag, 'When Festivals Turned Violent in Jeddah, 1880s–1960s' in N. Fuccaro (ed.), *Violence and the City in the Modern Middle East* (Stanford: Stanford University Press, 2016), pp. 63–74, 250–5; and Ulrike Freitag, '"Cosmopolitanism" and "Conviviality"?: Some Conceptual Considerations Concerning the Late Ottoman Empire', *European Journal of Cultural Studies*, 17 (2014), pp. 375–91, here pp. 377–80.

[58] Sami Zubaida, 'Middle Eastern Experiences of Cosmopolitanism' in S. Vertovec and R. Cohen (eds.), *Conceiving Cosmopolitanism: Theory, Context and Practice* (Oxford: Oxford University Press, 2002), pp. 32–41.

[59] Noah Sobe, 'Rethinking 'Cosmopolitanism' as an Analytic for the Comparative Study of Globalization & Education', *Current Issues in Comparative Education*, 12 (2009), pp. I–XX; and Mai Yamani, *Cradle of Islam: The Hijaz and the Quest for an Arabian Identity* (London and New York: I.B. Tauris, 2004), p. 18.

[60] John Willis, 'Azad's Mecca: On the Limits of Indian Ocean Cosmopolitanism', *Comparative Studies of South Asia, Africa and the Middle East*, 34 (2014), pp. 574–81, here p. 574.

non-Muslims, their presence remained a matter of apprehension and their movements were somewhat restricted, as the above quote by Niebuhr shows. If we extend the concept to the holy cities of Mecca and Medina, non-Muslims were, and are, even to this day, categorically excluded.

In Jeddah, no significant non-Muslim resident population developed until the mid-twentieth century, even if the numbers of resident non-Muslims increased with time. This only changed with the development of significant oil-extraction and the major influx of foreign labour after the 1950s. In this development, Jeddah clearly differs from many other Middle Eastern cities discussed under the rubric of cosmopolitanism, notably in the Ottoman context, where the term has on occasion acquired a fairly nostalgic quality.[61] The concept of cosmopolitanism can be helpful in the context of inviting comparison by drawing attention to particular strategies of actors, but also to the wider political contexts, notably in the imperial age. It can also help to think about the different actors and the repertoires which they developed to navigate and insert themselves into changing political and social environments.[62]

The ambiguity of the local meaning of *dihlīz* also reminds us of the use of cosmopolitanism not as a moral good but as a vice endangering

61 Among many others, Sibel Zandi-Sayek, *Ottoman Izmir: The Rise of a Cosmopolitan Port, 1840–1880* (Minneapolis: University of Minnesota Press, 2012) has the term 'cosmopolitan' in the subtitle of her book, for the use of cosmopolitanism in case studies cf. Ulrike Freitag and Nora Lafi (eds.), *Urban Governance under the Ottomans: Between Cosmopolitanism and Conflict* (Milton Park, Abingdon, Oxon: Routledge, 2014); and Derryl Maclean and Sikeena Ahmed (eds.), *Cosmopolitanisms in Muslim Contexts: Perspectives from the Past*, Exploring Muslim Contexts (Edinburgh: Edinburgh University Press, 2012). For a critique of the romantic notions, cf. Will Hanley, 'Grieving Cosmopolitanism in Middle East Studies', *History Compass*, 6 (2008), pp. 1346–67, Freitag, *'Cosmopolitanism' and 'Conviviality'?*. Incidentally, although there were more Europeans in Damascus (in addition to many Arab Christians, who were almost entirely absent from Jeddah), European influence there also remained restricted, and of little impact on public life, see Stefan Weber, *Damascus: Ottoman Modernity and Urban Transformation 1808–1918*, 2 vols. (Aarhus: Aarhus University Press, 2009) pp. 70–3.

62 Kai Kresse, 'Interrogating "Cosmopolitanism" in an Indian Ocean Setting: Thinking Through Mombasa on the Swahili Coast' in D. N. Maclean and S. K. Ahmed (eds.), *Cosmopolitanisms in Muslim Contexts: Perspectives from the Past*, Exploring Muslim Contexts (Edinburgh: Edinburgh University Press, 2012), pp. 31–50.

social cohesion and the nation. Politicians and scholars concerned with national identity and cohesion thus suspect cosmopolites of a lack of loyalty, reliability, and a clear identity. In nineteenth- and twentieth-century Europe, this sparked heated debates and cosmopolitanism could become a dangerous accusation in the wake of rampant nationalism.[63]

Among inhabitants of the central Saudi region of Najd, Jiddawis are known as *ṭurshat al-baḥr*. Interestingly, this was always rendered to me as 'spit of the sea' in Jeddah whereas, in Bedouin parlance, it actually refers more neutrally to travelling but has, in the context of the Hijaz, come to be considered an insult.[64] This seems comparable to the derogatory appellations used for people of an internationalist outlook or of diasporic origin called 'cosmopolitan' in late nineteenth- and early twentieth-century Europe. In the Saudi case, the difference is that it is not a specific social or political group but rather the population of an entire region, the Hijaz, which is thus denoted. The appellation has very real consequences as the genealogical discourse has become a kind of 'symbolic language of the Saudi rentier state' when it comes to general expressions of social hierarchy, as well as to more concrete distributive politics.[65] Hijazis, in turn, pride themselves on their more liberal and well-educated society. They attribute the fact that they played a prominent role in building the Saudi state both administratively and economically to their exposure to international trade and Ottoman rule. In the first years after the Saudi conquest, and in some ways even after the move of most ministries from the Hijaz to Riyadh in 1952–3, the Hijaz remained the 'nerve center' of the Saudi government, with Jeddah serving as a base for many embassies and companies until the 1980s. To this day, it is considered, by both foreigners and locals, to be the most liberal city in the Kingdom.[66] However, it has lost this comparative edge since the 1980s and there is an ongoing marginalization of Hijazi

[63] For the debate in Germany in the early nineteenth century, see Andrea Albrecht, *Kosmopolitismus: Weltbürgerdiskurse in Literatur, Philosophie und Publizistik um 1800* (Berlin and New York: Walter de Gruyter, 2005), particularly pp. 319–52.

[64] I thank Ibraheem al-Sinan for this insight.

[65] Samin, *Of Sand or Soil*, p. 203.

[66] Joseph Kostiner, *The Making of Saudi Arabia, 1916–36: From Chieftaincy to Monarchical State*, Studies in Middle Eastern History (New York: Oxford University Press, 1993), p. 174.

administrators and entrepreneurs in favour of people from Najd.[67] In reaction, local customs and traditions are celebrated and revived under the slogan of 'Jeddah is different', which epitomises local pride and identity.[68] Simultaneously, the demand to officially ban derogatory appellations such as 'spit of the sea' or 'remains of the hajj' (*baqāyat al-ḥajj*), brought forward in the context of the so-called 'Cultural Dialogue', reflects the deep anger and hurt felt by many Hijazis hailing from the 'old families'.[69] Since King Salmān has come to office, a social media debate about Hijazi identity has emerged which presents a new variation on this theme.[70]

'Jeddah ghayr' in many ways constitutes the quintessence of Jeddah's 'urban charisma' and 'soul', defended proudly by many locals and felt even by visitors today, in spite of the many changes the city has undergone since the period discussed in this book, which arguably constitutes the historical basis of the notion.[71] If we take 'Jeddah ghayr' as a shorthand for cosmopolitanism, we draw attention to the different ways in which diversity was part and parcel of life in the Hijaz. 'Muslim cosmopolitanism' helps explain exclusionary tendencies, while cosmopolitan practices are one way of approaching 'a set of practices, a disposition, and a specific cultural and social condition that allows Muslims to inhabit the contemporary

67 Mai Yamani, *Changed Identities: The Challenge of the New Generation in Saudi Arabia* (London: The Royal Institute of International Affairs, Middle East Programme, 2000), p. 13; cf. Yamani, *Cradle of Islam*; Soraya Altorki, *Women in Saudi Arabia: Ideology and Behavior among the Elite* (New York and Guildford, CT: Columbia University Press, 1986), p. 8; Madawi al-Rasheed, *A History of Saudi Arabia* (New York: Cambridge University Press, 2002), p. 153; and interview Riyadh, December 7, 2017.

68 For a scholarly elaboration on this, see Yamani, *Cradle of Islam*.

69 Mark Thompson, 'Assessing the Impact of Saudi Arabia's National Dialogue: The Controversial Case of the Cultural Discourse', *Journal of Arabian Studies*, 1 (2011), pp. 163–81, here p. 174; cf. Zina Sawaf, 'Encountering the State: Women and Intimate Lives in Riyadh, Saudi Arabia', PhD Thesis, Graduate Institute of International and Development Studies (2017), p. 55.

70 #Ḥuwwiyyat al-Ḥijāz, I thank Ahmed Alowfi for this information.

71 Thomas Hansen and Oskar Verkaaik, 'Introduction: Urban Charisma: On Everyday Mythologies in the City', *Critique of Anthropology*, 29 (2009), pp. 5–26. Urban sociologists have discussed this in a variety of ways which resemble each other, such as the habitus of cities or their inner logic. For a survey of these discussions with the relevant literature see Jens Wietschorke, 'So Tickt Berlin?: Städtische Eigenlogiken in der Diskussion', *Aus Politik und Zeitgeschichte*, 48 (2017), http://www.bpb.de/apuz/260056/so-tickt-berlin-staedtische-eigenlogiken-in-der-diskussion?p=all (accessed 11 Dec. 2019).

world'.[72] These notions will henceforth be referred to only for these purposes, as 'cosmopolitanism' works far less well as a tool when one seeks to explain how the diverse society of Jeddah functioned in everyday life, how hierarchies were established, and conflicts fought out or negotiated.[73]

A Focus on Conviviality

While cosmopolitanism helps draw attention to a multicultural setting otherwise ignored, the concrete practices of everyday interactions might be considered more usefully by employing the somewhat less politically charged term of conviviality. Its everyday use alludes to the joy of living expressed in 'Jeddah ghayr' but recent academic debates propose a more nuanced understanding of the term. While 'cosmopolitan practices' tend to focus on strategies employed by individuals, 'conviviality' emphasises the living 'with', and thus 'opens up the path to understanding human relations in a sense of interdependency'.[74] Like cosmopolitanism, 'conviviality' does have a strong normative strand, as is evident not only in what might be considered the constitutive text on the concept by Ivan Illich, but also in the subsequent attempts to appropriate the debate in order to establish solutions for future human development.[75]

Although the notion of 'cosmopolitan practices' does not per se exclude the middle class, it is striking that it has, so far, concentrated either on elites or, as a critique of this elitist approach, on highly mobile lower class members such as sailors, prostitutes, or petty criminals. Indeed, the comparatively lesser spatial mobility of the middle class has prompted Eldem to specifically exclude them from consideration as cosmopolitan.[76] One of the central arguments of this book is

[72] Mara Leichtman and Dorothea Schulz, 'Introduction to Special Issue: Muslim Cosmopolitanism: Movement, Identity, and Contemporary Reconfigurations', *City & Society*, 24 (2012), pp. 1–6, here p. 2.

[73] This argument is based on Cooper's warning against the overstretch of concepts, see Frederick Cooper, *Colonialism in Question: Theory, Knowledge, History* (Berkeley: University of California Press, 2005), notably pp. 7–12, 85.

[74] Nowicka and Vertovec, *Comparing Convivialities*, p. 342.

[75] Ivan Illich, *Tools for Conviviality*, Open Forum (London: Calder and Boyars, 1973); and Frank Adloff and Claus Leggewie, *Das konvivialistische Manifest: Für eine neue Kunst des Zusammenlebens* (Bielefeld: Transcript, 2014); cf. Nowicka and Vertovec, *Comparing Convivialities*, pp. 343–7.

[76] Edhem Eldem, 'The Undesirables of Smyrna, 1926', *Mediterranean Historical Review*, 24 (2009), pp. 223–7.

that we need to look at the social practices of interaction, discussed in Chapter 5, both within as well as between different social strata. They will help us understand the mechanisms by which people of different origins lived side by side on an everyday basis, even if this might be less spectacular than highbrow elite conversations across cultures or pub brawls in the harbour.[77] This would encourage us to consider anything from neighbourhoods to guilds as spaces and institutions in which everyday interactions constitute the basis for what we call society.[78] Paying attention to institutions, rather than individuals, also encourages taking a different approach to the notion of 'hospitality for the guests of God'. It furthers a perspective which considers the ways in which strangeness of pilgrims is mediated and controlled through the institution of the pilgrim guides (see Chapter 6), or how the spatial arrangement of house and quarter guides and channels interactions between people who are acquainted to different degrees and belong to different sexes (Chapter 4). These everyday practices are the building blocks which allow for conviviality.

A focus on ordinary social tools does not gloss over conflicts or the marking of boundaries and class. Such practices are inherent in many of the rituals which provided the social glue of Jiddawi society and can be related to different levels of social interaction from the household to the quarter, the city, and even the relations between the city and its surroundings. The added value of grouping such practices under 'conviviality' consists of the links to the broader contexts of public discourse, institutions, and material settings.[79]

Of course, this book does not aim to investigate all convivial practices. Rather, it pays special attention to those which are related to translocal connections of the inhabitants of Jeddah.[80] In particular,

[77] Freitag, *'Cosmopolitanism' and 'Conviviality'?*, pp. 380–1.

[78] This perspective is inspired by Michel Certeau, *The Practice of Everyday Life*, Paperback (University of California Press, 1988), particularly pp. 91–110, for a systematic interpretation of his approach Marian Füssel, *Zur Aktualität von Michel de Certeau: Einführung in sein Werk*, Aktuelle und klassische Sozial- und Kulturwissenschaftler-innen (Wiesbaden: Springer VS, 2018) pp. 95–122.

[79] Nowicka and Vertovec, *Comparing Convivialities*, p. 350; cf. Freitag, *'Cosmopolitanism' and 'Conviviality'?*; as well as the articles by Heil and Wise and Velayutham in the same issue.

[80] Ulrike Freitag and Achim Oppen, 'Introduction: 'Translocality': An Approach to Connection and Transfer in Regional Studies' in U. Freitag and A. v. Oppen (eds.), *Translocality: The Study of Globalising Processes from a Southern*

I refer here to connections which have a certain regularity, such as the pilgrimage or trade, where individuals might change but certain patterns remain. The 'local' in the term 'translocal' also means that the 'trans' does not need to be between politically distinct entities, such as in 'transnational' – it can range from the immediate surroundings of the locality, which was bounded by a wall, to other places within the same political system (in the case of the Ottoman Empire thus also reaching the Balkans), but also to geographically closer but politically distinct entities such as Ethiopia or Oman.

The Exceptionality of Jeddah in Perspective: Literature, Sources, and Approach

Of Nuggets and Gaping Holes: Sources and Approach

The history of a city which focuses on urban conviviality depends on sources that are available to a historian. Limitations are manifold and lie in the capacities and abilities of the researcher – in terms of available time, linguistic skill, and ability to process – as much as in the limited accessibility of some materials. I have had access to the Ottoman archives, albeit tempered by constraints of time and language, as well as to the British, French, and Dutch consular archives and to the collection of Leiden University Library. However, those of the Russian Empire and Iran, two states which established consulates, the records of which might provide a perspective quite different from those of the Western imperial powers, remained beyond my linguistic reach. Matters were also frustrating when it came to local archives. Neither court records – the staple source of Ottoman social and economic history for so many regions – nor proceedings of the various councils and municipal administrations have been available to me. I am grateful to friends and acquaintances for sharing the occasional legal document, notably wills, and *waqf* (endowment) documents, with me. This has allowed me to somewhat better understand the spaces in which people lived.[81] Nevertheless, this did not enable me to reconstruct in any

Perspective, Studies in Global Social History (Leiden and Boston: Brill, 2010), pp. 1–21.

81 A good example for the various sources available for urban social history in the Ottoman empire can be found in the articles in Daniel Panzac (ed.), *Les Villes dans l'Empire Ottoman: Activités et sociétés*, 1, Société Arabes et Musulmanes

comprehensive way the spatiality of the city, nor the composition of its inhabitants, as no census records are available such as those used by Büssow for Ottoman Palestine.[82] The archives of the Institute for Public Administration in Riyadh also proved extremely valuable with regard to matters regulated by the young Saudi state, while the King ʿAbd al-ʿAzīz Historical Center provided an important newspaper archive.

I hope to counter these imbalances to some extent through the use of local histories, which often incorporate memoirs, letters, and oral histories, as well as by family history interviews. These local histories, which have proliferated in recent years, not least in the run-up to the (successful) candidacy of Jeddah to become a world heritage site, can be divided into chronicles which include a contemporaneous account, and local histories. Among the former, the works by the Shāfiʿī mufti of Mecca, Aḥmad Zaynī al-Daḥlān, and by Aḥmad al-Ḥaḍrāwī al-Shāfiʿī, a scholar of Egyptian origin raised in Mecca, stand out as important sources for the nineteenth century.[83] Pioneers of local history writing, which was based on a variety of sources, even if these are not referenced according to modern academic standards, are al-Anṣārī, a journalist from Medina (1906–83), al-Sibāʿī, the Meccan historian known as the 'shaykh of historians' (1323–1404 h./1905–6 to 1983–4), and historian Maghrabī (d. 1996).[84] They all based their accounts on published and unpublished sources, as well as interviews, personal knowledge, and oral traditions.[85] al-Anṣārī, like a number of other

(Paris: Ed. du CNRS, 1991), vol. 5; and Daniel Panzac (ed.), *Les Villes dans l'Empire Ottoman: Activités et Sociétés*, 2, Société Arabes et Musulmanes (Paris: Ed. du CNRS, 1994), vol. 9.

82 Büssow, *Hamidian Palestine*.

83 Aḥmad Daḥlān, *Khulāṣat al-kalām fī bayān umarāʾ al-Ḥarām* (Cairo: al-Maṭbaʿa al-Khayriyya, 1305/1887–8); Aḥmad al-Ḥaḍrāwī, *al-Jawāhir al-muʿadda fī faḍāʾil Jidda*, ʿAlī Muḥammad ʿUmar (ed.) (Cairo: Maktabat al-Thaqāfa al-Dīniyya, 2002).

84 On al-Sibāʿī see Muḥammad Maghribī, *Aʿlām al-Ḥijāz*, 2nd edn., 4 vol. (vol. 4, 1st edn.) (Jeddah: Maṭābiʿ Dār al-Bilād, 1405/1985) vol. 3, pp. 10–21 and Manṣūr ʿAssāf (April 24, 2015). 'Aḥmad al-Sibāʿī. . .shaykh al-muʾarrikhīn'. Online article on *almrsal.com*. www.almrsal.com/post/231532.

85 ʿAbd al-Anṣārī, *Mawsūʿat tārīkh madīnat Jidda*, 2 (enlarged) (Jeddah: Maṭābiʿ al-Rawḍa, 1980); al-Maghribī, *Aʿlām al-Ḥijāz*. On al-Anṣārī, cf. Yamine Maḥmūd (November 01, 2015). Sīrat al-muʾarrikh ʿAbd al-Quddūs al-Anṣārī wa-ahamm injāzātuh. Online article on *almrsal.com*. www.almrsal.com/post/288338; on Maghrabī cf. Manṣūr al-ʿAssāf (December 01, 2017). 'Muḥammad Maghribī.Adīb al-Ḥijāz', al-Riyāḍ. Article on *alriyadh.com*. www.alriyadh.com/1642601 (accessed October 12, 2019).

early historians and authors of memoirs, was part of the emerging literary and journalistic environment of the first half of the twentieth century which is discussed in Chapter 5.

Although they were of a later generation, more recent authors such as Ṭrābulsī and Kābilī follow roughly the same methodology.[86] A number of other accounts, such as those by Raqqām, Bakur, Manāʿ and others reflect more closely the particular experience of their authors and their families, while notably the local histories by al-Faḍlī and al-Nimr are academic studies on the basis of local material.[87] Furthermore, interview-based biographies, as well as collections of local poetry and proverbs, have proven very useful.[88] While most of the above can be at least partly be considered as primary sources, there also is an increasing number of local and regional histories authored by professional historians using British, Ottoman, and local sources.[89]

Travelogues of Eastern, as well as Western visitors, photographs, and some local documents held by local people, have also proved important sources, at times containing rare insights into local relations or describing parts of the urban fabric. Their different drawbacks have been described by others, and I hope to avoid these by triangulating travelogues with other materials.[90] In spite of the individual positions

[86] Ṭrābulsī, *Jidda*; Wahīb Kābilī, *al-Ḥirafiyyūn fī madīnat Jidda: Fī ʻl-qarn al-rābiʿ ʿashar al-hijrī*, 3rd edn. (s.n.: s.n., 1425/2004); Muḥammad Diyāb, *Jidda: al-Tārīkh wa-l-ḥayyāt al-ijtimāʿiyya*, 2nd edn. (Jeddah: Maṭābiʿ Muʾassasat al-Madīna li-l-Ṣaḥāfa, 2003).

[87] Muḥammad Raqqām, *Jidda: Ḥikāyāt min al-zaman al-jamīl* (Jeddah: al-ʿĀmāl al-Thaqāfiyya, 1436/2014–5); Muḥammad Bakur, *ʿĀʾila jiddāwiyya* (Riyadh: Muʾassasat al-Turāth, 2013); ʿAbdallāh Manāʿ, *Baʿḍ al-ayyām baʿḍ al-layālī: Aṭrāf min qiṣṣat ḥayyātī*, 2nd edn. (Jeddah: Dār al-Funūn, 2009); ʿAbdallāh Manāʿ, *Tārīkh mā lam yuʾarrakh: Jidda, al-insān wa-l-makān* (Jeddah: Dār al-Marsā, 2011/1432).

[88] Hind Bā Ghaffār, *al-Aghānī al-shaʿbiyya fī ʻl-Mamlaka al-ʿArabiyya al-Saʿūdiyya* (Jeddah: Dār al-Qādisiyya li-l-Nashr wa-l-Tawzīʿ, 1994).

[89] For example Ṣābira Ismāʿīl, *Jidda khilāla ʻl-fatra 1286–1327 H./1869–1908 M.: Dirāsa tārīkhiyya wa-ḥaḍāriyya fī ʻl-maṣādir al-muʿāṣira* (Riyadh: Dārat al-Malik ʿAbd al-ʿAziz, 1418/1997–8); ʿAbdallāh b.ʿAbd al-ʿAzīz Bā Nāja,, *Tārīkh Jidda*; ʿAbdallāh Mansī, *Jidda fī ʻl-tārikh al-ḥadīth min 923 H. ilā 1344 H./1517 M. ilā 1926 M.* (n.p., 2015).

[90] The problematic nature of travelogues has been discussed extensively, for a good bibliographic overview of recent literature, see Katharina Lange, 'Histories of the Wulda: An Ethnographic-Historical Approach to Tribal Identity and Belonging in Syria, 19th–21st century', Habilitation, University of Leipzig (2017), pp. 91–2. On the possible use of photographs see Ulrike Freitag (2016). Urban Life in Late Ottoman, Hashemite and Early Saudi Jeddah, as documented

reflected in these sources, their authors or photographers were often keen observers, and thus enable us to grasp specific stories or describe minute details. They thereby help link the interaction of the specific and individual to wider social and political developments that emerge from other sources and the extant literature.[91]

One particular hole remains, however. Modern memoirs, as well as new fictional texts, give some insights into the dark side of households and quarters, such as female circumcision, rape, and violence.[92] These texts, not all of which are situated in Jeddah, offer an important counter-narrative to the more harmonising perspective on neighbourhoods and traditional institutions found notably in the local histories which are the main source on these institutions. The problem for the historian is the absence of verifiable historical sources on such topics, which would also allow critical assessment of the prevalence of such practices in different periods. It is nevertheless important to point out the high likelihood of their occurrence in Jeddah throughout the period discussed in this book in order to counter a somewhat nostalgic narrative of past urban harmony and point to the kinds of experiences and ruptures not readily available in the sources used. The one notable exception is the question of slavery due to the strong advocacy against the institution in some of the Western sources, and the systematic collection of slaves' narratives.

Given the time-span and range of topics covered in this book, my approach will mostly be a thematic one. Individual stories and institutions will often serve as entries into themes, and while care is taken to historicise, this study will only provide some building blocks instead of a comprehensive analysis of the development of all themes. This said, I still hope that, in this way, the historical development of Jiddawi society in its political and economic context from the mid-nineteenth to

in the Photographs in the Snouck Hurgronje Collection in Leiden. Working paper. www.zmo.de/publikationen/WorkingPapers/freitag_2016.pdf, pp. 2–5.

91 This approach is inspired by the discussion about the 'life course perspective', e.g. Richard Wall, Tamara Hareven and Josef Ehmer (eds.), *Family History Revisited: Comparative Perspectives*, The Family in Interdisciplinary Perspective (Newark, NJ: University of Delaware Press; Associated University Presses, 2001), p. 28.

92 Examples of this are the novels by Yusuf Muhaimid, *Wolves of the Crescent Moon: A Novel* (New York: Penguin Books, 2007) and Sulaiman Addonia, *Die Liebenden von Dschidda: Roman* (Hamburg: Atlantik, 2015) as well as the memoirs by Manal al-Sharif, *Losfahren* (Zürich: Secession Verlag, 2017).

the mid-twentieth century becomes intelligible. Furthermore, I will draw on, and narrate, the individual stories as microhistories of interaction in the urban space. These microhistories frequently point to wider global historical themes.[93] Through a 'thickened narrative' – a term which Peter Burke derived in analogy to Clifford Geertz' 'thick description' – I hope to contribute not only yet another Ottoman urban history, but to more precisely historicise the notion of 'Jeddah ghayr', as well as to help insert it into debates about life in diverse societies.[94] Finally, I hope that in such a 'global microhistory', Jeddah becomes visible as the gate through which those in the world had to pass who wanted to visit Mecca, as well as an important entrepôt in regional and international trade.[95]

'Jeddah Ghayr' – But Is It?

'Tyre is different', responded inhabitants of this smallish port city in southern Lebanon when asked about how they perceived of their city. By this, they not only referred to a perceived difference between the city and its hinterland, but also the wider country, which is characterised by widespread mistrust (and a vivid memory of past civil wars) between different confessional (and political) groups. The reason for this difference was attributed to Tyre's history with which, in their view, only original inhabitants could properly identify.[96]

This statement from Tyre is relevant to Jeddah in a number of ways. It demonstrates that the claim to differ from the wider environment made by Jeddawis is not unique and that, importantly, the question of conviviality of different people constitutes a matter of pride in more

[93] On microhistory, see Giovanni Levi, 'On Microhistory' in P. Burke (ed.), *New Perspectives on Historical Writing* (Cambridge: Polity Press, 1991), pp. 93–113; cf. Wladimir Fischer-Nebmaier, 'Introduction: Space, Narration, and the Everyday' in W. Fischer-Nebmaier, M. Berg, and A. Christou (eds.), *Narrating the City: History, Space, and the Everyday* (New York and Oxford: Berghahn Books, 2015), pp. 1–55.

[94] Peter Burke, 'History of Events and the Revival of Narrative' in P. Burke (ed.), *New Perspectives on Historical Writing* (Cambridge: Polity Press, 1991), 233–48, here pp. 240–5.

[95] Hans Medick, 'Turning Global?: Microhistory in Extension', *Historische Anthropologie*, 24 (2016), pp. 241–52, here particularly pp. 248–52.

[96] These findings are part of the ongoing doctoral work of Gabriele Bunzel-Khalil on historical memory in Tyre. I thank her for allowing me to quote from this unpublished material.

than one context. It also demonstrates the importance of an urban, rather than a regional or even national identification of urban dwellers, which demonstrates the link between 'citizen' and 'city', notably, but not exclusively in premodern contexts.[97] In the case of Jeddah, this city was locally known as *al-Balad*. This bears resemblance to the distinction which Lafi found with regard to Tripoli (Libya) where the term *al-bilād* denoted the walled town as space and urban community, while the more common word for city, *madīna*, was more specifically used for the built-up urban space.[98]

When urban space is discussed in this study, it is informed by the Lefebvrian notion of space as a complex conglomerate of physical environment (perceived space), of its abstract ordering in conceived space, and of the ways in which the physical space is inhabited (lived space).[99] Although the main focus of this study is on the ways in which people in Jeddah interacted and were governed, rather than on urban transformation as an expression of social change (as in Weber's study of Damascus) or the modernisation of an emerging provincial capital (as in Hanssen's study of Beirut), this interaction took place within a concrete city.[100] Fuccaro has suggested to consider cities as 'physical sites of political, social, and cultural interaction and exchange'.[101] Hence, the evolution of the urban space, and to some extent also contentions over its shape and use, are highly relevant to the topic at hand.[102]

97 This argument, which is based on historical research as well as Weberian thought, can be found, for example, in, for example Engin Isin, 'Who Is the New Citizen? Towards a Genalogy', *Citizenship Studies*, 1 (1997), pp. 115–32; Charles Tilly, 'Citizenship, Identity and Social History', *International Review of Social History*, 40 (1995), pp. 223–36.

98 Nora Lafi, *Une ville du Maghreb entre ancien régime et réformes ottomanes: Genèse des institutions municipales à Tripoli de Barbarie (1795 – 1911)*, Villes, histoire, culture, société Nouvelle série (Paris: L'Harmattan, 2002), pp. 119–24.

99 Henri Lefebvre, *The Production of Space* (Malden, MA, Oxford, and Carlton-Melbourn: Blackwell Publishing, 1991), pp. 33–9.

100 On this point cf. Nelida Fuccaro, *Histories of City and State in the Persian Gulf: Manama since 1800*, Cambridge Middle East Studies (Cambridge and New York: Cambridge University Press, 2009), vol. 30, pp. 1–2

101 Nelida Fuccaro, 'Introduction: Histories of Oil and Urban Modernity in the Middle East', *Comparative Studies of South Asia, Africa and the Middle East*, 33 (2013), pp. 1–6, 1,

102 Cf. Jens Hanssen, *Fin de Siècle Beirut: The Making of an Ottoman Provincial Capital*, Oxford Historical Monographs (Oxford: Clarendon Press, 2005), pp. 8–12, Weber, *Damascus*, pp. 15–23.

The statement by the people of Tyre is also interesting because Tyre, like Jeddah, has an Ottoman past. In both cities, the Ottomans restored their rule in 1840 and, over the following decades, implemented new provincial and urban institutions aiming to recalibrate the balance between local elites and centrally appointed administrations.[103] These reforms followed a pattern similar to that observable in better-studied cities such as Salonica, Beirut, Tripoli (Lebanon), Istanbul, Izmir, or Damascus.[104] Since the programme of the Ottoman reform era (*Tanzimat*) went far beyond a mere administrative reform and aimed to achieve a far-reaching modernisation of urban space and life, it is not surprising that in this field, too, Jeddah is comparable to other Ottoman cities, as will be shown in the course of this study. However, as a result of local and regional differences, as well as peculiar configurations of interest and power, there are also notable divergences between the ways in which reforms were implemented.

Here, the context of Jeddah's relation with the Red Sea and Indian Ocean comes into play. Arabs originating from Hadhramaut in Southern Yemen, who also had wide-ranging connections in the Indian Ocean from East Africa to India and increasingly to Southeast Asia, made up about half of the population of Jeddah.[105] Their leading economic and political role in the city and its trade throughout the period under investigation constituted one important link between the Red Sea and Indian Ocean worlds, as Pétriat's outstanding study has

[103] Nora Lafi, *Esprit civique et organisation citadine dans l'Empire ottoman (XVe–XXe siècles)*, The Ottoman Empire and Its Heritage (Leiden and Boston: Brill, 2018), vol. 64, pp. 228–97.

[104] Meropi Anastassiadou, *Salonique, 1830–1912: Une ville ottomane à l'âge des réformes*, The Ottoman Empire and Its Heritage (Leiden: Brill, 1997), vol. 11; Hanssen, *Fin de Siècle Beirut*; Layla Fawaz, *Merchants and Migrants in Nineteenth-Century Beirut*, Harvard Middle Eastern Studies (Cambridge, MA: Harvard University Press, 1983), vol. 18; Saßmannshausen, *Reform in Translation*; İlay Örs, *Diaspora of the City: Stories of Cosmopolitanism from Istanbul and Athens*, Palgrave Studies in Urban Anthropology (New York: Palgrave Macmillan, 2016); Zandi-Sayek, *Ottoman Izmir*; Weber, *Damascus*; Till Grallert, *To Whom Belong the Streets?: Property, Propriety, and Appropriation: The Production of Public Space in Late Ottoman Damascus, 1875–1914* (Berlin: FU Berlin (Microfiche), 2014).

[105] For an overview of the Hadhrami diaspora see Ulrike Freitag and William Clarence-Smith (eds.), *Hadhrami Traders, Scholars, and Statesmen in the Indian Ocean, 1750s–1960s* (Leiden, New York, Köln: Brill Academic Publishers, 1997).

demonstrated.[106] They were not alone: Indians and not least the sizable number of subsaharan Africans from the Red Sea coast and its hinterland, but also from further afar in East and West Africa, testify to such links (see Chapter 3), as do institutions such as the *shahbandar* or the distinctive local architecture, discussed in Chapter 4. The rhythm of the monsoon winds continued to influence travel since local navigation used the sail long after steamers had become a means of transport in the Red Sea, but had to struggle with the often difficult conditions.[107]

Thus, while cosmopolitanism in Ottoman port cities has been mostly discussed in terms of religious diversity, which increased in the context of urban growth of the nineteenth century in places such as Mersin, Salonica, Izmir, or Beirut through the immigration of Christian and Jewish merchants, Jeddah was distinctive in terms of its ethnic diversity.[108] The religious importance of the Hijaz as the holy land of Islam, the strong local power of the Emirs of Mecca, the physical distance from the Ottoman centre of power, the international connections, and a very diverse population with often multiple political affiliations, all influenced the ways in which local elites interacted with officials sent from the imperial centre and in which the Ottoman reform programme was implemented locally.[109] The different historical trajectories also meant that foreign attempts at intervention and at using foreign nationals as levers of influence played out somewhat differently, while in all cases resulting in enhanced efforts to clarify nationality, if possible by turning long-term residents into Ottomans (cf. Chapter 7).

106 Pétriat, *Le Négoce des Lieux Saints.*

107 Cf. William Facey, 'Trade and Travel in the Red Sea Region' in P. Lunde and A. Porter (eds.), *Trade and Travel in the Red Sea Region: Proceedings of Red Sea Project I Held in the British Museum, October 2002*, Society for Arabian Studies Monographs (London, 2004), pp. 7–17; William Facey, 'Jiddah: Port of Makkah, Gateway of the Indian Trade' in L. Blue, J. Cooper, T. Ross, and J. Whitewright (eds.), *Connected Hinterlands: Proceedings of Red Sea Project IV; Held at the University of Southampton, September 2008*, Society for Arabian Studies Monographs (London: Archaeopress, 2009), pp. 165–76; Miran, *The Red Sea*, pp. 159–61.

108 Meltem Toksöz, *Nomads, Migrants and Cotton in the Eastern Mediterranean: The Making of the Adana-Mersin Region 1850–1908* (Leiden: Brill, 2010) pp. 106–9; Anastassiadou, *Salonique, 1830–1912*, p. 58; Zandi-Sayek, *Ottoman Izmir*, pp. 50–63; Fawaz, *Merchants and Migrants*, pp. 28–43.

109 Both Weber, *Damascus*, pp. 17–21 and Johann Büssow, *Hamidian Palestine: Politics and Society in the District of Jerusalem*, the Ottoman Empire and Its Heritage (Leiden: Brill, 2011), vol. 46, pp. 309–432 also insist on the interactional dynamics between imperial and local elites.

When Jeddah (and the Hijaz) became a part of Saudi Arabia, the elite of which came from a region not integrated into the Ottoman domains, it also stood out as distinct from the Najd region – so much so that Najd and Hijaz were treated as distinct entities until 1932, when the Kingdom of Saudi Arabia was established. However, 'Jeddah ghayr' should not let us forget earlier contacts and a rather speedy integration of local elites into the economically leading group within the newly emergent Kingdom of Saudi Arabia. Nor should we ignore the influence of the former Ottoman administrative system on the emerging administration of the new Saudi state.[110]

Many Ottoman port cities expanded in the course of the nineteenth century due to the rise in exports from their agricultural hinterlands and of imports for local markets – which incidentally also increased religious heterogeneity.[111] Global economic developments played out differently in Jeddah, as Pétriat has shown. Jeddah initially benefitted from the growth in global trade – the rising number of Indians in Jeddah is one reflection of this trend. However, in the last quarter of the nineteenth century, it lost its role as major entrepôt in the trade between the Indian Ocean and the Mediterranean through the rise of Aden and the advent of steamshipping. This could not be compensated for by the increase in local (distributory) trade, although the same developments stimulated long-distance pilgrimage, which became cheaper and shorter. These developments might also explain the slower urban growth of Jeddah in comparison to other Ottoman port cities. After 1916, the language of modernisation, possibly as well as the overall vision of a modern city, still very much resembled comparable developments in the former Ottoman realms. Nevertheless, the divergences also became clearer, notably in regard to issues pertaining to notions of religious propriety.[112]

110 Frederick Anscombe, *The Ottoman Gulf: The Creation of Kuwait, Saudi Arabia, and Qatar* (New York and Chichester: Columbia University Press, 1997), p. 51f; Claudia Ghrawi, 'Saudi Arabia's Urban Revolution: Oil Urbanization and Popular Politics in al-Aḥsāʾ (the Eastern Province), 1938–1970', PhD Thesis, Freie Universität (2017), pp. 81–6, Toby Matthiesen, 'Centre–Periphery Relations and the Emergence of a Public Sphere in Saudi Arabia: The Municipal Elections in the Eastern Province, 1954–1960', *British Journal of Middle Eastern Studies*, 42 (2014), pp. 1–19, 1–2.

111 E.g. Toksöz, *Nomads, Migrants and Cotton* pp. 88–105.

112 This has been discussed in Ulrike Freitag, 'State-Society Relations through the Lens of Urban Development' in K. Fleet and E. Boyar (eds.), *Middle Eastern and North African Societies in the Interwar Period* (Leiden [etc.]: Brill, 2018), pp. 27–53.

Overall, the pace of this urbanisation was much slower and grew more organically than the type of oil urbanisation observable in the Gulf, notably in colonial contexts such as Bahrain.[113]

Pilgrims provided another vital link between Jeddah and the wider Muslim world. Excellent studies covering the organisation of the pilgrimage as well as, more specifically, particular pilgrimage routes, have been published in the past years.[114] They usually follow different imperial concerns and routes. This book reverses the approach by adopting a local perspective of the pilgrimage, as both a religious occasion and as a vital economic concern.

Overall, this book argues that Jeddah is different from other Saudi Arabian cities, notably those in the Najd, which have come to be considered the cultural norm, even if the tribal surroundings impacted on the city and its surroundings. It is also distinct among former Ottoman cities because of the influences from the Indian Ocean world, although it shared many features, and notably the political organisation and a certain notion of urban development, with other Ottoman cities. Finally, its connections to the wider Muslim world, coupled with the rather limited access for non-Muslim foreigners, contributed to the development of the particular form of conviviality outlined above. This interaction between Muslims of different origin is quite similar in Mecca and Medina, even if the specific configurations of Medina and Mecca mean that these cities have particular identities derived from their respective holy sites and place within the Muslim imaginary.

The Chapters of This Book

The scene of the book is set in Chapter 2. Here, a broad historical survey locates Jeddah as the port of Mecca within the new Islamic

113 Fuccaro, *Histories of City and State.*

114 E.g. Bianchi, *Guests of God*; Luc Chantre, *Pèlerinages d'Empire: Une histoire européenne de pèlerinage à la Mecque* (Paris: Éditions de la Sorbonne, 2018); Sylvia Chiffoleau, 'Le pèlerinage à la Mecque à l'époque coloniale: Matrice d'une opinion publique musulmane?' in S. Chiffoleau and A. Madoeuf (eds.), *Les Pèlerinages au Maghreb et au Moyen-Orient: Espaces Publics, Espaces du Public* (Beyrouth: Institut Français du Proche-Orient, 2005), pp. 131–63; Sylvia Chiffoleau, *Le voyage à la Mecque: Un pèlerinage mondial en terre d'Islam*, Collection Histoire (Paris: Berlin, 2015); Eileen Kane, *Russian Hajj: Empire and the Pilgrimage to Mecca* (Ithaca, New York: Cornell University Press, 2015); John Slight, *The British Empire and the Hajj: 1865–1956* (Cambridge: Harvard University Press, 2015).

polity and situates it in the wider world of trade in the region, but also between the Indian Ocean and the Mediterranean world, as can be seen on Map 1 of the Rea Sea at the beginning of this book. It shows the competition between the Portuguese and the Ottoman Empire in the early sixteenth century and traces growing Western interest in the trade in spices, textiles, and coffee. The closing of the Red Sea to Western shipping is understood as a result of religious, as well as mercantile, competition. The rise of the first Saudi state and its short-lived conquest of Jeddah prompted an Ottoman-Egyptian intervention until 1840. In contrast to the Gulf, European influence in the Red Sea region north of Jeddah only became palpable in the early nineteenth century and really took off with the opening of the Suez Canal. The improvement of steamshipping technology and the construction of the Suez Canal allowed for the re-routing of inter-oceanic trade to bypass Jeddah, which was made possible politically due to uneven trade agreements between the Ottoman Empire and European states. On the other hand, regional trade also increased and pilgrimage traffic grew fairly continuously, although it also created new European interest and intervention in the holy cities due to Western fears of anti-imperial propaganda and international concern about the spread of contagious diseases. Ottoman attempts at reform were set against this background of increased intervention. The Arab Revolt of 1916 ushered in nine years of Sharifian rule, which were ended by a military defeat against ʿAbd al-ʿAzīz Āl Saʿūd after a year-long siege. The defeat was also enabled by internal mobilisation by elite members against a ruling family that had over-exploited its political and religious position and thus antagonised the competing merchant elite.

Chapters 3 and 4 introduce the human and spatial dimensions of Jeddah's history. Using different family histories and sources on migration, Chapter 3 examines the different segments of the population of Jeddah and their establishment in the city, ranging from descendants of the Prophet Muḥammad (*sharīf*, pl. *shurafāʾ*) to slaves brought to Jeddah from the African coast and the Caucasus, in addition to merchants and stranded pilgrims from many parts of the Muslim world. Chapter 4 engages with the urban space and its development during and after the Ottoman reform period, including a number of suburbs that were intimately tied to the city but differed considerably in terms of the composition of their population.

Chapter 5 examines the urban institutions that provided the basis of interaction and integration on the level of quarters and the overall city, from household and quarter to guilds and religious or cultural gatherings and ceremonies. This includes the lowest level of urban government, the quarter administration. The chapter thus engages with the question of the social fabric of Jeddah, with its inclusionary as well as exclusive aspects. Chapter 6 investigates the economic bases of Jeddah, trade and pilgrimage, and casts a more in-depth glance at the institutions linked to these two professions, which, with their subsidiary branches, maintained the city economically. Chapter 7 considers how Jeddah was ruled on the level of the entire city, and the relationship between the city and provincial, as well as imperial and later national, authorities. It discusses institutions and practices such as councils and courts, stressing the influence and increasing power of elite members during Ottoman and Sharifian times, and the changes after Ibn Saʿūd's takeover and implementation of a new regime. In all periods at least some sections of local society were closely intertwined with public institutions. This could take multiple forms, most prominently perhaps membership of local notable families, such as merchants or pilgrims' guides, in the courts and councils established in the nineteenth century, but also the permanent settlement of officials and their engagement in the Jeddah trade, thus making them members of the local economic elite.[115]

The chapter also engages with the question of the implementation of law and order. Finally, it tackles attempts to regulate immigration from Ottoman times to the early Saudi nationality law and the different rationales behind attempts to limit or rather circumscribe the presence

[115] This analysis is based on the concept of urban notable developed by Albert Hourani, 'Ottoman Reform and the Politics of Notables' in Polk and Chambers (eds.), *Beginnings of Modernization in the Middle East: The Nineteenth Century*, Conference Proceedings (Chicago: University of Chicago Press, 1968), pp. 41–68; Philip Khoury, *Urban Notables and Arab Nationalism: The Politics of Damascus 1860–1920* (Cambridge: Cambridge University Press, 1983) and Philip Khoury, 'The Urban Notables Paradigm Revisited', *Revue des mondes musulmans et de la Méditerranée*, 55–6 (1990), pp. 215–30. For the larger question of state-society relations, see Benjamin Gourisse, 'Order and Compromise: The Concrete Realities of Public Action in Turkey and the Ottoman Empire' in M. Aymes, B. Gourisse, and É. Massicard (eds.), *Order and Compromise: Government Practices in Turkey from the Late Ottoman Empire to the Early 21st Century* (Leiden and Boston: Brill, 2015), pp. 1–24, notably pp. 7–13.

of strangers, driven in Ottoman times mostly by fears of imperial intervention and attempts at poverty limitation, while, in the Saudi period, the consolidation of and control over the populations seem to have been the core agenda.

The final outlook sketches out how old Jeddah has, in recent years, been reinvented in the double context of heritigisation and attempts at somewhat opening the country culturally and portraying it as tolerant to the outside. The celebration of diversity stands in distinct contrast to a hierarchical system distinguishing between nationals on the one side and expatriates and foreigners on the other, establishing much sharper distinctions than in the imperial age. Arguably, this could be seen as a success of the building of a nation-state, as such states tend to be far more exclusive than empires – even if the exclusionary tendencies began in the nineteenth century.

2 *Between Sea and Land: Jeddah through the Ages*

This chapter situates the history of Jeddah both in relation to the holy city of Mecca and its regional setting in the Red Sea between the Mediterranean and Indian Ocean. It then outlines in more detail the macropolitical history of Jeddah and the Hijaz during the nineteenth and twentieth centuries to set the stage for the subsequent chapters.

A Port of Pilgrims and Trade

According to Islamic tradition, Jeddah was founded by the third Caliph ʿUthmān b. ʿAffān in AH 26/AD 647 as the harbour best suited to supply Mecca and make it accessible to pilgrims arriving by sea.[1] The fact that it replaced an earlier port in the vicinity, be it al-Shuʿayba or the Ptolomeian Kentos, points to the strategic importance of the location:[2] seen from Mecca, the town was situated at the end of the shortest route to the sea. Its landing area, protected by coral reefs that were traversed by a canal and lagoons, offered shelter to small boats. Due to the wind regime in the Red Sea, ships from the Indian Ocean could sail about as far as Jeddah during the latter parts of the northeast monsoon. North of Jeddah, whereby persistent northerly winds and coral reefs were common, mostly smaller vessels which could sail closer to the coast were used. Jeddah also had disadvantages: fresh water had to be brought into the town as there were no springs in the vicinity. The coastal plain was only sparsely populated, with only a few oases situated in the foothills of the mountain range which separates the coastal plain (*Tihāma*) from the highlands.

1 Jārallāh al-Qurashī al-Hāshimī, *Faḍl Jidda wa-aḥwāluhā wa-qurbuhā min Makka: Li-l-ʿallāma al-Shaykh Jārallāh Muḥammad b. Fahd al-Qurashī al-Hāshimī al-mutawaffī sanat 554 H.* (Jeddah, 1433/2012–13), p. 17.

2 G. Hawting, 'The Origin of Jedda and the Problem of al-Shuʿayba', *Arabica*, 31 (1984), pp. 318–26; Facey, *Trade and Travel in the Red Sea Region*, for a summary of local traditions in ʿAbdallāh b.ʿAbd al-ʿAzīz Bā Nāja, *Tārīkh Jidda*, pp. 10–27.

At the time of Caliph ʿUthmān, the establishment of the port would have only facilitated the arrival of a few pilgrims headed for Mecca by boat as most pilgrims arrived by caravan until at least the eleventh century. The most sustained activity was commerce, although other towns such as Mocha and Hodeida on the Yemeni coast and Massawa and Suakin on the African shore competed with Jeddah both for a dominance as entrepôts in trade from the Indian Ocean passing through the Red Sea to the Mediterranean and vice versa, as well as in regional distributions centres. Its advantage over these other nodes consisted of the connection with Mecca as the newly established centre of Muslim pilgrimage.[3] Nevertheless, reports by travellers provide vivid images of the shifting fortunes of the city, often within a short time span. Thus, while Nāṣir-i-Khusraw reported in 1050 that Jeddah was a walled town with beautiful bazaars, Ibn Jubayr, travelling in 1183, writes of a village, composed mostly of reed huts and traces of the former walls.[4]

Although the centre of the emerging Islamic empire shifted from the Hijaz to Damascus, Baghdad and, from 1458, to Constantinople, the control of Mecca as the spiritual capital of the Muslim world remained an important legitimising factor for subsequent dynasties. Because of its relative proximity and trade connections, Cairo served as a hub transmitting and overseeing imperial orders. From approximately AD 960 onwards (and until 1925) strong local rulers emerged as the emirs (also known as *sharifs*) of Mecca.[5] They rivalled their nominal overlords for influence over the local Bedouin – crucial for the caravan trade in the interior – and the revenue from the pilgrimage and the customs of Jeddah. Hence, one of the important factors for Jeddah's economic prosperity were good relations between the emirs and their overlords, and a favourable customs policy to attract international shipping.

[3] For a survey until the twelfth century, see Timothy Power, 'The Red Sea under Caliphal Dynasties, c. 639–1171', *History Compass*, 16 (2018), for a more general overview of the political history; Ulrike Freitag, 'Jidda' in K. Fleet, G. Krämer, D. Matringe, J. Nawas, and E. Rowson (eds.), *Encyclopaedia of Islam*, 3rd edn., dx.doi.org/10.1163/1573-3912_ei3_COM_32823 (accessed May 07, 2019).

[4] Muḥammad Ibn Jubayr and M. de Goeje, *The Travels of Ibn Jubayr* (Leyden: Brill, 1907), vol. 1, pp. 76–9; and for Nāṣir-i Khusraw, see Pesce, *Jiddah*, p. 25.

[5] Christiaan Snouck Hurgronje, *Mekka: Die Stadt und Ihre Herren*, 2 vols. (The Hague: Martinus Nijhoff, 1888–89), vol. 1, pp. 53–9.

Another central factor were the ups and downs of international trade. Already during the crusades, a doctrine developed according to which only Muslim seafarers were allowed to sail the Red Sea and non-Muslims were forbidden to sojourn longer than three days in any one port.[6] This corresponds to the earlier noted specifically Muslim sensitivity regarding non-Muslim access to the holy cities, in addition, obviously, to trade interests. The Portuguese arrival in the Indian Ocean, and their first entry into the Red Sea in 1513, prompted the strengthening of Jeddah's sea defences. It also prompted increased Ottoman naval engagement in the Red Sea even before the defeat of the Mamluks at their hands. This paid off when the city, now also under Ottoman control, was defended against Portuguese attacks in 1517 and 1541.[7]

Muslim merchants benefitted from the establishment of this new empire spanning large parts of Europe, West Asia, and Northern Africa. An example is the Egyptian Ismaʿīl Abū Taqiyya, active in Cairo ca. 1580 to 1625, who participated in the declining spice and the emerging coffee trade.[8] He had agents in Jeddah and Mocha, as well as in Kano (Nigeria), Istanbul, and various parts of the Egyptian Delta region. Through contact with Jewish agents, his network extended even to Italy. His story also shows that both the caravan and the sea routes were used by merchants to reach Jeddah from Egypt, while pilgrims usually travelled with a caravan.[9]

The coffee trade in particular also attracted European merchants, and Mocha, seat of Ottoman admiralty since the 1550s, became the

[6] Subhi Labib, *Handelsgeschichte Ägyptens im Spätmittelalter (1171–1517)* (Wiesbaden: Franz Steiner, 1965), pp. 61–3.

[7] Labib, *Handelsgeschichte Ägyptens im Spätmittelalter (1171–1517)*, pp. 460–1; Andreu d'Alòs-Moner, 'Conquistadores, Mercenaries, and Missionaries: The Failed Portuguese Dominion of the Red Sea', *Northeast African Studies*, 12 (2012), pp. 1–28, here pp. 8–9 contains a survey of the Portuguese missions in the region. For an excellent overview of Ottoman Indian Ocean policies and events see Giancarlo Casale, *The Ottoman Age of Exploration* (New York and Oxford: Oxford University Press, 2010) p. 4.

[8] Nelly Hanna, *Making Big Money in 1600: The Life and Times of Isma'il Abu Taqiyya, Egyptian Merchant* (Syracuse, New York: Syracuse University Press, 1998), 1st edn. pp. 64, 71, 79–81.

[9] Hanna, *Making Big Money in 1600: The Life and Times of Isma'il Abu Taqiyya, Egyptian Merchant*, pp. 61; cf. in general terms Michel Tuchscherer, 'Activités des Turcs dans le commerce de la Mer Rouge au XVIIIe Siècle' in D. Panzac (ed.), *Les Villes dans l'Empire Ottoman: Activités et sociétés* (Paris: Centre national de la recherche scientifique, 1991), pp. 321–64, 322–3, 332–46.

main trade hub in the southern Red Sea. Merchants from Gujarat and Europe could settle there and conduct business without much interference. The trade to the north, via Jeddah and Suez, remained off limits for them.[10] This divide of the Red Sea, maintained throughout the eighteenth century, also meant a cultural divide. Cairene merchants hardly travelled south of Jeddah and even Muslim merchants from India and Iran hardly travelled to the north of it. Even the purchase of coffee seems to have been divided, with Jiddawi merchants preferring to purchase it in the northern Yemeni ports of Hodeida and al-Luḥayya.[11] Thus, Jeddah became the main centre of the coffee trade in the direction of Egypt and the Ottoman Empire.[12] On the Western side of the Red Sea and opposite Jeddah, Suakin seems to have also played a role, albeit a minor one, in the trade with India. Links between merchants of the two cities, as well as with the emirs of Mecca, seem to have been fairly sustained throughout the Ottoman period.[13] Writing in 1700, the Frenchman Poncet described the trade between Suez and Jeddah:

To which port [Suez] belongs about 40 sail of ships, who trade every year between that place and Judda [Jeddah]; their outward merchandise being little or nothing but provisions and pieces of eight, and their return all sorts

[10] Giancarlo Casale, 'The Ottoman Administration of the Spice Trade in the Sixteenth Century Red Sea and Persian Gulf', *Journal of the Economic and Social History of the Orient*, 49 (2006), pp. 170–98, here particularly pp. 184–97; Michel Tuchscherer, 'Trade and Port Cities in the Red Sea: Gulf of Aden Region in the Sixteenth and Seventeenth Century' in L. Fawaz and C. Bayly (eds.), *Modernity and Culture: From the Mediterranean to the Indian Ocean* (New York: Columbia University Press, 2002), pp. 28–45, here pp. 36–8; Andrew Peacock, 'Jeddah and the India Trade in the Sixteenth Century: Arabian Context and Imperial Policy' in D. Agius, E. Khalil, E. Scerri, and A. Williams (eds.), *Human Interactions with the Environment in the Red Sea: Selected Papers of Red Sea Project VI* (Leiden: Brill, 2017), pp. 290–322, 319.

[11] Nancy Um, *The Merchant Houses of Mocha: Trade and Architecture in an Indian Ocean Port*, Publications on the Near East (Seattle: University of Washington Press, 2009), pp. 6, 42–4.

[12] André Raymond, 'A Divided Sea: The Cairo Coffee Trade in the Red Sea Area during the Seventeenth and Eighteenth Centuries' in L. Fawaz and C. Bayly (eds.), *Modernity and Culture: From the Mediterranean to the Indian Ocean* (New York: Columbia University Press, 2002), pp. 46–57; Jane Hathaway, 'The Wealth and Influence of an Exiled Ottoman Eunuch in Egypt: The Waqf Inventory of ʿAbbās Agha'', *Journal of the Economic and Social History of the Orient*, 37 (1994), pp. 293–317.

[13] Andrew Peacock, 'Suakin: A Northeast African Port in the Ottoman Empire', *Northeast African Studies*, 12 (2012), pp. 29–50.

of spices, muslins, silks, precious stones, pearls and amber-grease, musk, coffee and many other drugs; which are brought by the trading vessels which come yearly from India to Mocha and Judda, and transported by land on camels to Cairo and Alexandria.[14]

The Ottoman traveller Evliya Çelebi described Jeddah, which he visited in 1670–71, as a large port serving India, Yemen, Aden, Basra, Lahsa (al-Aḥsā᾽), Habeş (the capital of which was Suakin[15]), and Suez. What he calls a large fortress must have been the city walls, within which a smaller fortress, seat of the governor and military, was situated. The town had 300 shops of various sizes. A new large *khān*, built by the then ruling governor, contained shops as well as warehouses. He also describes seven further *khān*-s and a number of mosques and smaller masjids.[16] Using the term 'oquel' (*wikāla*) for the building which Çelebi had termed *khān*, Poncet described an impressive structure 'built with a large apartment three stories high at each corner, with a court in the middle. The lowest story is to lay up the stores and provisions; passengers make use of the upper floors.'[17]

Given the apparently advantageous prices in Jeddah, European merchants since the late seventeenth century repeatedly tried to trade directly with the city. These attempts were initially repelled, probably due to the fear of competition by local merchants and the emir alike.[18]

14 William Foster, *The Red Sea and Adjacent Countries at the Close of the Seventeenth Century as Described by Joseph Pitts, William Daniel and Charles Jacques Poncet*, Works Issued by the Hakluyt Society (Nendeln: Kraus Reprint, 1967), 2nd ser., no. 100, pp. 63–4; c.f. Jane Hathaway, 'The Wealth and Influence of an Exiled Ottoman Eunuch in Egypt: The Waqf Inventory of ʿAbbās Agha'', *Journal of the Economic and Social History of the Orient*, 37 (1994), pp. 293–317.

15 For an account of Suakin in the seventeenth and eighteenth centuries; cf. Peacock, *Suakin*, pp. 38–43. On the administrative entanglements, cf. Shawqī al-Jamal, 'Wilāyat al-Ḥabash al-ʿuthmāniyya bayn Iyālat Jidda, wa-l-idāra al-miṣriyya (1881–1885)', *al-Dāra*, 22 (1417/1996), pp. 178–202.

16 Seyit Ali Kahraman, *Evliyâ Çelebi Seyahatnâmesi*, 2 vols. (Istanbul: Yapı Kredi Yayınları, 2011), vol. 2, pp. 870–1. On his journey, cf. Suraiya Faroqhi, 'Red Sea Trade and Communications as Observed by Evliya Çelebi (1671–72)', *New Perspectives on Turkey*, 5–6 (1991), pp. 87–105.

17 Foster, *The Red Sea and Adjacent Countries*, p. 157. cf. Chapter 4.

18 René Barendse, *Arabian Seas 1700–1763*, 4 vols. (Leiden [etc.]: Brill Academic Publishers, 2009), p. 211, gives 1680 as the date of the first British sailing to Jeddah; cf. André Raymond, *Artisans et commerçants au Caire au XVIIIe siècle* (Damas: Institut Français de Damas, 1973–4), pp. 120–3. Although he gives later (and for the massacre wrong) dates.

In 1719, a British merchant made it to Jeddah but was unsuccessful in selling his textiles. Six years later the Ottoman authorities seem to have accepted the presence of Western merchants as normal, ordering their local representatives not to demand special customs from them when they were purchasing coffee.[19] By 1725, both the Emir and the Ottoman governor sent an envoy to Mocha, requesting the British and Dutch to establish a factory in Jeddah. In spite of reservations, a Scottish supercargo sailed to Jeddah with great success. However, upon repetition of the expedition a year later, in June 1727, disaster struck: When lascars, who had died on board and were buried ashore were washed up by the sea, a rumour spread that the Christian merchants had murdered their Muslim employees. This resulted in the murder of seven Britons. In addition to a huge compensation, the British were forthwith assigned their own separate quarters, which were heavily guarded.[20] This separate factory still existed when Khoja ʿAbd al Karīm visited from Iran in 1742.[21] However, attempts by Indian and European merchants to break the monopoly of Cairene merchants over the run between Cairo and Jeddah in the eighteenth century failed, even when Egyptian authorities supported such European efforts in the 1770s, possibly to lower transport fares.[22] The Jeddah trade in the eighteenth century served Cairo, the pilgrims,

19 I owe this information to Professor Henning Sievert of Heidelberg University, email, November 20, 2017.

20 Barendse, *Arabian Seas 1700–1763*, pp. 212–4, who dates the event, however, to 1726. A first-hand account of the murder can be found in IOR, Orme Ms OV 183. vol. 5, fol. 103–46. The incident does not seem to have found its way into local chronicles, see ʿAbdallāh b.ʿAbd al-ʿAzīz Bā Nāja, *Tārīkh Jidda*, pp. 338–9.

21 Mohammed Abdul Karim, *Voyage de l'Inde à la Mekke: Par A'bdoûl-Kérym, favori de Tahmâs-Qouly-Khân extrait et traduit de la version anglaise de ses mémoires avec des notes géographiques, littéraires, & C.* (Paris: L'Imprimerie de Crapelet, 1797), pp. 200.

22 Raymond, *Artisans et Commerçants*, pp. 151–5; Mordechai Abir, 'The "Arab Rebellion" of Amir Ghalib of Mecca (1788–1813)', *Middle Eastern Studies*, 7 (1971), pp. 185–200, here pp. 190–1; and Daniel Crecelius, 'A Late Eighteenth-Century Austrian Attempt to Develop the Red Sea Trade Route', *Middle Eastern Studies*, 30 (1994), pp. 262–80. For the attempt by ʿAlī Bek al-Kabīr to open direct links between Egypt and India and the resistance of the Meccan Emir to this; cf. ʿAbdallāh b.ʿAbd al-ʿAzīz Bā Nāja, *Tārīkh Jidda*, pp. 345–9; and Ḥussām ʿAbd al-Muʿṭi, *al-ʿAlāqāt al-miṣriyya al-ḥijāziyya fī 'l-qarn al-thāmin ʿashar* (Cairo: al-Haiʾa al-Miṣriyya al-ʿĀmma li-l-Kitāb, 1999), pp. 37–44; Carsten Niebuhr, *Reisebeschreibung nach Arabien und andern umliegenden Ländern* (Zürich: Manesse, 1992/1774), pp. 279–81.

the other Red Sea ports from Suakin south, and finally, via the pilgrimage, the merchants of Aleppo.[23]

The increased European presence in the southern Red Sea and their interest in trading directly with Jeddah prompted the Ottoman government to assume a more direct role in the appointments of the governors of Jeddah. The administrative importance of Jeddah was further enhanced by the early eighteenth century, even if the governors of Egypt still seem to have maintained a say in the appointment of the governors of the Habeş province. Egypt also had to foot the bill for Jeddah's defence. The Ottoman troops that had been sent from Egypt to Jeddah played an important role in the provisioning of the Hijaz as well as in the Red Sea trade, not least because they were exempt from the customs of all harbours in the Red Sea. This added another source of competition for the sharifs of Mecca.[24]

The volatility of the economy of Jeddah and the Red Sea became evident during the turbulent end of the eighteenth century. The Napoleonic expedition to Egypt (1798–1801), the Ottoman re-conquest of Egypt and the expansion of Wahhabi forces in the Hijaz (1803–13) caused trade and pilgrimage to decline dramatically. This was in part due to the military events in Egypt, but also to the British blockade of the Red Sea trade.[25] Incidentally, in 1801 (i.e. immediately after the departure of the French forces from Egypt), the Red Sea trade once again picked up, although it suffered a number of setbacks until 1833/34 which corresponded to problems in the region, mostly caused by the fight against the Emir of Najd, but by also internal upheavals.[26] The close connection between Hijaz and Egypt beyond the level of political rule and trade become clear from an anecdote related by the contemporary Egyptian historian al-Jabartī. He documents how a Maghrebi *shaykh* called al-Kīlānī (probably the dialectic rendering of al-Jīlānī

[23] For details Barendse, *Arabian Seas 1700–1763*, pp. 215–21; cf. Niebuhr, *Reisebeschreibung nach Arabien*, p. 280.

[24] ʿAbd al-Muʿṭī, *al-ʿAlāqāt al-miṣriyya al-ḥijāziyya*, pp. 51–3. None of this is discussed in Abdulraḥmān Alorabi, 'The Ottoman Policy in the Hejaz in the Eighteenth Century: A Study of Political and Administrative Developments, 1143–1202 A.H./1731–1788 A.D.', PhD Thesis, University of Utah (1988).

[25] ʿAbd al-Muʿṭī, *al-ʿAlāqāt al-miṣriyya al-ḥijāziyya*, pp. 180–2.

[26] Charles Issawi, *The Fertile Crescent 1800–1914: A Documentary Economic History*, Studies in Middle Eastern History (New York: Oxford University Press, 1988), pp. 176–7. For an overview of historical events, see Alexei Vassiliev, *The History of Saudi Arabia* (London: Saqi Books, 2000), pp. 158–64.

and hence possibly member of a prominent Cairene and Jiddawi merchant family of Maghrebi descent) learned about the French occupation of Egypt while in the Hijaz, where the news had 'deeply disturbed' people, who 'raised a cry in the Sanctuary and stripped the Kaʿba. This shaykh began to preach to the people, summoning them to a Holy War ... '. According to him, a group of about 600 volunteers travelled to Egypt, joined other forces and fought the French, albeit to little effect.[27]

Between Saudi and Egyptian Rule (1803–1840)

In 1803, Wahhabi forces from Najd occupied Mecca and laid siege to Jeddah, which was only temporarily relieved by Ottoman forces. The respite was brief and in 1805–6, Emir Ghālib succumbed to Wahhabi pressure and surrendered. Until 1813 a peculiar constellation emerged, described by the Spanish explorer and soldier Domingo Francisco Jorge Badia y Leblich, aka Ali Bey, who visited Jeddah in 1807: The emir of Mecca exercised de facto control in Mecca and the Hijaz, the name of the Ottoman sultan was mentioned in Friday prayers, and the Saʿūdī emir controlled the situation militarily.[28] Locally, Islamic rules were applied stringently. al-Ḥaḍrāwī, writing in 1863/64 bemoaned that 'the Sharif ordered an end to the music played for him and the governor of Jeddah, until God ended this calamity'.[29] The Egyptian historian al-Jabartī reported more sympathetically on the resultant cancellation of 'unlawful taxes and acts of injustice' because the emir of Meccah ' ... had exceeded the (prescribed) limits in such things; they would even take five French riyāls from a dead man.'[30] Ali Bey confirms the widespread use of extortionary practices.[31]

27 ʿAbd al-Raḥmān al-Jabartī, *ʿAbd al-Raḥmān al-Jabartī's History of Egypt* (Stuttgart: Franz Steiner, 1994), vol. 3, p. 70; cf. pp. 90, 145.

28 Domingo Badia y Leblich, *Travels of Ali Bey in Morocco, Tripoli, Cyprus, Egypt, Arabia, Syria, and Turkey, between the Years 1803 and 1807*, 2 vols. (London: Longman, Hurst, Rees, Orme, and Brown, 1816), p. 63, for the period; see Snouck Hurgronje, *Mekka. Die Stadt und Ihre Herren*, pp. 144–55.

29 al-Ḥaḍrāwī al-Makkī al-Shāfiʿī, *al-Jawāhir al-muʿadda fī faḍā'il Judda*, p. 42, for the entire episode, pp. 36–42. For a contemporary Western account, see Louis Alexandre Olivier de Corancez, *The Founders of Saudi Arabia: The History of the Wahabis from Their Origin until the End of 1809* (Garnet: Reading, 1995); cf. Vassiliev, *History of Saudi Arabia*, pp. 98–105, 140–6.

30 al-Jabartī, *ʿAbd al-Raḥmān al-Jabartī's History of Egypt*, vol. 4, p. 6.

31 Badia y Leblich, *Travels of Ali Bey*, pp. 121–2.

Viscount Valentia, a British explorer and cartographer in the service of the East India Company visited Jeddah in 1805–6 (i.e. during Wahhabi dominance in the Hijaz) at a time when the Albanian officer Mehmed Ali (arab. Muḥammad ʿAlī) was establishing himself as governor of Egypt. Viscount Valentia reflects on the troubled political situation, showing the rivalling French, British, and Italian designs for the Red Sea. He documents that the East India Company (EIC) at that time already had a local agent, a certain Hammed Nasser, who was his assigned interlocutor, rather than a certain Ibrahim Jelani (Ibrāhīm Jīlānī), whom he describes as a leading merchant in Jeddah.[32] Jīlānī was a descendant of a merchant family from Fez, which had, like a number of other families from that town, migrated to Cairo in the early eighteenth century. Some family members moved from there into the lucrative Red Sea trade and settled in Jeddah and Mocha, where they acted as agents for Egyptian and Indian merchants.[33]

The EIC 'Agency' described by Onley was hence probably simply the presence of a local trade delegate who acted as an 'agent' (*wakīl*).[34] Whether the agent was permanently settled or only present during the trading season remains open. Incidentally, it would seem that Ali Bey, who apparently travelled in the service of the French, called on a certain Sidi Mohamed Nas, quite likely the same as the aforementioned Hammed Nasser (Muḥammad Nāṣir?).[35] It would not have been unusual for an agent to act for multiple interests, and the travelogues cited give us an early sense of the European competition in the Red Sea.

[32] Viscount Valentia, Earl of Mountnorris (George Annesley), *Voyages and Travels to India, Ceylon, the Red Sea, Abyssinia, and Egypt in the Years 1802,1803,1804,1805, and 1806*, vol. 3 (London, 1809), pp. 301–33; and the episode regarding the expulsion of the Ottoman governor probably occurred in 1800, see Abir, *The 'Arab Rebellion'*, p. 194. Viscount Valentia is discussed very briefly in Pesce, *Jiddah*, pp. 36–7, where an overview of other Western travellers can also be found in pp. 27–57.

[33] Ḥussām ʿAbd al-Muʿṭī, *al-ʿĀʾila wa-l-tharwa: al-Buyūt al-tijāriyya al-maghrabīyya fī Miṣr al-ʿuthmāniyya* (Cairo: al-Haiʾa al-Miṣriyya al-ʿĀmma li-l-Kitāb, 2008), pp. 272, 277; cf. Raymond, *Artisans et Commerçants*, pp. 470–6. A Jīlānī is mentioned in Gotha Ms. orient. A 2837, 134, letter to Ṣāliḥ Abū Qaṣīṣa, Shawwāl 10, 1210/April 18, 1796. I owe this reference to Boris Liebrenz.

[34] James Onley, *The Arabian Frontier of the British Raj: Merchants, Rulers, and the British in the Nineteenth-Century Gulf* (New York: Oxford University Press, 2007), p. 18, table 4. In 1800–1, British suggestions to open a factory were rejected by Sharif Ghalib, see Abir, *The 'Arab Rebellion'*, pp. 194–5.

[35] Badia y Leblich, *Travels of Ali Bey*, p. 39, on al-Jīlānī p. 44.

This foreshadowed the growing British interest in the Red Sea that eventually resulted in the occupation of Aden in 1839. It was crucial for the future development of Jeddah that the EIC fashioned itself as a protector of Indian merchant capital.[36]

The Wahhabi incursion severely affected the pilgrimage from Ottoman lands, and hence also the official subsidies.[37] In spite of al-Jabartī's measured comments, trade also suffered. Ali Bey noted that the earlier centre of Suez was a small town 'falling into ruins'.[38] In contrast, Jeddah was surrounded by a 'good wall' – unsurprisingly, as it had been restored to fight the Wahhabis – and its markets were 'well supplied', although the goods were expensive.[39] However, he remarked,

> These people were once much richer; but the war with the Wehhabites has impoverished them; because they have passed their nights and days during many years under arms. To this cause may also be added the war in Europe, which has paralyzed the commerce of the East; and the revolutions in Egypt, Arabia, Barbary, and also their own country . . . .[40]

The 'calamity' ended with the arrival of the new strong man of Egypt, Mehmed Ali, the powerful and very independent-minded governor of the Ottoman Empire. He came with several thousand soldiers to Jeddah in 1813, whereupon Sharif Ghālib once more changed sides and swore allegiance. al-Jabartī chronicles the more or less peaceful handover of the Hijaz which was made possible through the widespread bribery of local tribal shaykhs by the Egyptians at the instigation of Emir Ghālib.[41] This did not save the emir from arrest and exile in late 1813. He was replaced by a pliable relative of his. Jeddah became the Egyptian base for the fight against the Wahhabis. Mehmed Ali lifted a number of taxes and decreased customs in an effort to revive trade. He abolished the sharing of the Jeddah customs with the

36 On this development Reese, *Imperial Muslims*, pp. 40–63, on Mocha p. 45.

37 This might have applied more to the caravans than the sea routes, as the German traveller Ulrich Jasper Seetzen travelled from Jeddah to Mecca and Medina in 1809 and 1810, see Jutta Schienerl, *Der Weg in den Orient: Der Forscher Ulrich Jasper Seetzen: Von Jever in den Jemen (1802–1811)* Schriftenreihe des Staatlichen Museums für Naturkunde und Vorgeschichte (Oldenburg: Isensee Florian GmbH, 2000), pp. 90–1.

38 Badia y Leblich, *Travels of Ali Bey*, p. 29; and Vassiliev, *History of Saudi Arabia*, pp. 104–5.

39 Badia y Leblich, *Travels of Ali Bey*, p. 42.

40 ibid., p. 45.

41 al-Jabartī, *ʿAbd al-Raḥmān al-Jabartī's History of Egypt*, p. 239; cf. Daḥlān, *Khulāṣat al-kalām*, pp. 225–98.

emir and assigned him a monthly allowance.[42] The re-establishment of Egyptian rule revived the pilgrimage. The economic revival was further boosted by the reinstatement of Ottoman subsidies for the Bedouin, whose cooperation was needed for caravan transport and its safety. Incidentally, the Egyptian intervention resulted in the (temporary) re-assertion of the role of Egyptian merchants vis-à vis their European competitors.[43]

The almost three decades of Egyptian rule until the withdrawal in the 1840s were marked by much turbulence.[44] This was related to the war between the Egyptians and the Āl Saʿūd, but also to fighting in ʿAsīr and Yemen as well as the eventual attempt by Mehmed Ali to dispense of Sharifian rule altogether in 1836.[45] By the late 1830s, the caravan route from Egypt had been secured by Mehmed Ali, while in the interior, fighting with the revived Saudi emirate continued. Mehmed Ali established three centres of power in Medina, Mecca, and in the Yemen with a base in Mocha and then Hodeida.[46] When he withdrew in haste in 1840 and made way for a return to more direct Ottoman rule, many of the Indian merchant houses relocated to Aden, significantly accelerating this city's emergence as a major node connecting India with the Arab ports of the Red Sea.[47]

During the 'Egyptian period', the rapidly increasing number of foreign travel reports documents tensions between Cairo and Mecca and their impact of the prevailing unrest on trade.[48] They also inform us about the arrival of a number of Christians from the Ottoman world who, for the first time, settled in Jeddah. Thus, according to

42 Burckhardt, *Travels in Arabia*, pp. 417, 437.

43 Vassiliev, *History of Saudi Arabia*, pp. 147–9; and Fred Lawson, *The Social Origins of Egyptian Expansionism during the Muhammad Ali Period* (New York: Columbia University Press, 1992), pp. 74–82.

44 For an interesting documentary account for the period of Egyptian rule, see ʿAbd al-Raḥīm ʿAbd al-Raḥīm, *Muḥammad ʿĀlī wa-Shibh al-Jazīra al-ʿArabiyya 1819–1840*, 2 vols. (Cairo: Dār al-Kitāb al-Jāmiʿī, 1981).

45 The events are narrated from different perspectives in Daḥlān, *Khulāṣat al-kalām*, pp. 299–320; Ochsenwald, *Religion, Society, and the State*, pp. 131–2; and Vassiliev, *History of Saudi Arabia*, pp. 149–73.

46 Fulgence Fresnel, 'L'Arabie: Première partie', *Revue des Deux Mondes*, xvii (1839), pp. 241–57, here pp. 249–52.

47 Reese, *Imperial Muslims*, pp. 62–3.

48 For example, Eduard Rüppell, *Reise in Nubien, Kordofan und dem petträischen Arabien vorzüglich in geographisch-statistischer Hinsicht* (Frankfurt am Main: Friedrich Wilmans, 1829), pp. 234–5; and Rüppell, *Reise in Abyssinien*, p. 162.

Burckhardt, some Greek Christians erected a windmill outside of one of the gates to the North.[49]

While it seems that European vessels were now allowed to sail all the way to Suez, this did not imply that they were permitted to trade there. Rüppell writes in 1827 that a French merchant, who wanted to send coffee from Mocha to Suez and circumvent Jeddah customs, ran into serious trouble (although he attained his goal in the end). Ferret and Galinier confirmed in 1839 that foreign vessels were not allowed to take freight from Suez, while they also reported that local ships could be requisitioned in case of (military) need.[50]

The 1830–40s saw an increased Western interest in the Red Sea. The travelogues of the time abound with data on the trade of Jeddah and discussions about the potential to develop it further.[51] The British and French were busy exploring the geography of the region, as is testified by the surveys of Haines, Wellsted, and Ferret & Galinier.[52] The British in particular were actively investigating the prospects of steamshipping: In 1830, the steamer Hugh Lindsay made its first voyage to Jeddah, after the East India Company had already instituted a monthly connection from Bombay to Suez. In 1835 the British established the transport of coal between Cairo and Suez, which predicated their decision in 1837 to use the route via Suez for the mail service to India.[53] In 1843 the Peninsular and Oriental Steam Navigation Company instituted a regular mail run from India via Suez, now using larger vessels. Finally, in 1853, they abandoned smaller ships

[49] Burckhardt, *Travels in Arabia*, p. 383.

[50] Rüppell, *Reise in Nubien*, pp. 236–7.

[51] Maurice Tamisier, *Voyage en Arabie*, Reproduction of the Paris edition of 1840 (Graz: Akademische Druck- und Verlagsanstalt, 1840/1976), p. 121; and Charles d'Héricourt, *Voyage sur la Côte Orientale de la Mer Rouge, dans le Pays d'Adel et le Royaume de Choa* (Paris: Arthus Bertrand, 1841), p. 18.

[52] J. R. Wellsted, 'Observations on the Coast of Arabia between Rás Mohammed and Jiddah', *Journal of the Royal Geographic Society*, 6 (1836), pp. 51–96, Stafford Haines, 'A Description of the Arabian Coast, Commencing from the Entrance of the Red Sea, and Continuing as Far as Messenaat: ... with Some Observations Relative to Its Population, Government, Commerce and Culture', *Transactions of the Bombay Geographical Society*, 11 (1852/53), Ferret and Galinier, *Voyage en Abyssinie dans les provinces du Tigré, du Samen et de l'Ahmara* (Paris: Paulin, 1847).

[53] Jacques Jomier, *Le Maḥmal et la caravane égyptienne des pèlerins de la Mecque XIII. –XX. siècles*, Publications de l'Institut Français d'Archéologie Orientale Recherches d'Archéologie de Philologie et d'Histoire (Cairo: Imprimerie de l'Institut Français d'Archéologie Orientale, 1953), pp. 148–55.

altogether. However, steamshipping only really took off in the Red Sea with the opening of a rail connection between Suez and Alexandria in 1857. This was followed by the establishment of a range of new lines to the Indian Ocean and the Far East, as well as the opening of an Egyptian steam company in the Red Sea around 1858, initially called the Medjidieh, and later renamed as ʿAzīziyya or the Khedival line. It aimed to transport pilgrims, as well as goods to and from Yemen, Abyssinia, and the Hijaz, presumably including those which had come there from further East.[54] This development can be overstated: in 1861 only three steamers, in addition to 69 (large) sailing vessels (and an uncounted number of smaller ones), called at Jeddah.[55] With the opening of the Suez Canal in 1869, steam shipping intensified.

The French Orientalist Fulgence Fresnel was the first French consular agent and later consul in Jeddah in 1837. He noted bitterly that Mehmed Ali had given the British authorisation 'to deposit their coal wherever they wanted, and to attach to their coal-depots people of their choice'. Not only had they taken possession of Aden, they had also installed in Jeddah a 'European consul dressed in European fashion, and the canons of the Muslim fortress had to salute the English flag, hoisted above the consular building with twenty-one shots' in Jeddah.[56] Fresnel's concerns about the British coal depot do not seem to have been justified, as Aden was eventually chosen as the main coaling station where the mail run stopped regularly.[57] Jeddah probably served as a minor coaling station from the 1830s onward. This

[54] Great Britain, *Parliamentary Papers: Reports from Committees*, 18 vols. (London: Her Majesty's Stationery Office, 1831), vol. 10, pp. 743–54; P&O Heritage. 'P&O Steam Navigation Company', *poheritage.com*. www.poheritage.com/our-history/company-guides/peninsular-and-oriental-steam-navigation-company (accessed November 27, 2017); D. Kürchhoff, 'Alte und neue Handelsstraßen und Handelsmittelpunkte an den afrikanischen Küsten des Roten Meeres und des Golfes von Aden, sowie in deren Hinterländern', *Geographische Zeitschrift* ,14 (1908), pp. 251–67, here p. 253; and 'The Red Sea' in A. B. Becher (ed.), *The Nautical Magazine* (London: Brown Son & Ferguson), vol. 27, 1858, pp. 421–5, here pp. 422–3; cf. G. Dassy, *Notes on Sueis and Its Trade with the Ports of the Red Sea: With Tables of Exports and Imports, etc. for the First 6 Months of 1859* (London: Foreign and Commonwealth Office Collection, 1859).

[55] Muḥammad al-Shaʿfī, *al-Tijāra al-khārijiyya li-madīnat Jidda fī 'l-ʿahd al-ʿuthmānī 1840/1916* (Riyadh, 1428/2007), p. 49.

[56] Fresnel, *L'Arabie*, p. 256 (my translation).

[57] Henry Wise, 'Acceleration of the Overland Mails', *The Nautical Magazine and Naval Chronicle*, 13, pp. 104–5.

was initially organised through the British vice-consuls. Later, private merchants joined the business.[58]

During one of the visits of the Hugh Lindsay 1831, the then acting-agent of the EIC was replaced as the visitors found him 'in every aspect an improper person to be employed'. The new agent was 'an Armenian merchant, by name Alim Yusef', probably the same as Malem (*muʿallim* or master) Jousuf Jakoub el Bagdati (Baghdādī) who was encountered by Rüppell in the same year. Rüppell noted that el Bagdati did not know English.[59] The agent demanded and was granted a regular salary as well as the insignia of (vice-)consul. This marks the official establishment of the first Western (vice)consular agency in Jeddah.[60] The vice-consul remained the commercial agent of the EIC until 1858. When in 1838 a successor for the vice-consul arrived, this time from Britain, under the assumption that his predecessor had died, both were in for an unpleasant surprise.[61] While it was presumably al-Baghdādī's successor who donned Western clothes, the hoisting of the flag might have occurred at the date given by al-Ḥaḍrāwī, or possibly after Fresnel's arrival as consular agent. This would, however, only have been in early 1843. Before that date, another Armenian, named Georges Sarkiz and of Istanbuli origin, acted on behalf of the French whom he served later as auxiliary dragoman.[62]

58 William Ochsenwald, 'The Commercial History of the Hijaz Vilayet, 1840–1908', *Arabian Studies*, 6 (1982), pp. 57–76, here p. 72; TNA, FO 685/1/1, Stanley to Admiralty, January 26, 1860; FO 195/1415, Moncrieff to Foreign Office, May 4, 1882; FO 195/1451, Moncrieff to Foreign Office 28 July 1883; FO 195/2061 Devey to Foreign Office December, 1899; FO 195/2286, Monahan to Emb. Const., April 10, 1908; and MAE, CADN, Art. 4 Suret to Direction des Consulats March 1, 1879.

59 Minute of Earl Clare, Governor of Bombay, subscribed to by the Board, July 14, 1831, in Great Britain, *Parliamentary Papers: Reports from Committees*, 18 vols. (London: Her Majesty's Stationery Office, 1831), vol. 10, pt. 2, pp. 751–2, quote p. 752; and Rüppell, *Reise in Abyssinien*, vol.1, p. 159; cf. IOR, F/4/1440, 56916, cf. Pol. Dept. Bombay to Court of Directors, May 14, 1833; and TNA, FO 905/37 'History of British Representation in Jedda Up to 1930', Sir Andrew Ryan, March 22, 1936.

60 IOR, F/4/1440/56916, Sutherland, Bombay to Court of Directors, May 14, 1833; and R/19/1, Ogilvie to Campbell, March 31, 1838.

61 Ulrike Freitag, 'Helpless Representatives of the Great Powers?: Western Consuls in Jeddah, 1830s to 1914', *The Journal of Imperial and Commonwealth History*, 40 (2012), pp. 357–81, here pp. 359–60.

62 Fulgence Fresnel to Foreign Ministry, October 30, 1842, Archives du Ministère des Affaires Etrangères, Centre des Archives Diplomatiques de Nantes, Constantinople, Ambassade, Série D: Correspondance avec les Echelles, Djeddah 1.

The extent to which the establishment of the French consulate was an attempt to keep up with the British is reflected in de Fresnel's warning of the 'threat of a protectorate much more effective and persistent than that of the Turks, - the protectorate of the East India Company'.[63] His successor, Rochet d'Héricourt (consul 1849–54), echoed this view in an article written in 1842: 'This commerce [of the eastern coast of the Red Sea] is not rich enough to lure France with the bait of great profits; it has only the importance of its [and here one should add: geostrategic, U.F.] position, if I may express myself'.[64]

Ottoman Rule in the Age of Reform (Tanzimat)

Restoration and International Encroachment (1840–1858)

As a consequence of Ibrāhīm Pasha's defeat in Syria at the hand of Ottoman and Western forces, Egyptian forces withdrew from Yemen and Najd. In August of 1840, Emir Muḥammad b. ʿAwn, at the time a prisoner in Cairo, was returned to the Emirate of Mecca and witnessed the Ottoman restoration. The political history of the restored Ottoman rule in the Hijaz has already been well researched by scholars such as William Ochsenwald, al-Amr, and Numan. Thus the following historical account focuses on those events that are crucial for the following chapters. It covers the period known as the Tanzimat in Ottoman history for its thorough administrative reorganisation and attempts at modernising the Ottoman Empire, which manifested itself for example in massive projects of urban expansion and remodelling (cf. Chapter 4).

After the resumption of more direct Ottoman rule, the Hijaz initially formed the nucleus of an entity known as Ḥabeş Eyalet. Probably by 1865, it became the Vilayet of Jeddah and, in 1871, the Hijaz Vilayet.[65] The most salient features of renewed Ottoman control were

[63] Fresnel, *L'Arabie*, p. 256.

[64] Charles d'Héricourt, 'Lettre de M. Rochet d'Héricourt à M. d'Avezac Moka, le 26 mai 1842', *Bulletin de la Société de Géographie*, 19 (2ième série), pp. 118–27.

[65] Information on dates and borders varies greatly in the literature, c.f. Ochsenwald, *Religion, Society, and the State*; Saleh al-Amr, 'The Hijaz under Ottoman Rule 1869/1914: Ottoman Vali, the Sharif of Mecca, and the Growth of British Influence', PhD Thesis, University of Leeds (1974); and Nurtāç Numan, 'The Emirs of Mecca and the Ottoman Government of Hijaz, 1840–1908', License Thesis, Boğaziçi Üniversitesi (2006). On the administrative

the installation of a new line of emirs in Mecca, and the appointment of Ottoman governors who initially resided in Jeddah. Sometime after 1852 the then governor Aḥmad ʿIzzat Pasha was ordered to move the provincial capital to Mecca in order to exert more control over the Emir who was quite intent on pursuing an independent policy.[66] In 1860 the construction of a government building in Mecca started. Even if completion of the building took twenty years, in part due to opposition by the Emir, the governor began to spend more time in the holy city. According to French sources, from 1870–1 onwards the official seat of the governors became Mecca.[67] Their prolonged periods of absence from Jeddah resulted in the increased importance of the office of kaymakam (*qāʾimaqām; in* 1871: *mutaṣarrif*) of Jeddah.[68] As will be shown in Chapter 7, the urban governance of Jeddah was impacted by various waves of provincial and municipal reform. A range of other administrative measures, but also wider regional and global developments, impacted the Hijaz. This is most clearly exemplified in the Mecca uprising of 1855 and the Jeddah massacre of 1858, both of which will be discussed below.

During the Tanzimat era, Mecca remained important in terms of the Islamic legitimacy of the Ottoman Empire, both internally and externally. Its prominence increased notably in the latter decades of the century due to the development of pan-Islamism and the further extension of

changes, see Andreas Birken, *Die Provinzen des Osmanischen Reichs* (Unpubl., 1976), pp. 252–4, 4. I am following here Pétriat, *Le Négoce des Lieux Saints*, pp. 27. ʿAbdallāh b.ʿAbd al-ʿAzīz Bā Nāja, *Tārīkh Jidda* takes issue with the connection of Jeddah with the Ḥabeş eyalet, although his discussion, chronologically placed after the Napoleonic expedition, relates mostly to the sixteenth century, see pp. 243–9.

66 al-Amr, *The Hijaz under Ottoman Rule*, pp. 53–9; and Numan, *The Emirs of Mecca*, pp. 71–82. My reading of the relationship between emirs and governors is more conflictual than that recently put forward by M. Çiçek, 'Negotiating Power and Authority in the Desert: The Arab Bedouin and the Limits of the Ottoman State in Hijaz, 1840–1908', *Middle Eastern Studies*, 52 (2016), pp. 260–79.

67 Centre des Archives Diplomatiques de Nantes, 2_MI_3293, Étude sur l'organisation administrative et judiciaire de la ville de Djeddah, p. 1.

68 Ahmed Osmanoğlu, 'Hicaz Eyaletinin Teşekkülü (1841–1864)', MA Thesis, Marmara University (2004), p. 40; and Numan, *The Emirs of Mecca*, p. 61. For administrative transformations in the 1870s and 1980s see the documents in Suhayl Ṣabbān, *Murāsalāt al-Bāb al-ʿĀlī ilā wilāyat al-Ḥijāz (Makka al-Mukarrama, al-Madīna al-Munawwara) fī ʾl-fatra min 1283h ilā 1291h* (Mecca: Mu'assasat al-Furqān li-l-Turāth al-Islāmī, 2004), pp. 290–4, 302–3.

European rule over Muslims. Jeddah's importance as a port for pilgrims, merchants, and the military grew with the introduction of steamshipping although, as will be seen, unequally as regards these different functions. From the 1850s onward, steamers were used to transport pilgrims from Suez. In 1882/1884 the Egyptian *maḥmal*, a ceremonial litter containing a cover of the Kaʿba as well as gifts to the sharifs (see Chapter 5), was transported by steamer rather than with the traditional caravan for the first time. The new independence from the monsoon winds, as well as the opening of the Suez Canal, meant that the number of pilgrims increased, although not in a linear fashion.[69]

In the period after 1840, Jeddah's role in the Red Sea trade changed. Officially, the terms of the trade treaty of Balta Limanı now applied, reducing customs duties, though the British vice-consul reported difficulties with its implementation up until the mid-1850s.[70] More important was that, in the context of what Miran has called the 'Red Sea boom', Jeddah did not recover its earlier role as a major entrepôt in the trade between the Indian Ocean and the Red Sea.[71] It remained a major distributive port in the Red Sea region as well as a major port of call for the transit trade until the late 1870s, and as such even experienced an upturn. After this time, however, it lost a significant amount of its trade to Aden and Hodeida. This might be due to technological changes allowing smaller steamers to travel without coaling stops between Aden and Suez, but also reflects the ascendancy of British-controlled Aden. The trade of Jeddah recovered only after 1903.[72] This resulted in a reconfiguration of the merchant communities in the Red Sea area which also influenced the Jeddah elite, as discussed in Chapter 6.

Particularly noteworthy was the increasing number of British-protected Indian merchants. Whereas Burckhardt reported in 1814 that

69 Rita Stratkötter, *Von Kairo nach Mekka: Sozial- und Wirtschaftsgeschichte der Pilgerfahrt nach den Berichten des Ibrāhīm Rifʾat Bāšā: Mirʾāt al-Ḥaramain*, Islamkundliche Untersuchungen (Berlin: Klaus Schwarz, 1991), Bd. 145, pp. 78–9; Ochsenwald, *Religion, Society, and the State*, pp. 60–2; and Jomier, *Le Maḥmal et la Caravane Égyptienne*, pp. 150–1.

70 TNA, FO 195/375, Cole to Foreign Office, August 4, 1854.

71 Miran, *Red Sea Translocals*, p. 134.

72 Ochsenwald, *The Commercial History*; Colette Dubois, 'The Red Sea Ports during the Revolution in Transportation, 1800–1914' in L. Fawaz and C. Bayly (eds.), *Modernity and Culture: From the Mediterranean to the Indian Ocean* (New York: Columbia University Press, 2002), pp. 58–74; Pétriat, *Le Négoce des Lieux Saints*, particularly pp. 177–9; and Miran, *Red Sea Citizens*, pp. 66–9.

Banyans only visited Jeddah during the monsoon but did not settle, Rochet d'Héricourt remarked in 1842 that foreign trade in Jeddah, just as in Hodeida, Oleia (probably al-Luḥayya), Suakin, and Mocha, was represented by 'Hindu merchants known under the name of Banyans'.[73] This observation is echoed by Hamilton's observation that 'of the present population (1854) 1,500 are Indians, including many of the wealthiest merchants, nearly the whole trade of Jidda being in the hands of British subjects'.[74] While there were many Muslim traders of Arab and other descent, and while the religious affiliation of the Indian traders is unknown, Burckhardt had already noted the presence of more than 100 (non-Banyan, i.e. Muslim) Indian families. Given this wider trend, it comes as no surprise that in the 1850s an Indian named Faraj Yusr was the wealthiest merchant of Jeddah.[75]

The other change was the – arguably much slower and numerically far less significant – expansion of Greek merchants in the Red Sea. This seems to have occurred in the wake of the expansion of Mehmed Ali, when earlier discriminatory measures such as the wearing of a special dress were abolished.[76] By 1856 a Greek network based in Jeddah (see Chapter 6), is said to have controlled about a quarter of the Red Sea trade, causing considerable resentment among the Hadhrami merchants.[77] In addition, a number of travellers and adventurers seem to have arrived in the context of the Egyptian military presence in the Hijaz. Among them was, for example, a certain Thomas-Joseph Arnaud (1812–84), a pharmacist in the army of Ibrāhīm Pasha. He later served the Imam of Yemen and, between 1838 and 1843, operated a grocery store specialising in

[73] Burckhardt, *Travels in Arabia*, p. 15; and d'Héricourt, *Lettre de M. Rochet*, p. 121 (my transl.). For Suakin, cf. Elfateh, *Suakin (Sudan) and the Colonial Architecture*, vol. 1, pp. 214–5.

[74] James Hamilton, *Sinai, The Hedjaz, and Soudan: Wanderings around the Birth-Place of the Prophet and across the Aethiopian Desert, from Sawakin to Chartum* (Reading: Garnet Publishing, 1993/1856), p. 57.

[75] Pétriat, *Le Négoce des Lieux Saints*, pp. 32–4; and William Ochsenwald, 'The Jidda Massacre', *Middle Eastern Studies*, 13 (1977), pp. 314–26, here p. 315; cf. TNA, FO 78/1538, Stanley to Foreign Office, March 13, 1860, mentioning that 'the British Trade is nearly 3/4ths that of the whole trade of the place'. For Arab traders, cf. Mubārak al-Muʿabbadī, *al-Nashāṭ al-tijārī li-minā ʾ Jidda khilāla 'l-ḥukm al-ʿuthmānī al-thānī 1256 h./1840 m. –1335 h./1916 m.* (Jeddah: al-Nādī al-Adabī al-Thaqāfī bi-Jidda, 1993), pp. 190–200.

[76] Burckhardt, *Travels in Arabia*, pp. 14–15.

[77] Pétriat, *Le Négoce des Lieux Saints*, pp. 73–4.

candles in Jeddah before venturing on various explorations with Jeddah as his base until 1849.[78]

The French diplomat Arthur de Gobineau, who passed through Jeddah in 1854 en route to Teheran, gives an interesting description of the local situation and mood. He describes the increase in European style steamers owned and manned by Indians and Arabs. What, according to him, bothered the local population most was the enormous capacity of these new boats, together with their ability to sail all year round, which caused loss of employment.[79] To him, this, rather than religious resentment, was the real reason for the hatred of the (Western and Indian) foreigner which had been developing in the region for a few years. While de Gobineau's comments might well be reflective of what he observed and learned in Persia – given that his stay in Jeddah was extremely brief – his text certainly reflects a sense of anger and dissatisfaction also discernible elsewhere. This resulted, in his view, partly from the presence of Western representatives in the holy land of Muslims, especially at a time when Western powers became more visible in general, and were visible locally through steamships and the consulates. The occupation of Aden in 1839 had accentuated the European presence in terms of the wider Ottoman and Indian Ocean world, and European military interventions in places such as Greece or the Persian Gulf were widely known. Locally, the resurgence of Ottoman control did not go down well with the Meccan emirs, nor with the tribes of the Hijaz, a topic which will not be pursued further in the context of this book. Many Meccans in particular felt more at ease with Egyptian rule, not only because of the change of the ruling sharif but also for reasons of cultural proximity and expected economic benefit.[80] In addition, the Ottoman reforms, which partly amounted to increased central control and regionally translated into a war effort directed at the Yemen, caused significant disquiet.

78 See Claude Schopp, Chronologie de Thomas Joseph Arnaud, appended in the 2011 edition of Thomas-Joseph Arnaud, *Voyage au pays de la reine de Saba: Suivi de Thomas-Joseph Arnaud et Alexandre Vayssière en Égypte. Préface d'Alexandre Dumas*, Présenté par Claude Schopp (Paris: Pygmalion, 2011), pp. 259–63.

79 Arthur de Gobineau, *Trois ans en Asie* (Paris: Ernest Leroux, 1905), pp. 53–4, quotation p. 54 (my transl.).

80 See the interesting observations by Hamilton, *Sinai, The Hedjaz, and Soudan*, pp. 78–9.

Resulting from this larger panorama, the first palpable signs of protest were directed by members of the military against the hapless representatives of the great powers in Jeddah. In 1838, soldiers accosted the British vice-consul Ogilvie in the bazaar of Jeddah.[81] A decade later the French consul, Fulgence de Fresnel, was forced to leave Jeddah after an attack, again by soldiers.[82] That such acts were part of a wider sense of change and competition becomes clear when examining the following incident: In 1853 the British vice-consul reported that the chief tax collector and market inspector of Jeddah (the *muḥtasib*) ʿAbdallāh Agha was at the same time the agent of the Emir of Mecca, who was himself active in the India trade. The letter insinuates that it was at least partly as a result of commercial rivalry that the *muḥtasib* had repeatedly forced the Indian merchants to pay sums of money beyond any official dues, which the British representative was keen to prevent, causing 'a violent hatred' on the part of the *muḥtasib*.[83]

Matters came to a head in 1855. For a number of years, the Ottomans had begun to limit slave trade under massive foreign, notably British, pressure.[84] In a situation in which tensions between Emir ʿAbd al-Muṭṭalib and the Ottoman governors were already high and the Empire was weakened by the Crimean War, merchants in Jeddah contacted leading scholars and sharifs in Mecca in April 1855. They had received the worrying information that the slave trade might become completely prohibited by the Ottomans. Their letter expressed their concern and asked for guidance. The emir seized the moment to organise anti-Ottoman sentiment, resulting eventually in an open confrontation and a call for jihad against the Ottomans. According to the French consul, an Indian emigré by the name of 'Cheikh Fadl' was involved. This was none other than Shaykh Faḍl al-ʿAlawī b. Sahl, son

81 IOR, R/19/1, Ogilvie to Campbell (Cairo), October 31, 1838.

82 CADN, Const. Amb. D-Djeddah 1, de Montbrun to Amb. Const., June 8, 1856; TNA, FO 195/375, Page to Amb. Const., October 24, 1856; A. Dumas à Jules Martinet, pp. 7–35 in Arnaud, *Voyage au Pays de la Reine*, here pp. 19–21; and Freitag, *Helpless Representatives*, pp. 361, 368.

83 TNA, FO 195/375, Power of the Sherif's agent Abdallah Aga: Extract of Despatch from Consul C. Cole at Jeddah, November 11, 1853.

84 Ehud Toledano, *The Ottoman Slave Trade and Its Suppression: 1840–1890* (Princeton: Princeton University Press, 1982), pp. 91–123. For the following see also ʿAbdallāh b.ʿAbd al-ʿAzīz Bā Nāja *Tārīkh Jidda*, pp. 366–9. For Daḥlān who witnessed the events local rivalries and relations between Ottoman governors and emirs are more central, Daḥlān, *Khulāṣat al-kalām*, pp. 316–18.

of an influential Muslim leader in the Calicut region who had been forced into exile by the British in 1852.[85]

The revolt spread to other parts of the Hijaz, including Jeddah, a major entry point for slaves. Key demands of the insurgents were, besides their own exoneration and the retreat of Ottoman forces from Mecca, the expulsion of all Christians (who were accused of having violated the sacrality of the Meccan *ḥaram*), including their representatives, from the Hijaz. The revolt was eventually suppressed militarily and the Emir deported and replaced. Incidentally, and before the revolt was subdued, the Ottoman military commander was willing to agree to all demands except for the expulsion of the European consuls and their protégés.[86] The contentious question ostensibly at the heart of the troubles, the slave trade, continued unhindered after the events, which led contemporary observers as well as scholars to assume that the Ottomans had primarily intended to replace the Emir. They might have not dared to tackle the sensitive and economically important question of slave trade, which also served as a pretext for a similar revolt in the port of Massawa, leased to Egypt since 1846 and only for a brief period in 1864–5 reverted to the Hijaz.[87]

[85] CADN, Const. Amb. D-Djeddah 1, Dequié to Amb. Const., November 9, 1855. About Sayyid Faḍl, cf. Ulrike Freitag, *Indian Ocean Migrants and State Formation in Hadhramaut: Reforming the Homeland*, Social, Economic, and Political Studies of the Middle East and Asia (Leiden and Boston: Brill Academic Publishers, 2003), vol. 87, pp. 79–81; and Anne Bang, *Sufis and Scholars of the Sea: Family Networks in East Africa, 1860–1925*, Indian Ocean Series (London: Routledge Curzon, 2003), pp. 81–92.

[86] On these accusations which were presumably used to incite the population, see BOA, İD.22714 1 Ra 1272 (November 11, 1855). Interestingly, the Ottoman governor Kâmil Pasha (served in the Hijaz 1845 and 1853–6) had been ambassador to Berlin in 1838–9, see *Wikipedia*. 'Liste der Osmanischen Gesandten in Preußen', https://de.wikipedia.org/wiki/Liste_der_osmanischen_Gesandten_in_Preu%C3%9Fen (accessed December 26, 2017); cf. de Gobineau, *Trois Ans en Asie*, pp. 62–3.

[87] Toledano, *The Ottoman Slave Trade*, pp. 129–35; Ehud Toledano, *Slavery and Abolition in the Ottoman Middle East* (Seattle and London: Washington University Press, 1998), p. 205; Ochsenwald, *Religion, Society, and the State*, pp. 137–9; Pétriat, *Le Négoce des Lieux Saints*, pp. 28–32; and CADN, Const. Amb. D-Djeddah 1, Dequié to Amb. Const., November 4, 1855, November 9, 1855, November 16, 1855. For the link with Massawa, see Beillard to Amb. Const. December 7, 1855, and February 5, 1856; and TNA, FO 195/375, Page to Amb. Const., November 13, 1855, with the demands of the insurgents on pp. 7–8. Interestingly, Miran, *Red Sea Citizens*, does not connect the local revolt of 1853 with the slave issue.

Although the Ottomans regained the upper hand, the reports by the Western consuls indicate that the conflict between local, mainly Arab (and among them predominantly Hadhrami), merchants, and Indians protected by Britain continued. There was an attempt on the life of the British consul in May 1856 by an Albanian soldier.[88] When the Ottoman governor Kâmil Pasha, who had maintained friendly relations with the consuls, was replaced in 1856, the British acting Vice-Consul complained that he should have stayed for at least another year to calm down matters but was instead replaced by a former governor of Yemen, whom he described as ill, deaf, and 'mentally affected'. Worse still, the new governor took lodgings with ʿAbdallāh Agha (the *muḥtasib*), the very man who had, since 1853, been a suspected agent of the now-deposed emir, as well as a known opponent of the British consul.[89] It is hence not surprising that the harassment of consular officials and disputes over trade matters, such as the application of the British-Ottoman commercial treaty, continued.[90]

In June 1858 tensions exploded over the seemingly banal question of the flag under which a certain vessel was sailing.[91] Ṣāliḥ Jawhar, a merchant of Indian origin who was involved in a trade dispute with the former co-owner of the ship, changed the flag of his vessel from British to Ottoman in order to benefit from Ottoman protection. This act was endorsed by the newly created Merchant Council of Jeddah.[92]

88 CADN, Amb. Const. D-Djeddah 1, Lavalette de Monbrun to Amb. Const., June 8, 1856; and TNA, FO 195/375, Page to Amb. Const., June 9, 1856.

89 TNA, FO 195/375, Page to Amb. Const., October 27, 1856.

90 TNA, FO 195/375, Page to Amb. Const. February 13, 1857; Vice-Consul to Amb. Const., April 16, 1857; and CADN, Amb. Const. D-Djeddah 1, Lavalette de Monbrung to Amb. Const., November 20, 1856, January 19, 1857.

91 The events and sources have been discussed in detail in a number of works, so that I will give here only a very brief summary, see Ochsenwald, *The Jidda Massacre*; Pétriat, *Le Négoce des Lieux Saints*, pp. 71–122; Michael Low, 'The Mechanics of Mecca: The Technopolitics of the Late Ottoman Hijaz and the Colonial Hajj', PhD Thesis, Columbia University (2015), pp. 106–17; and Ulrike Freitag, 'Symbolic Politics and Urban Violence in Late Ottoman Jeddah' in U. Freitag, N. Fuccaro, N. Lafi, and C. Ghrawi (eds.), *Urban Violence in the Middle East: Changing Cityscapes in the Transition from Empire to Nation State*, Space and Place (New York: Berghahn Books, 2015), pp. 111–38. A contemporary local account is Daḥlān, *Khulāṣat al-kalām*, pp. 321–3; and a modern one ʿAbdallāh b.ʿAbd al-ʿAzīz Bā Nāja, *Tārīkh Jidda*, pp. 371–84.

92 Its creation is attested in BOA, A.AMD44/20 of 14 B. 1269 (April 4,1853); Suhayl Ṣabbān, *Jidda fī wathāʾiq al-arshīf al-ʿuthmānī*,(typescript, prepared as part of project of Encyclopedia of Jeddah) (n.d., 2005?), p. 87.

However, the merchant's opponent approached the British consulate for intervention. The acting Vice-Consul's substitute was the aforementioned Faraj Yusr, former head of the merchants (*shaykh al-tujjār*). As a long-standing resident of Jeddah with trading interests both with India and in the Red Sea, Faraj Yusr also held Ottoman nationality. Some of his business ventures were undertaken together with the Ottoman authorities.[93] In the years preceding 1858, he had bankrolled the Hijaz government as well as invested in a number of charitable projects, including the Jeddah water supply.[94] In contrast to Faraj Yusr, who did not achieve much and might not have been interested in a strong intervention given his entanglement with both Ottoman and British merchants, the Acting Vice-Consul had no such qualms upon his return. In a show of strength, he tried to seize the contested vessel and symbolically hoisted the British flag. Thereupon the kaymakam convened a meeting of leading merchants. That same evening all hell broke loose when a mob violently attacked the British and French consulates, as well as the trading house of Toma Sava & Co. Faraj Yusr's life was saved due to the intervention of ʿAbdallāh Naṣīf, who served as the Jeddah agent of the new Emir of Mecca. According to rumours, a connection between events in the Hijaz and the Great Indian Revolt of 1857 could not be ruled out.[95]

The violence left twenty-two people dead, among them the British and French representatives and many, mostly Christian, people under European protection. Furthermore, some were wounded and much property was looted. While the Ottoman governor hastily returned to Jeddah to restore order, the subsequent search for the culprits and their punishment was fraught by the intervention of a British captain who bombarded Jeddah, ignorant of the agreement between the Ottoman government and European embassies in Cairo. Hence two trials were held, resulting in the execution, exile, and imprisonment of commoners involved in the violence, as well as of suspected ringleaders, prime among them ʿAbdallāh al-Muḥtasib. Substantial compensation was paid to the businesses damaged by the affair.

93 Ochsenwald, *Religion, Society, and the State*, p. 172.
94 For a study of Faraj Yusr's trade and activities, see Pétriat, *Le Négoce des Lieux Saints*, pp. 42–9.
95 TNA, FO 195/579, Capt. Pullen to Sec. Admiralty, June 25, 1858.

Juan Cole was the first to draw attention to the wider conjuncture of revolts and uprisings during the mid-nineteenth century.[96] While such a broad brush necessarily obfuscates the complicated interplay of local, regional, and international factors, and while interlinkages even within the Ottoman context are often difficult to establish as Pétriat has shown, 1858 marks a symbolic shift in international power relations in the history of Jeddah and the Hijaz.[97] While the consequences for the Hijaz and for Jeddah were less dramatic than those for India or, for that matter, for Lebanon in terms of the impact of foreign rule, they marked a watershed in terms of imperial dominance. Neither the European presence nor the increasing dominance of European (or European-protected) merchants were seriously disputed again, despite the new wave of anti-Western sentiment in the late 1870s, as will be shown in the following section. Initially, however, there was a sigh of relief, with the French consul claiming in January 1859 that Europeans could now establish themselves freely on both coasts of the Red Sea, though it took a while until this actually occurred on any significant scale. Greek merchants, an important group of Western entrepreneurs, seem to have been deterred by the violence. One should, however, not overestimate proportions: visiting in 1852–3, Hamilton describes one Greek mercantile house, one wine shop and one Armenian broker as the only Christians of Jeddah.[98] Thus, the tale of the grandfather of the locally well-known Khawaja Yanni who had come to Jeddah in 1857 to establish a shipping company, escaped the massacre by swimming to an English ship, and then returned to Jeddah to open a bar somewhat romanticises the commercial importance of the Greeks.[99]

[96] Juan Cole, 'Of Crowds and Empires: Afro-Asian Riots and European Expansion, 1857–1882', *Comparative Studies in Society and History*, 31 (1989), pp. 106–33.

[97] Pétriat, *Le Négoce des Lieux Saints*, pp. 118–22. The consequences mentioned by ʿAbdallāh b.ʿAbd al-ʿAzīz Bā Nāja, *Tārīkh Jidda*, p. 384, seem less convincing: He ascribes the subsequent events in Syria and Lebanon to the Jeddah events, as well as the removal of the governorship to Mecca in order to protect him from the foreign powers (as outlined earlier, this had been decided already in the early 1850s.

[98] Hamilton, *Sinai, The Hedjaz, and Soudan*, p. 55.

[99] Hassna al-Ghamdi, 'al-Khawaja Yanni (Yanni the Westerner): An Example of Muslim-Christian Tolerance in Jeddah during the 20th Century', *Academic Journal of Interdisciplinary Studies*, 6 (2017), pp. 61–6, here p. 62. The author bases this part of her tale on a novel by Muḥammad Diyāb, *Khawāja Yannī: Riwāya*, 2nd edn. (Dubai: Madārik, 2016). I have not been able to find the name of Khristo or Dolo among those saved in 1858.

However, it is clear that after the massacre, no more international Greek merchants lived in Jeddah. The few Greeks and Italians who settled there were running bars, small shops, bakeries, or were employed by foreign companies, rather than establishing large scale merchant houses of their own. Consequently, they were not highly esteemed by the consuls.[100] In contrast, Ottoman subjects, whether of Hadhrami or Greek (often Muslim) origin, fared quite well, even if they sometimes faced fierce competition from British protected Indians and other foreign-protected traders (cf. Chapters 6, 7).[101] Overall, the massacre contributed to the image of Jeddah as a Muslim city, while Christian merchants preferred the Yemeni ports or those on the West coast of the Red Sea.

Consolidation, Transport Revolution, and Crisis (1860s to 1908)

The following two decades were marked mostly by calm and a relative dominance by the Meccan emirs over the Ottoman governors, facilitated by the long tenures of office of the former and the rapid turnover of the latter.[102] Changes in administrative personnel regularly reflected not only the usual rotation of bureaucrats but also the tensions between governors and sharifs. As will be discussed in Chapter 7, various measures of the Tanzimat were applied in the province during these decades, resulting in administrative re-orderings but also new institutions and mechanisms of governance.[103] This is reflected in the Ottoman archives which, besides a range of administrative issues, discuss relations with the Bedouin, the military measures resulting from the renewed Ottoman expansion in Yemen, and other regional issues. Nevertheless, the fear of renewed unrest lingered. This was

100 CADN, 2_MI_3228, Dubreuil to MAE, March 6, 1869; 2_MI_3229, Le Gay to Amb. Const., July 11, 1871, and September 22, 1872, Amb. Const. D-Djeddah 4, Buez to Amb. Const., March 12, 1875; TNA, FO 685/1, Stanley to Consul-General, Cairo, January 8, 1861; FO 195/1847, Richards to Amb. Const., March 14, 1894; and Pétriat, *Le Négoce des Lieux Saints*, p. 169.

101 Pétriat, pp. 169–72.

102 Ochsenwald, *Religion, Society, and the State*, pp. 164–5. A mostly reliable list of both can be found in al-Amr, *The Hijaz under Ottoman Rule*, pp. 253–4; and in al-Amr also a survey of the political history.

103 ʿAbdallāh b.ʿAbd al-ʿAzīz Bā Nāja, *Tārīkh Jidda*, pp. 386–92.

certainly a major concern not just to the foreign consuls but, more crucially, to the Ottomans. Consequently, when news of the massacre of Christians in Syria arrived in late summer 1860, the Ottomans sent extra troops to prevent another uprising.[104] Similarly, contentious questions regarding charges at the port remained and continued to occupy the foreign consuls.[105]

In the long term, the opening of the Suez Canal in 1869 can be regarded as a sea change. It improved the imperial Ottoman communications but also increased the Western presence, most notably perhaps after the British occupation of Egypt in 1882.[106] Together with the developments in steam technology, it furthered the rapid growth of sea-borne trade carried by steamers as opposed to sailing ships. While local merchants, as well as the Egyptian and Ottoman governments, invested in steamers for a time, it became clear by the 1880s that they could not compete with Western and, significantly, Indian companies, as well as private owners.[107] In the short term, the dhow traffic continued to carry an important part of the trade, notably where the distribution of goods in the region was concerned. Similarly, pilgrims did not immediately abandon the land route for the sea, and the choice was often determined by the state of security en route. Thus, there are frequent consular reports about the routes between either Mecca and Medina or between Medina and Yanbuʿ being cut by Bedouin (sometimes at the order of the sharifs) which prompted pilgrims to either take the sea route from Jeddah to Yanbuʿ and from there to Medina, or to travel by caravan.[108] Communications were much improved by the connection of Jeddah to the telegraph in 1882, although, once

[104] CADN, 2_MI3228, Rousseau to Direction Commerciale, Const., September 19, 1860, which contrasts with the optimism expressed by Sabatier a mere eighteen months earlier; cf. CADN, 2_MI_3228, Sabatier to Amb. Const., January 12, 1859.

[105] E.g. CADN, 2_MI_3228, Rousseau to Dir. des Consulats etc., Const., December 17, 1859; Monge to Amb. Const., April 23, 1863; and Pellissier to Amb. Const., September 30, 1864.

[106] The Ottoman dimension is emphasised by al-Muʿabbadī, *al-Nashāṭ al-tijārī li-minā' Jidda*, pp. 385–91.

[107] Pétriat, *Le Négoce des Lieux Saints*, pp. 142–55; cf. the figures in Ochsenwald, *Religion, Society, and the State*, p. 100, table 6.

[108] For example, CADN, 2_MI3229, Dubreuil to MAE, March 29, 1872; Buez to Min. du Commerce, February 7, 1877, February 24, 1877, December 22, 1877; and CADN, 2_MI3231, November 20, 1903, p. 19.

again, this measure did not go unchallenged by the Bedouin, who cut the cable or stole poles when in conflict with the government.[109]

Nevertheless, the carrying of pilgrims on steamers and attempts to limit this to specific companies or establish monopolies became a major issue notably after 1869. Yet this was only one aspect of a wider phenomenon that dominated international relations with regard to the Hijaz, another being the surveillance of pilgrims (and places, notably Jeddah and Mecca) with regard to hygiene and sanitation as well as to potentially anti-imperial politics.[110] The international concern with hygiene and sanitation had its background in the waves of cholera in Asia, the Middle East, and North America during the early nineteenth century (cf. Chapter 6).[111] In 1831 a Health Commission was set up in Egypt and in 1838 a Board of Health was instituted in Istanbul. Beginning in 1851, 'International Sanitary Conferences' debated how to control the global spread of diseases. Of particular importance for the Hijaz was the 1865 conference in Istanbul which decided on closer surveillance of the Red Sea route.[112] Particularly after the cholera epidemic of 1865, reports by Ottoman, Egyptian, as well as European doctors on the health situation in the Hijaz, notably during the hajj, were issued with increasing frequency, and a range of different measures to combat the disease was implemented. In this context, the consulates also employed Muslim doctors to serve in Mecca and observe conditions there, often extending their interest beyond health matters to a surveillance of political refugees from the empires and to potential anti-imperial agitation.

[109] BOA, Y.PRK.HR 89/1; and TNA, FO 195/1415, Monceriff to Dufferin, April 4, 1882, May 18, 1882, August 29, 1882; cf. Ochsenwald, *Religion, Society, and the State*, pp. 187, 214. For attacks on the telegraph see Ochsenwald, pp. 187, 214; and CADN, 2_MI3231, Letter of April 13, 1903.

[110] These issues have been thoroughly researched and will therefore be only presented very briefly here. See, for example, Huber, *Channelling Mobilities*, pp. 204–37; Chiffoleau, *Le Voyage à la Mecque*, pp. 49–200; and William Roff, 'Sanitation and Security: The Imperial Powers and the Nineteenth Century Hajj', *Arabian Studies*, 6 (1982), pp. 143–60; Michael Low, 'Empire and the Hajj: Pilgrims, Plagues, and Pan-Islam under British Surveillance, 1865–1908', *International Journal of Middle East Studies*, 40 (2008), pp. 269–90.

[111] For a survey of the different waves, see *Wikipedia*. 'Cholera Outbreaks and Pandemics', https://en.wikipedia.org/wiki/Cholera_outbreaks_and_pandemics (accessed December 28, 2017).

[112] John Baldry, 'Foreign Interventions and Occupations of Kamaran Island', *Arabian Studies*, 4 (1978), pp. 89–111, here p. 11.

While the consequences for Jeddah in terms of health facilities and better provision of drinking water will be discussed in more detail in Chapter 4, what is of interest here are the local repercussions of the new scale of global connections. The introduction of quarantine in the Red Sea through an agreement of international powers concerned about the spread of the cholera from 1867 onwards in al-Tūr, Wajh, and at the Moses Wells in the north, as well as at Jeddah in 1869 and Kamarān in the south (from 1882 onwards) had already caused serious grievances among the merchants.[113] The local populations of Jeddah and Yanbuʿ protested against interventions ordered by the first sanitary delegation sent by Istanbul to investigate health conditions and provisions for the pilgrimage in 1866. According to the French consul, this protest was incited by the Emir, who feared intervention in religious affairs as an infringement upon his authority and who thus spread the rumour that Christians were behind the Ottoman intervention. This confrontation between the Sharif and the Ottoman authorities might well have been only one dimension in more complex local intrigues.[114]

From the late 1870s until the end of the century, there were also serious economic concerns. British consul Jago, writing in 1886, goes as far as to say that it was the opening of the Suez Canal in conjunction with the quarantine measures which led to Jeddah losing its role as a trade emporium.[115] A French consular report from 1879 actually demonstrates the opposite, namely a significant growth of the volume in trade.[116] Pétriat has shown that the economic crisis of the 1880s and 1890s was more a crisis in the value of the goods exchanged and less one of their volume, resulting from the ever-increasing integration into the economic world system, which also made Jeddah more vulnerable to the depression between 1873 and 1896. The perhaps largest loss was the trade of Yemeni coffee which, during this period, became largely substituted by produce from Southeast Asia and America. Whatever

113 CADN, 2_MI_3228, Dubreuil to MAE, April 12, 1867, for Kamaran Baldry, p. 100. For reactions to the quarantine measures, see TNA, FO 78/2849, Wylden to FO, April 8, 1878; and FO 195/1451, Moncerieff to Vali, August 6, 1883.

114 CADN, 2_MI_3228, Schnepp to MAE, April 18, 1866.

115 TNA, FO 195/1547, Report by Consul Jago on revenue and taxation in the Vilayet of the Hidjaz, January 29, 1886.

116 CADN, 2_MI_3229, Lucciana to MAE, July 2, 1879.

coffee was exported from Yemen now passed by Hodeida and Aden. To some extent, losses could be compensated by the increasing numbers of pilgrims, which might well have added heat to the wrangle to control the transport of pilgrims. A number of other factors, such as contracts with the Ottomans, notably concerning the provisioning of the army as well shipments by dhow, might also have helped to keep the Jiddawi merchants afloat.[117] Local Bedouin tried to compensate for the loss of income from trade by attacking pilgrims and cutting the roads, while officials took to taking bribes and raising illegal levies.

The economic crisis, in conjunction with Ottoman political turmoil resulting from the war against Russia in 1877–8 and the short-lived constitutional experiment under the new Sultan Abdülhamid II, coincided with a number of other events, such fighting in Algeria, the second Anglo-Afghan war (1878–80), the ʿUrābī revolt in Egypt (1879–82), and the Mahdist movement in the Sudan (1881–99).[118] Aydin has argued that the years 1873–83, and in particular the Ottoman-Russian War 'featured a full mobilization of Muslim and Christian identities globally'.[119] Through pilgrims and refugees, as well as letters and news of these events arrived in Mecca, inevitably also impacting its *dihlīz*, Jeddah.[120] Thus, a number of Hijazis offered to volunteer in the Ottoman war against the Russians and several religious students travelled to the Sudan to join Mahdist forces.[121] Furthermore, some members of the Qādiriyya Sufi order, which was popular among slaves and others of African origin, attacked an Ottoman post on the route between Jeddah and Mecca, killing some officers.[122]

117 See Pétriat, *Le Négoce des Lieux Saints*, pp. 173–91. The figures in Ochsenwald, *The Commercial History*, p. 64, t. 2 show this most clearly for the period 1879–1902.

118 On the background of the Second Anglo-Afghan War (1878–80), see J. Norris, 'Second Anglo-Afghan War (1878–80)' in E. Yar-Shater (ed.), *Encyclopædia Iranica* (New York: Columbia University Center for Iranian Studies, 1996), www.iranicaonline.org/articles/anglo-afghan-wars (accessed December 29, 2017).

119 Cemil Aydin, *The Idea of the Muslim World: A Global Intellectual History* (Cambridge, MA: Harvard University Press, 2017), p. 59.

120 I have no information about the spreading of newspapers to the Hijaz in this period.

121 Ochsenwald, *Religion, Society, and the State*, pp. 202–3; and Christiaan Snouck Hurgronje, 'Some of My Experiences with the Muftis of Mecca', *Jaarsverslagen, Oostersch Instituut Leiden*, 4 (1941), pp. 2–16, here pp. 8–9.

122 Alfred Le Chatelier, *Les confréries musulmanes du Hedjaz* (Paris: Ernest Leroux, 1887), p. 46.

The widespread sense of danger to the Muslim world prompted concern among Western consuls. In August 1879, British consul Zohrab reported on 'statements of a serious nature having reached me from various and disconnected sources'. If true – which he somewhat doubted in spite of a variety of local, diplomatic, and Ottoman sources quoted – 'they prove the existence of ideas and plans which may give serious trouble in the future'. More specifically, this concerned the existence of a secret society, composed of 'Mollahs, Sheeks and Sheriffs', 'whose object is the removal of all Mohamedans from Christian control. This society is in communication with every Mussulman community throughout the world', where coordination seemed to be particularly strong with Syria.[123] This is probably a hint at connections to a movement of Syrian notables, supported by the exiled Algerian ʿAbd al-Qādir al-Jazāʾiri, whose aim was to incite revolt in a number of countries simultaneously. Dissatisfied with the increasing Western influence on the Ottoman Sultan, it was even considering to challenge the Ottoman caliphate.[124]

Zohrab explicitly linked his report to an earlier one of March 1879. At that time, Emir Ḥusayn b. Muḥammad (r. 1877–80) had informed the British consul's dragoman about plans by Indian Muslims to join the Afghans in their war against Britain. Another topic had been widespread disquiet among Muslims in Egypt and elsewhere concerning Western advances, increasing the danger of insurgency and war. Russia, the Emir was quoted to have said, was actively kindling discontent among Muslims. For once the Emir claimed to be acting in agreement with Istanbul on this matter.[125] In March 1880 the Emir visited Jeddah and the British consul intended to pursue the discussion on Afghanistan. This conversation never took place: Passing jubilant

[123] TNA, FO 195/1251 Zohrab to FO, August 6, 1879.

[124] On the Syrian movement, see Fritz Steppat, 'Eine Bewegung unter den Notabeln Syriens 1877–78: Neues Licht auf die Entstehung des arabischen Nationalismus', *Zeitschrift der Deutschen Morgenländischen Gesellschaft* Supp. 1, XVII. (Deutscher Orientalistentag Würzburg, 1968 [part 2:1969]), pp. 631–49. For further links see Tufan Buzpınar, 'Opposition to the Ottoman Caliphate in the Early Years of Abdülhamīd II: 1877–1882', *Die Welt des Islams*, 36 (1996), pp. 59–89, here pp. 69–73; Ochsenwald, *Religion, Society, and the State*, pp. 178–80. For further possible connections see Ulrike Freitag, 'Der Orientalist und der Mufti: Kulturkontakt im Mekka des 19. Jahrhunderts', *Die Welt des Islams*, 43 (2003), pp. 37–60, and 51–2, 62.

[125] TNA, FO 685/1, Consul Zohrab's Letter Book 1878, Zohrab to FO, March 12, 1878.

crowds on his arrival in Jeddah, 'a man of about 80 years of age dressed as a Derwish sprang at him and with an ordinary rusty clasp knife stabbed him just below the region of the heart.' The emir died shortly thereafter of inner bleedings.[126] The culprit turned out to be a visiting Afghan whose brother lived in Mecca.

Was this a repercussion of the Sharif's and the Ottoman's refusal to support the Afghan uprising against Britain? The Ottomans had, after all, tried to mediate between Afghans and the British, although in vain.[127] Did the murderer possibly even know of the Sharif's earlier conversations with the British, which, from an Afghan perspective, might have seemed treacherous? It is hard to know. Alavi has shown the intensity of the contact between Muslim activists in India, the Hijaz, and Istanbul, discussed how Indian insurgents installed themselves in the Hijaz and how anti-British calls for jihad were published in India. It is, however, equally true that the fear of anti-imperial uprisings in the garb of Islam led to a heightened fear of conspiracy in the West, which taints many of the available sources.[128] After all, it is no accident that the term pan-Islamism was probably coined in the late 1870s in Germany or Britain but became popularised in the 1880s in connection with Ottoman policies.[129] The late 1870s and early 1880s were one of those global moments during which local grievances and anti-imperial uprisings meshed with grand imperial schemes and rivalry in a way which is almost impossible for the historian to disentangle.

Be that as it may, notions of insurgency were also debated among Meccans in the context of the Egyptian ʿUrābī uprising (1879–91) and the Sudanese Mahdist movement (1881–99). The Shāfiʿī Mufti of Mecca, Aḥmad Zaynī Daḥlān, put forward the idea that even if Muḥammad Aḥmad was not *the* Mahdi expected at the end of the world, he still could be *a* mahdi in the sense of a Muslim leader

126 TNA, FO 195/1313, Zohrab to Amb. Const., March 16, 1880, and March 22, 1880.

127 For the Ottoman dimension of the Afghanistan question at this time, see Azmi Özcan, *Pan-Islamism: Indian Muslims, the Ottomans and Britain 1877–1924*, The Ottoman Empire and Its Heritage (Leiden: Brill, 1997), vol. 12, pp. 78–88.

128 Seema Alavi, *Muslim Cosmopolitanism in the Age of Empire* (Cambridge, MA and London: Harvard University Press, 2015), pp. 169–221, 196–320.

129 Umar Ryad, 'Anti-Imperialism and the Pan-Islamic Movement' in D. Motadel (ed.), *Islam and the European Empires*, The Past & Present Book Series, 1st edn. (Oxford: Oxford University Press, 2014), pp. 131–49, here pp. 131–2.

restoring faith and justice.[130] Thus, even if there was no coherent global plot in 1879 or in subsequent years by Muslims to fight against Western powers, there certainly was a heightened sense of urgency and an intensive exchange about global matters and the plight of Muslims in the Hijaz, in particular among Muslims in general and among Hijazis in particular. The murder of Sharif Ḥusayn b. Muḥammad in Jeddah can thus be seen as an indication thereof. These sentiments did not need to be coherent: In his discussions with Damascene notables considering secession of parts of Algeria from the Ottoman Empire, ʿAbd al-Qādir al-Jazāʾirī had explicitly demanded the continued spiritual recognition of the Ottoman caliph over North Africa. This mattered little for the Afghan shaykh who might (or might not) have thought about Kabul first and wider Muslim geopolitics second, if at all. Thus, one may indeed speak of a place and a moment of pan-Islamic sentiment, even if this was by no means as coherent and organized as its colonial observers feared, and if Pan-Islamism was not, as yet, a term widespread among Muslims themselves.

The effects of the crisis of 1880 continued into 1881 but were eventually subdued with the help of Osman Nūrī Pasha, initially commander of the troops and from 1882 to 1886 also governor of the Hijaz.[131] In 1882, ʿAwn al-Rafīq was appointed to the emirate. In his first years, he stood back and watched the centralising measures taken by a governor who would have liked to essentially deprive the emir of almost all his powers. However, from 1885 onwards, local opposition against health regulations and Ottoman modernisation measures started to crystallise once more and Emir ʿAwn certainly took part in the opposition by complaining to the Sultan. In autumn of 1886, he escalated the conflict by leaving for Ṭāʾif in protest, asking to be either released from his office or for the governor to be removed. The Sultan chose the latter option and ʿAwn al-Rafīq became the strong man of the Hijaz until 1905. He restored the powers of the Sharifate to the chagrin of many who had initially supported him (cf. Chapters 5 and 6).

130 Ochsenwald, *Religion, Society, and the State*, pp. 202–3; and Freitag, *Indian Ocean Migrants and State Formation*, pp. 204–7.

131 For the following, see Butrus Abu-Manneh, 'Sultan Abdulhamid II and the Sharifs of Mecca (1880–1900)', *Asian and African Studies*, 9 (1973), pp. 1–21. For an overview of Osman Nuri Paşa's life and activities Matīn Hülgū, 'Topal Osman Nuri Paşa Hayatı ve Faaliyetleri (1840–1898)', *Osmanlı Tarihi Araştırma ve Uygulama Merkezi Dergisi*, 5 (2005), pp. 145–53.

It was exactly during these already tense times that the fifth cholera pandemic (1881–96) struck Jeddah several times, bringing widespread death, but also increasing tensions between the population and the authorities. The Ottoman authorities tightened quarantine regulations even further through the erection of additional quarantine stations between Jeddah and Mecca, thus turning the two-day journey into a lengthy and uncomfortable trip and hindering trade. The governor also enforced the consumption of clean (but more expensive) drinking water, which most likely alienated those selling rainwater from cisterns (compare Chapter 4).[132] However, what provoked the particular wrath of the local population was the installation of two disinfecting machines to cleanse clothes and belongings of pilgrims in Jeddah and Mecca. On May 30, 1895, when a number of officials from various consulates went on an evening walk outside of Jeddah, they were attacked by Bedouin, who killed the British vice-consul Abdur Razzack and seriously wounded the Russian consul, also lightly wounding the British consul and French chancellor. The French account of events follows the official Ottoman explanation: The killing resulted from a popular fear that the machines poisoned those who were already ill. Thus, the population attacked the disinfecting machine and the hospital as well as, eventually, those whom they suspected to have prompted these health installations. The British reports add another element, namely the assumption that this was no simple outbreak of popular fear and frustration. According to this version, the British doctor and Vice-Consul, Abdur Razzack, who frequently visited Mecca, was deeply feared by the Emir. Abdur Razzack had repeatedly reported 'the numerous abuses and extortions from which the unfortunate pilgrims are annually exposed at the hands, or at least for the pecuniary advantage, of His Highness', meaning the emir.[133] This insinuated that the Bedouin had been acting at the command of the Emir. Even if the Ottoman governors were unable or unwilling to reign in Emir ʿAwn al-Rafīq, such reports also

[132] Ochsenwald, *Religion, Society, and the State*, pp. 68–9, 196–7; and Mark Harrison, 'Quarantine, Pilgrimage, and Colonial Trade: India 1866–1900', *The Indian Economic and Social History Review*, 29 (1992), pp. 117–44, here pp. 137–44.

[133] CADN, Const. Amb. D-Djeddah 7, Descouture to Amb. Const., June 1, 1895; on this also TNA, FO 195/1894, Richards to Amb. Const. June 17, 1895, quote from Lamb to Amb. Const., July 30, 1895.

cast them and their authority in a negative light. This might have contributed to their hesitation in pursuing the culprits.[134]

In addition to the increased ability of the Ottomans to move troops to the Hijaz by boat and the centralising reforms of the Tanzimat, there was the project of the Hijaz railroad. This promised improved imperial access to the holy cities. It also threatened the livelihood of the Bedouin, many of whom were the clients of the Emir. The railway never advanced beyond Medina, where construction ended in 1908. Plans to extend it and build a branch line from Jeddah to Mecca, for which parts were stored in Jeddah at least from 1912 onwards, were only given up with the advent of the First World War.[135]

The Young Turk Revolution, the End of the Empire, and the Long End of World War I in the Hijaz

News of the Young Turk revolution by military officers of the 'Committee of Union and Progress' (CUP) arrived in Jeddah by post on August 1, 1908, a good three weeks after the start and a week after the capitulation of the Ottoman sultan. The telegraph had been interrupted for almost three weeks, possibly by officials who were still loyal to the old regime.[136] On August 19, young Ottoman officers in Ṭāʾif formed a branch of the CUP and publicly declared the constitution reinstated, thus propagating one of the key demands of the revolutionaries. Ṭāʾif was a particularly symbolic venue: Midhat Pasha, a former Grand Vizier and governor of Syria and Izmir, known as the 'father' of the short-lived constitution of 1876, had, in 1881, been trialled and sentenced to death in Istanbul. As a result of British pressure, he was instead exiled to Ṭāʾif where he was assassinated in April 1883, probably on orders from the Sultan. The Young Turks in Ṭāʾif made good use of this symbol:

134 This point is particularly stressed by Low, *Empire and the Hajj*, pp. 280–5. For a well-informed Muslim account, see the comments on the relationship by Ibrāhīm Rifʿat, *Mirʾāt al-Ḥaramayn: al-Riḥlāt al-ḥijāziyya wa-l-ḥajj wa-mashāʾiruhu al-dīniyya muḥallātan bi-miʾat al-ṣuwar al-shamsiyya*, 2 vols. (Cairo: Maṭbaʿat Dār al-Kutub, 1344/1925), vol. 1, pp. 64–5.

135 BOA, DH.ID.42 24 Za 26, 1330/ November 6, 1912 and Ra 1, 1332/January 28, 1914. For the plans of that branch line, see Matīn Hūlākū, *al-Khaṭṭ al-ḥadīdī al-ḥijāzī: al-Mashrūʿ al-ʿimlāq li-l-Sulṭān ʿAbd al-Ḥamīd al-Thānī* (Cairo: Dār al-Nīl, 2011), pp. 201–7.

136 TNA, FO 195/2286, Husain to Amb. Const., August 7, 1908, TNA, FO 195/ 2286, Husain to Amb. Const., August 25, 1908.

The committee followed by a large crowd of the townpeople first proceeded to the tomb of the late Madhat Pasha of the same of the [sic!] first Turkish constitution who died in prison in Taif, and offered prayers to his soul, and then proceeded to the fort and released all the political prisoners, and marched to the military barracks. Here the soldiers were sworn to be true to the cause of the constitution and a detachment of soldiers with some officers was sent to bring to the barracks His Highness the Grand Sherif, who has been acting Vali there since Ahmed Ratib Pasha came to Jeddah.[137]

He then was made to stand between three people, among them a slave and a Bedouin, which indicates the humiliation of the procedure.

Upon this the Grand Sherif was sworn on Koran to follow the constitutional laws faithfully and sincerely in future in all his dealings with the public, including town people and the bedouin, and also to stop immediately all the illegal practices that were being perpetuated by his order on the people of Hijaz in general and on the pilgrims in particular and to take immediate steps to secure the safety of the roads in Hijaz.[138]

This interesting adaptation of constitutional demands to local needs was followed by speeches and three nights of illumination of the town. While their Meccan counterparts immediately followed suit, the Jeddah garrison reacted only a day later with a gun salute 'as a signal of the proclamation of the new form of Government'. The news spread rapidly, crowds gathered outside of the barracks and 'men embraced each other, speeches were made, prayers were offered for the Sultan, and deafening cheers were given.' The crowd proceeded to the seat of the kaymakam who had no choice but to receive them. The kaymakam swore an oath on the constitution. The governor, who had not attended any of the ceremonies on grounds of illness, was subsequently arrested and two prominent Hadhrami merchants only escaped the same fate because of the intervention of the Hadhrami community and leading merchants. After an initial period of excitement, when there was an 'understanding [of] the meaning of *Hurria* (liberty) to be freedom given to everybody to do as he liked', as a British report cynically commented, calm was restored.[139]

In October or very early November of 1908, elections for the Ottoman parliament were held in Jeddah and Mecca. Ostensibly due

137 TNA, FO 195/2286, Husain to Amb. Const., August 25, 1908. 138 Ibid.

139 Ibid. For this and the following cf. Pétriat, *Le Négoce des Lieux Saints*, pp. 196–204; and Ochsenwald, *Religion, Society, and the State*, pp. 216–7.

to a refusal of people to register as voters for fear of being drafted into the army, voting occurred through a system of 200 electors chosen for each quarter by the quarter headmen. These selected an electoral body of 25, which voted for Qāsim Zaynal ʿAlī Riḍā, son of one of the leading merchants of Jeddah. Qāsim, who had not succeeded in trade himself and worked as a journalist in Cairo, and planned to push for an improved water supply, harbour construction, and more and better schools.[140] Although the election was contested on the grounds that he was chiefly elected to save him from financial problems, it was later confirmed and Qāsim served in the Ottoman parliament until 1914, when he was replaced by Sharif Fayṣal, son of Emir Ḥusayn.[141]

Sharif Ḥusayn had been appointed to the emirate in summer 1908 against the wishes of the Young Turks, and sworn loyalty to Sultan Abdülhamid.[142] It is hence not surprising that he returned to ʿAwn al-Rafīq's policy of strengthening the emirate against the constitutional government, a policy which had some support among Meccans fearing the abolition or weakening of the emir's role.[143] Between 1909 and 1914 the Unionists variously sought to embarrass, weaken and eventually get rid of the Emir and only abandoned their plans with the onset of World War I. Conversely, Ḥusayn consolidated his connections to the Bedouin, hence opposition to the extension of the rail link, rejected by him for fear of Ottoman influence and by the Bedouin who feared for their livelihood, provided common ground. Ḥusayn also tried to prove his military prowess by fighting Ibn Saʿūd's newly recovered emirate. While the Young Turks might have hoped to exhaust him by sending him to fight the rebellious Sufi

140 This latter point is not unlikely, given that Qāsim's brother Muḥammad had founded a series of important private schools, see Ulrike Freitag (May 6, 2015). 'The Falah School in Jeddah: Civic Engagement for Future Generations?'. Article on *jadaliyya.com*. www.jadaliyya.com/pages/index/21430/the-falah-school-in-jeddah_civic-engagement-for-fu.

141 TNA, FO 195/2286, Monahan to Amb. Const., November 5, 1908, November 7, 1908, and November 10, 1908.

142 For this and the following; cf. Ernest Dawn, 'The Amir of Mecca Al-Ḥusayn Ibn-ʿAli and the Origin of the Arab Revolt', *Proceedings of the American Philosophical Society*, 104 (1960), pp. 11–34; and al-Amr, *The Hijaz under Ottoman Rule*, pp. 134–42; cf. ʿImād Yūsuf, *al-Ḥijāz fī 'l-ʿahd al-ʿuthmānī 1876–1918* (London: Alwarrak Publishing Ltd., 2011), pp. 139–207; and Wahīṃ Ṭālib Muḥammad, *Tārīkh al-Ḥijāz al-siyāsī 1916–1925* (Beirut: al-Dār al-ʿArabiyya li-l-Mawsūʿāt, 1427/2007), pp. 30–57.

143 TNA, FO 195/2286, Monahan to Amb. Const., December 2, 1908.

leader Muḥammad al-Idrīsī in ʿAsīr in 1911 and 1912, he returned even stronger.[144]

The Red Sea had become a subject of heightened imperial contestation after the Italian-Ottoman war of 1911–12, and World War I further intensified the conflict. The story of the Arab Revolt in 1916, which officially started with a shot by Sharif Ḥusayn from his balcony on the Ottoman barracks on June, 10, 1916 in Mecca, does not need to be retold here.[145] Sharif Ḥusayn's change of loyalty from the Ottoman sultan to the Arab nationalists was closely linked to his strained relations with the CUP government and British overtures, in addition to weariness of a war in which he feared the Peninsula to be in a particularly vulnerable position. He thus tried for some time to negotiate with the Ottomans as well as with the British in Cairo. In order to ward off increasingly urgent calls to openly support the Ottoman call for jihad, he pointed to the dangers of a British attack on the Hijaz.[146]

The British sea blockade of Ottoman ports proved to be another important argument for an alliance with the British, rather than with the Ottomans, from the second half of 1915 onwards. It is no accident that Sharif Ḥusayn, in addition to political demands, requested rice, flour, barely, as well as coffee and sugar in addition to weapons and money from the British in exchange for his support.[147] Although the Ottomans tried to secure the provisioning of the Hijaz, going so far as to divert vital grain from Syria and Yemen, famine spread along the

144 al-Amr, *The Hijaz under Ottoman Rule*p. pp. 143–58. For a detailed political history, see Anne Bang, *The Idrisi State in Asir 1906–1934* (London: Hurst Publishers, 1997).

145 For the history of the Sharifian state, see Joshua Teitelbaum, *The Rise and Fall of the Hashimite Kingdom of Arabia*, (London: Hurst & Company, 2001); Randall Baker, *King Husain and the Kingdom of Hejaz*, Arabia Past and Present (Cambridge, UK: Oleander Press, 1979), vol. 10. On the revolt cf. Hasan Kayali, *Arabs and Young Turks: Turkish-Arab Relations in the Second Constitutional Period of the Ottoman Empire; 1908–1918* (Berkeley and London: University of California Press, 1988), pp. 197–200.

146 For the diplomacy preceding the revolt, see E. Tauber, *The Arab Movements in World War I* (London and Portland, OR: Frank Cass, 1993), pp. 62–8, 78–82; and Yūsuf, *al-Ḥijāz fī al-ʿAhd al-ʿUthmānī*, pp. 176–7. The period 1916–25 is the focus of Ḥusayn Naṣīf, *Māḍī ʾl-Ḥijāz wa-ḥāḍiruhu* ([s.n.], 1349/ 1930); and Muḥammad, *Tārīkh al-Ḥijāz al-Siyāsī*.

147 Husayn to McMahon, February 18, 1916, see Letter No. 1 in 'Pre-state Israel: The Hussein-McMahon Correspondence', *jewishvirtuallibrary.org*, www.jewishvirtuallibrary.org/jsource/History/hussmac1.html#1.

coast. Even before food supplies became critical, speculation regarding food prices started to concern the authorities. [148] Indeed, some well-known merchant families even benefitted from the war by engaging in smuggling, hoarding, and benefitting from currency fluctuations. Furthermore, the war reduced the number of pilgrims dramatically, thereby impacting on a major source of income of the Hijaz.[149]

Jeddah was the first city to be attacked by Ḥusayn's forces on June 11, 1916. Given the comparatively strong Ottoman defences in a confrontation with tribal troops, British warships were called upon in support of his attack. They started bombarding Ottoman defences until these capitulated on June 16. This was accelerated by the intervention of notables who had been informed by the Sharif that British canons might well start bombarding the city itself.[150] Thereafter, the city became the major entry point for military supplies to the Sharifian troops, as well as for their provision by the British.[151] By early November, the Sharif felt secure enough to declare (or rather, have declared) himself king, thereby establishing the short-lived Arab Kingdom of the Hijaz.[152]

In winter 1918–19, while the peace conference of Paris was being prepared, the conflict between King Ḥusayn and ʿAbd al-ʿAzīz Āl Saʿūd (who in 1921 took on the title of Sultan of Najd and is commonly known as Ibn Saʿūd) erupted, with an attack by Ḥusayn's troops on the disputed town of al-Khurma. Ḥusayn was disastrously defeated in nearby Turaba.[153] In response, the British warned Ibn

148 This is well described by A. Musil, *Zur Zeitgeschichte von Arabien* (Wien and Leipzig: Manz Verlag, Verlag S. Hirzel, 1918), pp. 35–6; cf. U. Freitag, P. Pétriat and M. Strohmeier, 'La Première Guerre Mondiale dans la Péninsule Arabique … enquête de ses sources', *Arabian Humanities*, 6 (2016). On the famine in Medina see A. el-Bakri, 'Memories of the Beloved: Oral Histories from the 1916–19 Siege of Medina', *International Journal of Middle East Studies*, 46 (2014), pp. 703–18.

149 Pétriat, *Le Négoce des Lieux Saints*, pp. 205–10.

150 Naṣīf, *Māḍī 'l-Ḥijāz wa-ḥāḍiruhu*, pp. 49–50; and MECA, Memoirs by J. W. A. Young, GB165–0310, 'Three Months in Jedda', p. 1.

151 Mansī, *Jidda fī 'l-tārikh al-ḥadīth*, pp. 18–19; and Muḥammad, *Tārīkh al-Ḥijāz al-Siyāsī*, pp. 57–9.

152 Yūsuf, *al-Ḥijāz fī al-ʿAhd al-ʿUthmānī*, pp. 212–13, 232. For a detailed study of the internal organisation of the sharifate, see Muḥammad, *Tārīkh al-Ḥijāz al-Siyāsī*, pp. 73–152.

153 For a detailed discussion of Hijazi-Najdi relations see Muḥammad, *Tārīkh al-Ḥijāz al-Siyāsī*, pp. 249–440; cf. ʿAlī al-Wardī, *Qiṣṣat al-ashrāf wa-Ibn Saʿūd*, 3rd edn. (London: Alwarrak Publishing Ltd., 2007), pp. 191–5.

Sa'ūd not to advance further and sent reinforcements to Jeddah. This gave the Sharifian government another lease of life until 1924. However, the period from 1920 was marked by a growing alienation of the Hijazi merchant elites from King Ḥusayn. In February 1920, the kaymakam, 'Abdallāh 'Alī Riḍā, an appointee of Ḥusayn, met with the British agent. The latter reported:

> The old man was in a great talkative mood and opened his mind to me. His comments are rather spontaneous and outspoken .... He started relating in what an awful state of anarchy and chaos the country is. An undefinable discontent resigning in the Hedjaz and the poorer class is badly ill-treated as ever. He pointed out that the state of affairs is simply appalling, the administration drifting from bad to worse, and the King not only most unpopular but absolutely hated ... [154]

The fortnightly British reports abound with news of injustices, problems with water and food provision, and the spread of pro-Saudi views among the poorer population.[155] Nor did the increase in taxes and dues and the introduction for conscription for Takrūnīs (people of West-African origin, cf. Chapter 3) beyond Mecca increase the popularity of the King.[156] Even if one takes into account that the British reports might have been tainted by the increasingly impossible situation of Britain supporting both Sharif Ḥusayn and his foremost adversary, Ibn Sa'ūd, their exasperation partly resulted from the unwillingness of Ḥusayn to come to an agreement with Ibn Sa'ūd and partly reflects the views of their local interlocutors, such as 'Abdallāh 'Alī Riḍā.

The situation worsened after Ḥusayn declared himself caliph in March 1924 following the Turkish abolition of the caliphate.[157]

154 TNA, FO 686/26, Political and intelligence report for ten days ending February 1, 1920.

155 R. Jarman (ed.), *The Jedda Diaries 1919–1940: 1928–1934*, Political Diaries of the Arab World: Saudi Arabia (Slough: Archive Editions, 1990), vol. 1, Jeddah Report September 10–20, 1920, p. 379, December 11–20, 1920 and April 1–10, 1921, p. 528.

156 Ibid., vol. 2, Jeddah Report, January 1–20, 1922, p. 4; cf. Pétriat, *Le Négoce des Lieux Saints*, pp. 215–8.

157 The private letters by Reader Bullard provide an interesting if cynical perspective on events 1923–5 in which, for example, he accuses Jiddawis of a basically opportunistic attitude, see R. Bullard, *Two Kings in Arabia: Letters from Jeddah 1923–5 and 1936–9* (Reading: Ithaca Press, 1993), letter of October 19, 1924, p. 66.

In September of that year, Ibn Saʿūd's troops conquered Ṭāʾif, massacred hundreds of its inhabitants and plundered the town. At this stage, a group of leading Hijazi notables assembled in Jeddah and forced King Ḥusayn to abdicate in favour of his son (see also Chapter 7).[158] On October 6, 1924, Ḥusayn's son ʿAlī was declared king and his father left Jeddah three days later. Only a few days later, Ibn Saʿūd's troops, the famous Ikhwān, entered Mecca peacefully. In early December, Ibn Saʿūd himself arrived from Riyadh and took possession of Mecca after the European representatives (and most notably the British) had declared their neutrality as long as their property was respected.

Local delegations, as wells as foreign representatives and visitors such as the Arab American Amīn al-Rīḥānī and the British Arabist Harry St. John Philby, a self-styled intermediary, were involved in mediation attempts which did not yield any results.[159] From January to December 1925, Ibn Saʿūd's troops laid siege to Jeddah, where the economic situation worsened considerably.[160] On December 22, 1925, the city surrendered. On that date, King ʿAlī left the country for Iraq following a negotiated settlement. Two days later, Sultan ʿAbd al-ʿAzīz entered Jeddah and, after reassuring himself that everything was quiet, returned to Mecca. On January 7, 1926, Hijazi notables swore allegiance to him in Mecca and a day later he declared himself King of the Hijaz.[161]

[158] For the forced abdication of Ḥusayn, see Naṣīf, *Māḍī ʻl-Ḥijāz wa-ḥāḍiruhu*, pp. 120–31. The situation in Jeddah during the occupation is well reflected in the journals *Umm al-Qurā* and *Barīd al-Ḥijāz*. This is summarised in ʿA. al-Thubaytī, *Ḥiṣār Jidda min khilāl jarīdatay Umm al-Qurā wa-Barīd al-Ḥijāz* (Beirut: Jadāwil, 2015). For a more detailed analysis of the factional politics during this year Pétriat, *Le Négoce des Lieux Saints*, pp. 226–36.

[159] For a detailed chronology of Philby's life on the basis of his diaries see MECA, Philby Collection GB165–0229, Chronology of events in the life of Harry St. John Bridger Philby Abdullah Philby.

[160] For a chronicle of the occupation, the Saudi newspaper *Umm al-Qurā* is an important, albeit anti-Hashemite source. For a summary of the views presented therein, see al-Thubaytī, *Ḥiṣār Jidda*.

[161] Vassiliev, *History of Saudi Arabia*, pp. 260–4; and Mansī, *Jidda fī ʻl-tārīkh al-ḥadīth*, pp. 19–32. According to Jeddah Report November 28–December 31, 1925, Ibn Saud entered Jeddah on the morning of December 23, 1925, see R. Jarman (ed.), *The Jedda Diaries*, vol. 2, p. 357. From April 4, 1927, he took on the title King of the Hijaz, Najd and its Dependencies, see Jeddah Report April 1–25, 1927, p. 451.

The Establishment of Saudi Rule in Jeddah

On December 24, 1924 Ibn Saʿūd, Sultan of Najd and leader of an expanding emirate driven by a particularly strict interpretation of the Ḥanbalī interpretation of Islam, known as Wahhabiyya, issued a declaration to the population of the Hijaz. He reassured them of his intention to secure peace and stability for its population 'after this long period during which the people tasted the bitterness of life'.[162] The willingness of the local elite to give Ibn Saʿūd the benefit of the doubt surely helped to realise this primary goal. International recognition, first granted by the Soviet Union, was consolidated in the Treaty of Jeddah (1927) by the British. The treaty confirmed Saudi Arabian independence, as opposed to an earlier protectorate treaty of 1915. The most difficult part was to convince other Muslim rulers to accept the new ruler over the holy places of Islam. Once Ibn Saʿūd had gained control of the holy cities, demands for an internationalisation of said cities put forward mainly by Indian delegates, had been overtaken by events and the majority of delegates at a Muslim congress in Mecca in 1926 came to support the status quo.[163] This was in good part due to a successful – meaning largely peaceful and secure – pilgrimage in that year, although a number of changes to the hajj were introduced. In particular, those practices which Wahhabis regarded as polytheism (*shirk*) but which were acceptable in other interpretations of Islam were banned, meaning that disputes over religious practices erupted (see Chapter 5).[164]

Indeed, in terms of peace and stability, Ibn Saʿūd managed to establish a fairly stable regime. Thus, the crucial caravan routes between major cities became increasingly safer due to his support by and control of the Bedouin, whose shaykhs were made liable for security in their respective territories.[165] This was absolutely crucial notably in the 1930s when the pilgrimage tax was the main source of revenue of the emerging Saudi state.[166] Of course, a variety of local issues gave rise to controversies, from concrete administrative practices

162 Naṣīf, *Māḍī 'l-Ḥijāz wa-ḥāḍiruhu*, p. 212.
163 Vassiliev, *History of Saudi Arabia*, pp. 266–7; and Willis, *Azad's Mecca*.
164 R. Jarman (ed.), *The Jedda Diaries*, vol. 2, Jeddah Report, March 1–31, 1926, p. 381 and April 1–30, 1926, p. 386.
165 *Umm al-Qurā*, 60, February 19, 1926, p. 3.
166 Vassiliev, *History of Saudi Arabia*, p. 305.

to the seasonal appearance of the religious vigilance committees. The centrality of the pilgrimage for revenue, as well as for local and international legitimacy, also meant that this sector continued to be a major driving force in local development. Questions of security and transport that dominated the new state's agenda in the Hijaz, just as concerns with health, hygiene, and water had in the second half of the nineteenth century.

The political consolidation of the emerging state rested on the creation of two distinct political systems for Najd and the Hijaz, something which initially did not change with the declaration of the Kingdom of Saudi Arabia in September 1932. By this time, Ibn Saʿūd had successfully subdued a revolt by the Bedouin forces who had helped him secure victory in the first place (the so-called *Ikhwān*), quelled a stirring of dissatisfaction in the Hijaz and subdued the southern emirate of ʿAsīr which was annexed to the nascent Saudi state.[167] While the system in the central Najd region reflected both the religious claim to leadership (Ibn Saʿūd was commonly called by the title 'imam') as well as Bedouin traditions, the Hijazi institutions continued as established during Ottoman rule.[168] Given that Ibn Saʿūd's entourage included many Syrians, Iraqis, and Egyptians who held political office, the administrative system of the Hijaz was not fundamentally changed. In 1924 and 1925, Hijazis elected their Advisory Council. The 'Local Council' (*majlis ahlī)* elected in Mecca in 1925, already under Saudi rule, was then transformed into the *majlis al-shūrā* of the Viceroy and possibly enlarged by a few Members from Jeddah.[169] From 1926 onwards, this Advisory Council was appointed by the viceroy for the Hijaz, Prince Fayṣal.[170] To finance his policies, Ibn Saʿūd continued the time-honoured practice used by Ottomans and sharifs to oblige leading merchants to invest in government-led companies or to advance straightforward credits (cf. Chapter 4).

Although the 1930s marked the beginning of oil and mineral exploration, as well as a first oil concession signed in 1933, the more valuable

[167] Ibid., pp. 268–86. [168] Ibid., pp. 293–9.

[169] Kostiner, *The Making of Saudi Arabia*, p. 101; and on the elections in Mecca in 1925, *Umm al-Qurā*, 31, August 1, 1925. It is possible that this is identical with the Assembly mentioned in the Jeddah Report for January 1926, see R. Jarman (ed.), *The Jedda Diaries*, vol. 4, vol. 2, p. 372; cf. MECA, Philby Collection GB 165–0229, 1/4/5/1, January 13, 1926, p. 349.

[170] Kostiner, *The Making of Saudi Arabia*, p. 101.

concession in the short term was that of the gold mines of Mahd al-Dhahab. The first commercially viable oil field was found in 1938 in the east of the Peninsula, and the first cargo of oil exported on May 1, 1939. Much oil was detected in the following months and years, though World War II significantly slowed the development of oil extraction. Hence it was only from 1945 onwards that oil extraction reached levels which made a palpable impact on the Saudi economy. However, oil certainly drew American attention to Saudi Arabia. Hence, US aid commenced and, towards the end of the war, Ibn Saʿūd agreed to lease land for US airbases in a bid to balance British influence.[171]

While the political repercussions of these developments took until the 1950s and 1960s to become clear, the impact on the urban fabric of Saudi cities was felt more immediately. In the 1930s, motorised transport increased, albeit slowly. Cities like Jeddah registered a population growth, attracting rural to urban migrants, not just from Saudi Arabia but also from the Yemen and East Africa. While Mecca was the seat of the Hijaz government, the Foreign Ministry and the foreign consulates resided in Jeddah, as Mecca was off limits for non-Muslims. Jeddah also became the headquarter for a number of international firms due to its long-standing international links, relatively skilled labour force and openness in comparison to the much more conservative cities of the Najd. All of this attracted additional skilled labour and foreign experts from all over the world. Motorisation and urban growth prompted the demolition of the city wall, outside of which the suburbs had already begun to grow. This growth accelerated further as oil revenues increased, and a road network around and through Jeddah, as well as a connection to Mecca, improved communications considerably.[172]

Any epochal boundary is questionable. To choose the demolition of the Jeddah city wall in 1947 as the end date for this study is linked to

[171] Vassiliev, *History of Saudi Arabia*, pp. 312–27.

[172] Nūr Bā Qādir al-ʿAmūdī, *al-Hijra al-rīfiyya al-ḥaḍariyya: Dirāsa fī takayyuf al-muhājirīn ilā madīnat Judda* (Beirut: Dār al-Munthakhab al-ʿArabī, 1994), pp. 84–8; Rolf Krause, *Stadtgeographische Untersuchungen in der Altstadt von Djidda/Saudi-Arabien: Eine Dokumentation* (Bonn: Ferd. Dümmlers Verlag, 1991), pp. 24–7; and Mohammed Bagader, 'The Evolution of Built Heritage Conservation Policies in Saudi Arabia between 1970 and 2015: The Case of Historic Jeddah', PhD Thesis, University of Manchester (2016), p. 21.

the assumption that around this period, the character of the city began to change. Many factors can be listed here, from the changing transport network to the gradual move of the more affluent members of society to the suburbs, which offered the possibility of urban construction allowing for new amenities. They were replaced by rural migrants, who in turn gave way, by the 1980s, to poor immigrants from Yemen, Somalia, and Bangladesh. This changed the composition of the population of the old city, while in-migration altered the overall character of the urban populace which, in turn, became subject to new and more restrictive regulations. Of course, this would not have been possible without the provision of more drinking water, enabled by the ʿAzīzīya waterworks which opened in 1950. These not only provided the growing population and ever-increasing numbers of pilgrims with water, they also furthered a new style of construction using cement, rather than the traditional blocks cut from coral stone.[173]

[173] For details ʿAbd al-Anṣārī, *History of Aziziah Water Supply Juddah* (Jeddah, 1392/1972); and for the consequences on buildings cf. ʿAbd al-ʿAzīz Abū Zayd, *al-Miʿmārīyūn fī Jidda al-qadīma* (Jeddah: al-ʿĀmāl al-Thaqāfiyya, 14337/2012 or 2013), pp. 22–3, 117–21.

3 *The Changing Faces of Jeddah*

The aim of this chapter is to give a clearer sense of who the people from Jeddah were. It discusses the origins and changes of the population of Jeddah, commonly known as Jiddawis, during the nineteenth and early twentieth centuries. Using family histories, it illustrates some of the different paths by which people came to the city and settled there.[1]

The Population of Jeddah – An Overview

Both the size and the composition of the population of Jeddah pose a problem to the historian. There seem to exist no official population figures (which are often based on tax registers) from Ottoman times, which is partly due to the sacred character of the Hijaz, partly to the often protracted and complex manner in which a number of Arab provinces were incorporated into the Ottoman system, which involved a lot of bargaining, trial, and error.[2] We are thus dependent on consular sources as well as travelogues and oral history. Numbers increased during, but also before and after, the hajj and foreign visitors had only limited access to the women and children of a house. Thus, figures vary greatly.[3]

For the first half of the nineteenth century, the number of inhabitants mentioned in consular sources and travelogues varies between 12–15,000 and 22,000, while the estimates for the second half of the century are, on average, somewhat higher, suggesting a slight increase in population. The Ottoman yearbook for 1891–92 mentions 25,000

[1] The voluminous study by ʿAbd al-Razzāq Sulaymān Aḥmad Abū Dāʾūd, *Jidda wa-l-Jiddāwiyūn fī dhākirat al-insān*, 2 vols. (Jeddah: Dār Manṣūr al-Zāmil, 1438/2017), 2nd edn. appeared too late to be used in this book.

[2] On the problem of the missing statistics see Low, *The Mechanics of Mecca*, pp. 23–4. There were a number of different population counts in the second half of the nineteenth century; cf. Büssow, *Hamidian Palestine*, pp. 19–26.

[3] Rüppell, *Reise in Abyssinien*, vol. 1, p. 159, makes the first argument explicit.

Muslim inhabitants.[4] Numbers rose again during the twentieth century when there are mentions of around 30–50,000 inhabitants.[5] There are two anomalies in the figures, namely the low number mentioned by Ali Bey for 1807 (5,000 people) and the relatively low figure of 15,000 mentioned by Rathjens and von Wissmann in 1947.[6] Both could possibly be linked to instances of conflict, in the first case the war between the Ottomans and the Wahhabis, and in the second case World War II. Given that many leading merchants had family connections with other ports on the Red Sea coast, or at times even further away, they could move with relative ease and observe how conditions developed before deciding whether to return or resettle. For example, of the 547 family names listed for the old city by Ṭrābulsī, 35 could, during the late nineteenth century, also be found in Massawa, and 22 could be found in Suakin, indicating the existence of family branches.[7] Others had recourse to families in Cairo, Aden or the Hadhramaut, or even further afar. Thus, when Jeddah was beleaguered in 1925, some members of the ʿAlī Riḍā family took their wives and children to India until the new political order had been established, while yet others migrated to Sudan or Yemen where they could revive their businesses in cooperation with earlier business partners.[8] This practice can also be found elsewhere: The Massawan merchant of

4 *Hicaz vilâyeti salnâmesi*, defa 5 (Mecca: Vilayet Matbaası, 1309/1892–93), p. 275.

5 Compiled on the basis of Burckhardt, *Travels in Arabia*, p. 26; Rüppell, *Reise in Abyssinien*, vol. 1, p. 159; CADN, 2_MI_3228, M.E. de Sainte Marie to Min. of Commerce, May 13, 1865, and to MAE, December 20, 1865; 2_MI_3229, Buez to Min. of Commerce, December 31, 1877; 2_MI_3231, Bubief to MAE, September 29, 1903; *Hicaz vilâyeti salnâmesi*, defa 1 (Mecca: Vilayet Matbaası, 130/1883–84), p. 134; Muḥammad al-Batanūnī, *al-Riḥla al-ḥijāziyya li-walī ʾl-niʿm al-Ḥājj ʿAbbās Ḥilmī Bāshā al-Thānī Khidīw Miṣr sanat 1327*, 2nd edn. (Cairo: Maṭbaʿat al-Gamāliyya, 1329h./1911), p. 28; and David Hogarth, *Hejaz before World War I*, reprint of 2nd edn., 1917, with a new Introduction by R. L. Bidwell (Cambridge: The Oleander Press, 1978), p. 28.

6 Badia y Leblich, *Travels of Ali Bey*, p. 43; and Carl Rathjens and Hermann von Wissmann, 'Landschaftskundliche Beobachtungen im südlichen Hedjaz', *Erdkunde: Archiv für wissenschaftliche Geographie*, 1 (1947), pp. 61–89, 200–5, here p. 80.

7 This is based on a comparison of Ṭrābulsī, *Jidda*, pp. 83–94; with the index of Miran, *Red Sea Citizens*; and the findings of Elfateh, *Suakin (Sudan) and the Colonial Architecture*, vol. 1, pp. 229–30.

8 Interview, Jeddah, December 10. 2017; oral communication with ʿAbdallāh b. Zaqr, Jeddah, March 23, 2006; and MECA, Philby Collection, GB 165–0229, 1/4/5/1, Diary part 1, February 9, 1926, p. 396.

Egyptian origin, Aḥmad al-Ghūl, not only spent some of his life in Jeddah, where he married, but also considered relocating there during a commercial crisis in Massawa.[9]

Similar to the problem of numbers is that of the composition of the population. On the basis of the extant sources, some assumptions can be made. The first is that the changing economic and political fortunes of Jeddah are reflected in the composition of its population. Thus, there might originally have been a fairly small population of fishermen descended from local tribesmen. This possibly grew with the establishment of Jeddah as a port, and one can imagine a trickle of Bedouins to the city over the centuries, depending on the economic conditions. Nevertheless, it appears that much of the urban population of Jeddah was composed of immigrants from different places. The households of the wealthy probably included slaves and servants who helped run the various trades, as well as the shipping operations. The proportions of the early populations are difficult to gauge, but the urban elite seems to have been largely comprised of merchants. It furthermore included representatives of the sharifs of Mecca, who were, over centuries, both active traders and in control of a portion of the income from customs.

The sharifs, who claim descent from Prophet Muḥammad's grandson Ḥasan b. ʿAlī, were in a sense the quintessential Arab inhabitants of the region. Their status as Arabs was, as in all other cases, only transmitted through the fathers. While a number of sharifs lived in Jeddah, where there were also substantial religious and commercial endowments in their names, such as a *sūq*, cisterns, and houses that were rented out, the ruling emir resided in Mecca. He, as well as other family members in Mecca often conducted business in Jeddah through representatives called *wakīl* (pl. *wukalāʾ*).

As far as the merchant elite is concerned, which is documented as the group with whom many of the visitors, but also of the foreign consuls interacted the most, its composition seems to have changed considerably over the centuries. This was most likely linked to the different trends in international trade. Thus, while a number of merchants originating from Morocco, who had moved via Cairo to the Red Sea region, were regularly mentioned by visitors in the eighteenth and early nineteenth century, none of their names (al-Jīlānī, al-Saqāṭ, al-Khifrī,

[9] Miran and Layish, *The Testamentary Waqf*, p. 85.

al-Ghāzī) appear in sources consulted for the later nineteenth or the twentieth centuries.[10]

Furthermore, there are reports of changing settlement patterns in the Red Sea, notably from the 1840s until 1910 and especially in Massawa, during the period called the 'Red Sea boom' by Miran. Thus, increased numbers of Yemenis and Indians settled in that city, in addition to Greeks, Armenians, and even a few Western merchants.[11] In mid-nineteenth-century Jeddah, Indian, and Arab merchants owned the most important merchant houses. By this time, the number of Indians was probably already on the rise and might have contributed to the tensions in the Hijaz which resulted in the revolt in 1855 and the massacre of consuls in 1858 (see Chapter 2).[12] By 1860, Indians under British protection numbered around 500.[13] The reliability of these figures is questionable as, in 1871, the British consul complained that out of the many Indians resident in the Hijaz, only around 100 were registered with the consulate.[14] Nevertheless, many more would presumably claim British protection in case of conflict, if this promised a relative advantage (cf. Chapters 6, 7).

[10] ʿAbd al-Muʿṭī, *al-ʿAlāqāt al-miṣriyya al-ḥijāziyya*, p. 277; and Ṭrābulsī, *Jidda*, pp. 83–94; cf. ʿAbd al-Raḥmān al-Ṭayyib al-Anṣārī (ed.), *Dirāsāt tārīkh al-Jazīra al-ʿArabiyya* (Riyadh: Maṭbuʿāt Jāmiʿat al-Riyādh, 1399/1979), pp. 276–7, 283. Seetzen still met both al-Jīlānī and al-Sukkâth (probably al-Saqāt); cf. Ulrich Seetzen, 'Auszug aus einem Schreiben dess Russ. Kais. Kammer-Assessors Dr. U. J. Seetzen', *Monatliche Correspondence zur Beförderung der Erd- und Himmelkunde*, 27 (1813); and Ulrich Seetzen, 'Auszug aus einem Briefe des Kaiserl. Russ. Collegienassessors Herrn Dr. Seetzen an Herrn von Hammer aus Mocha den 14. November 1810', *Fundgruben des Orients*, 2 (1811), pp. 275–84, here p. 276.

[11] Dominique Harre, 'Exchanges and Mobility in the Western Indian Ocean: Indians between Yemen and Ethiopia, 19th–20th Centuries', *Les Chroniques du manuscrit au Yémen*, Special Issue 1 (2017), pp. 42–69, here p. 47; and Miran, *Red Sea Citizens*, pp. 118–44. For the term 'Red Sea boom', see Miran, *Red Sea Translocals*, p. 134.

[12] CADN, Amb. Const. D1, Outrey to Amb. Const., January 10, 1855, Beillard to Amb. Const., December 7, 1855; and 'The Jeddah Massacre' in A. B. Becher (ed.), *The Nautical Magazine* (London: Brown Son & Ferguson), vol. 27. babel.hathitrust.org/cgi/pt?id=nyp.33433066364872;view=1up;seq=446 (accessed December 23, 2017), pp. 426–8; *The Jeddah Massacre*, p. 428. For a differentiation of the Indian merchants see Pétriat, *Le Négoce des Lieux Saints*, pp. 42–3; and for the tensions Pétriat, pp. 72–5.

[13] TNA, FO 78/1538, Stalnley to FO, January 7, 1860; and FO 685/1, Stanley Letter Book, Stanley to FO, March 13, 1860.

[14] TNA, FO 78/2194, Raby to FO, February 13, 1871.

As mentioned in Chapter 2 and in contrast to Massawa or, even more clearly, to Aden, non-Muslim merchants remained a small minority in Jeddah. By contrast, migrants from the region of Hadhramaut in the Southern Arabian Peninsula played a prominent role as part of the merchant elite but were also well represented throughout the social hierarchy. While there was a fairly distinct wave of Hadhrami immigration in the 1920s and 1930s, it is more difficult to date the arrival of those families who became part of the merchant elites from the mid-nineteenth century. It can, however, be safely assumed that at least some of these families also arrived (or rose to prominence) with the more general economic upturn in the Red Sea region.[15] Although they pursued many trades and professions, it appears that the Hadhramis dominated the important slave trade.[16] They were such a large group that they were allowed not only an internal organisation presided over by their own shaykh, but also to bear arms and, in case of need, form a militia which was loyal to the emir of Mecca. Thus, in the context of the 1855 uprising, the British consul mentions more than 2,000 well-armed Hadhramis in Jeddah.[17]

Apart from the merchant elite, Burckhardt's observations on the many different ethnicities present in Jeddah have already been noted. A recent list of names of families living inside the city walls of Jeddah (i.e. presumably by the mid-twentieth century) published by Ṭrābulsī but reproduced by the municipality and circulated widely on social media confirms his findings: the names indicate that their bearers hail from various parts of the Arabian Peninsula from Yemen to Najd, as well as Iraq, Egypt, Syria, different parts of North Africa, but also Turkey, different parts of South and Southeast Asia, Afghanistan, Daghistan, Bukhara, West Africa (Takrūnī), and Greece.[18] Added to this must be those living in the suburbs of Jeddah which, although technically not part of the city (and not considered to be part of it by

[15] Pétriat, *Le Négoce des Lieux Saints*, p. 71 notes rightly that the 1858 massacre served to highlight the Hadhramis in the Western sources, which needs to be distinguished, however, from their emergence as an important merchant group.

[16] TNA; FO 195/375, Page to Amb. Const., November 13, 1855, August 4, 1856.

[17] Ibid., Page to Amb. Const., August 4, 1856; and Pétriat, *Le Négoce des Lieux Saints*, pp. 114–5. The Ottoman map of 1851 (see Chapter 4, Map 4.4) shows a tower in the wall called Burc-I Hadramî, whether this was sponsored or possibly defended by Hadhramis cannot be verified.

[18] Ṭrābulsī, *Jidda*, pp. 83–94. This is probably far from complete given that many Muslim names cannot be easily assigned to a specific place.

those within) were intrinsically bound to the urban economy while constituting a bridge to the surrounding regions and populations of Bedouin and villagers (see Chapter 4).

Stories of Voluntary Immigration – Or of Return?

Most of the retrievable family histories can only be traced back to the nineteenth century. Whether this is linked to a real change in population prompted, for example, by the struggle between the Āl Saʿūd and Mehmed Ali of Egypt in the early nineteenth century, to new economic possibilities as world trade expanded, to new administrative and political structures and limitations, and/or to the rise and fall of family fortunes cannot be verified. Furthermore, there is often little detail available, or parts of the histories are difficult to verify, as many of the accounts, written as well as oral, are based on memory rather than documents. Finally, the histories that were preserved are of individuals who were successful. Their names are preserved in endowment documents which testify to their growing wealth, they are listed among successful merchants, or are mentioned in consular archives or travelogues. Families which established themselves successfully during the nineteenth and early twentieth century have, over the past decades, begun to publish their family histories, often for the benefit (and edification) of their descendants and/or as a public testimony to their role in local history.[19] The following case studies, selected in order to demonstrate certain patterns and lines of self-presentation and therefore neither complete nor entirely representative, should thus be read without forgetting the probably more common cases of those who did not succeed and eventually returned to their homelands or scraped a living too small to be recorded in the sources examined for this book.

One example is the Qābil family which already enjoyed significant standing in the eighteenth century when one of its members was

[19] For these motivations, e.g. ʿAdnān al-Yāfī, *al-Nashʾa wa-l-takwīn: Dirāsa taṭbīqiyya min khilāl Āl al-Yāfi.* (Cairo: Dār al-Qāhira, 2005); Muḥammad Nūrwalī, *Ṣafaḥāt mūjaza min al-sīra al-mushriqa li-jaddinā ʿAbd al-Qādir Nūrwalī* (Jidda, 1431/2009), p. 5; Muḥammad al-Manqarī, *ʿAbd al-Majīd ʿAlī al-Shubukshī: Rajul al-amn wa-l-ṣaḥāfa wa-l-adab* (Jeddah: Maktab al-Aʿmāl al-Thaqāfiyya, 1432 h./2010), p. 23; Bakur, *ʿĀʾila jiddāwiyya*, p.7; and Aḥmad Āl Sībīh, *al-Muʿallim Muḥammad ʿAwaḍ bin Lādin* (Riyadh: Muʾassasat al-Turāth, 1341 h./2009), p. 17.

mentioned as the Ottoman governor of Jeddah in the 1770s.[20] Some family members seem to have entertained particularly close relations with the Meccan emirs of the Dhū Zayd line and acted as their commercial representatives in Jeddah. This position was probably comparable to that of the representatives of merchants (*wukalā'*) from other cities and reflects the distance between inland Mecca and its port.[21] In the early twentieth century, one of their members, Sulaymān, rose to prominence as a merchant, but also as administrator responsible for import permissions in Hashemite times and as the first president of the Merchant Court after the onset of Saudi rule.[22]

Another family which fulfilled such a function for the sharifs, this time from the Dhū ʿAwn branch, were the Naṣīfs. In the mid-nineteenth century, they were already counted among the foremost families of Jeddah and, throughout much of the nineteenth century, acted as agents of the emirs of Mecca. Little is known about the presumed founder of the family, Muḥammad Naṣīf, who, according to a family tree, died in 1101h./AD 1689–70. The father of ʿAbdallāh Naṣīf, a certain Abū Bakr, had endowed substantial properties in 1847.[23] Both Abū Bakr and his son ʿAbdallāh (d. 1288h./AD 1871–72) used the Ottoman title 'pasha', although it is unclear on what basis. At any rate, the family claims long-standing connections with Istanbul.[24] ʿAbdallāh as well as his grandson, ʿUmar (1822–1908) owned significant cisterns to the southeast of the old city, in an area called al-Sabīl.[25] The family also traded in grain and branched out into shipping and the transport of pilgrims. They invested their growing wealth not only in cisterns but

[20] James Bruce, *Travels to Discover the Source of the Nile in the Years 1768, 1769, 1770, 1771, 1772, and 1773: vol. 1*, 5 vols. (Edinburgh and London: J. Ruthven G. G. J. and J. Robinson, 1790), p. lxxii.

[21] Oral information from Sharīf Luayy b. ʿAbdallāh Āl Ghālib and his son Fahd, Jeddah, March 17, 2010. For an overview of the genealogy of the ruling *ashrāf* see the attached 'Stammtafeln' I-III in Snouck Hurgronje, *Mekka. Die Stadt und Ihre Herren*.

[22] Maghribī, *Aʿlām al-Ḥijāz*, vol. 1, pp. 43–4; and Kābilī, *al-Ḥirafiyyūn fī madīnat Jidda*, p. 39.

[23] This information is taken from a private waqf document, dated Dhū 'l-Qaʿida 7, 1395/November 10, 1975, which refers to the endowment of Dhū 'l-Qaʿida 14, 1263, consulted in Jeddah, March 2, 2015.

[24] Family tree contained in al-ʿAlawī al-Shanqīṭī, ʿAbduh Walad Aḥmad (ed.), *Dīwān al-majmūʿ al-laṭīf fī banī Naṣīf*, 2 vols. (Riyadh: Maktabat al-Tawba, 1423/2002); and interview with Dr. ʿAbdallā Naṣīf, March 20, 2011.

[25] Ṭrābulsī, *Jidda*, p. 142.

also in lands within the city walls, to the extent that by the 1890s they were said to own more than one quarter of the land within Jeddah.[26] ʿUmar, one of the wealthiest residents of Jeddah, for some time served as member of the provincial Administrative Council and possibly also as kaymakam.[27] In 1901 he is described as ʿUmar Naṣīf Pasha, head of the merchants of Jeddah.[28] He built the famous Naṣīf house in Jeddah in 1865 to host not only his own business partners and guests but also the Ottoman governor Ahmet Ratip Pasha and guests of the Meccan emir.[29] This tradition of hospitality was continued by his nephew Muḥammad Naṣīf (1885–1971). ʿUmar's brother Ḥusayn, Muḥammad's father, had died young so that Muḥammad was raised by his uncle. He became the most outstanding literary figure and an important notable of Jeddah (see Chapter 5).

One fascinating aspect of the family's history is the conflicting versions of origin. According to one tradition, the Naṣīfs descend from the Ḥarb tribe, living mainly between Jeddah and Medina, while according to another, they emigrated from Egypt. These were orally related to me by a family member who suggested that, perhaps, some family members had migrated to Egypt and later returned, a version which was also related to Philby by Muḥammad Naṣīf in 1924.[30] The connection to the Ḥarb, in contrast, would have possibly facilitated the transport of grain from Jeddah to the interior which was done by Bedouins.

In the course of the nineteenth century, there are also families from Persia who immigrated, among them the Zāhid and the ʿAlī Riḍā. The

[26] TNA, FO 195/1943, Alban to Herbert, August 3, 1896; Ṭrābulsī, Jidda, p. 142; and Muḥammad Aḥmad and Abdūh al-ʿAlawī, *Muḥammad Naṣīf: Ḥayyātuhu wa-āthāruh*. (Beirut, Damascus, and Amman: al-Maktab al-Islāmī, 1994), p. 119.

[27] TNA, FO 195/2061, Devey to FO, December 27, 1899, and TNA, FO 195/1451, September 26, 1883 Abdur Razzack an H. Wyndham Esq.; cf. CADN, 2MI 3243, Notes personnelles, notabilités musulmanes, p. 77, encl. in MAE to diplomatic and consular agencies, June 14, 1909. The role as *ḥākim*, ruler, which can only be translated into the office of kaymakam, was suggested to me by ʿAbd al-Raḥmān Naṣīf, March, 21 2011.

[28] Rifʿat, *Mirʾāt al-Ḥaramayn*, vol. 1, p. 20.

[29] Aḥmad and al-ʿAlawī, *Muḥammad Naṣīf*, p. 118–19; interviews with ʿAbdallāh al-Naṣīf, Jeddah, March 20, 2011; and ʿAbd al-Raḥmān al-Naṣīf, Jeddah, March 21, 2011; and for the date of the house Krause, *Stadtgeographische Untersuchungen*, p. 56.

[30] MECA, Philby Collection GB165–0229, 1/4/5/1, Philby Diary, part 1, November 29, 1924, p. 124.

latter trace their origins back to Arab tribes, possibly even the commander Amr b. al-ʿĀs (ca. 580–664), who went down in history as the Muslim conqueror of Egypt.[31] One of his sons conquered the region known variably as Khuzistan or Arabistan and mingled with Arab tribes known as Ḥawala.[32] From there, the ancestor moved first to Dushgan and from there to a village named Karmusta (arab. Karmūstaj) in southern Fars province. The family was involved in trade and led caravans to the port of Lingah. There are different versions of why young Zaynal (c. 1833–1929), the founding father of the Jeddah branch of the family, was taken from Lingah to Jeddah as a young boy approximately during the 1840s. The oral history of the family stresses that he had to flee Persia.[33] Zohrab, the British consul in 1879 had a much less romantic version. He claimed to have questioned Zaynal who 'states he was born in Aden where his parents landed while on their way to Mecca on account of illness, and he was brought up in India after leaving Aden'. According to this version, Zaynal came from Bandar Abbas rather than from Lingah.[34] No matter how he eventually arrived in Jeddah, Zaynal, after his arrival, was helped in his establishment by a fellow Arabo-Iranian family, the Zāhids, who traded in carpets and tobacco and who, like many South-Persian merchant families, maintained an office in Jeddah.[35] Hamilton reports that, in the early 1850s, about twenty Persian, mostly those trading in tobacco, resided in Jeddah in addition to a Persian consul who was under British protection.[36] According to Ochsenwald, Zaynal spent

[31] The connection to Amr b. al-ʿĀs was made by Yūsuf Aḥmad ʿAlī Riẓā, Jeddah, February 8, 2009; and by ʿAbdallāh Muḥammad ʿAbdallāh ʿAlī Riẓā, Jeddah, March 4, 2010.

[32] On the Hawala, see Ahmed al-Dailami, 'Purity and Confusion: The Hawala between Persians and Arabs in the Contemporary Gulf' in L. G. Potter (ed.), *The Persian Gulf in Modern Times: People, Ports, and History* (New York: Palgrave Macmillan, 2014), pp. 299–326.

[33] Michael Field, *The Merchants: The Big Business Families of Saudi Arabia and the Gulf States*, 2nd edn. (Woodstock, New York: Overlook Press, 1985), pp. 13–47.

[34] TNA, FO 195/1251, Zohrab to Amb. Const., November 12, 1879.

[35] Characteristically, the version, told from a Zāhid perspective, differs slightly: According to ʿAdnān Zāhid, their family hailed from Medina, but arrived 'anew' after a sojourn in southern Iran. In this version, Zāhids and three brothers of the ʿAlī Riẓā arrived together in Jeddah. Interview, Jeddah, March 6, 2006, the Jeddah connections of the local families were confirmed by ʿAbdallāh Muḥammad ʿAbdallāh ʿAlī Riẓā, Jeddah, March 4, 2010.

[36] Hamilton, *Sinai, The Hedjaz, and Soudan*, p. 57.

Table 3.1 *Family tree of the ʿAlī Riḍā family.*

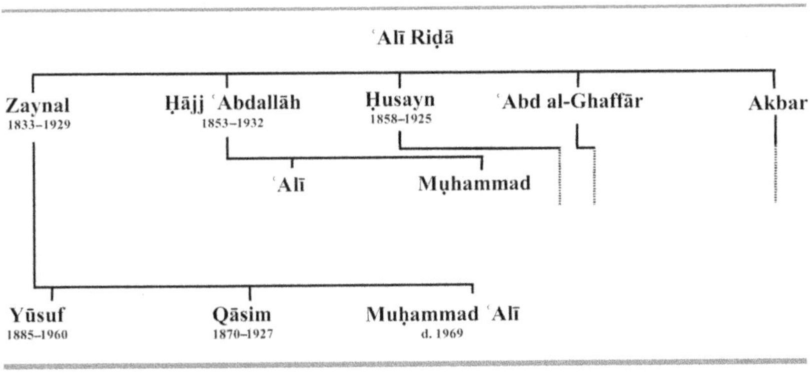

Drawn by Noël van den Heuvel.

fifteen years in Bombay, where he became prosperous.[37] He eventually established himself as an independent trader in food and cloth and brought two of his brothers, ʿAbdallāh and Ḥusayn, to Jeddah (see below, Table 3.1). His business flourished by the 1860s and the close link between his family and the Zāhids lasted well into the twentieth century, cemented by marital alliances. However, Zaynal also sought other connections: he married into the Naṣīf family and thus gained access to the sharifs of Mecca, eventually becoming their agent.[38] Like many prominent merchants, Zaynal spent part of his fortune on charity and became known as 'father of the poor'.[39]

The almost accidental way in which one or more brothers are said to have arrived, either together or individually, in Jeddah raises questions. In parallel, another relative, either a brother or, perhaps more likely, the son of ʿAlī Akbar who had remained behind in Persia, settled in Kuwait, while one of ʿAlī Akbar's sons moved to Bahrain.[40] Did he

[37] Ochsenwald, *Religion, Society, and the State*, p. 108.

[38] MAE, CADN, 2MI 3243, Notes personnelles, notabilités musulmanes, p. 60–1 (Zeinal Aly Reza and 61, Kassim Zeinal), encl. in MAE to diplomatic and consular agencies, 14.6.1909. According to ʿAbdallāh Naṣīf, he also acted as kaymakam, oral information Jeddah, March 21, 2011.

[39] Maghribī, *Aʿlām al-Ḥijāz*, vol. 1, p. 38.

[40] Carter, J. R. L, *Leading Merchant Families of Saudi Arabia* (London: Scorpion Publications; D.R. Llewellyn Group, 1979), pp. 160–1; and Field, *The Merchants*, pp. 16–18. A descendant of the Iranian family branch, Enayet Rezai, became the first director of the Teheran Opera House in 1967, L. O. Adams, *Notes on Roudaki Hall in Tehran, Iran*. www.operanostalgia.be/html/ROUDAKIHALL2016.html (accessed February 15, 2018).

have to leave, as is said to have been the case for Zaynal, or was him moving part of a conscious strategy of mercantile expansion in the Persian Gulf region during a period when a Pax Britannica was imposed on the Gulf in the early and mid-nineteenth century?[41] By the late nineteenth-century members of the Alī Riḍā family can be found as far afield as Bombay and Calcutta. This network surely facilitated their trade in foodstuffs from India to Iran and the Peninsula. With time they became involved in the transportation of pilgrims through the agency of the Moghul line. Profits were invested, inter alia, in houses in Mecca rented out to pilgrims during the season.

Zaynal's younger brother ʿAbdallāh, in addition to taking part in the family business of Hajji Abdullah Alireza Co., also became the first Sharifian governor or kaymakam. His term in office lasted until his death in August 1932, well into Saudi reign.[42] It was thus him who officially handed over the city to Ibn Saʿūd, as can be seen in Figure 3.1. The eldest of Zaynal's sons from an Ethiopian (i.e. probably slave) mother also had political ambitions: Qāsim became deputy to the Ottoman parliament after the Young Turk revolution of 1908 and was behind the construction of the first coal-fired seawater desalination plant.[43] His younger brother Muḥammad is today mainly remembered for founding the Falāḥ schools in Jeddah (founded in 1905) and Mecca (founded in 1912), with later branches established in Bombay, Bahrain, and Dubai, as well as, briefly, in al-Mukallā.[44] He financed these by becoming one of the foremost pearl and diamond traders in Bombay, where he processed pearls bought from Bahrain and exported to Paris and London.[45]

The family of Nūrwalī resembles that of the ʿAlī Riẓā in their claim to Hijazi origin, as well as in that of their travel, except that in their case it was between India, more precisely Patan in Gujarat, and the Hijaz.

41 For the economy of the Gulf region in the eighteenth and early nineteenth century, see Fuccaro, *Histories of City and State*, pp. 43–60; and for the British in the Gulf Onley, *The Arabian Frontier*, pp. 43–4.
42 Maghribī, *Aʿlām al-Ḥijāz*, vol. 1, pp. 136–44.
43 Field, *The Merchants*, p. 22.
44 Abkar, *Ṣuwar min Turāth Makka*; Maghribī, *Aʿlām al-Ḥijāz*, vol. 1, pp. 316–30; *Madāris al-Falāḥ: al-Ḥaḍāra wa-l-Turāth* (hectographed copies of testimonials, newspaper articles and interviews, often without precise indication of source) (n.d.); and Maḥmūd Riḍwān, *Qālū ʿan Muḥammad ʿAlī Zaynal* (hectographed collection of articles and interviews, often without precise indication of sources) (n.d.).
45 Oral communication, Amna Muḥammad ʿAli Riẓā, Jeddah, February 21, 2009.

Figure 3.1 Ibn Saʿūd and Shaykh ʿAbdallāh ʿAlī Riḍā.
Leiden University Libraries, Or. 12.288 J: 4, date 1925

They finally settled in Jeddah in late Ottoman times, initially importing rice from India, where they had agents in Bombay, Surat, and Burma via Aden.[46] Later, probably sometime during the first half of the twentieth century, they added perfume and traditional medicines, which were then complemented by the import of modern medicine. ʿAbd al-Qādir Nūrwalī (d. 1977), whose biography was written by his great-grandson as a memoir for the family, invested, like the other families, in real estate, in his case in Jeddah, Medina, Mecca, and Ṭaʾif.[47] Interestingly, his grandson biographer reports not only how the pious merchant consulted local scholars before making business decisions but also cultivated connections with visiting Indian scholars, offering them accommodation in his house in Medina and benefiting from their counsel as well as their reputation, thus enhancing his own social and cultural standing.[48] While the Nūrwalīs did not rise to the same

46 al-Muʿabbadī, *al-Nashāṭ al-tijārī li-mināʾ Jidda*, p. 2010.
47 Nūrwalī, *Ṣafaḥāt Mūjaza min al-Sīra al-Mushriqa*, pp. 18, 21, 24; and interview with D. ʿAbd al-Wahhāb ʿAbd al-Raḥmān Nūr Walī, Jeddah, March 27, 2010.
48 Nūrwalī, p. 27.

economic and political position as the Naṣīf or ʿAlī Riḍā, they counted among the wealthy merchants. This found expression in their acquisition of a large house in the Yemen quarter of Jeddah near the *sūq*.[49]

The families discussed above would appear to be Egyptians, Persians, and Indians, except that their own claim is to Arab descent. They share an argument, though each family has its own variation, stated explicitly in Adnan Yafi's study *The Arab Family*, in which he uses his own family history as an example.[50] He embeds the family's story into a wider discussion of Arab migrations from the Arabian Peninsula as far as Andalusia and Persia in the wake of the Islamic expansion.[51] According to Yafi, the migration of his ancestors from the Maghreb to Egypt and Syria and from there to the Hijaz needs to be considered as a reverse migration to the heartlands of the Arabs. In the particular case used as an example, Yafi's ancestor ʿAbd al-Badīʿ arrived in the late nineteenth century and established himself as a textile merchant. His first son ʿUmar achieved the positions of head of the guild of textile merchants (*shaykh al-qummāshīn*) in the 1920s or 1930s.[52] Such histories are, Yafi argues, particularly well preserved among the descendants of the Prophet, the *ashrāf*, due to their concern with family and genealogy. For him, the Sharifian concern with descent is an outstanding example of the wider Arab culture which gives much importance to genealogy and tribal origins.[53]

Quite independently of the veracity or otherwise of the individual family histories, the insistence on Arab origins and their explicit connection to tribal genealogies seem like an answer to those who called Jiddawis 'spit of the sea', a name which was discussed in Chapter 1. In the context of an increasingly tribally and ethnically conscious nation-state, in Saudi Arabia as much as in the Arab Gulf States, Yafi's

49 Kābilī, *al-Ḥirafiyyūn fī madīnat Jidda*, p. 178. Their importance was stressed by Khaled al-Maena, Jeddah, February 21, 2010.

50 ʿAdnān al-Yāfī, *The Arab Family: Origin and Formation. An Applied Study through the Al-Yafi Family* (Jeddah, 2437/2016); and al-Yāfī, *al-Nashʾa wa-l-Takwīn*, English version al-Yāfī, *The Arab Family*.

51 al-Yāfī, *al-Nashʾa wa-l-Takwīn*, pp. 3–12.

52 al-Yāfī, *The Arab Family*, p. 209; cf. Kābilī, *al-Ḥirafiyyūn fī madīnat Jidda*, p. 134. On the longer history of Syrian cloth merchants in Cairo and Jeddah; cf. Raymond, *Artisans et Commerçants*, vol. 2, pp. 478–83; and ʿAbd al-Muʿṭī, *al-ʿAlāqāt al-miṣriyya al-ḥijāziyya*, p. 171.

53 al-Yāfī, *The Arab Family*, pp. 61–5. He has added a copy of the (recent) certificate from the *naqīb al-ashrāf* in Damascus to confirm the veracity of the claims put forward, p. 283.

argument of a genealogically proven descent from not only the Arabian Peninsula, but the House of the Prophet, asserts the place of his family as one with deep roots in the Hijaz. al-Dailami makes a similar argument about the debates on the Ḥawala, evoked in Jeddah by the ʿAlī Riḍā genealogy outlined above, when arguing that the Arab identification of the Ḥawala 'examines how people have chosen to invalidate, reassemble, and strategically redeploy their cultural identifications in nation-states in which the relationship between the political and the ethnic, or more accurately between political citizens and ethnic subjects, remains unresolved.'[54]

In Jeddah, this means that while plurality is celebrated in a demonstrative manner, individual families nevertheless refer to the hegemonic discourse by presenting their national credentials as tribal Arabs.[55] Anecdotal evidence of the adoption of new names to veil the origin betrayed by *nisba*s, adjectives denoting origin (such as 'al-Dāghestānī') confirms such an interpretation.[56] As for the large Hadhrami community, the Arab origin of which is undisputed, the *sāda* (descendants of the Prophet via his grandson al-Ḥusayn) also have a link to the Hijaz. Others point to their ancient South Arabian tribal origins. Thus, the biography of Muḥammad ʿAwaḍ Bin Lādin (Bin Laden), founder of a leading construction company in Saudi Arabia in 1931, devotes two pages to the tribal origin of the family. This is traced back to the South Arabian tribe Kinda, whose prominent role in Arabian pre-Islamic history is then explained.[57] The book thus provides a prestigious lineage for somebody who was raised in a family of builders, a group which, in the rigidly stratified society of the Hadhramaut, did not enjoy a high reputation.[58] It provides a remarkable contrast to the subsequent story of a young orphan who learned his trade but quickly went abroad to earn money, first in Abyssinia, then in Aden and finally in Jeddah around 1920.[59] In terms of a narrative highlighting the

54 al-Dailami, *Purity and Confusion*, p. 299; cf. Onley, *Transnational Merchant Families*, p. 47.
55 al-Dailami, *Purity and Confusion*, p. 315.
56 Interview, Khaled al-Maena, Jeddah, March 21, 2010. The exemplary *nisba* has been chosen at random.
57 Āl Sībīh, *al-Muʿallim*, pp. 18, 20.
58 Linda Boxberger, *On the Edge of Empire: Hadhramawt, Emigration, and the Indian Ocean, 1880s–1930s*, SUNY Series in Near Eastern Studies (Albany: State University of New York Press, 2002), pp. 32–3.
59 Āl Sībīh, *al-Muʿallim*, pp. 24, 26.

remarkable achievement of becoming the prime government contractor in construction (and in the remodelling of the *ḥarams* of Mecca and Medina) for half a century, the rise from abject poverty to great wealth follows a script equivalent to the American dream. The fact that the director of the prestigious religious college of Tarīm in Hadhramaut has authored a recent booklet on the family, highlighting both the tribal origin and the affinity of certain family members to the Hadhrami religious elite suggests changing perspectives on social hierarchies in relation to migration, economic success, and the passing of time.[60] It should be added that Bin Lādin is only one of a number of remarkable entrepreneurs with similar trajectories. An almost parallel history is that of Sālim Bin Maḥfūẓ, founder of the National Commercial Bank of Saudi Arabia.[61]

Whether this tendency to emphasise (or to focus one's research on) one's Arab origin is more predominant amongst elite families would warrant further investigation. It is made possible by genealogical practices which focus on the patronym and which allow both the acculturation in different spaces through intermarriage as well as the reclaiming of a specific – Peninsular – heritage through the patronym and a genealogy leading back to the Prophet or – in the cases of Naṣīf, ʿAlī Riẓā and Bin Laden, reference to a particular tribal heritage. Migration at times helped to obfuscate the more mundane details of a family's genealogy.[62]

Not all migrants are, however, equally concerned with presenting themselves as original Arabs. There are other cases where, for example, the Indian origin is presented in a matter-of-fact manner. Thus, the Bakhsh family, originating in Agra, has made its genealogy available

60 Sālim al-Shāṭirī, *Risāla mukhtaṣira fī tārīkh qabīlat Āl Bin Lādin* (Tarīm, 2011).

61 On the company see Field, *The Merchants*, pp. 75, 105–6; Carter, *Leading Merchant Families of Saudi Arabia*, pp. 108–11; and *sbg.com*. 'Almualem/ Mohammed Awad Binladin; A Word by Engineer Bakr Bin Mohammed Binladin'. www.sbg.com.sa/profile.html (accessed February 16, 2018). For Sālim Bin Maḥfūẓ see Khālid Bā Ṭarfī, *Sālim bin Maḥfūẓ … yatadhakkar* (Jeddah, 1435/2014). For a slightly different version; cf. Thomas Pritzkat, *Stadtentwicklung und Migration im Südjemen: Mukalla und die hadhramitische Auslandsgemeinschaft*, Jemen-Studien (Wiesbaden: Reichert, 2001), vol. 16, pp. 86–7.

62 On the question of migration and genealogy in the case of Hadhramis, see Engseng Ho, 'Names beyond Nations: The Making of Local Cosmopolitans', Études Rurales, *Comparative Studies in Society and History*, 163/164 (2002), pp. 215–31.

online.[63] Karīm Raḥīm Bakhsh migrated to Mecca with his family and young sons in 1854, where he studied in the *ḥaram*. Around 1940 one of his grandsons moved from there to Jeddah and became a noteworthy mercantile agent.[64]

So far, the question of (im)migration has been told as a male story. This is due to a number of factors. For one, women, particularly those of higher status, travelled considerably less frequently than men in times when long-distance travel was difficult. Those who travelled, mostly in the context of the hajj, left few narratives. This differs to some extent for women who were brought to the Hijaz, usually as slaves, as will be discussed below. One prominent exception for this rule is a lady of Indian origin, Ṣadīqa Sharaf al-Dīn. Her father was a book merchant in India and maintained business relations with Muḥammad Naṣīf, the aforementioned notable and *homme de lettres*. He sent his daughter on the pilgrimage (interestingly, little is known about who accompanied her) and she was hosted in Jeddah by Muḥammad Naṣīf. Naṣīf, too, was obsessed with learning and was so impressed by her piety and mastery of the Koran that he married her to his son ʿUmar. Ṣadīqa, an accomplished *dāʿiya* (a term used for people propagating Islam), first taught in her house and subsequently established the Madrasa Naṣīfiyya, the first girls' school of Jeddah (licensed in 1956).[65]

While the marriage of a notable's son to a foreign woman was not unusual, as has already been mentioned in the introduction, there are also a number of cases where this did not occur. Famously, Sālim Bin Maḥfūẓ, another poor Hadhrami boy arriving in the 1920s, first had a number of different jobs before starting to work for a Meccan money-changer of Indian origin, ʿAbd al-ʿAzīz Kaʿkī. Kaʿkī's children showed no real passion for the profession, so that he eventually offered his daughter to Bin Maḥfūẓ in marriage, which laid the foundation for the

[63] *tribalpages.com*. 'Bakhsh family'. https://atef47.tribalpages.com/tribe/browse?userid=atef47& view=0&pid=5 (accessed February 16, 2018).

[64] Interviews, ʿAdnān al-Yāfī, Jeddah, March 22, 2006; and Atef Bakhsh and cousins, Jeddah, February 18, 2009.

[65] Ṭrābulsī, *Jidda*, p. 441; and interview with Ṭrābulsī, March 13, 2010. The school Dār al-Ḥanān was founded a year earlier by Queen Effat, but then Ṣadīqa had already taught some years at her home, and it is not unlikely that it needed a royal project to be licensed before a private school could be opened; cf. *dhs.edu.sa*. 'Tārīkh Dār al-Ḥanān'. www.dhs.edu.sa/pages.aspx? pageid=3 (accessed February 19, 2014).

latter's immense wealth after he successfully founded a bank.[66] This story is an example of marriage as a form of alliance, which was often used to join two families sharing a business, as suggested by Altorki.[67] She herself gives an example of two approximately equally ranked families intermarrying. The interesting aspect of the marriage between Bin Maḥfūẓ and Kaʿkī's daughter is, however, that the latter had simply been an employee. In an interesting twist, descendants of another Hadhrami employee of Kaʿkī claim that he had offered him the daughter first but that the boy's family had refused because she was of Indian, and not of Arab descent. The marriage of Zaynal ʿAlī Riḍā to a daughter of the Zāhid's might be considered more like one of equals, given possible earlier business relations in Persia. In contrast, his aforementioned conjugal union with a daughter of the Naṣīfs is another prominent example of the marriage of a newcomer without established local family credentials to a girl from the local elite, something which departed from the central Arabian norms discussed in the introduction. The tendency to out-marry seems to have decreased markedly in the second or third generation for both men and women. However, by the time Altorki was conducting her research in the 1980s, marriage outside the family was on the rise once again due to socio-economic change.[68]

Jeddah also featured a fairly large sub-Saharan population, about which much less is known. It was constituted of people of different origins including both East Africans, such as people from the Sudan and Suakin, as well as West Africans. These are known as Takrūrīs or Takrūnīs (pl. Takār(i)na) and hailed from West Africa. However, there are also a number of other appellations which were at times confounded with, or summarised under, the name of Takrūrī. There were the Shanāqiṭa (sing. Shinqīṭī), travelling with the pilgrimage caravans starting in Shinqīṭ (present-day Chinguetti in the Adrar-region of Mauretania).[69] Another name given to West Africans, more specifically

66 In addition to the literature in fn. 50, this and the following is also based on interviews with Muḥammad Bā Quʿr, grandson of Sālim Muḥammad Bā Quʿr, Jeddah, February 16, 2015; and Khayriyya ʿAbdallāh, former slave of Muḥammad Bā Quʿr, February 22, 2009.

67 Altorki, *Women in Saudi Arabia*, pp. 123–47, especially pp. 140–1.

68 Altorki, p. 143; and Interview, ʿAbdallāh Muḥammad ʿAbdallāh ʿAlī Riḍā, March 4, 2010.

69 ʿUmar al-Naqar, 'Takrūr: The History of a Name', *Journal of African History*, 10 (1969), pp. 365–74.

those called Fulbe or Fulānī, is Fallāta, a term that has become largely conflated with Takārna.[70] Further distinctions were sometimes made for those from Bornu, as well as for speakers of Haussa.[71] While many of the Takārna are said to have fled the French imperial expansion in West Africa, other West Africans arrived as pilgrims or scholars.[72] Of course, these were not mutually exclusive trajectories: One Shaykh al-Fallāṭa in Jeddah in the Saudi period originated from a learned family in Sokoto (or Kano). The family emigrated via Chad and Sudan to the Hijaz when the British occupied Nigeria. Their initial settlement in Mecca was possibly supported by *awqāf* for African pilgrims (and/or paupers). Eventually, a descendant became the pilgrims' guide for West African pilgrims in Jeddah, organising their transfer from the harbour to Mecca.[73] The scholarly background is also prominent in the history of the Barqāwī family, which claims to originate from Barqa in present-day Libya. Its eponymous ancestor moved to Chad as a missionary and played a role in a local Muslim emirate. He then went on pilgrimage to the Hijaz and settled in Jeddah. One of his descendants, the (great-?)grandfather of my interviewee, became a leader of hajj-caravans during Sharifian rule. He moved from his house in the old city to the suburbs, presumably, because he needed armed retainers for the position.[74]

The less fortunate among the African migrants often lived in the suburbs of Jeddah, notably al-Ruways and Nakutu (see Chapter 4), which they shared with local fishermen, slaves, as well as poor Indians, Yemenis, and Sudanese.[75] Many of the Takārna in Jeddah worked as

[70] Peter Holt, 'Fallāta' in P. J. Bearman, T. Bianquis, C. E. Bosworth, E. J. van Donzel, and W. P. Heinrichs (eds.), *Encyclopaedia of Islam*, 2nd edn., 12 vols. (Leiden: Brill, 1960–2005). dx.doi.org/10.1163/1573-3912_islam_SIM_2261 (accessed February 19, 2018).

[71] Oral information Talal Bakur, Jeddah, March 19, 2011.

[72] The story recounted by Tamisier, *Voyage en Arabie*, pp. 132–6. That they were sent to the Hijaz because of overpopulation, seems rather spurious, but attests to a significant Takrūrī population already by the 1840s.

[73] Interview, Prof. Muḥammad Fahīm, Jeddah, January 7, 2009. For an account of scholars of West African origin, see Chanfi Ahmed, *West African 'Ulamā' and Salafism in Mecca and Medina: Jawāb al-Ifrīqī-the Response of the African*, Islam in Africa (Leiden and Boston: Brill, 2015), vol. 17; for the migration following colonisation particularly pp. 13–23.

[74] Interview with ʿAbd al-Raḥmān al-Barqāwī, Jeddah, March 26, 2010. The information was too sketchy to reconstruct any details.

[75] Rathjens and Wissmann, *Landschaftskundliche Beobachtungen*, p. 82; and Kābilī, *al-Ḥirafiyyūn fī madīnat Jidda*, p. 80.

boatmen and porters.[76] Others specialised in making large mats.[77] According to one source, numerous Takrūnī pilgrims stayed outside of the walled city because they did not speak Arabic (in contrast to, for example, Sudanese pilgrims).[78] However, the spacious Jamjūm house in Ḥārat al-Shām, the most prestigious quarter in the late nineteenth century, featured a terrace known as the 'terrace (*dikka* or *dakka*) of the Shanāqiṭa'. According to living memory (probably going back to the mid-twentieth century), this was used by pilgrims from West Africa during the period of the hajj. They resided in an annexe to the building in the evenings. It attracted members of the local population, who loved to listen to the stories these visitors had to tell about their homeland and journey.[79] Philby's diary has an interesting description of a procession of slaves with some musical instruments which culminated in the performance of a dance. This was explained to him as a regular feature of slave society, linked to some kind of fetish worship and hailing from the Sudan. He ends his description with the particularly interesting note that 'The slave society here appears to have a regular organisation of Shaikhs etc.'[80]

Ottoman officials did not constitute a clear ethnic group (although they are often labelled as 'Turkish'), as they came from different geographical and ethnic backgrounds but had, through education, been socialised into Ottoman culture. As representatives of the ruling power, they exercised fiscal, judicial, and military authority. Thus, their presence was probably not universally welcomed.[81] However, they also stood out in terms of dress (as the photograph of the Jeddah court scribe in Figure 3.2 illustrates) and lifestyle.

Thus, the traveller Keane, whose account very openly reflects his own notions of civilisational hierarchy, nevertheless might have had a

[76] TNA, FO 195/1451 Moncrieff to FO, July 27, 1883. In Mecca, many also were involved in menial labour during the pilgrimage, CADN, 2_MI_3229, Suret to Min. of Commerce, December 3, 1879, Dr. Morsly to Min. of Commerce, November 6, 1882.

[77] TNA, FO 195/2174, Devey to Amb. Const., Report on the Hejaz Vilayet, September 9, 1903, p. 4.

[78] Oral information Ṭalāl Bakur, Jeddah, March 19, 2011.

[79] Oral communication, ʿAbīr Abū Sulaymān, Jeddah, March 10, 2017.

[80] MECA, Philby Collection GB165-0229, 1/4/5/1, Philby Diary, part 1, November 28, 1924, p. 121.

[81] E.g. Hamilton, *Sinai, The Hedjaz, and Soudan*, pp. 70–1; TNA, FO 195/879, Calvert to Amb. Const., June 3, 1865; FO 195/1251, Zohrab to FO, August, 1879; and FO 179/1313, Zohrab to FO, March 16, 1880.

Figure 3.2 Hasan Efendi, Scribe of the Court.
Leiden University Libraries, Or. 26.368: 19

point when he mentioned that Ottomans (in his parlance: 'Turks') were hated not only because of their exercise of power but also 'on account of their adoption of European costume and their introduction of such Christian innovations as forks, chairs, and, it is whispered, even wine into the holy Meccah'.[82] While Turkish soldiers in particular were at times associated with drinking, there are occasional hints in the consular reports which would support the idea that at least some of the Ottoman officials sent from further away considered Jeddah a kind of uncivilised outpost, almost like some of the European consuls.[83] Such

[82] T. F. Keane, *Six Months in the Hejaz: An Account of the Mohammedan Pilgrimage to Meccah and Medinah*, 2nd. edn. of Six Months in Mecca: An Account of the Mohammedan Pilgrimage to Meccah, London: Tinsley Brothers 1881. (London: Ward and Downey, 1887), p. 90.

[83] For alcohol consumption by soldiers, e.g. Rüppell, *Reise in Abyssinien*, vol. 1, p. 169; TNA, FO 195/1104 Beyts to Emb. Const., December 20, 1876. For the mention of an Ottoman discourse of lack of civilisation, see FO 195/1314,

imagery notwithstanding, some Ottoman officials did speak good Arabic. One example of this is kaymakam ʿAlī Pasha, appointed in 1879. Others were of Arab origin or even locals who rose to higher positions in the Ottoman administration.[84] These seem to have been more widely accepted by the local population. Thus, a British report in October 1899 mentions that sanitary measures taken in Jeddah were met with 'mild approval' due to the high standing of a 'local' kaymakam. Besides the local origin, a long local training in different government departments might have contributed to the success of this former secretary to the provincial governor.[85]

Slavery in Jeddah – A Case of 'Coerced Migration'?[86]

In 1888 the French consul in Jeddah estimated that about one-fifth of the population were slaves.[87] Like the remainder of the population, slaves came from different regions and were imported on the basis of specific criteria. Contrary to the Gulf, where Hopper has been able to discern a distinct growth in demand for (male) labour on date plantations and in the pearl industry during the second half of the nineteenth century, the gender balance for those who remained in Jeddah is less clear. Pearling in the Red Sea was far more circumscribed than in the Gulf, and agriculture was only possible in the mountains to the East of Jeddah, or in Medina.[88] According to a 'high Turkish official', slaves were the only solution to the question of domestic work as 'Mussulman women cannot be engaged as servants for they could not work with their faces concealed and if they expose them they would be breaking the law of the Koran. Christian women cannot be engaged

Burrell to FO, August, 1880; and on local perceptions of Turks, see John Burckhardt, 'Observations sur les habitants de la Mecque et de Djidda', *Nouvelles Annales des Voyages*, 50 (=2e série, 20) (1831), pp. 5–37, 129–63, 134–7.

84 TNA, FO 195/1251, Zohrab to Emb. Const., November 11, 1879.

85 TNA, FO 195/2060, Devey to Emb. Const., October 30, 1899; for his background, see Hussain to O'Conor, September 1, 1899.

86 Ehud Toledano, *As If Silent and Absent: Bonds of Enslavement in the Islamic Middle East* (New Haven, CT: Yale University Press, 2007), p. 24.

87 MAE, CADN, Const Amb D4, Djeddah, Consul to Amb. Const., December 31, 1888, p. 5.

88 Matthew Hopper, *Slaves of One Master: Globalization and Slavery in Arabia in the Age of Empire* (New Haven, CT: Yale University Press, 2015), p. 8.

as it would be a pollution'.[89] This type of work was, with a few exceptions, a female domain, both because household work was considered a female task, and in order to maintain strict gender segregation. The British consul's observation regarding the preponderance of male slaves in Jeddah thus seems highly unlikely and was perhaps caused by the large number of slaves resold to the Gulf, Egypt, and Syria, as well as to his limited access to the women's quarters. Jeddah is probably more comparable to Massawa, where Miran also noted a preponderance of female over male slaves, although a systematic investigation of the entire period would be necessary to confirm this.[90]

While women were thus often imported to serve as domestic workers, they were also sought after for sexual pleasure and procreation. Some were destined exclusively for the latter task. Thus, the most sought-after and highly-priced slaves were Georgian and Circassian women who were bought to produce fair-skinned offspring.[91] One notable of Jeddah in the late nineteenth century is said to have owned dozens of slaves because he was desperate for a son. Because he himself was fairly dark-skinned, he bought Syrian, Armenian, and other Caucasian slaves. If they had children, he manumitted the women and they remained in the household. Those who did not become pregnant were resold.[92] For Massawa, Miran has noted that those men who could not afford Circassian or Georgian slaves preferred Ethiopian women, often of

[89] TNA, FO 685/1 Consul Zohrab's Letter Book 1879, Zohrab to FO, May 14, 1879. On domestic service in the Middle East; cf. Maldine Zilfi, 'Servants, Slaves, and the Domestic Order in the Ottoman Middle East', *Hawwa*, 2 (2004), pp. 1–33. For the legal status of Muslim slaves, see R. Brunschvig, ''Abd' in P. J. Bearman, T. Bianquis, C. E. Bosworth, E. J. van Donzel, and W. P. Heinrichs (eds.), *Encyclopaedia of Islam*, 2nd edn., 12 vols. (Leiden: Brill, 1960–2005), dx.doi.org/10.1163/1573-3912_islam_COM_0003 (accessed February 22, 2018).

[90] TNA, FO 195/1313, Zohrab to Foreign Office, March 13, 1880. It is quoted by Y. Erdem, *Slavery in the Ottoman Empire and Its Demise, 1800–1909*, St. Antony's Series (New York: St. Martin's Press, 1996), pp. 63–4; and Jonathan Miran, 'From Bondage to Freedom on the Red Sea Coast: Manumitted Slaves in Egyptian Massawa, 1873–1885', *Slavery & Abolition*, 34 (2013), pp. 135–57, p. 138. For slaves being predominantly women; cf. TNA, FO 685/1, Stanley Letter Book, Stanley to Amb. Const., January 21, 1862. Although such statements are always only momentary impressions and would need to be followed systematically through time.

[91] For a case of mistreatment of a Georgian slave, see TNA, FO 195/1251, Zohrab to FO, December 22, 1879.

[92] Interview with ʿAbd al-Raḥmān Naṣīf, Jeddah, March 21, 2011.

Oromo origin.[93] This certainly also applied in Jeddah. The religious affiliation of slaves was often obscured by their captors, 'they are sold as Christians to Moslem purchasers, and as Moslem to Christians', observed one colonial official based in Zanzibar in a report on slavery in the Red Sea.[94] In both cases, slavery implied the more or less forced conversion of the enslaved.

Many of the fair-skinned girls were brought as slaves with pilgrimage caravans from Syria. Yemeni girls and women also often arrived with or as pilgrims. Thus, I was told about a girl who had entered a second marriage in Yemen, probably in the 1940s. Her new husband proposed to take her on hajj, whereupon she left the children from her first marriage with her parents and travelled to Mecca with him. In Jeddah, he brought her to a house and left her under the pretext of attending to some business. When he did not return, she enquired and found out that she had been sold to this household. Her story ended more happily than most: Because she kept crying, her new master contacted the pilgrims' guide of the Yemenis. He arranged for the woman to be returned to Yemen at the end of the pilgrimage season – to which fate we do not know.[95] The enslavement of Muslims, which was a common practice, contradicted Islamic Law which forbids such enslavement. Non-Muslim slaves were converted by their masters, although such conversions do not seem to have required a major ceremony, judging by the silence of sources on the topic.

Interestingly, some domestic tasks which one might have expected wives or slaves to perform were outsourced. Among them was the washing of clothes, probably a particularly tedious affair in a city with a permanent water shortage. While slaves were sometimes imported specifically for this chore, washing was also performed by free Takrūnī women presumably living in the African settlements on the outskirts of Jeddah.[96] Perhaps this outsourcing was one way by which women tried to limit the employment of slaves who might turn out to be their rivals.

93 Miran, *From Bondage to Freedom*, p. 138.

94 TNA, FO 881/2270, Sir Bartle Frere to FO, May 29, 1873; and Anita Burdett, *The Slave Trade into Arabia 1820–1973*, 5 vols. (Slough: Archive Editions, 2006), vol. 2, pp. 757–74, here p. 758.

95 Interview with Khayriyya ʿAbdallāh, Jeddah, February 22, 2009.

96 Alaine Hutson, 'Enslavement and Manumission in Saudi Arabia, 1926–38', *Critique: Critical Middle Eastern Studies*, 11 (2002), pp. 49–70, 62; fn. 46; and interview with Khayriyya ʿAbdallāh, Jeddah, February 22, 2009.

Another strategy was for women to prefer the acquisition of female slaves with darker skins 'to those more attractive in appearance' (here the reporting consul seems to share the beauty standards of the local men).[97] Given the perceived right of men to the sexual services of domestic servants, the ladies of Jeddah may be forgiven for attempting to limit this as much as possible.

Most of the enslaved men came from across the Red Sea, although there are many stories of kidnapping in the Hijaz. The latter practice seems to have peaked in the period between 1910 and 1924 when the slave trade was decreasing and World War I, the Arab Revolt, and the wars between Sharifian and Saudi forces increased demand for military labour.[98] Thus, there is a trustworthy report about Nigerian pilgrims who were seized in Mecca and transported to the Sharifian barracks in 1923 in order to join the army.[99]

A typical story of African captivity, which can be found in the consular archives where slaves sought manumission, was as follows:

> Before me this 16th day of August 1877 Farruk, a Nubian boy aged about 20 years declares that he was captured in his Country about 9 years ago, and brought with 129 other slaves via Khartum to Suakin, and from there by an Arab Dhow to Jeddah, he was landed in the harbour, and marched to the slave market in the town, where he was sold to an Arab named Mustapha Ramadan, a Turkish Subject resident at Jeddah.[100]

Although there were many slaves bought to help in their owner's business or household, others were

> bought for purposes of profit. The Arab having obtained as many slaves as his means will permit, sends them out to earn money by labor. These slaves are bound to hand daily to their master 5, 8 or 10 Piastres according to the labor they are permitted to engage in, and they must earn also sufficient to keep themselves, when they fail to give the required sum, whatever they may have earned is taken from them [,] they are flogged and left to starve.[101]

97 TNA, FO 195/1451, Monceriff, February 19, 1883, Memorandum: Red Sea Slave Trade 1882.
98 Hopper, *Slaves of One Master*, p. 208.
99 Bullard, *Two Kings in Arabia*, letter of September 9, 1924, pp. 55–6.
100 TNA, FO 84/1482, from Jeddah Consulate, August 15, 1877.
101 TNA, FO 84/1571, Consul Zohrab, Jeddah, to FO, March 13, 1880, Despatch Slave Trade no. 3; and Burdett, *The Slave Trade into Arabia*, vol. 3, pp. 509–10.

This report, dated 1880, is important in so far as sources on slave labour in Jeddah are rare. From the documents concerned with slavery, a range of occupations can be surmised. One was the transport of salt to Jeddah, another one pearling. While the pearl banks of the Red Sea could not compete with those of the Persian Gulf, they were nevertheless exploited for pearls as well as mother of pearl.[102] Boatman and porter were other frequent occupations.[103] Individual slaves worked in shops and coffee shops as well as flour mills, where they carried water or cut blocks from coral stone.[104] In the manumission documents analysed by Hutson bodyguards, servants of Ottoman officials and military occupations are also mentioned.[105] Professions such as milk-boy, shepherd, and camel driver point to ownership by Bedouins, who played a very active role in slavery. Since they were usually based outside the city and often also beyond the suburbs, they do not form a systematic part of this study. It seems that slaves working for wages often did not live in the houses of their masters, in contrast to the overwhelming majority of female slaves as well as those boys and possibly men involved in either domestic work or – possibly – the trading business. They usually lived in the neighbouring villages, often among the Takārina discussed above.

Manumission documents tend to tell us about the suffering of slaves. A particularly dramatic escape was that of the wife of the dragoman of the French consulate in 1847. In a reversal of the usual narrative of slaves seeking refuge with the consulates, Nour-es-Sabâh sought refuge with the Ottoman authorities, who considered her the slave of the dragoman. She claimed conversion to Islam, which precluded any efforts by the French consul and his dragoman to reclaim her as the dragoman's wife (due to the prohibition of Muslim women being

102 TNA, FO 541/22 Memorandum by Mr. Wylde, late British Vice-Consul, Jeddah, September 25, 1878; Burdett, pp. 327–8; CADN, 2_MI3229, Lucciana to MAE, July 2, 1879; Philippe Pétriat (ed.), *Une Histoire Partagée. Sources Françaises sur l'Histoire de l'Arabie: Hedjaz et Najd 1839–1943* (2014), p. 147; and for 1856, CADN, 2_MI3244, Note sur la pêche des huitres et des macres dans le mer Rouge, May 10, 1910, which mentions mostly Port Sudan, Massawa, Hodeida, Djibouti, and Aden; cf. Burdett, *The Slave Trade into Arabia*, vol. III, p. 309.

103 TNA, FO 195/1451, Consul Jeddah to FO, July 27, 1883.

104 Burdett, *The Slave Trade into Arabia*, vol. 3, pp. 658, 720–3 on slave cases in Jeddah 1882.

105 Hutson, *Enslavement and Manumission in Saudi Arabia*, p. 62; and fn. 46.

married to non-Muslims). The consul did not succeed in reclaiming the valuables which the dragoman claimed she had stolen. Whether her fate improved thereafter remains unknown.[106]

There are also accounts of extraordinary success. For example, Ṣufyān b. ʿAbdallāh al-Ḥabashī, who seems to have had a special acumen for business, was eventually manumitted by his master, ʿAbdallāh b. Yūsuf Bā Nāja, one of the foremost Hadhrami merchants of Jeddah. He was included in the family endowment which granted him a house in the family compound, and his descendants became known as the more successful of the two branches of the Bā Nāja family. This story is similar to those discovered by Terence Waltz about the careers of (ex-)slaves in Cairo.[107] No matter how exceptional or representative these different examples are, it is striking that the majority of cases of runaway slaves documented in the British consulate of Jeddah in 1882 ended with the reconciliation of master and slave. Only relatively few among such slaves insisted on manumission or were manumitted as a result of their bad physical condition resulting from malnutrition and abusive treatment. Those freed were usually re-assigned as workers to officials or notables, as repatriation was usually not an option given the often unknown origins and the young age of enslavement.[108]

In some ways, narratives of voluntary migrants and of slaves are comparable: very often, they arrived at a young age, they could work their way up the social ladder, marry, and settle down.[109] Since

[106] CADN, Constantinople, Ambassade, Série D, 1, French consul to Amb. Const., December 16, 1847. The case bears much resemblance with one told by George La Rue, 'Seeking Freedom in Multiple Contexts: An Enslaved Sudanese Woman's Life Trajectory, ca. 1800–1834', *Journal of Global Slavery*, 2 (2017), pp. 11–43. I wish to thank Benedetta Rossi for this reference.

[107] Pétriat, *Le Négoce des Lieux Saints*, pp. 269–75; and Terence Walz, 'Sudanese, Habasha, Takarna, and Barabira: Trans-Saharan Africans in Cairo as Shown in the 1848 Census' in T. Walz and K. M. Cuno (eds.), *Race and Slavery in the Middle East: Histories of Trans-Saharan Africans in Nineteenth-Century Egypt, Sudan, and the Ottoman Mediterranean* (Cairo: The American University of Cairo Press, 2010), pp. 43–76.

[108] Burdett, *The Slave Trade into Arabia*, vol. 3, pp. 658, 720–3. For an interesting account; cf. Saʿīd al-Surayḥī, *al-Ruways* (Beirut: Jadāwil, 2013), pp. 37–8.

[109] The young age was, for example, noted by Hamilton, *Sinai, The Hedjaz, and Soudan*, p. 63. The similarity in age between migrants and slaves is also noted by Hopper, *Slaves of One Master*, pp. 3–4.

manumission was considered a pious act, many slaves were freed at some stage, ideal-typically after they had repaid their purchase price, more commonly upon the death of their owners.[110] Furthermore, they remained linked to the households of their former owners in a patronage relationship, while free immigrants married into local families and thus became part of the social fabric of the city. Women, who had born their owners' children (who were then free persons), became known as *umm walad* (mother of the son). They could no longer be sold and were usually manumitted, in exceptional cases even married. This ideal-typical integration into the social unit of the household forms the basis of Toledano's observation of the relative absence of slaves from the historical records in the former Ottoman Empire. He therefore likens slavery to an 'instance of forced migration' and locates it institutionally in a society functioning through hierarchical relationships.[111] One could also take his reflections as a prompt to comparatively assess the life-courses of young migrants and young slaves, and thus open a perspective on the changing roles of them in local society over the period of their lives. This is not to blur the important distinction that at least in the case of men, the fact that they lacked control over their whereabouts and labour remained a central distinguishing trait of slaves, as long as they were not freed. This does not mean that dependency on their former master ceased automatically with their manumission, though.[112] This latter observation is particularly pertinent in the case of women, who were generally more restricted in their movements. For them, the question might have been more one related to the establishment of stable social relations that could no longer be disrupted by them being sold.[113] Yet even

[110] John Hunwick, 'The Same but Different: Africans in Slavery in the Mediterranean Muslim World' in J. O. Hunwick and E. T. Powell (eds.), *The African Diaspora in the Mediterranean Lands of Islam*, Princeton Series on the Middle East (Princeton, NJ: Markus Wiener Publishers, 2002), pp. ix–xxxvii, here p. xviif; cf. TNA, FO 685/1 Consul Zohrab's Letter Book 1879, Zohrab to FO, May 14, 1879.

[111] Toledano, *As if Silent and Absent*, pp. 9–59, here p. 24. As research on the potential existence of a culturally constituted diaspora exists for the Gulf, but not for Jeddah, I cannot engage with this part of Toledano's argument here.

[112] For inspiring suggestions on this topic for West Africa, see Benedetta Rossi, 'Migration and Emancipation in West Africa's Labour History: The Missing Links', *Slavery & Abolition*, 35 (2014), pp. 23–46.

[113] Interview, Khayriyyah ʿAbdallāh, Jeddah, February 22, 2009.

marriage was not entirely safe as it did not preclude unilateral divorce. Hence they only achieved real security if they had a number of grown-up children who could protect them if their husbands abandoned them.

Toledano himself has noted the 'risk of downplaying' slavery's 'harshness' through this type of conceptualisation.[114] The harshness manifested itself in the frequently reported cases of maltreatment or sale of an *umm walad* in spite of the legal prohibition.[115] It was also blatantly evident for those who lost the protection of 'their' households, either through a voluntary break or because they no longer proved useful to their masters. Hutson recounts the case of Khadija bin Gummiog, who owned some possessions but lived apart from her (female) master – most likely in one of the villages outside of Jeddah. Khadija, sixty years of age, was ill and therefore unable to defend herself against attempts of Takārna to steal her property. She therefore sought the support of the British Consulate.[116] While social relations could go wrong among freeborn men and women and cause great hardship, they usually had a better legal position as well as more powerful social networks to fall back on. The greatest advantage of the conceptualisation of slavery as coerced migration thus seems to be that it forces us to think through the different possible experiences of both, slaves as well as free migrants.

The practice of slavery continued throughout the period under consideration, although the importation of slaves was curbed. However, the institution of slavery was only abolished in 1962.[117] In 1927, Ibn Saʿūd had committed in the Treaty of Jeddah to co-operate with the British consulate in fighting the trade. When the treaty was renewed in 1936, Saudi Arabia prohibited the importation of slaves by sea and limited the entry of slaves by land to those whose enslavement prior to 1936 could be proven. In turn, Bullard, British minister at Jeddah at

114 Toledano, *As if Silent and Absent*, p. 258.
115 TNA, FO 881/3439, Beyts to FO, June 20, 1877.
116 Hutson, *Enslavement and Manumission in Saudi Arabia*, p. 58.
117 Suzanne Miers, 'Slavery and the Slave Trade in Saudi Arabia and the Arab States on the Persian Gulf, 1925–63' in G. Campbell (ed.), *Abolition and Its Aftermath in Indian Ocean Africa and Asia*, Studies in Slave and Post-Slave Societies and Cultures (London and New York: Routledge, 2005), pp. 120–36, here p. 130.

the time, gave up the right of manumission.[118] Aware of possible criticism, Bullard argued that this law was more useful as a step on the way to ending slavery than the British right of manumission.[119] There are no indications that the actual treatment of slaves changed significantly during the period of Saudi rule.

[118] Suzanne Miers, 'Diplomacy versus Humanitarianism: Britain and Consular Manumission in Hijaz 1921–1936', *Slavery & Abolition*, 10 (1989), pp. 102–28, here p. 122; and Hutson, *Enslavement and Manumission in Saudi Arabia*, p. 49.

[119] Bullard, *Two Kings in Arabia*, letter of October 5, 1936, p. 113.

4 *The Changing Urban Space of Jeddah*

In conjunction with the increase in population and pilgrims, the urban space of Jeddah changed considerably over the course of the nineteenth and early twentieth century. Even if this change pales in comparison to the dramatic urban expansion and reconfiguration which took place in the imperial capital Istanbul, in Mediterranean ports such as Salonica, Izmir, Beirut, Tripoli, or inland centres such as Damascus, let alone such newly founded port cities as Port Said and Mersin, it nevertheless reflects the wider project of modernising Ottoman cities in the period of the *Tanzimat*.[1] As in the case of these other cities, Jeddah's urban development was a reflection of the growing demands on the port linked to the increase in trade and the introduction of steamers. It also mirrored notions of urban modernisation introduced both by Ottoman governors and local residents familiar with urban development elsewhere.[2] However, in contrast to the other cases mentioned, foreign companies were not involved in the Hijaz, probably due to Muslim sensitivities over possible non-Muslim presence.

Maps and travel reports constitute an important source of information regarding this transformation. The relative scarcity of such sources, notably of maps, means that periodisation before the 1870s must remain approximate. Thereafter, both Ottoman and consular documentation become more regular. The discussion of the concrete structures comprises a variety of sources. Many of these are either photographs or often fairly recent documents and oral accounts.

[1] The framework of the Ottoman urban reform project is discussed by Cengiz Orhonlu, *Osmanlı imperatorluğunda şehircilik ve ulaşım Üzerine araştırmalar* (Izmir: Ticaret Matbaaçılık, 1984). For Salonica, see Anastassiadou, *Salonique, 1830–1912*, pp. 39–200, for Izmir, cf. Zandi-Sayek, *Ottoman Izmir*, for Beirut, Hanssen, *Fin de Siècle Beirut*, for Tripoli, Saßmannshausen, *Reform in Translation*, for Damascus, Weber, *Damascus*, and for Mersin, Toksöz, *Nomads, Migrants and Cotton*.

[2] A detailed description for Izmir can be found in Zandi-Sayek, *Ottoman Izmir*, pp. 115–49.

In spite of the variety of written, oral, and visual sources, a precise reconstruction the historic development of the built heritage will be impossible until serial accounts from the court records or from individual owners become available. Architecturally as well as in terms of functional buildings, Jeddah resembled other Red Sea towns such as Yanbuʿ further north and Mocha and Hodeida on the Yemeni Red Sea Coast, but also Massawa and Suakin, with which the city was in close contact.[3] Therefore, occasional reference will be made to developments in these other cities for comparative purposes and to help in the establishment of a plausible timeline. Nevertheless, each city differed from the other, depending on necessities as well as on predominant architectural and political influences in specific periods. These differences extend even to the urban terminology.[4]

Overview: The Urban Growth of Jeddah

Burckhardt's travelogue of 1814 provides a convenient starting point to consider the urban growth of Jeddah in the nineteenth and early twentieth century:

> The area inclosed by the new wall (about three thousand paces in circuit) and the sea, is not entirely covered with buildings. A broad piece of open ground extends the whole length of the interior of the wall; and there is, besides, a good deal of waste ground near the Báb el Medina, and on the southern extremity. Having traversed this open space in coming from the gate, you enter the suburbs, comprising only huts formed of reeds, rushes, and brushwood, and encircling the inner town, which consists of stone buildings. The huts are chiefly inhabited by Bedouins, or poor peasants and labourers, who live here completely after the Bedouin fashion. Similar quarters for people of this description may be found in every town of Arabia. The interior of Djidda is divided into different districts. The people of Sowakin, who frequent this place, reside near the Báb el Medina; their quarters are called Haret è Sowakiny. Here they live in a few poor houses, but principally under huts, to which the lowest class of people frequently resort, as many public women reside here, and those who sell the intoxicating beverage called Boosa.[5]

[3] Um, *Reflections on the Red Sea Style*.
[4] Thus, *wikāla* is used frequently in Suakin to denote buildings which in Jeddah would be called *ḥawsh*, see below.
[5] Burckhardt, *Travels in Arabia*, pp. 16–17.

Burckhardt's description mostly confirms the impression given by Carsten Niebuhr in his 1774 map based on the visit in 1762 (Map 4.1). This map combines a built-up area along the coastline with hut settlements. The engraving by Niebuhr's companion Baurenfeind (Figure 4.1) seems to overextend the wall somewhat. More importantly, however, it shows that Niebuhr's sketch is incomplete in terms of the solid buildings it shows. According to al-Anṣārī, Jeddah featured at least

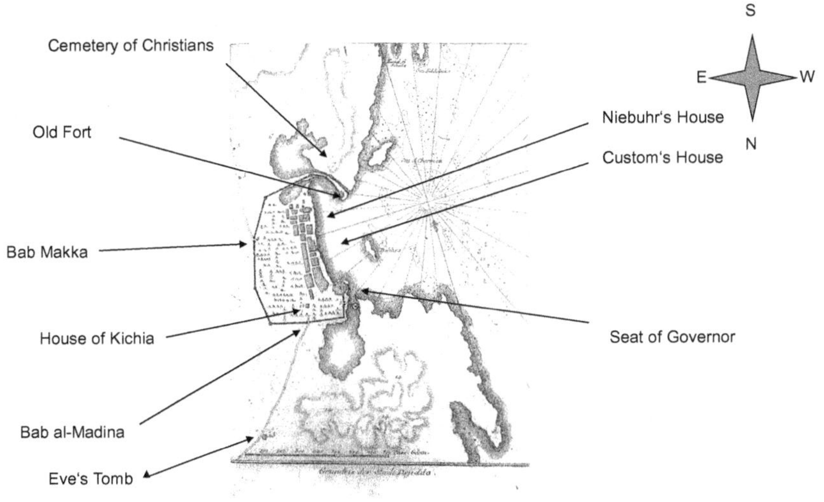

Map 4.1 Ground plan of Jeddah, drawn by Carsten Niebuhr (1774).
Reisebeschreibung nach Arabien und andern umliegenden Ländern, table LV.

Figure 4.1 Engraving of Jeddah by G.W. Baurenfeind (1774).
Carsten Niebuhr, Reisebeschreibung nach Arabien und anderen umliegenden Ländern, table LIII

three, possibly four mosques when Niebuhr visited. At least three of the towers on Baurenfeind's image seem to be mosques, the fourth one possibly being either a mosque or a lighthouse.[6]

Hut settlements inside the wall, but away from the main *sūq* area, such as those that can be seen on Niebuhr's map, were also described by Eduard Rüppell in 1831. According to Rüppel, they were mostly inhabited by black sailors and prostitutes.[7] However, the city centre, meaning mostly the *sūq* (market streets) and its immediate environs, is uniformly described by travellers in the first decades of the nineteenth century as 'well built' with 'many lofty and spacious houses' (Sadlier 1819), constructed 'of large blocks of very fine madrapore' with 'handsomely arched' doorways and 'covered with fret work ornaments carved in the stone' (Valentia 1805–6). From the descriptions, most buildings in the centre were probably two to three stories high and did not rise much higher, even in the early 1850s.[8]

Pétriat has shown how the Bā Nāja family acquired properties next to the Ḥanafī Mosque at the northern end of the main *sūq* from 1834 onwards to eventually develop a major complex of imposing houses.[9] This probably coincided with the expansion of what became the most affluent quarter of Jeddah, the Ḥārat al-Shām (northern quarter), ostensibly after the foreign consulates and government offices moved there in the second half of the nineteenth century.[10] The increase in building activities on hitherto undeveloped land eventually pushed the poorer population of the huts, locally known as *ʿushsha* (pl. *ʿushash*) either to the settlements outside the wall or prompted them to rent small apartments (known as *ʿuzla*) in the stone houses. Throughout the nineteenth century, these seem to have increased in

6 al-Anṣārī, *Mawsūʿat tārīkh madīnat Jidda*, pp. 426–9; and Giovanni Finati, *Narrative of the Life and Adventures of Giovanni Finati*, William John Bankes (ed.), 2 vols. (London: John Murray, 1830), vol. 2, p. 42, see note 5 for mosques for 1807.

7 Rüppell, *Reise in Abyssinien*, vol. 1, p. 172.

8 Finati, *Narrative of the Life and Adventures*, vol. 2, p. 42; George Foster Sadlier, *Diary of a Journey across Arabia* (Bombay, 1866), p. 100; M. Bové, 'Voyage aux Côtes de l'Arabie Heureuse', *Bulletin de la Société de Géographie*, 2e série (1834), pp. 145–65, here p. 155; Rüppell, *Reise in Nubien*, p. 234; and Hamilton, *Sinai, The Hedjaz, and Soudan*, p. 53.

9 Pétriat, *Le Négoce des Lieux Saints*, pp. 165–7.

10 Abū 'l-Jadāʾil, Khālid Ṣalāḥ Sanūsī, *Rawā lī wālidī wa-ṣaḥibuh* (Jeddah: Dār Manṣūr al-Zāmil, 1438/2017), p. 35. For this urban shift; cf. Freitag, *Symbolic Politics and Urban Violence*, p. 131.

height to five or six floors. This height was achieved partly by adding onto older buildings and partly through the construction of new buildings. These developments were a reaction to the growth in population, to the greater affluence, and to the increase in the number of pilgrims in need of accommodation. This put pressure on the basic infrastructure for water and health, which was provided partly by local entrepreneurs, partly by the state.

Both the Egyptian and the Ottoman rulers were primarily concerned with basic infrastructure vital for defence and the basic functions of the city. Thus, the Egyptians built or restored a number of government buildings within the wall and constructed new barracks to the north of the town.[11] An Ottoman map of Jeddah in 1851 (Map 4.2) shows an outline of the walled city with seven gates and fourteen towers. Prominent features on the seaside are the former citadel, marked as a hospital for the regular troops and the artillery, and a military dockyard. The office of the *vali* of Jeddah (this could at the period refer to the provincial governor, but also to the kaymakam), was situated next to artillery barracks to the south of the customs' gate. In the north-eastern part of the city was an ammunition storage with a guardhouse and a gate. To the north of the city, the barracks built by Mehmed Ali are visible near the Medina Gate, and to their north-east the large Cemetery of Eve. A number of windmills can be seen near a large lagoon, buildings apparently first introduced by Mehmed Ali, possibly to supply the army with grain.[12] Although this innovation was criticised by local scholars who blamed it for an outbreak of the plague in 1815 and demanded the destruction of the windmills. Apparently, the original windmills were destroyed, or fell into disrepair due to lack of maintenance, and were eventually turned into barracks for irregular troops. However, by the 1860s, Sikandar Begum once again describes twenty to twenty-five windmills outside of Jeddah, though they did not function during her visit in 1863–4.[13]

11 The new barracks were built on land bought from a Jiddawi who had sheds to keep goods on it. Oral information, Māzin ʿAbdallāh al-Saqqāf, Jeddah, November 26, 2012.

12 al-Batanūnī, *al-Riḥla al-ḥijāziyya li-walī al-niʿm*, p. 15.

13 Burckhardt, *Observations sur les Habitants*, here p. 144; Charles Didier, *Séjour chez le Grand-Chérif de la Mekke* (Paris: Librairie Hachette et Cie, 1857), p. 130; Tamisier, *Voyage en Arabie*, p. 74; and Sikandar Begum, *A Princess's Pilgrimage*, pp. 30–1.

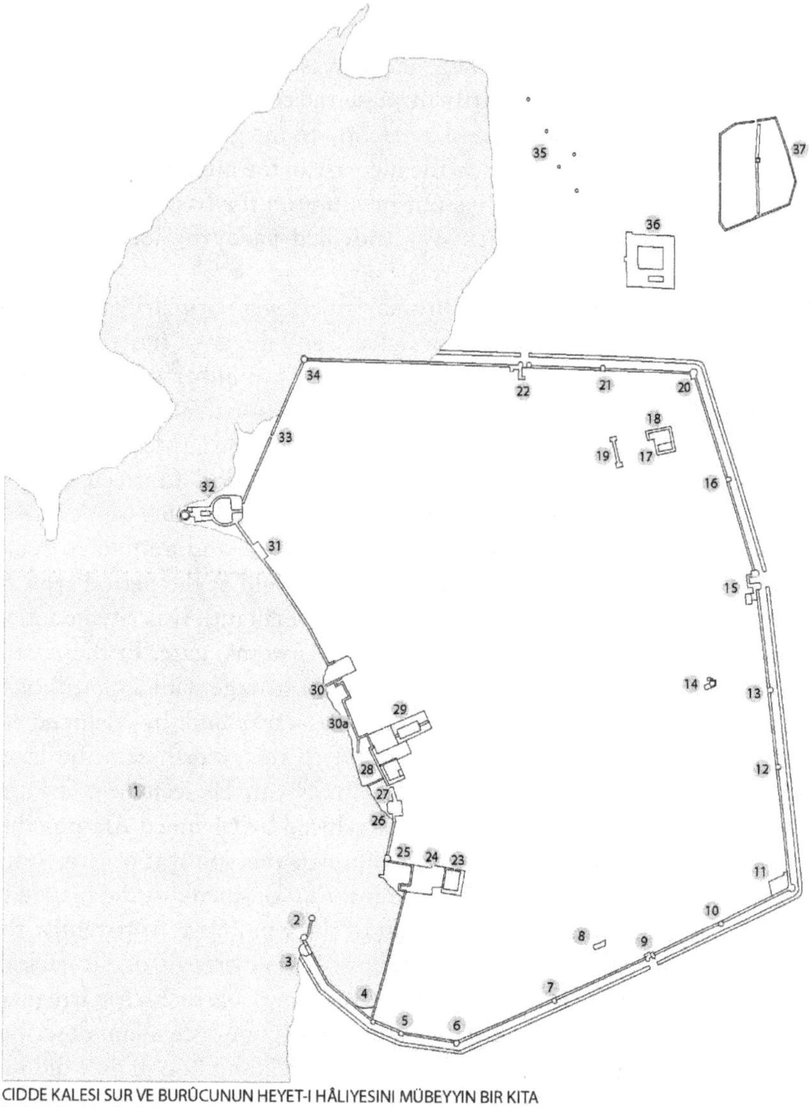

CIDDE KALESI SUR VE BURÛCUNUN HEYET-I HÂLIYESINI MÜBEYYIN BIR KITA
RESM-I MUSATTAHIDIR. Fî 25 Ca. [1]267 [28 Mart 1851]
ZIRÂ'-I MIMÂRÎ MIKYÂSIDIR

Map 4.2 Ottoman map of 1851. (1) Red Sea, (2–5, 6–7, 10–14, 20–1, 34) Towers (5) Fort, (8) Şerîf Fort, (9) Şerîf Gate, (15) Mecca Gate, (17) Gate, (18) Ammunition Depot, (19) Ammunition Guardhouse, (22) Medina Gate and New Gate, (23) Artillery Barracks, (24) Dîvân of the Vali, (25) Vesîr Gate, (26) Ruined Fort, (27) Şevne Gate, (28) Customs' Gate, (29) Ruined Fort, (30) Maghrebinian's Gate, (30a) Dockyards, (31) Fort, (32) Military Hospital, (33) Martyr's and Sır, (?) Gate, (35) Ruined Windmills, (36) Infantry Barracks, (37) Eve's Tomb.
Drawn by Melody Mosaver on the basis of BOA PLK p. 45.

The map offers a military view of the city, which reflected the Ottoman imperial perspective. This was to change in the second half of the nineteenth century, which is better documented. The military was still a major concern, so that repairs of barracks and the wall regularly feature in the documents.[14] Another major topic was the health of the military. Around 1868 a new hospital, probably due to both military and civilian needs, was opened.[15] In 1910 a British doctor visited it and described a relatively basic structure consisting of two stone rooms and a wooden structure of poor quality. The wooden building was 'formerly the Municipal Hospital, the above-mentioned stone building having been used till last year as Military Hospital.'[16]

Interestingly, the Ottoman administration did not seem to own substantial buildings in Jeddah beyond military ones. Thus, complicated negotiations with the Emir of Mecca had to take place to ensure the repair of the residence of the governor of Jeddah, as he was the owner of the house.[17] In 1872 a rented government building collapsed during attempts to dig a well (or, more likely, a cistern) inside of it.[18] Eventually, the local authorities were allowed to buy a house for government employees.[19] In the early twentieth century, the kaymakam was housed in the northern quarter near the Medina Gate.

The Development of the Port and Market Areas

In contrast to other Ottoman cities of the period, it would seem that in Jeddah, it was not the municipality but a variety of different governmental agencies who, in conjunction with local notables, often convoked in ad-hoc commissions, undertook public works.[20] Thus, the crucially important port area was a joint concern of the military and

[14] BOA, İ.MVL 223 7699–01–01/02–01; Y.PRK.ASK. 80 59 (March 21, 1892); and Ṣabbān, *Murāsalāt al-Bāb al-ʿĀlī ilā Wilāyat al-Ḥijāz*, pp. 70–1.

[15] MAE, CADN, Article 3 (2MI3228), 'Mesures prises dans les villes saintes pour le Pélerinage de cette année. Améliorations obtenues depuis 1867, dans le Hedjaz, et surtout à Djeddah', in Dubreuil to MAE, March 6, 1869, p. 11.

[16] TNA, FO 195/2350, Municipal Hospital, in Monahan to Emb. Const., March 10, 1910.

[17] BOA, İ.MVL 223 7699224–7638–01–01, 02–01.

[18] Ṣabbān, *Jidda fī Wathāʾiq al-Arshīf al-ʿUthmānī*, pp. 16–17; based on BOA, Ayyinyat 871/51.

[19] Ṣabbān, *Murāsalāt al-Bāb al-ʿĀlī ilā Wilāyat al-Ḥijāz*, p. 315.

[20] Compare Weber, *Damascus*, pp. 83–8, for Damascus.

local merchants and people active in the pilgrimage business. Jeddah was protected by coral reefs which required vessels to anchor about one mile offshore and have passengers and cargo transported by small boats through a labyrinth of small passages to the shore. These were secured by signals and lights to improve safety in December 1860.[21]

Due to falling sea levels, some passages were so shallow at times that passengers had to wade through the water to reach dry ground.[22] Apparently, in a joint initiative by the then kaymakam Nūrī Effendi and a 'council' of Jeddah (possibly this refers to a newly created health council mentioned in the documents) comprising *'ulamā'*, notables, and merchants, a major programme of port and urban improvement was devised in 1866–7. The debris accumulated from the *sūq* was collected and thrown into the sea to construct an improved landing area and corniche, and the channel leading to the quay area was dredged.[23] A major incentive for the merchants to contribute substantially to financing the construction was that, due to the low water levels, their freight became exposed to theft. Furthermore, passengers, mostly pilgrims, experienced difficulties upon disembarking as they had to wade through shallow water. The new structure was later named 'Azīziyya Quay in honour of the Sultan, which resulted in a decoration and later promotions for Nūrī Effendi. It also seems that the lagoon to the south of Jeddah, still visible on Niebuhr's map, was filled in as its filthy waters were believed to contribute to the spreading of disease. In a similar combination of concern for health and comfort, the *sūq*s were covered to provide shade and houses whitewashed.[24] The slaughterhouse was moved so that the remains of the carcasses could hitherto be disposed of in the sea rather than left lying around. Access to the port was also broadened. Much of the costs of these works were raised locally by the merchants and the kaymakam himself. This prompted the citizens of Jeddah to ask the Sultan 'to regard us above our peers' (*ṭālibīn bihi imtiyāzan bayna amthālinā*).[25]

21 BOA, DH İ. 466 311125–02/03 of R. 5, 1277/October 21, 1860.
22 Tamisier, *Voyage en Arabie*, p. 116.
23 BOA, İ.MVL. 565 25421 of 1283, 1866–7.
24 Ṣabbān, *Murāsalāt al-Bāb al-'Ālī ilā Wilāyat al-Ḥijāz*, pp. 52–3, 70–1, 128; and al-Ḥaḍrāwī al-Makkī al-Shāfi'ī, *al-Jawāhir al-mu'adda fī faḍā'il Judda*, pp. 45–6.
25 Sinān Ma'rūfughlū, *Najd wa-l-Ḥijāz fī 'l-wathā'iq al-'uthmāniyya* (London: Dār al-Sāqī, 2002), pp. 119–23. For the letter; cf. ibid. pp. 94–6. The original language of the petitions might well have been Arabic, at least judging by the

It may be assumed that the subsequent decorations of a number of leading merchants were linked to their participation in the works.[26] A comparison of the map of 1851, shown above in Map 4.2, with a plan of the coastline, prepared in conjunction with works described below and with Map 4.3 of 1881, shows how much land was reclaimed in the brief period between the preparation of the two maps.[27] It is noteworthy that the works in Jeddah occurred around the same time as those in Beirut, although the immediate context, as well as the measures taken, differed considerably.[28] This synchrony shows that the Ottoman response to new demands, in this case of the changing shipping industry and trade developments, had an empire-wide scope even if different actors were involved and concrete measures and approaches differed according to local conditions.

According to Tamisier, this was not the first time that land was reclaimed: He describes a tower attached to what was formerly the old citadel and claims that at the extreme end of the wall, a new citadel had been constructed. In the middle, a gate was still discernible which had been the one leading to the port but which in 1834, when he visited, was about 200 meters from the current quay. Based on his description it also seems that part of the land which was to become the northern quarter had been reclaimed from the adjacent lagoon at that time.[29]

The works in the entire harbour area were continued in an even more ambitious manner in 1879 by Governor Nāshid Pasha and the kaymakam Nūrī Pasha.[30] In September or October of 1879, the *vali* convoked a 'town improvements Commission', to quote the British Acting-Consul, which included local notables as well as representatives

facsimile of 1890 shown in Philippe Pétriat, 'For Pilgrims and for Trade: Merchants and Public Works in Ottoman Jeddah', *Turkish Historical Review*, 5 (2014), pp. 200–20, p. 215, which also discusses such public works; cf. Ṣabbān, *Jidda fī Wathā'iq al-Arshīf al-'Uthmānī*, p. 40; Ṣabbān, *Murāsalāt al-Bāb al-'Ālī ilā Wilāyat al-Ḥijāz*, pp. 148, 202; and CADN 2_MI_3228 Djeddah, March 6, 1869, Dubreuil to MAE, Direction du Consulats, Ministre du Commerce, Ambassade de C.ple «Mesures prises dans les villes saintes pour le Pélerinage de cette année. Améliorations obtenues depuis 1867, dans le Hedjaz, et surtout a Djeddah».

26 Ṣabbān, *Murāsalāt al-Bāb al-'Ālī ilā Wilāyat al-Ḥijāz*, pp. 148, 202.

27 BOA, PLK p. 4618.

28 Hanssen, *Fin de Siècle Beirut*, pp. 87–92.

29 Tamisier, *Voyage en Arabie*, pp. 114–6. This would confirm findings by Māzin 'Abdallāh al-Saqqāf on the basis of old land documents; cf. oral communication, Jeddah, November 26, 2012.

30 BOA, İ.ŞD. 48 2615 (August 8, 1879).

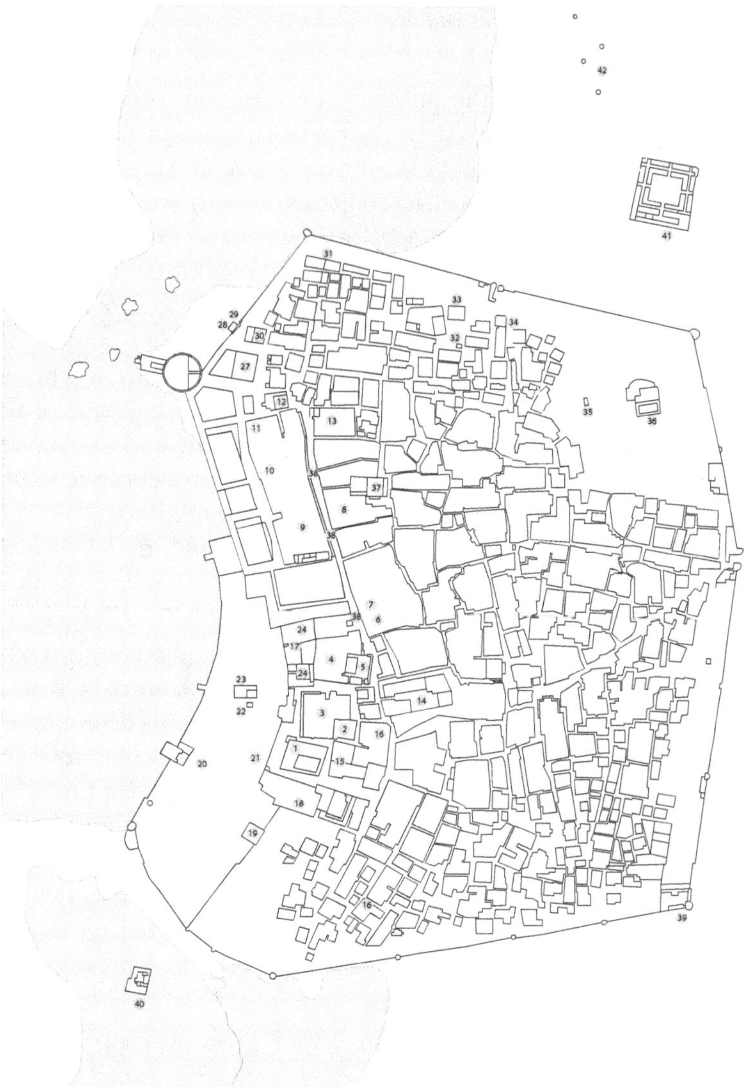

Map 4.3 Map of Jeddah in 1880–1. (1) Ḥawsh Abu Lilghaz /Abu Laila?, (2) Ḥawsh Dallāl, (3) Ḥawsh al-Sharīf, (4) Ḥawsh al-ʿAkkāsh, (5) ʿAkkāsh Mosque, (6) Ḥawsh Haşim, (7) Ḥawsh Bardastani, (8) Ḥawsh Bā Nāja, (9) Ḥawsh Šarbatlī, (10) Ribāṭ al-Sāda, (11) Ribāṭ Bā Dīb, (12) Bakir Pasha Mosque, (13) Bakir Pasha Ḥawsh, (14) Provincial Şevne, (15) Ḥawsh al-Bilād, (16) Ḥawsh al-Wazīr, (17) Postal Şevne, (18) Ḥawsh Dhūwī Zayd, (19) Gaz Depot, (20) Quarantine, (21) Police Station, (22) Prayer Space, (23) Municipality Coffeehouse, (24) Customs' Office, (25) Maghrebi Gate, (26) Rüşdiyye School, (27) Sayyid Saqqaf Effendi Musa, (28) Martyr's Cemetery, (29) al-Arbaʿīn Gate, (30) Bā ʿAshan, (31) French Consulate, (32) Prayer Space, (33) British Consulate, (34) Government Offices, (35) Guardpost, (36) Cemetery, (37) Ḥawsh Masjid al-Ḥanafī, (38) Sūq, (39) Hospital, (40) Türbe of Şaykh Abū 'l-ʿUyūn, (41) Barracks, (42) Ruined Windmills.
Drawn by Melody Mosaver on the basis of an Ottoman map.

of the consulates. This seems to have been a body which probably combined leading merchants and other community leaders but was not identical with any of the existing institutions of urban governance discussed in Chapter 7. They were asked to make suggestions for the improvement of the town, port, and wharf, how such improvements could be carried out, and, perhaps most importantly, how to raise the necessary funds. 'The Governor-General invited it to form a new Municipality consisting of members who could be trusted to carry out the duties of their office. This was done and the town is rapidly assuming a more healthy appearance.'[31] A new seawall was built, more land reclaimed and the busy space between the sea and the town, where goods and passengers were landed and passed through customs as well as health checks, extended. The harbour area was laid out anew, a quay arranged, and space made for the needs of customs and quarantine.[32] The municipal coffeehouse (Map 4.3, no. 23) in the port area probably served as a meeting place for the municipal council and a place where city officials received and answered requests by the population, at least until the construction of a designated municipality building.[33] This is important in so far as it was situated outside of the walled urban space while serving as the city's major political space. This notwithstanding, it seems that there also existed a room for more confidential political meetings. Thus, in the critical confrontation of 1858, a meeting by city officials and notables was held in the old customs house, also situated in the port area.[34] The municipal coffeehouse probably also served as a hub for those in the transportation industry (see Chapters 6 and 7).

The Provincial Council of the Hijaz also sought to repair the wall which threatened to collapse, presumably in the same context. The council proposed to pay for this by selling some state lands occupied by old barracks.[35] The discussion also came to involve the Ministry of War, which saw the need to repair the barracks for the imperial soldiery. The Ministry eventually gave green light to the project. Thereupon

[31] TNA, FO 195/1251, Zohrab to Emb. Const., October 23, 1879.
[32] Ochsenwald, *Religion, Society, and the State*, p. 180.
[33] For a similar institution in Tripoli see Lafi, *Une ville du Maghreb*, pp. 148–51.
[34] TNA, FO 195/579, Walner to Acting Consul, Cairo, August 17, 1858, encl. 1, deposition by Myrialaki d'Antonio, pp. 3–4.
[35] BOA, I.MMS 64-3015-001-(45), March 21, 1879.

A special commission ... was set up with the participation of high-ranking military officers of Mecca and Jeddah, a state engineer [memleket mühendisi] as well as the local officials, the members of the administrative council and some others to discuss the means to realize the project. After long discussions, the council decided to prepare an auction bill of sales after visiting the aforementioned places and buildings. After an inspection, a map was drawn and the length and width of each building was measured. The auction bills were drafted by the above-mentioned council and sent to the chief crier of the city to announce and advertise the auction.[36]

The idea of an auction was abandoned in the process. Instead, the council sold the land of the old barracks and, with that money as well as funds raised through (probably more or less voluntary) donations from leading merchants, carried out the urban renewal plans. Unfortunately, the details of this process remain somewhat obscure.

By 1890 further works were demanded by local notables and, according to British and French reports, carried out by 1895.[37] Further land was reclaimed from September 1894 onwards.[38] A new pilgrim shelter was erected and a small kiosk for the passport officers built. This kiosk was surrounded by a (tiny) garden. This was an almost ostentatiously luxurious feature in a city suffering from chronic water shortage and a testimony to the attempt to provide Jeddah with a semblance of a park, i.e. a quintessential emblem of Ottoman urban modernisation elsewhere.[39] Another large building, meant to serve jointly as a casino and hotel, was planned, although the British consul was rather doubtful whether it would actually be erected and we have no further testimony as to the outcome of the plan.[40] Instead, a large building (on the very right-hand side of Figure 4.2) was later used by the health and quarantine services, as well as the Municipal Council (see Chapter 7).

[36] BOA, İ. DH. 826/66580–01, January 17, 1881, transl. by Ayşel Yıldız. The original map was prepared by Erkan-i Harb.
[37] Pétriat, *For Pilgrims and for Trade*, pp. 212–19.
[38] TNA, FO 195/1847, Abdur Razzack to Emb. Const., September 25, 1894.
[39] Weber, *Damascus*, pp. 164–6.
[40] TNA, FO 195/1894, Richards to Emb. Const., February 14, 1895, March 19, 1895, about the visit of a sanitary commission with further proposals for cleaning up the town; and May 20, 1895 for the visit of the marine engineers. For the French report, see CADN Amb. Const. Série D 6, Descoutures to Amb. Const. April 30, 1895.

Figure 4.2 The port in 1895.
Encl. in CADN, Const. Amb. Série D 6, Descoutures to Amb. Const. 30.4.1895

The large scale extension and remodelling of the port area between 1866 and 1895 is probably the closest Ottoman building activities ever came to approaching the scale of the far more extensive construction carried out in cities such as Alexandria, Beirut, Damascus, or, of course, Istanbul itself during the same period.[41] It is no surprise, then, that the completion of the construction was celebrated by decorating the new buildings with flags, a large public dinner as well as a 'very handsome display of fireworks' ('for Jeddah', as the British consul remarked tersely).[42]

Works on the *sūq*s were somewhat more limited and can in no way be compared to the large-scale building and remodelling programme

[41] For Alexandria, see Robert Ilbert, *Alexandrie, 1830–1930: Histoire d'une communauté citadine*, Bibliothèque d'Étude (Cairo: Institut Français d'Archéologie Orientale, 1996), vol. 112; for Beirut, see Fawaz, *Merchants and Migrants*; for Damascus, see Grallert, *To Whom Belong the Streets?*; and for Istanbul as well as an empire-wide comparative perspective, see Zeynep Çelik, *Empire, Architecture, and the City: French-Ottoman Encounters, 1830–1914*, Studies in Modernity and National Identity (Seattle and London: University of Washington Press, 2008).

[42] TNA, FO 195/1894, Richards to Emb. Const., February 14, 1895.

carried out in Damascus, for example.[43] In 1866/67, the kaymakam Nūrī Effendi, together with the merchants, initiated a programme (which was then used for the aforementioned port works a few years later) to clean debris from the markets. He also initiated the whitewashing of the adjacent walls and the covering of the *sūq* to provide shade.[44]

An interesting episode in terms of private and public ownership of urban space is the story of Qābil Street. King Ḥusayn had taken over the Ottoman provincial store (no. 14 on Map 4.2) after the Arab Revolt and converted it into a thoroughfare bordered by shops. He thereby divided the space of a public building into several ones which generated profit for the state or, since coffers were not really divided, for himself. In urban terms, he opened a new and direct connection between the harbour and the Mecca Gate. The mayor (*ra'īs al-baladiyya*) of Jeddah, Sulaymān Qābil, bought this (public) property from King ʿAlī in 1924 during the siege of Jeddah in return for the delivery of grain for his troops. This allowed him, during early Saudi times, to expand the buildings, which were now rented out for private profit. The provision of electricity from generators, at the time a novelty, added further value.[45]

Water and Other Public Works

Historically a major problem in Jeddah was a lack of natural water supplies within or near the confines of the city. Given the scarcity and unpredictability of rain, this problem was only partly solved by cisterns in the large houses which collected the run-off from the seasonal rains. Outside of the city, mud walls collected the runoff from large areas and channelled it to underground cisterns, estimated to number around 800 in 1880.[46] In addition, a number of attempts were made to bring

43 Weber, *Damascus*, pp. 179–201.

44 Ṣabbān, *Jidda fī Wathā'iq al-Arshīf al-ʿUthmānī*, p. 4; BOA, Ayniyat 871/18-19, CADN 2_MI_3228 Djeddah, Amb. Const. to MAE March 6, 1869; and Maʿrūfughlū, *Najd wa-l-Ḥijāz fī al-wathā'iq*, pp. 119–22.

45 al-Anṣārī, *Mawsūʿat tārīkh madīnat Jidda*, p. 567; and Ṭrābulsī, *Jidda*, p. 235.

46 This is described well in Rathjens and Wissmann, *Landschaftskundliche Beobachtungen*, pp. 84–5; cf. Muḥammad Ṣādiq Bāshā, *al-Riḥlāt al-ḥijāziyya*, ed. Muḥammad Hammām Fikrī (Beirut: Badr li-l-Nashr wa-l-Tawzīʿ, 1999), p. 304.

piped water to the city, which, however, eventually always dried up.[47] The first notable initiative in the period being discussed occurred in 1852–3 and is closely associated with the name of Faraj Yusr. He was one of the wealthy Indian merchants of Jeddah, owning up to eight boats sailing under the British flag in 1857.[48] By the mid-1850s he had become *shaykh al-tujjār* or representative of the merchants (see below, as well as Chapter 6). His wealth meant that he had to bankroll the local Ottoman authorities in times of need. In the 1850s, Faraj Yusr initiated and partly financed the construction of a pipe to bring water from a source in the mountains to Jeddah. The project included the installation of water tanks and distribution points at various places in the city, including – unsurprisingly – the harbour where ships could be supplied. It seems that this project was funded mostly through voluntary contributions by merchants, although the state was involved in some way, as can be seen by the decoration of an officer on account of his support for this project and the construction of a military hospital.[49]

By 1878 the Ottoman government initiated major works to provide water in Mecca due to the increasing number of pilgrims and the concurrent rise of Ottoman and international concern about the sanitary conditions of the pilgrimage (cf. Chapter 6). In parallel, works in Jeddah commenced in the early 1880s to improve the existing water channels and build additional water tanks, as the scheme by Faraj Yusr had fallen into disrepair by this time. By 1887 the state had built pipes to a source now named ʿAyn al-Ḥamidīyya (or al-Wazīriyya) and freshwater reservoirs at the foot of the mountains.[50] The water was brought to a large tank outside of the city wall. It was funnelled into pipes to different distribution points in the city and near the harbour.[51]

[47] The first such attempt is said to go back to the last Mamluk Sultan Qansaw al-Ghauwri; see, for example, al-Anṣārī, *Mawsūʿat tārīkh madīnat Jidda*, pp. 141–53.

[48] TNA, FO 195/375, Vice Consul Jeddah to Ambassador Istanbul, October 2, 1856, and January 13, 1857. On Faraj Yusr and the project; cf. Maghribī, *Aʿlām al-Ḥijāz*, vol.1, pp. 433–5.

[49] al-Anṣārī, *Mawsūʿat tārīkh madīnat Jidda*, p. 147; ʿAbd al-Anṣārī, *Tārīkh al-ʿAyn al-ʿAzīziyya bi-Jidda: Lamaḥāt ʿan maṣādir al-miyāh fī ʾl-Mamlaka al-ʿArabiyya al-Saʿūdiyya* (Jeddah, n.d.), p. 45; Ṣabbān, *Jidda fī wathāʾiq al-arshīf al-ʿuthmānī*, 48; and ʿAdnān al-Yāfī, *Jidda fī shadhrāt al-Ghazzāwī* (Jeddah, 1431/ 2010), pp. 139–42.

[50] BOA, I.DH. 1253–98331–01, R. 30, 1309/December 3, 1891. It is difficult to identify the different sources retrospectively.

[51] al-Anṣārī, *Mawsūʿat tārīkh madīnat Jidda*, pp. 147–9.

Low has discussed this episode very much from a perspective in which there was a rival concern for the health of pilgrims between the British and Ottoman Empires, as well as a concern by the Ottoman rulers in Istanbul to demonstrate to its subjects its ability to provide services associated with a higher degree of civilisation.[52] While this line of reasoning doubtlessly reflects the official perspective, it tends to neglect the agency of local residents: as Low himself notes, the initial steps in this major project were taken by the Ḥanafī *muftī* of Mecca, a shaykh of Indian origin who raised a workforce in order to conduct the works.[53] He is much more likely to have acted out of a local concern – something that I would call 'civic engagement', which complemented probably very nicely the grander imperial vision.

Even if this new scheme of water provision did not entirely satisfy the need for water, it was met with major opposition by the owners of private reservoirs outside of the town. They had earned 'vast profits' from selling this water during the pilgrimage season.[54] In consequence, they apparently collaborated with the Bedouins (who had otherwise brought water to town with their animals) in blocking the new system, something which seems to also have contributed to the quick demise of earlier schemes such as the one by Faraj Yusr. The state continued investing in the pipes, probably urged to do so by the health department and motivated by the need for clear water during the pilgrimage season.[55] Thus, by 1901 Ibrāhīm Rifʿat Pasha noted that many of the cisterns were no longer used due to the provision of piped water.[56]

The installation of the first seawater desalination plant in 1907, or possibly its replacement in 1911, increased the variety of available water sources. For the first time, Jeddah had sufficient, even an excess

52 Michael Low, 'Ottoman Infrastructures of the Saudi Hydro-State: The Technopolitics of Pilgrimage and Potable Water in the Hijaz', *Comparative Studies in Society and History*, 57 (2015), pp. 942–74, for the argument see notably pp. 945–50.

53 Low, *Ottoman Infrastructures*, p. 957.

54 Ṣādiq Bāshā, *al-Riḥalāt al-Ḥijāziyya*, p. 304.

55 Gülden Sarıyıldız, *Hicaz karantina teşkilâtı (1865–1914)* (Ankara: Türk Tarih Kurumu Basımevi, 1996), pp. 118–19. For a status quo in 1906, see Francis Clemow, *Les eaux de Djeddah: Communication faite au Conseil Supérieur de Santé le 11 Septembre 1906* (Constantinople: Imprimérie Loeffler, 1906).

56 Rifʿat, *Mirʾāt al-Ḥaramayn*, vol. 1, p. 23.

amount of water, so that it was able to build an ice factory.[57] By 1908 the Emir of Mecca demanded the rehabilitation of the ʿAyn al-Ḥamīdiyya, although it remains unknown whether this request was successful.[58] However, it seems the system of piped water was improved further in the first decade of the twentieth century. During Hashemite times these systems were kept running, although the conflict with Ibn Saʿūd, and particularly the year-long siege of Jeddah, led to a serious deterioration of supplies.[59] With the establishment of Saudi Rule, a new condenser was installed in 1927 (Figure 4.3). However, due to ongoing technical problems, the connections with the natural sources at the Meccan foothills were once again rehabilitated in 1933.[60] The restoration was celebrated lavishly and the 'men of the state and the notables' were invited. Subsequently, water pipes to the different quarters were laid (or rehabilitated).[61]

This double strategy of using rainwater and desalination continued well into the second half of the twentieth century, with major construction completed on the, now renamed, ʿAyn al-ʿAzīziyya in 1947. Sea-water condensation, for a short period considered obsolete, made a major comeback in light of the ever-growing demand for water in the kingdom, which nowadays depends almost exclusively on desalinated water.[62]

Other infrastructural measures included the planned connection of the Hijaz, notably of Jeddah and Mecca, to Cairo and Istanbul by telegraph. The Ottomans initially planned their own lines via Suakin, but, due to political unrest, instead collaborated with the British, who

[57] Ṣabbān, *Jidda fī Wathāʾiq al-Arshīf al-ʿUthmānī*, p. 49. For the ice factory, see Ṣabbān, p. 49; BOA, I.Hus.R.1325/40, Ḥihāz ṣihhiye idaresi, Sanawi Rāpūr 1330, p. 42.

[58] Ṣabbān, *Jidda fī Wathāʾiq al-Arshīf al-ʿUthmānī*, p. 49.

[59] Jarman (ed.), *The Jedda Diaries*, vol. 1, Jeddah Report, January 1922, pp. 3–4; Dalāl al-Ḥarbī, 'al-Awḍāʿ al-dākhiliyya fī Jidda fī fatrat al-ḥiṣār 1343–144 h./ 1925 m. min khilāli ṣaḥīfat "Barīd al-Ḥijāz"', *al-Darʿiyya*, 47–8 (2010), pp. 123–84, here pp. 140–1; and ibid., vol. 2, Jeddah Report, July 21–August 10, 1925, p. 325.

[60] TNA, FO 371/11442, Jeddah Report, April 1926, p. 385; FO 371/12250, *Jeddah Report,* July 1927, p. 466; FO 371/13010, Jeddah Report, December 1927, p. 486; and IOR, L/PS/12/2073, Jedda Report, August 1933, p. 2.

[61] *Ṣawṭ al-Ḥijāz,* September 5, 1933, and February 26, 1934.

[62] For a detailed account, see al-Anṣārī, *Tārīkh al-ʿAyn al-ʿAzīziyya bi-Jidda*; cf. Pesce, *Jiddah*, pp. 137–8.

Figure 4.3 Photograph of saltwater condenser 1926.
Leiden University Libraries, Or. 12.288 B: 31

had lines running via Suez.[63] From 1909 onwards, motor traffic was used for the mail service between Mecca, Jeddah, and Ṭāʾif. In early 1914 the roads were so unsafe that armoured vehicles were requested to guarantee the safety of the letters and passengers.[64] Between 1911 and 1914 plans were made for the construction of a railway line from Jeddah to Mecca, intended to eventually connect to the Hijaz Railway. Equipment and building materials were brought to

[63] BOA, Y.PRK.HR 89/1; TNA, FO 195/1415, Monceriff to Dufferin, April 4, 1882, May 18, 1882, August 29, 1882; Y.PRK.UM. 115/32 (1896); and DH. İD. 145 1 5 (April 22, 1912). On the telegraph, cf. Mostafa Minawi, *The Ottoman Scramble for Africa: Empire and Diplomacy in the Sahara and the Hijaz* (Stanford, CA: Stanford University Press, 2016), pp. 104–15.

[64] BOA, DH.İD. 194 15 (March 3, 1914). The idea was to pay for these vehicles through the postage dues.

and stored in Jeddah. This project was abandoned in 1914, together with yet further construction on the harbour.[65] This central installation was only extended significantly between 1949 and 1951 with the construction of a large pier, which did away with the need for transhipment and thus revolutionised the organisation of port labour (cf. Chapter 6).[66]

In contrast to other parts of the Empire, where foreign contractors undertook many of the public constructions, the authorities in the Hijaz were keen on keeping direct control over the provision of services – notwithstanding their acceptance of more or less voluntary contributions by merchants and notables who could be considered 'local'. This can be seen from the insistence, in 1911/12, that the Ottoman authorities – rather than a British company – construct the municipal gas depot at Jeddah.[67] Once again, this type of choice was most probably related to sensitivities concerning Western involvement in the *dihlīz* of Mecca.

Notable Features of Urban Jeddah: A Close Reading of Maps and Photographs

The map of 1880–1 (Map 4.3) is remarkable for its detailed depiction of the walled city of Jeddah, but also of a number of major features outside of the wall which were closely linked to the city, at times performing similar functions of a *dihlīz* for Jeddah as Jeddah itself did for Mecca. This is true notably for the area just outside of the Mecca Gate, as well as for the large suburb to the south, called Nakutu. A number of roads can be seen leading to (or from) the gates both to the structures outside, but also to the east (towards Mecca), the north (towards Medina), and the south. Military installations were situated between the barracks northeast of the Medina Gate and the Mecca Gate, and graves dotted the landscape around Jeddah. The map also points to an increasingly professionalised approach to town planning. For the first time, it gives a detailed account of the interior of the city, and thus also of the numerous commercial and religious buildings.

[65] For the motor traffic, see BOA, DH.MUİ 28/2 2 (November 24, 1909); for the train construction, see BOA, DH.İD. 9 7 (March 12, 1911); DH.İD. 42 24 (November 6, 1912); DH.İD. 191 9 (January 28, 1914) and for works in the harbour, see DH.İD. 199 4 (February 17, 1914).

[66] Pesce, *Jiddah*, p. 142. [67] BOA, DH.İD. 1526 (1911–12).

Another important source regarding urban development from the 1880s are photographs by contemporary observers and visitors. While the French consul in particular documented the works on the harbour, many of the architectural photographs were taken during the first decades of the twentieth century. They were taken by consuls and consular officials, by military personnel, but also by travellers and foreigners residing in the Hijaz. A systematic study and comparisons of photographs by Western and by Eastern travellers would require finding copies of the often badly reproduced images of Arab travelogues such as Batanūnī's, which was beyond the scope of this study.

As elsewhere in the Muslim world, pious endowments or *awqāf* were a major institution through which public – as well as private – buildings were withdrawn from the property market. The donor, who had his deed registered in the religious court, thereby donated his property either for public charitable purposes, such as mosques, pilgrims' hostels, water supplies, care for the poor etc., or, in the case of private endowments, to his or her own family until the extinction of the line, at which time the property reverted to a designated charitable cause. Thus, any income derived from the property, for example through renting it as a shop, apartment, *wikāla* or the like, went to the designated purpose, with the exception of a certain portion allocated to the caretaker and maintenance.[68] Krause estimated that, by the late 1980s, about 35 per cent of property in the old city was registered as *waqf*.[69]

The following discussion of notable features, first within and then outside of the wall, focuses on particularly noteworthy institutions and buildings. In some cases, where detailed discussions of functions form part of later chapters, they will be only mentioned, in other cases a more detailed discussion is necessary.

68 On the legal foundations, see R. Peters, 'Waḳf' in P. J. Bearman, T. Bianquis, C. E. Bosworth, E. J. van Donzel and W. P. Heinrichs (eds.), *Encyclopaedia of Islam, 2nd Edition*, 12 vols. (Leiden: Brill, 1960–2005). dx.doi.org/10.1163/1573-3912_islam_COM_1333 (accessed January 02, 2019); Weber, *Damascus*, pp. 75–81, on family endowments in late Ottoman Palestine Beshara Doumani, 'Endowing Family: *Waqf*, Property Devolution, and Gender in Greater Syria, 1800 to 1860', *Comparative Studies in Society and History*, 40 (1998), pp. 3–41.

69 Krause, *Stadtgeographische Untersuchungen*, p. 57.

al-Balad: The Walled City of Jeddah

All existing maps of the city confirm the centrality of the port area described above. Nevertheless, this major gate to the outside world was separated from the town by a wall. This served security concerns, although the city was – due to its coral reefs – well protected from the seaside.

The 1880–1 map resembles Niebuhr's sketch in so far as, beyond the sealine, there was the major market street which was lined by large structures. Two thoroughfares lead to the eastern (Mecca) gate, from where those people and wares headed for Mecca and the interior departed. The names of the urban quarters on the map of 1880–1 are given as Yaman, Shām, and Maẓlūm Maḥallesi, i.e. the Southern and Northern quarters and the 'Quarter of the Oppressed'.[70] At some time during the thirteenth ḥijrī century (i.e. between 1785 and 1882 CE), the south-western part of the Yemen quarter became Ḥārat al-Baḥr (the Quarter of the Sea), although it did not have its own *'umda* and thus might not have constituted a separate administrative unit (cf. Chapter 5).[71] As this change of name could be linked to an expansion of the city after the reclamation of part of the land gained from the southern lagoon, this might well have happened in or even after the 1880s, which could explain the absence of the name from the 1880 map. Ḥārat al-Baḥr was initially the richest quarter, as it was inhabited by boatmen, sailors, and pilgrims' guides, i.e. people working in professions crucial to the local economy.[72] Each of the quarters consisted of large residential units and had some share of the urban commercial spaces. In contrast to many contemporary cities such as Aleppo and Sana'a, quarters were not separated by walls and internal gates, although, as will be shown in Chapter 5, their limits were well known to their inhabitants, who closely surveyed strangers

70 The name is said to drive from the execution of a certain Sayyid ʿAbd al-Karīm al-Barzanjī by the Ottomans, Ṭrābulsī, *Jidda*, p. 179. Hamilton, *Sinai, The Hedjaz, and Soudan*, p. 54, still calls it 'Hedjaz'.

71 al-Nimr, *Ḥārat al-Baḥr*, p. 19 and Abū 'l-Jadāʾil, Khālid Ṣalāḥ Sanūsī, *Rawā lī wālidī wa-ṣaḥibuh*, p. 35. A British report on measures taken to control the plague of March 1899 only mentions three quarters, see TNA, FO 195/2061, Hussain to Amb. Const., March 23, 1899.

72 Abū 'l-Jadāʾil, Khālid Ṣalāḥ Sanūsī, *Rawā lī wālidī wa-ṣaḥibuh*, p. 35.

(including inhabitants of other quarters) straying from the main thoroughfares.[73]

A closer comparison of the maps of 1851 and 1880 shows the growing size and importance of the northern quarter. For example, the governor's office had moved there and was no longer situated near the port area as it had been in 1851. This might be linked to other developments in the new quarter, such as the new governmental school (no. 26) being established there as well as this being the quarter in which the European consulates could now be found (see nos. 31, 33). At least as far as the European consulates were concerned, this change of location was possibly not only due to the northern quarter being considered better, but rather because it seemed safer than the more 'popular' quarter of the port and *sūq*, where the consulates had been so violently attacked in 1858.[74]

Commercial, Communal, and Religious Buildings

In 1840 Tamisier described the 'grand bazar', nowadays known as Sūq al-Nadā, as a large street lined with high houses. These were decorated with wooden screens, locally called *rawshān* (pl. *rawāshīn*). However, by the 1850s most houses outside of the *sūq* were still 'externally mean' and without such screens, which must have been quite expensive.[75] The shops, according to Tamisier, were slightly elevated and displayed the goods which were kept in depots behind the shop. He describes the goods available in the different sections of the *sūq*, from the northern end where bakers and small restaurants provided nourishment, to the south where dried fruit, oil, grains, and pulses were sold. In between, one could acquire weapons, potteries, glass, or, indeed, visit a coffee shop.[76]

The market area, or *sūq*, was lined with huge structures called *ḥawsh* (pl. *aḥwāsh*, Turk. *havş*) on the map. A *ḥawsh* in the old city of Jeddah

[73] On the distinction between main thoroughfares and 'private' quarter roads; cf. Cem Behar, *A Neighborhood in Ottoman Istanbul: Fruit Vendors and Civil Servants in the Kasap İlyas Mahalle*, SUNY Series in the Social and Economic History of the Middle East (Albany: State University of New York Press, 2003), p. 47.

[74] TNA, FO 195/1251, Consul Zohrab to FO, November 13, 1879.

[75] Hamilton, *Sinai, The Hedjaz, and Soudan*, p. 54.

[76] Tamisier, *Voyage en Arabie*, pp. 80–3.

could be a number of different structures: a courtyard around which rooms were built for housing purposes, a courtyard adjacent to a house and enclosed by a wall, a mere enclosure to store goods, or, indeed, a commercial structure combining a number of these functions.[77] Thus, a young migrant arriving alone in Jeddah with no prior connections could find lodgings in a *ḥawsh*, possibly even for free at the outset of his stay. This enabled the person to make initial contact, while others could see from the way he engaged in shared work whether he was a worthy potential employee. There might even have been designated *aḥwāsh* for the accommodation of such itinerant bachelors.[78] Single rooms were at times called *ʿuzla* (pl. *ʿuzal*), a term also used for apartments in larger houses that were rented out separately.

The large *aḥwāsh* in the *sūq* area of Jeddah often seem to have combined a number of functions around a courtyard in that they accommodated shops and storage on the ground floor while offering living space on the upper levels.[79] Thus, the endowment document (*waqfiyya*) of Yūsuf Bā Nāja (d. 1864–5) refers to properties endowed in the Ḥawsh al-Ḥalwānī in detail. These comprised nine rooms, most of which were rented out though one was used by two people without rent.[80] Interestingly, two of these *ʿuzal* were rented to (apparently single) women and another one given to a couple free of rent. The property in the *ḥawsh* also comprised two interior courts, ten shops, and seven storage rooms.[81] As the *wikāla*s on the map line the main market street of Jeddah, the shops were presumably open to the street and might or might not have had access to the courtyard or to storage

[77] For a description of *aḥwāsh* in Greater Syria, which served similar functions, see Saßmannshausen, *Reform in Translation*, pp. 76–8. For the *ḥawsh* as a poor communal dwelling; cf. André Raymond, 'The Spatial Organization of the City' in S. K. Jayyusi, R. Holod, A. Petruccioli and A. Raymond (eds.), *The City in the Islamic World* (Leiden and Boston: Brill, 2008), vol. 1, pp. 47–70, here p. 66.

[78] Interview, Muḥammad Bā Quʿr, Jeddah, February 16, 2015.

[79] Oral information, Talāl Bakur, February 29, 2012. On the commercial *aḥwāsh*, see al-Thaqafī, *al-ʿImāra bi-madīnat Jidda*, vol. 1, pp. 260–4, under the title 'al-khānāt'. In Suakin, these were presumably called wikāla, e.g. Elfateh, *Suakin (Sudan) and the Colonial Architecture*, vol. 1, pp. 166–7.

[80] Khālid Bā Ṭarfī, *Ibrāhīm al-Muḥammad al-Hassūn … yatadhakkar* (Jeddah, 1435/2014), pp. 63–4 for the story of how poor immigrants from Najd settled in Jeddah.

[81] Philippe Pétriat, 'Les Grandes Familles Marchandes Hadramies de Djedda, 1850–1950', PhD Thesis, Université Paris 1 (2013), p. 449. For the storage function of *aḥwāsh;* cf. CADN, 2_MI_3229, Le Gay to Amb. Const., August 12, 1872.

facilities either behind or above the stores. The mercantile character of Jeddah is confirmed by the (strangely round) numbers of 30 *khān* buildings (presumably the commercial *aḥwāsh*) and 900 shops (*dukkān*) overall, listed by the Ottoman yearbook for 1891–2.[82]

A sales document of 1859 confirms that *aḥwāsh* could also be private property and that their ownership was often shared between a number of people, presumably as a result of both inheritance and sales. The *ḥawsh* referred to in this document, situated in Ḥārat al-Shām, and included a building of clay and stone.[83] Burton, who visited Jeddah in 1853, gives a lively description of the Ḥawsh al-Sharīf (no. 3) as 'a vast pile of madrepore ... once the palace of Mohammed bin Aun, and now converted into a Wakalah'.[84] He was not the only pilgrim to have stayed there.[85]

Due to this combination of functions, the *aḥwāsh* often fulfilled the functions of a caravanserai in Jeddah, a term which is indeed found in Western accounts.[86] Burckhardt, in his description of Jeddah, speaks of khān as a place where he as a cash-strapped traveller could find accommodation and mentions a great gateway, serving as the entrance, providing welcome shade.[87] Another term used in Jeddah is that of

82 *Hicaz vilayeti 1309*, p. 275.

83 Private document dated 4 Rajab 1275, referring to properties of Ruqayya bte Uthmān al-ʿAmūdī, private archive of Māzin ʿAbdallāh al-Saqqāf, Jeddah, consulted November 26, 2012.

84 Richard Burton, *Personal Narrative of a Pilgrimage to el Medinah and Meccah* (ed. Isabel Burton), 2nd edn. (London: Longman Brown Green Longmans and Roberts, 1857), vol. 2, p. 266. According to al-Ḥaḍrāwī al-Makkī al-Shāfiʿī, *al-Jawāhir al-muʿadda fī faḍāʾil Judda*, p. 53, it still contained „*quṣūr*' (palaces).

85 CADN, 2_MI_3229, Le Gay to Amb. Const., August 1, 1872, Buez to Min. of Agriculture and Commerce, March 4, 1873.

86 Pétriat (ed.), *Une Histoire Partagée*, p. 109. In this, it resembles the medieval Mediterranean *funduq*, cf. Olivia Constable, *Housing the Stranger in the Mediterranean World: Lodging, Trade, and Travel in Late Antiquity and the Middle Ages* (Cambridge: Cambridge University Press, 2003), pp. 68–106. On the terminological conundrums; cf. Nancy Um, 'Spatial Negotiations in a Commercial City: The Red Sea Port of Mocha, Yemen, during the First Half of the Eighteenth Century', *Journal of the Society of Architectural Historians*, 62 (2003), pp. 178–93, here pp. 180–1.

87 Burckhardt, *Travels in Arabia*, pp. 2, 9; cf. al-Thaqafī, *al-ʿImāra bi-madīnat Jidda*, vol. 1, p. 261. He confirms that what was called a *khān* in Syria was identical to a *ḥawsh* in Jeddah. The term *khān al-bunn*, the coffee warehouse, also appears in a land document of the Bā Nāja family pertaining to Mecca, dated Dhū 'l-Qaʿida 21, 1350/March 31, 1932, in the possession of Māzin ʿAbdallāh al-Saqqāf, consulted Jeddah March 2, 2015; cf. Ṭrābulsī, *Jidda*,

wikāla, which technically designated offices of a merchant house, but was often physically located in a *ḥawsh*. Some of the *aḥwāsh* functioned as locations where goods could be auctioned, as is indicated most prominently by the Ḥawsh al-Dallāl (no.2).[88]

Local historian al-Kābilī defines a *wikāla* as 'the center for wholesale trade in the sūqs of Jeddah, because the goods were stored there, sold and distributed. It was furthermore the place for the foreign merchants and travellers. The wikāla took the place of the (khān) and some wikālas were specialised for the activities of the guilds.'[89]

The latter point means that *wikāla*s also provided spaces of production, in this function resembling what is elsewhere known as a *qayṣariyya*, or, in Yemen, a *ṣamṣara*. A final meaning of *ḥawsh* in Jeddah was the courtyards surrounding mosques, such as those of the Ḥanafī, ʿAqqāsh, and Bakır Pasha Mosques.

Incidentally, there was another term used for large storage spaces, namely the Egyptian word *shūna* (turk. *şevne,* storage or warehouse). These spaces were initially used to store the grain used to provision pilgrims. The map of 1851 features a *şevne* gate (no. 27), pointing to a nearby government storehouse. In 1880–1, the map explicitly mentions such a provincial storehouse (no. 14) where foodstuffs (mostly grain) provided through alms from other parts of the empire were kept for the pilgrimage season.[90] The term *şevne* is, however, also used for the telegraph and post office (*cevap şevnesi*, no. 17) in the port area and thus seems to be as flexible as *ḥawsh*.

Further prominent features on the map in terms of their location are the two *ribāṭ*s which are labelled, representing only a fraction of total of the twelve *aribṭa* (pl. of *ribāṭ*) present in 1885.[91] A *ribāṭ* in the Hijaz was basically a hostel for pilgrims which was usually endowed by rich people from particular regions for the benefit of

pp. 240–1. On the use of *ḥawsh* for *khan;* cf. Albert Kazimirski, *Dictionnaire Arabe-Français: Contenant toutes les racines de la langue Arabe, leurs dérivés* ... (Cairo: Imprimérie Khédivale, 1875), vol. 1, p. 653.

[88] This is mentioned as 'khan al-dallālīn' by al-Anṣārī, *Mawsūʿat tārīkh madīnat Jidda*, p. 560.

[89] Kābilī, *al-Ḥirafiyyūn fī madīnat Jidda*, p. 69.

[90] Interview, Māzin ʿAbdallāh al-Saqqāf, March 2, 2013.

[91] al-Thaqafī, *al-ʿImāra bi-madīnat Jidda*, vol. 1, p. 198; for the following pp. 197–223. The number sounds plausible as Manāʿ, *Tārīkh Mā lam Yuʾarrakh*, gives the number of fourteen, p. 266.

their compatriots.[92] One example is the *ribāṭ* of the Bohras, a branch of the Ismāʿīlī sect whose visitors did not mix much with other pilgrims or the locals.[93] They could have had another function, namely the care of those wanting to stay in or near the holy cities who had no regular income or funds and could not afford to rent rooms. Sufis often congregated in the *arbiṭa* which might also explain why local scholars taught there on a regular basis at times.[94] This gave rise to the current meaning of *ribāṭ* in the Hijaz, which is an institution providing care for poor people, often women. According to al-Nimr, the *arbiṭa* housed poor people who vacated their rooms during the hajj season. This indicates a mixed-use, or perhaps a transitional later phase when pilgrims only came for a very short period.[95]

It is difficult to gauge the number of *arbiṭa* in old Jeddah, but the large number of twenty-nine such structures existing in 1993 in the old city suggests that there were a fair number of these types of pilgrims' hostels available in the period under investigation.[96] A typical *ribāṭ* in the old city, depicted in Figure 4.4, consisted of rooms grouped around a small courtyard, which could be covered by a roof. It could comprise one or two stories and usually had communal facilities. Although some *arbiṭa* consisted entirely of private spaces accessible individually from the street.

According to the Ottoman yearbook of 1891–2, Jeddah had five large mosques, only three of which are identifiable on the map.[97] Besides mosques, Jeddah featured a number of *zawāyā* (sing. *zāwiya*), which could serve both as local prayer rooms as well as Sufi convents.[98] Thus, the large Hadhrami community maintained both a *ribāṭ*

[92] Suʿād Bin ʿAfīf, 'Mujtamaʿ al-ribāṭ: Dirāsa waṣfiyya li-asālīb al-riʿāya al-ijtimāʿiyya fī buyūt al-fuqarāʾ bi-madīnat Jidda, al-Mamlaka al-ʿArabiyya al-Saʿūdiyya', MA Thesis, King ʿAbd al-ʿAzīz University (1993), pp. 50–1. For other types of arbiṭa, see pp. 45–52. For an early discussion of ribāṭ as inn or hostel for needy travellers, often specifically religious travellers, see Constable, *Housing the Stranger*, pp. 48–51, 61–3.

[93] Oral communication, Talāl Bakur, Muḥammad Raqqām, February 29, 2012.

[94] al-Yāfī, *The Arab Family*, p. 55, discusses them as Sufi hospices. For the teaching, see al-Anṣārī, *Mawsūʿat tārīkh madīnat Jidda*, p. 355.

[95] al-Nimr, *Ḥārat al-Baḥr*, pp. 264–6.

[96] Bin ʿAfīf, *Mujtamaʿ al-Ribāṭ*, p. 71, table 3.

[97] *Hicaz vilayeti, 1309*, p. 275.

[98] Ochsenwald, *Religion, Society, and the State*, p. 43, counts well over twenty-seven *zawāyā* for Jeddah. The Ottoman yearbook for 1891 counts seven türbes and thirty masjids (small mosques). It does not have the category of *zawiya*,

Figure 4.4 Ribāṭ al-Khunjī al-Kabīr.
Photographed by François Cristofoli, www.unesco.org/new/fileadmin/MULTIMEDIA/HQ/ERI/images/whc2014_saudi_arabia07.jpg

as well as two *zāwiya*, one next to the main *sūq* known as Zāwiyat al-Ḥaḍārim and another one in Ḥārat al-Yaman knowns as Zāwiya ʿAlawiyya. These names point to the importance of these spaces as gathering points not only for the larger community (i.e. at times of prayer, but possibly also on other occasions) but also for the adherents to the ʿAlawī Sufi order.[99] Some of these *zawāya* contained a tomb of a saint (*türbe*) or even had a few graves around them, others were simple rooms. In contrast, the Sanūsī Zāwiya near Bāb al-Sharīf resembled a proper mosque and had an adjacent hostel for pilgrims. Indeed, in the late 1880s, it functioned predominantly as a pilgrims' hostel.[100]

Hicaz vilayeti 1309, p. 275. Presumably because of the sensitivity of the theme of Sufism, al-Thaqafī, *al-ʿImāra bi-madīnat Jidda* discusses the prayer rooms of the *zawāya* under 'small mosques', pp. 168–71.

[99] Pétriat, *Le Négoce des Lieux Saints*, p. 254; cf. ʿAbdallāh al-Sharīf, *Dhikrayāt Muḥammad Darwīsh Raqqām: Jidda dākhil al-sūr* (Jeddah: al-Maṭbaʿa al-Maḥmūdiyya, 2013), p. 137.

[100] Interviews, ʿAbdallāh Manāʿ, Jeddah, February 28, 2012; Talāl Bakur, Muḥammad Raqqām, February 29, 2012. On the Sanūsī zawāyā in the Hijaz

The Zāwiyat al-Hunūd also predominantly served a particular ethnic community, in this case Indian merchants. It was situated right next to the *wikāla* (probably another *ḥawsh*) known as Qaṣbat al-Hunūd.[101] Usually, the link of a *zāwiya* to a specific Sufi order was more important than that to an ethnic group, although these categories did often overlap.[102] Some of the *zawāyā* were founded by Sufi pilgrims to serve primarily as pilgrims' hostels.[103]

On the southeastern edge of town, a hospital can be discerned, to the northeast, inside the wall, a graveyard as well as a police station. The majority of the remaining structures, however, were residential and will be discussed somewhat more thoroughly in the following section.

Domestic Spaces in the 1880s

Beyond the port and *sūq* areas extended Jeddah's residential quarters, though the *sūq* was formally part of these. By 1880, *al-Balad* probably contained hardly any, perhaps even none, of the huts typical of the Red Sea coast. Although the map still depicts free spaces which allowed further building activities until the 1940s, a comparison of the structures inside to those shown in the southern suburb of Nakutu shows that the houses inside were significantly larger (and thus presumably more solid) than those on the outside. This notwithstanding, the houses inside varied significantly in size and, presumably, in height depending on the wealth of the owner as well as the size of the occupying family.

As described in Chapter 1, the ground floor of a typical Jeddah house served as a reception area, office, and storage space, but could also be used to accommodate servants or slaves. Most of the larger houses had a second, less conspicuous, entrance that could be used by women who thus did not have to pass by the men's offices or reception

see Ochsenwald, *Religion, Society, and the State*, pp. 46–7 and Le Chatelier, *Les Confréries Musulmanes du Hedjaz*, p. 275.

101 Kābilī, *al-Ḥirafiyyūn fī madīnat Jidda*, pp. 66, 90. Possibly there were even two Indian zawāyā in the old city, oral information, Māzin ʿAbdallāh al-Saqqāf, Jeddah, February 28, 2013.

102 This becomes very evident in Le Chatelier, *Les Confréries Musulmanes du Hedjaz* when he describes the different orders, the countries where they are spread, and their presence and adherents in the Hijaz.

103 Ibid., pp. 188–9, for the *zawāyā* founded for Indian pilgrims of the Bayyūmiyya order.

halls.[104] A staircase connected the ground floor to the higher levels, where the living spaces, forming small apartments with one or more rooms and complete with bathrooms, were separated from the stairwell by doors. Wherever possible, there were at least two rooms, one for sleeping, the other one for the reception of – usually female – guests, who assembled in the houses while the men met outside. The kitchen was situated at the top of the house, or sometimes between different floors so that they were accessible to servants directly from the staircase.[105] Balconies protruded, covered entirely by *rawāshīn*,, shown in Figure 4.5, which allowed for ventilation, but also for sound to travel from the streets and small squares below. A number of both smaller and larger terraces on different levels allowed the inhabitants to breathe fresh air while performing tasks such as cleaning the laundry and preparing food. It also allowed inhabitants to sleep outside during the hot summer months. There were many variations in detail depending on the size of the land, the wealth of the owner, and the personal needs and preferences of the inhabitants. Interestingly, the famous Naṣīf house has four floors with very high ceilings at the front, but eight at the back where the servants' quarters and service functions of the house were situated.[106]

As mentioned previously, some houses also had a *ḥawsh* or courtyard, used for commercial or recreational purposes. Indeed, while the *ahwāsh* in Jeddah provide a distinct commercial space (something largely absent in historical Mocha), some of the larger merchant houses clearly combined commercial space for storage and offices with living quarters.[107] A prime example of this is the Bin Ḥimd house in the Shām quarter (Figure 4.6) which actually consists of two houses on either side of a courtyard, with large covered storage spaces and an office next to the main entrance gate. It points to the profession of its owner, who was active in the grain trade.[108]

[104] For descriptions of different types of houses, see Bagader, *The Evolution of Built Heritage Conservation Policies*, pp. 171–7; Maneval, *The Architecture of Everyday Life*, pp. 69–75; Bokhari, 'Jeddah', pp. 183–5; and al-Thaqafī, *al-'Imāra bi-madīnat Jidda*, vol. 1, pp. 321–401.

[105] al-Thaqafī, *al-'Imāra bi-madīnat Jidda*, vol. 1, pp. 333–4.

[106] Krause, *Stadtgeographische Untersuchungen*, p. 56.

[107] Um, *Spatial Negotiations*, pp. 182–3.

[108] On the family and trade network see Freitag, *A Twentieth-Century Merchant Network*.

Figure 4.5 Houses with wooden *rawashīn* and a *mirkāz*.
Leiden University Libraries, Or. 12.288 J: 28, date unknown

Some of the houses featured stone benches immediately adjacent to the walls.[109] However, joint seating areas in front of houses, often leading onto little squares (*barḥa*), were more common. These seats were known locally as *mirkāz* and consisted of wooden benches, sometimes covered, where groups of (male) friends, known as *shilla*, would meet regularly.[110] Some of these *marākiz* developed into neighbourhood coffeeshops which, in contrast to the coffeeshops in the port and *sūq* area, were only semi-public in that access to the quarters, and hence to the *barḥāt*, was informally monitored (and controlled) by neighbourhood youth, who also used the *barḥa* for sports.[111] It is probably around these *barḥāt* and clusters of family dwellings that

109 Burckhardt, *Travels in Arabia*, p. 14.
110 On the squares and seating arrangements for *shilal*, see Ṭrābulsī, *Jidda*, pp. 190, 202–6; and Manāʿ, *Tārīkh Mā lam Yuʾarrakh*, pp. 34–5.
111 al-Sharīf, *Dhikrayāt Muḥammad Darwīsh Raqqām*, pp. 139–41; and Ṭrābulsī, *Jidda*, p. 190.

Figure 4.6 Storage halls in Bin Ḥimd house.
Photograph by the author

the neighbourhood as an informal subdivision of the more formal unit of the quarter developed.[112] Thus, a sales document mentions a *Ḥayy al-ashrāf* (quarter of the sharifs) as the property's location. This was part of Ḥārat al-Yaman, in which the Zāwiya ʿAlawiyya and graveyard were situated and a large portion of the Hadhramis resided. Not only the seller and buyer of the particular property but also the neighbours, were of Hadhrami origin.[113] To what extent much land in the quarter belonged to the Meccan sharifs, who thus might have been responsible for the naming, is difficult to gauge. Today, the general

112 On such neighbourhoods within a quarter; cf. Behar, *A Neighborhood in Ottoman Istanbul*, p. 17.

113 al-Thaqafī, *al-ʿImāra bi-madīnat Jidda*, vol. 1, p. 242 even claims that the Yemen quarter consisted of Ḥārat al-Baḥr and Ḥārat al-ʿAlawī. On the Sūq al-ʿAlawī; cf. Ṭrābulsī, *Jidda*, p. 235.

passageway leading to Bāb Makka, which borders on the neighbourhood (and constitutes the boundary between the Maẓlūm and Yaman quarters) is known as the ʿAlawī Sūq and has acquired as much importance as the Sūq al-Nadā.[114] Besides the Ḥayy al-Ashrāf (whose residents were also known as *ahl al-ʿAlawī*, the people of al-ʿAlawī) the Yemen quarter also had an area known by the name of the Sanūsiyya mosque near Bāb al-Sharīf, and one named after the al-ʿUqaylī mosque.[115]

During the pilgrimage season, the lower floors, or even entire houses, were rented out to pilgrims while the families withdrew to the upper floors or to houses they might have owned in the suburbs or in Ṭāʾif. The marked presence of strangers in the city, who at times even camped in the squares, was, at least partly, mediated by the pilgrims' guides and/or the immediate hosts (cf. Chapter 6).

Building styles in Jeddah had always varied to some degree. In the late nineteenth century, open balconies became fashionable, although they could hardly be used by families and could thus not replace the shielded roof terraces. In 1929/30 the Zaynal ʿAlī Riḍā family was the first to introduce concrete and cement to Jeddah, about the same time that the Khozāma Palace in al-Nuzla al-Yamaniyya was built with the same materials.[116] Given the need for imported steel from Egypt or Europe, as well as for much water, this technology only took off after the end of World War II and the opening of the ʿAzīziyya waterworks in 1948. This was to revolutionise construction in Jeddah.[117] Beyond such rather scarce observations, the sources used for this study tell us fairly little about the type of more profound transformation in lifestyle that has been documented in Weber's study of art and architecture as evidence of social change with regard to Damascus due to the relatively fewer maps, photographs, travelogues, and newspapers and other sources containing relevant information.[118]

[114] Krause, *Stadtgeographische Untersuchungen*, p. 41.

[115] Abū 'l-Jadāʾil, Khālid Ṣalāḥ Sanūsī, *Rawā lī wālidī wa-ṣaḥibuh*, pp. 32–4.

[116] Abdulla Difalla, 'Jeddah's Slum Areas: The Attempt to Redevelop al-Nuzla al-Yamania', MA Thesis, Ball State University (2015), p. 37.

[117] al-Anṣārī, *Mawsūʿat tārīkh madīnat Jidda*, pp. 34–5; and Abū Zayd, *al-Miʿmārīyūn fī Jidda al-qadīma*, pp. 22–3, 117–21.

[118] Weber, *Damascus*, pp. 22–6.

Jeddah extra Muros

Part of the importance of the 1880–1 map is that it depicts some of the immediate vicinity of Jeddah. Map 4.4 shows a number of military installations, religious sites, and settlements. Interestingly, we can see a slaughterhouse to the south (no. 3). As it is quite close to the track leading south, as well as to the suburb Nakutu, this seems to be the old one which was either given up in conjunction with the aforementioned works of 1866–7, or – if it continued functioning (it is not marked as

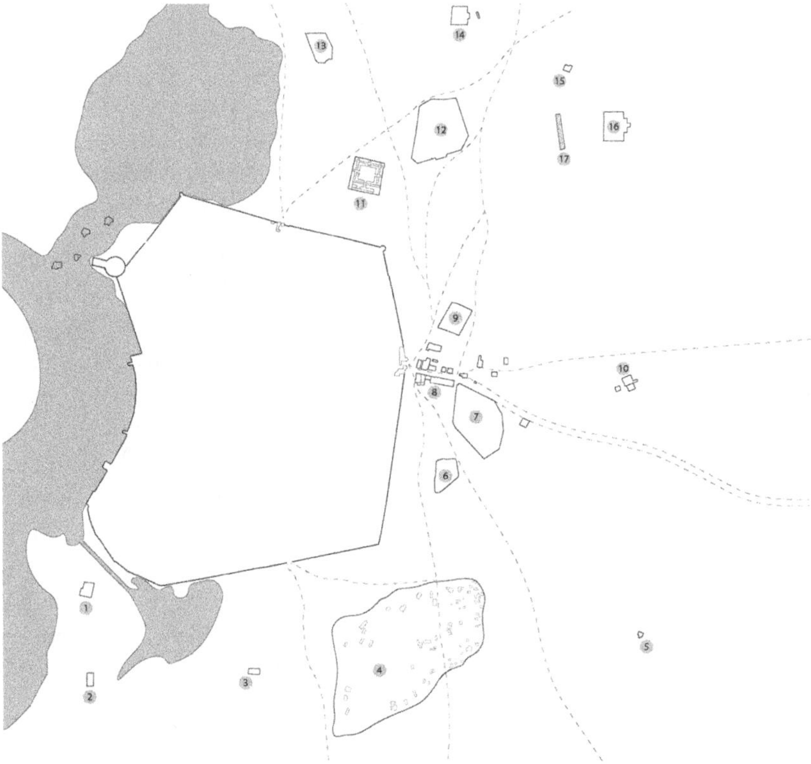

Map 4.4 Map of the surroundings of Jeddah 1880–1. (1) Türbe of Shaykh Abū 'l-ʿUyūn, (2) Christian Cemetery, (3) Slaughterhouse, (4) Nakutu, (5) Türbe of Sayyid Maḥmūd, (6) Cemetery (?), (7) Asad Cemetery, (8) Coffeehouses, (9) al-Mashhad, (10) Cistern, (11) Barracks, (12) Cemetery of Eve, (13) Derelict Windmills, (14) Military (?), (15) (?), (16) (?), (17) Military (Shooting Range?). Drawn by Melody Mosaver on the basis of the Ottoman map of 1880–1.

defunct on the map) – we have an indication that the building of a new slaughterhouse was only planned.

The Suburbs

Two settled areas are clearly discernible, one directly outside of the Mecca Gate, one to the south. Formally, they did not belong to the walled city, the gates which opened at sunrise and closed at sunset for visitors even from the immediately adjacent settlements.[119] The 'coffeehouses' outside the Mecca Gate, possibly one of the structures visible in Figure 4.7, had their roots in a Bedouin settlement which was described by Burckhardt as an assembly of huts

> inhabited by the camel-drivers who traffic between that city and Djidda; by poor Bedouins, who earn a livelihood by cutting wood at a considerable distance in the mountains; and by Negro hadjis, who adopt the same means of supporting themselves during their stay at Djidda. Here is held the market for live cattle, wood and charcoal, fruits and vegetables in wholesale.[120]

In Burckhardt's time, this settlement was not just a liminal space between the city and its environs, and between Jeddah and Mecca – another *dihlīz*, so to say. It was also a space in which news and goods were exchanged and transportation deals struck. Pilgrims passed through this gate and met with their guides and mounts to Mecca either inside or directly outside of it. According to Hamilton, there was an extensive grain bazaar inside the wall, and a suburb composed of straw huts directly outside of it, inhabited by people of African origin 'and the resort of all the bad characters of the town'.[121] In the memoir of a merchant born in 1910, the coffeehouse located outside Bāb Makka was 'a center and meeting place for all those who had business in Bāb Makka, particularly the camel drivers upon arrival and departure, and this was also due to its proximity to the vegetable,

119 Oral information, ʿAbd al-Wahhāb Abū Zināda and ʿUmda ʿAbd al-Ṣamad, Jeddah, November 17, 2011.

120 Burckhardt, *Travels in Arabia* (p. 20 of German edition), cf the description by Badia y Leblich, *Travels of Ali Bey*, p. 46. For a description of 1806, see Muḥammad Farāhānī and Hafez Farmayan (eds.), *A Shi'ite Pilgrimage to Mecca 1885–1886: The Safarnâmeh of Mirzâ Moḥammad Ḥosayn Farâhâni*, 1st edn. (Austin: University of Texas Press, 1990), p. 199.

121 Hamilton, *Sinai, The Hedjaz, and Soudan*, p. 65.

Figure 4.7 Outside of Bāb Makka.
Photograph Wilfred Thesiger (Copyright Pitt Rivers Museum, Univ. of Oxford, 2004 130 31792 1–0)

wood, and herb markets which were held daily.'[122] With time, the huts were complemented – if not replaced – by more solid buildings.[123] In 1883 a British report described some shops outside the gate that were submitted to plunder by Bedouin, which speaks to the dangers to which the suburbs extra muros were exposed during this period.[124]

Another marketplace is mentioned, apparently inside of the walls, presumably selling both provisions to the urban population and goods for the Bedouin such as pots and tools, but also imported grain and

[122] Unpubl. memoirs by Saʿīd b. Muḥammad b. ʿUbayd b. Zaqr, dated 1984, p. 9. I thank Philippe Pétriat for this information.

[123] Farāhānī and Farmayan (eds.), *A Shi'ite Pilgrimage to Mecca*, p. 199; TNA, FO 195/1689, Abdurrazzack to Amb. Const., October 27, 1890, with a description of the Mecca Gate as thoroughfare; and FO, 195/2061, Devey to FO, March 6, 1899 on the quarantine barracks. The map indicates no hut structures. Given the continued need for Bedouin and pauper accommodation, and lacking information as to the comprehensiveness of the information, their absence seems somewhat unlikely. See also left edge of image RGS 091411, B 10583, Clemow 1906.

[124] TNA, FO 195/1451, Moncrieff to FO, July 27, 1883.

other foodstuffs.[125] Additional quarantine installations at the Mecca Gate, erected in the context of the cholera epidemics in 1897 and 1898 (see below, Chapter 6), doubled as stores selling merchandise for Mecca.[126] When motorised transportation for pilgrims was introduced in earnest in 1926, the space outside became even more congested.[127] Given that by that time security had been established, the gate seems to have remained open most of the times and photographs indicate that the outside of the wall became more densely built up.[128] Although the topography of the area and the position of the Mecca Gate has changed, the space, enclosed by Sūq al-Badū, Sūq al-ʿAlawī and the current position of the Mecca Gate, still evokes the hustle of travelling with its garages, gas, and bus station, though it is now only a connecting space, and the earlier, very real, divide by wall and gate is difficult to imagine any longer.

Another large suburb, Nakutu (Figure 4.8), is indicated on the map to the Southeast of Bāb al-Sharīf (no.4) a little northeast of the current Hindāwiyya quarter. It consisted of huts built from reeds and debris. According to the map, there were three sections, namely (from West to East) Naquṭu, Bīsha, and Takārna. While Western travellers seem to consider all three parts of Nakutu, and mention its African inhabitants, which included freed slaves, local histories mention Ḥārat Bīsha and Ḥārat al-Takārna, but rarely Nakutu.[129] Given the different origins as well as the available building materials, the styles of the huts varied considerably. The French intelligence officer, and later Jesuit priest, Savignac, who visited in 1917 and to whom we owe a number of photographs, estimated that the suburb comprised between two and

125 TNA, FO 195/1894 Alban to Amb., Constantinople, November 11, 1895. For a lively description based on memory, see Abū ʻl-Jadāʾil, Khālid Ṣalāḥ Sanūsī, *Rawā lī wālidī wa-ṣaḥibuh*, p. 20.

126 TNA, FO 195/2061, Devey to FO, March 6, 1899. A photograph taken by Clemow in 1906 shows the solid nature of the buildings outside, RGS, 091413, D 402.

127 *Umm al-Qurā*, 151, October 4, 1927; and IPA 9289/02, 16 R.A. 1365 (February 18, 1946).

128 Rathjens and Wissmann, *Landschaftskundliche Beobachtungen*, pp. 81–2; Carlo Nallino, *Raccolta di Scritti Editi e Inediti*, Pubblicazioni dell'Istituto per l'Oriente (Rome: Istituto per l'Oriente, 1939), p. 65, figure 12; and RGS, Thesiger collection photo 2003.130.31784.1 of June 23–4, 1945.

129 Kābilī, *al-Ḥirafiyyūn fī madīnat Jidda*, p. 53.

Figure 4.8 Photograph of Nakutu.
Van Voorthuysen 1926. Leiden University Libraries, Or. 12 288 B: 36

three hundred huts.[130] Many of the inhabitants worked in the harbour or in quarries, while women carried water, worked in households, or as prostitutes.[131] European travellers seem to have visited it for its exotic appearance, so that we have more photographs of Nakutu than of the other suburbs. In contrast to the villages described below, which do not figure on the map, Nakutu is designated a *mahalle*, a quarter, although I have no sources on whether such an *extra muros* quarter had its own administrative logics or was in some way integrated into urban politics. The picturesque use of reet and twigs had its price:

[130] Raphaël Savignac, 'Carnet de guerre de 1914–1918: Épisode de son voyage au *Hedjaz*, comme officier de renseingement dans la marine', 1917, unpub. Manuscript, Ècole biblique et archéologique française de Jérusalem, p. 10. For another description, see TNA, CO 879/119, H.R. Palmer, 'Report on a Journey from Maidugari, Nigeria, to Jeddah in Arabia', August 1919.

[131] Rathjens and Wissmann, *Landschaftskundliche Beobachtungen*, p. 82; Oral information, ʿAbd al-Raḥmān al-Barqāwī, Jeddah, March 19 and 26, 2010; and Nallino, *Raccolta di Scritti*, p. 186; cf. TNA, FO 195/1251, Zohrab to FO, November 13, 1879.

Figure 4.9 Arial photograph of Jeddah and its surroundings in 1948.

According to a Dutch report, Nakutu experienced at least one major fire in 1916. Such fires might well have been a fairly frequent occurrence in such villages.[132]

Two small settlements to the north of Jeddah (beyond the scope of the map, but discernible on the aerial picture of 1948, Figure 4.9) by the name of Upper and Lower Ruways supplied Jeddah with fish.[133] By the 1940s their population and settlement type was similar to that of

[132] The Indonesian Hajj, Documents from the Archive of the Dutch Consulate at Jidda, Saudi Arabia, Rapport eener dienst-reis naar Djeddah, November 15, 1916, p. 45.

[133] al-Anṣārī, *Mawsūʿat tārīkh madīnat Jidda*, p. 86; and Nallino, *Raccolta di Scritti*, p. 186.

Nakutu, though the upper village had a number of stone buildings that were destroyed during Ibn Saʿūd's siege of Jeddah in 1925.[134] Ruways was one of the villages in the surroundings of Jeddah through which Ethiopian slaves were imported in 1922.[135] A booklet on Ruways, published by a descendant of its earlier inhabitants in 2013 and resembling a stream of nostalgic lamentation, describes the settlement as one on the margins of the city, as well as of the villages, and contrasts the inhabitants, whom he calls Bedouin (*badū*), with the *ḥaḍar* or urbanites in a very Khaldunian style.[136] 'The *ḥaḍar* of Jeddah did not know us, and our relations in the desert were suspicious of us, we lived between those and these, we ended as Bedouin in the eyes of the ḥaḍar, and ḥaḍar in the eyes of the Bedouin and did not know who we were' – except, one could add, extremely poor.[137] This also increased their vulnerability in times of conflict, as is shown by the almost complete exodus during the siege of Jeddah in 1925.[138] However, after this time, and with the establishment with peace by the new ruler, the quarter expanded rapidly and housed many new arrivals from different parts of the Kingdom.[139]

Outside of the 1880–1 map, which was prepared to assist urban planning inside the wall, but clearly discernible to the Southeast of Jeddah on the aerial photograph taken in 1948, was the village of al-Nuzla al-Yamāniyya. It started as a Bedouin settlement and goes back to at least the mid-eighteenth century, according to the oldest extant land documents.[140] Its inhabitants mostly worked in the pilgrim trade by providing camels and organising the caravans (the so-called *mukharrijūn*). Later many of them became drivers and thus continued to transport pilgrims and goods. Others owned large water cisterns and sold the water in town. Some agriculture and animal husbandry completed the original economic portfolio of this village.[141] When Philby visited in November 1924, he found a place of 'whitewashed square single-storey houses and reed-huts' which was, due to Ibn

134 Rathjens and Wissmann, *Landschaftskundliche Beobachtungen*, pp. 82–3.
135 TNA, FO 371/7718, Jeddah Report, January 1922, p. 7.
136 al-Surayḥī, *al-Ruways*, pp. 6–7.
137 Ibid., for the poetic description p. 9, for poverty p. 10.
138 Ibid., pp. 53–61.
139 ʿAdnān al-Yāfī, 'al-Ruwais: A District in the Heart of Jeddah' in *The Story of Ten –Ḥikāyat 10* (Jeddah, 2013), pp. 10–16, here pp. 14–16.
140 ʿAbbās al-Faḍlī, *al-Nuzla al-Yamāniyya: Ḥayy fī dhākirat Jidda* (Jeddah: Maktabat Dār Zahrān, 2010), p. 13.
141 al-Faḍlī, pp. 37–64.

Sa'ūd's occupation of Mecca, almost deserted, with most inhabitants seeking shelter behind the walls of Jeddah.[142] al-Nuzla's moment of fame came when Ibn Sa'ūd started to have the Khuzām palace built there between 1928 and 1932, which probably encouraged a number of the rich families, such as the family of Muḥammad 'Abdallāh 'Ali Riḍā, to move to this new quarter as well.[143] It is presumably in this period that the buildings started to change from huts (*'ushash* and *bakākīr*, sing. *bakkār*) and houses made from unburnt bricks to those constructed from coral stone and – after the 1940s – cement.[144] Nevertheless, land in al-Nuzla remained fairly cheap, so that families at times also moved there in order to rent out their houses to pilgrims' guides or directly to pilgrims for profit.[145]

al-Nuzla al-Yamāniyya shared with al-Kandara, another suburb situated on the northeast of the old city and probably similar in the original composition of the population and appearance, that inhabitants from inside the walled city, who could not escape the heat by moving to Ṭā'if in the mountains, spent hot summer nights in these villages in the late nineteenth century.[146] Both villages, situated at about half a mile in the case of Kandara and one mile in the case of Nuzla from the town, were among the first destinations of well-to-do families who wanted to expand beyond the old town from the third decade of the twentieth century onwards.[147] An interesting comment on the early gentrification is the description of the new palace of Sayyid 'Umar al-Saqqāf by 'Ayyūb Ṣabrī in 1886. According to him, it was replete with ornaments from India and China and more splendid than

142 MECA, Philby Collection GB165–0229, 1/4/5/1, Philby Diary, part 1, November 18, 1924, p. 97.

143 al-Faḍlī, *al-Nuzla al-Yamāniyya*, pp. 188–90; Difalla, *Jeddah's Slum Areas*, p. 37. On the 'Alī Riḍā house in Nuzla, see Marianne Alireza, *At the Drop of a Veil: The True Story of a California Girl's Years in an Arabian Harem* (Boston: Houghton Mifflin Company, 1971), p. 212.

144 al-Faḍlī, *al-Nuzla al-Yamāniyya*, pp. 33–4. For the slow transition in building techniques in al-Nuzla, see Difalla, *Jeddah's Slum Areas*, pp. 38–9.

145 Muḥammad al-Jifrī, *'Umar 'Abd Rabbuh: Ḥayyāt … wa-sīra* (Jeddah: Maṭābi' Saḥar, 1438/2017), p. 68.

146 TNA, FO 195/2061 Hussain to Amb. Const., September 18, 1899. According to Abū 'l-Jadā'il, Khālid Ṣalāḥ Sanūsī, *Rawā lī wālidī wa-ṣaḥibuh*, p. 51, al-Kandara began its life as a summer resort.

147 This was confirmed to me in many interviews in Jeddah between 2009 and 2015.

the palaces of Istanbul.[148] In 1907 the merchant Aḥmad Ẓāhir was involved in a dispute about a house in Kandara, which his father had owned in addition to a house in the old town.[149] It is not unlikely that this was another case of a merchant owning the equivalent of a country house. Given these observations, it is probably not an accident that Kandara also was the location of the first factory to cut marble, i.e. produce luxury tiles, which was established by Muḥammad Bin Lādin, the Ḥadhrami building magnate introduced in Chapter 3.[150] North of Jeddah lay another tribal settlement, Bānī Mālik.[151]

While the settlements were closely tied to the urban economy and population in different ways, as has been indicated, they were considered as extraneous to the city. Most urban historians from Jeddah mention only a few of these settlements and villages, if any, as Jeddah for them was *Jidda dākhil al-sūr* – Jeddah inside the wall, as is the title of one of these books.[152] This is made quite explicit in al-Shaqafī's dissertation in which he describes them as follows: 'As far as her suburbs are concerned, they were dominated by informality, and lack of order' (*ammā ḍawāḥīhā fa-qad ghalaba ʿalayhā 'l-ʿashwāʾiyya, wa-ʿadam al-tartīb*).[153] To this day, these former suburbs, by now all built over with more recent constructions, are considered *ʿashwāʾiyāt*, i.e. informal (and almost by implication only semi-legal) settlements in need of a planned reconstruction. From this perspective, the city gates were the true border between the city and the outside.[154] The extent to which the outside was considered dangerous is reflected in the legend of the *Hawl al-Layl*, the nightfright lurking outside the city walls and accosting the unsuspecting traveller who had to move outside the protective walls after nightfall.[155]

Not unsurprisingly, the perspective of al-Faḍlī as historian of al-Nuzla al-Yamāniyya differs considerably and constitutes an interesting comment on both the position of the suburb and the composition of

148 Ayyūb Ṣabrī, *Mirʾāt al-Ḥaramayn: A History of Mecca and Medina*, vol. 3 (s.l., 1886), pp. 194–5. For a photograph of the house, see Rifʿat, *Mirʾāt al-Ḥaramayn*, vol. 1, plate 17.

149 TNA, FO 195/2254, Monahan to Amb. Const., September 30, 1907.

150 al-Anṣārī, *Mawsūʿat tārīkh madīnat Jidda*, p. 472.

151 Ibid., p. 554.

152 al-Sharīf, *Dhikrayāt Muḥammad Darwīsh Raqqām*.

153 al-Thaqafī, *al-ʿImāra bi-madīnat Jidda*, vol. 1, p. 245.

154 al-Sharīf, *Dhikrayāt Muḥammad Darwīsh Raqqām*, p. 8.

155 ʿAbd al-ʿAzīz Abū Zayd, *al-Usṭūra fī madīnat Jidda* (Jeddah: Maktabat Kunūz al-Maʿrifa, 2016).

the urban population in a way which is very different from the booklet on Ruways cited above.[156] On the one hand, he lays claim to the historicity of the suburb both through the publication of the work and its content, referring to old land documents as well as to its history and properties. On the other hand, an image of a diverse but intimately connected population is presented which prominently included the Bedouin, who were considered a threat by people from inside the wall (and are still perceived as aliens by members of old families to this day).[157] The population also included *ashrāf* as well as '*buyūt wa-afrād*'. The *buyūt* ('Houses') refer to people from known (urban) families, such as Batarjī. The *afrād* ('individuals') were not linked to either tribe or known urban family, many bearing the *nisba* '*al-'uthmānī*', suggesting that they might have descended from Ottoman employees. In al-Faḍlī's words,

> in these two parts of the quarter, history registered the most delightful images of co-habitation and fusion between different groups and sections of inhabitants of al-Nuzla irrespective of the different strata, in so far as ties of understanding, coherence, affinity and intermarriage extended between them. They all fused in one melting pot consisting in the end of a novel social fabric with all types of appearance, so that one cannot find a family in al-Nuzla al-Yamāniyya which did not intermarry over generations with all people from the quarter, and it is questionable whether this type of intermarriage is reached in the city of Jeddah.[158]

The ideal of the tightly integrated city, already known from the introduction as a characteristic of Jiddawi identity, is thus extended to al-Nuzla. It is, however a society which somewhat differs from that of Jeddah, at least upon closer inspection. In contrast to Jeddah itself, where Bedouin influence is downplayed to this very day, the author of the history of al-Nuzla confidently emphasises the combination and, indeed, fusion of the urban and rural, or *ḥaḍar/tamaddun* and *badū* populations. In a sense, this is more reflective of the high status of a tribal origin in Saudi society than the way in which Jiddawis describe their identity, and it is perhaps also telling that

[156] al-Surayḥī, *al-Ruways*, p. 24 mentions the feeling of superiority by inhabitants of al-Nuzla vis-à-vis Ruways.
[157] al-Faḍlī, *al-Nuzla al-Yamāniyya*, pp. 14–26, quotation p. 24.
[158] Ibid., p. 13.

the history of al-Nuzla was written by somebody tracing his family's origins in the rural areas.[159]

When, in 1947, the wall between the old city and the suburbs was demolished to make room for cars and further urban development, some of the old families had started to establish houses in the more prestigious suburbs, mostly in the direction of al-Nuzla and Kandarah.[160] Urban development outside the Medina Gate consisted, at that time, of what the British Minister in Jeddah mockingly called a two-lane 'miniature Champs Elysées', namely a kind of boulevard 'marked out with oil drums and neatly bordered with drains' 'to carry traffic, one-way of course, to and from the desert'.[161] The distinction between the old city and what were to become first its plush suburbs, later its adjacent slums, did not disappear so easily. It lives on in the distinction between *al-Balad*, the old town, and the surrounding areas considered to be *ʿashwāʾiyyāt* in spite of the fact that *al-Balad* is almost void of Saudi inhabitants these days. It also lives on in the almost legendary status of the families hailing from the old town as the true Jiddawis, and it is echoed when members of the 'Houses' comment on certain places being unsuitable due to the presence of 'Bedouin'.

Religious Sites

The 1880–1 map shows a number of interesting religious sites outside the city wall. To the north of the Mecca Gate is a fairly large rectangular structure, seemingly an enclosure, known as al-Mashhad (no. 9). This is where people assembled for the morning prayer of ʿĪd al-Fiṭr at the beginning of Shawwāl.[162]

Until its demolition in 1926, the cemetery surrounding the so-called Tomb of Eve was the primary religious attraction beyond the walls of Jeddah and many of those who left travelogues paid it a visit.[163]

[159] Ibid, p. 16.
[160] According to al-Jifrī, *ʿUmar ʿAbd Rabbuh* p. 132, the demolition continued for two years.
[161] IOR, L/PS/12/2073, Jeddah Report January 1936, pp. 2–3.
[162] MECA, Philby Collection GB165–0229, Diary Part 1, p. 97 speaks of Al Mishhad. Ṭrābulsī, *Jidda*, p. 330, writing about a time when it took place in a mosque outside Bāb Makka; cf. Diyāb, *Jidda*, p. 92.
[163] al-Anṣārī, *Mawsūʿat tārīkh madīnat Jidda*, pp. 424, 484–5. concentrates on different views on its authenticity. For a detailed description of how it looked like before its demolition see Philby Diary Part 1, p. 74, p. 193; cf. Nallino, *Raccolta di Scritti*, pp. 177–8.

Another major site is the large Asad-Cemetery outside of the Mecca Gate (no. 7). According to al-Anṣārī, it was named after a certain ʿAbd al-Raḥmān al-Asad, a 'man of jabartī origin, i.e. of the Muslims of Ethiopia'.[164] According to al-Anṣārī, he lived in a hut. 'People asked for his blessings, and thought he possessed piety. He gave them charms, wrote amulets and gave them incense against the jinns. When he died in his hut they built a dome over it, and then a wall around it. This place became known as the Asad Cemetery'.[165]

The map of 1880–1 shows two further graves: Shaykh Abū 'l-ʿUyūn (no. 1), to the Southwest of the old city, and one of a certain Sayyid Maḥmūd (no. 5) to the West of Nakutu. In addition, Wissmann and Rathjens also mention a tomb of Shaykh Fadah near the cemetery of Eve.[166] Practices associated with the graves will be discussed in Chapter 5.

The Christian Cemetery

Both the map by Niebuhr (no. 7) and the map by the Ottomans (no. 2) mark the Christian, or, more precisely, the non-Muslim cemetery to the south of Jeddah, depicted in Figure 4.10. This attests to a longer history than the one acknowledged in consular circles in the nineteenth century when Mehmed Ali was credited with the establishment of the cemetery.[167] It is possible that it was in his time that the cemetery was walled to protect the graves against dogs, vandalism, and the nearby sea, which occasionally flooded it.[168] Historically, it would seem that it served foreign merchants and sailors who did not survive their stay in Jeddah. In 1878 British consul Zohrab managed to identify thirteen British graves (among them the 'Body of an English woman name not

164 al-Anṣārī, *Mawsūʿat tārīkh madīnat Jidda*, p. 563; cf. *Wikipedia*. 'Jeberti people'. https://en.wikipedia.org/wiki/Jeberti_people (accessed March 8, 2018).

165 al-Anṣārī, pp. 563–4. For a miracle associated with him, see Abū 'l-Jadāʾil, Khālid Ṣalāḥ Sanūsī, *Rawā lī wālidī wa-ṣaḥibuh*, pp. 111–2.

166 Rathjens and Wissmann, *Landschaftskundliche Beobachtungen*, p. 77. The name Abū 'l-ʿUyūn was confirmed to me by Talal Bakur and Muḥammad Raqqām, February 29, 2012.

167 TNA, FO 78/1538, Stanley to Foreign Office, January 28, 1860; cf. CADN, Djeddah, Consulat, 2 MI_3248, French Consul, Jeddah to Amb., Cairo, January 3, 1912. On the cemetery, see Nallino, *Raccolta di Scritti*, pp. 171–7.

168 TNA; FO 78/1538, Stanley to FO, January 28, 1860.

Figure 4.10 Photograph of the Christian cemetery in Jeddah, March 1926.
Van Voorthuysen. Leiden University Libraries, Or. 12.288 B: 38

known'), five Austrians, more than ten 'sundry' graves, four French Vice-Consuls, and two Jews.[169]

In the absence of houses named after non-Muslims, or non-Muslim places of worship, the cemetery is hence the only lasting physical monument of Jeddah's long connection with non-Muslim visitors and residents. As such, it could have acquired symbolic importance at different points in the period being discussed, and certainly did well into the twenty-first century.[170] For example, both the question of the official honours given to deceased French consul Rochet d'Héricourt (d. 1854) for his funeral cortège, as well as a commemorative plaque for a British Vice-Consul Moncrieff who died in 1884 while on post in Suakin, gave rise to complaints about Ottoman reluctance to

[169] TNA, FO 195/1251, Zohrab to Foreign Office, December 11, 1879.

[170] For modern discussions, see IOR, MSSEUR/F370/805, Joint Resolution, Jeddah, October 17, 1983; and Yaroslav Trofimov, 'Saudi Arabia Welcomes Foreigners to Work in Nation – but Not to Die', *The Wall Street Journal*, April 9, 2002.

acknowledge the death of prominent Christians.[171] This shows that, for Western consuls as well as for visitors, the cemetery became a *lieux de mémoire* for the history of Western presence. A particularly popular grave to visit and to take photos of was that of the French explorer Charles Huber who discovered a famous stele with Aramaic inscriptions in Taymāʾ and was murdered in July 1884 by Bedouin not far from Jeddah. His remains, or at least parts thereof, are interred in the cemetery.[172] It also testifies to the large presence of Eritreans, Filippinos and others in the second half of the twentieth century, with a remarkably large number of infant graves pointing to the downsides of the present-day labour regime.

171 TNA, FO 195/1482, Jago to Earl Dufferin, May 29, 1884; and CADN, Const Amb 1841–57, Dequié to Amb. Const., March 11, 1854; cf. TNA, FO 195/1767, AbdurRazzack to Amb. Const., August 20, 1892.

172 Mark Caudill, *Twilight in the Kingdom: Understanding the Saudis*, foreword by Steve Coll (Westport, CT and London: Praeger Security International, 2006), pp. 8–9.

5 *Solidarity and Competition: The Socio-Cultural Foundations of Life in Jeddah*

The Saudi writer ʿAbdallāh Manāʿ was born in Ḥārat al-Baḥr in 1939.[1] In his autobiography, he recounts an episode from his youth that touches on a number of aspects central to this chapter, which discusses those urban institutions that provided social cohesion, such as family, quarter, professional associations, or guilds.

Manāʿ's grandfather was a wealthy member of the important guild of *maʿādī*, the boatspeople who transhipped people and goods from their ships to the shore before a large pier was opened in 1951 and rendered their task superfluous.[2] At some stage, he had been the guild's shaykh and, according to his grandson, quite wealthy, as 'his household comprised two servants, a female slave (*jāriya*) and three *muzāwiriyya* – helpers – at least, and a number of sambuks [arab. sanbūq] and launches [small steamboats]. And my grandfather bought two houses in Ḥārat al-Baḥr'.[3] ʿAbdallāh's father continued the business and provided boat services to the government. Matters changed when the father died, leaving behind his wife and two young sons.[4] The elder brother of his father inherited the business, 'leaving us the "crumbs" ... and perhaps less than that'.[5] Consequently, Abdallāh's mother had to turn to sewing and his grandmother to teaching children the Koran in order to make ends meet.[6] Apparently, the family had fallen on such hard times that they received *zakāt* (alms) on the occasion of *ʿāshūrāʾ* to be able to afford fresh clothes and sweets for the children. Unfortunately, Manāʿ is silent on the identity of the benefactor. In Jeddah, *ʿāshūrāʾ*, celebrated by Shi'i Muslims to

[1] For a short biography, see *Wikipedia*. "ʿAbdallāh Manāʿ". https://ar.wikipedia.org/wiki/ عبدالله_مناع (accessed March 30, 2018); cf. al-Nimr, *Ḥārat al-Baḥr*, pp. 140–1. On the family Raqqām, *Jidda*, pp. 75–6.

[2] Pesce, *Jiddah*, p. 142.

[3] Manāʿ, *Baʿḍ al-Ayyām Baʿḍ al-Layālī*, p. 21.

[4] Ibid., pp. 22–3. Given the age of the father (67), this might have been a second or third wife.

[5] Ibid., p. 23.

[6] Ibid., pp. 23–4.

commemorate the death of Ḥusayn b. ʿAlī and often honoured by Sunni Muslims through fasting and almsgiving, was a day of celebration during ʿAbdallāh's youth.[7] Indeed, Abū 'l-Jadāʾil also mentions a special sweet for this day, named *ʿāshūriyya.*[8]

At some point, ʿAbdallāh's mother and grandmother found themselves in a situation where they had problems collecting the rent from tenants to whom they had rented part of their house.[9] This was, of course, a vital issue for a poor widow. She therefore sent her son to Shaykh Sulaymān Abū Dāʾūd, a friend of her deceased husband and his grandfather's successor as shaykh of the *maʿādī.* ʿAbdallāh went to the large house, which had two or three stories. His description grants a vivid image of a house in this quarter, which was probably typical for large dwellings in *al-Balad*:

> I was surprised that in front of his house was a large platform (barza) consisting of two large benches (dikka) ... and next to them a pigeon tower, next to which a shed for the chickens ... and on another side a wooden 'box' for the sheep and many lambs ... in front of all this slept a large dog ... and next to him a cow eating clover.[10]

Shaykh Abū Dāʿūd told the boy to talk to the co-owner a few days later. By that time, the affair had already been settled. When the mother heard of this, she is quoted saying 'did I not tell you, that "nobody can settle it but its men"'.[11] While this proverb praises the performer of a good deed, it has a gendered implication which is very pertinent in a segregated society where the woman could not approach the intermediary directly.

Manāʿ's childhood tale, though set at the very end of the period under discussion in this book, illuminates a range of issues which will be explored further in this chapter, namely the question of family and household, as well as that of neighbourhoods and quarters and of

[7] Ibid., p. 33. On *ʿāshūrāʾ*, see A. Wensinck and Ph. Marçais, "ʿĀshūrāʾ" in P. J. Bearman, T. Bianquis, C. E. Bosworth, E. J. van Donzel and W. P. Heinrichs (eds.), *Encyclopaedia of Islam*, 2nd edn., 12 vols. (Leiden: Brill, 1960–2005). dx.doi.org/10.1163/1573-3912_islam_COM_0068 (accessed March 29, 2018). For *ʿāshūrāʾ* in Mecca, see Snouck Hurgronje, *Mekka. Aus dem Heutigen Leben*, p. 51.

[8] Abū 'l-Jadāʾil, Khālid Ṣalāḥ Sanūsī, *Rawā lī wlidī wa-ṣaḥibuh*, p. 92.

[9] The story is also recounted in al-Nimr, *Ḥārat al-Baḥr*, p. 133, where some details become clearer.

[10] Manāʿ, *Tārīkh Mā lam Yuʾarrakh*, p. 38. [11] Ibid., p. 40.

professional associations or guilds. The chapter also discusses religious and cultural activities, which provided opportunities for interaction between different sectors of the population, and which were crucial to defining a sense of belonging to Jeddah and hence of being a Jiddawi.

These institutions and activities constituted the building blocks of the society of Jeddah, bound together by a host of mutual obligations, as well as shared traditions and religious life. It is these social bonds and convivial practices that will be explored in this chapter. This requires some detail because, while most elements of this social order can be found in many Middle Eastern societies of this period, there were important variations between different cities, as shows the comparative discussion by Mermier, who reviewed the literature from North Africa to the Peninsula, while himself describing the situation in Sana'a, Yemen.[12] These differences were rooted in the different ethnic and religious composition of populations which impacted on their cultural life, as well as on notions of hierarchy. As a comparison of Jeddah before and after 1925 shows, politics also influenced social life to an important extent.

The Household

As mentioned in Chapter 3, families (*ʿawāʾil)* constituted the backbone of local society in Jeddah, as elsewhere in the Middle East and beyond, fulfilling a range of social, cultural, economic, and at times even political functions.[13] As the rhetoric on families indicates, they consist of specific people related to each other in a variety of ways as much as they form a powerful 'social and cultural framework' which at once legitimises and purports to explain certain historical developments.[14] As social historians have shown, families were not only constructed in different ways as social and economic units but their

[12] Franck Mermier, *Le cheikh de la nuit: Sanaa; Organisation des souks et société citadine*, Bibliothèque Arabe Collection Hommes et Sociétés (Arles and Paris: Actes Sud; Sindbad, 1997), notably pp. 115–8.

[13] al-Yafi, *The Arab Family*, p. 162. Preceded by the definite article, *al-ʿawāʾil* denotes the leading elite families, this is how anthropologists Altorki and Yamani use the term.

[14] Iris Agmon, 'Women, Class, and Gender: Muslim Jaffa and Haifa at the Turn of the 20th Century', *International Journal of Middle East Studies*, 30 (1998), pp. 477–500, see pp. 493–5.

members could also pursue quite different interests, politically as well as economically.[15]

Soraya Altorki describes the typical (elite) families of Jeddah as follows:

The predominant pattern of residence for the older generation was viripatrilocal, i.e., a woman moved to her husband's father's house, where she had a room, an apartment on a floor, or a whole floor to herself, depending on the size of the house. This arrangement was advantageous insofar as sons usually joined their father's business. The father continued to provide the budget for the whole household . . . .[16]

As Altorki also explains, households could vary in size depending on social status and wealth, as well as a range of other factors, and they could split if they grew economically or in numbers.[17] Apart from immediate family members, households were comprised of servants and – probably more common until the early twentieth century – slaves who had been acquired both for domestic service and for work. In the absence of census material, there is little reliable information on polygamy, or indeed the sizes of individual households. Manāʿ's description of his grandfather's household would seem typical of a well-to-do family in a quarter inhabited predominantly by those whose work was related to port and the sea, while the leading merchant households might well have been somewhat larger.

Marriage strategies seem to have varied between households. While most interviewees stressed that their families preferred first cousin marriages, there are – besides the exogamous marriages already discussed in Chapter 3 – also cases of longstanding family alliances, such as between the ʿAlī Riḍā and the Zāhid. Polygamous and subsequent marriages, as well as the acquisition of female slaves often allowed for both the consolidation of family or business ties and the establishment of new links within and without professional, ethnic, or quarter communities.

15 Doumani, *Endowing Family*; Weber, *Damascus*, pp. 48–50.
16 Altorki, *Women in Saudi Arabia*, pp. 31–2.
17 Altorki's considerations for the period under discussion do not differ too much from what she writes about the later period, see her Soraya Altorki, 'Some Considerations on the Family in the Arabian Peninsula in the Late Ottoman and Early Post-Ottoman Period' in A. e.-A. Sonbol (ed.), *Gulf Women* (Syracuse, New York and London: Syracuse University Press; Eurospan [Distributor], 2012), pp. 277–309, here pp. 283–7.

Households were the most important settings for women, who not only managed the internal machinations of daily life but, through teaching and participation in social and religious life, contributed greatly to the standing of a household in the social fabric of the quarter and city.[18] This can be deduced from the criteria which Altorki singles out as attributes of elite status, but which were also important to non-elite families. An elite family was known for its reputation which was based on descent, piety, wealth, and individual achievement.[19] Pétriat has shown in much detail, with regard to the Bā Nāja, how a merchant family established itself and its 'house' in economic and political terms, as well as the incorporation (or rather proximity, as he calls it) of the freed slave. He further discusses how, through marriage, relations within the family as well as with business partners and other allies in the city were strengthened.[20] In Jeddah, merchants and pilgrims' guides formed the economic elite of the city (cf. Chapter 6).

One important way of becoming a recognised Jiddawi family, and a member of the elite, was investment in real estate. Indeed, it would seem that wealth, in addition to a good reputation, social, and political engagement would lead to the qualification of somebody as a member of the *ʿawāʾil*, a group classified in earlier scholarship often as 'notables'. This term is also used here to denote politically influential members of elite families, albeit without the politically exclusivist and somewhat mechanical functionalist understanding which has been attributed to the concept.[21]

Elite membership could take different forms, and there might have been different strategies pursued by different families, although the sources do not suffice to make definite statements on this issue. It seems that a few families invested very heavily in property. In the case of the Bā Nāja, Pétriat has documented how, over a period of 34 years, the

[18] This comes also out nicely in the biographies compiled by Muḥammad Ṭrābulsī, *Rāʾidāt min ahālī Jidda* (Al Madinah Printing & Publishing Co., 1439/2018). Since these biographies deal mostly with the period from the 1940s, they have not been systematically used for this study.

[19] Altorki, *Women in Saudi Arabia*, pp. 14–18.

[20] Pétriat, *Le Négoce des Lieux Saints*, pp. 251–324.

[21] Hourani, *Ottoman Reform and the Politics of Notables*, for critiques see Khoury, *The Urban Notables Paradigm* and, more radically, James Gelvin, 'The "Politics of Notables" Forty Years After', *Middle East Studies Association Bulletin*, 40 (2006), pp. 19–29; for a useful working description Weber, *Damascus*, pp. 50–1.

initial unbuilt property was developed and expanded into a fairly large complex of adjacent houses and stores next to the Ḥanafī Mosque in the northern quarter.[22] The family also possessed a number of further properties, as well as the *ribāṭ* Bā Nāja, all situated in the Shām quarter.[23] Even large landowners in Jeddah did not necessarily reside in Jeddah for all their life: Faraj Yusr, the aforementioned Indian-Ottoman merchant seems to have relocated part of his business to Calcutta, where he died in 1873, and possibly went as far as to shift his main residence there some time after the massacre of 1858, in which he was among those targeted.[24] He had owned, and endowed, numerous houses in Jeddah. Most, if not all, of these were sold after his death, possibly in payment of his debts there, so that one of his larger houses is known today as that of Jamjūm.[25] Consequently, the list of present-day owners of houses in the old city gives a number of further interesting clues. However, it names only a fraction of the owners of buildings existing when it was compiled, and, furthermore, does not indicate who endowed the approximately twenty to 30 per cent *awqāf* which are nowadays under the administration of the Ministry of Endowments. In addition, some allowance must be made for changing ownership after 1947.

In spite of these lacunae, the list indicates that, besides the Bā Nāja, the families of Naṣīf, Bā ʿIshn, al-Hazzāzī and Shaḥḥāta own four properties or more (or have endowments in their name) to this day, while the families of Ṭaha and ʿAshmāwī own three properties each. Interestingly, the term *bayt*, house, is also often used locally to denote the household, and thus the people associated with a notable physical structure in the old city. Most of the houses which are still preserved and owned by these families form clusters in the northern quarter, while only Naṣīf and ʿAshmāwī own houses in the southern part of Ḥārat al-Shām or even in the Maẓlūm quarter. In many cases, families own a number of adjacent properties, indicating a process of gradual

[22] Pétriat, *Le Négoce des Lieux Saints*, pp. 165–9.

[23] This and the following is based on the analysis of a map with numbered houses prepared in the context of the present-day conservation project in Jeddah and available in the municipality. I thank ʿUmda Malak Bā ʿĪsā for a copy.

[24] Pétriat, *Le Négoce des Lieux Saints*, pp. 42–9; and TNA, FO 195/375, Page to Emb. Const., January 1857.

[25] CADN 2_MI3246, Castro to Bougarel, Jeddah, October 9, 1873, and December 8, 1873; and tour of the old city with ʿAbīr Abū Sulaymān, March 10, 2017.

growth and consolidation within the same neighbourhood. The names of alleyways and squares point to many more such clusters, or at least to large houses formerly owned (or inhabited) by prominent families. The presence of most of the preserved large holdings in Ḥārat al-Shām would seem to confirm that this quarter housed the most affluent residents, who were often active in commerce and trade, while the other quarters catered more to craftsmen and people working in the port.[26] To what extent the remaining information on property distribution indicates that no such clusters existed in the other quarters, or that people there more commonly rented than owned accommodation cannot be even reasonably guessed on the basis of the existing sources. However, al-Nimr asserts for *Ḥārat al-Baḥr* that some families owned much property, both within this quarter as well as elsewhere, to the extent that some lived exclusively off the income derived from them.[27] Thus, the notion of all families owning the houses they occupied, as claimed by Bokhari, seems somewhat naive.[28]

The naming of passages and squares after the Bā ʿIshn and Naṣīf suggests that other squares named after local families were also next to clusters of property owned by them. Examples are ʿĀshūr and Sunbul squares or the Khunjī passageway, named after a family of Iranian origin with a branch in the Gulf that endowed two *arbiṭa*.[29] Both the Bā Nāja and the Naṣīf family properties comprise a significant proportion of buildings, which are marked as (family) *awqāf*, meaning that they would support descendants of the endower until their extinction when the *waqf* would revert to a charitable purpose. Such family endowments can constitute a field of study in themselves, as has been recently discussed for greater Syria by Doumani, pointing to the different ways in which they could be used to shape family fortunes and relations.[30] While this requires material different from that investigated in this study, namely much more insight into both endowments and court litigation related to them is required, Doumani's study shows how endowments provoked manifold contestations and conflicts within wider families.

[26] al-Thaqafī, *al-ʿImāra bi-madīnat Jidda*, vol. 1, p. 233.
[27] al-Nimr, *Ḥārat al-Baḥr*, p. 26. [28] Bokhari, Jeddah, p. 147.
[29] al-Thaqafī, *al-ʿImāra bi-madīnat Jidda*, vol. 1, pp. 244–5.
[30] Beshara Doumani, *Family Life in the Ottoman Mediterranean: A Social History* (Cambridge, New York, Melbourne, Delhi, and Singapore: Cambridge University Press, 2017).

This connects well to Manāʿ's story, which illustrates the oftentimes difficult situation of women who were widowed. Here, it was the brother of the husband who left the widow and her children in a state of precarity, and the episode with the co-owner of the house also shows the troubles women could face when trying to keep and protect their property. Indeed, family here emerges not only as an entity of support but also of competition. Doumani's study shows that this tendency to preserve a patriline's inheritance was no prerogative of Jiddawi society but could be also observed in Nablus.[31] Based on Snouck Hurgronje's discussions of Mecca, Altorki shows that women often feared not only wider relations but also their husbands' attempts to control or even appropriate their assets.[32] In this context, it is interesting to see that private houses were endowed not only to safeguard them against confiscation by the state but often also to secure the inheritance of female heirs.[33] Both practices were also known elsewhere in Ottoman lands.[34]

Arguably, the endowment of commercial properties, such as the large *awqāf Āl Ghālib* (by the Sharifian family) in the Sūq al-Nadā inscribes the family name in a prominent way into the urban landscape, while, of course, also serving to protect the property and secure long-term income for the family.[35] Although this was, as Pétriat rightly shows, by no means a prerogative of the Hadhramis or other migrants, it could acquire particular significance for newly settled migrants. In particular, investment in different forms of charity and religious institutions increased the prestige, and hence the social capital, of the benefactors. For example, the arguably most important collection of Jeddah biographies for the time under consideration names Zaynal ʿAlī Riḍā 'father of the poor' for the extent of his charitable engagement.[36] The families of Bā Nāja, Bā ʿIshn, Naṣīf, and Shaḥḥāta endowed one or

31 Ibid., pp. 65–83.

32 Altorki, *Some Considerations on the Family*, pp. 298–9; and Snouck Hurgronje, *Mekka. Aus dem Heutigen Leben*, vol. 2, p. 113.

33 Interviews with Atef Bakhsh and cousins, February 18, 2009 and Māzin ʿAbdallāh al-Saqqāf, Jeddah, February 28, 2013.

34 Doumani, *Endowing Family*.

35 On the endowment of commercial properties, see Ulrike Freitag, 'Arab Merchants in Singapore: Attempt of a Collective Biography' in H. de Jonge and N. Kaptein (eds.), *Transcending Borders: Arabs, Politics, Trade and Islam in Southeast Asia* (Leiden: Brill Academic Publishers, 2002), pp. 109–42.

36 Maghribī, *Aʿlām al-Ḥijāz*, vol. 1, p. 38.

more *arbiṭa*, as did the prominent Indian-Ottoman merchant Faraj Yusr and the families of Khunjī, Bā Dīb, Bā Junayd, and al-Nimr.[37] Faraj Yusr also became known for his investment in the provision of water, as was shown in Chapter 4. The Hadhrami banker Sālim bin Maḥfūẓ endowed a mosque, admiringly depicted and described in the Kuwaiti journal *al-ʿArabī* as a 'masterpiece of beauty and art' and the largest mosque of Jeddah in the 1960s.[38]

A special case is the endowment of the Falāḥ school by Muḥammad ʿAlī Zaynal ʿAlī Riḍā. He, together with his friends, provided the initial endowment of the Falāḥ school and over time many other families contributed smaller and larger properties to support this school. It thereby became a real embodiment of public civic spirit, not merely a project to increase the prestige of one family, but a community project – an Arab language school teaching religious as well as secular sciences – that is still alive.[39]

These examples support Isin's argument that endowments can be considered acts of citizenship, and hence demonstrate a civic spirit in the Ottoman Empire.[40] From an urban perspective, they clearly marked the public presence of the respective families. Miran has argued that in Massawa the rise from 'small time teenage peddlers to wealthy merchants, owners of immovable and moveable property and leading citizens in the urban political and public arena' constitutes an important act of integration into local society. A perspective which focusses on the diasporic nature of Arabs, Indians, and others might obscure such practices of place-making due to the focus on the translocal connections rather than the insertion into local societies.[41] The same can safely be said about Jeddah.

[37] al-Thaqafī, *al-ʿImāra bi-madīnat Jidda*, vol. 1, p. 11.

[38] Salīm Basīyū, 'Jidda: Bāb al-ḥajj ilā bayt Allāh al-ḥarām', *al-ʿArabī* (1964), pp. 83–114, pp. 100–1 (quote p. 100).

[39] On the school, see Freitag, *The Falah School*. The endowed properties are distributed throughout old Jeddah, some were shown to me by Māhir al-Khulaydī, February 26, 2015.

[40] Engin Isin, 'Ottoman Waqfs as Acts of Citizenship' in P. Ghazaleh (ed.), *Held in Trust: Waqf in the Islamic World* (Cairo and New York: American University of Cairo Press, 2011), pp. 209–26.

[41] Jonathan Miran, 'Endowing Property and Edifying Power in a Red Sea Port: Waqf, Arab Migrant Entrepreneurs, and Urban Authority in Massawa, 1860s–1880s', *The International Journal of African Historical Studies*, 42 (2009), pp. 151–78, p. 158.

Around the elite families were grouped other families who were linked to the elite through social relations, expressed through visits as well as *zakāt* (a religiously prescribed tax).[42] In turn, the elite families could rely on the social and political support of these satellite families, something which Altorki does not really incorporate into her account. What she does do, however, is to show in detail the crucial role played by women in the construction and maintenance of such networks. Life cycle events from birth to death were accompanied by intricate rituals and an etiquette of visits and gift exchanges, which had absorbed influences of the different elements of the population of Jeddah, and probably also varied depending on social class. Among these were circumcision, the memorisation of the Koran, and marriage, but also more individual celebrations such as the celebration of the first pilgrimage or the first annual trip to Medina (see below).[43] Regardless of the details, these social traditions expressed and cemented social relationships within and between households. In many of these ceremonies, which usually comprised parallel male and female events, the female part of the ceremony was more elaborate and, though less well documented, at least as important as that of men, if not more so.[44]

A detailed analysis of urban factions, which resulted from such physical and social clusters of families, cannot be systematically reconstructed. However, there were certain instances of urban mobilisation, for example in 1858, which give some indication of how retainers could, through a variety of networks, be mobilised to commit violent street action. While neighbourhoods and professional networks

[42] Altorki, *Women in Saudi Arabia*, p. 5. Altorki presents it as a one-sided dependency, but scholarship on other cities shows clearly the mutuality of such relations, e.g. Khoury, *Urban Notables and Arab Nationalism*; and Linda Schatkowski-Schilcher, *Families in Politics: Damascene Factions and Estates of the 18th and 19th Centuries* (Stuttgart: Franz Steiner, 1985).

[43] On these traditions, see al-Anṣārī, *Mawsūʿat tārīkh madīnat Jidda*, pp. 243–51; Ṭrābulsī, *Jidda*, pp. 353–83; and Muḥammad b. Nāṣir al-Asmarrī, 'Tārīkh al-ḥayyāt al-ijtimāʿiyya fī Jidda: 1300–43 h./1882–1925 m.', MA Thesis, King ʿAbd al-ʿAzīz University (2008/1429), pp. 88–97. Snouck Hurgronje gives a good description of circumcision in his diary, probably based on his own observation, see UBL, Cod. Or. 7112 Snouck Hurgronje Jeddah Diary, p. 44.

[44] For a description of many of these ceremonies, see Ṭrābulsī, *Jidda*, pp. 353–82; al-Anṣārī, *Mawsūʿat tārīkh madīnat Jidda*, pp. 245–53; and Abū 'l-Jadāʾil, Khālid Ṣalāḥ Sanūsī, *Rawā lī wālidī wa-ṣaḥibuh*, pp. 79–92.

probably played a role in this, the satellite family of prominent families were most likely also mobilised.[45]

Quarters and Neighbourhoods

By the end of the nineteenth century, Jeddah consisted of four quarters which, in turn, comprised a number of locally known, distinct neighbourhoods, as has been shown in Chapter 4. These quarters were formal units of urban governance over each of which an *ʿumda* (head of quarter) resided. He answered to the *muḥtasib*, who was responsible for public order. Such urban quarters, called *mahalle* in Turkish and *ḥayy* in Arabic, have a long history in the Middle East. Basically, they were, and still are to this day, the lowest formal level of urban governance, and a crucial link between higher state institutions and the population of quarters. The quarter's functions in imperial Ottoman governance became redefined in the context of urban reforms in 1826 and 1864 and included the registration of births and deaths, the supervision of local guards and the prevention of illegal land transfers. Tax collection, usually mentioned as a task of quarters in the Ottoman Empire, seems not to have figured, possibly due to the quite haphazard nature of taxation in the Hijaz which was characterised by many exceptions.[46] The transformation of the quarter's functions during the reform period also marked the transition from

[45] I explore this issue in some detail in Freitag, *When Festivals Turned Violent*; cf. Pétriat, *Le Négoce des Lieux Saints*. pp. 84–118.

[46] Ed., 'Maḥalle' in P. J. Bearman, T. Bianquis, C. E. Bosworth, E. J. van Donzel and W. P. Heinrichs (eds.), *Encyclopaedia of Islam*, 2nd edn., 12 vols. (Leiden: Brill, 1960–2005). doi.org/10.1163/1573-3912_islam_SIM_4775 (accessed March 28, 2018); Mahmoud Yazbak, *Haifa in the Late Ottoman Period, 1864–1914: A Muslim Town in Transition* (Leiden, Boston, and Köln: Brill, 1990), pp. 83–6; Behar, *A Neighborhood in Ottoman Istanbul*; and specifically for the functions of a *muhtar* (arab.: mukhtār) in the late 19th c., pp. 160–71; Élise Massicard, 'The Incomplete Civil Servant?: The Figure of the Neighbourhood Headman (Muhtar)' in M. Aymes, B. Gourisse, and Élise Massicard (eds.), *Order and Compromise: Government Practices in Turkey from the Late Ottoman Empire to the Early 21st Century*, Social, Economic, and Political Studies of the Middle East and Asia (Leiden: Brill, 2015), pp. 256–90. For Jeddah, see Ṭrābulsī, *Jidda*, pp. 180–90; and al-Nimr, *Ḥārat al-Baḥr*, pp. 237–41. On taxation in the Hijaz see FO 195/1547, Report by Consul Jago on Revenue and Taxation in the Vilayet of the Hedjaz, February 4, 1886 and Low, *The Mechanics of Mecca*, pp. 23, 61.

leadership by the local imam to that of a *muhtar* (the Turkish denomination) or *ʿumda* as a secular authority.[47] The following account of quarters in Jeddah shows that, in spite of regional variations, they followed a more general pattern observable in much of the Ottoman Empire.[48]

According to the oral accounts of today as well as the (modern) local histories which reflect the reality in the first half of the twentieth century, the population of a quarter proposed a candidate (or more than one) for *ʿumda* to the sancak authorities, who needed to sanction the choice. This is very close to the regulations stipulated by the Ottoman Provincial Law of 1864.[49] Thereafter, the *ʿumda* was paraded through the quarter, accompanied by songs and given presents by the rich of the quarter. During the period under consideration, it seems to have been an honorary office, so that these presents were the major remuneration of the *ʿumda*.[50] The office was an elective function – governmental agreement provided – although, de facto, it seems to have often run in particular families.[51] It was filled by trustworthy members of the local community, who were, however, normally not members of the most prominent merchant elite. This resembles practices in other Ottoman cities such as Haifa.

A Saudi decree in October 1927 defined the tasks of the *ʿumda*, who had to be literate, older than twenty-five years and knowledgeable about the quarter. During the Saudi era, major functions were, again, the security of the quarter, its basic services (including the comfort of pilgrims) and mediation in neighbourhood conflicts. Violations of the religious norms were to be persecuted by the religious police (see

[47] Behar, *A Neighborhood in Ottoman Istanbul*, pp. 65–7.

[48] As the study by Behar is particularly detailed and well-documented, it serves as a privileged site of comparison.

[49] Massicard, *The Incomplete Civil Servant*, pp. 259–60; c.f. C. Findley, 'Mukhtār' in P. J. Bearman, T. Bianquis, C. E. Bosworth, E. J. van Donzel and W. P. Heinrichs (eds.), *Encyclopaedia of Islam*, 2nd edn., 12 vols. (Leiden: Brill, 1960–2005). dx.doi.org/10.1163/1573-3912_islam_SIM_5472 (accessed January 12, 2019).

[50] Oral communication, ʿUmda ʿAbd al-Ṣamad, March 21, 2011; cf. Abū 'l-Jadāʾil, Khālid Ṣalāḥ Sanūsī, *Rawā lī wālidī wa-ṣaḥibuh*, p. 43, for the Ottoman period Massicard, *The Incomplete Civil Servant*, p. 260.

[51] For names of *ʿumad*, see Abū 'l-Jadāʾil, Khālid ṣalāḥ Sanūsī, *Rawā lī wālidī wa-ṣaḥibuh*, pp. 35–6, 37–8; al-Nimr, *Ḥārat al-Baḥr*, pp. 237–42; and Ṭrābulsī, *Jidda*, pp. 184–90.

Chapter 7). The *ʿumda* was also to pass on government decisions to the local population and inform the relevant authorities about incidents such as fires or serious crimes, as well as help authorities in apprehending culprits. He was to be assisted by a neighbourhood council consisting of four volunteers.[52]

Be that as it may, it is clear that the quarters, clearly shown in Map 5.1, fulfilled important administrative functions on the lowest level, notably in terms of guarding the quarter at night by employing the night guards (*ʿusas*) headed by the *ʿumda*'s deputy, policing minor criminal offences (the quarter had the right to arrest suspects), mediation in conflicts, and the maintenance of public spaces and hygiene (i.e. waste disposal).[53] Besides the *ʿumda*, local religious leaders and elders of the neighbourhoods, often those presiding the informal gatherings in the *maqāʿid* (indoors) and *marākīz* of the neighbourhood squares, formed the elite of the quarter and thus can also be seen as an important set of mediators between the urban government, discussed in Chapter 7, and the local population.[54] The most notable elders and the *ʿumda* formed an informal council which would, for example, compensate debtors in the case of a deceased neighbourhood member who left debts after their deaths.[55] In other cases, such as the support by Sulaymān Abū Dāʾūd for Manāʿ's mother, individual elders acted. This is counted by al-Nimr as one of many incidents during which this influential notable exercised his position as (unofficial) *shaykh al-ḥāra*, i.e. most respected elder of the quarter.[56] In contrast to the situation in Istanbul described by Behar, I have no information regarding endowments by locals for the specific benefit of their neighbourhood, which does not mean that this did not occur or was implied in wills and *awqāf* providing, for example, for the support of the poor or a local *ribāṭ*.[57]

52 *Umm al-Qurā*, 159, November 23, 1927, p. 3.

53 I have explored the formal and informal quarter organisation in comparison to the wider Middle East in Freitag, *When Festivals Turned Violent*. For Jeddah, much information was gleaned from the works of Ṭrābulsī, *Jidda*; Manāʿ, *Tārīkh mā lam yuʾarrakh*; and insights gained from interviews with ʿUmda Ṣamad ʿAbd al-Ṣamad,Jeddah, March 21, and November 17, 2011; and a conversation with ʿUmda Malak Maḥmūd Bā ʿĪsa, March 4, 2013.

54 al-Nimr, *Ḥārat al-Baḥr*, pp. 325–33; and Ṭrābulsī, *Jidda*, pp. 202–6.

55 Oral information, Dr. ʿAdnān al-Yāfī, Jeddah, March 22, 2006.

56 al-Nimr, *Ḥārat al-Baḥr*, p. 133.

57 Behar, *A Neighborhood in Ottoman Istanbul*, pp. 31–2.

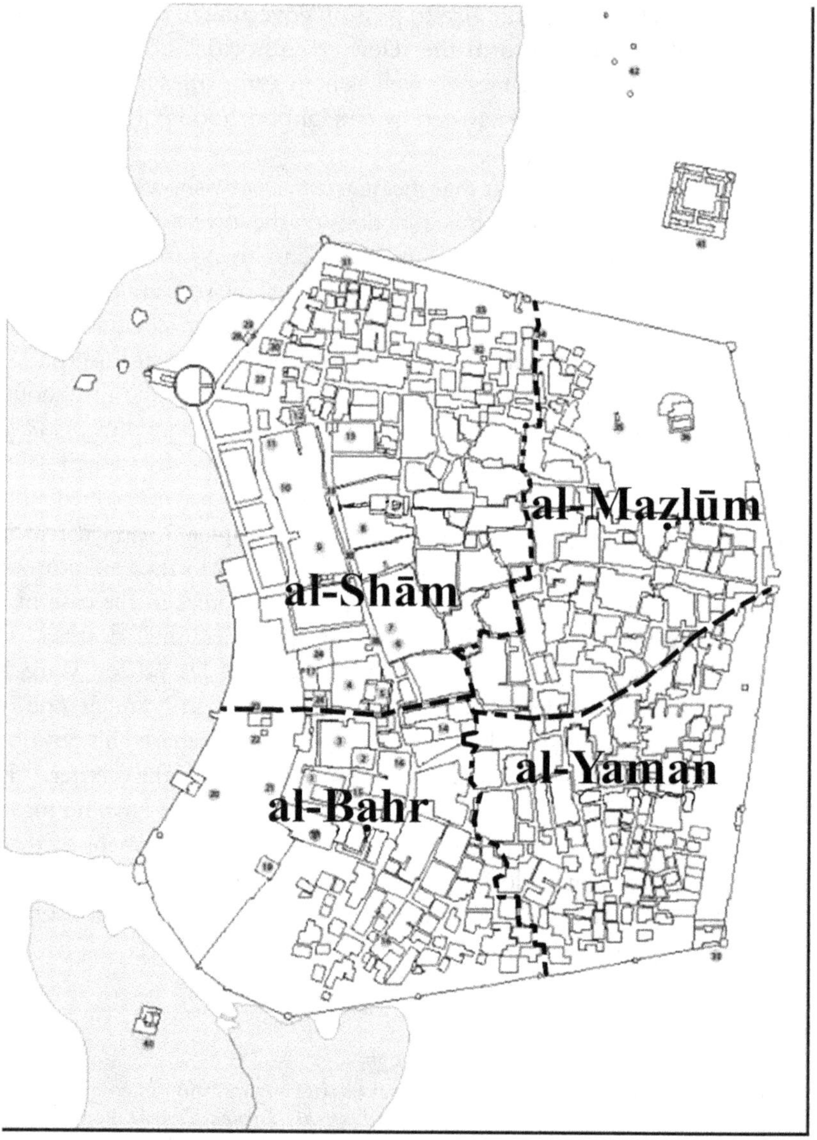

Map 5.1 Jeddah within the walls.
Drawn by Dr. Muḥammad Bā Qādir

Another important urban institution was the coffeehouse.[58] This could, once again, serve different functions, depending on its location. Coffeehouses situated along the main *sūq*s or in the port area offered their services to both local customers and visitors to the city. As we have seen in the case of Bāb Makka, in coffeehouses near transport hubs, information was circulated and transport of people and goods arranged.[59] The municipal coffeehouse was thus situated in the economic and political hub of the port (cf. Chapter 4).

Certain important inhabitants of quarters could choose a coffee shop, rather than a *mirkāz*, as their regular location. Thus, it seems that, between 1931 and 1971, Shaykh Ḥasan Bakur, shaykh of the seamen (*baḥḥāra* or *ma ʿādī*)[60] had

> a special corner in the coffeehouse of Muḥammad Ibrāhīm ... for meetings in the morning (ḍaḥī) with the seamen[61] and the heads of groups of workers, whereas the afternoon (ʿaṣr) was reserved for the reception of the needy, and the meeting of his friends . . .'[62]

Thus, this coffee shop partly served a professional function, although the shaykh kept the records and the money for the workers and others on the ground floor of his house in the *maqʿad*. Other coffeehouses were famous for attracting customers of a particular type, such as literary people, workers of particular professions, or particular age groups. Often, storytellers would frequent the coffeehouses to entertain the guests. Many travellers commented on the widespread

58 On Ottoman coffeehouses in the nineteenth century, see Cengiz Kirli, 'Coffeehouses: Public Opinion in the Nineteenth-Century Ottoman Empire' in A. Salvatore and D. F. Eickelman (eds.), *Public Islam and the Common Good*, Social, Economic, and Political Studies of the Middle East and Asia, 1385–3376 vol. 95, (Leiden and Boston: Brill, 2004), pp. 75–97 with a special focus on the exchange of information and surveillance, for earlier periods see the contributions in Dana Sajdi (ed.), *Ottoman Tulips, Ottoman Coffee: Leisure and Lifestyle in the Eighteenth Century* (London and New York: Tauris, 2007) and Betül Başaran, *Selim III, Social Control and Policing in Istanbul at the End of the Eighteenth Century: Between Crisis and Order* (Boston: Brill, 2014), pp. 148–58.

59 On the coffeehouses, Ṭrābulsī, *Jidda*, pp. 196–201; and al-Nimr, *Ḥārat al-Baḥr* pp. 315–24.

60 The two terms are used to describe the same profession, e.g. Kābilī, *al-Ḥirafiyyūn fī madīnat Jidda*, p. 179; and Raqqām, *Jidda*, pp. 166–9.

61 The term used is *rijāl al-baḥr*, which seems to include a variety of the sea-related professions.

62 Bakur, *ʿĀʾila jiddāwiyya*, p. 82.

Figure 5.1 Coffeeshop besides the Dutch consulate, 1926.
Photographer Van Voorthuysen, Leiden University Libraries, Or. 12 288 B: 26

presence of this urban institution in Jeddah, and the Ottoman year-book of 1305/1888 diligently lists forty coffeehouses.[63] Some of these, such as the one depicted in Figure 5.1, probably were more frequented by the men of the neighbourhood.

My sources say little about how the nature of the coffeehouses might have changed. In one case, a squabble erupting between a Turkish coffee shop owner of Greek owner (and presumably Christian) and a Persian subject in 1882. The latter started to threaten the former with an attack on Christians if the latter did not sell him liquor. This somewhat paradoxical intervention – to attack a Christian for refusing to act against the Islamically decreed prohibition on alcohol – resulted in a trial and a prison sentence for the Persian.[64] In 1935, there is a report about the *Hai'at al-amr bi-l-ma'rūf wa-l-nahy 'an al-munkar* (the

[63] *Hicaz vilâyeti salnâmesi*, defa 3 (Mecca: Vilayet Matbaası, 1305/1887–8), p. 213.
[64] FO 195/1415, Moncrieff to FO, July 7, 1882.

organisation to command right and forbid wrong) ushering coffeeshop visitors into mosques at prayer time.[65] While this also fits with the anti-smoking campaigns of the *Hai'a* discussed in Chapter 7, there is no hint at the overall closure of these public and semi-public coffeehouses.

As an intermediate space between the house and the larger city, it was usually within the confines of the quarters that women visited each other, and that children and young girls were socialised. Ritualised visits at the end of the month of Ramaḍān involved not only family members, who visited each other on the first day of the ʿĪd, but also the quarters. Thus, the second day of ʿĪd was reserved for visits of people in the quarters Yaman and Baḥr, while, on the third day, people visited friends and relatives in the Shām and Maẓlūm quarters.[66]

When young boys reached adolescence, they joined in the *alʿāb shaʿbiyya*, the popular 'games' that involved competitions between young men. The most important of these was the *mizmār*, a competition between two teams around a fire during which the brandishing of sticks was accompanied by drums and singing. The most successful performers on the level of the neighbourhood then competed on the level of the quarter and gained much prestige as local youth leaders. Local historian ʿAbdallāh Abkar, discussing the importance of this dance in the quarters of Mecca, notes that it was considered a practice through which masculinity was constituted (*maṣnaʿ al-rijāl*). This happened on a number of levels. Winning boosted not only the reputation of individuals, but also that of neighbourhoods within a given quarter, and quarters, when the competition took place on the level of the city.[67] These took place during weddings, celebrations marking the end of Ramaḍān, and official visits when the whole city would turn out to greet a new governor or the emir of Mecca. Although such practices were partly superseded by new sports such as football competitions, which began in the late 1920s, and the ceremonial use of dances and music was toned down after the Saudi takeover of Jeddah, they dominated for most of the period under consideration.

The *mizmār* was not the only way in which quarters competed. Thus Snouck Hurgronje, who stayed in Jeddah in 1884–5, describes how the Ottoman governor arrived in Jeddah in early January 1885 and was

[65] IOR/L/PS/12/2073, Jedda Report, December 1934, p. 3.
[66] al-Asmarrī, *Tārīkh al-ḥayyāt al-ijtimāʿiyya*, pp. 97–8.
[67] Abkar, *Ṣuwar min turāth Makka*, p. 206.

received by visitors, while the town was illuminated. Part of the greetings consisted of the quarters marching past behind banners, and Snouck Hurgronje points to a brawl that erupted because one person had joined the procession of another quarter. He also mentions a competition between the different quarters about who had the most beautiful *maḥmal* (ceremonial litter accompanied by the distribution of sweets). Apparently, the quarters also paraded behind banners.[68] It is very likely that similar events occurred during other official celebrations such as a sultan's birthday or inauguration, when the municipality and the army put up decorations and lighting and festivities included fireworks, and not only the foreign consuls but also the ordinary people came to celebrate and 'show their happiness and joy'.[69]

Abkar also refers to the link between the groups of players, who formed youth gangs (also known as *futuwwa*, *al-yābā* and *shuj'ān)*, and the security of the quarter.[70] al-Nimr describes how the youth of Ḥārat al-Baḥr served as guards, approaching any stranger to find out what he needed. If they could help him with directions, they would, but if he acted suspiciously, they proved a 'good deterrent, and some of the sons of the Baḥr quarter were marked by their severity and bodily strength', hinting that at times there were violent confrontations with the intruders.[71]

Obviously, the two functions could intersect, and brawls between quarter youth tended to break out, particularly during ceremonial processions when people crossed from one quarter into the next.[72] An especially prominent case is that of a wedding ceremony where the wedding procession had to cross from one quarter into another.

68 UBL, Cod. Or. 7112 Snouck Hurgronje Jeddah Diary, pp. 44–5. Unfortunately, it remains unclear to which official he refers as the title pasha could be used in different ways, although on a later occasion, he uses the term for the Hijaz governor, p. 54b.

69 Ismā'īl, *Jidda khilāla 'l-fatra 1286–1327*, p. 144. For festivities related to the Empire in Izmir, which was visited twice by the Sultans, c.f. Zandi-Sayek, *Ottoman Izmir*, pp. 180–5.

70 On the protection of neighbourhoods; cf. Bokhari, Jeddah, p. 150. For these groups; cf. 'Abd al-'Azīz Abū Zayd, *Ḥikāyāt al-'aṭṭārīn fī Jidda al-qadīma: Dirāsat tārīkhiyya wa-ṣuwar ijtimā'iyya li-l-mu'taqidāt wa-l-waṣfāt al-sha'biyya*, 2nd edn. (al-'Āmāl al-Thaqāfiyya, 1433/2012), pp. 111–3. The term *al-yābā* seems more closely related to builders and carpenters, see Diyāb, *al-Mufradāt al-'āmmiyya fī madīnat Jidda*, p. 153.

71 al-Nimr, *Ḥārat al-Baḥr*, p. 29. He also continues to describe the youth as excelling at the *mizmār*.

72 Sa'īd bin Zaqr, *[unpublished memoires]* (1984), p. 9. I thank Philippe Pétriat for this information.

Apparently, the groom, who was a relative of Muḥammad Ṭawīl, one of the notables of Jeddah (or, in the words of one of the local chroniclers, '*kabīr Jidda*' – the most important one), had overlooked discussing proceedings with the local *'umda*. The procession comprised the groom

> surrounded by famous singers of the time and preceded by large gas lights ... carried by men. The groom was preceded by carriers of *'ūd* [a particular type of incense]. When the procession in which many notables of the city, as well as men and youth reached the borders of the Yaman quarter in front of the al-Mi'mār mosque next to the house of the Jamjūm family at that time, some members of the Yaman quarter opposed the procession and asked them to return to where they came from. They said – this is our quarter and we won't permit you to enter. The people from the Shām quarter insisted to enter as they could not return with such a large procession. The men from both sides lost their temper and insulted each other, then they used their sticks and beat each other. The procession dissolved and the people dispersed fearing for their safety as a result of the crazy battle which had erupted without warning.[73]

Eventually, elders from both sides managed to calm the excitement and allowed the groom to reach his bride, but only with the help of the police who arrested some of the young men.[74] There existed a protocol for the settlement of inter-quarter disputes of this and other types, regulating who participated in mediation meetings, as well as time and place of such gatherings.[75]

While this episode is perhaps an extreme case of quarter tension, it is quite typical of traditional quarter organisations both in the Middle East and in Europe, as I have argued elsewhere.[76] While neighbourhood rivalry could take distinctly confessional aspects in Ottoman cities such as Izmir in which neighbourhoods were at least partly associated with religious affiliations, the case of Jeddah shows that such distinctions were not needed for the constitution of neighbourhood identities, and their at times even violent expression.[77]

73 Maghribī, *A'lām al-Ḥijāz*, vol. 1, p. 47.
74 Ibid., pp. 47–8; and Manā', *Tārīkh mā lam yu'arrakh*, p. 201.
75 Abū 'l-Jadā'il, Khālid Ṣalāḥ Sanūsī, *Rawā lī wālidī wa-ṣaḥibuhi*, pp. 43–4.
76 Cf. Snouck Hurgronje, *Mekka. Aus dem Heutigen Leben*, vol. 2, on violent quarter competitions there, p. 810. For this as a wider phenomenon; cf. Freitag, *Symbolic Politics and Urban Violence.*
77 Zandi-Sayek, *Ottoman Izmir*, pp. 154–60.

In Jeddah, the *ṣuhba* is described as a pastime associated with collective chanting. Given that the *ṣuhba* was performed in groups, it could become a rallying point for quarter solidarity.[78] While Ṭrābulsī describes it in very neutral terms as 'collective chant' mostly accompanied by the clapping of hands, it was a religiously inflected past-time closely associated with Sufism (see below).

From the 1920s onwards, football became another major preoccupation of the young men. The interesting aspect for the purposes of this study is that this type of youth culture and organisation was inclusive of those quarter residents who chose to participate irrespective of their origin. Hence, while neighbourhoods and quarters could be exclusive to non-residents, they provided a format through which new residents or their descendants could become active members of local society, similar to their participation in professional organisations and religious ceremonies.[79]

Abū 'l-Jadā'il, who conducted oral history with elders, makes two additional interesting points which underline the crucial social function of quarters. According to his interviewees, newcomers to a quarter (locally known as *nazīl*), no matter if 'only' from another quarter or from afar, were expected to organise invitations to get to know the other residents, and thus become part of local society. Furthermore, he mentions that certain quarters in Jeddah maintained alliances with quarters in Mecca. Given the importance of the pilgrimage, and the frequency with which people from Jeddah went to Mecca and vice versa, membership in the quarter of the other city mediated the presence of strangers by associating them with a known and trusted entity, the allied quarter. These examples are another pointer to the social importance of the quarters in the overall management of diversity in the city.[80]

Ethnic Associations

In the wider (late) Ottoman system, religious minority communities had their own representatives, often with a mandatory representation in communal councils, as Yazbak has shown for Haifa.[81] This system

[78] Ṭrābulsī, *Jidda*, pp. 421–2; and Raqqām, *Jidda*, p. 209.
[79] For example, al-Nimr, *Ḥārat al-Baḥr*, p. 30, mentions a Sindī among those excelling in *ṣuhba* in Ḥārat al-Baḥr.
[80] Abū 'l-Jadā'il, Khālid Ṣalāḥ Sanūsī, *Rawā lī wālidī wa-ṣaḥibuh*, p. 42.
[81] Yazbak, *Haifa in the Late Ottoman Period*, pp. 84–5.

existed in partial overlap with the functions of the quarters described in the last section. While Jeddah had no religious minorities to speak of, the existence of shaykhs representing different ethnic communities seems to have followed a similar logic. This system of ethnic representation could be found in many ports of the Indian Ocean world.[82]

The material on this institution is, overall, very scarce, with the exception of information on the numerically most important group, the Hadhrami community. Local traditions recount a decree (*firmān*), issued by Sultan Mahmud II in 1820/21 which stipulated that Hadhramis could regulate all their internal affairs, including inheritance disputes and sales, in front of the *shaykh al-ḥadhārim* rather than involving local legal or political authorities.[83] Snouck Hurgronje's account of Mecca indicates that their competence was similar to that of the *ʿumda* in speaking for their own community. He also mentions that, in Mecca, the Afghans had a similar communal organisation.[84] For Jeddah, one local history mentions (without any additional information), similar representatives for the Africans (though it is not clear which ones), Yemenis, and Central Asians (Bukhārā).[85] It was also suggested to me that other large groups such as Indians and Southeast Asians were represented by the consuls of the imperial powers ruling there, while British documents mention the existence of a Persian *shāhbandar* in 1861. This institution is otherwise mainly known from ports in the Indian Ocean as the representative of specific communities. The term was, however, also used in Jeddah to denote the head of the merchants (see Chapter 6). Presumably, these community organisations, in conjunction with the quarter representatives, helped ease the settlement of migrants. Often, they would have been the first point of call, providing shelter and possibly employment or social help, and

[82] This has been discussed by Michael Pearson, *The Indian Ocean*, Seas in History (London and New York: Routledge, 2003), pp. 95–112; cf. Christine Dobbin, *Asian Entrepreneurial Minorities: Conjoint Communities in the Making of the World-Economy 1570–1940*, Monograph series/Nordisk Institut for Asienstudier, Digital print (London: Routledge Curzon, 2005), vol. 71, who emphasises the aspect of entrepreneurial minorities.

[83] Documentation on Jeddah is somewhat scarce, see Pétriat, *Le Négoce des Lieux Saints*, pp. 114–8; for Mecca by Snouck Hurgronje, *Mekka. Aus dem Heutigen Leben*, vol. 2, p. 7. The Arab accounts seem to confuse some institutions, e.g. al-Anṣārī, *Mawsūʿat trīkh madīnat Jidda*, p. 231.

[84] Snouck Hurgronje, *Mekka. Aus dem Heutigen Leben*, vol. 2, p. 7.

[85] al-Sharīf, *Dhikrayāt Muḥammad Darwīsh Raqqām*, p. 164.

easing integration into particular professional communities and quarters.[86] It is very possible that groups considered 'foreign' thus all had their own internal organisations. The complication in Jeddah arose from the fact that these 'foreigners' could acquire Ottoman nationality after five years of residence, so that the distinction between 'Ottoman' and 'foreign' became much more blurred than the institutional arrangements suggest. This also gave people a certain choice as to where to turn in case of problems (see Chapter 7).

Guilds and the Organisation of Labour

As already mentioned, professional groups, usually organised in guilds (locally called *ḥirfa*), formed another backbone of Jiddawi society. Unfortunately, the term *ḥirfa* can also be used to denote a profession without implying guild membership, and the ways in which the term *ṭāʾifa* is used is also far from clear.[87] For Damascus, Weber renders *ṭāʾifat al-miʿmāriyya* as 'co-operative' of 'architects' while, for Jeddah, I would argue that the same terminology would more correctly denote a guild of builders (who were designing and building the houses with no clear separation between these tasks).[88] Similarly, descriptions of the ways in which the *ḥirafiyyūn* operated in Jeddah also indicate a guild-like character. These guilds ranged from the *wukalāʾ*, responsible for receiving pilgrims and organising their onwards journey to water carriers, to builders and the proud guild of boatmen. André Raymond found a list of 245 Cairo guilds in the year 1801.[89] A range of local

86 Behar, *A Neighborhood in Ottoman Istanbul*, pp. 121–5, can show in detail how local communities in conjunction with the *muhtar* helped navigate Ottoman internal settlement restrictions, and one may well imagine comparable processes for international migration.

87 For the Ottoman guilds see Donald Quataert, 'Labor History and the Ottoman Empire, c. 1700–1922', *International Labor and Working-Class History*, 60 (2001), pp. 93–109, here p. 101, also on the great local differences in guild organisation within the Ottoman Empire. Suraiya Faroqhi, *Artisans of Empire: Crafts and Craftspeople under the Ottomans*, Library of Ottoman Studies (London: Tauris, 2009), vol. 17 gives a comprehensive overview of the state of the art, particularly interesting is her comparative chapter on Ottoman and European guilds, pp. 208–20.

88 Weber, *Damascus*, p. 83, for Jeddah see Abū Zayd, *al-Miʿmārīyūn fī Jidda al-qadīma*.

89 André Raymond, 'Une liste des corporations de métiers au Caire en 1801', *Arabica* 4 (1957), pp. 150–63.

histories list different guilds, numbering around sixty overall, although it would seem that distinctions between related professions are remembered, and hence recorded, vary between the sources of the different local histories.[90] Furthermore, some professions, such as that of merchant, were highly subdivided according to the matters they traded in, and yet others contend that this large and economically important group did not constitute a *ḥirfa* at all.[91] There were probably more than fifty guilds, though the saying according to which Jeddah was known as the city of one thousand guilds seems largely exaggerated.[92]

The guilds, together with many of the crafts, disappeared in the 1960s as a result of the oil boom, i.e. about a century after their – slow and regionally very uneven – demise began in much of the Ottoman Empire.[93] In Saudi Arabia, it was their collective bargaining power, notably of the transport guilds, which was seen by both the government and the merchants as an obstacle to their own interests and gains.[94] As only very few written sources, beyond local histories and memoirs, on the guilds were available for this study, the following survey based on interviews and recent historiography mostly refers to the early to mid-twentieth century.[95] Although one would assume that guilds functioned in similar ways in earlier and later periods, this would need to be verified should additional sources become available. Similarly, the question of ethnic specialisation in particular professions, and its connection to migratory patterns, remains an important question for future research because, apart from photographic evidence pointing to a

[90] Diyāb, *Jidda*, pp. 40–67; Kābilī, *al-Ḥirafiyyūn fī madīnat Jidda*; and Abū 'l-Jadā'il, Khālid Ṣalāḥ Sanūsī, *Rawā lī wālidī wa-ṣaḥibuh*, pp. 122–61. An example for unclear distinctions is Abū Zayd, *al-Mi'mārīyūn fī Jidda al-qadīma*; and Bā Ṭarfī, *Sālim bin Maḥfūẓ* p. 25, where it seems that those who measured and cut stone were potentially organised separately, while the description in Khālid Bā Ṭarfī, *Jidda: Umm al-rakhā' wa-l-shidda*, 2nd edn. (Madīna: Mu'assasat al-Madīna li-l-Ṣaḥāfa wa-l-Ṭibā'a wa-l-Nashr, 1435/2014) p. 130 suggests that this was part of the builders' training.

[91] Kābilī, *al-Ḥirafiyyūn fī madīnat Jidda*, pp. 32–41, for possible divisions, according to 'Abdallāh Bin Zaqr, trade was no *ḥirfa*, Jeddah, March 23, 2006.

[92] This was related to me by Sāmī Nawwār, Jeddah, March 9, 2011.

[93] Anastassiadou, *Salonique, 1830–1912*, pp. 334–58 can show for Salonika major changes for the period 1840–1900, I have not been able to find similar material for Jeddah.

[94] Kiren Chaudhry, *The Price of Wealth: Economies and Institutions in the Middle East* (Ithaca: Cornell University Press, 1997), pp. 74–6.

[95] Oral information, 'Abdallāh Bin Zaqr, Jeddah, March 23, 2006; and Sāmī Nawwār, March 9, 2011.

preponderance of African labour (free or unfree cannot be judged from photographs), there is little material to go by.[96]

The organisation of the professions in guilds seems to have followed a common scheme, which was based on a wider model that could also be found in other parts of the Ottoman Middle East, with the guilds serving as another link between state and population regarding standards (of quality and measures), but also the provision of services and labour for the state and the distribution of goods.[97] Given the sacred status of the Hijaz, the extent to which the guilds were responsible for gathering and paying taxes remains obscure (see Chapter 7).[98] Notably, the Emir of Mecca found ways to benefit from the service industry surrounding the pilgrimage beyond the 'voluntary contributions' paid by pilgrims. Thus, admission to a *hirfa* needed a license for which fees were paid. In times of fiscal need, pilgrims' guides, but possibly also members of other trades, were asked to renew their licenses regularly (instead of obtaining them once for life).[99] From the period of King Ḥusayn onwards, this developed into more regular taxation by the state (see Chapter 6).

The central obligation of the guilds was training and the guarantee of professional standards. Boys, who often took up their father's profession, usually started training between the ages of ten and thirteen, often after finishing Koran school. The levels and formalisation of training varied from profession to profession, but it seems that training in the workshops and businesses of partners was preferred to that in the father's own business. One shaykh of the guild of upholsterers remembered that his training was considered complete when his uncle served him coffee. This symbolic recognition of his maturity meant that he was now in a position to open his own business and take on

96 This question, which is obvious in an immigrant society such as Jeddah, has been discussed for Istanbul by Cengiz Kirli, 'A Profile of the Labor Force in Early Nineteenth-Century Istanbul', *International Labor and Working-Class History*, 60 (2001), pp. 125–40.

97 This is described well in Gabriel Baer, 'The Administrative, Economic and Social Functions of Turkish Guilds', *International Journal of Middle East Studies*, 1 (1970), pp. 28–50.

98 On the tax exemption Selçuk Somel, 'Osman Nuri Paşa'nın 17 temmuz 1885 tarihli Hicaz raporu', *Ankara Üniversitesi Dil ve Tarih-Coğrafya Fakültesi Tarih Bölümü Tarih Araştırmaları Dergisi*, 18/29 (1996), pp. 1–38, here pp. 13–14; and Low, *Empire and the Hajj*, p. 61.

99 Snouck Hurgronje, *Mekka. Aus dem Heutigen Leben*, vol. 2, pp. 98–100.

apprentices.[100] This recognition seems to have taken the place of an earlier examination, which had already been abolished by the time of Snouck Hurgronje's visit in the mid-1880s.[101] The training of merchants who, according to one member of the profession, did not consider themselves a *ḥirfa,* nevertheless followed a similar pattern (cf. Chapter 6).[102]

Members of specific guilds had regular meeting places, often coffee-houses. Thus, the boatmen met in a coffee shop near the harbour, below the meeting room of the municipality. The *mukharrijūn*, those who organised the transport of goods from the harbour or storage spaces to other towns and cities by contracting camel drivers (*jammāla*) and vouching for the safe delivery of goods, frequented a coffeehouse in Qābil Street, near the harbour.[103] In one local history, the guild meetings in the coffee shop of Saʿīd Ḥātm are described in a way which explains the functioning of these organisations well, comparing the space to a parliament for the guilds:

> These groups of craftsmen[104] [the butchers, white-limers (*nawwārūn*), and builders etc.] met when they needed to decide on the admission of a new person to their trade, or if the *ʿumda* of a quarter needed to be changed, or their deputies, or if matters coming from specialised bodies like the municipality needed to be decided. The municipality was responsible for all professions with regard to their performance and the wages they deserved. All these things happened through this coffeehouse, which had a wide inside space where the shaykh of the guild could meet its members.[105]

One should add that these coffeehouses could also serve as a place where craftsmen and clients met.

100 Bā Ṭarfī, *Jidda.*, pp. 131–3.
101 UBL, Cod. Or. 7112 Snouck Hurgronje Jeddah Diary, p. 55.
102 Oral information, ʿAbdallāh Bin Zaqr, Jeddah, March 23, 2006; and Muḥammad Bin Ḥimd, Jeddah, February 24, 2016. Baer also emphatically argues for the inclusion of merchants in the consideration of guilds, although of course in general terms without reference to Jeddah, see Baer, *The Administrative, Economic and Social Functions*, p. 31.
103 Bā Ṭarfī, *Jidda*, p. 14; and al-Faḍlī, *al-Nuzla al-Yamāniyya*, pp. 37–8. Possibly, the *jammāla* had yet another designated coffeehouse, see al-Nimr, *Ḥārat al-Baḥr*, p. 316.
104 The term here is *ṭawāʾif al-ḥirafiyyīn*, which could also mean 'guilds of craftsmen'.
105 al-Sharīf, *Dhikrayāt Muḥammad Darwīsh Raqqām*, pp. 150–1.

The person went to the popular coffeehouse and searched for a local master builder (*mu ʿallim baladī*) who would study with him this idea, and together with the other master builders help him with advice and guide him towards somebody among them who could work with him.[106]

Although the municipality oversaw the workings of the guilds and could intervene if they saw that something was amiss, it was the guild which, in the first instance, set the standards and prices. In trade disputes, for example between the builder of a house and the client, the shaykh of the guild, together with other masters was asked to judge the validity of the complaint. He would then decide on the appropriate course to settle the dispute. In extreme cases, offending builders could be forced to leave the profession. There also existed an internal moral code governing the interaction between competing guild members.[107]

The shaykhs of the guilds were elected by their members. Like the *ʿumda*, the shaykh needed official endorsement which, in Ottoman times, was done either through the *muḥtasib*, in professions linked to commerce and trade, or through the *qāḍī* for professions such as muezzins, teachers etc.[108] In the Saudi period, the *shaykh* was endorsed by royal decree.[109]

The seamen were a special case, as they were an especially important group in a port city such as Jeddah. Abū ʻl-Jadāʾil argues that, while the Baḥr quarter did not have separate *ʿumda* from the Yaman quarter, the seamen, most of whom lived in the Bahr quarter, had their *shaykh al-baḥr*, i.e. their head of guild. According to Raqqām, the *shaykh al-baḥr* held this office and also served as the *ʿumda* of this quarter until the two offices were separated after the death of one particularly influential shaykh.[110]

There seems to have existed a stiff competition between two factions of seamen, and hence there were two contenders for the leadership of the *maʿādī*, in the first half of the twentieth century, even if the background to this rivalry remains absent from the existing accounts.[111] In the case of the seamen, the shaykh was responsible for overseeing a fair

106 Abū Zayd, *al-Miʿmārīyūn fī Jidda al-qadīma*, pp. 22–3, and pp. 23–4 also for the further process of completing a building.
107 Ibid., pp. 45–51.
108 UBL, Cod. Or. 7112 Snouck Hurgronje Jeddah Diary, p. 55.
109 IPA, 12/1/54 of Muḥarram 6, 1356/March 18, 1937.
110 Abū ʻl-Jadāʾil, Khālid Ṣalāḥ Sanūsī, *Rawā lī wālidī wa-ṣaḥibuh*, p. 35; and Raqqām, *Jidda*, p. 168. I could not establish the date.
111 Raqqām, *Jidda*, pp. 168–9.

distribution of work. Thus, the *shaykh al-maʿādī* had an office in the harbour, led by a *bāshkātib*, or chief secretary. He allocated the work of transporting goods and people in their sambuks from the ships anchoring about one mile off shore to the port. He also collected the dues from the merchants and company representatives and later distributed them among the owners of and workers on the sambuks according to the shares they were owed.[112] As there seem to have been complaints about overloading, the Saudi government intervened in 1931, attempting to regulate the trade further by limiting the weight allowed and introducing closer inspections, thereby de facto limiting the self-regulatory regime of one of Jeddah's most important guilds.[113] In general, the host of documents related to regulations concerning guilds in the archives of the Institute of Public Administration shows that, during the period until the 1950s, the Saudi Arabian government was actively involved in regulating the different guilds on matters ranging from the unification of the dress of the boatmen on the sambuks to the organisation of the profession of money-changers.[114] To what extent this is a continuation of earlier practice or a sign of an increasing centralisation in the wake of building a new state cannot be answered on the basis of the available material.

How did the cooperation between guild members and newcomers work in practice? From interviews, it is clear that new arrivals could practice their trade without joining the guild. While Ottoman officials are known to have ordered craftsmen from Istanbul to work in the holy cities, there seem to have also been itinerant craftsmen in certain professions.[115] Thus, both local and itinerant carpenters seem to have participated in the construction of the Naṣīf house in the late 1870s.[116] Was it the Turkish architect who brought these carpenters or were

112 Bā Ṭarfī, *Jidda*, pp. 98–100; and al-Nimr, *Ḥārat al-Baḥr*, pp. 53–4.

113 al-Nimr, p. 54.

114 IPA 160 of Shaʿbān 2, 1358/September 16, 1939 (*sambūks*), 695/518 of Rabīʿ al-Awwal 28, 1350/August 12, 1931 (money changers) to the regulation of the relationship between merchants and camel drivers, 37571/10 of Rajab 29, 1368/May 26, 1949.

115 BOA, A.DVN 90/77, Za 5, 1269/August 10, 1853 for one Ottoman example of stonemasons being employed in Medina.

116 Aḥmad and al-ʿAlawī, *Muḥammad Naṣīf*, p. 192. The house was built between 1872 and 1881, see *Archnet*, 'Bayt Nassif', https://archnet.org/sites/3794 (accessed April 5, 2018). It needs to be pointed out that according to the local history, the master builder was an illiterate local, whereas the above account follows the Archnet description.

there travelling groups (or individuals) touring the Hijaz (or the Red Sea region) for employment? Were these individual and thus exceptional cases or a frequent occurrence? While these questions are important to better understand the integration of migrants into local society, they cannot be answered at present.

Mutual help and the organisation of social cohesion clearly formed an integral part of the guilds' tasks. Thus, the story of Abū Dā'ūd helping Manā''s mother, recounted at the beginning of the chapter, can be read not only in terms of neighbourhood but also in terms of the support of the guild for its members, given that Manā's father had been in the same profession. Besides supporting dependants of guild members who fell ill or died, they also paid advances if members had a period of low or no business. For example, when no ships arrived, boatmen received credit in terms of advance on future earnings.[117] Helping with debt was another form of support. Writing about Dutch guilds between 1550 and 1800, van Leeuwen describes this function of the guilds as 'a system of middle-class welfare'.[118]

When it comes to the significance of welfare arrangements of guilds for the functioning of society, it is difficult to compare the above-cited Dutch study to the scattered (and mostly oral or local history) sources available on the Jiddawi guilds. From what we know so far, the system in Jeddah seems closer to that of the smaller or earlier guilds described by van Leeuwen. These offered 'informal assistance in the case of illness and burials, and sometimes help for widows and elderly masters no longer able to work', which would also seem a fair description of al-Manā''s case.[119] Notably, in the early days of Saudi rule, dependants of guild members, mostly women, appealed directly to the state authorities for support of their claims, often with success.[120]

A final important task of the guilds is similar to that of the quarters, namely the organisation of activities enhancing group solidarity. Once again, the evidence pertains mostly to the boatmen and seamen, who were considered to be particularly rich. 'We were', one boatman is reported saying, 'called 'the Barmakids', referring to the Barmakids in the age of Caliph Harun al-Rashid, for their widespread 'generosity''

[117] Manā', *Tārīkh mā lam yu'arrakh*, p. 37; and Bā Ṭarfī, *Jidda*, p. 101.

[118] Marco H.D. van Leeuwen, 'Guilds and Middle-Class Welfare, 1550–1800: Provisions for Burial, Sickness, Old Age, and Widowhood', *The Economic History Review*, 65 (2012), pp. 61–90, here p. 86.

[119] Ibid., p. 79.

[120] Chaudhry, *The Price of Wealth*, p. 75; and fn. 66.

(or, indeed, squandrous tendencies).[121] Thus, during the night before the ʿĪd celebration, the

> '*maʿādī* went to 'al-qabwa', a place in the grand bazaar, and each of them had his children with them. They bought for each of them what they wanted, sandals for a pound, and a turban, or belt, or . . . different kinds of turbans of valuable silk, in addition to the material for the cummerbund of the ʿanbar type. Sometimes the money did not suffice and they incurred a debt to be repaid from the income from the hajj. All these clothes were worn only once. . .'[122]

Finally, the guilds helped organise social events, although not very much is known about this. However, the *maʿādī* are said to have played an important role in the organisation of a boat race, which took place right after the pilgrimage season.[123] According to one local history, this was a new tradition introduced by British sailors in the first quarter of the twentieth century and was then taken up locally.[124]

This discussion of the guilds has thus far focussed exclusively on men, due to the bias in the available evidence. However, we know from photographs and fleeting comments in a variety of sources that women worked as water carriers and were present in the harbour (perhaps as porters). They earned money by sewing, as Manāʿ reports about his mother and taught in Koranic schools (as did his grandmother), they brewed alcohol, prepared and sold food, worked as prostitutes, washerwomen and entertainers, and were experts in traditional medicine, in midwifing, but also in the *zār* cult.[125] Midwives, who also cared for young children, were known as close associates of the druggists (*ʿaṭṭārūn*). While they are discussed and even named in a booklet on the profession, there is no indication of how they were organised or, indeed, what compensation they received for their services.[126] Some

121 The term *fanjarī* in local parlance means somebody generous, or squandrous, Diyāb, *al-Mufradāt al-ʿāmmiyya fī madīnat Jidda*, p. 111. The latter meaning is supported by Abū 'l-Jadāʾil, Khālid Ṣalāḥ Sanūsī, *Rawā lī wālidī wa-ṣaḥibuh*, p. 35.

122 Bā Ṭarfī, *Jidda*, p. 102.

123 Oral information, Talāl Bakur and Muḥammad Raqqām, Jeddah, March 19, 2011. Such a boat race is mentioned for 1938 in Jarman (ed.), *The Jedda Diaries*, vol. 4, Jeddah Report, February 1938, p. 267.

124 al-Nimr, *Ḥārat al-Baḥr*, pp. 82–3.

125 Altorki, *Some Considerations on the Family*, pp. 299–306. The link to sewing is also made in Ṭrābulsī, *Jidda*, p. 434.

126 Abū Zayd, *Ḥikāyāt al-ʿaṭṭārīn*, pp. 53–4.

of these tasks were performed by slaves, others by free women, and some by both. Unfortunately, there is currently not much more information available on issues such as pay, organisation, or the proportion of women involved in profitable occupations.

The above discussion of quarters, ethnic groups, and guilds shows that there was probably a multi-tiered system. This might have afforded a Hadhrami seaman in the Baḥr quarter certain choices as to whom he had recourse in certain affairs, such as conflicts or social support, while, in others, the *ʿumda*, the community representative or the guildmaster was unequivocally responsible.[127] These choices could reflect interest, but arguably also different levels of integration into local society. Indeed, while it is recounted locally that the Hadhramis and Indians in Jeddah constituted somewhat separate communities – nowadays remembered in terms of dress, language, and marriage – there is also mention of those who became full *ahl al-balad* (lit.: people of the city) by adopting local dress and customs.

Religious and Cultural Life in Jeddah

Religious Practices and Holidays

Life in Jeddah was structured according to the Islamic calendar. While the Ottoman capital and important provincial cities experienced some degree of industrialisation and while modernisation was symbolised not least by the erection of clock towers, such as in the mosque of Mehmed Ali in the Cairo citadel (completed in 1858) and, notably from the 1860s, throughout the empire, these developments largely bypassed Jeddah.[128] If anything, the introduction of coal modernity – and thus pilgrimage journeys occurring closer to the actual dates of the hajj – allowed multiple smaller rites outside of the pilgrimage season to be observed without the distraction of large numbers of guests in town.

127 Snouck Hurgronje, *Mekka. Die Stadt und Ihre Herren*, p. 187, describes a similar situation for Mecca.

128 On the ostentatious presence of clocktowers, see Mohammad al-Asad, 'The Mosque of Muhammad ʿAli in Cairo', *Muqarnas*, 9 (1992), pp. 39–55; and Avner Wishnitzer, *Reading Clocks, Alla Turca: Time and Society in the Late Ottoman Empire* (Chicago: University of Chicago Press, 2015), pp. 180–2. Wishnitzer also gives a detailed analysis of the different ways, politics and the development of time-keeping, relevant for the following are particularly pp. 20–5.

The daily rhythm of life for most people was determined by the *adhān*, the call for prayer. People started working shortly after the Morning Prayer (*ṣalāt al-fajr)* and continuing to do so until sunset *al-maghrib*), with breaks for the midday (*al-ẓuhr*) and afternoon prayers (*al-ʿaṣr*) as well as lunch. The period until the night prayer (*al-ʿishāʾ*) was a prime time for socialising. On Fridays, people worked before the communal prayer. Officials had the Fridays off, and their working hours were determined by Ottoman (*alla turca*) time, known locally as *zawālī*, which survived in Jeddah until the 1970s.[129]

The following account provides a chronological overview of the year which highlights the rich texture of religiously inflected practices and customs. Of course, these varied to some extent between different groups and families. Nevertheless, the cumulative effect of these traditions and practices provided an overall structure for spiritual and social exchange and comfort, involving both family, quarter, and the entire city. A number of other religious institutions and traditions will then be discussed before the last section of this chapter, which is devoted to new types of cultural and associational life that emerged mostly in the twentieth century.

The Yearly Religious Cycle

The first month of the Islamic year, *muḥarram*, was welcomed with a special *ifṭār* (breakfast according to the *zawālī* calendar which starts a day after sunset), consisting of honey, *ṭaḥīna* (sesame cream) and milk for a 'white' new year, as well as a lunch of mulukhiyya.[130] The tenth of *muḥarram*, the *ʿāshūrāʾ*, is mentioned by Manāʿ and is the day when *zakāt* was given to the poor and sweet rice sprinkled with nuts was prepared. Some people fasted either on the 9th and 10th or on the 10th and 11th of *muḥarram*.[131]

Jeddah did have some, though not many, Shi'i inhabitants as well as visitors, mostly of Iranian or South Asian origin. Dutch Orientalist Snouck Hurgronje has left us a rare account of a Shi'ite *ʿāshūrāʾ* celebration in November 1884 in his diary.[132] Visitors of the ceremony on the 9th of *muḥarram*, who also seem to have raised funds to cover

[129] Abū 'l-Jadāʾil, Khālid Ṣalāḥ Sanūsī, *Rawā lī wālidī wa-ṣaḥibuh*, pp. 80–1.
[130] al-Sharīf, *Dhikrayāt Muḥammad Darwīsh Raqqām*, p. 99, for different food.
[131] Oral information, Dr. Anwar al-ʿIshqī, Jeddah, January 6, 2009.
[132] UBL, Cod. Or. 7112 Snouck Hurgronje Jeddah Diary, pp. 26–31.

the costs, were wealthy resident Persian merchants and rich pilgrims who had lingered in Jeddah after the pilgrimage, while poor pilgrims and poor Persian residents performed in the presence of the Persian Vice-Consul and some foreign visitors, among them Snouck Hurgronje and the Dutch consul with boxes, drapes, and sofas, where a theatre-like setting had been arranged from which the onlookers partly watched recitations and partly joined in by chanting. The next evening, ceremonies resumed in a somewhat expanded fashion, with the kaymakam paying a visit. This official Ottoman presence at a ceremony that had been, according to Snouck Hurgronje, previously forbidden is possibly less surprising in light of the fact that the kaymakam had, in the 1860s, also acted for the Persian Vice-Consul during his prolonged absences.[133]

The start of the month of *Ṣafar* was, once again, marked by a special meal. As the month was seen as one during which calamities were likely to happen, people did not marry during this period.[134] Snouck Hurgronje reports that, while some people felt that the last day of the month was particularly ominous, others in Jeddah celebrated it by leaving the old town and walking, picnicking, or camping in the vicinity of the town. He observed horse, donkey, and camel races, and a good many women and slaves moving around outside of the old city.[135]

Rabīʿ al-awwal and *Rabīʿ al-thānī* saw a return to normal life, with weddings, but also nightly Koranic readings. Some people celebrated the Prophet's birthday (*mawlid nabawī*) on the 12th of *Rabīʿ al-awwal*. According to Snouck Hurgronje, the *mawlid* was more commonly celebrated on the 11th *Rabīʿ al-awwal*, by recitations of the *mawlid*. Children were dressed up an a special pastry filled with honey prepared. There was some official attention given to the occasion, though, with illuminations on war-boats and official buildings including the barracks and a recitation of the *mawlid* in the Ḥanafī Mosque,

133 For the prohibition, see UBL, Cod. Or. 7112 Snouck Hurgronje Jeddah Diary, p. 30. For the Vice-Consul's representation, see TNA, FO 685/1, Stanley to Amb. Const., June 20, 1861. The Persian Vice-Consul seems for many years to have come to Jeddah mostly for the pilgrimage season, oral information, Prof. Hossein Abadian, Berlin, April 3, 2018.

134 Abū 'l-Jadāʾil, Khālid Ṣalāḥ Sanūsī, *Rawā lī wālidī wa-ṣaḥibuh*, p. 92; and UBL, Cod. Or. 7112 Snouck Hurgronje Jeddah Diary, pp. 31–2.

135 UBL, Cod. Or. 7112 Snouck Hurgronje Jeddah Diary, p. 42.

which was frequented by officials. He also observed a Sufi procession through the town.[136]

The next two months, *Jumādā al-ūlā* and *Jumādā al-ākhira*, were, once again, considered ill-fated. Thus, no marriages took place for fear that they might not last long if contracted during these months.[137] In *Rajab*, however, a major event took place which many Jiddawis participated in, namely the collective visit (*rakab*) to Medina or, more specifically, to the Prophet's tomb and mosque.[138] One leg of the journey would take about six to eight days by donkey and ten or more days by camel, which made it a major undertaking.[139] Hence, preparations began at the beginning of the month and were, once again, organised according to the respective quarters, who appointed shaykhs for the purpose. First-time participants in the *rakab* were promenaded through their quarters on horses or camels upon their return, while women showered them with sweets thrown from the windows and a dinner was arranged in their honour.[140] In 1903 the French consul estimated a participation of 4–5,000 people while the newspaper *Umm al-Qurā* reported that the number of those participating in the 'Medina caravan' numbered 2,721 persons in April 1926.[141]

Sha'bān was another month during which people liked to spend time outside of the old city, in the suburbs or on the islands off the coast. These '*Sha'bān* excursions' (*nuzhāt sha'bāniyya*) were an occasion for picnics, often accompanied by music and other merriment, probably not dissimilar from what Snouck Hurgronje described for the end of *Ṣafar*.

Ramaḍān was ushered in by the cannons of the garrison and by prayers for blessings.[142] People divided the month into three sections. The first, *maraq*, was devoted to the preparation of special dishes that

136 Ibid., p. 43.
137 Abū 'l-Jadā'il, Khālid Ṣalāḥ Sanūsī, *Rawā lī wālidī wa-ṣaḥibuh*, pp. 92–3.
138 A similar procession took place from Mecca, Ḥasan Qazzāz, *Ahl al-Ḥijāz bi-'abqihim al-tārīkhī* (Medina: Maṭābi'al-Madīna li-l-Ṣaḥāfa, 1415/1995–6), pp. 53–61.
139 Abū 'l-Jadā'il, Khālid Ṣalāḥ Sanūsī, *Rawā lī wālidī wa-ṣaḥibuh*, p. 96, also mentions that one of his family once got lost, which might indicate that he was kidnapped when staying behind the caravan for a short while. On the *rakab*; cf. Ṭrābulsī, *Jidda*, pp. 525–6, 538–42.
140 al-Anṣārī, *Mawsū'at tārīkh madīnat Jidda*, p. 252.
141 CADN, 2_MI_3231, Dubief to Emb. Const., October 31, 1903; and *Umm al-Qurā*, 68, April 23, 1926, p. 4.
142 For *Ramaḍān* see al-Sharīf, *Dhikrayāt Muḥammad Darwīsh Raqqām*, pp. 96–9, for a Meccan perspective Qazzāz, *Ahl al-Ḥijāz*, pp. 104–21.

were exchanged between families, the second, *khalq*, to the preparation of new clothes and the last, *sharq*, to the ritual cleaning of the houses in preparation for the ʿĪd, which began on the first day of *Shawwāl* and lasted four days. Preparations for this occasion had, of course, started earlier and could include the fattening of sheep over months, but also the preparation of elaborate dishes. As soon as the ʿĪd was announced by cannon shots, people congratulated each other. After the Morning Prayer, they dressed in fine clothes and went to al-Mashhad outside Bāb Makka for the ʿĪd Prayer (see Chapter 4). According to the traveller Tamisier, who visited Jeddah in 1840, this lasted about an hour and a half and ended with a sermon by the city's *qāḍī*. Afterwards, the women visited the graves of their ancestors to ask for forgiveness.[143] After a family meal, the children went out to the fairgrounds that had been set up in the squares of the Shām, Maẓlūm, and Yaman quarters (later separate sections were put up for girls and protected against glances from outsiders). Figure 5.2 depicts one of a number of different types of swings that were erected for the occasion.

Dhū al-Qaʿida was known as the month of 'getting up and sitting down' (*al-qawma wa-l-qaʿda*), as many people de-camped from their apartments and houses to make room for the pilgrims who started to arrive. Cooks set up stalls in the streets for the pilgrims, adapting to their regional cuisines, reflecting the position of various regionally specialised pilgrims' guides across town.[144] Particular groups of pilgrims, which were usually accompanied by officials and often military from the respective governments, brought with them the so-called *maḥmal*, a richly decorated palanquin containing covers for the *Kaʿba* (the so-called *kiswa*), which were annually changed, and/or presents from the rulers to the Emirs and scholars of Mecca. The most famous *maḥmal* came from Cairo, although, at different periods, there were others sent from Yemen, Syria, Iraq, the Maghreb, West Africa, and Anatolia.[145] As mentioned in Chapter 2, after 1884, the Egyptian

143 Tamisier, *Voyage en Arabie*, pp. 136–7; and al-Sharīf, *Dhikrayāt Muḥammad Darwīsh Raqqām*, p. 170.

144 Rifʿat, *Mirʾāt al-Ḥaramayn.*, vol. 2, pp. 304–8.

145 al-Nimr, *Ḥārat al-Baḥr*, p. 84; Fr. Buhl and J. Jomier, 'Maḥmal' in P. J. Bearman, T. Bianquis, C. E. Bosworth, E. J. van Donzel and W. P. Heinrichs (eds.), *Encyclopaedia of Islam*, 2nd edn., 12 vols. (Leiden: Brill, 1960–2005). dx.doi.org/10.1163/1573-3912_islam_SIM_4789 (accessed October 5, 2018); and Ṭrābulsī, *Jidda*, pp. 527–35.

Figure 5.2 Children celebrating *ʿĪd.*
Leiden University Libraries, Or. 12.288 M: 36

maḥmal arrived usually by sea. In the early twentieth century, the route changed several times. For example, from 1910 onwards, the Hijaz Railway was used until Medina, which must have ended again with World War I.[146]

Upon arrival in Jeddah, the *maḥmal* was greeted by crowds, as can be seen in Figure 5.3. It was then brought to a *ḥawsh* in Ḥārat al-Baḥr, near the port. Ibrāhīm Rifʿat Bāshā, an Egyptian commander of the hajj in 1901, describes how, on the second day of its presence in Jeddah, 600 regular and irregular Ottoman soldiers turned up for a celebration of the *maḥmal.* Accompanied by eighty musicians of the local military corps as well as the Egyptian musicians accompanying the *maḥmal,* it was paraded across town, where everyone appeared in

[146] For details, see Jomier, *Le Maḥmal et la Caravane Égyptienne*, pp. 149–70.

Figure 5.3 Arrival of the *maḥmal*.
Leiden University Libraries, Or. 12.288 J: 10

their best clothes.[147] According to a memoir reflecting Hashemite and very early Saudi practices, people very much looked forward to this event. According to the local memoir, the officials accompanying the *maḥmal* distributed food and sometimes even coins to the people until it left.[148] During the presence of the Egyptian delegation, people came daily to visit the *maḥmal*, listen to the (military) music and perform the *mizmār*.[149]

In Ottoman times, the festivities accompanying the *mahmal*'s presence in Jeddah combined religious anticipation of the pilgrimage with a more political aspect of fostering loyalty to the larger empire of which Egypt was still an important part. This explains the highly political nature of disputes surrounding the Egyptian *maḥmal* after the disintegration of the Ottoman Empire. In 1923 a first dispute arose between the Egyptian and Hashemite governments, which resulted in the

[147] For a vivid description of the arrival of the Egyptian *maḥmal* in 1901, see Rifʿat, *Mirʾāt al-Ḥaramayn*, vol. 1, pp. 19–20. He and his company camped near the tomb of Eve, presumably at that time, that was also where there *maḥmal* was kept, Rifʿat, p. 17; cf. vol. 2, p. 186, for the experience in 1907.
[148] al-Nimr, *Ḥārat al-Baḥr*, p. 84. [149] Rifʿat, *Mirʾāt al-Ḥaramayn*, p. 20.

immediate return of the *maḥmal* to Egypt. The background was the Egyptian insistence on sending an unauthorised medical team to Jeddah and Mecca with the aim of preventing the spread of disease, not least by warning pilgrims not to drink the water of the Zamzam well. Fearing a negative impact on the pilgrimage, the Hashemite government refused to authorise the team. This occurred against the wider background of fear of foreign intervention in the Hijaz through the backdoor of medical concerns. At the time, the Egyptians planned a far-reaching intervention in the Hijaz, through the support of the Hashemites, aimed against the Āl Saʿūd. At any rate, the attempts negotiate a solution to the conflict failed and the *maḥmal*, as well as payments and food intended to be distributed among the local population, was ordered back to Egypt.[150]

In 1926 the *maḥmal* reached Mecca for the last time, just as the pilgrimage started to recover after two years of wartime disruption.[151] According to British sources, Wahhabi *ʿulamāʾ* had insisted that the *maḥmal* should only be allowed to accompany the Egyptian pilgrims if no music was performed past Jeddah, nobody smoked in public, and no graves were visited.[152] Although the local newspaper *Umm al-Qurā* had published *fatāwā* disapproving of the visits of graves, of music, and of dance, the schedule of the *maḥmal* and its progress were reported diligently, as was the royal visit to its resting place in Mecca.[153] When it reached Mina to the blasts of trumpets, Najdi pilgrims threw stones at it. Egyptian guards accompanying it opened fire and killed twenty-five of the attackers.[154] Thus ended the visits of

150 For details, see Dirk Boberg, *Ägypten, Nağd und der Ḥiğāz: Eine Untersuchung zum religiös-politischen Verhältnis zwischen Ägypten und den Wahhabiten, 1923–1936, anhand von in Kairo veröffentlichten pro- und antiwahhabitischen Streitschriften und Presseberichten*, Europäische Hochschulschriften. Reihe XXVII, Asiatische und Afrikanische Studien (Bern and New York: P. Lang, 1991), vol. 28, pp. 39–50 and Naṣīf, *Māḍī ʾl-Ḥijāz wa-ḥāḍiruhu*, pp. 94–6.

151 Boberg, *Ägypten, Nağd und der Ḥiğāz*, pp. 69–109.

152 Jarman (ed.), *The Jedda Diaries*, vol. 2, Jeddah Report, May 1–31, 1926, pp. 387–8.

153 *Umm al-Qurā,* 73, May 28, 1926, p. 1 for the *fatāwā,* no. 75, June 11, 1926, p. 3 for the programme, for the events in Mecca no. 78, June 29, 1926, p. 1. A somewhat more pro-Egyptian account is Jarman (ed.), vol. 2, Report on Events in the Hejaz for the Period June 1–30, 1926, pp. 393–4.

154 Jomier, *Le Maḥmal et la Caravane Égyptienne*, pp. 67–8; and Joseph Kostiner, *The Making of Saudi Arabia, 1916–1936: From Chieftaincy to Monarchical State,* Studies in Middle Eastern History (New York: Oxford University Press, 1993), p. 106.

the *maḥmal* in the Hijaz, although it was still produced and paraded in Cairo and apparently occasional attempts were made to send it to Jeddah until 1952 when the Egyptian Grand mufti also outlawed it and declared it idolatrous.[155]

With the start of *Dhū al-Ḥijja,* the pilgrims began to make their way to Mecca, often accompanied by Jiddawis who worked in the transport business. Families in town also prepared special foods, although the preparations were fewer as many of the men were away in Mecca. Those who had no professional obligations often participated as groups in the pilgrimage.[156] The season of the ʿĪd was known as the *khulayf*, the season of those left behind.[157] These 'left behind' were mostly women, who in turn organised a carnival of their own, known as *al-Qays*. They donned male clothes and took to the streets where they lit fires and danced.[158] First time pilgrims from Jeddah were celebrated in a way similar to the ones returning from the Medina *rakab* for the first time.[159]

Other Religious Traditions

The Visiting of Tombs

The map of Jeddah from 1880, discussed in Chapter 4, points to a number of domed tombs (known as *türbe* (Turkish) or *qabr* (Arabic) in the immediate vicinity of Jeddah. Each of these tombs, the most famous of which was arguably that of Eve, had its own story, but, in essence, they were considered to be the graves of virtuous men and, in the case of Eve, women who were therefore venerated.[160] Some of these

155 Jomier, *Le Maḥmal et la Caravane Égyptienne*, pp. 67–73.
156 Ṭrābulsī, *Jidda*, pp. 543–5.
157 Diyāb, *al-Mufradāt al-ʿāmmiyya fī madīnat Jidda.*, p. 48.
158 For details on this tradition and its later interpretations see Ulrike Freitag, 'Playing with Gender: The Carnival of *al-Qays in Jeddah*' in N. Maksudyan (ed.), *Women in the City: A Gendered Perspective on Ottoman Urban History* (New York: Berghahn Books, 2014), pp. 71–85; cf. Ahmad Nasr and Abu Bakar Bagader, 'Al-Gēs: Women's Festival and Drama in Mecca', *Journal of Folklore Research*, 38 (2001), pp. 243–62.
159 al-Anṣārī, *Mawsūʿat tārīkh madīnat Jidda*, pp. 251–2.
160 For the practice, see Richard McGregor, 'Grave Visitation/Worship' in K. Fleet, G. Krämer, D. Matringe, J. Nawas, and E. K. Rowson (eds.), *Encyclopaedia of Islam*, 3rd edn. (Leiden: Brill, 2007). dx.doi.org/10.1163/1573-3912_ei3_COM_27519 (accessed April 19, 2018).

graves were also located in mosques, such as that of Abū 'l-ʿAnaba in the northern quarter, or in some of the *zawāya* discussed in Chapter 4.[161]

In each case, specific legends and beliefs were related to the deceased, as has been described in Chapter 4 with regard to ʿAbd al-Raḥmān al-Asad, who was known to give out charms and amulets. The tombs were visited in the hope that, with the aid of the deceased, problems could be solved, but they also served as important places for meetings and/or joint rituals. While such practices were shunned in Saudi Arabia and thus not much written information on them can be found locally nowadays, a number of recent publications give at least a glimpse of what was probably a richly textured calendar of religious events and practices, which took place until the early twentieth century. Thus it is difficult to know whether the visits to these tombs took, during some time in the past, the form of regular processions, as known, for example, for the Hadhramaut, or if they were organised on a smaller scale and possibly in conjunction with particularly auspicious days in the Islamic calendar.[162]

The most prominent tomb for Jiddawis, as well as for international visitors, was certainly that of Eve, which was visited by men and women alike. Most of those who left travelogues went to see the grave, though often only mentioning this fact, or discussing the shape of the grave or the shape or likelihood of Eve actually being buried there.[163] According to tradition, it was here where, in the past, seamen expected to learn (by way of the genus loci) whether ships delayed in their return journey from India were safe.[164] On Thursday afternoons women seem to have visited the grave in large groups. Ibrāhīm Rifʿat particularly noted the female beggars loitering near the tomb, while Philby noted the important social function of visiting the tomb.[165]

161 ʿAbd al-Qādir al-Shāfiʿī, *Bride of the Red Sea: A 10th/16th Century Account of Jeddah*, Translation of: al-Silāḥ wa-l-ʿuddah fī tārīkh bandar Judda, Occasional Papers Series (University of Durham, 1984), vol. 22, pp. 18–21, see also p. 22. For a modern account, see Abū Zayd, *al-Usṭūra fī madīnat Jidda*, pp. 85–6.

162 According to ʿUmda ʿAbd al-Ṣamad, for example, there were no such large-scale *ziyārāt* in Jeddah, oral communication, March 21, 2011.

163 For examples, see Maḥmūd, *Riḥalāt al-Ḥajj*, vol. 1, pp. 32, 78, 138, 364; and Muḥsin al-Amīn, *Riḥlāt al-Sayyid Muḥsin al-Amīn* (Beirut: Dār al-Turāth al-Islāmī li-l-Ṭibāʿa wa-l-Nashr wa-l-Tawzīʿ, 1974), p. 32.

164 al-Shāfiʿī, *Bride of the Red Sea*, p. 15.

165 MECA, Philby Collection GB165–0229, Philby Diary part 1, 1/4/5/1, p. 193; The Indonesian Hajj, Documents from the Archive of the Dutch Consulate at Jidda, Saudi Arabia, Rapport eener Dienstreis naar Djeddah, November 15, 1916, pp. 110–1; and Rifʿat, *Mirʾāt al-Ḥaramayn*, vol. 1, p. 22.

The tomb of al-ʿAlawī in the Yaman quarter was considered locally to be a refuge from the authorities. Hence, this was a place to which people brought food, even in the early twentieth century.[166] In contrast, Shaykh Abū 'l-ʿUyūn, buried to the south of the wall and after whom the adjacent sea inlet was named, was known for his ability to heal. Thus, people came to wash themselves, and in particular their eyes, in the sea, hoping for healing. They brought millet and candles, which were thrown into the sea to strengthen their requests. Women, in particular, came to demand fertility, which offered a chance for communal bathing in the sea.[167]

It is well known that these practices were anathema to the Wahhabi establishment and those influenced by their austere views on what they considered a deviation from monotheism, and thus *shirk* (polytheism).[168] The Meccan Emir ʿAwn al-Rafīq (1882–1905), whose long run in office was characterised by the strengthening of the emirate vis-à-vis his Ottoman overlords and a rather ruthless quest for power, reportedly influenced by *salafī* ideas brought to Mecca by the scholar and merchant in textiles, Shaykh Aḥmad b. ʿĪsā (see Chapter 6).[169] He thus ordered the destruction of a number of tombs in Mecca.[170] In December 1901 ʿAwn al-Rafīq visited Jeddah with a government delegation including the Governor to open the new telegraph connection to

166 Abū 'l-Jadāʾil, Khālid Ṣalāḥ Sanūsī, *Rawā lī wālidī wa-ṣaḥibuh*, p. 32.
167 Ibid., p. 49, Oral communication by Talāl Bakur, Muḥammad Raqqām, February 29, 2012.
168 It is important to heed Sedgwick's warning about both temporal as well as social distinctions among those commonly classified as 'Wahhabi'. As this is not a detailed study of religious developments, though, these distinctions are more implied here than spelt out, see Mark Sedgwick, 'Saudi Sufis: Compromise in the Hijaz, 1925–40', *Die Welt des Islams*, 37 (1997), pp. 349–68, here p. 352.
169 On ʿAwn al-Rafīq's rule and his relations to the Ottomans, see Ochsenwald, *Religion, Society, and the State*, pp. 186–214. For a decidedly pro-Ottoman perspective see Rifʿat, *Mirʾāt al-Ḥaramayn*, vol. 2, pp. 275–88. On his salafism, see ʿAbdallāh Bassām, *ʿUlamāʾ Najd khilāla thamāniyat qurūn*, 2nd enlarged edn., 6 vols. (Riyadh: Dār al-ʿĀṣima, 1419/1998–9 [1397/1977]), vol. 1, p. 440; cf. Aḥmad al-Sibāʿī, *Tārīkh Makka*, 2 vols. (Mecca: Maktabat Ihyāʾ al-Turāth al-Islāmī, 1999), vol. 2, p. 553; fn. 1; and al-Sibāʿī, *Tārīkh Makka*, pp. 550–7, on his rule.
170 al-Batanūnī, *al-Riḥla al-ḥijāziyya li-walī al-niʿm*. I would like to thank Dr. Saʿūd al-Sarḥān for these references. For the measures taken by the Emir; cf. TNA, FO 195/2126, Consul Jeddah to Amb. Const., October 14, 1902, Confid. Memorandum respecting His Highness the Grand Sherif, notably p. 2; cf. Abu-Manneh, *Sultan Abdülhamid II and the Sharifs*, here pp. 19–20.

Rābigh. He met with the scholars and jurists, enquiring about the state of religious affairs. As a result of these consultations he ordered the demolition of all shrines (*'kull mazār wa-maqām'*) in order to 'safeguard the true religion from the blemishes of superstitions and the disbeliefs of the masses'.[171] Thus, the shrines of Shaykh ʿAlawī, Shaykh Abī Sarīr, Shaykh Abū ʿAynih, Shaykh Maẓlūm, Shaykh al-Arbaʿīn, Shaykh al-ʿAqlī, and Shaykh Abū 'l-ʿUyūn were destroyed.[172] In Jeddah, the tomb of Eve was exempted, as were the tombs of Khadīja and Ibn ʿAbbās in Ṭāʾif, supposedly because the Emir feared that the Ottomans might depose him if he went too far.[173] According to Ochsenwald, the Emir enjoyed considerable local popularity for measures such as curbing certain noisy Sufi practices, eliminating the term *sayyid* and also passing sumptuary legislation.[174]

In late January 1926 Philby reports that the entrance to the actual dome over Eve's tomb had been blocked to stop people visiting.[175] In April 1926 the British consul reported that the dome of the tomb of Eve had been destroyed and that people were no longer permitted to visit it for worship.[176] Dutch consul van der Meulen remembers that 'the dome was demolished and when pilgrims, and especially women, continued to visit the place the government ordered every stone to be carried away'.[177] The newspaper *Umm al-Qurā* was more circumspect: It carried two long articles by the same author on the prohibition to visit or, indeed, build over tombs without, however, referring to the concrete event. Perhaps this was due to some concern about

171 al-Ahrām no. 7234, January 3, 1902, p. 1, with a report from Jeddah of Ramaḍān 13, 1319/December 23, 1901.

172 On Shaykh al-Arbaʿīn, see Abū Zayd, *al-Usṭūra fī madīnat Jidda*, pp. 73–7, 273–5. For some of the other graves, see Abū Zayd, pp. 84–7.

173 ʿAbdallāh Āl al-Shaykh, *Mashāhīr ʿulamāʾ Najd wa-ghayrihim* (Riyadh: Dār al-Yamāma, 1392/1972), p. 188.

174 Abū 'l-Jadāʾil, Khālid Ṣalāḥ Sanūsī, *Rawā lī wālidī wa-ṣaḥibuh*, p. 50. The Indonesian Hajj, Documents from the Archive of the Dutch Consulate at Jidda, Saudi Arabia, Rapport eener Dienstreis naar Djeddah, November 15, 1916, p. 111, names also the tombs Aboe Hanna, Sanūsī and Abū ʿAlwān; cf. Ochsenwald, *Religion, Society, and the State*, p. 213. For the abolition of the title sayyid; cf. TNA, FO 195/2061, Devey to Amb. Const., February 1, 1899.

175 MECA, Philby Collection, GB 165–0229, 1/4/5/1, January 19, 1926, p. 361.

176 Jarman (ed.), *The Jedda Diaries*, vol. 2, Jeddah Report, April 1–30, 1926, p. 385.

177 Daniël van der Meulen, *The Wells of Ibn Sa'ud* (London: Murray, 1957), p. 104.

local anger over the destruction.[178] Nevertheless, according to a British report in 1930, Muslims apparently still wanted to visit the site, so that they had to be prevented from doing so and the doors were walled up to deny them access.[179] Incidentally, the tomb of Eve attracts visitors to this day, even if the cemetery is now walled off and there is little to see beyond repetitive concrete slabs. In 2009, this triggered the suggestion by the chairmen of the Committee for the Promotion of Virtue and the Prevention of Vice to erase this site completely, which caused a heated debate for a few days and was then laid to rest once again.[180]

It would seem that some of the minor tombs continued to be worshipped for some time, as a report from 1936 recounts the destruction of the 'tomb of a Yemeni holy man and reputed miracle worker who died many years ago', including the removal of his skeleton which was then transferred to another cemetery.[181]

While we have little information on whether or not Sufi orders were involved in some of these activities, they were quite active with regard to holding sessions of *dhikr* (meetings during which religious texts are recited) and *mawlid* (celebrations of the Prophet's birthday, or that of certain saints). Hamilton noted in the early 1850s that *dhikr*s were still being held, which, according to him, were a popular entertainment.[182] Some of these displays of religiosity seem to have been quite public in nature: Sometime between 1916 and 1925, a Sufi procession passed the place where Muḥammad Naṣīf and his friends were conversing. Annoyed, they threw stones at the procession – something quite impolite for a prominent young notable and learned person in his early thirties.[183] Even if *dhikr* and other Sufi sessions were held indoors, the wooden window screens allowed not only the noise of the street, but also the calls of the muezzin to enter the houses. Charles Didier who

178 *Umm al-Qurā*, 67, April 9, 1926 and 68, April 23, 1926. The differences about the religious policies between Ibn Saʿūd and the Ikhwān shine through in the British reports, Jarman (ed.), *The Jedda Diaries*, vol. 2, Jeddah Report, May 1926, p. 387 and June 1926, pp. 393–4.

179 Jarman (ed.), vol. 3, Jeddah Report, May 1930, p. 131.

180 Ḥajjī Jābir (January 28, 2009). 'Inqisām fī al-Saʿūdiyya bi-Shaʾn Izālat 'Maqbarat Umminā Ḥawā'', article on *alJazeera.net*, https://bit.ly/2MhuQlR.

181 IOR, L/PS/12/2073, Jeddah Report, April 1936.

182 Hamilton, *Sinai, The Hedjaz, and Soudan*, p. 67.

183 Maghribī, *Aʿlām al-Ḥijāz*, vol. 1, p. 237.

passed through Jeddah in 1854, describes how he heard 'the grand religious fantasias: songs, prayers, sermons, all with music – but what kind of music! Accompanied by flutes and tambourines.'[184] Of course, the wide variety of Sufi orientations and practices, which was present in the Hijaz due to it attracting Muslims from all countries and orientations, needs to be noted – not all Sufis followed or would have approved of the same practices.

In 1887 the French colonial official and Orientalist Alfred Le Chatelier who had, until then, mostly worked in Algeria and travelled in North and sub-Saharan Africa, published a book on the Sufi orders of the Hijaz, mainly on the basis of reports by returning pilgrims.[185] According to their perspective, all orders with the exception for the Sanūsiyya had come under the tight control of the local authorities, possibly at the initiative of Emir ʿAwn al-Rafīq.[186] Le Chatelier gives the number of orders as twenty-five and mentions the existence of thirty *zawāyā* in Jeddah, before entering a more detailed discussion of eighteen of them.[187] It becomes clear that some orders had been successful in recruiting local adherents while others comprised mainly of immigrants from particular regions. Some *zawāyā*, such as that of the Naqshabandiyya in Jeddah and Mecca, were only frequented during the pilgrimage as the order had practically no local followers in these cities – in contrast to Medina.[188] This also means that the orders could become – at certain moments – the representatives of specific ethnic or tribal groups, or act according to the (real or perceived) interest of specific outside powers or groups, as has been seen in the case of the excitement surrounding the rise of the Sudanese Mahdi (cf. Chapter 2).[189] As for the Sanūsiyya, according to Le Chatelier it was the dominant order among the Bedouin, who were, he argues,

[184] Didier, *Séjour chez le Grand-Chérif*, p. 136 (my translation).

[185] Le Chatelier, *Les Confréries Musulmanes du Hedjaz*. On Le Chatelier, see the lengthy entry in *Wikipedia*, 'Alfred Le Chatelier', https://en.wikipedia.org/wiki/Alfred_Le_ Chatelier (accessed April 20, 2018). A much shorter list can be found in Abū 'l-Jadāʾil, Khālid Ṣalāḥ Sanūsī, *Rawā lī wālidī wa-ṣaḥibuh*, pp. 109–10.

[186] Le Chatelier, *Les Confréries Musulmanes du Hedjaz*, pp. 7–9. In his account of ʿAwn al-Rafīq's rule, see Rifʿat, *Mirʾāt al-Ḥaramayn*, vol. 2, pp. 276–93. He reprints a long complaint by ʿAlawī sayyids about the Emir, which might indicate that he had a general problem with potentially competing religious organisations.

[187] Ibid., p. 20. [188] Ibid., p. 159. [189] Ibid., p. 189.

prone to ally themselves with the Āl Saʿūd.[190] Such an alliance needs to be understood not merely on the basis of Bedouin alliances, the Sanūsiyya also had a fairly austere (or, adherents would argue, reform-minded) approach to Sufism, sometimes described as neo-Sufism, even if its founder, Muḥammad ʿAlī al-Sanūsī, contradicted Muḥammad b. ʿAbd al-Wahhāb on some central issues such as *takfīr* (accusation of unbelief) and the validity of Sufism.[191] This approach was particularly widespread among orders based on the teachings of Ahmad b. Idris (d. 1837).[192] Furthermore, according to Le Chatelier, large parts of the urban population were attracted by this order. He does not mention another very important order, notably popular among the Hadhramis, namely the ʿAlawiyya.

Mark Sedgwick has shown convincingly that ʿAbd al-ʿAzīz b. Saʿūd sought compromise, not the imposition of pure doctrine, after the conquest of the Hijaz, although the period of early Saudi rule is perhaps better known for radical actions such as the destructions of domes or the exchange of religious personnel and teaching, notably in Mecca and Medina.[193] Certainly, *dhikr* sessions which included music and dance were officially forbidden and many Sufi shaykhs preferred to go abroad, similar to some of the merchants. However, a number of shaykhs continued to teach, more discretely and in private, or returned after some time. This concerned particularly those who were based on the neo-Sufi tradition and, once again, specifically the Sanūsiyya. In addition, the respect for the privacy of houses meant that these

[190] Ibid., pp. 286–90. He goes on to argue that the emirs of Mecca preceding ʿAwn al-Rafīq had favoured this order and sees in it the nucleus of a pan-Islamic movement, pp. 288–94.

[191] On these issues, see the comparative article by Ahmad Dallal, 'The Origins and Objectives of Islamic Revivalist Thought, 1750–1850', *The Journal of the American Oriental Society*, 113 (1993), pp. 341–59.

[192] For a debate about this concept, see Rex O'Fahey and Bernd Radtke, 'Neo-Sufism Reconsidered', *Der Islam*, 70 (1993), pp. 52–87. On the Idrīsī tradition, see Rex O'Fahey, *Enigmatic Saint: Ahmad Ibn Idris and the Idrisi Tradition* (London: Hurst, 1990).

[193] If not indicated otherwise, the following is based on Sedgwick, *Saudi Sufis*; and Guido Steinberg, *Religion und Staat in Saudi-Arabien: Die Wahhabitischen Gelehrten 1902–1953* (Würzburg: Ergon, 2002). See Steinberg, pp. 552–61, 511–78 for an overall assessment of religious policies in the Hijaz. For an overview of the Islamic policies between 1926 and 1939; cf. William Ochsenwald, 'Islam and Loyalty in the Saudi Hijaz, 1926–1939', *Die Welt des Islams*, 47 (2007), pp. 7–32.

provided fairly safe environments for all sorts of practices, as long as they were not transmitted to the street.

Le Chatelier mentioned that a number of Sufi lodges in the Hijaz were mainly active during the pilgrimage season because the number of their local members was fairly low. Raqqām recalls that during the 1940s or 1950s, Egyptian and Yemeni Sufis would look for a particular person who normally acted as broker in the vegetable market. However, he had memorised the Koran and was a known reciter of the holy text as well as of Sufi recitations. Upon the request of the visitors, he would furnish particular neighbourhood squares and then lead the crowd in their recitations. From Raqqām's description, it is clear that locals joined in these sessions.[194] Besides the hosting of the pilgrims and the joint activities in Mecca, this is another example of the larger Islamic *communitas* between pilgrims and locals in the wider context of the pilgrimage, as discussed in the introduction.

Special Prayers

Near the Asad cemetery was a space for the 'prayer for help' (*ṣalāt al-istighātha*) in the vicinity of a number of cisterns and wells.[195] Based on its location it seems to be the space which Snouck Hurgronje described as the area for the rain prayer (*ṣalāt al-istisqāʾ*) which he witnessed in December 1884. According to him, people, including school children with banners as well as Sufis, arrived in their best clothing. The communal prayer was followed by a sermon and the ceremony was repeated on the next evening when rain did not appear as had been expected.[196]

Many of the religious practices described served spiritual as well as social needs, indeed, it might have been the very combination of the two that gave them their special role in the social life of the city. They need to be seen in conjunction with the other activities described above which centred around family and quarter as well as professional life.

[194] al-Sharīf, *Dhikrayāt Muḥammad Darwīsh Raqqām*, pp. 107–8. Raqqām does not seem to have mentioned proper dates.

[195] Abū 'l-Jadāʾil, Khālid Ṣalāḥ Sanūsī, *Rawā lī wlidī wa-ṣaḥibuh*, p. 51.

[196] UBL, Cod. Or. 7112 Snouck Hurgronje Jeddah Diary, pp. 38–40. For a similar prayer in 1903, see Devey to Amb. Const., January 15, 1903, p. 2. In 2010, I was shown a place near the Khuzām-Palace in Jeddah which was also said to be used for such prayers.

During the late nineteenth and early twentieth century, these practices were supplemented through the appearance of some new forms of sociability, prime among them different types of sports.

Educating the Young

In Jeddah, as in many other Middle Eastern cities, most children received some basic education at home. They then trained on the job, depending on the professions of their fathers, as has been discussed in the context of the guilds. Many boys and girls also attended private Koranic schools for a few years, some separate and some mixed, memorising parts of the holy book and acquiring basic literacy and numeracy skills. While Mecca had a large body of religious teachers for advanced studies in the field of religion, the sources are silent about higher Islamic teaching in Jeddah.[197] Although, as will be shown, state education started to be introduced gradually from the late Ottoman period onwards, private education continued to dominate throughout the period under consideration, which is why education is discussed in this chapter.

By 1874 ʿUmar Naṣīf and other notables seem to have pressed (and volunteered to partly pay) for the establishment of one of the higher elementary (or middle) schools (*rüşdiye*) which were due to be established in provincial cities after the Ottoman education law was passed in 1869.[198] This occurred at the same time as a number of private elementary schools were opened by Indian Muslims in Mecca. However, instruction at the school was in Ottoman Turkish, at least predominantly, and hence it was frequented mostly by the children of Ottoman officials and only the sons of a few notables, such as the Naṣīfs. Probably for that reason, but possibly also due to the limited capacity of this school, some Egyptians and locals founded another school by the name of *al-Najāḥ* in 1900. The curriculum seems to have

[197] For cursory surveys, see Ochsenwald, *Religion, Society, and the State*, pp. 74–9; Muḥammad al-ʿAmūdī, *Min tārīkhinā*, 2nd edn. (Beirut: al-Dār al-Saʿūdiyya li-l-Nashr, 1967), pp. 144–50; and al-Asmarrī, *Tārīkh al-ḥayyāt al-ijtimāʿiyya*, pp. 138–47.

[198] Ṣabbān, *Jidda fī wathāʾiq al-arshīf al-ʿuthmānī*, p. 42; Suhayl Ṣabbān (ed.), *Nuṣūṣ ʿuthmāniyya ʿan al-ʿawḍāʿ al-thaqāfiyya fī al-Ḥijāz: al-Awqāf, al-madāris, al-maktabāt* (Riyadh: Maktabat al-Malik ʿAbd al-ʿAziz al-ʿĀmma, 1422/2001), pp. 154–5; and BOA, MF.MKT. 37 11 of 2 C./Ca. 1293/May or June 26, 1876.

been quite close to that of the religious school. *al-Najāḥ* school was mostly financed privately, not least by Muḥammad ʿAlī Zaynal of the Zaynal ʿAlī Riḍā family. When it ran into financial troubles, it received Ottoman support on the condition that the language of instruction would be changed to Ottoman Turkish. This was in line with Ottoman policies elsewhere and a recognition of the state's limitations at providing a service which was increasingly in demand.[199] Official support did not suffice to save the school from attrition and it had to close in 1907 or 1908.[200] Muḥammad ʿAlī Zaynal was also the leading force behind the establishment of another private school, *al-Falāḥ*, shown in Figure 5.4. Because of the insistence on Arabic as the language of instruction, the school, established some time before 1905, only obtained its license then.[201] While resembling Koranic schools on the elementary level, the intermediary and higher levels came to include history, geography, accounting, engineering and, probably only later, English. The school proved such a success that branches were opened in Mecca and, in the 1920s, Dubai and Bahrain as well as, in 1931, in Bombay. Students were sent from the Hijazi schools to Bombay to study and be trained in Muḥammad ʿAlī Zaynal's pearl business. When the school ran into financial difficulties in the early 1930s and private support did not suffice, the merchants suggested a new import tax to King Ibn Saʿūd to keep the school running.[202] To this day, it is among the leading schools in Jeddah (and the Meccan school ranked among the top schools in Saudi Arabia in 2015), relying on the income of many religious foundations (*awqāf*) and support by business families, which largely surpasses government funding and allows the school to offer many extra-curricular activities.[203] The Indian heritage of the school's founders was inscribed architecturally into the urban fabric of the school. The

199 Weber, *Damascus* pp. 154–5, describes similar occurrences for Damascus.
200 Muḥammad al-ʿAbd al-Raḥmān al-Faḍl, 'Madrasat al-Najāḥ qabl Madrasat al-Falāḥ fī Jidda', *al-Manhal*, 21(6) (December 1970), p. 65.
201 Maghribī, *Aʿlām al-Ḥijāz*, vol. 1, pp. 318–9; and Riḍwān, *Qālū ʿan Muḥammad ʿAlī Zaynal*, p. 66. According to Nallino, *Raccolta di Scritti*, p. 127. The school opened officially in 1908. The following is based on Freitag, *The Falah School*.
202 IOR, L/PS/12/2085, Saudi Arabia Annual Report 1935, p. 42.
203 Interviews with Khālid Yūsuf ʿAlī Riḍā, Jeddah, February 15, 2015; Bakur Baṣfar and Māhir al-Khulaydī, February 22, 2015; and Māhir al-Khulaydī, February 26, 2015.

Figure 5.4 al-Falāh school.
Photograph by the author, 2007

cupolas of the old school building, as well as the shape of the main entrance, still stand out in the architecture of old Jeddah and testify to the Indian roots of the architect.

The success of *al-Falāḥ* overshadowed that of the *rüşdiye* which, under different names, remained the main government school until the end of the period under consideration. When al-Batanūnī visited in 1908–9, *al-Falāḥ* had twice as many students as the *rüşdiye*.[204] In 1924 Philby reported that it normally had about 8–900 pupils though, due to the war conditions, the number of attendees had dwindled to 300 or less.[205] A British report in 1933 listed one primary and one

204 al-Batanūnī, *al-Riḥla al-ḥijāziyya li-walī al-Ni'm*, p. 9. He talks of a school called al-Iṣlāḥ, which must be a misunderstanding.
205 MECA, Philby Collection GB165-0229, Philby Diary part 1, November 2, 1924, p. 45.

secondary governmental school in Jeddah, while the main school was *Madrasat al-Falāḥ* with 700 pupils and 24 teachers.[206]

While the main school was a boys' school, there was a girls' school attached to *al-Falāḥ* from 1930 onwards, established at the initiative of Muḥammad Ṣalāḥ Jamjūm.[207] This must have been highly innovative for the time, as the next notable girls' schools were only founded in the mid-1950s by Ṣadīqa Sharaf al-Dīn, the India-born wife of Muḥammad Naṣīf's son ʿUmar and, a year later, by the Turkish-raised wife of Prince (later King) Fayṣal.[208] During this period, and at least until the onset of state education for women in 1960–1, there seem to have been a significant number of private schools run by women in Jeddah, mostly Koranic schools, though they possibly also taught other subjects.[209] While these schools mostly catered to girls only, Ṭrābulsī and a number of other men remember attending a (probably mixed) Koranic school run by a woman.[210]

Cultural Gatherings

Relatively little is known about other social and cultural activities, such as salons, in Jeddah. For example, in Mecca scholars regularly met to discuss religious matters. In light of the descriptions of frequent visits to the houses where prominent pilgrims stayed, it is highly likely that such – perhaps more informal and perhaps also more seasonal – salons developed in Jeddah, in addition to the already mentioned informal circles of the *maqāʿid* and *marākiz*. They could consist of neighbours, but also of business partners and other friends, 'serving their mutual interests and deepening the bonds, friendship and brotherhood' among participants.[211] Certainly, there were circles of friends who made it into local histories, such as a youth group which met regularly near the barracks to discuss religious and literary matters.[212] The barracks

206 IOR, L/PS/12/2085, Saudi Arabia Annual Report 1933, p. 37.
207 Ṭrābulsī, *Jidda*, p. 330.
208 Interview, Dr. Fāṭima Naṣīf, Jeddah, May 16, 2015; and Rāniya Sulaymān Salāma, *Dār al-Ḥanān*, Jeddah 1429/2008–9.
209 While Ṭrābulsī, *Jidda*, pp. 432–5 and 441–2 is rich in names and details, the book unfortunately lacks dates and references.
210 Ibid., pp. 432–3.
211 Unpublished memoirs by Saʿīd b. Muḥammad b. ʿUbayd b. Zaqr, dated 1984, p.7.
212 al-Anṣārī, *Mawsūʿat tārīkh madīnat Jidda*, pp. 237–8.

might well have been a favourite spot not only due to the presence of a number of large trees offering shade and small fruit but also because the military band practised there each afternoon and thus provided some otherwise rare musical entertainment.[213]

One central personality of the twentieth century who probably maintained such a circle of his own in addition to hosting many visitors – Muslim and foreign alike – was Muḥammad Naṣīf.[214] Raised by his grandfather ʿUmar, Muḥammad Naṣīf was socialised into the role of a leading notable from his childhood. At the same time, he stood out for his passion for learning, assembling an impressive library over his lifetime. In keeping with the family tradition, mentioned briefly in Chapter 3, he offered wide-ranging hospitality to scholars and others passing through Jeddah. Muḥammad Rashīd Riḍā, visiting Jeddah during his 1916 pilgrimage, described the incessant stream of people coming to see him in Naṣīf's house and (probably often) engaging in learned debates.[215] Naṣīf himself was of *salafī* leanings, apparently through the intervention of the cloth merchant ʿAbd al-Qādir al-Tilmisānī. The latter had been influenced by the same Najdi scholar and merchant who had swayed ʿAwn al-Rafīq to destroy the tombs (cf. Chapter 6).[216] Like Tilmisānī, Naṣīf used his wide intellectual and political network in the Arab world, India and beyond to print books by scholars such as Ibn Taymiyya and Ibn Qayyim al-Jawziyya. However, Naṣīf's circle also comprised Western scholars and diplomats and thus became a meeting place of people of different interests and orientations. According to Philby, Naṣīf resented 'being called a Wahhabi but is nearer to that persuasion than to any other'.[217]

213 Unpublished memoirs by Saʿīd b. Muḥammad b. ʿUbayd b. Zaqr, dated 1984, p. 13.

214 If no other references are given, the following is based on the biography of Aḥmad and al-ʿAlawī, *Muḥammad Naṣīf*; as well as on Ulrike Freitag, 'Scholarly Exchange and Trade: Muḥammad Ḥusayn Naṣīf and His Letters to Christiaan Snouck Hurgronje' in M. Kemper and R. Elger (eds.), *The Piety of Learning: Islamic Studies in Honor of Stefan Reichmuth*, Islamic History and Civilization (Leiden and Boston: Brill, 2017), pp. 292–308.

215 Yūsuf Ībish (ed.), *Riḥalat al-Imām Muḥammad Rashīd Riḍā*, Jamaʿahā wa-ḥaqqaqahā Yūsuf Ībish (Beirut: al-Muʾassasa al-ʿArabiyya li-l-Dirāsāt wa-l-Nashr, 1971), pp. 85–7.

216 Bassām, *ʿUlamāʾ Najd*, Vol. 1, p. 439.

217 MECA, Philby Collection GB165–0229, 1/4/5/1, Philby Diary, part 1, November 29, 1924, p. 124.

Muḥammad Naṣīf was also a member of a rather singular club called *Nādī al-Ṣalāt* (prayer club), described by the Lebanese-American traveller Amin al-Rihani when he visited Jeddah in 1922, as a small group of seven men who met informally every evening at sunset on the beach. They first prayed the Maghrib prayer together, then played with an iron ball (the description insinuates a game similar to the French 'Boules') and finally discussed literature, poetry, and history. The aim was apparently a combination of bodily, intellectual, and spiritual exercise (*riyāḍa*). The group was made up of members of the Jeddah elite: its most senior member was Zaynal ʿAlī Riḍā, his brother, the kaymakam (Rihani calls him *muḥāfiẓ*) of Jeddah, al-Ḥājj ʿAbdallāh, Sulaymān Qābil, the head of the municipality, and his brother ʿAbd al-Qādir, as well as Muḥammad Ṭawīl, described as the banker of King Ḥusayn. The last, and perhaps a somewhat puzzling, member was al-Mullā Ḥusayn al-Shīrāzī, 'a scholar of the secrets of mechanics and Sufism, who repair(ed) the lamps and sewing machines and recite(d) the poetry of Jalāl al-Dīn al-Rūmī in Persian'.[218] al-Shīrāzī was possibly an acquaintance of the ʿAlī Riḍās who did not establish himself in Jeddah, which we know because the name does not appear on the (questionable) list of families of the old city nor seems to be mentioned in the volumes of biographies.[219] Thus, he was not a member of the notability, but perhaps a resident or itinerant Sufi and craftsman with an outstanding intellectual profile. Be that as it may, it is noteworthy that the group – with the exception of ʿAbd al-Qādir Qābil and al-Shīrāzī – formed the Jeddah nucleus of one of the very few political parties the Hijaz ever had, the National Party (see Chapter 7).

A Nascent Journalistic and Publishing Scene

Even in the early twentieth century, Muḥammad Naṣīf, with his distinctive interest in books and publishing, was an exception in Jeddah, and in the wider Hijaz. There was a modest trade in books, notably in Mecca, and a number of writers who authored manuscripts on various subjects. One notable example was the Shāfiʿī

[218] Amīn al-Rīḥānī, *Mulūk al-ʿarab*, vol. 1 (Beirut: Maṭābiʿ Ṣādir Rīḥānī, 1951), pp. 46–8, quote p. 48. On the basis of al-Rīḥānī's account, the club was also remembered in an article by ʿAbdallāh Salmān, 'Nādī al-Ṣalāt awwal nādin taʾsīsan fī 'l-Ḥijāz', *al-Nādī*, 1322, April 27, 2011.

[219] Maghribī, *Aʿlām al-Ḥijāz*; and Ṭrābulsī, *Jidda*, pp. 83–94.

mufti of Mecca, Aḥmad Zaynī Daḥlān, who is also one of the first Hijazi authors whose works were printed in the government press. This press had been installed during the reign of Osman Nūrī Pasha in 1883 to print the provincial yearbooks, but also books in the (religious) sciences. It published books in Arabic, Malay, and Ottoman.[220] The yearbooks ceased to appear in 1892–3, but it seems that the press continued to print some religious material. All of this is a far cry from the burgeoning publishing houses which existed in Cairo or Beirut in the late nineteenth century.[221]

After the Young Turk Revolution, the press published the bilingual official newspaper *Ḥijāz* (probably from November 1908 until 1916), as well as the first issues of the independent bilingual weekly *Shams al-Ḥaqīqa* (Sun of Truth).[222] After a few issues, a special publishing house was established for this newspaper, which vanished once more in 1909.[223] The publishing house was bought by a Meccan intellectual, who published educational material in addition to short-lived newspapers. The first printing house in Jeddah was established in May 1909 in order to publish the journal *al-Iṣlāḥ al-Ḥijāzī* (Hijazi Reform).

These newspapers mark the beginning of journalism in the Hijaz.[224] *Al-Ḥijāz* was an official newspaper which primarily published political news, but also, notably in the first issues, calls for reform of the Hijaz whilst sidelining controversial issues. *Shams al-Ḥaqīqa* seems to have been a clearly partisan organ of the Young Turk movement. As for the first newspaper in Jeddah, *al-Iṣlāḥ al-Ḥijāzī*, it was directed by Rāghib Muṣṭafā Tawakkul, a man of Syrian origin, while the editor was Adīb

220 Ochsenwald, *Religion, Society, and the State*, pp. 79–80, for more details on the early printing presses Muḥammad al-Shāmikh, *Nash'at al-ṣiḥāfa fī 'l-Mamlaka al-ʿArabiyya al-Saʿūdiyya* (n.p.: Dār al-ʿUlūm li-l-Tibāʿa wa-l-Nashr, 1982), pp. 11–31, for Daḥlān Freitag, *Der Orientalist und der Mufti*, p. 43. The following account mentions developments in Mecca as well as Jeddah due to their proximity but omits Medina because of the distance between the cities.

221 E.g. Hanssen, *Fin de Siècle Beirut*, p. 1, for a survey of the Arab press.

222 al-Shāmikh, *Nash'at al-ṣiḥāfa fī 'l-Mamlaka*, pp. 41–4 discusses possible other publication dates that were mentioned in earlier publications. The Arabic name was initially *al-Ḥijāz*, the article was dropped after the first issues, ibid., p. 44.

223 al-Shāmikh, pp. 18–19, 50–8.

224 In addition to the detailed account of al-Shāmikh, the brief account Bakrī Amīn, *al-Ḥaraka al-adabiyya fī 'l-Mamlaka al-ʿArabiyya al-Saʿūdiyya* (Beirut: Dār Ṣādir, 1392/1972), pp. 106–7 and the somewhat longer one by al-ʿAmūdī, *Min Tārīkhinā*, pp. 96–104 as well as Mansī, *Jidda fī 'l-tārikh al-ḥadīth*, pp. 258–61 have been consulted for the following account of the development of the press.

Dā'ūd Harārī, whose origins were Lebanese. According to memories of Muḥammad Naṣīf, this short-lived paper was supportive of Sharif Ḥusayn, quite in contrast to the Meccan *al-Iṣlāḥ al-Ḥijāzī*.[225] Another Arab in Jeddah by the name of Aḥmad Rāfat al-Iskandarānī, probably of Egyptian origin, tried his hand at a daily called *Ṣafā' al-Ḥijāz* (Clarity or Purity of Hijaz) in the summer of 1909, although this newspaper disappeared even more quickly than *al-Iṣlāḥ al-Ḥijāzī*.

Little is known about the impact of these newspapers, and their quite rapid disappearance (with the exception of the official one) points to financial difficulties quite typical of this period. In addition, the period of freedom of the press which started with the Young Turk Revolution was brief, with a law in July 1909 reintroducing much tighter controls.[226] Given the limited availability of copies of these newspapers and the absence of a thorough analysis of their contents, neither the reasons for their disappearance nor their impact on local society can really be judged.

During the Sharifian rule, the newspaper *Ḥijāz*, which closed shortly before the withdrawal of Ottoman forces from Mecca, was revived as a more or less official publication named *al-Qibla* in August 1916.[227] Its first editor was the Syrian journalist Muḥibb al-Dīn al-Khaṭīb (1886–1969) who had already a reputation as an Arab and Islamic activist and was drawn to Mecca to support Sharif Ḥusayn.[228] The newspaper targeted a broader Hijazi audience and can thus be seen as a kind of (proto-)national newspaper. Meanwhile, an Arab language newspaper with the name *al-Ḥijāz* appeared in Medina until 1918, possibly as a kind of successor to the earlier Meccan newspaper.[229]

When the National Party, many of whose leaders had been members of *Nādī al-Ṣalāt* discussed in the previous section, forced Ḥusayn's abduction, those within it who were loyal to King ʿAlī founded *Barīd al-Ḥijāz* (Hijaz Post) as its mouthpiece. Muḥammad

225 al-Shāmikh, *Nash'at al-ṣiḥāfa fī 'l-Mamlaka* pp. 60–3.

226 This is discussed with regard to Damascus by Grallert, *To Whom Belong the Streets?*, pp. 59–63.

227 On this issue al-Shāmikh, *Nash'at al-ṣiḥāfa fī 'l-Mamlaka* pp. 105–6. The name alludes to the direction of the Kaʿba, towards which Muslims pray.

228 On al-Khaṭīb's career, see Khayr al-Dīn al-Ziriklī, *al-Aʿlām: Qāmūs tarājim li-ashhar al-rijāl wa-l-nisā' min al-ʿarab wa-l-mustaʿribīn wa-l-mustashriqīn*, 15th edn. (Beirut: Dār al-ʿIlm li-l-Malāyīn, 2002) vol. 5, p. 282, on the sequence of editors al-Shāmikh, *Nash'at al-ṣiḥāfa fī 'l-Mamlaka*, pp. 107–8.

229 al-Shāmikh, *Nash'at al-ṣiḥāfa fī 'l-Mamlaka*, p. 117.

Ṣāliḥ Naṣīf, who during these months also became mayor, undertook the publication, with a former editor of *al-Qibla*, al-Ṭayyib al-Sāsī, later joining as editor.[230]

With the Saudi takeover, *al-Qibla* was succeeded by *Umm al-Qurā* (Mother of Villages, i.e. Mecca) as the new official weekly which exists to this day.[231] Besides featuring news about international, Saudi and local affairs, it became an important outlet for a variety of cultural themes, featuring articles by leading local intellectuals and writers until the emergence of more specialised publications from the late 1930s onwards. This notwithstanding, its editors saw their role as educators of the nation.

In April 1932 Muḥammad Ṣāliḥ Naṣīf opened *Ṣawt al-Ḥijāz* (Voice of Hijaz) in Mecca as a newspaper with a focus on cultural and literary topics.[232] Its aim was to provide the newly educated youth with an outlet for their intellectual output, as well as a source for further inspiration. The idea to establish the weekly (from 1939 onwards bi-weekly), Naṣīf stated in a later interview, developed in 'private and public gatherings (*majālis*)' and with the aim to serve the cultural advancement of the nation.[233] Indeed, the majority of articles, particularly during the first years, were authored by the emerging intellectual elite and thus reflect local debates more closely than the educational contributions in *Umm al-Qurā*. With its further establishment and changing editors, this orientation lessened somewhat even if the newspaper continued to circulate mainly within the rather limited educated circles, something which caused continuous financial problems.[234] The newspaper was printed in the former press of *al-Manār*, which had been imported from Cairo by Naṣīf in 1931–2 for *al-Maṭbaʿa al-Salafiyya*. His initial aim was to publish *salafī* texts – which indicates a close link to the intellectual project of his cousin Muḥammad Ḥusayn Naṣīf.[235]

230 Muḥammad al-Qashʿamī, *Muḥammad Ṣāliḥ Naṣīf: al-rāʾid al-ṣahafī* (Jeddah: al-Nādī al-Adabī al-Thaqāfī bi-Jidda, 2010), pp. 17–21.
231 al-Shāmikh, *Nashʾat al-ṣiḥāfa fī ʾl-Mamlaka*, pp. 149–52, Nallino, *Raccolta di Scritti*, p. 138.
232 al-Shāmikh, *Nashʾat al-ṣiḥāfa fī ʾl-Mamlaka*, pp. 153–62; al-Qashʿamī, *Muḥammad Ṣāliḥ Naṣīf*, pp. 43–115. In 1935, the ownership structure changed, al-Shāmikh, p. 155; c.f. Nallino, *Raccolta di Scritti*, p. 138.
233 al-Shāmikh, *Nashʾat al-ṣiḥāfa fī ʾl-Mamlaka*, p. 154.
234 al-Shāmikh, pp. 159–60.
235 al-Qashʿamī, *Muḥammad Ṣāliḥ Naṣīf*, pp. 43–4.

From 1937 onwards the literary and cultural field was further enriched by *al-Manhal* (The Spring), a journal more closely resembling a cultural magazine than a newspaper, established by the journalist and historian ʿAbd al-Qaddūs al-Anṣārī in Medina. Besides publishing articles about history and literary developments, the journal also published literary works such as short stories, as well as translations.[236] For a short period (1938–41), an Islamic journal called *al-Nidāʾ al-Islāmī* (Islamic Call), published in Arabic and Malay, appeared in Mecca.[237]

The Second World War with its economic constraints caused the government to close all newspapers, with the exception of *Umm al-Qurā*, in July 1941 and elevated *Umm al-Qurā* to its previous role as an official newspaper. *Ṣawt al-Ḥijāz* resumed publication in 1946 as *al-Bilād al-Saʿūdiyya* (Saudi Lands), eventually loosened its literary orientation.

The newspapers reflect an emerging sphere in which debates left the cultural gatherings and were increasingly transported into a Hijazi and, after 1925, wider Saudi sphere. In spite of censorship, their beginnings as official mouthpieces and the involvement of journalists from other parts of the Arab (and Muslim) world, particularly in the initial phases, the press in the interwar period reflects the evolving local intellectual sphere. Many of the leading writers and historians of the time were also journalists, and thus the press gives some impression of the wider cultural scene. Thus, many of the notable poets, authors and learned people discussed by Nallino in 1939 also feature among the journalists, editors, and educators of the Hijaz.[238] Many of them, such as al-Anṣārī, al-Sibāʿī and al-Kutubī, also wrote histories or memoirs which in turn have informed this work. While a detailed newspaper analysis was beyond the scope of this book, the debates provide an interesting reflection of the evolving socio-cultural concerns. One issue pertaining to youth and changing past-times in the urban context stands out in particular and will therefore be explored in the next section.

The Emergence of Football

In the mid-1920s a new game began to garner the attention of the Jeddah male youth. During about 1925 football was introduced by

[236] al-Shāmikh, *Nashʾat al-ṣiḥāfa fī ʾl-Mamlaka*, pp. 170–6.
[237] Ibid., pp. 176–9. [238] Nallino, *Raccolta di Scritti*, pp. 132–7.

young Malay and Indonesian pilgrims. In 1926 or 1927, their clubs obtained a special license in Mecca. The weekly *Umm al-Qurā* defended the game, the popularity of which spread very rapidly, but regretted the use of foreign (*ʿajamī*) terms. One commentator wrote

> I heard recently that some writers in Jeddah Arabized all its terms and use them. I would like to thank these people for this sentiment ... and the feelings that motivated them to do this .... I call on the Hijazis to care as much as their brothers, and to use the Arab terms ... by which they will serve their language and homeland. I also ask the newspaper *Ṣawt al-Ḥijāz* in which we have place many hopes (may God realised them) to obtain these terms and publish them, as it has a section devoted to sports.[239]

It seems that almost in parallel, namely in summer 1926, Muḥammad (ʿAlī) Riḍāʾ founded the Hijazi Sports Club (al-Ḥijāz al-Riyāḍī). Within a few weeks, however, its members disagreed on whether its memberships should be open to all social groups. Hence, in January 1927 a group (itself consisting of members of wealthy families) split off and founded the Union Club (*Nādī al-Ittiḥād*), which is now the oldest football club in Saudi Arabia. Their aim was to widen the game beyond elite circles[240]

Both clubs apparently practised outside of the city walls.[241] In 1931 the first proper match between the two was held, with enthusiastic support by young men of the different quarters.[242] In 1935/36 a third club, al-Hilāl al-Baḥrī, was founded, which counted locals, as well as resident Indonesians and Adenis among its members.[243] It seems that football had quickly become a very popular pastime for young men, to some extent following in the tradition of neighbourhood groups competing with each other, like in the *mizmār*.

[239] *Umm al-Qurā*, 387, May 13, 1932, p. 4.

[240] This account is based on the club's history and will hence be probably controversial, Yūsuf al- Saʿātī Sayyid and Bā ʿĪsā Ṣāliḥ Amīn, *Nādī al-Ittiḥād: Iṣdār khāṣṣ bi-munāsabat murūr tisʿīna ʿāman ʿalā al-taʾsīs* (Jeddah: Mansour Al Zamil, 1438/2017), pp. 14–15. For a slightly different account see *Wikipedia*. 'Al-Ittihad Club (Jeddah)'. https://en.wikipedia.org/wiki/Al-Ittihad_Club_(Jeddah) (accessed October 10, 2019).

[241] al-Anṣārī, *Mawsūʿat tārīkh madīnat Jidda*, p. 267; and Ṭrābulsī, *Jidda*, p. 503.

[242] Ṭrābulsī, *Jidda*, p. 503; cf. Sayyid and Amīn, *Nādī al-Ittiḥād*.

[243] al-Anṣārī, *Mawsūʿat tārīkh madīnat Jidda*, p. 268. According to Sayyid and Amīn, *Nādī al-Ittiḥād*, p. 32, this occurred already in 1931. The name could be rendered as 'Half-Moon of the Sea'.

An enthusiastic local historian also recalls the first 'international' matches against members of foreign groups like the Indonesians living in Jeddah, as well as the attempt to introduce paid tickets for matches in May 1932. This move failed because the enthusiastic crowds were unable to pay for tickets but insisted on watching the matches.[244] By June 1932 *Umm al-Qurā* listed eight football clubs. The author of the earlier article felt the urge to defend the sport against attacks from both *Ṣawt al-Ḥijāz* and people who had written to him complaining of a growing obsession with the sport, causing craftsmen and even merchants to neglect their work in order to attend matches. He concluded that while he still does not recommend a ban on the sport, he suggests to take it less seriously, notably because of the hate it created between adherents of different teams.[245] Perhaps the article praising the virtues of and need for hard work in the next issue was an indirect continuation of this theme, without, however, mentioning any connection to the disturbances allegedly caused by the new craze.[246]

The enthusiastic crowds soon resorted to early incidences of hooliganism, with players attacking each other. Overly excited spectators are reported to have suffered heart attacks.[247] It thus does not come as a surprise that the authorities became worried. In summer of 1932 the British reported:

> It is not the football itself which has fallen under suspicion, but the fact that it brings young men together in clubs. One of those interested explained gravely about the end of June that the King, deferring to the views of a liberal entourage, had not prohibited the game, but that it was uncertain whether those who persisted in playing it might not be arrested.[248]

Two years later the game was banned in Jeddah (but not in Mecca), where, a few months later, there was even talk of arranging a match between young sportive Iraqi pilgrims and locals.[249] A possible reason for the ban might have been a competition for (and possible confrontations over) a gold-plated medal between four Jeddah clubs, namely al-Ittiḥād, the newly founded al-Hilāl al-Baḥrī, al-Mukhtalaṭ

244 Ṭrābulsī, *Jidda*, pp. 504–6.
245 *Umm al-Qurā*, 392, June 17, 1932, p. 4. The newpaper *Ṣawt al-Ḥijāz* ran almost daily articles on football and sports until 1935.
246 *Umm al-Qurā*, 393, June 24, 1932, p. 4. 247 Ṭrābulsī, *Jidda*, pp. 507–8.
248 IOR, L/PS/12/2073, Jedda Report, May–June 1932, pp. 2–3.
249 IOR, L/PS/12/2073, Jedda Report, July 1934, March 1935, p. 2.

('the mixed one'), and Shabāb Indūnīsya (Indonesian Youth), which could have aroused protest by Wahhabi scholars. At any rate, the history of al-Ittiḥād only mentions one further match thereafter, which took place in 1935 (against the crew of a British steamer called the 'Hastings').[250]

In 1939 there was still a ban on football in Jeddah, in spite of the local press arguing that regular exercise helped to keep young men away from mischief.[251] Indeed, the ban could not stop the ever-growing popularity of the sport. ʿAbdallāh Manāʿ recalls, unfortunately without giving dates nor his own age, how boys began to roam the city in search of open spaces to play football. They probably had to frequently change spaces as a result of the official prohibition.[252] Football also became a sport played in schools and permitted outside of the town's confines.[253] However, larger matches seem to have been halted until 1947.[254]

This early history of the football clubs is interesting as it sheds light on issues otherwise not addressed much in the local history, namely social distinction and the issue of the integration of outsiders. The game – as manifested in terms of formal organisation – started as one of the sons of the elite (*abnāʾ al-dhawāt*) although it opened up quickly.[255] Thus, among the members of the first 'administrative committee' of al-Ittiḥād, only the name of ʿUthmān Bā Nāja stands out as a member of one of the richest families, while al-Riyāḍī was sponsored by Naṣīf and ʿAlī Riḍā. Nevertheless, the social history of Saudi football would require a more detailed prosopographic study of both clubs, sponsors as well as players, for which the currently available data is insufficient.[256]

It is furthermore interesting to see that some of the teams and their players were mostly or exclusively local residents, while two of the teams of the 1933 competition were characterised as 'mixed' and

[250] Sayyid and Amīn, *Nādī al-Ittiḥād*, pp. 33–5.
[251] TNA, FO 371/ 23271, Jedda Report, August 1939, p. 2; and *Ṣawt al-Ḥijāz*, August 30, 1939.
[252] Manāʿ, *Baʿḍ al-Ayyām Baʿḍ al-layālī*, pp. 36–44.
[253] Ṭrābulsī, *Jidda*, p. 508; and al-Anṣārī, *Mawsūʿat tārīkh madīnat Jidda*, p. 269.
[254] Sayyid and Amīn, *Nādī al-Ittiḥād*, p. 35. [255] Ibid., p. 14.
[256] al-Anṣārī, *Mawsūʿat tārīkh madīnat Jidda*, p. 267; and Sayyid and Amīn, *Nādī al-Ittiḥād*, p. 23. While there is fairly detailed information on al-Ittiḥād, it is far patchier for Riyāḍī which forbids a proper comparison.

'Indonesian'. This is not surprising, given that the sport was introduced by pilgrims, and it might be that the Indonesian team was among the pilgrim groups that had arrived a bit early for the hajj. After all, the tournament took place at the very end of *Shawwāl*, i.e. just over a month from the actual pilgrimage. The names could, however, also point to a distinction made between in- and outsiders, i.e. long-term and short-term residents.

6 *The Economic Lifelines of Jeddah: Trade and Pilgrimage*

As has been shown in Chapter 2, Jeddah's very existence was closely tied to the Mecca pilgrimage and to trade. These two activities were closely interlinked with regard to the seasonal rhythm of maritime travel and concerning the logistic needs of providing food for a large number of visitors in an environment that did not produce much locally. The growth and development of international trade correlated with the desire of the emirs as well as empires and states to control this trade and raise customs.

This chapter intends to examine these two economic foundations of Jeddah, which fundamentally linked it to the outside world. Both trade and, to an even greater extent, the pilgrimage have been the subjects of detailed studies before, notably, for the period under investigation, the one by Pétriat.[1] They will hence only be discussed briefly while the focus of the chapter will be on the merchants (the *tujjār*) and pilgrims' guides (called *mutawwif* in Mecca, *wakīl* (pl. *wukalā'*) in Jeddah and *nā'ib* in Medina), who constituted the economic elite of Jeddah. Economic life in Jeddah cannot, of course, be reduced to the said groups – boatmen, porters and water carriers, builders, cooks and bakers, some of whom have been mentioned in the preceding chapters, formed part of a wider economic and social fabric that cannot be explored in exhaustive detail. Rather, the overall aim of the chapter is to gain a better understanding of how relations between Jeddah and its surroundings were organised and changed throughout the nineteenth and the first half of the twentieth century.

Trade and Transport

Major Trends in the Period 1850–1950

Ochsenwald's survey of trade in the period from 1840 to 1908 discusses a number of the source-related problems of documenting

[1] Pétriat, *Le Négoce des Lieux Saints.*

Jeddah's trade. These are partly linked to the figures itself, which are not equally available for the entire period, and partly to the fact that only goods were registered for which customs had to be paid. With the opening of trade in the Red Sea, and hence Jeddah's loss of the customs monopoly, this probably excluded a growing number of goods imported by sea, which came in addition to possible under-reporting and, of course, smuggling. Nor does the slave trade, discussed in Chapter 3, appear as part of the trade records. Additionally, land trade was never systematically recorded.[2]

For the mid-1850s Pétriat has shown that the main ports with which Jeddah traded were Calcutta, Bombay, Aden, and Suez, as well as, regionally, Suakin and Hodeida, and, in Southeast Asia, Singapore. The main imports (in terms of value) were coffee, cotton materials, rice, grain, sugar, carpets, and shawls, as well as spices and wood. Coffee and spices were largely transhipped, together with the regional products of hides, gum, Arabic henna, incense, and salt. Most of the rice, grains, and sugar was intended for local and regional consumption, to a large extent the provisioning of the pilgrims, something which was also true of the smaller scale imports of dates and butter (probably ghee). About half of the cloth imports remained in the Hijaz.[3] Until the crisis of 1882, the value of (registered) re-exports by sea was about half of the value of overall imports, which gives at least a vague idea of the importance of Jeddah as a trade emporium.[4] Through these figures, one can discern a complicated web of local and international trade which varied depending on the prices of commodities and currencies.[5] Thus, Suez needs to be taken as a cypher for all maritime trade from the Mediterranean as well as northern Europe,

2 Ochsenwald, *The Commercial History*, here p. 63. A more detailed study, based solely on (sadly very poorly referenced) British sources and literature is al-Shaʿfī, *al-Tijāra al-khārijiyya li-madīnat Jidda*.

3 Pétriat, *Le Négoce des Lieux Saints*, pp. 32–40. For a more detailed account; cf. al-Muʿabbadī, *al-Nashāṭ al-tijārī li-minā' Jidda*, pp. 200–13. For a contemporary list of merchandise, see Hamilton, *Sinai, The Hedjaz, and Soudan*, p. 61.

4 Ochsenwald, *The Commercial History*, p. 64; and Pétriat, *Le Négoce des Lieux Saints*, pp. 37–8. For 1857, see also TNA, FO 685/1, Stanley (Alexandria) to FO, May 3, 1859, and Stanley to Consul Cairo, February 22, 1861. This seems more realistic than the (half year) figures cited by Pétriat for 1854, which indicate a perfect balance of trade, pp. 35–6.

5 On these issues; cf. Ochsenwald, *The Commercial History*, pp. 63–70.

while Aden was effectively an entrepôt through which goods arrived from East Africa, the Gulf, as well as India and further east.

The claims for compensation raised in the aftermath of the massacre of 1858 probably give the best insight into how the wide-ranging trade of the mid-nineteenth century could be organised. Although the following case is somewhat atypical in that it describes one of the Greek merchant houses which, at this time, had expanded in the Red Sea and did not remain in Jeddah for long after the 1858 attacks, it is worthwhile to briefly consider it. Burton mentioned encountering a certain Khawajah Sower, characterised as 'a Greek' and a M. Anton ('a Christian from Baghdad') and others, adding that many of these died in 1858.[6] The link to the date of the massacre of 1858 allows us to identify Sower as Sava Moscoudi, head of a merchant house operating out of Lemnos and acting as the Jeddah representative of Toma Myrialaki and A. D'Antonio and Company, who had their headquarters at Cairo. The organisational diagram of this conglomerate in Table 6.1 shows a network which was centred on Cairo. It was connected to Istanbul, Marseilles, and Liverpool, as well as to Calcutta via Suez. Its Jeddah branch, run by Sava Moscoudi, who was the foremost European merchant of Jeddah, traded with Mecca and Bethlehem, served the port of Aden and further onwards to Muscat and Bombay. Yet another agent in Hodeida was active in (different) Red Sea ports as well as Basra and, finally, there was a trade associate in the Sudan at Takka, between Khartum and the Red Sea.[7] By 1856 this trade network was said to control about one quarter of the Red Sea trade, thus having obtained a significant share in a trade conducted predominantly by Muslim merchants as recently as a few decades earlier.[8] Significantly, the powerful Hadhrami merchants of Jeddah who, according to Didier, were controlling almost all the trade of Jeddah (in contrast to some of the

[6] Burton, *Personal Narrative of a Pilgrimage*, p. 272.

[7] Takka is the old name for the region around Kassala, and possibly designates the present city. It is mentioned in Hermann von Pückler-Muskau, *Aus Mehemed Alis Reich: Ägypten und der Sudan um 1840*, vol. 3 (Stuttgart: Hallberger'sche Verlagshandlung, 1844) p. 298. According to this account, Takka was larger than Khartum. I thank Muhammad Elfateh for this reference.

[8] TNA, FO 195/579, Jeddah claims 1858, A. Inclosure on Messrs Myrialaki A. d'Antonio and Company, August 12, 1858; cf. Ochsenwald, *The Jidda Massacre*, here p. 315; and Pétriat, *Le Négoce des Lieux Saints*, pp. 56–60. For more on the firm of Sava Moscoudi; cf. Didier, *Séjour chez le Grand-Chérif*, pp. 160–1.

Table 6.1 *Organisational chart of Myrialaki and A. D'Antonio and company.*

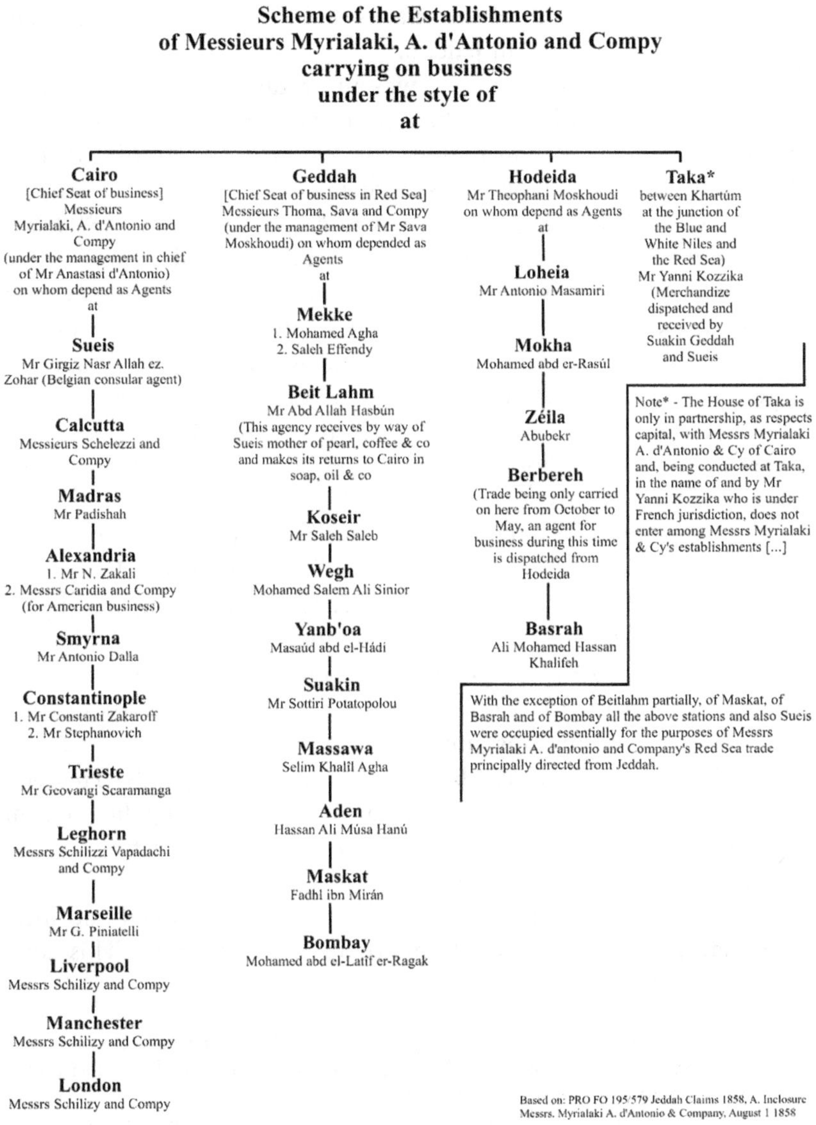

Drawn by Noël van den Heuvel based on TNA, FO 195/579, Jeddah claims 1858, A. Inclosure on Messrs Myrialaki A. d'Antonio and Company, August 12, 1858.

earlier-quoted sources that saw the Indians in this role) attempted to boycott the house of Sava Moscoudi, which shows the tensions provoked by the rise of this new force in local trade.[9] As has been discussed in Chapter 2, one result of the attacks of 1858 was to stop significant future Greek investment in Jeddah.

Ochsenwald argues that there was an overall growth of imports, as well as exports, until 1881. Thus, contrary to British predictions, the Suez Canal did not immediately impact on the trade of Jeddah.[10] However, from 1882 onwards both imports and exports dropped dramatically. While imports started to recover slowly in 1890, and then more significantly around 1903, international exports never quite picked up again. This was partly linked to a global depression, partly to local events, as discussed in Chapter 2.[11] One aspect of the trade crisis was that Suez, Bombay, and Aden slowly took over the international *entrepôt* function of Jeddah. This is reflected in an 1894 British trade report which noted that many British goods now reached Jeddah via Port Said, Suez, or Bombay, rather than being shipped there directly.[12]

The fairly brief recovery was followed by the prolonged crisis of World War I and the consecutive conflict between the Emir (later King) of the Hijaz and Ibn Saʿūd. Merchants were hampered by the British sea blockade of the Ottoman Empire (until 1916), limitations on Indian exports by the colonial government and the closure of the Suez Canal. From 1916 onwards, the Sharifs raised levies on their income, and, perhaps most importantly, created a government agency controlling prices and distribution of all imported goods. This does not preclude that some were able to profit from the smuggling of arms and other goods, as well as the rise in prices for foodstuffs. Pétriat has shown that, in spite of significant losses, Jeddah merchants managed to keep afloat not least by mobilising their regional and international networks and long-term credits without return. This could

[9] Didier, *Séjour chez le Grand-Chérif*, p. 161; and Pétriat, *Le Négoce des Lieux Saints*, pp. 73–4. For a comparable Greek network in the Mediterranean, cf Toksöz, *Nomads, Migrants and Cotton* , pp. 106–8.

[10] TNA, FO 78/2194, Consul Raby (Bath) to Foreign Office, February 13, 1871; and Ochsenwald, *The Commercial History*, p. 64.

[11] On the crisis of the 1880s and 1890s and the subsequent recovery, see Pétriat, *Le Négoce des Lieux Saints*, pp. 173–94.

[12] Foreign Office, *Foreign Office 1984*, p. 2.

even involve periods without profits during which they managed to preserve their networks. Variations in regional economies, such as very profitable trading environments in Cairo and Basra during the last war years, further contributed to their ability to recover after the war, using methods similar to those of Western merchants during the same period.[13]

King Husayn continued the earlier practice of the emirs to derive considerable income from levies on pilgrims' services, derived mostly from the pilgrims' guides and transport business.[14] He also increased extractions from merchants and combined this with a cut in subsidies for the tribes in the areas surrounding the holy cities. Consequently, banditry by the tribes increased and resulted in the almost complete standstill of trade. The population of Medina, already reduced by the famine of World War I, declined further, and due to the insecurity, Hashemite officials withdrew from secondary cities and ports.[15] The then British consul, Bullard, attributed the economic troubles to 'the diminished demand from Medina, owing to the disturbed state of the roads, but mainly to the King's action in messing about with prices and above all with rates of exchange'.[16]

With the integration into the emerging Saudi state, levies on the pilgrimage became the largest source of income for the Saudi state. Ibn Saʿūd also did his best to pressurise merchants into support for his ventures, thereby in some ways continuing Ottoman and Sharifian practices 'as a bad payer [of debts] but a good client'.[17] Merchants had to balance their need to cultivate good contacts with the new ruler, for example by participating in an abortive state company that was to organise motor transport of pilgrims to Mecca, while dodging demands to provide government loans where possible.[18] Nevertheless, the resumption of the pilgrimage, as well as Saudi government

[13] Pétriat, *Le Négoce des Lieux Saints*, pp. 208–18. I thank Philippe Pétriat for pointing me to the different rhythms of trade and the advantages this could have for merchants.

[14] On his ways of revenue extraction, see Teitelbaum, *The Rise and Fall*, pp. 152–82.

[15] Chaudhry, *The Price of Wealth*, pp. 56–7.

[16] St. Antony's College Oxford, MECA, Ryan papers GB165-0248, VI/5, Sir Reader Bullard, July 20, 1924, p. 3.

[17] Pétriat, *Le Négoce des Lieux Saints*, p. 325; cf. pp 326–9.

[18] Jarman (ed.), *The Jedda Diaries*; Jeddah Report, February 1–29, 1928, vol. 3, p. 8; and Ibid., August 1–31, 1929, vol. 3, p. 83.

contracts, meant that the Jeddah merchants gained a respite before the world economic crisis hit Saudi Arabia with a vengeance. Although Chaudhry rightly argues that, during this period, different communities within the new country were hit differentially due to the lack of overarching institutions, both the Hijaz and the national government were clearly affected by the crisis.[19] The number of pilgrims had returned to an average of 100,000, not least because of the quick restoration of security after 1925–6. In 1930 pilgrim numbers dropped quite dramatically to around 40,000 and stagnated at that level during the following two years. Financial speculations exacerbated the crisis but, in 1933, Ibn Saʿūd decided to attempt to attract Indian capital to revive plans of building a railway between Mecca and Jeddah to further ease the pilgrimage and thus increase its reach.[20] As shown in Chapter 2, matters only significantly changed with the onset of the commercial extraction of oil. Due to the economic decline caused by World War II, its real impact on economic development coincides with the end of the period under investigation here.[21]

Revolutionising Transport

During the period under discussion, three transport revolutions occurred. The first was the introduction of steam shipping (cf. Chapter 2). While Jeddah merchants, some of whom owned significant numbers of dhows, initially invested in steamers, it seems that they could not, in the medium and long term, compete sufficiently to remain in this business. The competition of the large companies, mostly British or British-Indian, but also European and Egyptian, seems to have deterred local merchants from investing significantly into this new means of transport.[22] Although a few of the leading merchants, such as Bā ʿIshn and Muḥammad Fāḍil ʿArab, acquired small steamers, most local merchants continued to use sailboats for re-exports in the Red Sea area (which for some time expanded). From the 1870s onward they relied

19 Chaudhry, *The Price of Wealth*, p. 6.
20 St. Antony's College Oxford, MECA, Philby Collection GB 165–0229, 5/2/11/7 Economics in Arabia, Jeddah, March 8, 1933. On the commercial crisis, see Pétriat, *Le Négoce des Lieux Saints*, pp. 335–40.
21 Vassiliev, *History of Saudi Arabia*, pp. 317–20.
22 For a detailed analysis of the different countries' share in steam transport, see al-Shaʿfī, *al-Tijāra al-khārijiyya li-madīnat Jidda*, pp. 43–84.

instead on transport agencies offering steam service, even, to an increasing extent, for the Red Sea trade.[23] A notable exception was the business of the Mecca-based Hadhrami merchant, ʿAbd al-Raḥmān al-Saqqāf who had established a branch office in Singapore in 1848. His descendants managed to maintain a share in the important business of transporting pilgrims between Southeast Asia and the Hijaz until some time before the onset of World War I.[24] Others, like the company of Ḥajjī Zaynal ʿAlī Riḍā, acted as local agents of steam companies, in their case the Bombay and Persia Steam Navigation Company, and were also willing to make investments in a coal depot.[25]

From the 1860s onward there were plans to improve the connection between Jeddah and Mecca. The initial idea was to introduce animal-drawn carts, later the abortive railway line.[26] While both would have improved the transport of goods and pilgrims, they would also have completely transformed not only the urban geography and economy but also posed a serious challenge to the Bedouin and their transport and trade business. Some Bedouin, fearing for their livelihoods and resenting increased control, had already sabotaged both the telegraph and, more crucial in regard to transportation, the Hijaz railway line. Furthermore, as outlined earlier, the Emir of Mecca was not happy about an increased Ottoman influence in his realms.

It is thus not surprising that the introduction of motorised transport was a slow affair. Initially, cars were only used from 1909 onwards for the mail service between Mecca, Jeddah, and Ṭāʾif, to which must be added a very small number of privately owned vehicles.[27] A steam

23 al-Anṣārī, *Mawsūʿat tārīkh madīnat Jidda*, pp. 224–5; Pétriat, *Le Négoce des Lieux Saints*, pp. 77, 126, 140–51, 177–9; and al-Muʿabbadī, *al-Nashāṭ al-tijārī li-mināʾ Jidda*, p. 223.

24 William Clarence-Smith, 'Hadhrami Entrepreneurs in the Malay World, c. 1750 to c. 1940' in Ulrike Freitag and W. G. Clarence-Smith (eds.), *Hadhrami Traders, Scholars, and Statesmen in the Indian Ocean, 1750s–1960s* (Leiden, New York, and Köln: Brill Academic Publishers, 1997), pp. 297–314, here pp. 300–1; cf. Pétriat, *Le Négoce des Lieux Saints*, pp. 148–9.

25 TNA, FO 195/2198, Devey to Amb. Const. August 4, 1905 and November 6, 1905.

26 MAE, CADN, Article 3 (2MI3228), 'Mesures Prises Dans les Villes Saintes pour le Pélerinage de Cette Année. Améliorations obtenues depuis 1867, dans le Hedjaz, et surtout à Djeddah', in Dubreuil to MAE, March 6, 1869; and Mehmed Şakir, *Hicaz'ın ahvâl-i umûmiye-i sıhhiye ve ıslahât-ı hazırasına dair bazı müşahedat ve mülahazât-ı bendeğami hâvi bir layiha-i tıbbiye* (Constantinople, 1303/ 1890).

27 BOA, DH.MUI 28/-2-2, Za 11, 1327/November 24, 1909.

omnibus, imported in 1911 to shuttle passengers between Mecca and ʿArafāt, arrived in a state of irreversible disrepair.[28] The conflict between the Sharifian government and Ibn Sa'ūd complicated transport between Mecca and Jeddah anyhow, so that motorised transport only seriously commenced from 1926 onwards, when Philby obtained the permission to import Ford cars.[29] Ibn Saʿūd seems to have briefly attempted to protect caravan transport by not allowing pilgrims to travel by car.[30] This did not, however, apply to private vehicles, and the development of motorised transport could not be halted. Only three years later one third of all pilgrims used buses and cars to travel between Mecca and Medina. The government attempted to organise the aforementioned joint stock company to syphon off profits, causing frictions with local merchants who saw their own interests endangered. The scheme did not survive for long which illustrates the strength of local capital vis-à-vis the state as long as the merchants cooperated with one another.[31] In spite of local struggles over control, the number of cars and buses increased quickly. Furthermore, lorries, designed to transport goods, were also imported.[32] By 1947 there were still official lists giving the prices for camel hire during the pilgrimage, but their share in the overall transport business had dwindled to insignificance.[33] This caused problems with the Bedouin in the surrounding areas. In 1930 one British report described the Bedouin as 'a depressed and discontented class.'[34] There were some instances of protest, for example, in 1930, all cars that had been designated for the transport of pilgrims were turned over and torched.[35] In contrast to earlier periods, however, Ibn Saʿūd mostly managed to impose control due to his

28 TNA, FO 195/2376, Consul Jeddah to Amb. Const., March 8, 1911.

29 Ṣabrī al-Ḥamdī, *Ḥarakat al-taḥdīth fī 'l-Mamlaka al-ʿArabiyya al-Saʿūdiyya 1926-1953* (Beirut: Arab Scientific Publishers, 1435/2014), p. 112. On the motorisation of the pilgrimage in Saudi times; cf. Chantre, *Pèlerinages d'Empire*, pp. 266–69.

30 MECA, Philby Collection, GB 165–0229, 1/4/5/1, Philby Diary Part 1, p. 366.

31 *Umm al-Qurā*, 151, October 4, 1927; Jarman (ed.), *The Jedda Diaries*, vol. 3, p. 8; Jeddah Report, February 1928, p. 82; and Jeddah Report, July 1929, p. 80. A similar experiment in terms of a single company for the transport of all pilgrims was conducted in 1946, IPA 9782/02, Rabīʿ al-awwal 16, 1365 (February 18, 1946).

32 Jarman (ed.), *The Jedda Diaries*, vol. 4, Jedda Report, September 1937, p. 213.

33 Chiffoleau, *Le Voyage à la Mecque*, p. 77.

34 IOR, L/PS/12/2085, Hejaz-Nejd Annual Report 1930, p. 49.

35 Jarman (ed.), *The Jedda Diaries*, vol. 3, Jeddah Report, May 1930, p. 130.

Figure 6.1 Office in the Bin Ḥimd house.
Photograph by the author, 2017

alliance with many tribal leaders, and thus avoid the return of the insecurity that had riddled the routes under Ottoman and Sharifian rule.[36] A proper road to Mecca, financed by the *awqāf al-Ḥaramayn*, was only completed in 1938 by the Bechtel Corporation.[37] Incidentally, these changes also spelt the end of the guild of the *mukharrijūn* who had been organising transport by caravan for merchants and pilgrims' guides. Merchant caravans, one of which is depicted in Figure 6.2, continued to play a role in the trade between the Hijaz, Najd, and the Gulf throughout the 1930s and 1940s.

Finally, air traffic made its appearance at the very end of the period under discussion. In October 1930 a school of aviation was founded in Jeddah and five years later ten students were sent to Italy to train as pilots. In 1936 Egypt Air offered to transport pilgrims to Jeddah, while an internal connection between Jeddah and Medina was opened in

[36] An interesting question which cannot be explored further here is the extent to which these economic transformations also fed into the tribal unrest of the period 1927–30, often summarised as Ikhwān uprisings; cf. Kostiner, *The Making of Saudi Arabia*, pp. 117–40.

[37] al-Ḥamdī, *Ḥarakat al-taḥdīth fī 'l-Mamlaka*, p. 112.

Figure 6.2 Caravan to Mecca.
Royal Geographical Society PR 091419

1937.[38] By 1370/1950 the camel was hardly used to transport pilgrims any more.[39]

The Merchants of Jeddah

As the changing fortunes of particular groups of merchants, such as the Moroccans in the eighteenth and Greek and Indian merchants in the nineteenth century have already been addressed at different points of this book, and as Pétriat provides, within his well-documented history

[38] *Umm al-Qurā*, 307, October 24, 1930; Stratkötter, *Von Kairo nach Mekka*, p. 283; and al-Ḥamdī, *Ḥarakat al-taḥdīth fī 'l-Mamlaka*, p. 120.
[39] Long, *The Hajj Today*, pp. 46–9.

of Hadhrami merchants, a quite comprehensive picture of different aspects of merchant activities, life, and socio-political involvement in urban life, the following section will be limited to a number of more general observations. It will then briefly introduce one example of sea- and one of land-borne trade.

The Organisation of the Merchants

Jeddah merchants did not consider themselves to be a *ḥirfa* (here presumably meaning 'craft') but constituted a *ṭāʾifa* (i.e. a guild). Irrespective of the term used, their organisation resembled that of the guilds described in Chapter 5.[40] Their chief representative was the *shaykh al-tujjār*, also called *shāhbandar*, or, in Ottoman, *baş tuccar*, in obvious concurrence with terminology in the Indian Ocean rim, where, however, the term usually referred to the representatives of specific merchant communities (cf. Chapter 5). Like the *shāhbandar* in Cairo, which existed since Napoleonic times, and like the shaykhs of guilds in Jeddah, the *shaykh al-tujjār* was elected by the members of the profession. He fulfilled an honorary function, mediating, and settling disputes. His appointment had to be confirmed by the Ottoman authorities, though the merchants or local stakeholders at times tried to circumvent this rule.[41] This seems to have been connected to the payment of a considerable sum to the authorities, this presumably being one of the many fees raised to supplement the state (or provincial) coffers.[42] During 1852 or 1953, Hamilton described how 'according to old custom, when a forced loan war required of the town, the Indian merchants were forced to contribute a large

[40] Oral information, ʿAbdallāh Bin Zaqr, Jeddah, March 23, 2006, Muḥammad Bin Ḥimd, Jeddah, February 24, 2016. Baer also emphatically argues for the inclusion of merchants in the consideration of guilds, although of course in general terms without reference to Jeddah, Baer, *The Administrative, Economic and Social Functions*., here p. 31.

[41] Pétriat, *Le Négoce des Lieux Saints*, p. 101.

[42] al-Muʿabbadī, *al-Nashāṭ al-tijārī li-mināʾ Jidda*, p. 191; Kābilī, *al-Ḥirafiyyūn fī madīnat Jidda*, p. 66. On Cairo, see Omar Cheta, 'Rule of Merchants: The Practice of Commerce and Law in Late Ottoman Egypt, 1841–1876', PhD Thesis, New York University (2014) p. 23; and fn. 36. Pascale Ghazaleh, 'Trading in Power: Merchants and the State in 19th Century Egypt', *International Journal of Middle East Studies*, 45 (2013), pp. 71–91, here p. 78, argues that before Napoleon, the Cairene *shahbandar* was far more independent and powerful.

proportion as their quota', thereby describing another common practice of surplus extraction.[43]

In 1853 a *majlis tijārī* (Commercial Council, sometimes also called *maḥkama* or court)[44] was established in Jeddah. Membership was honorary and no unlawful dues were to be raised for the cases debated there.[45] This new body, the establishment of which was part of the Tanzimat reforms, was similar to the development of this institution first in Egypt and then in the Ottoman Empire, where these new councils were meant to adjudicate in commercial disputes both between Ottomans and between European plaintiffs and Ottoman defendants. While their legal grounding only developed throughout the course of the century, it was clear from the beginning that these councils would not apply Islamic law. They usually also included representatives of foreign communities.[46] Ghazaleh has argued that for Egypt the introduction of these councils, which were headed by the *shāhbandar* of the merchants, nevertheless contributed to the weakening of the latter's role as he was now forced to act in co-operation with a group of peers.[47] The Jeddah council is first mentioned in a letter of 1854. There, the Ottoman governor had asked the court to settle a conflict between Ahmed Meshat (Mashāṭ) and Hajee Salah Syed Johar (Jawhar).[48] While we learn little about the actual matter, the two opponents were the later representative of the Khedival Company in Jeddah and (probably) the Indian/Ottoman Muslim who triggered the 1858 violence by changing the flag of a merchant vessel, in other words fairly prominent members of Jeddah's merchant community.[49] The consular archives regularly mention disputes, which usually involved one of their protégées, and, as will be discussed in

[43] Hamilton, *Sinai, The Hedjaz, and Soudan*, p. 58.

[44] For reasons of coherence, I will only use Commercial Council for this body.

[45] BOA, A.AMD. 44 20 of Receb 14, 1269/April 23, 1853; and Pétriat, *Le Négoce des Lieux Saints*, pp. 100–3.

[46] For Egypt, see Cheta, *Rule of Merchants*, pp. 33–64. For the Ottoman Empire, see Stanford Shaw and Ezel Shaw, *History of the Ottoman Empire and Modern Turkey: Volume 2: Reform, Revolution, and Republic: the Rise of Modern Turkey, 1808–1975* (Cambridge: Cambridge University Press, 1977), pp. 118–9.

[47] Ghazaleh, *Trading in Power*, pp. 78–9.

[48] TNA, FO 195/375, Cole to Amb. Const., March 29(?), 1854.

[49] On Mashāṭ, see al-Muʿabbadī, *al-Nashāṭ al-tijārī li-mināʾ Jidda*, p. 209, and Maghribī, *Aʿlām al-Ḥijāz*, vol. 3, pp. 160–1.

Chapter 7, it seems that this council was also used as location for the negotiation of urban politics.[50]

In one interesting case, the jurisdiction of the *majlis* was at stake. In a dispute about the amount of taxes to be paid on sugar, coffee, and tea, the customs' officials refused to accept the interference of 'the merchants', i.e. most likely the Commercial Council or the *shāhbandar*.[51] One may safely assume that the unanimous rejection of high taxes by the merchants was anticipated, with both governor and Emir, backing the customs' officials who, after all, secured their revenues. In another dispute before the court reported in the French consular archives, where landownership was concerned, both sides to the conflict tried to rally local political support: The French protégée sought support from the Governor, while the claimant appealed to the Emir (who apparently had interests of his own in the case). Eventually, the case was deferred to Istanbul.[52]

The Commercial Council continued to be mentioned in the context of a variety of cases. With the establishment of Hashemite rule, a new Chamber of Commerce was inaugurated.[53] This was, however, tied to a 'national company' which effectively controlled all prices in order to prevent profiteering during wartime. According to a French report, this stated aim was undermined by the unstated alliance of the king with one particular group of merchants at the expense of others.[54] Neither this nor the attempt to entice the shaykhs of the guilds to buy shares of an 'Industrial Enterprise Company', which was meant to run steamers in order to revive the trade of Jeddah, seem to have borne much fruit.[55]

Yet another attempt to re-launch the Commercial Council was made in 1926, i.e. a few months after the fall of the Hashemite Kingdom and the incorporation of the Hijaz into the realms of Ibn Saʿūd. The merchants drew up their own statutes based on the Ottoman model,

[50] TNA, FO 195/375, Cole to Amb. Const., March 29(?), 1854; FO 685/1. Stanley Letter Book Stanley to Amb. Const., April 11, 1863; cf. FO 195/1313, Burrell to Amb. Const., August 21, 1880.

[51] TNA, FO 685/1, Stanley to Amb. Const., April 11, 1863.

[52] CADN, 2_MI_3229, Le Gay to Amb. Const., August 12, 1872, August 20, 1872, August 29, 1872, September 10, 1872, and September 11, 1872.

[53] *al-Qibla*, 15, Dhū al-Ḥijja 5, 1334/October 3, 1916, pp. 2; and 16, Dhū al-Ḥijja 8, 1334/October 6, 1916.

[54] Pétriat, *Le Négoce des Lieux Saints*, pp. 215–6.

[55] Jarman (ed.), *The Jedda Diaries*, vol. 2, January 1922 p. 3.

which were confirmed by the Consultative Council, in which they, together with the guilds, were prominently represented.[56] Besides Hijazi merchants, the Council was comprised of a Najdi, a Lebanese, and two Indian merchants, as well as a Dutch convert and banker. Its tasks included litigation in different types of disputes between merchants, brokers, ship owners, and others involved in commerce, as well as problems arising from currency exchange and disputes over contracts.[57] In the context of the economic crisis and the implementation of a new commercial code, a new Commercial Council was appointed in 1930. It comprised a government representative, as well as Sulaymān Qābil, Aḥmad Bā ʿIshn, Muḥammad b. Ḥimd, the Najdi merchant ʿAbdallāh Ibrāhīm al-Faḍl, and a certain Muḥammad Ismāʿīl.[58]

The internal classifications of the merchants, and the question of whether they formed sub-associations (*ṭāʾifa*) as they did in Egypt, remains somewhat elusive. Kābilī differentiates between those who imported from abroad, the wholesale merchants redistributing goods within the Hijaz (called *ḥabāba* who, according to Kābilī, had their own shaykh), and the retailers selling within the city of Jeddah.[59] With the possible exception of small groceries in the quarters, most retailers were organised in the relevant market streets (*sūq,* pl. *aswāq)*, thus forming associations which either were formal guilds or functioned in analogy to them. Thus, Kābili mentions shaykhs for some of the *sūqs*, such as Sūq al-ʿAlawī. In the case of Sūq al-Badū, one of the main shop owners, the Hadhrami Ḥamūd b. Aḥmad Bin Hārūn was appointed to the position of *shaykh al-sūq* in 1871–2, whereas the main *sūq* (al-Sūq al-Kabīr) had Ṣāliḥ Ibrāhīm Jawhar as shaykh. He was a merchant of Indian origin whose ship was crucially involved in the 1858 commercial dispute that prompted the massacre.[60]

The examination of one particular merchant business, that of Muḥammad b. Aḥmad b. Ḥimd (d. 1946), whose office is shown in

[56] Chaudhry, *The Price of Wealth*, p. 71; and fn. 55–6.
[57] Vassiliev, *History of Saudi Arabia*, pp. 302–3; and *Umm al-Qurā*, 102, November 26, 1926.
[58] *Umm al-Qurā*, 300, September 5, 1930, p. 2; cf. Pétriat, *Le Négoce des Lieux Saints*, p. 331.
[59] Kābilī, *al-Ḥirafiyyūn fī madīnat Jidda*, pp. 34–41. The name implies that these were grain merchants. For the comparison with Egypt, see Cheta, *Rule of Merchants*, p. 33. Unfortunately, he gives no clue as to how these different groups were made up.
[60] Kābilī, *al-Ḥirafiyyūn fī madīnat Jidda*, pp. 56, 62.

Figure 6.1, illustrates for the late Ottoman and the interwar period that the export and regional redistribution of different types of goods could certainly be combined in one business, in addition to a merchant also acting as trade representative for others and as a money lender.[61] Thus, grouping wholesale merchants based on the goods they traded would have posed some problems. Nevertheless, in some cases, such as that of the cloth merchants (*al-qummashūn*, Kābilī is clear that their organisation was a separate *ḥirfa* with its own shaykh.[62] Among the cloth merchants, some were actually engaged in wholesale imports from Egypt, Syria, India, and elsewhere, while others were presumably engaged in both, wholesale, and retail trade. From the names and descriptions of the *tujjār*, it appears to be fairly certain that institutions such as the Commercial Council mostly represented those engaged in international wholesale trade.

Sea and Landborne Trade in the Early Twentieth Century

Grain supply for the holy cities, and the Hijazi hinterland, was the major import of the Hijaz in the period discussed here. Pétriat's study of the Bā Nāja has shown the close links of one such family with, notably, Cairo, from where much of the wheat was imported.[63] He has furthermore demonstrated the changing regional scope of trade in the century between the 1850s and 1950s, which depended on overall political and economic conditions. During World War I Sharifian rule, as well as in the early days of the Ibn Saʿūd's rule, a number of leading merchants took the precaution of leaving Jeddah temporarily by moving to Cairo, various Red Sea ports or to India. They often left behind a family member or business partner to continue the business while others, men as well as women and children, were taken to what was considered a safer environment.[64] Pétriat describes this phenomenon as an expression of the elasticity of families who had dependencies in a range of neighbouring ports and could hence react flexibly to a temporary (or less temporary) turn in their fortunes, thereby

[61] Freitag, *A Twentieth-Century Merchant Network*.
[62] Kābilī, *al-Ḥirafiyyūn fī madīnat Jidda*, pp. 134–7.
[63] Pétriat, *Le Négoce des Lieux Saints*., pp. 242–4.
[64] Ibid., pp. 242–7. For a number of Hadhrami families, see *Umm al-Qurā*, 33, August 16, 1925; and interview with Layla al-Nuʿmānī ʿAlī Riḍā and Salmā ʿAlī Riḍā, Jeddah, December 10, 2017.

incidentally strengthening their positions by entering new alliances for the period ahead.[65]

Muḥammad b. Aḥmad Bin Ḥimd's papers reveal this partial re-orientation of trade, with a strong focus on the Red Sea for the interwar period.[66] Bin Ḥimd's father seems to have provisioned Ottoman troops in the Hijaz with food and arms, although, so far, there is no indication as to the regions from which he acquired the goods.[67] The son established himself as a grain merchant with a strong network in the southern Red Sea, mostly in Yemen, but also Eritrea and the Sudan. The large house in Ḥārat al-Shām was built in 1844, according to the plate next to the door. As it is actually a combination of at least two houses, this might well reflect a process of enlargement similar to that described by Pétriat for the Bā Nāja properties in Chapter 5, although the history of the building has yet to be documented. At any rate, it contains large storage halls on the ground floor, with a back door in order to ease loading and unloading of supplies. To the right of the front entrance and overlooking the hallway is the old office from which business was directed. The separation of living quarters, office and warehouse which Cheta observed in Alexandrian merchants in the second half of the nineteenth century and which, according to him, was quite typical of the Mediterranean world and beyond, was clearly alien to Muḥammad Bin Ḥimd and many of his contemporaries in Jeddah. This does not exclude that merchants may have rented warehouse space in addition to their own houses, as has been shown in Chapters 4 and 5.[68]

While his correspondence shows that he bought grain from Yemen, he also imported rice, chickpeas and other foodstuffs, tea, coffee, spices, and cloth, presumably for consumption both by locals and by pilgrims. These goods came mostly from India, either directly through business partners in Bombay and Calcutta, or via Aden, where Bin Himd

65 In French: 'plasticité', see Pétriat, p. 247.

66 On the Hadhrami networks in the Red Sea; cf. Janet Ewald and William Clarence-Smith, 'The Economic Role of the Hadhrami Diaspora in the Red Sea and Gulf of Aden, 1820s to 1930s' in U. Freitag and W. G. Clarence-Smith (eds.), *Hadhrami Traders, Scholars, and Statesmen in the Indian Ocean, 1750s–1960s* (Leiden, New York, and Köln: Brill Academic Publishers, 1997), pp. 281–96.

67 The following is based on the more detailed examination of sample papers from Bin Himd's collection in Freitag, *A Twentieth-Century Merchant Network*.

68 Cheta, *Rule of Merchants*, p. 168.

maintained a significant number of partners and correspondents. Importantly, Muḥammad Bin Ḥimd also maintained quite a large volume of correspondence with merchants in Mecca and Medina. To what extent he actually traded with them requires further investigation, but the fact that a Najdi merchant in Medina, ʿAbdallāh M. Bassām, asked him to transfer a large sum of money to Bombay indicates that they conducted significant business with each other.[69] This typically also involved some measure of providing credit. The separation between merchants trading by sea and by land suggested by Kābilī must hence be questioned or, perhaps, be located more precisely in time which is difficult with the information currently available.[70]

Bin Ḥimd's papers also contain a handwritten booklet with rules in Arabic grammar. This was probably used to train apprentices who had to learn how to write proper business letters. It is a further illustration of the fact that merchants, like members of other guilds, preferred to train their sons in the offices of their colleagues once they had obtained basic skills in reading and writing from the small neighbourhood Koranic schools. This continued even after the establishment of the Ottoman middle school (*rüşdiye*) in 1876 and the private (Arabic) *al-Falāḥ* school in 1905. Consequently, the *Falāḥ* school introduced a fine for parents who withdrew their children during a cycle of education.[71] The typescript biographies of four members of the al-Faḍl family (see below) illustrate how, in the late nineteenth and early twentieth century, children between the ages of ten and fifteen were sent to business branches in faraway cities on the Peninsula and in India to be trained by relatives. Even if the children went to school they could be sent abroad to business partners during the vacations, although, according to the memoir of one of them, the aim of this was a more general exploration of the self and the world, rather than the immediate study of bookkeeping and work ethics.[72] The scepticism towards formal

[69] Dārat al-Malik ʿAbd al-ʿAzīz, Papers of Muḥammad b. Aḥmad Bin Ḥimd. When consulted in 2015, these papers were not yet catalogued, hence no exact reference can be given.

[70] On the lack of documentation for the inland trade; cf. Pétriat, *Le Négoce des Lieux Saints*, p. 191.

[71] Conditions of Acceptance, dated Muḥarram 26, 1341/September 18, 1922 copy in al-Falāḥ school, Jeddah, as well as in Riḍwān, *Qālū ʿan Muḥammad ʿAlī Zaynal*, p. 167.

[72] Bin Zaqr, *unpublished memories*, p. 3. I thank Philippe Pétriat for this information.

education among merchants differs significantly from the approach taken by the merchants of Alexandria in the latter part of the nineteenth century, as described by Cheta.[73] It is noteworthy, however, that it was precisely the members of the merchant families with Indian connections who initiated and sponsored the *Falāḥ* school, presumably after having witnessed the benefits of formal instruction in mathematics, English, and other subjects abroad.[74]

Bin Himd's connection with Bassām alerts us to the fact that, with the change of regime, a new group of administrators and merchants, composed of the Najd as well as international supporters of Ibn Saʿūd, competed with the old families. However, trade with Najd had a long history. Some of the Najdi 'newcomers' to the scene of Jeddah merchants, such as the al-Faḍl and al-Bassām, were merchants who had already established themselves in Jeddah in late Ottoman times, and not all of them were early supporters of Ibn Saʿūd. In 1887–8 Aḥmad al-Bassām was an elected member of the Administrative Council of Jeddah and a relative of his, Sulaymān b. ʿAbdallāh al-Bassām, met the Egyptian *amīr al-ḥajj*, Ibrāhīm Rifʿat Pasha in 1901. Ibrāhīm Rifʿat describes him favourably as 'the representative (*wakīl*) of the Emir of Najd and a merchant of good character, manliness and respectability'.[75] His father had been the head of the merchant house in ʿUnayza and his business was already established in Jeddah, while also maintaining close relations with India. They were so prominent in Jeddah that, according to Doughty, Najdi traders in Jeddah, if not called '*sharqiyyīn*', were commonly known as Bassām.[76] Like the Bassāms, the Faḍl family from ʿUnayza was already established in the Hijaz in late Ottoman or early Saudi times. Similar to Bassām, they also had an Indian branch. This dealt in pearls, most likely in cooperation with the Quṣaybī family, which

[73] Cheta, *Rule of Merchants*, p. 136. On the training of merchants' sons; cf. Pétriat, *Le Négoce des Lieux Saints*, pp. 300–6.

[74] Thus, Muḥammad ʿAbd al-Raḥmān ʿAbdallāh al-Faḍl, himself a graduate of the private al-Najāḥ school, was among the first sponsors of *al-Falāḥ* (typescript biography obtained from ʿUthmān al-Faḍl, Jeddah, March 15, 2010).

[75] Rifʿat, *Mirʾāt al-Ḥaramayn*, vol. 1, p. 20; and plate 14 for an image; cf. Pétriat, *Le Négoce des Lieux Saints*, p. 191.

[76] Charles Doughty, *Travels in Arabia Deserta*, 2 vols. (London and Boston: Philip Lee Warner, new edn. 1901 [1888]), vol. 2, p. 350 and passim. To this day, a number of houses in old Jeddah are known as the '*buyūt al-sharqiyyīn*' (and not by the names of the owners).

had a branch in Bahrain. The profits from this business were re-invested in trade in Jeddah.[77] At the same time, the family encouraged other Jiddawi merchants such as the Bā Nāja to invest in the Indian pearl business.[78]

The story of Shaykh Aḥmad b. Ibrāhīm b. Ḥamad ʿĪsā al-Sudayrī (1837/38–1911), mentioned in Chapter 5, is particularly instructive regarding the way in which the trade in goods contributed to the flow of ideas.[79] Born in the town of Shaqrāʾ, halfway between Riyadh and ʿUnayza, Aḥmad b. Īsā had a basic religious education in his hometown after which he moved to Riyadh, where he studied with ʿAbd al-Raḥmān b. Ḥasan b. Muḥammad b. ʿAbd al-Wahhāb and his son ʿAbd al-Laṭīf, the foremost Wahhabi scholars of their time.[80] He then went on the pilgrimage and used the time in Mecca to study. Among his teachers in the Ḥaram was Muḥammad b. Sulaymān Ḥasab Allāh, a conservative-minded scholar, rumoured to have maintained sympathies for the Wahhabiyya, and rival of the Shāfiʿī mufti Aḥmad Zaynī Daḥlān.[81] Another noteworthy teacher was Nuʿmān Effendi al-Ālūsī in Baghdad, whose interest in Ibn Taymiyya constituted an important link between *salafi* and Wahhabi scholars.[82] Like many scholars, Aḥmad b. ʿĪsā needed to pursue a gainful profession, which in his case

[77] Interview with Aḥmad ʿAbdallāh al-Faḍl, Jeddah, March 12, 2010.

[78] Pétriat, *Le Négoce des Lieux Saints*, p. 213.

[79] The following account is based on Bassām, *ʿUlamāʾ Najd*, vol.1, pp. 436–52; and the somewhat shorter biography in Āl al-Shaykh, *Mashāhīr ʿulamāʾ Najd*, pp. 185–8. I think Prof. Werner Ende for this reference. For a shorter biography, see al-Ziriklī, *al-Aʿlām*, vol. 1, p. 89.

[80] For a list of his teachers, see Bassām, *ʿUlamāʾ Najd*, vol. 1, pp. 442–3. On the two descendants of Muḥammad b. ʿAbd al-Wahhāb, see Esther Peskes, *Muḥammad B. ʿAbdalwahhāb (1703–92) im Widerstreit: Untersuchungen zur Rekonstruktion der Frühgeschichte der Wahhābīya*, Beiruter Texte und Studien (Stuttgart: Steiner, 1993), vol. 56, p. 128.

[81] On Ḥasab Allāh and his relationship with Daḥlān, see Muḥammad Bā Dhīb, 'Ḥasab Allāh, usra' in A. Z. Yamānī and ʿ. Ṣ. Tashkandī (eds.), *Mawsūʿat Makka al-Mukarrama wa-l-Madīna al-Munawwara* (London: Mu'assasat al-Furqān li-l-Turāth al-Islāmī), vol. 7, pp. 446–8, here pp. 446–7; Christiaan Snouck Hurgronje, *Verspreide Geschriften* (Bonn and Leipzig: Schroeder, 1924), vol. 3, p. 72–5. A British report of 1882 interestingly describes Hasab Allah as a converted Copt who had been in favour of the destruction of the grave of Abī Ṭālib and somebody acknowledging the claim to the caliphate by 'the Wahabee Chief Saoud', see TNA, FO 1951415, Monceriff to Amb. Const., April 30, 1882.

[82] David Commins, *The Wahhabi Mission and Saudi Arabia*, Library of Modern Middle East Studies (London and New York: I.B. Tauris, 2006), pp. 132–3.

was cloth trade. On the authority of Muḥammad Naṣīf, Bassām reports the following, which will be cited in full for it illuminates the land trade on which we have relatively little information:

> Shaykh Aḥmad b. ʿĪsā bought cloth from Shaykh ʿAbd al-Qādir b. Muṣṭafā al-Tilmisānī, one of the merchants of Jeddah, for the sum of one thousand gold pounds. He would pay him four hundred directly, and the remainder in instalments. The last instalment would be paid when Shaykh al-Tilmisānī came to perform the pilgrimage each year, and then they would start the new year with a new contract. The guarantor (*kafīl*) of Shaykh Aḥmad b. ʿĪsā was Shaykh Mubārak al-Musāʿid, a client (*min mawālī*) of the Āl Bassām.[83] Shaykh Aḥmad b. ʿĪsā always paid the instalments at their exact time ... so that Shaykh ʿAbd al-Qādir told him: I have worked for over forty years with people and never met anyone with whom cooperation was better than with you, oh Wahhabi. It seems that what is spread about you people of the Najd is exaggerated by their enemies.[84]

According to Bassām, this sparked a conversation about whether Wahhabis actually prayed to God, and then led to a discussion on religious matters which lasted for three days until 'God opened my heart to the *salafī* creed (*al-ʿaqīda al-salafiyya*)'. The discussion about the names and properties of God continued for another 15 days between the two until Shaykh al-Tilmisānī was completely won over. Shaykh al-Tilmisānī then began not only to sponsor the printing of books by *salafī* authors but also won over Muḥammad Naṣīf to the *salafī* way – a story which probably only captures one of the different influences on Naṣīf.[85] An interesting aside is the last reported comment about the trustworthy business practices of Wahhabis, which might, in the business-minded Jeddah merchant community, have been as important an argument as the more abstract theological issues debated. Indeed, it might have had long-term effects with regard to the willingness of Jeddah merchants to stand up against Shairīf Ḥusayn b. ʿAlī and eventually support the submission to Ibn Saʿūd.

[83] The usage of *mawlā* in this context is odd, it might be a legal dependent (slave).

[84] Bassām, *ʿUlamāʾ Najd*, vol. 1, pp. 437–8. According to Āl al-Shaykh, *Mashāhīr ʿulamāʾ Najd*, p. 186, it was thirty years.

[85] Bassām, *ʿUlamāʾ Najd*, vo. 1, pp. 439–40. For influences on Muḥammad Naṣīf; cf. Aḥmad and al-ʿAlawī, *Muḥammad Naṣīf*, p. 140; and Nallino, *Raccolta di Scritti*, p. 137.

As already pointed out in Chapter 5, Aḥmad b. ʿĪsā also influenced the Emir of Mecca where he resided until 1899.[86] Ironically, Aḥmad b. ʿĪsā had refused at some unstated earlier time to take on a position as judge offered by the then Saʿūdī Emir Fayṣal b. Turkī (r. 1834–8, 1843–65). Instead, he became a judge in the town of Mujamaʿa and for the Sudayr region, then under the rule of Ibn Rashīd of Ḥāʾil. When the notables of al-Mujamaʿa offered ʿAbd al-ʿAzīz their submission in 1326/1908, the shaykh who had quite successfully spread Wahhabi views among the merchants and rulers of the Hijaz lost his job and is said to have died in poverty.[87]

Merchants and Rulers

Relations between the Jeddah merchant elite and the rulers – both Ottoman governor and emir of Mecca – were fraught with complications. While governors came and went at different rhythms, many emirs served either multiple terms, such as Muḥammad b. (ʿAbd al-Muʿīn) b. ʿAwn (1827–36, 1840–51, 1856–8) and ʿAbd al-Muṭṭalib b. Ghālib (1827, 1851–7, 1880–1) or had long consecutive terms of office, such as ʿAbdallāh b. Muḥammad (1858–77) and ʿAwn al-Rafīq (1882–1905). As already discussed in Chapter 2, the emirs, as well as other sharifs, engaged in trade and were thus in direct competition with the merchants of Jeddah. Moreover, one of the prominent Jeddah merchants was usually picked as the emir's *wakīl* to deal with all matters that had to be settled in Jeddah. For many years ʿUmar, Ḥusayn, and Muḥammad Naṣīf acted in this function.[88] This was a volatile position as the agent – who also had his own commercial interests and local political alliances – could be dismissed at will. For example, in September 1883 ʿUmar Naṣīf was replaced by his bitter rival Mūsā al-Baghdādī, at the same time as a new kaymakam for Jeddah was appointed by the governor. A few days later Naṣīf was

[86] Bassām, *ʿUlamāʾ Najd*. According to Āl al-Shaykh, *Mashāhīr ʿulamāʾ Najd*, p. 188, he only retuned after ʿAwn al-Rafīq's death in 1323/1905.

[87] There is some confusion about the date of the submission of al-Mujamaʿa under the rule of the Āl Saʿūd. The proper date seems to be 1908, see ʿAbd al-ʿAzīz al-Tuwayjirī, *al-Malik ʿAb dal-ʿAzīz, Dirāsa wathāʾiqiyya*, Beirut 1997, pp. 659–61. I thank Dr. ʿAwaḍ al-Bādī for this reference.

[88] TNA, FO 195/2061, Mohammed Hussain to Devey, January 10, 1899; CADN, 2_MI_3243, no. 44, Notes de renseignement sur les notabilités musulmanes, 1909, p. 77.

accused by the governor of complicity in an uprising by the Ḥarb Bedouin.[89] He was jailed and sentenced to exile but released shortly thereafter due to his excellent connections.[90] Similarly, in December 1899 the British consul reported that 'Omar Nassif Effendi . . . has been practically disgraced' due to disagreements over the Emir's accounts. Although the Governor of the Hijaz stayed at Nasīf's house for four weeks at the expense of the Emir, the kaymakam (ʿAlī Yamanī), described as a local who had worked his way up in the Hijaz administration, had become the interim agent of the Emir. He expected ʿAbdallāh Bā Nāja to be awarded the job.[91] Similarly, in 1909 Muḥammad Naṣīf was the agent of the Emir while in 1916 he is described as an opponent of the sharifs.[92]

In spite of their shorter tenures, many of the governors also engaged in business, often in cooperation with merchants who had the necessary local knowledge and connections to obtain credit. Pétriat documents a case of the governor Ahmed Ratip Pasha (1893–1908) and his interactions with ʿAbdallāh Bā Nāja in the transfer of large amounts of currency from Istanbul, via their ex-slave Ṣufyān, and possibly Cairo. This allowed for a safe as well as a discrete transaction, quite important not only for reasons of safety but also possible enquiries as to the sources of the governor's wealth.[93] Obviously, a close relationship with the Ottoman governor could prove advantageous for business, and if one enjoyed equally good relations with both the highest Ottoman official in the region and the emir, as the Bā Nājas did, this was doubly beneficial.

Not much is known about the involvement of lower rank officials in business transactions. One notable exception was the *muḥtasib*

89 TNA, FO 195/1451, Abdur Razzack to Amb. Const., September 26, 1883. On the rivalry between Naṣīf and Baghdādī Aḥmad and al-ʿAlawī, *Muḥammad Naṣīf*, pp. 118–9.

90 Numan, *The Emirs of Mecca*, p. 141.

91 TNA, FO 195/ 2061, Devey to Amb. Const., December 27, 1899. About ʿAlī Yamanī's career, see FO 195/2061, Hussain to Amb. Const. September 1, 1899; and FO 195/2254, Memorandum about the career of Ali Yumni Effendi, encl. in Monahan to Amb. Const., April 26, 1907. An earlier incident of a similar sort seems to have occurred in 1880, see below. On an earlier rivalry between Naṣīf and ʿAbdallāh Bā Nāja, see Pétriat, *Le Négoce des Lieux Saints*, p. 85. For more rotations, see al-Anṣārī, *Mawsūʿat tārīkh madīnat Jidda*, pp. 328–9.

92 CADN, 1_MI_3243, no. 44, Notes de renseignement sur les notabilités musulmanes, 1909, p. 77; and Hogarth, *Hejaz before World War*, p. 66.

93 Pétriat, *Le Négoce des Lieux Saints*, pp. 198–200.

ʿAbdallāh Agha in the 1850s, mentioned in the context of the merchant rivalries of the 1850s and the massacre of 1858 (Chapter 2). Responsible for urban order, but also for the collection of taxes from shopkeepers, he furthermore acted as the agent of the Emir of Mecca.[94] Finally, he was involved in the monopoly of the salt trade, a re-export from Suakin which served, together with pilgrims, as an important ballast on the voyage to India where it could be resold at a profit.[95] He thus collaborated, but also competed, with a number of merchants and greatly opposed the foreign consulates for their attempts at protecting their protégés from undue levies (which he was in a position to extract) as well as from attempts at monopolising lucrative trades.[96]

This should not distract us from noting that, until 1858, the French and British consuls were themselves part of the merchant community. Thereafter, the only exception was the appointment of Captain Beyts, a British East India Company merchant, from 1874-78, when the local economy was very weak.[97] The most pertinent example for consequences of appointing professional diplomats are the controversies concerning the transport of pilgrims, a large business from which a number of parties, including the emir of Mecca, wanted to derive maximum profit. It is not surprising that Beyts as a merchant did not take kindly to the monopoly on pilgrims' transport which had been established by 'One or two English, and several Indian subjects of more doubtful character … acting more or less in concert with the Dutch firm of Van der Chys and Co., and with the Turkish authorities'.[98] While the British officials asserted that their man was faultless, they nevertheless suggested to restore a paid consul to the job to avoid future complications.

However, the replacement of Captain Beyts as vice-consul did not end controversies over who was allowed to transport pilgrims. In late

[94] TNA, FO 195/375, Extract from Consul Cole's letter to Amb. Const., December 11, 1853 in Page to Amb. Const., October 27, 1856.

[95] TNA, FO 195/375, Cole to Amb. Const., August 4, 1854; and CADN, 2_MI_3228, Sabatier to MAE, December 17, 1859. On the monopoly, see TNA, FO 78/2194, Raby to FO, February 13, 1871; cf. FO 195/956, Raby to Amb. Const., September 3, 1869. On the ballast function; cf. Pétriat, *Le Négoce des Lieux Saints*, pp. 39–40.

[96] For more detail Pétriat, pp. 81–4; and Freitag, *Helpless Representatives*, here p. 368.

[97] Freitag, *Helpless Representatives*, p. 360.

[98] TNA, FO 881/3801, Confidential Print 3801, Memorandum respecting State of Affairs connected with the Jeddah Consulate, pp. 2–3.

1878/early 1879, we find the company of Mssrs Wylde Beyts & Co. engaged in a bitter controversy with the dragoman of the British consulate and other British subjects about who was entitled to British consular protection and, implicitly, to consular support in their aims to transporting pilgrims.[99] A year later this company was mentioned as an agent of the Emir, while the Emir's former agent, ʿUmar Naṣīf, was suddenly in danger of being arrested by his former client. By 1880 Beyts engaged in a bitter controversy with the dragoman of the British consulate (and his own former employee), who was now part of a business partnership with the Dutch Vice Consul, ʿUmar Naṣīf, 'and other influential people', among them ʿAbdallāh Bā Nāja.[100] Apparently, membership in such monopolistic consortia shifted considerably and fallouts regularly resulted in lawsuits and accusations of illegal doings. Such was the case in 1884, when the firm of Mr Oswald, also engaged in providing coal to the British navy and grain to the Ottomans, fell out with their former partners.[101] In 1888, it was Thomas Cook who complained about a monopoly in the Malaysian pilgrims' transport, which was said to involve the

> Chief Sheik of Malays, Dutch Vice Consul Mr Van der Chys, Sayd Omar Sagof, a British subject native of Singapore, and lastly Yusef Kudse, the paid Dragoman of the British Consulate who is the prime mover in the scheme and whose position and influence in the consulate keep the whole thing going. Very large sums are paid by the co-partners to High officials for their support of the monopoly.[102]

Given that Thomas Cook & Son had themselves been appointed to a monopoly on the transport of Indian merchants by the British Indian government in the preceding year, a contract which ended in 1893 by which time the firm's share in the Indian pilgrimage transport had fallen to a share of less than 10 per cent, it seems fair to assume that

99 TNA, FO 195/1251, Woods to Amb. Const., December 9, 1879 and Wylde Beyts & Co to Consul Zohrab, December 7, 1879.

100 TNA, FO/1314, Burrell to Amb. Const, September 20, 1880.

101 TNA, FO 195/1415, Monceriff to FO, April 5, 1882, FO 195/1482, Report on the pilgrimage; Jago to FO, September 27, 1884; and Pétriat, *Le Négoce des Lieux Saints*, p. 182. Ca. 1886, and possibly earlier, Mr. Oswald also acted for the company Gellatly Hankey in Suakin and Jeddah, which was to become the first bank of the Hijaz, George Blake, *Gellatly's 1862–1962: A Short History of the Firm* (London: Blackie & Son Ltd, 1962), p. 110.

102 TNA, FO 685/2, part III, Thos. Cook & Son to secretary to the Government of India, July 21, 1888.

the complaints were aimed to eliminate a business rival rather than advocate for more general fair play.[103] Thomas Cook must have been particularly embittered by the group's attempt to extend the monopoly to the Indian pilgrims. Another plaintiff was the governor, who was left out of this new scheme and hence tried to abolish it. Instead, he lost his post due to the intervention of the Emir's friends in Istanbul.[104] Nevertheless, in 1894 there seems to have been a serious attempt to eliminate particular abuse of those who had completed the pilgrimage. Specifically, pilgrims' guides tried to extract extra dues for camel hire, force pilgrims to book particular return passages, or pay invented extra fees. As this practice was particularly used on Javanese pilgrims, a decree that was posted all over Jeddah stated 'that the post of Javanese pilgrim sheikhs, and that of the chief pilgrim-sheikh are and remain totally abolished'.[105] The effectiveness of these measures can be doubted, as, in the letter accompanying a copy of the decree, the British consul noted new complaints from Indian and Bahraini pilgrims.[106]

The list of examples of rivalling business interests could be continued. Pétriat has shown how this could lead to the formation of merchant factions who strengthened their links through intermarriage and acted collectively, most notably during the violent attack on consuls and foreign merchants in 1858.[107] Nevertheless, the cultivation of good relations with the main powers in the Hijaz, governor and emir, remained a crucial element of success. Concurrently, alienating them could have grave consequences. Thus, Mūsā Baghdādī, the aforementioned short-term agent of the Emir and rival of ʿUmar Naṣīf, seems to have fallen out with the political elite in 1887. Consequently, he was exiled to Baghdad with the active support of the Emir, the governor, the kaymakam, and ʿUmar Naṣīf.[108] According to local lore,

[103] Ibid., part II, Extract from the Proceedings of the Government of India, Simla, May 3, 1887. On the appointment; cf. Thos. Cook & Son, *The Mecca Pilgrimage: Appointment by the Government of India of Thos. Cook & Son* (London, n.d.: [1893]). On the course of events, see Low, *The Mechanics of Mecca*, pp. 304–14.

[104] Numan, *The Emirs of Mecca*, pp. 139–40.

[105] TNA, FO 195/1847, Copy of Announcement (in Arabic and translation) of April 7, 1894, encl. in Richards to Amb. Const., May 1, 1894.

[106] TNA, FO 195/1847, Richards to Amb. Const., May 1, 1894.

[107] Pétriat, *Le Négoce des Lieux Saints*, most explicitly pp. 107–9, pp. 286–92 and passim.

[108] Numan, *The Emirs of Mecca*, pp. 142–3.

it is not unlikely that this was Naṣīf's revenge for his own earlier exile in which he suspected Baghdādī to have been involved.[109]

The Turnover of Elites

Dependence on the ruling elites and their changing policies and replacement was one among a number of factors which contributed to the slow change in the dominant merchant elite over the 100 years being discussed. Another was the changing pattern of trade and migration. Had there always been some important Najdi merchants in the Hijaz and Jeddah? Or was their more noted presence in the late nineteenth century a reflection of political changes, or of the growth of east Arabian trade in horses, grain, dates, and pearls? Finally, the larger pattern of merchant houses also played a role, whereby family enterprises often could not sustain themselves for more than three generations.[110]

Pétriat has documented the process of elite change by scrutinising the membership of the commercial councils in its different emanations. Even where the name remained the same, he has carefully traced the emergence of new branches of old families and, eventually, the transformation of merchants into entrepreneurs in an oil-driven society in which royal patronage was an important ingredient of success.[111] As discussed in Chapter 5, the emir had introduced a comprehensive system of licensing fees for guild members. Furthermore, as has been shown using the example of the pilgrim transport, merchants depended on official good-will, which included a de facto willingness to share their profits with the emir or Ottoman authorities. This very much resembles Ghazaleh's observations on nineteenth-century Egypt, where she observed merchants becoming increasingly dependent on the state.[112]

Sharifian rule was marked by quite substantial levies on the merchants and a rise of discontent, as has been shown in Chapter 2. This eventually caused the notables of Jeddah to unite and overthrow King Ḥusayn, as will be discussed in more detail in Chapter 7,

109 Maghribī, *A'lām al-Ḥijāz*, vol. 3, pp. 350–2.
110 Pétriat, *Le Négoce des Lieux Saints*, pp. 293–8, 363–7; and Freitag, *Arab Merchants in Singapore*.
111 Pétriat, *Le Négoce des Lieux Saints*, pp. 107, 215–6, 279, 295, 331, 363–6.
112 Ghazaleh, *Trading in Power*, pp. 73–4.

although matters only really changed with the onset of Saʿūdī rule and the arrival of a new group of administrators and merchants, from the Najd as well as from international supporters of Ibn Saʿūd in the Hijaz. Among these was the former British diplomat Philby, who had started a trading company in Jeddah in 1926. This only took off after Philby had converted to Islam in 1930 and become an important advisor to the king until, by the mid-1930s, local competitors started to emerge.

Some of the new business leaders, such as the al-Faḍl and al-Bassām, were Najdi merchants who had already established themselves in Jeddah in late Ottoman or early Sharifian times, as has been shown.[113] They now experienced a strong career boost. It is noteworthy that they were, until very recently, considered by Jiddawis to be as much outsiders (or newcomers) as Syrians, Indians, or Africans. In spite of ʿUnayza's reputation as the 'Paris of Najd'[114] and the far-ranging trade connections with the Gulf, Iraq, India, and Greater Syria, Altorki compares the Jiddawi *ahl al-balad*, 'a metropolitan city with a cosmopolitan population', with 'the culture of the nomadic tribes' when speaking of them, but also of Najdis arriving in the 1950s.[115] This is a reflection of a deep-rooted suspicion which could still be discerned in interviews in the first decade of the twenty-first century when asking how these relative newcomers to the Jeddah scene were perceived. Partly, this might have been linked to the urban fear of people who were still very much emphasising their tribal origin, but it probably also reflected the political and economic contestations on the Arabian Peninsula. In the years after the Saudi take-over, this feeling might have been further strengthened by the rapid ascendance of merchants of Najdi origin, such as the al-Quṣaybī, al-Khurayjī, al-Juffālī, al-Turkī, Sulaymān (al-Ḥamdān), al-Zughaybī, and al-Nāniyya.[116] In addition, other newcomers established close relations with the new king, such as

113 According to Altorki, *Women in Saudi Arabia*, p. 12, they were only 'owners of humble grocery stores' until the time of the Hashemites, but this might well reflect a current local perspective on these new immigrants.

114 al-Rīḥānī, *Mulūk al-ʿArab*, p. 606.

115 Altorki, *Women in Saudi Arabia*, p. 11.

116 If not indicated otherwise, the following is based on ʿAbd al-Raḥmān al-Shibīlī, 'Min usra rāʾida fī 'l-tijāra wa-l-shūrā wa-l-siyāsa wa-l-tarḥāl', al-Sharq, Dhū 'l-Qaʿida 1425/December 2004, pp. 52–3; as well as on a typescript set of biographies given to me by ʿUthmān b. ʿAbd al-Raḥmān b. ʿAbdallāh Ṣāliḥ al-Faḍl, Jeddah, March 15, 2010.

the new Hadhrami immigrants Bin Lādin and Bin Maḥfūẓ. It is thus worthwhile to briefly recount the trajectory of one of the Najdi families, the al-Faḍl, and shows the structural similarities of their immigration and eventual integration to the earlier generations of immigrant merchants.

The author of a biography of ʿAbdallāh b. Muḥammad al-Faḍl (ca. 1880–1969) firmly inserts his history into that of the regional trade network alluded to above. In late Ottoman times, a number of families from the Qaṣīm region in Najd settled in Mecca, Medina, Ṭāʾif, and Jeddah, being motivated by either religion, trade, or service in the Ottoman army. The aforementioned case of Aḥmad b. ʿĪsā illustrates that these professions could be combined, and also how the connection to Najd could be maintained.

In the last quarter of the nineteenth century the ʿUnayza merchant Ṣāliḥ b. ʿAbdallāh b. Ṣālīh al-Faḍl (d. 1923) established a family branch in Bombay, trading in foodstuffs together with his brother, ʿAbd al-Raḥmān. During World War I, he spent some time in Medina, supplying the Ottomans with grain during the siege by Sharif Ḥusayn and the British, causing some trouble to their Jeddah branch (see below).[117] He then returned to Bombay. The Bombay branch of al-Faḍl also supplied the Emir of Najd, ʿAbd al-ʿAzīz b. Saʿūd, with much-needed grain during his campaigns to establish his rule over Najd and then present-day Saudi Arabia.[118] This seems to have occurred with the compliance of the British, as the al-Faḍl business obtained a recommendation from Harry St. John, alias ʿAbdallāh Philby, to the customs' officials of Bombay, which seems to have allowed for an exception to the embargo of exports to the Peninsula. It came in particularly handy when, in 1920, Ibn Saʿūd ordered three cars. The go-between was incidentally ʿAbdallāh al-Quṣaybī, with whom the al-Faḍls had prior dealings in Bahrain.[119]

When Prince Fayṣal passed through Bombay en route to a royal visit to London in 1919, he met the family. Besides owning property and having a business in Bombay, Ṣāliḥ established business branches in

[117] Muḥammad al-ʿAbd (!) al-Raḥmān al-Faḍl, 'Akhī al-marḥūm ʿAbdallāh al-Muḥammad (!) al-Faḍl', *al-Manhal,* March–April 1969, pp. 92–3.

[118] Interview with ʿUthmān b. ʿAbd al-Raḥmān b. ʿAbdallāh Ṣāliḥ al-Faḍl, Jeddah, March 15, 2010.

[119] Muḥammad al-ʿAbd (!) al-Raḥmān al-Faḍl, 'Min dhikhrayāt al-māḍī', *al-Manhal,* May 1961, pp. 704–5.

Karachi (where he died), Mecca, Medina, and Jeddah. Ṣāliḥ's brother ʿAbdallāh (1880–1968) left the Najd with his family for Bombay in 1891–2 when Ibn Rashīd conquered Qaṣīm. In 1906–7 ʿAbdallāh, who, meanwhile, had been trained in English, Urdu, accounting, and trade, joined Ibn Saʿūd's court in Riyadh.[120] Eventually, he settled in Mecca as a merchant. However, much of his business seems to have actually occurred through his Jeddah branch.[121] It is likely that he cooperated with his half-brother Muḥammad b. ʿAbd al-Raḥmān (1888/9–1972), who attended *al-Najāḥ* school in Jeddah and then probably worked in his uncle's business. It was most likely one of the al-Faḍls who, in 1908, was dealing in coal and attempted to convert his business into a 'privileged coal store in which coal for bunker purposes may be stored free of import and export duty'.[122]

Due to their contacts with the Ottomans, Sharif Ḥusayn closed the al-Faḍl business in 1913–4. He imprisoned ʿAbdallāh b. Muḥammad as well as his cousin ʿAbdallāh b. Ṣāliḥ and eventually deported them.[123] Muḥammad b. ʿAbd al-Raḥmān thereupon left for Karachi, where he entered into a partnership with a large trading house. He also seems to have maintained political contacts with the Khilāfa-movement, propagating Ibn Saʿūd's rule.[124] After Ibn Saʿūd's rule over the Hijaz had been secured, he returned in 1926 to the Jeddah business. Perhaps due to the decline of the pearl industry, possibly due to the Nagpur riots, during which one family member was killed[125], the Indian branch of the firms seems to have been on the verge of collapse then and had to close a few years later, once again in connection with the decline of the value of natural pearls.[126]

120 Typescript collection of biographies obtained from ʿUthmān al-Faḍl, Jeddah, March 15, 2010.

121 Interview, ʿUthmān al-Faḍl, Jeddah, March 15, 2010.

122 TNA, FO 195/2286, Monahan to Emb. Const., April 10, 1908.

123 According to the typescript, this was due to the accusation of the two men being supporters of Ibn Saʿūd and the Ottomans, which would make a date of 1916 ff. more likely. According to Muḥammad b. ʿAbd al-Raḥmān al-Faḍl, 'Filbī ka-mā ʿaraftuhu', *al-Manhal*, November 1960, pp. 309–11, here p. 310. This was due to accusations of their proximity to the Ottomans, which makes more sense at that time.

124 Muḥammad b. ʿAbd al-Raḥmān, 'Baʿḍ dhikrayātimin qabl rubʿ qarn', *al-Manhal* 10; 7, April/May 1950, pp. 232–3.

125 Interview, ʿUthmān al-Faḍl, Jeddah, March 15, 2010. He probably refers here to the Nagpur riots of 1927.

126 IOR, L/PS/12/2085, Hejaz-Nejd, Annual Report, 1931, pp. 68–9.

With Ibn Saʿūd's conquest of Mecca, ʿAbdallāh al-Faḍl became his advisor. He joined Ibn Saʿūd's forces in the fight for Medina and later went to Aden, from where he guided pilgrims to Mecca via the land route, since Jeddah was under siege. In 1927, he resumed his merchant activities and dealt in foodstuffs in Mecca, and, two years later, was appointed deputy head of the Consultative Council, representing the merchants. By 1931 he was head of the government during the periods of absence of Prince Fayṣal.[127]

ʿAbdallāh al-Faḍl was co-founder of the first abortive state motor transport company in 1925–6. He also became a chief supplier of the Royal Palace in 1926, was responsible for allocating the *ṣadaqa* (1928), and became administrative inspector in Medina and al-Aḥsāʾ. In 1934, he founded the first welfare organisation of the Hijaz and in 1949 he resigned in order to obtain medical treatment in Cairo, where he died two decades later. He also returned to this merchant business for some time. His half-brother Muḥammad was appointed a member of the Administrative Council of Jeddah in 1931 and a member of the *majlis al-shūrā* in 1942.

The al-Faḍl were thus duly rewarded for their early and significant support of Ibn Saʿūd. They were also awarded a piece of land to the north-west of the old city. This had been filled in during Sharifian times and initially used as a recreational site. However, the al-Faḍl did not keep it for long and it returned to the hands of the Āl Saʿūd, who developed it into a hotel and shopping facilities.[128]

The trajectory of ʿAbdallāh's other half-brother, Ibrāhīm b. ʿAbd al-Raḥmān (1892–1940), was not dissimilar, except that he was trained in Bombay from c.1902/3 and sent to the firm's Mecca branch in 1912/13, where he traded in foodstuffs, clothes, and pearls. Besides the businesses in Jeddah, Bahrain, India (presumably Bombay and Karachi), and ʿUnayza, a branch in Medina is also mentioned as a trading partner.[129] In 1930 Ibrāhīm became a member of the *majlis al-shūrā* and joined the government a year later, thereafter repeatedly serving in different positions. Other family members were also

[127] The biographies vary somewhat on the dates. On dates, I am following the typescript biography, on titles, the article by al-Shibīlī who has researched on the basis of the official journal *Umm al-Qurā*.

[128] Bin Zaqr, *unpublished memories*, p. 13.

[129] Typescript biography of Ibrāhīm b. ʿAbd al-Raḥmān b. ʿAbdallāh b. Faḍl.

appointed to the government, possibly due to their relatively high level of education. The family intermarried with the then almost almighty Finance Minister, ʿAbdallāh Sulaymān, but also maintained close relations with the Zaynal branch of the well-established ʿAlī Riḍās, whom they knew from Bombay.

While the rise of the al-Faḍl was thus linked to their royal connections, this should not overshadow their links to local families, notably those also engaged in the India and pearl trade, such as the ʿAlī Riḍā, Jamjūm, or Hazzāzī and their integration into local society. This occurred through charity, but also through joint political activities. Examples are ʿAbdallāh b. Muḥammad al-Faḍl's membership in the new Merchant Council formed in November of 1926 and the various administrative functions he exercised.[130] Finally, such collaborations also resulted in joint business ventures, such as the attempt to establish a local syndicate for motorised pilgrims' transport with ʿAbdallāh Zaynal, Sulaymān Qābil, Ibrāhīm al-ʿAmmānī, and a member of the al-Dihlawī family from Mecca.[131]

The Pilgrimage

The centrality of the pilgrimage for the very existence of Jeddah but also for its rulers and inhabitants has already been pointed out. Systematically, this can be subdivided into a number of different factors which were, of course, interlinked. Besides the different fees demanded of pilgrims, and their spending on housing, food, transport etc., they also enlivened the local trade through the goods (and slaves) which they brought in order to pay for their voyage, and through their own acquisition of goods to take home.[132] Finally, many of the vessels

130 *Umm al-Qurā*, 102, November 26, 1926, p. 3.

131 MECA, Philby Collection GB165–0229, Diary part 1, February 7, 1926, p. 398. The eventual concession went to a slightly different consortium, see MECA, Philby Collection GB165–0229, Diary part 1, February 28, 1926, p. 364. The numbering of the diary is odd as Philby kept pages empty and later used them.

132 For example, a French report in 1873 noted that the Persians, who had problems with their currency, brought carpets and fabrics to cover their costs, see CADN, 2_MI_3229, Buez to MAE, February 27, 1873; cf. Buez to Min. of Agriculture and Commerce, March 31, 1873. For the general dependence of most people on the hajj; cf. TNA, FO 195/1514, Jago to FO, March 5, 1885.

and caravans which carried pilgrims also bought goods for the local merchants, something which notably occurred before the dominance of steamshipping.[133] Thus, a good pilgrimage such as that in 1865, when 48,000 pilgrims passed through a town of approximately 15,000, was much desired.[134] Years with low numbers, caused for example by crises or the plague, not only endangered the livelihoods of townspeople and Bedouin but, from a consular perspective, increased the danger of 'fanaticism'. Specifically, this presumably meant unrest and/or a decrease in the security of roads as Bedouin tried to compensate for loss of income by raiding merchants and travellers.[135]

Not all pilgrims were equally appreciated: Algerian and Tunisian pilgrims were reputed to be quite wealthy.[136] In contrast, there are repeated reports about beggars whom the Ottoman authorities deported at their own expense if they could not force the consuls to take charge of them.[137] A particular concern was destitute Indian pilgrims, who often had to be housed and returned at the expense of the British government (cf. Chapter 7).[138] Hamilton noted in 1852–3 that the British consul had provided free passage back for as many as 6,000 pilgrims.[139] This was one of the reasons why the British had tried to establish the aforementioned monopoly for Thomas Cook, who was meant to ensure that a return journey was booked beforehand. This situation was not helped by the fact that, even in the early twentieth century, many pilgrims were reported to arrive early for the pilgrimage, which indicates that they had opted for sailing boats or early steam passages rather than for the steamers timed more exactly for the pilgrimage.[140]

133 CADN, 2_MI_3229, Dubreuil to MAE and others, December 16, 1871.

134 For approximate pilgrimage numbers, see Ochsenwald, *Religion, Society, and the State*, p. 61.

135 TNA, FO 195/1514, Jago to FO, March 5, 1885; and FO 195/1987, Devey to Amb. Const., April 18, 1897.

136 CADN, 2_MI_3231, Guès to Amb. Const., March 2, 1898.

137 CADN, 2_MI_3229, Buez to Min. of Agriculture and Commerce, March 31, 1873; April 9, 1873; and 2_MI_3231, Dubief to Amb. Const., May 13, 1903.

138 See, for example, TNA, FO 78/2194, Raby to FO, February 13, 1871; FO 195/2174, Dewey to Amb. Const., April 3, 1904; cf. Low, *The Mechanics of Mecca*, pp. 267–83.

139 Hamilton, *Sinai, The Hedjaz, and Soudan*, p. 56.

140 CADN, 2_MI_3231, Dubief to Emb. Const., October 31, 1903.

Organising the Pilgrims: The Institution of the Pilgrim's Guides (ṭawwāfa)

The pilgrimage was organised through the guild of the *muṭawwifūn*, or pilgrims' guides, based in Mecca.[141] The guides were responsible for pilgrims from particular regions, for example Egypt, India, or Central Asia, often subcontracting, in order to deal with the large numbers of pilgrims, and forming sub-guilds. They organised not only accommodation in Mecca but also assisted the pilgrims in the rites of the pilgrimage, as well as in more mundane daily tasks, often also serving as interpreters. Each *muṭawwif* had a representative (*nā'ib*) in Medina who was responsible for catering to the needs of those pilgrims visiting that city before or after performing their duties in Mecca. Furthermore, they had deputies (*wakīl*, pl. *wukalā'*) in Jeddah. These, often also called *muṭawwif* in Western sources, were responsible for caring for the pilgrims during their arrival in Jeddah and organising their onward journey to Mecca.

The network of the *muṭawwifūn* extended into the countries of origin of the pilgrims. Thus, after the end of the pilgrimage, *wukalā'* would travel to the countries for which they were responsible in order to engage with their local counterparts to cultivate their contacts and get a sense of the number of pilgrims that were to be expected.[142] While it is not clear when this practice began, it certainly still existed during World War II, when Ibn Sa'ūd even advanced money to the *muṭawwifūn* in order to boost the declining numbers of pilgrims.[143] The entire system, which, according to a French guess in 1896, comprised about a 1,000 people, was supervised by the emir.[144]

141 The origins of the *ṭawwāfa* as a paid function, and as a guild, have not yet been researched thoroughly. The most precise information can be found in Ḥasan Salīm, 'al-Ṭawwāfa wa-l-muṭawwifūn fī 'l-'aṣr al-mamlūkī' in Kursī al-Malik Salmān (ed.), *al-Ṭawwāfa wa-l-muṭawwifūn: Iṣdār nadwat al-ṭawwāfa wa-l-muṭawwifīn*, 3 vols (Riyadh, 2017), vol. 1, pp. 245–70. According to F. Peters, *Jerusalem and Mecca: The Typology of the Holy City in the Near East*, New York University Studies in Near Eastern Civilization (New York: New York University Press, 1986), vol. 11, p. 230, there are pre-Islamic precedents.

142 This practice is referred to in Rif'at, *Mir'āt al-Ḥaramayn*, vol. 1, p. 63; and Raqqām, *Jidda*, p. 164.

143 Michael Miller, 'Pilgrims' Progress: The Business of the Hajj', *Past and Present*, 191 (2006), pp. 189–228, here 219.

144 For a very good description of the system, see Snouck Hurgronje, *Mekka. Aus dem Heutigen Leben*, pp. 28–33; and CADN, 2_MI_3231, Querry to Amb. Const., August 10, 1896.

It seems that Emir ʿAwn al-Rafīq and, to some extent, the Ottoman authorities contributed significantly to the increase in prices by demanding a regular renewal of the licenses of *muṭawwifūn* which had, earlier, been valid for a lifetime. Furthermore, responsibility for the different regions was auctioned to the highest bidder.[145] In 1890 the licenses of five British Indians were withdrawn, though later reinstated.[146] Obviously, *muṭawwifūn* wanted to recover their fees, which meant that all members of the chain of people employed needed to calculate their fees accordingly. Ibrāhīm Rifʿat, the Egyptian *amīr al-ḥajj*, gave the following description which resonates with numerous other travelogues, consular accounts and studies:

In Jeddah, six and a half Egyptian qirsh – rupee – was taken for each sedan (*shuqduf*). Even if it was taken from the seller in reality it was paid by the buyer because it was part of the price and was taken from the [overall] price. For each camel, which transports the pilgrim from Jeddah to Mecca, two *riyāl*s were for the Sharif, and five Ottoman *qirsh* (four Egyptian *qirsh*) for the [Ottoman] government and another *riyāl* for the *wakīl* of the *muṭawwif* in Jeddah and the one who contracted the camel (*al-muqawwim*) – taxes which were not sanctioned by God. The price of a camel from Jeddah to Mecca was six *riyāl 'barim'* (about ten Egyptian *riyāl)* in the beginning of this year's season. If we deduct from this the taxes, the remainder, less than three *riyāl*, was for the camel-driver and his beast.[147]

According to Ibrahim Rif'at, this prompted the camel-drivers to exploit the pilgrims as much as possible, raising prices until they reached thirty *riyāl*. Low inserts this specific practice into the wider schemes of monopolising the pilgrimage that were discussed above and links them to the presence of European extraterritorial influence, removing the hajj from exclusive Ottoman control.[148] Certainly, both imperial powers and profit-oriented Muslims were happy to exploit the opportunity of the pilgrimage. Thus, in a move to privatise the responsibility

145 For a detailed description, see Snouck Hurgronje, pp. 99–100. According to Hadhrami shaykh who was in contact with the French consulate, the *ṭawwāfa* was sold, CADN, '_MI_3231, Labosse to unknown recipient, no. 20, dated Jeddah, July 22, 1890.

146 TNA, FO 195/1689, Wood to Amb. Const., May 30, 1890.

147 Rifʿat, *Mirʾāt al-Ḥaramayn*,vol. 1, p. 65. See also, for example, TNA, FO 685/2, Translation from the Arabic Journal of Mohammed Abou-Elewa's Pilgrimage, Cairo to Meccah, Medinah, and Back, 1886.

148 Low, *The Mechanics of Mecca*, pp. 314–8 and 332.

for poor pilgrims, one of the British suggestions was to have pilgrim agents at all Indian seaports.[149] Nevertheless, Low's argument presumes a largely uncorrupted functioning of the pilgrimage prior to the 1880s. Given the involvement of Ottoman officials in merchant rackets in the 1850s, this seems somewhat optimistic, even if the increasing scale of the pilgrimage obviously also increased both the temptation to exploit pilgrims and the profits that could be obtained. Furthermore, in light of reports from the 1870s which describe scenes of chaos and violence during departure not only due to lack of space on the ships, but also due to regulations related to new sanitation measures, the demands for a somewhat more planned approach by consular officials appears not entirely irrational.[150] A French consul who had previously written much about the exploitation of pilgrims, wryly commented on (presumably local) Muslim fears about the disappearance of the pilgrimage due to the presence of Western ships in 1900.

> If ever the pilgrimage to Mecca was to disappear, one would not need to blame the Christian nations, as some suggest, but those who live off it, those who have transformed it into a most lucrative business.[151]

Although the consul primarily directed his blame at the Sharif and the Ottomans, one could also accuse the non-Ottoman Muslims and Westerners, who all competed to obtain a share of the profits.

The system of the *tawwāfa* has remained in place to this day. Sharif Ḥusayn aimed, once again, to re-divide responsibilities for different parts of the Muslim world in order to increase his revenues. Although the plan failed and his relentless drive to raise revenues backfired, complaints about high prices and bad conditions soared. The confiscation of medical supplies and the attempt to place the Egyptian medical mission under the Sharif's supervision even sparked a major crisis in the

[149] IOR, R/19/7, L/P&S/7/30, no. 15, Circular to Local Governments and Administrations, August 24, 1881. The need for regulation was also stressed by French officials, e.g. CADN, 2_MI_3231, Dubief to Emb. Const., February 3, 1904.

[150] CADN, 2_MI_3227, Dubreuil to MAE, March 26, 1870. A major crisis occurred in 1881 when due to the cholera, transport of pilgrims from Jeddah was suspended both past Suez and Aden, and tens of thousands converged on Jeddah in the hope of catching a boat (2_MI_3229, letters from October 19 to December 19, 1881).

[151] CADN, 2_MI_3231 (Dubief to Emb. Const.?) No. 25, May 25, 1900; cf. 2_M_3231, Télégramme chiffré, June 13, 1895 to Emb. Const.

relationship between Egypt and Hijaz.[152] One must also consider the decline of security on the overland routes and, in 1925, the blockade of Jeddah by Saudi troops which only allowed a few pilgrims to make the journey overland or through other ports, notably Rābigh.[153]

Once security was established after the Saudi takeover, the system seems to have been somewhat relaxed.[154] When entering Mecca, Ibn Saʿūd committed to the preservation of the profession. In 1926 a new law (*niẓām idārat al-ḥajj*) was enforced, in which the king once again licensed specific *muṭawwifūn* to organise the hajj for specific groups 'according to the old traditions'. The responsibilities of the *muṭawwif* regarding the religious duties as well as the worldly concerns of the pilgrims were defined, specifying that the *muṭawwif* had to instruct his pilgrims in the rites of the pilgrimage 'according to their [i.e. the pilgrims'] religious school'. Female *muṭawwifa*s had to make sure that they got trustworthy people serving 'their' pilgrims – which indicates that they were not meant to perform these duties themselves. The highest offices were those of *raʾīs mashāʾikh al-jāwā* (head of the Southeast Asian pilgrims' guides) and *raʾīs li-ʿumūm al-muṭawwifīn* (head of the general pilgrims' guides) which were responsible for the behaviour of the remainder of their guild members.[155] The decree also regulated the tasks of the *zamzam* water distributors, the *mukharrijūn*, health officials, and others.[156] The *wukalāʾ* of the *jāwā* and general pilgrims' guides in Jeddah had to receive pilgrims at the harbour, register them, cater for their transport and that of their luggage to their abode, get the permit for, and organise the onwards journey. The *wukalāʾ* were in turn supervised by *nuqabāʾ* (delegates), who mediated in cases of conflict and reported to the heads of the *muṭawwifūn* in Mecca.[157]

In 1927 a decree stipulated that the accommodation of pilgrims had to fulfil certain standards of furnishing and cleanliness that were to be inspected prior to registration with the sanitary inspectorate. The *muṭawwifūn* (and consequently the *wukalāʾ*) had to ensure that the regulations were respected.[158] In order to improve services, the king

152 Chiffoleau, *Le Voyage à la Mecque*, pp. 266–7. 153 Ibid., p. 270.

154 On the rising costs during Hashemite times, see Chantre, *Pèlerinages d'Empire*, p. 228; Chaudhry, *The Price of Wealth*, p. 55 also p. 13; and for early Saudi times IOR, L/PS/12/2085, Hejaz-Nejd Annual Report 1930.

155 *Umm al-Qurā*, 101, November 19, 1926, p. 3. 156 Ibid., pp. 3–4.

157 Ibid., p. 4. 158 *Umm al-Qurā*, 117, March 11, 1927, p. 3.

opened a school for *muṭawwifūn* in 1927/28. In 1949/50, a directorate of the *muṭawwifūn* was created and put under the supervision of the Ministry of the Interior and later to the Ministry of Pilgrimage. Since 1981/82, there are also special organisations for the *wukalāʾ* (and other pilgrimage related groups).[159]

In addition to these organisational measures, a number of practical steps were taken. These included the erection of tent cities for the pilgrims at the main stations of the hajj, which were fitted with the necessary sanitary installations. A special radio station was to inform and instruct pilgrims.[160]

Housing and Feeding the Pilgrims

Once the pilgrimage season started, the *wukalāʾ* in Jeddah would be on the watch for arriving ships from the top of their houses and rush to the harbour when these began to disembark.[161] When pilgrims had found their *wakīl*, he would take over and more or less organise the passage through quarantine (more on which later) and customs, guiding the pilgrims via the 'Sea Gate' (Bāb al-Baḥr) to their respective accommodation, which depended very much on the pilgrim's status and place of origin.

Very prominent visitors were usually housed with leading notables. The mansion most famously receiving many guests, including King Abd al-Aziz Al Sa'ud, was that built by ʿUmar Naṣīf in 1298–9/1881 (1872–81) and inherited by his grandson Muḥammad (discussed in Chapter 3). Some *wukalā* owned entire houses that were rented out to the pilgrims. The probably more common model, which old people in Jeddah still remember, was that families moved to the top floor of their houses or, if they had houses in Ṭāʾif, even to Ṭāʾif. This allowed them to rent out a maximum number of rooms to pilgrims. In busy years, pilgrims' accommodation could include the stone benches in front of

159 Sulṭān al-Ḥujaylī, "al-Ṭawwāfa' mihna ḥufiẓat li-ahl Makka … wa-400 malyūn', al-Ḥayyāt, August 31, 2017. For a detailed account of the development in Saudi times; cf. Īnās al-Khālid and Muḥammad al-Raḥḥāla, 'Qirāʾat fī tārīkh anẓimat al-ḥajj wa-l-ʿumra fī ṣaḥīfat Umm al-Qurā', *Kursī al-Malik Salmān b. ʿAbd al-ʿAzīz* 1436/2010.

160 Khayr al-Dīn al-Ziriklī, *Shibh al-Jazīra fī ʿahd al-Malik ʿAbd al-ʿAziz* (Beirut: Maṭābiʿ Dār al-Qalam, 1970), vol. 3–4, p. 1336.

161 Explanation during guided tour to Bayt Naṣīf, March 13, 2006.

houses. In some instances, pilgrims also resorted to renting benches in coffee shops or to camping in the streets.[162] At times, women would even invite strangers in if they saw them sleeping rough.[163] Sometimes, pilgrims who had no personal connections also found a place in a *ribāṭ*, in a *wikāla*, or a *zāwiya*, spaces discussed in more detail in Chapter 4.

It seems that the first hotels in Jeddah were only built in the early twentieth century. The Egyptian traveller al-Batanūnī, who performed the Hajj in 1909, mentions that he heard of a 'small inn' (*nazlan saghīran - lūkānda*) near the customs office, but that he had not seen it.[164] By 1933 the Italian Nallino describes two hotels, one in and one outside of the old city, thereby incidentally indicating the increased state of security.[165] Subsequently, more hotels were built which suffered, however, from economic problems due to the seasonal fluctuation in visitors. Only in 1950–1 and 1956 were the large pilgrims' hostels at the port, the old airport, and near the quarantine built, which became known as pilgrims' cities.[166] If these facilities did not suffice, tents were pitched outside of the city wall, a practice that was already common in the first decades of the nineteenth century.[167]

What seems important for the theme of diversity in terms of housing is that the *ṭawwāfa* provided an effective way of mediating the impact of strangers in the city. Although, as has been shown, not all pilgrims came through this organised system and were allocated accommodation by designated guides, the overwhelming majority did. Even if pilgrims stayed in private houses, which would normally have created various problems, for example in terms of the movement of women through the house, they were strangers who were part of a known system and were thus made to fit existing categories.[168] The *muṭawwif* acted as their guarantor vis-à-vis the hosts, comparable, perhaps, to the role a *maḥram* (unmarriageable legal escort of women) plays when

162 Pilgrims camping outdoors are mentioned for example in CADN, 2_MI_3229, Suret to Min. of Agriculture, January 7, 1879; and documented by RGS 091397, C 2392, Clemow 1906, Nallino, *Raccolta di Scritti*, p. 171.
163 Oral information, Dr. ʿAdnān al-Yāfī, Jeddah, March 22, 2006.
164 al-Batanūnī, *al-Riḥla al-ḥijāziyya li-walī al-niʿm*, p. 10.
165 Nallino, *Raccolta di Scritti*, p. 169.
166 al-Anṣārī, *Mawsūʿat tārīkh madīnat Jidda*, pp. 435–8.
167 Interviews, Dr. ʿAdnān al-Yāfī, March 22, 2006; Aḥmad ʿAbdallāh al-Faḍl, March 12, 2010; and Foster Sadlier, *Diary of a Journey*, p. 100.
168 On such tensions, see Shryock, *The New Jordanian Hospitality*, especially p. 36.

representing women in their dealings with strangers. He and the hosts he contracted also kept a close eye on the pilgrim who was thus under a sort of surveillance. The fact that this occurred in a way which benefitted the hosts materially was certainly another way to sweeten the presence of strangers.

The pilgrims were mostly provisioned by their respective hosts. However, it seems that there existed a de facto a variety of models. Thus, little booths would spring up next to the houses of important pilgrim guides (*busṭat al-hajj*), which catered to the specific regional tastes of the pilgrims of those *wukalā*ʾ. At times, these booths remained for up to eight months, which also shows the potential length of pilgrimage seasons, and then packed up until the next season.[169] Similarly, the business of the likes of water carriers and sellers in the *sūq* increased markedly, hence the common saying that Jeddah (as well as Mecca) lived off pilgrimage season.

As far as the onwards-transportation is concerned, the most important hub was the area around Bāb Makka, as already discussed in Chapter 4. It was here where the pilgrims met their camel drivers and, increasingly from the 1920s onwards, their busses and cars. The second hub was Bāb al-Madīna, from where the caravans in the direction of Medina started and arrived.

Pilgrims as an International Concern

We have seen in Chapter 2 how the establishment of the British and French consulates in Jeddah in the 1830s occurred in the context of imperial rivalry out of a tradition of trade with the Indian Ocean. By the 1860s, and with the growth of Muslim populations under Western rule and the growth in steamshipping and plans to open the Suez Canal, they became concerned with the Hijaz as a destination for pilgrims.[170] This reflected an anxiety about 'Sanitation and Security', described as a kind of 'twin infection' in a pioneering article by William Roff, that has been echoed many times since.[171] As both aspects have

169 Raqqām, *Jidda*, pp. 157–8.
170 Chiffoleau, *Le Voyage à la Mecque*, pp. 109–20.
171 Roff, *Sanitation and Security*, p. 143; e.g. Michael Low, 'The "Twin Infection": Pilgrims, Plagues, and Pan-Islam under British Surveillance, 1865–1924', Paper at Graduate Conference: Crossing Boundaries, Spanning Regions: Movements of People, Goods and Ideas, March 10, 2006; Low, *Empire and the Hajj*;

obtained much attention in academia, the following very brief summary will focus exclusively on aspects of direct relevance for Jeddah.

One important consequence of these concerns was a certain rush to open consulates. In 1872 the Dutch established a consulate, partly, out of concern for the growing numbers of Southeast Asian Muslims under their protection who travelled to the Hijaz. In 1876 the Swedish king appointed a consul, in 1880 Austria and Greece followed suit, and in 1891, Russia with its Central Asian population, joined in.[172] By 1884 there was also a Persian consulate in Jeddah, which is where Snouck Hurgronje witnessed the *ʿāshūrāʾ* celebrations.

The political concerns of the consuls were twofold. Most importantly, they felt that they needed to supervise pilgrims from their countries. One aspect was the need to control and possibly prevent the long-term presence of impoverished pilgrims in the Hijaz (and in the transit countries) to make sure that they complied with the Ottoman regulations and the demands to deport those overstaying their welcome. Furthermore, they felt that they needed to protect pilgrims from the kinds of abuses and extortionate practices described above. Finally, pilgrims and merchants were in need of consular representation in the not infrequent cases of robbery and theft in the Hijaz, either during their sojourn in the cities or, perhaps more frequently, during travel between Jeddah, Mecca, and Medina.[173] From a Muslim perspective this last reason was, of course, a mere pretext: On the occasion of the arrival of a Muslim Russian consul in 1891, Sayyid Faḍl al-ʿAlawī warned of the presence of Muslim consuls who were furthering Western control over the holy land of the Hijaz. Consuls, Sayyid Faḍl advised, should not be allowed to settle in the holy city but should only be allowed in Jeddah.[174]

Saurabh Mishra, *Pilgrimage, Politics, and Pestilence: The Haj from the Indian Subcontinent, 1860–1920* (Oxford: Oxford University Press, 2011); Chantre, *Pèlerinages d'Empire*, pp. 67–74 and passim; and John Slight, 'British Colonial Knowledge and the Hajj in the Age of Empire' in U. Ryad (ed.), *The Hajj and Europe in the Age of Empire*, Leiden Studies in Islam & Society (Leiden and Boston: Brill, 2017), pp. 80–111.

172 Freitag, *Helpless Representatives*, p. 360. On the Russian consulate see Kane, *Russian Hajj*, pp. 68–9.

173 Random examples for this practice are mentioned in CADN, 2_MI_3229, Malpertuy to MAE, June 16, 1881; 2_MI_2_3231, Labosse to Emb. Const., March 7, 1891; and Dubief to Emb. Const., March 4, 1904.

174 BOA, I.DH 1237/96875 of 16 Z. 1308 (July 23, 1891). I thank On Barak for this reference.

More pressing, from an imperial perspective, was the second issue, namely the political supervision. Ever since the massacre of foreign consuls and merchants in 1858, when the British suspected a connection to the Great Indian Revolt, they had lingering fears of the Hijaz serving as a hotbed of anti-imperial and what would later become known as pan-Islamic sentiment.[175] There were a number of occasions when such fears intensified, such as on the occasion of the murder of Grand-Sharif Ḥusayn b. Muḥammad in 1880, when there were anti-imperial revolts from Algeria to Afghanistan (see Chapter 2). Dutch officials were particularly troubled by the Hadhrami scholar ʿAbd al-Raḥmān al-Zāhir al-Saqqāf (1833–1996) and his attempts to rally Ottoman military support for the anti-colonial uprising in Aceh in 1873. While this took the indefatigable activist to Istanbul, ʿAbd al-Raḥmān could use his family links in Jeddah and Singapore (both in the pilgrim's business and in religious circles) to muster Arab backing for the anti-colonial struggle.[176] Anti-imperial activists did indeed often pass through the Hijaz, which regularly alerted the consular officials of the countries from which these persons stemmed. Worse still than possible pan-Islamic alliances of activists was the potential danger of their mobilisation of Ottoman support. While political agitation required presence in Istanbul, the relative inaccessibility of Mecca for Western powers meant that activists, but also others who had a brush with colonial officials, could take refuge there. Perhaps the most striking case is the mass-emigration of Muslims from the Muslim Sahel region between Mali and Bornu to the Hijaz in the very early twentieth century, fleeing French and British expansion.[177] While the image of Mecca as a refuge was perhaps not entirely accurate, it was certainly one which kept officials of colonial and foreign offices busy. Indeed, it was a combination of health and political issues that prompted the British to appoint a Muslim vice-consul in Jeddah in 1882, i.e. in the

[175] For an early sense of such pan-Islamic solidarity under an Ottoman umbrella see Hamilton, *Sinai, The Hedjaz, and Soudan*, pp. 76–7.

[176] On this, see Anthony Reid, 'Habib Abdur-Rahman Az-Zahir (1833-1896)', *Indonesia*, 13 (1972), pp. 37–60; Freitag, *Indian Ocean Migrants and State Formation*, pp. 195–7; and Aydin, *The Idea of the Muslim World*, pp. 58–64 on the period 1873–83. For the link of these fears to the Sufi brotherhoods, see Chantre, *Pèlerinages d'Empire*, pp. 47–52.

[177] Ahmed, *West African 'Ulamā' and Salafism*, pp. 9–10. On the issue of refuge by Muslims in the wider Ottoman Empire; cf. Alavi, *Muslim Cosmopolitanism.*, pp. 22–30 and passim.

midst of fears of Muslim anti-imperial agitation.[178] In France, fears of pan-Islamic agitation sparked considerations of limiting or even banning the hajj, even if health reasons were used as a pretext.[179] This also shows how entangled the engagement for pilgrims was with other, from an imperial perspective, more pressing issues, namely imperial security and the health of the empire and of Europe.

Health Matters: Water, Quarantine, and Hospitals

Even if European concerns with health were often emphasised to cover up political interventions regarding the pilgrimage, health was an issue of concern to both Ottoman authorities and pilgrims. On average, about 20 per cent of them died during pilgrimage, but in bad years it could be many more. However, it should not be forgotten that the provision of health services in a city like Jeddah had three different, although clearly interrelated, aspects: the health of the military, the health of the urban inhabitants, and the health of the pilgrims, and that an improvement of such services formed part of the wider programme of urban modernisation pursued during the Tanzimat period. This is evidenced by widespread investments in various aspects of health care and sanitation found in a broad range of cities.[180]

One prime issue was the provision of clean drinking water (cf. Chapter 4). The measures taken by the Ottoman authorities were in part due to the pressure of local merchants, but they were also a response to international concerns. Thus, it was the British representative on the Istanbul Board of Health who first suggested the installation of a seawater condenser to the Hijaz Sanitary Administration.[181] It was probably this aspect which finally swayed the Board of Health in Istanbul to finance the desalination plants of Yanbuʿ and Jeddah in 1907, as well as the almost immediate replacement of the

178 TNA, FO 685/1, III, Sec. To the Gvt. of India to Assistant Surgeon Abdul Razak, H.B.M's Vice Consul at Jeddah, August 25, 1882.

179 Chiffoleau, *Le Voyage à la Mecque*, pp. 133–6; in 1903, consul Dubief engaged with the argument, reasoning that the pan-Islamic role of Mecca was exaggerated, CADN, 2MI3231, Dubief to Emb. Const., May 13, 1903.

180 See, for example, Anastassiadou, *Salonique, 1830–1912*, pp. 103–9, Weber, *Damascus*. pp. 147–53.

181 Clemow, *Les Eaux de Djeddah*, pp. 10–16; and Birsen Bulmuş, *Plague, Quarantines and Geopolitics in the Ottoman Empire* (Edinburgh: Edinburgh University Press, 2012), pp. 165–6.

Jeddah plant in 1911.[182] With the establishment of Saudi rule, there was a perceived need to improve pilgrimage provisions, not just for reasons of Islamic legitimacy, but also for the vital income generated through pilgrimage. It was partly this concern for the pilgrimage which prompted the investments in new sea-water condensers as well as into the rehabilitation of ʿAyn al-ʿAzīziyya. As the concrete measures have been discussed in Chapter 4, they will not feature in the following in spite of also being important in context.

The Ottoman administration was mostly concerned with the provision of health services to the military and to pilgrims, although de facto, services were often put to multiple uses.[183] At the beginning of the period under consideration, there were hardly any modern medical services in Jeddah. Cholera appeared repeatedly in the Hijaz from 1831 to the 1850s, with devastating effects.[184] Following the Paris Sanitary Conference of 1851, the Ottoman government began to apply basic quarantine measures and sent a physician and pharmacist to Medina as well as inoculators to the Bedouin. However, when the devastating cholera epidemic of 1865 swept through the Hijaz, there was no surveillance of sea arrivals, who constituted the vast majority of pilgrims, nor was there a quarantine station, lazarets or hospitals to treat the sick. The following survey will consider quarantine, hospitals, and the provision of sanitation, always with a special focus on Jeddah and its development.

Quarantine[185]

Following the great cholera epidemic of 1865, which reached as far as California, a French report described the spread of the disease via

182 Low, *The Mechanics of Mecca*, pp. 259–60; and Kasım İzzeddin, *Hicaz'da Teşkilât ve Islahât-ı Sıhhiye ve 1330 Senesi Hacc-ı Şerifi: Hicaz Sıhhiye Idâresi, Senevi Rapor* (Istanbul: Matbaa-yi Amire, 1330/1911), pp. 39–50.

183 Mehmed Şakir, *Hicaz'ın Ahval-i Sıhhiye Müşahedat.*

184 Cornelia Essner, 'Cholera der Mekkapilger und internationale Sanitätspolitik in Ägypten (1866–1938)', *Die Welt des Islams*, 32 (1992); and Chantre, *Pèlerinages d'Empire*, pp. 67–9.

185 For more general surveys, see Essner, *Cholera der Mekkapilger*; Valeska Huber, 'The Unification of the Globe by Disease?: The International Sanitary Conferences on Cholera, 1851–1894', *The Historical Journal*, 49 (2006), pp. 453–76; Ochsenwald, *Religion, Society, and the State*, pp. 64–73; Mark Harrison, 'Disease, Diplomacy and International Commerce: The Origins of International Sanitary Regulation in the Nineteenth Century', *Journal of*

al-Mukallā on the South Yemen coast to the Hijaz. There had been no inspection of arrivals, as would be implemented later, no quarantine nor lazarets for the ill, no hospitals, pharmacies, dispensaries or doctors.[186] Some 30,000 pilgrims were said to have died at Munā alone during the epidemic.[187] It is hence not surprising that the International Sanitary Conference in Istanbul proposed to establish a sanitary station at the southern entrance of the Red Sea, even if there are indications that a basic medical infrastructure for poor pilgrims had been established earlier (see Chapter 7).[188]

By 1866 it was clear that the sea route was the cause of the transmission of infectious diseases, as the lengthy caravan travel from the Hijaz itself served as a sort of quarantine. In the same year, an Ottoman sanitary commission came to Jeddah to make arrangements for the inspection of arrivals, as well as health provisions in the adjacent ports. It is possible that it was in this context that a local Health Council was established which became involved in the urban works described in Chapter 4. The sanitary commission also arranged a basic medical service in Mecca, Medina, Yanbuʿ, al-Qunfudhah, Hodeidah, and Mocha, as well as al-Wajh. Another commission, headed by a French physician, was charged to find a convenient site for quarantine stations for the pilgrimage, suggesting al-Tūr at the northern and Camaran Island at the southern end of the Red Sea.[189] Two years later quarantine stations in el-Tūr, al-Wajh and at the Moses Wells were operational, apparently checking pilgrims on the maritime return route.[190]

A French report of 1869 also hints at serious restrictions on the housing of pilgrims. House owners in Mecca and Medina were obliged to whitewash their houses and their pilgrims' accommodation was supervised by the police. In Jeddah, pilgrims were only allowed to

Global History, 1 (2006), pp. 197–217; and Chiffoleau, *Le Voyage à la Mecque*, pp. 153–200.

186 CADN, 2_MI_3228, Consul, Jeddah to MAE, December 20, 1865.

187 Baldry, *Foreign Interventions and Occupations*, p. 17.

188 Ibid., p. 11. For the following; cf Stratkötter, *Von Kairo nach Mekka*, pp. 100–6.

189 René Tresse, *Le pèlerinage syrien aux villes saintes de l'Islam* (Paris: Chaumette, 1937), p. 281; and John Baldry, 'The Ottoman Quarantine Station on Kamaran Island 1882–1914', *Studies in the History of Medicine*, 2 (1978), pp. 3–137, here p. 21.

190 CADN, 2_MI_3228, Consul Jeddah to MAE, April 12, 1867.

move in certain areas and camps outside of town were patrolled day and night. The French consul's satisfaction with these measures once again shows the close intertwinement of health and political containment, as he explicitly voiced his satisfaction with this control of 'religious exaltation of the fanatics'.[191]

To what extent these measures actually helped prevent the disease, or whether poor conditions and sloppy practices actually contributed to it spreading further, remained contested for many years.[192] As works on Kamaran Island were delayed, various quarantine stations and lazarets were set up around Jeddah by 1869 and a number of health officials were appointed to various cities.[193] Nevertheless, European observers considered these measures to be so ineffective that in 1874 the newly re-opened British consulate was directed to control passengers on British vessels.[194]

In 1882 Kamaran Island was made an obligatory quarantine stop and pilgrims were charged hefty fees for their involuntary stay. Furthermore, sanitary conditions were less than ideal and prompted fairly immediate complaints by Indian pilgrims. The *Bombay Gazette* even claimed that 'more sickness occurs on the island of Kamaran than during the voyage'.[195] Additionally, the long wait also increased the risk that pilgrims might miss the pilgrimage, leading, at times, to rebellions on ships, as well as to significant resentment by merchants fearing for their goods. The British government, anxious to present a pro-pilgrimage attitude in order not to alienate its British-Indian Muslim subjects, responded by attempting to subvert quarantine rules.[196] In parallel, quarantine barracks were put up outside the Jeddah walls in the expectation that the quarantine fees paid by pilgrims would eventually cover the costs.[197]

Consequently, in May 1884 the French consul reported that permanent outposts of the Kamaran quarantine station with lazarets for

[191] Ibid., Dubreuil to MAE, March 6, 1869.

[192] Huber, *Channelling Mobilities*, pp. 228–9; and TNA, FO 195/1767, Correspondence printed in 'The Times of India', July 26, 1891.

[193] Baldry, *Foreign Interventions and Occupations*, p. 27.

[194] Ibid., p. 29.

[195] Bombay Gazette, August 7, 1883, quoted after Harrison, *Disease, Diplomacy and International Commerce*, p. 125; cf. Mishra, *Pilgrimage, Politics, and Pestilence*, p. 56.

[196] Mishra, *Pilgrimage, Politics, and Pestilence*, pp. 57–8. For al-Tūr, see Huber, *Channelling Mobilities*, p. 229.

[197] BOA, Y.PRK.ASK. 12 57, B. 19, 1299/June 6, 1882.

sick pilgrims were established on the two islands of Abū Sa'd and Wasṭa just off the port of Jeddah. This would decrease the waiting time at Kamaran by six days.[198] In 1897 and 1898 additional quarantine stations were also set up between Jeddah and Mecca, possibly in response to a plague outbreak in Bombay in 1896.[199] This caused unrest due to fears of merchants that their income in trade might suffer.[200]

Foreign governments, distrusting local provisions, started to send doctors from various places with the pilgrims. These treated pilgrims and reported on the health conditions during the pilgrimage.[201] Thus, we have a long list of health and sanitation reports by Egyptian, French, British, and Dutch health specialists. In spite of the attempts to check pilgrims and maintain an acceptable level of hygiene, cholera returned in 1877–8, prompting more stringent measures of quarantine and sanitation. For example, during the Hajj of 1884, a temporary hospital (probably more a lazaret) for pilgrims was set up in Jeddah outside the Mecca Gate.[202] However, it proved difficult to control the spread of disease and hence such measures had to be repeated regularly. By 1910 a separate Hijaz Sanitary Administration was put in place to minimalize foreign involvement in local health decisions.[203] A series of prefabricated German quarantine barracks were set up, presumably south of old Jeddah, to replace old installations.[204]

The quarantine of the Hijaz during Hashemite rule was judged disastrous by the British, to the extent that they reinstated the quarantine of Kamaran.[205] Although services improved under the Saudi government, which established its own Public Health Authority in 1926 in

198 CADN, 2_MI_3229, Article 7, Consul Jeddah to Min. of Commerce, May 26, 1884.
199 Harrison, *Disease, Diplomacy and International Commerce*, pp. 137–41.
200 CADN, 2_MI_3231, Djeddah, Guès to Emb. Const., July 6, 1897, August 25, 1897. For a similar incident in 1902, Baldry, *Foreign Interventions and Occupations*, p. 77.
201 E.g. CADN, 2_MI_3228, Article 3, Dubreuil to MAE, January 12, 1870.
202 MAE, CADN, 2MI_3229, Article 7, Consul de Lostalot to Min. of Commerce, January 16, 1883.
203 Bulmuş, *Plague, Quarantines and Geopolitics*, pp. 163–5.
204 Kasım İzzeddin, *Hicaz Sıhhiye Rapor*, pp. 77–8.
205 Baldry, *Foreign Interventions and Occupations*, p. 113. For more detail on the Sharifian and Saudi management of the hajj; cf. Chiffoleau, *Le Voyage à la Mecque*, pp. 264–71; and Chantre, *Pèlerinages d'Empire*, pp. 213–78.

close coordination with the International Sanitary Conferences, it was only in 1956 that Saudi Arabia took control of the entire health management of the pilgrimage, including quarantine.[206]

Hospitals and Sanitation

The first hospital for (foreign) pilgrims and paupers (*al-ghurabāʾ*) was built in 1861 by the Ottoman government, although discussions for the need of a pilgrim's hospital by the British in 1890 indicated that this satisfied neither demand nor their expected level of care.[207] As a result of the devastation caused by the 1865 epidemic, and of the subsequent Ottoman attempts to improve services, the Ottoman government decided to build a hospital with a disinfecting service.[208] It could be the one that was opened in 1868, which probably catered to military and civilian needs. According to French reports, it was still active in the 1880s.[209] In the context of the port improvements of 1895, lazarets for cholera-stricken pilgrims were established.[210] Temporary lazarets or hospitals were also set up in Jeddah when the bubonic plague struck in 1896.[211] In 1898 the Governor of the Hijaz came for his annual inspection visit and opened a hospital for pilgrims.[212]

206 Baldry, *Foreign Interventions and Occupations*, p. 118; John Willis, 'Governing the Living and the Dead: Mecca and the Emergence of the Saudi Biopolitical State', *American Historical Review*, 122 (2017), pp. 346–70, here p. 368; and al-Ḥamdī, *Ḥarakat al-taḥdīth fī 'l-mamlaka*, p. 203; and IPA, 3135/04 of Ramazan 2, 1351/December 30, 1932.

207 The hospital is mentioned in BOA, A.MKT.UM 490/36 of Safer 3, 1278; cf. TNA, FO 685/2, Abdour Razzak to HM Acting Consul, May 7, 1883. Weber, *Damascus*, pp. 147–53, mentions a hospital with the same name for Damascus. This is likely to have also been connected to the pilgrims departing from this city.

208 Ochsenwald, *Religion, Society, and the State*, pp. 64–6; and CADN, 2_MI_3228, 'Mesures prises dans les villes saintes pour le Pélerinage de cette année. Améliorations obtenues depuis 1867, dans le Hedjaz, et surtout à Djeddah', in Dubreuil to MAE, March 6, 1869.

209 CADN, 2_MI_3229, Suret to Min. of Commerce, October 19, 1881, and November 10, 1881.

210 Pétriat, *For Pilgrims and for Trade*, pp. 207–19; TNA, FO 195/1847, Richard to Emb. Const., February 15, 1894, Abdur Razzack to MOF, September 25, 1894; FO 195/1894, Richards to FO, February 14, 1895; and CADN, Constant. Amb., D, Djeddah 6, Report of April 30, 1895.

211 Baldry, *Foreign Interventions and Occupations*, pp. 64–5.

212 CADN, 2_MI_3231, Article 13, Guès to Amb. Constantinople, January 3, 1898.

These efforts notwithstanding, the British consul still made scathing remarks about the available hospital facilities.[213] In 1910 British-Indian doctor Abdur-Rahman described the Municipal Hospital, which by then had merged with the former military hospital, as being 'in a deplorably filthy condition and neglected in every way'.[214] It is thus not surprising that the British even considered the construction of a special hospital for Indian pilgrims in 1910.[215] In October 1911 the British consul reported the opening of a new pilgrim hospital catering to both pilgrims and local patients, albeit somewhat inconveniently located outside of town.[216] It is probably identical with the modern hospital and quarantine barracks shown in a Sanitary report of 1912, although the hospital plans date back to 1899.[217] Given the lax British regulations regarding overloaded British pilgrim ships, as well as their opposition to the quarantine, these harsh critiques of Ottoman sanitary conditions raise questions as to the true reasons for the criticism, which could be used to argue for stronger foreign intervention.

Neither in Hashemite nor in early Saudi times did the situation change dramatically, first due to the war situation, but then also for lack of resources. Nevertheless, the more stringent application of extant public health regulations, and better care for existing facilities, contributed to a much more effective overall provision of health services.[218]

Besides quarantine and actual medical care, the general sanitary conditions of the Hijazi cities, as well as water, were primary concerns of both Ottoman and international health officials and observers. While earlier travellers differ in their impressions of Jeddah, many

[213] TNA, FO 195/1943, Alban to Emb. Const., March 5, 1896 and July 27, 1896.

[214] TNA, FO 195/2350, Monahan to Emb. Const., March 10, 1910; cf. TNA, FO 685/3, Jeddah VIII, Draft Confidential Report Consul Jeddah to Emb. Const., March 12, 1909.

[215] TNA, FO 195/2350, Monahan to Emb. Const., May 30, 1910.

[216] TNA, FO 195/2376, Consul Jeddah to Emb. Const., October 16, 1911.

[217] See the plans (of 1899) and photographs (undated) in Mustafa Güler, Ömer Yılmaz, and İlhan Ovalıoğlu (eds.), *Belgelerle Osmanlı Devrinde Hicaz*, 2 vols. (Istanbul: Çamlıca, 2008), vol. 2, pp. 306–9 (plans) and pp. 312–3 (photographs). The photographs are reproduced from the Hijaz Health Administration, BOA, Kütüphane no. 2028.

[218] Willis, *Governing the Living and the Dead*, pp. 351–5; cf. Ochsenwald, *Islam and Loyalty*, pp. 10–18.

visitors mention that the state of cleanliness left much to be desired.[219] As discussed in Chapter 4, the kaymakam Nūrī Effendi initiated a major programme to cleanse Jeddah and improve it in 1866–7. Subsequently, the municipal council was charged with the upkeep of cleanliness in the city. However, this did not solve the issue. By 1880 the French consul complained once again that measures such as disinfection, street cleaning, control of the state of hygiene in pilgrims' hostels, etc., which had been recommended by the International Sanitary Conference of Istanbul in 1866, were not implemented in a satisfactory way.[220] It remained a topic of concern for the foreign consuls, as British reports from the 1890s show.[221] Thereafter, the topic fades from the consular reports. Nevertheless, an article in the newspaper *Umm al-Qurā* about the necessity of inspecting pilgrims' accommodations in 1927 hints at the continued existence of sanitary concerns for quite some time.[222]

Bedouin: An Indispensable Element of Trade and Pilgrimage

In the discussion of port cities their relation to the sea and to cities and populations beyond the oceans very often takes centre stage.[223] The extant histories of Jeddah are no exception to this rule, as can be seen in the local historiography. Regarding the Bedouin, discourses dominate which emphasise the Khaldunian contrast between urban dweller and Bedouin. As has been shown in this chapter, the economic lifelines of Jeddah, trade and pilgrimage, were intrinsically linked not only to the sea, but also to the interior of the Hijaz, i.e. the 'hinterland' of Jeddah, and its inhabitants, most notably the Bedouin.

As has been seen, some of those engaged in organising relations to the Bedouin, namely the *mukharrijūn*, often themselves of Bedouin

219 For example Bové, *Voyage aux Côtes de l'Arabie Heureuse*, p. 155; and Saleh Soubhy, *Pèlerinage à la Mecque* (Le Caire: Imprimerie Nationale, 1894), pp. 59–60.

220 CADN, 2_MI_3229, Suret to Min. of Agriculture and Commerce, November 15, 1880.

221 TNA; FO 195/1730, Abdur Razzack to Amb. Constantinople, August 27, 1891; and FO 195/1894, Richards to Amb. Const., March 19, 1895

222 *Umm al-Qurā*, 117, March 11, 1927, p. 3.

223 The literature survey in Onur İnal, 'A Port and Its Hinterland: An Environmental History of Izmir in the Late Ottoman Period', PhD Thesis, University of Arizona (2015), pp. 23–44, is instructive; cf. Wouter Jacobs, 'Rotterdam as a World Port City', *Port Planning, Design and Construction*, 65 (2015), pp. 78–80.

origin, lived a settled life in the extra-muros suburbs of Jeddah such as al-Nuzla (cf. Chapter 4). The relative absence of the discussion of relations with the hinterland from histories of Jeddah might be partly due to the aforementioned prejudices. It is, however, also due to the fact that, at least according to extant studies, the relations with the Bedouin were a main point of contention between the Ottoman governors and the emirs of Mecca. While the Ottoman government was anxious to ensure the safety of the pilgrimage, and for this reason sent regular payments to the Bedouin in order to guarantee safe-passage of caravans, the execution of the Bedouin policy lay in the hands of the emirs of Mecca, who were in regular contact with the local Bedouin shaykhs. If they were at odds with the Ottoman governors, they could thus incite the tribal leaders to block the roads or, worse, perform attacks such as those on the foreign consuls in 1895 (see Chapter 2). Consequently, the Ottomans tried to develop relations with tribal leaders, which only added another layer of intertribal conflict.[224]

Furthermore, there were instances when tribal leaders acted of their own accord against both the emir and the Ottomans, such as in 1883 when fighting erupted in Mecca and Jeddah suburbs were raided.[225] On occasions like these the physical defence the Jeddah wall provided proved to be more solid than the religious sanctity of the Mecca area – although the Great Mosque does not seem to have ever been violated.

From the material available so far, it seems that both pilgrims and merchants were very much at the mercy of the Bedouin. One example is the merchant ʿAbd al-Qādir al-Tilmisānī, who has been mentioned earlier in the context of trading with Najd and being converted to *salafī* ideas. He was a French subject and thus the French consuls of Jeddah were repeatedly asked to assist him in cases of theft and robbery. In August 1890 he had sent goods from Jeddah to Medina, using a boat until Yanbuʿ and then switching to a caravan. This caravan was attacked by Bedouin and the French consul intervened with the governor to reclaim the value, which Tilmisānī claimed to be 27,000

224 These issues are discussed in Ochsenwald, *Religion, Society, and the State*; and Ali al-Kholaif, 'The Hijaz Vilayet 1869–1908: The Sharifate, the Hajj, and the Bedouins of the Hijaz', PhD Thesis, University of Wisconsin (1986).

225 Ochsenwald, *Religion, Society, and the State*, p. 187; and TNA, FO 195/1451, Moncrieff to Amb. Const., July 27 and 28, 1883.

Franc.[226] A correspondence over four years developed, during which Tilmisānī suffered further losses: in 1893 a barge of goods was captured near Yanbuʿ, leading to the loss of the goods. Somewhat later a caravan was attacked between Mecca and Jeddah and some boxes of sugar owned by Tilmisānī were lost and, in November, Tilmisānī lost a load of materials en route to Mecca. Compensation was promised repeatedly, which was partly financed from the subsidies otherwise due to the Bedouin, but although these were not paid out it remains unclear if Tilmisānī was ever fully reimbursed for his losses. However, the French reports also show that the Ottoman government itself lost goods during some of the raids, which might explain their lack of enthusiasm for reimbursing a French subject for losses caused by a party outside government control.

There were also regular attacks on pilgrim caravans. When tensions between the emirs and governors or among the Bedouin ran high, such attacks even took place in the holy city of Mecca.[227] The consuls regularly tried to intervene, often feeling frustrated and at times even suggested a collusion between emir and Ottoman governor.[228]

As has been pointed out before, matters got worse under Sharif Ḥusayn, and even the guild of the transporters, the *mukharrijūn*, seems to have joined those who supported banditry. A major reason was that Ḥusayn discontinued the regular allowances which had originally been paid by the Ottomans and then continued by him. Apparently, this was not counterbalanced by his refusal to introduce motor traffic in order to protect the tribal transport economy.[229] Chaudhry shows that the conflict led to an almost complete collapse of the population of the Hijazi cities and the withdrawal of Sharifian forces from smaller towns and villages.[230]

In spite of widespread scepticism against Wahhabi doctrines in the Hijaz, the quick return of security to the countryside and the prospect

[226] The first letter in this matter is CADN, 2_MI_3231, Labosse to Emb. Const., March 7, 1891. Further letters and telegrams dated July 11 and 21, 1891, December 1, 1891, February 22, 1892, March 18, and 24, 1892, October 11, 1893, November 30, 1893, March 15, 1894, and June 7, 1894.

[227] Examples are TNA, FO 195/1313, Burrell to Goschen (?), July 30, 1880; FO 195/1653, Wood to Amb. Const., December 9, 1889; and FO 195/1689, Wood to Amb. Const., February 1, 1890.

[228] TNA, FO 195/1894, Alban to Amb. Const., August 18 and 23, 1895.

[229] Chiffoleau, *Le Voyage à la Mecque* p. 75.

[230] Chaudhry, *The Price of Wealth*, pp. 56–7.

of a less exploitative pilgrimage was a significant factor in Ibn Saʿūd's internal as well as for international recognition of legitimacy. For this reason, the affair surrounding the Egyptian *maḥmal*, which Ibn Saʿūd tried to protect without alienating the Bedouin attackers too much, proved to be such a complicated affair. With the suppression of the subsequent series of revolts by the *Ikhwān* and in the Hijaz (1928–32), Ibn Saʿūd managed to establish himself as the undisputed lord of the land, as well as creating peace on the Peninsula.[231]

What would need to be investigated further is the question to what extent individual merchants, or other urban brokers, managed to establish their own links with the tribes and hence secure an advantage in trade. What role, if any, did the *mukharrijūn* play in this game during Ottoman times? How did the Bedouin perceive their own role, and how did they justify their raids on pilgrims? Is there more evidence of Bedouin investment in cities, of intermarriage, or of loan relations between the city and its hinterland? These questions will require further research but are crucial in order to fully explore the theme of city-hinterland connections.

[231] Of course, tribal policies under Ibn Saʿūd were far less straightforward and more complex than can be discussed in the context of an urban history of one of the Hijazi towns. On this, see Kostiner, *The Making of Saudi Arabia.*, pp. 100–40.

7 Governing and Regulating Diversity: Urban Government in Jeddah

An account of the urban governance of Jeddah needs to discuss the different levels on which power and influence in the city were exercised. First and foremost was the central Ottoman government in Istanbul, represented locally by the governors who often also had command of the troops. The next layer were the emirs of Mecca, the long-established local powerholders. Finally, organs in which local notables were represented and cooperated with the government at various levels need to be considered. The institutional setup in the Hijaz, and in Jeddah in particular largely followed wider Ottoman patterns even if it might have been less highly differentiated. This will be followed by a brief description of the criminal justice system and of measures taken to maintain moral standards in a vibrant port city.[1] Vagrants were seen as a threat to the maintenance of order and raised the additional question of who could legitimately claim to be a Hijazi. This question was linked to worries about foreign intervention and, in Saudi times, to increasing attempts at securing a stable Hijazi population, reducing, wherever possible, fluctuation in the resident population and consolidating their nationality. Once Saudi control had been established a host of measures were taken to ensure at least basic conformity with Wahhabi notions of propriety and to foster the creation of a joint Najdi-Hijazi identity.

Imperial Presence and Local Notables: The Institutions of Jeddah

As the main port of the Hijaz, and hence as a central node for communication, the Ottomans, rather than the emirs of Mecca, dominated

[1] For example, it would seem that there was no cadastre started for Jeddah, something quite central in the urban development of many cities of that period, such as Damascus or Izmir. The general Ottoman framework is discussed in İlber Ortaylı, *Studies on Ottoman Transformation*, Analecta Isisiana (Istanbul: Isis Press, 1994), vol. 10.

Jeddah from the 1840s onwards.[2] The governor of Jeddah (*vali*), as he was called until 1882 when the title was changed to governor of the Hijaz, only moved to Mecca around 1870, as has been discussed in Chapter 2. Even before that date, he spent prolonged periods of time in Meccan and Ṭāʾif in order to keep control over the emir. In the meantime, the kaymakam of Jeddah stood in for him, which explains why the kaymakam was at times also called governor of Jeddah.[3]

In 1879 the foreign consuls protested against the long periods of absence of the governor, which greatly aggravated their tasks of supporting foreign nationals and their concerns. This indicates that by this time the kaymakam had lost many of his prerogatives and effective interventions needed the authority of the governor who, by then, resided in Mecca.[4] In 1885 the British consul complained that the governorship of Jeddah had been 'practically abolished by the governor general of the Hedjaz', meaning that all important matters had to be sent to Mecca or Ṭāʾif, the usual residences of the *vali*.[5] The Meccan emirs visited the city from time to time and, as has been discussed in Chapter 6, when they were in Mecca, they maintained a presence through their representative, who was usually one of the most important merchants, or, at times, even the Ottoman kaymakam. While this representation was officially mostly commercial, the emirs could command the loyalty of part of the Jiddawi notability and thereby influence politics in the city.

It is difficult to gauge from the sources when and if the civil and military authority of the *vali* was firmly separated. In the early 1840s, one of the main tasks of the governors was the military re-establishment of Ottoman rule.[6] A sample check reveals that, as in Baghdad, most governors had a military background and were possibly military as well as civil appointments.[7] However, the military stationed in and just

[2] An overview is given in al-Amr, *The Hijaz under Ottoman Rule*, pp. 69–73, 76–7.

[3] Numan, *The Emirs of Mecca*, p. 61.

[4] TNA, FO 195/1251, Zohrab to FO, May 12, 1879; cf. Zohrab to Governor General of the Hedjaz, May 9, 1879, FO 685/1, II, Consul Zohrab's letterbook, Zohrab to FO, May 28, 1879.

[5] TNA, FO 195/1514, Jago to Emb. Const., February 20, 1885.

[6] Osmanoğlu, *Hicaz Eyaletinin Teşekkülü (1841–1864)*, p. 26.

[7] Sinan Kuneralp, *Son Dönem Osmanlı Erkân ve Ricali: (1839–1922): Prosopografik Rehber* (Istanbul: İsis, 1999). The statement is based on a comparison of the list of governors, p. 32, with short biographies pp. 51–127.

outside Jeddah seems to not have played a major role in urban politics. One exception were the frequent instances of protest during which soldiers who had not been paid or were overdue for release from their service took to the streets and occupied the ʿAkkāsh Mosque. It proved consistently difficult to find troops willing to serve in the Hijaz, even after the establishment of the 6th army of Iraq and the Hijaz.[8] According to a British report, protests of soldiers occurred about once every eight years. This almost ritualised protest did not cause particular excitement in the city. After all, it did not take the dimension of the plundering of the *sūq*, as was the case repeatedly in Iraqi cities during the late nineteenth century, i.e. when the regular army was expanded without sufficient governmental resources.[9] To what extent the position of the barracks outside of the old city played a role in this remains a matter of speculation (see Number 11 of Map 4.3).

Until 1862, the governor appointed the provincial administrative staff himself, thereafter only the guards were appointed by him, whereas the more important administrators (such as the kaymakam) were appointed by Istanbul. Nevertheless, they were under his supervision and the governors often had a say in the appointments. The governor was supported by a small staff. Besides the offices of governor and kaymakam, the office of *ḥisba* was of particular importance. The *muḥtasib* as supervisor of markets, main tax collector, and enforcer of public order (hence also called, at times, head of the police) was under the supervision of the governor.[10] Interestingly, this list of tasks, as well as the economic roles played by the *muḥtasib* due to his preferential access to key

For the situation in Baghdad; cf. Christoph Herzog, *Osmanische Herrschaft und Modernisierung im Irak: Die Provinz Bagdad, 1817–1917*, Bamberger Orientstudien (Bamberg: University of Bamberg Press, 2012), vol. 4, pp. 214–9.

8 Osmanoğlu, *Hicaz Eyaletinin Teşekkülü (1841–1864)*, pp. 29–34.

9 Herzog, *Osmanische Herrschaft und Modernisierung*, pp. 243–4.

10 For the office of *muḥtasib* in the longue durée see Lafi, *Esprit civique et organisation*, pp. 54–5, pp. 124–5 and Robert Mantran, 'Ḥisba – Ottoman Empire' in P. J. Bearman, T. Bianquis, C. E. Bosworth, E. J. van Donzel, and W. P. Heinrichs (eds.), *Encyclopaedia of Islam*, 2nd edn., 12 vols. (Leiden: Brill, 1960–2005). dx.doi.org/10.1163/1573-3912_islam_COM_0293 (accessed October 7, 2019); for modern history see Jörn Thielmann, 'Ḥisba (Modern Times)' in K. Fleet, G. Krämer, D. Matringe, J. Nawas, and E. K. Rowson (eds.), *Encyclopaedia of Islam*, 3rd edn. (Leiden: Brill, 2007). dx.doi.org/10.1163/1573-3912_ei3_COM_30485 (accessed July 03, 2018). The appellation of chief of police is evoked in the context of the violence of 1858, e.g. FO 195/579, Pullen to Secretary of the Admiralty, June 25, 1858.

economic institutions, suggests a great likeness between the *muḥtasib* in Jeddah in the 1850s and the *shaykh al-bilād* described by Lafi for Tripoli for the first half of the ninetenth century.[11]

Most of what is known about the office of *muḥtasib* in Jeddah comes from descriptions of one particular official who held this position: ʿAbdallāh, a *muḥtasib* of Egyptian origin who might have been an appointee from the time of Muḥammad ʿAlī Pasha. He became an important figure in Jeddawi politics due to his dual function as official and leading merchant, due to which he became a leading notable. ʿAbdallāh was involved in hostility towards the French consul Fresnel in 1848, was accused of pursuing illicit trading practices in 1854 and therefore dismissed from his official administrative functions, supported the revolt of Emir ʿAbd al-Muṭṭalib in 1855 and was said to have been a major player in the 1858 massacre.[12] Interestingly, the office of *muḥtasib* could have different foci depending on local circumstances: ʿAbdallāh's counterpart in Mecca seems to have been mostly responsible for overseeing the pilgrimage, although that might have offered similar chances at enrichment.[13] Theoretically, the office disappeared with the introduction of Provincial Councils after 1849, although this administrative reorganisation arrived in Jeddah somewhat later, as will be discussed below.[14]

The Institutional Locus of Ottoman Urban Politics: Councils and Courts

Johann Büssow has noted how the Tanzimat reforms gradually increased local participation in the wider context of an intensification

[11] Lafi, *Une ville du Maghreb*, pp. 133–82. This would tally with her observation that the role of this official changed in different ways during Ottoman rule, see Lafi, *Esprit civique et organisation*, p. 125.

[12] Osmanoğlu, *Hicaz Eyaletinin Teşekkülü (1841–1864)*; Pétriat, *Le Négoce des Lieux Saints*, pp. 40–1, 80–8, 94–6 and passim.

[13] On the *iḥtisāb* in Mecca see Osmanoğlu, *Hicaz Eyaletinin Teşekkülü (1841–1864)*, p. 118, on the state control of the office since 1827, Bernard Lewis, 'Baladiyya' in P. J. Bearman, T. Bianquis, C. E. Bosworth, E. J. van Donzel, and W. P. Heinrichs (eds.), *Encyclopaedia of Islam*, 2nd edn., 12 vols. (Leiden: Brill, 1960–2005), dx.doi.org/10.1163/1573-3912_islam_COM_0095 (accessed October 7, 2019).

[14] M. Saraçoğlu, 'Economic Interventionism, Islamic Law and Provincial Government in the Ottoman Enmpire', *Journal of the Ottoman and Turkish Studies Association*, 2 (2015), pp. 59–84, 60–2, 77–81.

of the reach of the state or, put differently, of state-society relations, in Ottoman Palestine. He has also warned us not to underestimate the earlier consultative mechanisms that had existed in the form of more or less informal circles of notables, guest houses and religious institutions.[15] As so often, it is the formal institutions that have left the greatest paper trail and are thus the easiest to trace, Jeddah being no exception of this rule. They, as will be seen below, constituted a formal venue for an exchange between Ottoman officials and local leadership.

While new style city councils were first established in Istanbul in 1854, it seems that in Jeddah there were earlier, possibly sporadic meetings of a council or *diwān* when important matters in the city needed to be discussed. It is quite possible that these were remnants of a reorganisation during Egyptian rule.[16] These meetings increasingly took on a more regular character.[17] The Merchant Council (see Chapter 6) possibly took on this function in the early days, something which will be discussed below.

The provincial reforms of the Tanzimat period provided a host of new institutions. It would seem that a key difference between provincial reform in the Hijaz and in other Arab provinces was the exemption of the Hijazi population from military service. Otherwise, it was mostly the pace of reform and the specific ways in which local notables and appointees interacted with those sent by the imperial centre which differed.

In the 1850s, the plan to install a provincial council, conceived as a kind of provincial parliament, encountered staunch resistance by the Emir of Mecca. In the end, the governors resorted to convening a council, formed by government employees, to make important decisions.[18] It thus seems that Ochsenwald's contention, namely that the reforms were of little consequence in a province where 1840 marked the restoration of Ottoman rule rather than the onset of something new, is overly pessimistic.[19] The new provincial laws of 1864,

[15] Büssow, *Hamidian Palestine*, pp. 62–5, 72–3.

[16] Weber, *Damascus*, p. 33, notes such a process for Syria, where a *dīwān al-ḥisba*, characterised as an 'advisory body of notables . . . and top officials' was introduced.

[17] Osmanoğlu, *Hicaz Eyaletinin Teşekkülü (1841–1864)*, p. 43.

[18] Ibid., pp. 45–6. The establishment of such a council was decreed in March 1855, see BOA, A.MKT.UM 187 17 of Receb 6, 1271/March 25, 1855.

[19] Osmanoğlu, *Hicaz Eyaletinin Teşekkülü (1841–1864)*, p. 45; and Ochsenwald, *Religion, Society, and the State*, pp. 132–3.

1867 and 1870 created a new structure, aiming to strengthen the authority of imperially delegated officials, but also eventually expanding specialised civil service.[20] Below the level of governorate (*eyalet*, from 1867 *vilayet*), with its own provincial council, there were *sancak*s, *kaza*s and *nahiye*s. Jeddah, ruled by a kaymakam (also variously called *vali* or *mutasạrrıf*), became the centre of a *sancak* (Arab. *liwāʾ*) comprising the *kaza* of al-Līth and the *nahiye* of Rābigh.[21] The *sancak* of Jeddah had its own administrative council. Furthermore, a municipality was created in early 1873.[22] Rābigh and al-Līth each had their own kaymakam and administrative councils, at least by the time the provincial yearbooks were published in the 1880s.[23]

In 1884, Jeddah was home to an Administrative Council for the *sancak*, comprising both officeholders and appointed members, to a Judicial (*tamyīz*) Council for the *sancak*, a Merchant Council (here called court, *mehkeme*), with permanent and temporary members, and finally, and Municipal Board (*heyet*), later called Municipal Council (*meclis*, Arab. *majlis*), with ex officio and other members. While some of these offices also catered for the surrounding areas, the latter two specifically served Jeddah.[24] As has been shown in Chapter 6, the Merchant Court can be traced back to 1853. From 1854 onwards, the consular archives mention that disputes were settled there.

The provincial yearbook of 1887 specified that some members of the Administrative Councils of the *sancak* were elected, though, in 1892–3, such a council is only mentioned in descriptions of Medina, not Jeddah.[25] The French description of 1916 again mentions it, so

[20] Weber, *Damascus*, pp. 35–7 for Damascus.

[21] A French report of 1916 (CADN, 2_MI_3293, *Étude sur l'organisation administrative et judiciaire de la ville de Djeddah [ca. 1916]*, p. 2) claims that Yanbuʿ also was ruled from Jeddah, which does not conform with the presentations in the extant provincial yearbooks which place it in the district of Medina. Unless there was a change in the early twentieth century, this information might be erroneous.

[22] CADN, 2_MI_3229, Le Gay to Min. des Fonds, September 8, 1873.

[23] Ochsenwald, *Religion, Society, and the State*, pp. 167–9; cf. Fuāʾd Ḥamza, *Qalb Jazīrat al-ʿArab*, 2nd edn. (Riyadh: al-Dāra, 1968), p. 323. For the texts of the various laws, see George Young, *Corps de Droit Ottoman: Recueil des Codes, Lois, Règlements, Ordonnances et Actes les Plus Importants du Droit Intérieur, et d'Études sur le Droit Coutumier de l'Empire Ottoman*, 6 vols. (Oxford: Clarendon Press, 1905), vol. 1, pp. 36–95, 99–105; and *Hicaz vilâyeti salnâmesi*, defa 2 (Mecca: al-Matbaa al-Miriye al-Kaine, 1303/1885–6), pp. 220–1.

[24] *Hicaz vilayeti,* 1301, pp. 96–7.

[25] Ibid., 1309, p. 232 for Medina.

that it may be that this council was inactive for some time.[26] Meanwhile, the 1892–3 yearbook specified that some members of Jeddah's Merchant Court were elected.[27] To what extent this increase in elective members reflects a certain evolution after the introduction of these bodies, as stipulated by the Municipal Code of 1867, and to what extent it may be due to the increasingly detailed nature of the yearbooks is impossible to verify at this point.[28]

The kaymakam was responsible for public security, the customs' administration and the overall administration of the district. It seems that the administrative council, which brought together the heads of the court, the mufti, the accountant, and other officials including, at times, the head of the Jeddah municipality, mostly served this purpose. Some other functions, such as the Ottoman debt administration, sanitary issues, religious jurisdiction, education, post and telegraph office etc. all depended on ministries in Istanbul. A successful kaymakam could try to coordinate them but had ultimately little authority.[29] The multitude of institutions in Jeddah, which also included the passport office, the administration of the imperial storehouse (presumably the *şevne* discussed in Chapter 4), the administration of religious endowments, etc., exemplifies the expansion of state activities noted by Büssow as typical of the transformation the Ottoman provinces underwent during the reform period.[30]

From an imperial perspective the municipality of Jeddah was the lowest level of administration, although, as was shown in Chapter 5, the quarters constituted an essential building block for its work. It was thus also the quarters through which the representatives of the Municipal Council were elected, while its head was appointed. The tasks of the municipality comprised the upkeep of the city, internal security, the prevention of begging and petty crime, market supervision, and the

[26] CADN, 2_MI_3293, Étude sur l'organisation administrative et judiciaire de la ville de Djeddah (ca. 1916), p. 2.

[27] *Hicaz vilayeti,* 1305, pp. 206–7; and *Hicaz vilâyeti salnâmesi*, defa 4 (Mecca: Vilayet Matbaası, 1306/1888–89), pp. 261–2.

[28] On this transition, see Malik Sharif, *Imperial Norms and Local Realities: The Ottoman Municipal Laws and the Municipality of Beirut (1860–1908)*, Beiruter Texte und Studien (Beirut and Würzburg: in Commission at Ergon Verlag, 2014), vol. 105, pp. 54–7.

[29] CADN, 2_MI_3293, Étude sur l'organisation administrative et judiciaire de la ville de Djeddah (ca. 1916), pp. 1–3; and *Hicaz vilayeti,* 1305, p. 206.

[30] Büssow, *Hamidian Palestine*, pp. 60–71, cf. Weber, *Damascus*, pp. 35–41.

upkeep of roads and, later, lighting, though, as has been shown in the context of the discussion of the pilgrimage, some of the sanitary measures were actually induced and possibly also implemented by the Sanitary Council. The entries for the Municipal Council in Jeddah in the provincial yearbooks are very interesting because, for some reason, the 'Municipal Council' is portrayed as basically comprising the entire municipal administration. It was headed by the mayor and included an ever growing number of people: the inspector of the market and main tax collector, those responsible for cleaning the city, the city doctor (who was distinct from the quarantine staff), and engineer, in addition to twenty-two so called *baṣṣāṣīn* ('observers, agents, spies', there is no specification of their tasks).[31] It is unlikely that they all met for deliberations. Thus, the personnel entries of the 'Municipal Council' are most instructive for observing ways in which the personnel of the Empire during the Tanzimat increased in volume and diversified with regard to their tasks. Much of this reflected the new municipal legislation.[32] Perhaps the most fascinating – and singular – detail is the mention of a midwife (*qābila*) by the name of Fāṭima in 1888–9. Were her services not accepted by local women and the office made redundant after a short time, or did the government not find any women willing to serve in a provincial backwater? Or was this a service for female pilgrims, which was quickly discontinued?[33] The apparently ever-expanding tasks of the municipality were funded through revenue derived from fishing and the sale of corals, the income of municipal buildings such as the municipal coffeehouse, certain storage spaces, and from a tax on houses imposed in 1873.[34]

[31] *Hicaz vilayeti,* 1309, pp. 263–4.

[32] Saßmannshausen, *Reform in Translation*, pp. 222–8, also notes this increase in personnel. For the tasks, see Sharif, *Imperial Norms and Local Realities*, pp. 80–90.

[33] *Hicaz vilayeti,* 1306, p. 251. Neitheri Sharif, *Imperial Norms and Local Realities*; nor Büssow, *Hamidian Palestine*; or Saßmannshausen, *Reform in Translation*, pp. 222–8, all working on Greater Syria, mention such a position. The state regulations on medical services mention that medical personnel subordinate to the doctor could be appointed where required, see Young, *Corps de Droit Ottoman*, vol. 3, p. 205.

[34] CADN, 2_MI_3293, Étude sur l'organisation administrative et judiciaire de la ville de Djeddah (ca. 1916), p. 3; and 2_MI_3229, Le Gay to Min. des Fonds, September 8, 1873. On the tasks of municipalities, Sharif, *Imperial Norms and Local Realities* cf., pp. 57–8.

Ottoman Urban Politics in Practice: The Changing Locus of the Notables

The central role of merchants and pilgrims' guides in Jeddah's economy and politics has already been noted on a number of occasions. A more detailed study of Jeddah politics would need much more local information from the different councils and therefore cannot be executed adequately in this section. However, some examples are fairly well documented and will therefore be used in the following to describe the overall functioning of urban politics under the different regimes.

The Municipal Council

It seems that, during Ottoman times, Jeddah merchants and pilgrims' guides, for which the shorthand 'notables' will be used, did not see the Municipal Council as an adequate place in which to engage to influence the future of their city. Additionally, it is not clear to what extent the electoral process was always implemented rigorously. The following British report shows that, when in 1879 a 'towns improvement Commission' was formed by the Governor of the Hijaz, this commission was

> 'invited to form a new Municipality consisting of members who could be trusted to carry out the duties of their office. This was done . . . .'[35]

While the yearbooks from 1883/84 to 1892/93, which were consulted for this work, often give varying names for the municipal councillors, none of those listed were obvious members of the group of leading merchants.[36] Thus, it seems that the municipality provided basic services, but was apparently not seen as the most significant place for conducting urban politics. This was instead done either at the level of the quarters – often by important members of the guilds, or other leading figures of the quarter – or in the interplay between merchants, Ottoman officials, sharifs, and consuls, i.e. in the institutions in which these groups were represented. This seems quite different from what Saßmannshausen observed in nineteenth-century Tripoli, Hanssen in

[35] TNA, FO 195/1251, Zohrab to Amb. Const., October 23, 1879.

[36] This is based on a search in al-Anṣārī, *Mawsūʿat tārīkh madīnat Jidda*; and the registers in Maghribī, *Aʿlām al-Ḥijāz*. The yearbooks used are those of 1301 (1183–4), 1303 (1885–6), 1305 (1887–8), 1306 (1888–9), and 1309 (1892–3).

Beirut, and Zandi-Sayek in Izmir, and might be due to the fact that, while the municipality was responsible for urban development, this de facto also always involved higher powers.[37] The municipality of Jeddah seems to have mostly served as the interface between the lowest level Ottoman appointees and the representatives of the quarters, not as a major policy-making body. This notwithstanding, at the end of the nineteenth century the Municipal Council resided in an impressive building on the seafront built in the course of the harbour works in 1894–5 for the health and quarantine services.[38]

The joint residence of municipality and sanitary authorities did not preclude rivalries between these two institutions. Street cleaning was a core task of the municipality. Perhaps because this provided the opportunity to employ sweepers, and thus cultivate a certain group of clients, the Municipal Council was not inclined, in 1896, to cede this task to the sanitary inspector who had been dissatisfied with the performance of the service.[39]

Under Sharifian rule, the hierarchy changed in so far as the imperial layer disappeared and the head of the municipality now reported to the Sharif's representative in Jeddah.

The Commercial Council (Majlis al-Tijāra)

As has been discussed in Chapter 6, the merchants were part of the Commercial Court, which adjudicated in cases in which foreign subjects were involved, which occurred frequently. In 1857, its head was the famous India merchant Faraj Yusr, who had apparently been appointed by the Ottoman governor until he was replaced by ʿAbd al-Ghaffār Bā Ghaffār in 1857 upon the demand of a group of merchants.[40] In 1878, the court comprised ʿUmar Naṣīf, Ḥasan Bā Hārūn, and Muḥammad Ṣāliḥ Bā Ghaffār and, during the period until the early 1890s, the yearbooks regularly mention well-known names such as Mashāṭ, ʿĀshūr, and Bā ʿIshn as council members. In 1892–3 the Najdī merchant al-Bassām and the Iranian Khunjī appear as

[37] See Saßmannshausen, *Reform in Translation*, pp. 28–225; Hanssen, *Fin de Siècle Beirut*, pp. 139–55; Zandi-Sayek, *Ottoman Izmir*, pp. 94–101. Yazbak, *Haifa in the Late Ottoman Period*, does not comment much on membership in the municipality, except for the sectarian dimension, pp. 81–3.

[38] Rifʿat, *Mirʾāt al-Ḥaramayn*, vol. 1, p. 22.

[39] TNA, FO 195/1943, Alban to Amb. Const., March 3, 1896.

[40] Pétriat, *Le Négoce des Lieux Saints*, pp. 48, 101.

members.[41] Although, as Pétriat has pointed out, a slow turnover of generations and families is visible even without a detailed prosopographic analysis of the composition of the council, there is also a great deal of continuity. King Ḥusayn re-instituted the court in late 1919, appointing Qāsim Zaynal as its head.[42] In 1926, the well-known notables Sulaymān Qābil, Aḥmad Muḥammad Ṣāliḥ Bā 'Ishn, and Muḥammad Ṣāliḥ Jamjūm sat next to converted Dutchman and banker van de Pol, and the names of Bā 'Ishn, Bā Ghaffār, 'Alī Riḍā, Bā Nāja, and Bin Zaqr are present in the Chamber of Commerce, the successor to the Commercial Council, until the late 1950s.[43]

The Commercial Council brought together old and new merchants and high-ranking Ottoman officials. It thus served as one of the venues of urban political integration. While one might argue that in the Ottoman system it was meant to solve conflicts between locals and foreigners (see Chapter 6), the situation in Jeddah was different in so far as the 'strangers' involved could often claim Ottoman nationality. Although European merchants appear as members of this body later on, Faraj Yusr, a British subject, was also considered an Ottoman by virtue of his long residence in Jeddah. al-Bassām from Najd and 'Abd al-Ra'ūf Khunjī, presumably linked to the family of Iranian origin which had endowed two *arbiṭa* (see Chapter 5), probably had no such links to Europe, although both might also have had some claim to Ottoman nationality. A British report of 1880, which complains about the council, notes that many English and Indian merchants had hoped to have their cases solved in a consular context, which was not possible. However, it also notes that British attempts to have permanent 'British Assessors', presumably members, of the Commercial Council had not met with success.[44] It might be this very fact which made the council an important venue for more local issues. This notwithstanding, it also functioned as a regular court in the late 1880s.[45]

Pétriat has shown how merchant factionalism and local politics were often closely intertwined. Thus, the infamous affair of the Irani, the flag of which Ṣāliḥ Jawhar had changed in 1858, was discussed in the Commercial Council, which had condoned his action. Upon the British

41 *Hicaz vilayeti,* 1309, pp. 261–2. 42 Teitelbaum, *The Rise and Fall*, p. 133.
43 Pétriat, *Le Négoce des Lieux Saints*, p. 364.
44 TNA, FO 195/1313, Burrell to Goschen, August 21, 1880.
45 TNA, FO 195/1653, Wood to Amb. Const., April 15, 1889, about procedural issues.

consul's renewed change of flag, the kaymakam once again convened this council. Among those present at that meeting were the *shaykh al-sāda*, the head of the Merchant Council and a number of further merchants.[46] Is it conceivable that the kaymakam had actually reconvened the very same council which had already condoned the hissing of the Ottoman flag? The only real doubt comes from the almost exclusive presence of Hadhrami merchants who, according to Pétriat, formed a 'clique'. Since we do not have, at present, any list of the members of the Council at the time, the question has to remain open, although the answer would give an important clue as to the Commercial Council's institutional role in local politics.

Sometimes trade disputes were solved by extrajudicial means such as mediation. This could involve people who were current, former, or future members of the Commercial Council. Thus, the claims of British Indian merchants from Mecca and Medina that goods were lost in Bedouin raids were referred for negotiation by the governor to 'Aliyemeni Effendi his maktubji, Omar Nasif Effendi the agent of the Grand Sharif, and Abdulla Banaja Effendi a respectable merchant of this place'.[47] In other words, the mediators were a trusted administrator and future kaymakam (ʿAlī Yamanī), the head of the merchants and long-term member of the Administrative Council (ʿUmar Naṣīf), and ʿAbdallāh Bā Nāja from the well-known Hadhrami merchant family.[48]

The Commercial Council was also called upon to settle labour conflicts which could not be resolved within guilds or which involved more than one professional group. The most obvious place in Jeddah for such conflicts was the harbour, where disputes between merchants, porters, and the customs administration seem to have been fairly frequent. In a case in 1886, the Commercial Court decided that merchants were entitled to employ their own porters (presumably slaves or menial labourers from their warehouses) to move goods from the ships through customs and to the warehouses.[49]

46 TNA, FO 195/579, Walner to Act. Consul Cairo, August 17, 1858, encl. No. 1.
47 TNA, FO 195/2061, Muhammed Hussain to Devey, January 10, 1899.
48 On Naṣīf's membership in the Administrative Council, which is not reflected in the yearbooks; cf. TNA, FO 195/2061, Devey to Amb. Const. December 27, 1899.
49 TNA, FO 195/1943, Albans to Amb. Const., January 17, 1896. In the long letter, the consul also mentions the Administrative Council (p. 18), possibly by mistake, as he otherwise discusses the role of the *Majlis al-Tijara*.

Apparently, the guild of porters appealed to the kaymakam, who called a meeting in the Custom House, the minutes of which read as follows:

So in the presence of all merchants foreign and Turkish subjects as well as Yusuf Kudzi the dragoman of the British Consulate it was put forth by the Caimakam that the porters were poor men and in many cases had to support large families, and taking all this into consideration a new rate of porterage ought to be fixed, consequently the annexed tariff was prepared and approved of by the merchants and the porters. Also it was made a condition that the porters should give every satisfaction in the discharge of their duties and showing civility to the merchants, and the goods should be removed from the Custom House in order of their arrival and that no delay should on any account be made to allow the goods to accumulate on the Bundu [port] and so cause damage.

More care should be taken in expediating the removal of goods in the rainy season and when the sea is high as also in the pilgrimage season. That the porters agree that they will not demand any extra charge on such occasions. That the claim of porters to raise the porterage charges after this will not be entertained by the Court. That if any inconvenience will arise after this the authorities will be obliged to take steps to punish the porters and deal them according to law. Dated 8 April 1885.[50]

This settlement was sealed by the kaymakam, the treasurer, the shaykh of the *sāda*, the *qāḍī,* and two more officials. It does not seem to have achieved the intended peace.

Ten years later, a similar conflict erupted in which the earlier agreement was evoked. In this instance, the kaymakam dismissed the shaykh of the Custom House porters (i.e. of their guild) and appointed another one on the condition 'that some of the prices of porterage should be reduced and that a uniform scale should prevail throughout the year, no distinction being made during certain months as was the case before.'[51]

However, and this is an interesting testimony to the relative independence of officials, the customs superintendent, or 'Nazir' (rüsumat nazırı), contested the right of the kaymakam to appoint or dismiss the porters' shaykh. One may assume that the superintendent derived some benefit from the prerogative and that in this conflict he coordinated his

[50] TNA, FO 195/1943, Copy of Agreement between officials and porters, dated April 8, 1886.

[51] TNA, FO 195/1943, Alban to Amb. Const., April 18, 1896. For the prehistory, see Alban to Amb. Const., January 17, 1896.

actions with the porters. Although the kaymakam declared to act on the authority of the Governor and the superintendent was eventually swayed, matters did not proceed smoothly. According to the British report, the power-struggle between the two officials continued, with the superintendent complaining to Istanbul and rumours spreading that the kaymakam had accepted a bribe from the new shaykh of porters.[52] The intervention by the kaymakam solved the problem of the porters only until the advent of the pilgrimage season when demand for porters increased and the new shaykh of the porters once again demanded higher porterage fees. Yet even their payment did not result in the speedy removal of perishable goods from the open space of the harbour where they were temporarily stored, causing renewed complaints about the matter.[53] Similar disputes continued well into the twentieth century.[54] Even in 1928, i.e. under Saudi rule, the question arose as to who was responsible for unloaded goods during their passage through customs.[55]

If one compares the Commercial Council of Jeddah with what has been written about equivalent institutions in Baghdad, Beirut, Damascus, Haifa, and other Ottoman cities, it seems that it had a particularly prominent role in urban politics in the wider sense, notably if compared with the municipality.[56] Even if we consider that, in some cases, it is not entirely clear whether 'Council' referred to the Merchant Council or to the Administrative Council discussed in the following section, the very powerful position of merchants, and the need for the Ottoman authorities to come down on the side of other local contestants in order to secure some kind of balance of interests, becomes very obvious.

The Administrative Council

We also find prominent notables in the Administrative Council. This was another elite body in terms of membership, comprising regular

[52] TNA, FO 195/1943, Alban to Amb. Const., February 18, 1896.

[53] TNA, FO 195/1943, Mohammad Hussayn to Amb. Const., September 16, 1896.

[54] TNA, FO 195/1943, Alban to Amb. Const., March 23, 1896; FO 195/2286, Monahan to Chargé d'Affaires, July 2, 1908; and FO 195/2320, Monahan to Amb. Const., February 23, 1909.

[55] Oral information, ʿAbdallāh al-Zaqr, Jeddah, March 23, 2006.

[56] Works consulted for this comparison were Büssow, *Hamidian Palestine*; Grallert, *To Whom Belong the Streets?*; Herzog, *Osmanische Herrschaft und Modernisierung*; Saßmannshausen, *Reform in Translation*; Sharif, *Imperial Norms and Local Realities*; and Yazbak, *Haifa in the Late Ottoman Period*.

member such as the kaymakam, his deputy, the chief accountant, the tax director, and in 1888–9, the director of religious endowments in addition to notables. Presumably, it was in such company that decisions of larger importance for the city were taken, and it is hence not surprising that we find important names represented there. Thus, in 1883/84 the elected members were Mūsā al-Baghdādī, the rival of ʿUmar Naṣīf, Ibrāhīm Nāẓir, Ṣāliḥ Bā Ghaffār, ʿAbd al-Qādir Bā Dīb, and Muḥammad Mirdād (in 1887/88 listed as member of the Commercial Council).[57]

On two occasions in 1879, the British consul reports discussing matters of economic importance and local sensitivity with the kaymakam. In the first instance, the consul protested against the still ongoing slave trade in the presence of 'the Majlis'. It is not clear whether this was the Administrative or Commercial Council. Certain measures were agreed upon to increase the supervision of the harbour and instruct the tribes about the illegality of the trade.[58] The second time, the issue concerned currencies: While wholesale merchants used silver for their transactions, retailers dealt in copper. In July 1879, the kaymakam decreed the devaluation of Turkish copper coins, upon which the retailers closed their shops in protest. The reason behind this was the high price of silver in the Yemen, and since the wholesale merchants needed silver, they wanted to force retailers to no longer pay them in copper, or, if they did so, to compensate them for their transaction losses. When the British consul came to protest this measure, he found the kaymakam 'in council with the Chief Merchants of the town'.[59] The kaymakam blamed the devaluation on the *majlis*, which one remains unclear. The complicated fiscal situation was only resolved through protracted negotiations between different groups of merchants, heads of guilds, and the Ottoman authorities.[60] The sources do not tell us if the initial decision was taken by the Merchant Council or the Administrative Council, which is what Pétriat assumes.

57 *Hicaz vilayeti,* 1301, p. 95; and *Hicaz vilayeti,* 1306, p. 250.

58 TNA, FO 685/1, II Consul Zohrab's Letter book, Zohrab to FO, May 3, 1879.

59 TNA, FO 685/1, II: Consul Zohrab's Letter Book, July 11, 1879. Neither al-Amr, *The Hijaz under Ottoman Rule*, p. 77, nor William Ochsenwald, 'The Financial Basis of Ottoman Rule in the Hijaz, 1840–1877' in W. W. Haddad and W. L. Ochsenwald (eds.), *Nationalism in a Non-National State: The Dissolution of the Ottoman Empire* (Columbus: Ohio State University Press, 1977), pp. 129–49, here p. 59, explain this any further.

60 Pétriat, *Le Négoce des Lieux Saints*, p. 176.

According to the British consul, the situation had been so tense that the military had to patrol the markets for some time to prevent the outbreak of renewed unrest. When the British consul, this time together with his Dutch colleague, called on the kaymakam after an interim solution had failed to calm the situation, 'the Medjlis was called and the principal merchants and heads of guilds were summoned, a very animated discussion was raised'.[61]

The negotiations seem to have resolved the issue for Jeddah, even if, in Mecca, it sparked a riot. At the very least the consul no longer felt the need to report the situation.[62] While the issue is of importance to economic historians working on the differential values of diverse currencies in international trade at a time when the flow of information was still relatively slow and a major economic crisis was in the making, what is of importance in our context is the insight into the workings of local politics. No matter which council was active, the episode reveals the power of the leading wholesale merchants. It illustrates the ways in which consuls and guildsmen could be mobilised (and themselves mobilise support), be heard and, in this case, sway the view of the most important decision-maker on the level of the *sancak*, namely the kaymakam. It is also interesting to see how, in this situation at least, the wholesale merchants, the group which contributed so much to the financing of public works, voluntarily and at times forcibly, could be disregarded when the public security seemed threatened.

The importance of the coordination between kaymakam and local notables also became apparent in the summer of 1883, when, during the Bedouin uprising which was briefly mentioned in Chapter 6, the kaymakam of Jeddah held another council meeting. Since 'several useful measures were decided on for defence against both attack from outwards, and internal disorder', it is highly likely that the kaymakam had convened a relatively large circle, as both quarter headmen and guilds might have been closer to the question of street security than the wholesale merchants.[63] This was likely not an internal meeting, given that the British consul was quite aware of the discussions, even if he does not mention whether or not he was present.

[61] TNA, FO 685/1, II: Consul Zohrab's Letter Book, July 11, 1879.

[62] For the Mecca riot, TNA, FO 195/12511, Zohrab to Amb. Const., August 7, 1879.

[63] TNA, FO 195/1451, Moncrieff to FO, July 27, 1883.

An interesting undated anecdote related by Muḥammad Naṣīf illustrates how the kaymakam tried to use the Administrative Council in order to exert pressure on specific notables. In one particularly dry year, the only notable who had water left in his cisterns demanded a much higher price for his water than usual. The water carriers complained to the kaymakam, who convoked the Administrative Council, hoping it would decide to force the notable to sell his water at the usual, lower price. However, the notable refused, probably because others had been unwilling to have a similar decision imposed on them in comparable cases. Luckily, a heavy rainfall resolved the dispute before it could escalate.[64]

In summary, it is worthwhile noting that even in a faraway province like the Hijaz, and in a small city like Jeddah, the extension of state activity, marked inter alia by the establishment of new institutions and participatory avenues, however limited, left its mark.[65] As shall be seen shortly, it even implanted new ideas about political legitimation and constitutionalism.

Intervention in Times of Crisis: The Brief Interlude of the National Party in Sharifian Times

During the brief Sharifian interlude, the local elite seems to have been integrated rather less in the decision-making processes. The Ḥanafī mufti of Mecca, ʿAbdallāh Sarrāj, served as Minister of Justice and Aḥmad b. ʿAbd al-Raḥmān Bā Nāja, as his Minister for Finance. The Council of Elders, *majlis al-shuyūkh*, included representatives of a number of different groups, scholars, merchants, *ashrāf*, and tribal leaders. Among these was the head of the Jeddah Chamber of Commerce, ʿAbdallāh b. Zaynal ʿAlī Riḍā.[66] This rather symbolic council did not preclude the quick disillusionment of its members with the king and his attempts to centralise power.[67]

The various consultative mechanisms described above, as well as the informal gatherings of notables discussed in Chapter 5, and, in

[64] Muḥammd Ḥusayn Naṣīf, 'Min azamāt al-māʾ fī Jidda', *al-Manhal*, 28 (1967), pp. 484–5.

[65] Büssow, *Hamidian Palestine*, pp. 63–5. Aspects of increased infrastructural power were debated in Chapter 4 and below.

[66] Teitelbaum, *The Rise and Fall*, pp. 184–5. On the appointment of Aḥmad Bā Nāja Pétriat, *Le Négoce des Lieux Saints*, pp. 206–8.

[67] Teitelbaum, *The Rise and Fall*, pp. 187–98.

particular, the *Nādī al-Ṣalāt* provided ample opportunities for leading figures in Jeddah to meet and discuss politics and related matters.[68] In spite of their early complaints to the British consul, it required an extraordinary crisis, namely the war between King Ḥusayn and the Sultan of Najd, ʿAbd al-ʿAzīz Āl Saʿūd, for them to decide on an act which has remained singular in the history of Jeddah and the Hijaz.[69] A group of leading notables, mostly from Jeddah but also comprising some refugees from Mecca, decided on October 3, 1924 to demand the abdication of Sharif Ḥusayn and the enthronement of his son ʿAlī. They argued that after the so-called Ṭāʾif-incident, when hundreds of residents were massacred after the occupation of Saudi forces in September 1924, people feared war and bloodshed. The historian Ḥusayn Naṣīf, son of Muḥammad Naṣīf, boldly calls those who took action '*ahālī Jidda*', the people of Jeddah, probably reflecting the way in which the notables saw themselves as the real spokespeople of the local population.[70] When Ḥusayn did not immediately agree to all demands, a second letter was sent by said notables, which went so far as to claim that they constituted 'the nation' (*al-umma*). Given that yet another telegram imploring Ḥusayn to agree to the demands was signed by 140 persons, one may assume that most leading Jiddawi personalities, in addition to refugees from Mecca, had indeed taken part in the meetings.[71]

In the context of this correspondence, and before the ascent of ʿAlī b. Ḥusayn to the throne, the self-styled 'notables of the nation' (*aʿyān al-umma*) assembled and invited 'the people' (*al-ahālī*) to meet in the house of Muḥammad Naṣīf 'to elect a party which represents them'.[72] The result of these elections, in which more than 600 votes were cast, reflects the 'who is who' of Jeddah at that time. Among the thirteen people elected, eight hailed from Jeddah.[73] These were the customs

[68] For this and the following cf. mainly Naṣīf, *Māḍī 'l-Ḥijāz wa-ḥāḍiruhu*, pp. 120–40; and Pétriat, *Le Négoce des Lieux Saints*, pp. 226–36.
[69] Teitelbaum, *The Rise and Fall* quotes a 1920 British report on this, p. 191. For the following, cf. Teitelbaum, pp. 210–8.
[70] Naṣīf, *Māḍī 'l-Ḥijāz wa-ḥāḍiruhu*, p. 120.
[71] Ibid., p. 122; and Pétriat, *Le Négoce des Lieux Saints*, p. 227.
[72] Naṣīf, *Māḍī 'l-Ḥijāz wa-ḥāḍiruhu*, p. 132.
[73] Ibid., p. 133, gives the numbers of votes which, if one adds those not elected but mentioned, comes to somewhere above 600. We do not know, however, how many votes each person had, so that Pétriat's assumption (p. 229) of 583 voters not only neglects the votes for those who did not become part of the committee but also assumes that each person had only one vote.

superintendent, Muḥammad Ṭawīl, the chief finance officer of Jeddah, Muḥammad Ṭāhir al-Dabbāgh, the mayor, Sulaymān Qābil, the kaymakam, ʿAbdallāh (ʿAlī) Riḍā, and the merchants Qāsim Zaynal (ʿAlī Riḍā, the former deputy to the Ottoman parliament), ʿAlī Salāma, and Muḥammad (Ḥusayn) Naṣīf and his relative, Muḥammad Ṣāliḥ Naṣīf, characterised as 'one of the rich people of Jeddah' (*aḥad aghniyāʾ Jidda*).[74] The aim of the party was to preserve the nation from the impending war with Ibn Saʿūd and to guard the country in a constitutional Islamic way, protecting it from all suspicious plots and foreign influence'.[75] Both the proceedings and the terminology are very interesting: They indicate that the notables felt that elections would bestow upon them the legitimacy to execute an as of yet unheard of act: The replacement of the ruler and the assumption of responsibility for what was left of an independent Hijaz. The choice of vocabulary which included a constitutional (*dustūrī*) approach confirms this and, at the same time, bears testimony to the impact the Ottoman reforms had left on the local elite. This is quite irrespective of how exclusive Ottoman elections and the elite circles were and how selective their own understanding of a constitutional approach might have been. The notables also formed a government headed by the mufti of Mecca, although secret negotiations by members of the National Party with Ibn Saʿūd in December 1924 and their subsequent punishment by King ʿAlī must have considerably weakened their influence.[76]

It would be interesting to know, in this context, how strong the influence of Qāsim ʿAlī Riḍa was in this circle, as he surely brought the most intimate understanding of parliamentarianism to the forum.[77] Indeed, Philby compares the relationship of Muḥammad Ṭawīl and

[74] Ibid., p. 133. ʿAlī Salāma went on to become a member of the *majlis al-shūrā*, see ʿAbd al-ʿAzīz al-ʿĪsā, *Arshīf Mamlakat al-Ḥijāz wa-Salṭanat Najd wa-Mulḥaqātihā, 1343h–1346h* (Beirut: Dār al-Jadāwil, 2013), p. 448.

[75] Naṣīf, *Māḍī 'l-Ḥijāz wa-ḥāḍiruhu*, p. 134. For a rather less generous characterisation of Muḥammad Ṭawīl and ʿAbdallāh ʿAlī Riḍā see MECA, Papers by Sir Andrew Ryan, GB165–0248, 6/5, Sir Reader Bullard's Jeddah letters, 1923–4 and 1936–7, letter of July 20, 1924, p. 7, where he describes them as interested in their own business interest.

[76] Baker, *King Husain*, pp. 208–12.

[77] On Qāsim's active participation in debates in the Ottoman parliament and press; cf. Sabine Prätor, *Der arabische Faktor in der jungtürkischen Politik: Eine Studie zum osmanischen Parlament der II. Konstitution (1908–1918)*, Islamkundliche Untersuchungen (Berlin: Schwarz, 1993), vol. 170, pp. 40–1, 117–8, 119–20, 273 (his classification as *ʿālim* by Prätor is very odd).

Qāsim ʿAlī Riḍā in December 1924 to that of 'Prime Minister' and 'Leader of the Opposition'.[78] According to Philby,

They had been in agreement for the deposition of Husain but Qasim is now in opposition because he is out for a progressive policy schools for boys and girls, foreign (if possible Muslim) experts to supervise various branches of the administration, a republic etc. Mhd Tawil had no difficulty in making out his case being entirely agreement with Qasim on all points (except that he prefers a constitutional monarchy to a republic) though existing difficulties made it quite out of the question to do anything until peace is established by agreement or the war fought out.[79]

In spite of such disagreements, a number of those in the executive committee of the party took part in ʿAlī's government. Meanwhile, Qāsim and some of his allies tried to impose their views, through advice as well as the publication of letters in Egyptian newspapers. They even incurred trial and punitive payment.[80] It seems that under the pressure of siege, the National Party frayed further and, as pressure on King ʿAlī mounted, not only Najdi merchants, but also notables like Muḥammad Naṣīf were suspected of treason, in the latter case resulting in imprisonment.[81]

An interesting detail is the composition of the committee appointed by Ibn Saʿūd to run the affairs of the city in early January 1926. It consisted of some of the leading politicians like Muḥammad Naṣīf, ʿAbdallāh, and Qāsim Zaynal and the new head of the municipality, ʿAlī Salāma. Muḥammad ʿAlī Qābil was the nephew of Sulaymān, although nothing is known of his political orientation. To these were added Nāṣir al-Turkī, a Jeddah shopkeeper from ʿUnayza, who went on to have a career in the administration of Medina, and ʿAlī al-Turkī, presumably a relative of his.[82] Their presence in this circle is another indication of the rise of Najdi merchants, noted in Chapter 6, into elite circles, even if the exact role and duration of this committee beyond the

78 According to Teitelbaum, *The Rise and Fall*, p. 214, Ṭawīl in the period of transition from Ḥusayn to ʿAlī had become 'in reality governor of Jeddah'.

79 MECA, Philby Collection GB165–0229, 1/4/5/1, Philby Diary, part 1, December 13, 1924, p. 147.

80 Ibid., November 4, 1924, p. 56, and November 13, pp. 82–3.

81 Ibid., December 31, 1924, p. 159, October 17, 1925, p. 184, and October 26, p. 201.

82 *Umm al-Qurā*, 54, January 8, 1926. Muḥammad Naṣīf is most likely Muḥammad Ḥusayn Naṣīf. Some indications of Nāṣir al-Turkī's further public trajectory can be found in the index of names in al-ʿĪsā, *Arshīf Mamlakat al-Ḥijāz wa-Salṭanat Najd*.

transitory period remains unclear. It was probably surpassed by the establishment of the municipality.

The Resumption of (a New) Normality

The Saudi state took some time to establish its institutions which were, in 1925, themselves still evolving given the almost constant state of war and expansion since the reconquest of Riyadh by Ibn Saʿūd in 1902. During the first years of Saudi rule, the Hijaz was an administratively distinct entity, with institutions which merely modified what had existed before. The Constitution of the Hijaz of 1926, amended in subsequent years to accommodate the establishment of the Kingdom in 1932 as well as further institutional changes over the following years, set out the organisational structure of the new state-in-formation.[83] It provided for a Consultative Assembly (*majlis shūrā* is rendered as Legislative Assembly in the translation, art. 28–31), as well as for appointed Administrative Councils for Medina and Jeddah (art. 32–7).

In Jeddah, the first such council consisted of well-established notables: ʿAbdallāh b. Muḥammad al-Faḍl, Sulaymān al-Qābil, Aḥmad al-Hazzāzī, and Muḥammad Ṣāliḥ Bā Nāja.[84] Curiously, Mecca, the capital (art. 3), did not have such a council, thus continuing, to a certain degree, the administrative distinction of Mecca which had existed during Ottoman times.[85] In addition, general municipal councils were to be formed in Jeddah, Mecca, and Medina, comprising 'landlords, members of special crafts and professions ... and notables, who will be appointed by His Majesty the King or His Viceroy after their names have been put ford' (art. 65). In any case, the municipal institutions were supervised by the Department of Internal Affairs or, respectively, its local administrators (art. 13).[86] In 1937, a detailed statute came to

83 For translations of the relevant documents see IOR, L/PS/12/2099, the cover letter (Gill to FO, May 18, 1932) enlists these changes; cf. al-Ziriklī, *Shibh al-Jazīra*, vol. 1, pp. 353–4.

84 *Umm al-Qurā*, 145, October 4, 1927.

85 The yearbooks list Mecca's religious functionaries and specific urban institutions such as schools, police, or poorhouse. Else, provincial institutions such as the provincial Administrative Council were put in place, rather than separate ones for the city or district, e.g. *Hicaz vilayeti,* 1309, pp. 148–58.

86 It is not entirely possible to date possible changes to the constitution before it was communicated to the British Foreign Office in 1932, see IOR, L/PS/12/2099 Gill to FO, May 18, 1932.

regulate the work of the municipalities, reiterating the previous rules for the selection of the members of city councils.[87] This resembles the course of events in the other formerly Ottoman districts of Saudi Arabia in al-Aḥsāʾ.[88] It would seem that this system was kept in place until the early 1960s and even extended to other parts of the country. In the late 1950s, the administration was comprehensively reorganised, with Hijaz losing some of the administrative structures, such the position of viceroy of the Hijaz, which had distinguished it from the rest of the country, while some of the formerly Ottoman institutions were absorbed into the overall Saudi Arabian administrative system.[89]

While not very much is known thus far about the activities of the municipal councils, which were mostly concerned with concrete matters of urban development, the work of the Hijazi (from 1927: Hijazi and Najdi) Advisory Council was regularly reported in the newspaper *Umm al-Qurā*.[90] After the 1926 constitution had been approved, it initially consisted of thirteen, then from 1927 onwards of eight appointed members.[91] This assembly was to be consulted on a wide range of matters, from the budgets of the state and municipalities, via concessions for economic and building projects, to the drafting of laws and statutes.[92] Over the years, the Advisory Council also dealt with a host of practical issues. These ranged from how to lower marriage costs to economic projects such as the transport monopoly, electrification, or passports.[93]

Little comment on these developments can be found in the official press. An unusually open admission of criticism, probably at the lack

[87] For the entire statute, see al-Ḥamdī, *Ḥarakat al-taḥdīth fī 'l-Mamlaka*, pp. 184–200, for the council, pp. 189–90.

[88] Matthiesen, *Centre–Periphery Relations*, pp. 4–5.

[89] Vassiliev, *History of Saudi Arabia*, pp. 444–9.

[90] For the statutes of the Council, see *Umm al-Qurā*, 135, July 15, 1927, pp. 2–3.

[91] This number is given by Kostiner, *The Making of Saudi Arabia*, p. 101 for 1926, while *Umm al-Qurā*, 135, July 15, 1927 lists eight new members, which is in line with the new regulation of July 15, 1927, see IOR, L/PS/12/2099, Regulation concerning the Legislative Assembly.

[92] al-Ziriklī, *Shibh al-Jazīra*, vol. 2, pp. 571–2 and pp. 572–3 for the further development until 1950.

[93] *Umm al-Qurā*, 299, July 11, 1930, for an instructive list of topics during the last session see *Umm al-Qurā*, 299, August 29, 1930, p. 2. The following issues contain similar lists of topics. However, it should be noted that the Jiddawi members who joined the 'Assembly' in January 1926 were also not elected but, at least according to a British report, 'went by common assent' in Jarman (ed.), *The Jedda Diaries* , vol. 2, Jeddah Report, January 1926, p. 372.

of legitimacy of an appointed rather than an elected council, a long article in February 1927 argued that the king was very wise in taking the advice of the people (*al-umma*) seriously. Even if the current system (which unfortunately was not explained) was not perfect, it was the best that could be realised under the prevailing circumstances because

> every country has its character and nature and is not [necessarily] suited for systems which do not fit its scientific and intellectual nature.[94]

An important practical change was the slow but marked replacement of Hijazi personnel by people from the Najd, as has already been noted during the discussion of the al-Faḍl family in Chapter 6. In 1927, a modification to the regulations of the Advisory Council stipulated that of its eight members, four were appointed after 'consultation with men of excellence and experience', while a further four were appointed by the government, two of which had to be Najdis.[95] There was no comparable provision for Hijazis. Given the apparent sensitivity of Hijazis to this situation, it is perhaps not surprising that the office of kaymakam of Jeddah left in the hands of ʿAbdallāh ʿAlī Riḍā had held it since Sharifian times. Only after his death an official from the Najd was appointed who had prior experience in the Hijaz: ʿAbd al-ʿAzīz b. Muʿammar.[96]

Although a number of the notables leading the National Party were involved in advising Ibn Saʿūd on local affairs and finances after the takeover, they were clearly relegated to secondary roles. This becomes apparent from Philby's diaries, as well as from the lists of people occupying official positions who are named in the regular British reports from Jeddah. Although Qāsim Zaynal, Muḥammad Naṣīf, and Muḥammad Ṭawīl were in the wider orbit of the government, and certainly asked to bankroll the government in ways very similar to Ottoman and Sharifian times, the strong man with regard to finances was now ʿAbdallāh Sulaymān.[97] The abortive movement of the 'Party

94 *Umm al-Qurā*, 112, February 4, 1927, p. 1.
95 IOR, L/PS/12/2099, Regulation concerning the Legislative Assembly, July 15, 1927. Art. 3
96 IOR, L/PS/12/2073, Jeddah Report, July–August 1932, p. 5; cf. al-Anṣārī, *Mawsūʿat tārīkh madīnat Jidda*, p. 327. It seems that Maghribī, *Aʿlām al-Ḥijāz*, vol. 1, p. 137 errs when claiming that he was already appointed by the Ottomans.
97 Kostiner, *The Making of Saudi Arabia*, p. 145.

of Free Hijazis' (Ḥizb al-Aḥrār al-Ḥijāzī), formed by Hijazi exiles in Cairo and featuring two leading names of the earlier National Party, namely Muḥammad Ṭāhir al-Dabbāgh and ʿAbd al-Raʾūf Ṣabbān from Mecca, can be seen as a last ditch attempt to not only re-establish Sharifian rule, but also to salvage the influence of the merchants on Hijazi politics. The short-lived rebellion incited in collaboration with forces in ʿAsīr and tribal forces failed utterly.[98]

At any rate, most of the merchants preferred to accommodate themselves with the new regime. With time and the onset of oil extraction, entrepreneurship such as that shown by Bin Lādīn and Bin Maḥfūẓ became a new road to economic ascendancy and most of the older merchant families turned to import via concessionary agreements, notably after World War II.[99] They now had to share their fortunes with the new arrivals from Najd and no longer held significant political influence. Thus, one may argue that, while the economic power may still have resided largely with the Hijazi merchants, their political influence, expressed in the Ottoman reform councils and finding its culmination in the National Party, began to wane with the Saudi takeover. This notwithstanding, members and descendants of the Hijazi merchant elite continued to occupy leading offices in the administration built by Ibn Saʿūd for quite some time.

Crime and Punishment

As in all port cities, the diversity of the population and the presence of many temporary visitors from different walks of life caused a number of challenges to the internal security and the upholding of what was considered morally acceptable. There were different levels of policing in the city: the *ʿumda* and his guards were responsible for the security of the neighbourhoods and had the right to detain people overnight while a second tier of urban police was responsible for more serious offences. The following section will chart the urban crime-scape in a fairly brief manner due to the severe limitations of the available sources for the topic. In addition, many of the available studies, as well as the consular sources, focus primarily on the matter of the security of pilgrims, which seems to have also been the Ottoman's main concern.

98 Kostiner, pp. 158–73; and Pétriat, *Le Négoce des Lieux Saints*, pp. 340–3.
99 Pétriat, *Le Négoce des Lieux Saints*, pp. 370–91.

As much of the Bedouin attacks took place outside of the cities, this topic will be mostly sidelined.[100]

The Urban Police

Recent studies by Ergut, Lévy, and Schull have shown that the Ottoman police in the nineteenth century was very much an institution in the making.[101] The janissaries had acted as an urban police force until their destruction in 1826.[102] From 1845 onwards, a distinct police administration was gradually installed in Ottoman cities and police stations erected in different quarters. In the course of the provincial re-organisation of the empire in 1864/65, this *zaptiye* (gendarmerie), was meant to be controlled by a special council.[103] From 1892 to 1893 onwards one finds the distinction between *zaptiye* which was mostly responsible for villages and rural areas, and police, mostly acting in cities.[104]

How did these developments play out in Jeddah? Fairly little is known about the early police force, apart from the fact that the *muḥtasib* was sometimes also called Chief of Police in the context of 1858. The post of Chief of Police, albeit without an indication of the Arabic or Ottoman terms used, also appears a number of times in the following decades in the consular archives. Presumably, this force was under the authority of the kaymakam.[105] In 1860, the British Vice-Consul reported that Egyptian troops had 'hitherto formed the police of the town'.[106] It is possible that this was an exceptional state of

100 Ismāʿīl, *Jidda khilāla 'l-Fatra 1286–1327*, pp. 31–5; and al-Asmarrī, *Tārīkh al-ḥayyāt al-ijtimāʿiyya*, pp. 41–2, with the last paragraph of p. 41 being identical to Ismaʿīl, last paragraph of p. 32, but giving different sources.

101 Ferdan Ergut, 'The State and Social Control: The Police in the Late Ottoman Empire and the Early Republican Turkey, 1839–1939', PhD Thesis, New School for Social Research (1999); Noémi Lévy, 'Une institution en formation: La police ottomane à l'époque d'Abdülhamid II', *European Journal of Turkish Studies. Social Sciences on Contemporary Turkey*, 8 (2008); and Kent Schull, *Prisons in the Late Ottoman Empire: Microcosms of Modernity* (Edinburgh: Edinburgh University Press, 2014).

102 Lévy, *Une Institution en Formation*, §§ 8–10.

103 Ibid., §§ 14, 26.

104 On the rural focus of the *zaptiye*, see Schull, *Prisons in the Late Ottoman Empire*, p. 23.

105 TNA, FO 195/131 Zohrab to FO, March 13, 1880; and FO 195/1767, Abdur Razzack to Amb. Const., August 20, 1892.

106 TNA, FO 685/1, I. Stanley Letter Book, Stanley to Consul-General, Cairo, September 18, 1860.

affairs following the massacre of 1858, although the nature of the force which had been under the command of the *muḥtasib* remains unclear. It is thus possible that, after the abolition of the janissaries, some soldiers had been commissioned with police work.[107]

The map of 1880, discussed in Chapter 4, indicates the existence of urban police stations (i.e. no. 21). The yearbooks from the late 1880s and thereafter mention the existence of a gendarmerie. However, they give no idea of the size of this force, which at this point was presumably still responsible for urban security. Neither did they hint at the existence of the Supervisory Council which, theoretically, should have exercised control – although it is easily possible that in smaller cities such as Jeddah, this function was assumed by the District Administrative Council.[108] Thus, the emergence of the police force as an institution independent of the armed forces could be found in Jeddah during the Hamidian period, although with variations from the ideal-type set out in imperial legislation.[109]

This legislation further differentiated the tasks of the police force: 'administrative police' was meant to patrol neighbourhoods and public spaces for security and good moral conduct. It further controlled population movement and vagrancy. A 'political police' was to guarantee the security of the regime, acting against any conspiracies and controlling publications, and the 'judicial police' presumably supported the judiciary.[110] After the Young Turk revolution of 1908, the gendarmerie was dissolved. In Jeddah, the control of neighbourhood security remained in the hands of the *ʿumda*. One focus of police work was the harbour, where the focus was on the control of population movements and of goods. This was so prominent that, in Sharifian times when the local administration partly or fully overlapped with the Hijazi one, the Harbour Master was also the 'Super-Chief of Police, Commandant (Jeddah) of Jeddah to some extent Minister of Marine, and Minister for Air'.[111] It should be noted that the consular archives mention the police, probably most often in the context of either

107 This had been the case in Izmir, for example, Zandi-Sayek, *Ottoman Izmir*, pp. 88–90.
108 *Hicaz vilayeti*, 1305, p. 208; and *Hicaz vilayeti*, 1309, p. 264.
109 Lévy, *Une Institution en Formation*, § 3. 110 Ibid., § 18.
111 Jarman (ed.), *The Jedda Diaries*, vol. 2, Jeddah Report, September 28–October 31, 1923, p. 170.

combatting or secretly supporting the slave trade.[112] The political police is not mentioned as such in the yearbooks, however, it might be that the aforementioned *baṣṣāṣīn* (spies) employed by the municipality were this force.

Murder, Robbery, and Theft

Jeddah was a fairly safe town for its residents, although somewhat less so for pilgrims. One British consul wryly described this situation as follows:

> those who want an absolutely safe place to live in should avoid Jeddah but it would be somewhat safer and very much more respectable if nine tenths of the Europeans were to leave it.[113]

This was written during the tense period of 1882–3 when there was a confrontation between the Bedouin of the Ḥarb tribe and the Ottoman government. A large contingent of villagers and tribespeople from neighbouring villages had sought refuge in the city. They were considered to be uncivilised by the townspeople and hence fear of attacks and plundering spread, although no incidents occurred. This moment of crisis is a rare incident which gives detailed information about the military and police forces of the town. The consul lists about 250 soldiers, policemen, and 'some armed inhabitants', of whom 3–400 were ready to guarantee the upkeep of order in their quarters.[114]

The most notable crimes seem to have been linked to the presence of foreigners and their real and perceived interference with local politics and interests, as well as with larger imperial politics. They also demonstrate the extent to which Jeddah was a nodal point in translocal networks and could become, on specific occasions, a stage where transnational politics with only a partial or even no connection to the city was played out. This is, to some extent, true of the violent, politically motivated attacks on consuls and foreign merchants in

[112] E.g. TNA, FO 195/1251, Zohrab to FO, June 28, 1879; FO 195/1375, Zohrab to FO, December 30, 1880; Zohrab to FO, May 4, 1881; and FO 195/1767, Abdur Razzack to Amb. Const., September 24, 1892.

[113] TNA, FO 195/1451, Moncrieff to FO, July 28, 1883. For a possibly less ironically inflected similar statement of 1909, see FO 685/3, Jeddah VIII, Draft Confid. Report Consul Jeddah to Amb. Const., March 12, 1909.

[114] TNA, FO 195/1451, Moncrieff to FO, July 27, 1883.

1858 and for the murder of British vice-consul Abdur Razzack in 1895. Both reflected larger concerns of imperial interference with trade and pilgrimage, as well as regional and local concerns and rivalries. The murder of Sharif Ḥusayn b. Muḥammad in 1880, as well as that of the uncle and cousin of the Agha Khan in 1896, which was committed by a Persian in the Baghdādī house, could be considered examples for almost de-territorialised crimes. The first can be linked to disagreements about Ottoman-British relations with regard to policy in Afghanistan as explained in Chapter 2, while the second seems to have been committed for sectarian reasons.[115]

Apart from these crimes, only three more murders made it into the consular archives, the first because it had a link with the slave trade, the second, because the victim was a Christian, and the third because the French dragoman was detained briefly. In the first case, a slave girl was killed by an influential local man. He had been 'Examiner in one of the Tribunals' of Jeddah in 1880. 'The murderer being a man of influence and well off [one could add: quite in contrast to the victim, U.F.], the crime was concealed and was soon forgotten'. The culprit committed the mistake of picking a fight with a fellow (free and probably influential) Arab who seems to have remembered the case and informed the Governor of the Hijaz. Consequently, 'the man was immediately arrested, tried and convicted.'[116] However, the case was referred to Istanbul, whether by a higher tribunal or a kaymakam fearing the influence of the culprit is not elaborated in the sources. However, more than two years later the case reappeared in the British files because the sentence of '14 years of penal servitude' was confirmed. Consequently, the culprit 'was marched along the Bazaar with chains on his legs and a copy of the sentence and its confirmation hanging from his neck. He was the subject of much attention.'[117]

It is interesting to see that, once the verdict was confirmed, the sentence was not only applied but the culprit was publicly shamed in

115 TNA, FO 195/1943, Alban to Amb. Const., June 6, 1896.

116 TNA, FO 195/1313, Zohrab to Amb. Const., March 13, 1880. On the criminal court system in the late Ottoman Empire, cf. Schull, *Prisons in the Late Ottoman Empire*, pp. 22–5 who also discusses, in the subsequent pages, the development of criminal law and punishment.

117 TNA, FO 195/1415, August 4, 1882, Monceriff to Amb. Const., the murder was first mentioned, where the initial sentence is also mentioned.

spite of his apparent prominence. Such public shaming seems to have constituted an integral part of the penal system applied in Jeddah. This is at least suggested by one of the images taken by the member of the French expeditionary force to the Hijaz in 1917, Père Raphaël Savignac: It shows two men in shackles, supposedly guarded by a third. Although the image focuses on the people and hence does not give the overall setting, the photograph seems to depict a public pillory.[118]

The second murder was that of an Ottoman Armenian Christian. He was reputedly fairly wealthy and lived alone. His murder occurred in the context of a robbery. In spite of the victim being an Ottoman subject, the Western consulates wrote to the Governor of the Hijaz, pressing for a speedy investigation.[119] We can see how European representatives felt obliged to intervene on behalf of Christians in the heartland of Islam, even if the crime did not concern their own subjects.

In the final case, the French dragoman seems to have had only accidental contact with one of two people involved in a brawl which ended in a fatality.[120] The French reports give no information on the actual crime – if it was not an accidental killing. Rather, they concentrate on the apparently almost random association of their dragoman with the event.

While most robberies occurred outside of Jeddah and the victims were usually caravans of merchants and pilgrims, theft was a fairly common crime within the walls of old Jeddah too. Obviously, the consular records concentrate on the plight of pilgrims who, like present-day tourists, seem to have been easy prey for criminals. Thus, there were instances where they were relieved of their valuables in their accommodations.[121] In one case, the accusation was levelled against the landlady of an Algerian and her servant, which is a rare case not only documenting possible female criminal energy but also their independent economic agency (as both: landladies and criminals).[122] The prison sentence for one of the two ladies confirms the existence of a female prison in Jeddah.

[118] Savignac Collection, Jerusalem, image 02811-3326.
[119] TNA, FO 195/1313 Johur to Amb. Const. June 4, 1880; and CADN, 2_MI_3229, Mardrus to MAE, May 26, 1880 and June 3, 1880.
[120] CADN, 2_MI_3231, Djeddah, October 10, 1894.
[121] E.g. CADN, 2_MI_3229, Le Gay to Amb. Const., August 1, 1872.
[122] CADN, 2_MI_3256, Affaires judiciaires, pp. 317–22.

Theft also occurred in other houses, including the consular buildings that were usually protected by hired guards.[123] It was quite common for servants or slaves to be accused of having committed the crime, possibly to incriminate them when they were seeking protection or manumission.[124] Sometimes even the guards came to be accused of theft.[125] Another common space for theft seems to have been the Customs House which was, until 1896, an open space.[126] Thieves came from different walks of life, and included Ottoman officers, as in a case when an officer, accompanied by a soldier, stole salted meat from a Greek store. While in many cases the culprits were apprehended and tried, in this case, the authorities tried to cover up and help the officer flee the country.[127]

Of course, there were a host of other crimes large and small that found their way into the records. Thus, in 1879 the British consul reported that a grave in the Christian cemetery outside of Jeddah had been violated in search of valuables buried with the corpse.[128] More common were disputes about inheritance and, notably, attempts at defrauding widows of their rightful inheritance.[129] This further increased the need to secure women's inheritance by endowing property in their name (see Chapter 5).

Endangered Morality: Prostitution and Alcohol

Morality in Jeddah was of major concern to authorities, as it was on the one hand a port city with many men arriving and staying for short periods, on the other the gate to the holy cities of the Hijaz. The two themes most closely associated with morality were alcohol consumption and prostitution, which is typical for port cities. Although the two seem to have been linked to some degree, the sources on them differ

123 CADN, 2_MI_3229, Le Gay to Amb. Const., September 11, 1872. On theft in the French consular building, Buez to MAE, February 26, 1878.
124 CADN, 2_MI_3229, Le Gay to Amb. Const., September 11, 1872; and Mardrus to MAE, July 5, 1874; 2_MI_3231, Djeddah, July 3, 1889 where the argument is explicitly made.
125 TNA, FO 195/1313, Burrell to Amb. Const., August 21, 1880.
126 CADN, 2_MI_3229, Le Gay to Amb. Const., October 8, 1872; and TNA, FO 195/1943, Alban to Amb. Const., March 23, 1896.
127 CADN, 2_MI_3229, Suret to Amb. Const., March 1, 1880.
128 TNA, FO 195/1251, Zohrab to FO, November 13, 1879.
129 TNA, FO 195/1943, Alban to Amb. Const., February 6, 1896.

considerably in that the consular records show a clear preoccupation with the question of alcohol and shy away from engaging with prostitution. The latter practice is more clearly documented in travelogues. With regard to Beirut, Hanssen has argued that the discourse on public morality adopted after the 1860s was an attempt to condemn any practices considered deviant, notably in places which were seen as emblematic for the modernity to which Beirut aspired.[130] In Jeddah, such notions might have exercised high ranking Ottoman officials, but the more common perspective was that deviance and morality were particularly abhorrent due to the vicinity of the holiest cities of Islam.

The consular preoccupation with alcohol is not just linked to the consuls' own desire for regular alcohol supplies, but also to the fact that they represented the Christian population which was, at times, allowed to import alcohol. For example, governor Namık Pasha (1857–8) had forbidden the importation of wine and spirits until the arrival of his successor at the end of his term of office. A number of Europeans turned to the French consul, asking him to intervene with the new governor to lift the ban. The governor refused on the grounds that Jeddah was an essentially Arab (Islamic) city with a mere thirty Europeans, by which he meant to imply that alcohol, the sale of which to Muslims was forbidden, could not constitute a viable business. Furthermore, the governor argued, it endangered public order.[131]

The issue remained on the agenda. In 1862 and 1863, the British vice-consul seems to have managed to negotiate some special permissions for Christian residents in and visitors passing through Jeddah. This rather restrictive arrangement caused an outcry from merchants who had hoped to make a living selling alcohol.[132] The real market seems to have exceeded the limited number of Christians by far, and illegal sales (to Muslims and in particular to the garrison) were quite common. While the consuls were trying to defend what they considered to be a right by Christians to consume alcohol, they were, at the same time, embarrassed by those merchants who refused to accept the limitations on the sale of alcohol. 'And why these miserable fights? Do they

130 Hanssen, *Fin de Siècle Beirut*, p. 193.
131 CADN, 2_MI_3228, Jeddah, May 2, 1859.
132 TNA, FO 195/754, Brit. Consul to Caimacam, October 31, 1862; Stanley to Amb. Const., January 10, 1863; FO 685/1, I. Stanley Letter Book, Stanley to FO, January 14, 1863; and Stanley to Amb. Const., February 18, 1863.

truly befit the Vice-Consulate of France!', exclaimed Vice-Consul Buez in March 1875.[133] Meanwhile, alcohol, in particular a local brew called 'Araki', was readily available on the market.[134] This 'Araki' is probably similar to the brew described by Burckhardt as being produced by the female inhabitants of the Harat al-Soakiny.[135] By December 1876, the British vice-consul reported that the person in charge of supervising the enforcement of rules regarding alcohol sales, a young kaymakam, was addicted to the very stuff he was meant to ban.[136]

The question of alcohol continued to trouble Ottoman authorities and foreign consuls alike during the next decades. Sometimes its sale was fully forbidden, sometimes it was allowed to non-Muslims, sometimes the amount which could be taken from a government-controlled store to houses was closely regulated.[137] The fact that there was strong competition on the market suggests that it was a lucrative business.[138] Concerns connecting alcohol to public disorder were no mere speculation, as the following example shows: In 1897, the acting French consul expelled a French-protected Greek subject for being not only a drunkard but also for engaging in a brawl with an Austrian seaman and insulting the police officers who came to intervene. From a consular perspective, this could potentially incite anti-European sentiment and therefore was perceived as a security threat.[139]

After 1925, the regulations governing the import of alcohol became, if anything, even stricter. Once again, Europeans started to complain about difficulties of obtaining their favourite drug.[140] However, they

133 CADN, 2_MI_3245, E. Gasparoli to French Consul, December 1, 1867; and Const. Amb., Série D, Djeddah 4, Buez to Amb. Const. March 12, 1875.
134 CADN, 2_MI_3229, Buez to Amb. Const., February 1, 1876.
135 Burckhardt, *Travels in Arabia*, p. 17.
136 TNA, FO 195, 1103, Beyts, June 14, 1875 to Amb. Const.; and FO 195/1104, Beyts to Amb. Const. December 20, 1876.
137 CADN, 2_MI_3229, Buez to Amb. Const., November 20, 1878; TNA, FO 195/1847 Richards an Currie, March 14, 1894.
138 CADN, 2_MI_3229, Luccina to Amb. Const., June 15, 1879; Suret an Ambassade à Constantinople Djeddah, January 28, 1881; TNA, FO 195/1847, Richards to Amb. Const., May 3, 1894; FO 195/1894, Richards to Amb. Const. February 20, 1895; and FO 195/1943, Alban to Amb. Const., May 7, 1896.
139 CADN, 2_MI_3231, Djeddah, March 14, 1897.
140 Jarman (ed.), *The Jedda Diaries*, vol. 3, Jeddah Report, July 1928, p. 29; ibid., Jeddah Report, May 1930, p. 131and IOR, L/PS/12/2073, Jedda Report, February 1935, p. 2.

also reported that alcohol, like other prohibited 'vices' such as gramophones, abounded.[141]

In contrast to alcohol, prostitution is at best very discreetly hinted at in the consular records. One possible example is the report about a public outrage at the presence of an Egyptian lady in the house of a European in 1885, recorded by the French consul.[142] Burckhardt's observation about 'public women' (i.e. presumably prostitutes) from Suakin (i.e. on the other coast of the Red Sea and possibly the Horn of Africa) residing in Jeddah and selling alcohol is discreetly confirmed by a British report of 1879 talking about the banishment of 'bad female characters' to an outlying village.[143] Since most of these settlements were inhabited by Bedouin or Africans, and since Rathjens and Wissmann also describe prostitution in Nakutu in the 1940s, it is reasonable to assume that many prostitutes were either of East African or Egyptian origin.[144] Presumably, many of these women catered either to sailors or to the poor, as richer men could satisfy their sexual needs by buying slaves and (ab)using them as concubines.

Controlling Movement and Vagrancy

The control of population movements was an integral part of the tasks of the Ottoman police forces. For the Hijaz, one can distinguish a number of partly overlapping concerns: The policing of vagrants and poor people, with an emphasis on poor pilgrims who tended to get stranded (cf. Chapter 6), checking for potential agents of rival imperial powers, the prevention of contraband (including the slave trade) arriving and the control of illnesses brought in by pilgrims. Some of these, notably questions of political influence, but also of the control of trade and illness, have already been dealt with, at least partly, in earlier chapters when such issues as slave trade and quarantine were addressed. The entire question of foreign influence will be taken up in the following subchapter on nationality. Hence, the discussion here will focus mainly on the question of the policing of vagrants and poor

141 IOR, L/PS/12/2073, Jedda Report, February 1935, p. 2.

142 CADN, Const. Amb. Série D, Djeddah 4.

143 TNA, FO 195/1251, Zohrab to FO, November 13, 1879.

144 Burckhardt, *Travels in Arabia*, p. 17; Rathjens and Wissmann, *Landschaftskundliche Beobachtungen*, p. 82; and interview Muḥammad al-Ṭrābulsī, Jeddah, March 21, 2006.

people. This has already been discussed quite extensively for the Ottoman Empire at large.

Herzog gives a good survey of the legal basis of passports, both internal and external. 'Internal passports' or travel permits, called *mürur tezkeresi*, were at least theoretically required by anyone travelling within the empire throughout much of the nineteenth century. While in much of Europe external passports were abolished around the middle of the nineteenth century, entry to the Ottoman Empire required such a passport, as well as a *mürur tezkeresi*. Although this rule seems to date back to 1844, the passport was included in a list of Ottoman laws and regulations only in 1867.[145] While this might have been a mere quirk linked to administrative (re-)ordering, it also seems to have reflected a wider awareness of an increasingly perceived need to control the population, and some attempts at translating this into practice, if we consider the not at all comprehensive evidence from the Hijaz.

In Jeddah, the numbers of pilgrims in the 1840s and the duty to support them might have made stringent checks somewhat difficult. The British authorities seem to have convinced the Ottomans to exempt pilgrims travelling from British controlled territories, most notably India, from such checks.[146] This attitude changed during the following decades. This was partly due to fears about the spread of contagious diseases and partly to imperial concerns about controlling Muslims, politically as well as to prevent expenses related to repatriation. Often enough, this concerned Indians.

Imperial powers consequently began imposing passports on pilgrims, albeit at different paces and with hugely varying efficiency. They also attempted to control 'their pilgrims' by registering them, collecting their passports, or return tickets.[147] The Government of India even alerted pilgrims by imprinting on their passports a warning that it

[145] Christoph Herzog, 'Migration and the State: On Ottoman Regulations Concerning Migration since the Age of Mahmud II' in U. Freitag, M. Fuhrmann, N. Lafi, and F. Riedler (eds.), *The City in the Ottoman Empire: Migration and the Making of Urban Modernity*, SOAS/Routledge Studies on the Middle East (London and New York: Routledge, 2011), pp. 117–34, here pp. 118–29.

[146] Roff, *Sanitation and Security*, here p. 146.

[147] E.g. CADN, 2_MI_3229, Le Gay to Min. des Consulats, November 21, 1873; and 2_MI_3231, Dubief to Amb. Const., May 1, 1901.

would not necessarily return them home.[148] This topic has already been discussed at some length in the literature.[149] On the Ottoman front, the concerns were not entirely different from the Western imperial ones, although with different foci: Large numbers of poor pilgrims, who depended on charity or begging, were considered a threat to public order. If pilgrims hailed from territories under Western imperial rule, they were feared to open a door for unsolicited intervention by these foreign powers. Furthermore, the spread of cholera caused growing anxiety. Last but not least, the nineteenth century saw a small but rising number of European travellers posing as Muslims and attempting to reach Mecca, which the authorities were keen to prevent.[150]

Although a comprehensive study of Ottoman policies regarding vagrancy seems to be missing, literature suggests that these fluctuated between a more interventionist and a more laisser-faire attitude, with implementation also varying between the capital, which was at the centre of attention, and different provinces. The first tendency seems to be noticeable during the late eighteenth century and again from the late nineteenth century onwards.[151] In Istanbul, renewed attention for the issue of the dislocated poor rose in the context of refugees from the Russian Empire after the Russo-Turkish War of 1877–8. In 1896, Sultan Abdülhamid II founded a poor house which not only provided temporary shelter, but also training for the poor and for

148 Radhika Singha, 'Passport, Ticket, and India-Rubber Stamp: "The Problem of the Pauper Pilgrim" in Colonial India c. 1882–1925' in A. Tambe and H. Fischer-Tiné (eds.), *The Limits of British Colonial Control in South Asia: Spaces of Disorder in the Indian Ocean Region*, Routledge Studies in the Modern History of Asia (London: Routledge, 2009), pp. 49–83, here pp. 53–44.

149 For different imperial policies, e.g. Singha, Luc Chantre, 'Le Pèlerinage à La Mecque à l'époque coloniale (v. 1866–1940): France-Grande-Bretagne-Italie', PhD Thesis, Université de Poitiers (2012), pp. 183–99; Kane, *Russian Hajj*, pp. 55–7.

150 al-Muʿabbadī, *al-Nashāṭ al-tijārī li-minā ʾ Jidda*, pp. 130–2.

151 See Başaran, *Selim III, Social Contro*; Özbek, *'Beggars' and 'Vagrants'*; and Ferdan Ergut, 'Policing the Poor in the Late Ottoman Empire', *Middle Eastern Studies*, 38 (2002), pp. 149–64. The variations between contexts are particularly clearly pointed out in Mine Ener, 'Religious Prerogatives and Policing the Poor in Two Ottoman Contexts', *The Journal of Interdisciplinary History*, 35 (2005), pp. 501–11.

orphans, which complemented attempts to police and, where possible, remove the poor from the city.[152]

There are no studies of passport practices associated with the pilgrimage for the first decades covered in this study, as extant literature in Western languages and in Arabic tends to rely on consular sources (which only begin to discuss the issue systematically from the 1870s onwards) or on Ottoman documents from the 1880s and later. In turn, earlier travelogues have much to say on customs and little to nothing on passport controls. Due to this situation, we also know more about people coming from European Empires than about internal travellers. There are also certain conjunctures as to when the passport question seems to have become particularly acute, such as in the early to mid-1880s and the late 1890s. These correspond to distinct crises, which have been discussed in Chapter 2. For the first period, this was the fallout of the Russo-Turkish War, the ʿUrābī uprising, British occupation of Egypt, and internationally, the Mahdi uprising in the Sudan, as well as, locally, the dispute between the Ottoman governors and the new Emir of Mecca. The assassination of the British vice-consul in 1895 marked the height of local suspicions of British imperial aims in the Hijaz, possibly also reflecting closer Ottoman-British cooperation in the period. The following brief survey, which cannot but reflect these lacunae, will need to be complemented from hitherto unmined Ottoman or local sources in the future.

We have early reports of passport problems by Southeast Asian and Algerian pilgrims, although the exact nature of the problems is not quite clear.[153] In February of 1881, the British ambassador was informed that the Ottoman authorities intended to expel unidentified foreigners and that

> all persons arriving in the ports of the Hedjaz after the 1st of April 1880 (sic!), whether Indians, Javanese, Algerians, &c., will not be permitted to land if they do not possess proper identifying papers.[154]

This was ostensibly due to the increasing number of 'vagabonds' and vagrants in the Hijaz.[155] In spite of the conveyance of this information

152 Ener, *Religious Prerogatives and Policing the Poor*, pp. 509–11.

153 TNA, PRO, FO 78/2357, Wylde to Consul of Netherlands, January 10, 1877; and CADN, 2_MI_3229, Buez to MAE, February 21, 1873.

154 IOR, L/P&S/7/30, encl. 3 to No. 15, Zohrab to Viceroy and Governor-General of India, February 17, 1881.

155 IOR, L/P&S/7/30, encl. 3 to No. 15, Zohrab to Viceroy and Governor-General of India, February 17, 1881.

to the British-Indian authorities, many pilgrims were apparently caught unawares.[156] A petition by the 'Muftis and Ulemas and the Guardians of the temple at Mecca' to the Ottoman Governor deplored this situation. The petitioners described the plight of pilgrims, who had to leave their luggage at customs and were semi-interned until their documents had been issued. Furthermore, they also needed an additional pass from the Turkish authorities. This, the petitioners argued, was preventing Muslims from completing the pilgrimage and was totally contrary to Muslim customs. If indeed passports were necessary, they should have been issued by the home countries.[157] Even if the last point sounds as if it had been written by a consular official, the petition reflects some genuine concerns of the pilgrims, even if those who signed might also have been worried about their own sources of income from the pilgrims. As regards consular officials, the changes inspired them to come up with a host of new ideas about future hajj management, from passport fees to the presence of pilgrim agents in India and tighter medical inspection.[158] The major underlying fear was that Ottoman authorities could potentially demand that the consulate pay for the repatriation of the pilgrims.[159]

Was this panic singular in the history of the Hijaz? In 1883, the consul reported that, since the pilgrimage of 1881, pilgrims had no longer been asked for passports, contrary to legal provisions. Instead, the *wukalāʾ* procured travel permits from the authorities, apparently a profitable business for both the pilgrims' guides and the clerks, perhaps due to its doubtful legality.[160] A year later, the system was put back into place. Foreigners now needed a visa issued at a port outside the Hijaz. If they had no such visa or, worse, no passport they incurred high fees. British imperial authorities applied this rule when dealing with people aiming to travel to the Hijaz. As this ruling was propagated only shortly before the Hajj, pilgrims arrived without proper

[156] TNA, FO 195/1375, Moncrieff to Amb. Const., July 14, 1881.

[157] TNA, FO 78/3314, Petition from the Muftis etc. The enclosed Arabic copy does not refer to muftis, *ʿulamāʾ*, and 'guardians' but to those who put their seals to the petition – the names and titles are, however, lacking.

[158] IOR, L/P&S/7/30, No. 15, Circular to Local Governments and Administrations, August 24, 1881.

[159] IOR, L/P&S/7/30, encl. 3 to No. 15, Zohrab to Viceroy and Governor-General of India, February 17, 1881.

[160] TNA, FO 195/1451, Monceriff to Gvt. Of India, May 13, 1883.

papers and, eventually, were permitted to proceed to Mecca without extra payment.[161]

Four years later, a young Englishman contracted by a Dutch firm was not as lucky. Arriving without proper papers, he had to pay 100 piastres in fines.[162] In late 1890, the British circulated the blueprint of pilgrims' passports to their dependencies and the consulate in Jeddah.[163] The introduction of visas led to a rapid increase in visa fees which by 1895 were more than triple that of a simple local *mürur tezkeresi.*[164] However, if this introduced a relative advantage for Ottoman subjects and local residents, this was not to last: by 1897, the costs of the *mürur tezkeresi* had doubled.[165]

It seems that rules were applied much earlier on the route via Suez. French reports from the 1870s onwards mention passports and visas. For example, in February 1873 the French consul reported that Algerians paid two 'talaris' if they obtained their visa in Alexandria or Suez, while Javanese paid three if they arrived without a visa in Jeddah.[166] The taxes imposed on pilgrim visas seem to have differed, depending on the place of origin, as transpires from a French report from 1895.[167] However, on neither route, anything amounting to full control was ever implemented. Thus, in 1876, French consul Buez voiced his concern that the local authorities should demand passports from arriving passengers. 'The city', he claimed, 'is full of Tunisians, many of whom ex-convicts', for whom Jeddah was an 'Eden'.[168] When France tried to limit the number of Algerians travelling on the hajj, their Algerian subjects had the possibility to obtain a 'teskeré ou passeport arabe', i.e. a travel document, in Tunis or Tanger.[169] This also points to an issue which caused an increase in anxiety for all

161 TNA, FO 195/1482, Abdur Razzack to Amb. Const., July 15, 1884, August 27, 1884.
162 TNA, FO 195/1610, Jago to Amb. Const., April 18, 1888.
163 TNA, FO 685/3, Miscellaneous VI, Deputy Secretary of the Gvt. of India to Consulate Jeddah, January 20, 1891.
164 TNA, FO 195/1894, Richards to Amb. Const., April 4, 1895.
165 TNA, FO 195/1987, Devey to Amb. Const., January 1, 1897, January 14, 1897.
166 CADN, 2_MI_3229, Buez to MAE et al., February 27, 1873. Another report mentions a fee of two 'talaris' for Alexandria and Suez, and three for Javanese who arrived in Jeddah without a visa.
167 CADN, 2_MI_3231, Descoutres to Amb. Const., April 10, 1895.
168 CADN, 2_MI_3229, Buez to Amb. Const., February 1, 1876.
169 CADN, 2_MI_3229, Buez to Min. of Commerce, December 22, 1877.

imperial powers involved, namely the issue of people with multiple nationalities, as will be discussed below.

As has already been noted, many poor pilgrims were stranded in Mecca and in Jeddah after the end of the hajj. According to a French doctor working for the Ottoman Sanitary Service about twenty to 25 per cent of the pilgrims were unable to pay a newly introduced sanitary tax.[170] While these might not automatically have been paupers, a portion of them certainly were. A fairly detailed description by the British consul in 1897 discusses how about 350 poor pilgrims were stranded in Mecca. When the British-Indian authorities refused to help, 250 members of the group returned to Mecca 'where they can obtain food and shelter at the rubats or almshouses, and sometimes even a little work and wages'. Some found shelter in Jeddah, while 70–80 ended up camping in the harbour area where 'they can scrape up some means of existence from the driblets of rice and grain escaping from the damaged sacks.' They did not move until a local shaykh and some other people, as well as some of the *arbiṭa* took some of them in, thus also providing for them. A local relief fund bought tickets for 50 pilgrims and the British consul, under pressure from the local authorities, humbly asked whether they might be taken back on a steamer that was passing by at the time.[171]

Indeed, the primary approach to the regular presence of large numbers of poor pilgrims after the end of the hajj was their deportation, if the relevant authorities were willing to comply. These were keen on passing on the costs of this to the pilgrims in different ways.[172] Where no colonial officials were at hand, the Ottomans had to act themselves, as in 1888 when they hired a ship from Jeddah to Hodeida to return 126 pilgrims to Yemen.[173]

In addition to poor pilgrims, droughts or conflict in the countryside could swell the population of Jeddah. Following a lengthy drought, the British consul reported the presence of large numbers of Bedouin in both Mecca and Jeddah. The Jeddah authorities appeared helpless and took no steps to alleviate the suffering of the starving Bedouin, nor to expel them from the city.[174]

170 Chiffoleau, *Le Voyage à la Mecque*, p. 62.
171 TNA, FO 195/1987, Devey to Amb. Const., 14 Dec. 1897.
172 For an example, see the letters from April 2 and 3 from the Sanitary Inspector and the British Consul on this matter in TNA, FO 195/2174.
173 al-Muʿabbadī, *al-Nashāṭ al-tijārī li-minā' Jidda*, p. 128.
174 TNA, FO 195/1653, Wood to Amb. Const., December 9, 1889.

As the reports show, relief for the poor was generally considered a private matter, even if performed by public figures.[175] As such, it had a long tradition in the Hijaz, with the *arbiṭa* forming a cornerstone of poor relief for residents and pilgrims alike. They were built by wealthy merchants, as well as by wealthy pilgrims and, until nationality became a major issue, also by foreign rulers for the benefit of pilgrims from their countries (see below). This was complemented by private charity providing food and clothes for the poor and by official attempts at limiting the number of poor people.[176]

The fear of the spread of disease as well as the Muslim duty to cater to pilgrims were twin concerns of the Ottoman government and reflected on its international reputation. Hence, in the Hijaz, the above-mentioned private efforts were coupled with some investment by the government. This concerned, first and foremost, the care of the sick, which began, it is important to note, before the massive international efforts after the Sanitary Conference of Constantinople, as has been shown in Chapter 6. It also extended to the construction of very substantial shelters for poor pilgrims in Mecca and Jeddah.[177]

In Sharifian times, the issue of poor pilgrims gained further attention in the light of the generally impoverished state of the now independent Hijaz. While in 1921, when pilgrim numbers were still down due to the effects of the war, only 500 pilgrims could not pay for their return journey, this number rose to 2,765 in 1923. The British consul Bullard describes vividly how, in 1923, the British consulate, as well as a local committee, tried to limit the number of those they assisted by buying return tickets.[178] Sharif Ḥusayn suggested to establish a permanent repatriation fund, something fiercely resisted by the consuls, who preferred to act on a case-by-case basis in order to avoid additional incentives for poor pilgrims.[179] Consequently, he decreed that the passengers of each ship consist to 10 per cent of poor pilgrims.[180]

When, in 1926, another Sanitary Conference convened in Paris, article 93 of the final convention stipulated something that had been

[175] Ener, *Religious Prerogatives and Policing the Poor*, p. 504.
[176] Chiffoleau, *Le Voyage à la Mecque*, p. 78.
[177] Kasım İzzeddin, *Hicaz Sıhhiye Rapor*, pp. 52–66. The report illustrates well the motivations and details measures taken, images of the Jeddah hostel for the poor pp. 59, 63.
[178] Bullard, *Two Kings in Arabia*, letter of September 16, 1923, pp. 14–55.
[179] Chantre, *Le Pèlerinage à La*, pp. 378–84. [180] Ibid., p. 392.

attempted many times but been rejected not least by the British Government of India: Namely that each pilgrim should either prove that he was in possession of a return ticket or depose an equivalent sum of money before setting off. To impose better control, passages by sail were forbidden. The number of return tickets issued increased continuously from 56 to 98.62 per cent of all tickets issued in 1932, probably as the result of an economic crisis which made a lengthy stay in the Hijaz a rather unpleasant prospect. In addition, Ibn Saʿūd also attempted to prevent the immigration of poor people by land. Thus, he warned the British government in August of 1942 that he would no longer allow destitute Yemenis and Hadhramis (as well as other foreign subjects) to enter the Kingdom.[181] The number of poor pilgrims stranded in the Hijaz, and of those deported, also decreased.[182] These efforts notwithstanding, the problem of people overstaying their welcome remains an issue to this very day.

Who is a Hijazi: Legal Distinctions and Their Local Consequences

As has been seen in the discussion of the control of movement, which played an important role throughout the entire period under discussion, legal distinctions were made between Ottoman (and later Sharifian and Saudi) subjects and foreigners. I will argue in this section that the Ottoman rationale behind enforcing stricter separations was due to fear of foreign imperial interference. This is in line with the argument developed by Akcasu that the Ottoman government was concerned to naturalise foreign Muslims, or else to explicitly exclude them.[183] The Saudi government's priority in the period until 1947 was the establishment of a new political entity with a more or less stable population. Present-day discussions about limiting access to redistributive income from oil, or even the kind of genealogical concerns about 'Arabness' discussed in the introduction and conclusion, seem to have played only a minor role in this formative period of the Kingdom.

[181] IOR, L/PS/12/752, Telegram Jeddah to FO, August 26, 1942.

[182] Chantre, *Pèlerinages d'Empire*, pp. 246–48 and passim; cf. the regulations and cases in IOR, L/PS/12/2077.

[183] A. Akcasu, 'Migrants to Citizens: An Evaluation of the Expansionist Features of Hamidian Ottomanism, 1876–1909', *Die Welt des Islams*, 56 (2016), pp. 388–414.

Ottoman Concerns: Foreign Influence

Who was considered Ottoman? The problem with definitions of nationality is, as Hanley has shown, that they only really emerged in the course of the nineteenth century. Furthermore, this development, which to some extent preceded formulations of national identities, occurred in the colonial and imperial context. An important context in the Ottoman case was the tradition of written protection for specific groups, which were further developed in the capitulations.[184] While foreign Muslims came under Ottoman jurisdiction, Europeans and, increasingly, local non-Muslims working for Europeans were granted capitulatory privileges. From the eighteenth century onwards, demands to protect these individuals became a tool for exerting pressure on the Ottoman government. In various local contexts, Muslims in foreign service could also obtain this status and thus undermine Ottoman authority over all resident Muslims.[185] The list of persons protected by the British consulate in Jeddah in 1891 includes four Muslim employees of the consulate in this category.[186] They had a similar status to subjects from the British Empire.

In the Hijaz, the conflict of 1858 over the flag flown on the ship of Ṣāliḥ Jawhar, which resulted in the Jeddah massacre (see Chapter 2), exemplifies the kind of conflicts that could arise from foreign (in this case British) attempts to extend their 'protection' and influence over people and properties that could equally be identified as Ottoman. A second major issue was that of land in the Hijaz once the Ottoman law permitting private land ownership by foreigners was passed in 1867. Fearing foreign intervention, it was argued that the Hijaz should

184 These categories are explored by Will Hanley, *Identifying with Nationality: Europeans, Ottomans, and Egyptians in Alexandria* (New York: Columbia University Press, 2017), pp. 173–216. In spite of Isin's considerations, I will use the term 'subject' rather than 'citizen', without aiming to establish inherent distinctions but in analogy to the British terminology, Isin, *Ottoman Waqfs as Acts*, here pp. 32–40.

185 Gianluca Parolin, *Citizenship in the Arab World: Kin, Religion and Nation-State*, IMISCOE Research (Amsterdam: Amsterdam University Press, 2009), pp. 71–3. The question of protection has been well explored, e.g. Maurits van den Boogert, *The Capitulations and the Ottoman Legal System: Qadis, Consuls, and Beratlıs in the 18th Century* (Leiden: Brill, 2005).

186 TNA, FO 195/1730, Wood to Amb. Const., April 28, 1891, p. 4.

be exempt from this rule as the province in which the two most holy cities of Islam were situated.[187]

The Ottoman Nationality Law of 1869 is, compared to other nationality laws, an early attempt to clarify the distinction between 'nationals' and 'foreigners' from the perspective of imperial governance. It must be seen as an attempt to curb this increasing European encroachment and had, at the time, no ambition to incorporate issues of citizenship rights or identity.[188] The law was fairly inclusive: children born to an Ottoman father were automatic subjects and those born on Ottoman soil to foreign parents could be naturalised three years after coming of age. After a residence of five years, or in recognition of specific merits, individuals could be awarded nationality. A letter from the French consul to the kaymakam in 1889 shows that he had been consulted about possible objections to the naturalisation of a certain Muḥammad Ṣāliḥ Jīlānī.[189] French officials themselves seem to have been confused as to what the legal requirements in cases of the adoption of a new nationality were. Could the French consulate award an Ottoman subject French nationality simply on the basis of French rules and could the Ottomans do the inverse, or was an Ottoman or French approval required? Unfortunately, the French file does not answer this question. It also gives no clue as to whether Jīlānī kept his status as a French subject.[190]

Finally, and in reflection of earlier practices, all residents of the Empire were to be considered Ottomans until the opposite was established. A later regulation clarified that all those holding foreign nationality prior to the law could retain it. A treaty with Persia specified that Persians were treated as foreigners in spite of their religion.[191]

Unfortunately for the Ottomans, the law did little to mitigate the problems arising in the Hijaz. For analytic purposes, one can distinguish between a number of different categories of problematic cases:

187 On the law, see Abdul-Karim Rafeq, 'Ownership of Real Property by Foreigners in Syria, 1869–1873' in R. Owen and M. P. Bunton (eds.), *New Perspectives on Property and Land in the Middle East*, Harvard Middle Eastern Monographs (Cambridge, MA: Harvard University Press, 2000), pp. 175–239.

188 Hanley, *Identifying with Nationality*, p. 58, for the categories of 'national' and 'foreigner' pp. 5–9, 56–8, 63–4; and Parolin, *Citizenship in the Arab World*, p. 73.

189 CADN, 2_MI_3240, no. 25 to Caïmmacam, June 8, 1905.

190 CADN, 2_MI_3231, no. 4 to Amb. Const., Jeddah, February 3, 1891.

191 Parolin, *Citizenship in the Arab World*, p. 74.

First, Muslims from regions which had never been under Ottoman rule, second, Muslims from former Ottoman realms, and third, Hijazis who laid claim to foreign nationality or protection and thus fell under the far-reaching concessions granted to foreign consuls.[192] The first group consisted mainly of British Indians and Southeast Asians. As a British-Indian merchant resident in Jeddah, Ṣāliḥ Jawhar had been able to claim Ottoman nationality (even prior to the Nationality Law).[193] British Indians could find refuge from British authorities pursuing them for political or criminal offences in the Hijaz and the authorities would refuse their rendition on the basis that they were Ottoman subjects.[194] The wildly differing numbers of British subjects given by the consulate – from 'nearly ten thousand' to a list of just over 100 – probably indicates that many Muslims were not keen on British protection, instead of pointing to massive population fluctuations. Thus, in 1879, consul Zohrab complained that there were less than 1,500 British subjects, as not all those entitled to claim it actually asked for it and registered with the consulate.[195] This number is interesting as it is actually divided into different categories, listing 4 British-born persons (among them the consul and his wife), 6 Maltese, 109 British Indian subjects, typically working as merchants, clerks, shipping or pilgrim agents or brokers, tailors, and druggists, as well as the above-mentioned 4 (local) Muslim employees of the British consulate, who would fall in the last of the three categories of protected people.

Foreign protégés from territories formerly under Ottoman control, mainly in North Africa and regions occupied by Russia at times considered the Hijaz a refuge from their new governments. Thus, a group of Algerians living in Medina stayed away from the Algerian consulate. This alarmed the consul, who feared their potential influence on pilgrims from their home country.[196] The Ottoman authorities were in turn keen to extend protection to such people, even if they

192 On this issue, e.g. Zandi-Sayek, *Ottoman Izmir*.
193 This was true regardless of Jawhar's possible Greek Muslim origin, Ochsenwald, *Religion, Society, and the State*, p. 143 and Low, *The Mechanics of Mecca*, p. 117.
194 E.g. TNA, FO 195/879, Stanley to Amb. Const., April 26, 1864.
195 The large number is mentioned in TNA, FO 685/1, I. Stanley Letter Book, Stanley to Amb. Const., June 20, 1861; the lower one in FO 195/1730, Wood to Amb. Const., April 28, 1891; and FO 685/1, II: Consul Zohrab's Letter Book, Zohrab to FO, July 20, 1879.
196 CADN, 2_MI_3231, No. 92, Djeddah, July 25, 1899.

came from places such as Afghanistan, arguing that as Muslims they were entitled to Ottoman protection, regardless of their nationality. Sometimes, these were classified as Muslim foreigners, but quite often they were granted Ottoman nationality based on their residence in Ottoman domains. The main aim was to avoid yet another increase in the numbers of foreign-protected persons which could have opened a door to interventions.[197]

The Ottoman passport, obtainable for Algerians in Tunis and Tangiers, allowed them to perform the pilgrimage in years when the French authorities had forbidden it.[198] This contention over who was responsible for Russian or French protégés, considered by the Ottomans to be under their legislation, was by no means confined to the Hijaz.[199]

Another thorny issue in which nationality came into play was the question of inheritance. In the case of foreign Muslims dying in Ottoman lands – a frequent occurrence during pilgrimage due to the often high age of pilgrims and disease, their legacy could be claimed by the state. Because of this, consuls were repeatedly involved in trying to salvage the claims of a protégé's relatives to his (or her) inheritance.[200]

As elsewhere in the Ottoman realms and beyond, those who were meant to be controlled by the extension of nationality found multiple ways to turn this to their advantage, both legally and socially.[201] Zaynal ʿAlī Riḍā, for example, was described by the French in 1909 not only as the most important merchant but also as a former Persian turned Ottoman.[202] From a British perspective, Zaynal was a 'respectable British subject', a claim which they were quite willing to defend against the Persian consul who claimed his country's authority

[197] These questions are discussed in detail by Lâle Can, 'The Protection Question: Central Asians and Extraterritoriality in the Late Ottoman Empire', *International Journal of Middle East Studies*, 48 (2016), pp. 679–99; Akcasu, *Migrants to Citizens*, pp. 397–8.

[198] CADN, 2_MI_3229, Buez to Min. of Commerce, December 22, 1877.

[199] For the competition to control Algerians and Tunisians in Syria see Pierre Bardin, *Algériens et Tunisiens dans l'Empire Ottoman de 1948 à 1914* (Paris: Ed. du Centre National de la Recherche Scientifique, 1979), cf. Hanley, *Identifying with Nationality*, pp. 173–95 for the situation in Alexandria.

[200] For example, CADN, 2_MI_3229, Suret to Amb. Const., February 17, 1881.

[201] Hanley, *Identifying with Nationality*, pp. 189–90 and passim.

[202] CADN, 2_MI_2342, Notes de Renseignement sur les Notabilités Musulmanes de Djeddah, 1909.

over Zaynal.[203] Matters were even more complicated with ʿAlī b. Muḥammad Bā Nāja who, in 1903, appeared with a British passport issued in the consulate in Zanzibar. According to the British reports, he attempted to thus realise claims to inheritance which had already been refused under Ottoman law. After consultation with the India and Foreign Offices, the claim was rejected. Not only had the claimant, as well as his father and grandfather, been born in Jeddah as Ottoman subjects, he himself had also left Hadhramaut five years before the Protectorate treaty of 1888. Worse still, his grandfather had participated in the 1857 massacre.[204] In this case, the legal argument was clearly compounded by a moral judgement on the family.

While merchants such as Zaynal actively sought out foreign protection, others did the opposite, and, in either case, could make use of the possibility of multiple affiliations. Apart from escaping colonial control, there was another, increasingly strong incentive to opt for Ottoman nationality, namely land and property. In the early 1860s, the Ottoman Council of Ministers had warned both the Emir of Mecca and the Ottoman governor that foreign protection of long-term residents of the holy cities should not be permitted and that foreign Muslim residents there had to abide by Islamic Law. Foreigners residing in the holy cities, but also in Jeddah had, for a long time, invested in real estate, either by posing as Ottomans or through local women. Consequently, this law caused considerable apprehension and resistance, mostly among those directly concerned, but also among local power-holders, who had their own reasons to treat this group of foreign residents well.[205] As already mentioned, the Ottoman law allowing the acquisition of private property by foreigners explicitly exempted the Hijaz. This does not seem to have changed local practice immediately. Hence, a series of decrees from Istanbul was issued to remind local authorities and consuls of the rules.[206] Although the law

[203] TNA, FO 195/1313, Zohrab to Amb. Const., March 16, 1880. For the dispute with the Persian consulate, see FO 195/1251, Zohrab to Amb. Const., November 12, 1879.

[204] TNA, FO 195/2224, the nationality question of Ali bin Mohamed Banaji, May 25, 1906.

[205] On these earlier practices Young, *Corps de Droit Ottoman*, vol. 1, p. 334, for the law of 1867 and relevant protocols of 1868 and 1876, see Young, pp. 337–45.

[206] Can, *The Protection Question*, pp. 688–90; and Ṣabbān, *Jidda fī wathāʾiq al-arshīf al-ʿuthmānī*, p. 55.

continued to be honoured more by its breach than by observance, as Can shows with regard to Central Asians, it also seems to have induced a fair number of people to seek Ottoman nationality. In 1882, the British consul opined on this matter: While poor Indians might change their nationality, he wrote, 'the better to do will probably be unwilling to sacrifice British protection'.[207] North Africans were also affected, as is shown by the example of an Algerian who had not even been registered as a French protégé, but now explicitly aimed to change his status in order to buy property in Medina.[208]

Most of the individual cases mentioned in the consular archives, as well as in Can's article, concern private property acquisition by foreigners in Mecca and Medina.[209] Can has shown that the prohibition also applied to charitable institutions in Mecca. A comparable case from Jeddah had a particularly high profile: The Nawab of Rampur intended to establish a rest house for Indian pilgrims in the city as many pilgrims had to sleep rough for lack of funds to rent accommodation. To this purpose, she deposited 2,020,000 rupees with the British consulate, which was asked to realise the project. An obvious path was to establish a pious foundation. The consul came up against the usual argument, also encountered by Central Asian benefactors, namely that this was prohibited by law.[210] Given that the request therefore would have aroused suspicion and was unlikely to be granted, the consul was advised to 'find an honest Arab in whose name the property might stand'.[211] He responded by consenting and informing the British Ambassador in Istanbul that he suggested Abdullah Effendi Banaji (Bā Nāja), 'one of the most respected citizens of this town' and, nota bene, a member of the same family of which members would be denied nationality with great moral impetus six years later.[212]

An interesting sideshow in this wider context were the attempts by Emir ʿAwn al-Rafīq to exclude 'foreign' pilgrims' guides and

207 TNA, FO 195/1415, Monceriff to Amb. Const., May 7, 1882.
208 CADN, 2_MI_3221, No. 40 of October 28, 1895.
209 This was also an issue pre-1867 elsewhere in the Empire, and some of the tactics employed resembled very much the strategies used in Jeddah, cf. Zandi-Sayek, *Ottoman Izmir*, pp. 53–67.
210 TNA, FO 195/2083, Devey to Amb. Const., March 7, 1900. For the Central Asian comparison, see Can, *The Protection Question*, p. 689.
211 TNA, FO 195/2083, note dated March 22, 1900.
212 TNA; FO 195/2083, Devey to Amb. Const., July 8, 1900.

monopolise the *ṭawwāfa* for Ottoman subjects, thus aiming to increase earnings for himself and preclude foreign interventions.[213] As this seems to have been occurring in a legal grey zone, the British consulate managed to defend the licenses of some Indian pilgrim guides in 1890 by threatening to increase the consulate's involvement in choosing brokers and agents.[214] In the long run, ʿAwn al-Rafīq seems to have persisted in his attempts to make the *ṭawwāfa* an Ottoman affair.[215]

One final group should be mentioned at least briefly: Christians under consular protection. These were mostly individuals of Greek and Maltese origin. While the European consuls felt more affinity to them than to their Muslim protégés, Hanley's notion of the 'accidental equality' of imperial subjects to the European imperial powers describes well the uneasy relationship between these Christians and their protectors.[216] The Maltese in Alexandria were even explicitly excluded from the category of 'Europeans'. In Jeddah, it was the Greeks, Armenians, and Italians (of varying nationalities), in addition to the Maltese, who were considered to not be quite of equal social status. This was, on the one hand, partly the result of the social distinction between consuls and merchants and, on the other, due to frequent clashes of tavern keepers with local norms, but also legal and political hierarchies.[217] The case nicely illustrates Hanley's view that legal and social meanings of nationality often intersected in uneasy ways.

The Post-Ottoman Hijaz: Early Saudi Concerns

It seems that Sharifian rule, established in the midst of World War I and dominated by the War's aftermath and the subsequent conflict with Ibn Saʿūd, was too short for considerations of a nationality law. Ibn Saʿūd had a different approach: only nine months after the Saudi takeover of the Hijaz, a first nationality law for the Hijaz was issued on 29 September 1926. The law was adapted in August 1930 to clarify some minor issues, but mostly to accommodate the union of

213 This is discussed in Low, *The Mechanics of Mecca*, pp. 315–8.
214 TNA, FO 195/1689, Wood to Amb. Const., May 30, 1890.
215 TNA, FO 195/1943, Alban to Amb. Const., February 17, 1896.
216 See Hanley, *Identifying with Nationality*, pp. 176–81.
217 E.g. TNA, FO 685/1, I Consul Stanley's Letter Book, Stanley to Consul-General, Cairo, January 8, 1861; and CADN, Const. Amb. D-Djeddah 4, Buez to Amb. Const., March 1, 1875.

Najd and Hijaz.[218] In 1938, the last nationality law for the period under discussion was issued, now firmly speaking of Saudis, rather than Hijazis or Najdis.[219]

Muslims residing in the Hijaz and borderland regions were, ever since the end of the Ottoman Empire, considered to be Hijazi nationals together with everyone else who did not hold another nationality. Hijazi nationality could be granted by a royal decree after only three (instead of five) years of residence. The adoption of foreign nationalities required official consent. Women of Hijazi men became Hijazi, while men could not acquire nationality through marrying local women. Children born to foreign parents in the Hijaz held the nationality only when residing in the country.[220] An interesting new regulation stipulated that the nationality could be revoked for those who entered military service of other countries without prior consent (art. 7, 1926; art. 11, 1938). This seems an indication of the as yet instable political identities of former Ottoman territories (and their tribal 'hinterlands') which meant that many former Ottoman officers (and other former soldiers and politicians) were hired in the services of different emergent states at different times.[221] It would seem that, in the dynamic geopolitical environment of the 1920s and 1930s, this caused greater anxiety than a possible British or French imperial leverage over subjects of dual nationality, which had dominated Ottoman policies on nationality in the context of the capitulatory regime. Indeed, article 5 of the Anglo-Saudi Treaty of Jeddah (1927) stipulated mutual

[218] For the amendment, see Ettore Rossi and U.F., 'Arabia', *Oriente Moderno* 11 (1931), pp. 156–7, here p. 156; and for the Arabic text *Umm al-Qurā* giving August 18, 1930 as the date of change. For criticisms that concerned regulations that were consequently appended, see IOR, L/PS/12/2073, Jeddah Report, January–February 1931, p. 15–18; cf. Parolin, *Citizenship in the Arab World*, p. 89.

[219] The text is contained in Nallino, *Raccolta di Scritti*, pp. 244–6; Parolin, *Citizenship in the Arab World* seems to have overlooked this text. I have not been able to access the issue of *Umm al-Qurā*, of December 16, 1938 where the law was published in Arabic.

[220] The full text can be found in Ettore Rossi, 'Arabia', *Oriente Moderno*, 11 (1931), pp. 189–92, here p. 190; Parolin, *Citizenship in the Arab World*, p. 88; cf. Jarman (ed.), *The Jedda Diaries*, vol. 2, Jeddah Report, October 1926, p. 418.

[221] This is a major theme in Michael Provence, *The Last Ottoman Generation and the Making of the Modern Middle East* (Cambridge: Cambridge University Press, 2017).

protection of the countries' subjects.[222] The modifications to the earlier Ottoman law show that the Saudi concern in this period was clearly to consolidate the population of the Hijaz, and, after 1927, that of the Kingdom. It wanted to – gradually – reduce the possibilities afforded by multiple nationalities, and hence eventually reduce the mobility of its population for the sake of greater control.

Another controversial issue which had caused friction in Ottoman times was also resolved in this treaty. It stipulated in article 4 that the property of deceased British subjects without relatives or legal representation had to be handed to the consulate after the necessary dues had been paid.[223] The question of land remained a thorny issue: On September 9, 1934, Ibn Saʿūd signed a decree banning foreigners from buying real estate in the Hijaz while allowing it elsewhere in the Kingdom. This continued the earlier Ottoman stipulation. The division of the Ottoman Empire after 1918, as well as the more liberal practice of land sales under Sharifian rule, meant, however, that now many more people were actually affected. Consequently, provisions were made to allow those who had legally acquired land but were now barred from ownership, to continue its use.[224]

Entrance into the Kingdom, and particularly travel to places beyond Jeddah and the holy cities, now required government permission and thus became, if anything, more complicated, according to Nallino's account of 1938.[225] Such permission was refused if criticism had been voiced by the applicants. New converts had to prove their religious conviction through prolonged residence in Jeddah where they needed to obtain certificates testifying to their conversion. If political or military aims were suspected, even ordinary believers were barred from visiting Mecca and Medina. Non-Muslims remained barred from the holy cities and required permission to visit even the ports of the Hijaz, although this could be obtained on the spot if the country of origin did not have a Saudi embassy or consulate. Muslims could obtain leave to stay in the country for a year upon payment of ten thalers, which could

222 Jacob Hurewitz, *Diplomacy in the Near and Middle East: A Documentary Record: 1914–1956*, vol. 2 (Princeton, NJ: Nostrand, 1956), p. 150.

223 Ibid., pp. 149–50.

224 Ettore Rossi, 'Arabia', *Oriente Moderno*, 15 (1935), pp. 95–7, here pp. 95–6; and Ochsenwald, *Islam and Loyalty*, here p. 31.

225 Nallino, *Raccolta di Scritti*, pp. 144–9. The entire paragraph follows his account.

be withdrawn in case they became undesired. Non-Muslims needed special permits which were usually linked to diplomatic work or mineral explorations. In another interesting move, a local merchant who held an Egyptian passport was barred from leaving the Hijaz because he was considered a Hijazi subject, having been born in the area. This shows that there was a certain concern to increase the number of Hijazis and exert control over them.[226]

On a more practical level, Hijazis apparently resented the significant numbers of foreigners employed by Ibn Saʿūd. Consequently, from September 1926 onwards, state employees had to be Saudi subjects. The large number of foreigners in government service were given the choice of becoming Saudis, being dismissed or, if their services were indispensable, being employed on fixed-term contracts. Among the four customs officials who contacted the British consulate for advice, one Sudanese decided to take on Saudi nationality, while three Indians resigned from their posts. Two Indian engineers retaining their positions, but also their nationality had to sign a clause stipulating that they would not involve the British consulate in cases of dispute. Nevertheless, the level of application of these regulations remained somewhat unequal when very high officials were concerned.[227]

Overall, it seems fair to state that the new Saudi government pursued a quite inclusive strategy in terms of nationality, as far as (mainly Arab) Muslims were concerned. Its main aim was to keep out potential trouble-makers and political adversaries, while the fear of imperial subversion faded into the background.

Prescribing Religion and Lifestyle

In contrast to the austere environment of the Najd, many people in the port city of Jeddah smoked, listened to music, shaved their beards, and did not mind photography unless they were, like Muḥammad Naṣīf in his early years, fervent adherents of Wahhabi interpretations of Islam.[228]

[226] Jarman (ed.), *The Jedda Diaries*, vol. 2, Jeddah Report, September 1926, pp. 412–33.

[227] Ibid., September 1926, p. 412; cf.; ibid p. 372; and MECA, Philby Collection GB165-0229, 1/4/5/1, Philby Diary, part 1, February 2, 1926, p. 389.

[228] In his youth, Naṣīf even destroyed his only photograph of his father; cf. Freitag, *Scholarly Exchange and Trade*, here pp. 301–22 and 307–88 with a translation and facsimile of a letter by Naṣīf on this topic.

While King Ḥusayn had attempted to combat prostitution, alcohol consumption, music, and dancing in Mecca and, to some extent, in Medina, no such efforts were made in Jeddah.[229] Furthermore, prostitution and the consumption of alcohol were by no means restricted to passing sailors and non-Muslims. Rather, it was 'almost as easy to buy whisky as to buy any other commodity in the market, and Moslems had been drinking freely', the British consul remarked upon the prohibition of alcohol imports for Europeans in 1928.[230] The Sufi practices discussed in Chapter 5 and such new phenomena as football further compounded the image of Jeddah as a veritable hotbed of vice in the eyes of Wahhabi scholars. The years following the conquest of the Hijaz were hence marked by attempts to impose a stricter religious regime, first on an ad hoc basis and, increasingly, in a more sustained manner.[231] Matters became particularly tense during the pilgrimage seasons because of the added influx of people of different orientations. Thus, in March 1926, barbers were 'instructed not to shave the faces of pilgrims or residents completely' and only the Wahhabi imam could lead the evening prayers.[232] Two months later, the conditions for the visit of the Egyptian *maḥmal* included a ban on accompanying music, public smoking, and circumambulating and worshipping tombs (cf. Chapter 5).[233] By summer, Philby reported that the number of male and female prostitutes had greatly receded and by autumn, the attendance of prayers had become more or less compulsory.[234]

In August 1928, the British consul compiled a comprehensive list of regulations which show in how much detail the new lords of the land intended to regulate, or rather modify, local practices. Everyone had to pray all prayers in the mosque and business transactions were halted during prayers. No man's religious beliefs or nation were to be cursed and abusive language was banned. All forms of amusement or sports, alcohol consumption, smoking and shaving, as well as, in the case of men, wearing of gold and silver ornaments and silk, were forbidden, as

229 For Mecca see Teitelbaum, *The Rise and Fall*, pp. 131–3.

230 Jarman (ed.),*The Jedda Diaries*, vol. 3, Jeddah Report, July 1928, p. 29.

231 This is discussed in great detail in Steinberg, *Religion und Staat in Saudi-Arabien*, pp. 511–79. For shorter overviews, see Ochsenwald, *Islam and Loyalty*; and Freitag, *State-Society Relations*, here pp. 39–41.

232 Jarman (ed.), *The Jedda Diaries*, vol. 2, Jeddah Report, March 1926, p. 381.

233 Ibid., May 1926, p. 387.

234 MECA, Philby Collection GB165–0229, 1/4/5/2, Philby Diary, part 2, November 12, 1926, p. 7 and November 16, 1926, p.14.

was appearance with insufficient clothing in public. Wailing for the dead, mixing of genders, fortune-telling, and divining were banned. Women were not allowed to visit tombs or leave the house in the evenings without a male escort. Sufi practices (*dhikr*, *mawlid*), almsgiving for the deceased (*isqāṭ*), the *zār* cult, and the *mizmār* were outlawed. Singing and swearing, dishonesty in business transactions and demanding interest became illegal, as well as sending welcome parties for caravans. Finally, the ill-treatment of animals was sanctioned.[235]

While religious re-education through the (increasingly exclusive) teaching and preaching of the Wahhabi doctrine, as well as through educational articles in the newspaper *Umm al-Qurā*, was bound to take some time to change behaviours, the main tool used to impose the measures was an Islamic institution which was also at the heart of the extension of local police, namely the *ḥisba*, which here was taken to mean 'commanding right and forbidding wrong' rather than 'market inspection'.[236] The institution founded to enforce this dictum was the *Hai'at al-amr bi-l-maʿrūf wa-l-nahy ʿan al-munkar*, often referred to as the religious police. As a collective duty, 'forbidding wrong' had existed in the Najd for some time, certainly at least since the second Saudi state. However, the *Hai'a* was founded for the Hijaz in the late summer of 1926 in an attempt to impose and police certain regulations, particularly during the pilgrimage but also, and more importantly, to reign in interventions by the Ikhwān and other self-proclaimed defenders of the faith.[237] Initially, under Hijazi command, the committees in the Hijaz were put under the supervision of the Najdi scholar ʿAbd al-Malik

235 Jarman (ed.), *The Jedda Diaries*, vol. 3, Enclosure 2 of Jeddah Report, August 1928, p. 34. The report mentions Nezmar (No. 14) which I think is a misreading of *mizmār*.

236 E.g. *Umm al-Qurā*, 14, March 13, 1925 (article about *bidʿa* and against the celebration of the Prophet's birthday and his *miʿrāj*); 16, March 27, 1925 (article against smoking); 330, October 10, 1931 (article against *al-tawassul bi-l-nabī*).

237 DARA, Wathāʾiq Waṭaniyya 2295, Letter by Raʾīs Dīwān al-Niyāba al-ʿĀmma, Ṣafar 16, 1346/August 15, 1927; cf. undated document no. 192; cf. Steinberg, *Religion und Staat in Saudi-Arabien*, pp. 411–4. For restrictions on other religious interpretations in Mecca see Jarman (ed.), *The Jedda Diaries*, vol. 3, Jeddah Report, July 1929, p. 78, for Medina pp. 82–3. For an account of the development of the concept in general see Michael Cook, *Commanding Right and Forbidding Wrong in Islamic Thought* (Cambridge: Cambridge University Press, 2000). For developments in the Najd, see Cook, pp. 165–91, and for the founding of the 'Committee', pp. 182–5.

b. Ibrāhīm al-Shaykh, possibly in order to alleviate any Najdi suspicions regarding Hijazi religious laxness.

The activities of the *Hai'a* were not always of equal intensity, which was partly a function of political needs. While, during the pilgrimage, rules were often more strictly enforced, this was less the case during the King's absence or during special occasions when visitors were expected. Thus, while not much happened in early September 1928, this lull was followed by an intense anti-smoking campaign in which sixty persons were arrested in one night, 'the commandant of police leaning on his balcony the while placidly smoking a cigarette', which did not pose a problem as smoking was no crime inside the police station.[238] In some parts of the Hijaz, such apparently arbitrary rules caused violent backlashes, such as in Ṭā'if where a judge refusing to condemn a smoker was killed, sparking riots.[239] In Jeddah, the *Hai'a* tried, at the beginning of Ramadan of 1934, to forcibly move people from coffee shops to the mosque. This resulted in a brawl during which two members of the *Hai'a* were beaten and about eighty civilians arrested.[240] Probably more frequent were private complaints about the restrictions.[241]

Yet again, during the celebrations of the accession of King ʿAbd al-ʿAzīz in 1930, restrictions were eased. For example, an official photographer from Egypt was invited, Egyptian journalists were brought in to witness the occasion, and even public smoking could be observed. This was, the British consul noted, in line with 'a desire to get away from the irksome restrictions which, in Jedda at any rate, have never been popular'.[242] This indicates that there was some truth to a repeatedly stated British assertion that Ibn Saʿūd was actually more liberal than the Wahhabi establishment.[243] However, he had to be careful not to alienate them. Thus, when he expressed interest in obtaining a camera, he felt he had to 'take expert advice from the 'Ulama as to whether

238 Jarman (ed.), *The Jedda Diaries*, vol. 3, Jeddah Report, September 1928, p. 36. This was in line with the official prohibition on smoking, Steinberg, *Religion und Staat in Saudi-Arabien*, pp. 419–20.

239 Jeddah Report, December 1928, p. 48.

240 IOR, LP/S/12/2073, Jeddah Report, December 1934, p. 3.

241 MECA, Philby Collection GB165–0229, 1/4/5/2, Philby Diary, part 2, November 21, 1926, p. 20.

242 Jarman (ed.), *The Jedda Diaries*, vol. 3, Jeddah Report, January 1930, p. 112.

243 E.g. IOR, L/PS/12/2073, Jeddah Report, January–February 1931, p. 4.

photos are Haram' and shrugged off Philby's attempt to dismiss such doubt off hand.[244]

Only two months later, religious police, allegedly brought in from the Najd, crashed any such expectations at relaxation, confiscating mouth organs (and apparently reselling them in the market) and penetrating the urban quarters to control smoking, the playing of music, and lax prayer attendance.[245] This occurred in the context of an expected visit of several Najdi tribal chiefs. By December of 1930, these strict rules had once again been eased and the governmental school even featured a school choir.[246] By 1938, there was actually an advertisement for radios (admitted in 1935, although when it was discovered that they could be used to play music, their use was restricted to news) and mouth organs (discreetly termed 'toys').[247]

From time to time, new regulations were announced – such as the ban on football discussed in Chapter 5, on gramophones in 1934, and on three–dimensional representations of living creatures – and old ones reiterated.[248] For example, in 1938, unmarried men were banned from living in the same houses as married couples.[249] In 1940, hefty fines were imposed on men defying the ban on shaving.[250] Judging by the density of articles criticising local customs and traditions, religious and moral anxiety seems to have reached a peak in the autumn of 1938 and in early 1939.[251] Most of the topics addressed formed part of the 1928 list of prohibitions. Besides religiously questionable practices, conspicuous consumption, for example in the

[244] MECA, Philby Collection, GB 165-0229, 1/4/5/1, Philby Diary part 1, March 3, 1926, p. 358.

[245] Jarman (ed.), *The Jedda Diaries*, vol. 3, Jeddah Report, March 1930, pp. 120–1; cf. Jeddah Report, May 1930, p. 131.

[246] Jarman (ed.), vol. 3, Jeddah Report, December 1930, p. 169.

[247] Ibid., February 1938, vol. 4, p. 256; and IOR, LP/S/12/2073, Jeddah Report, February 1935, p. 2, August 1935, p. 5.

[248] IOR, LP/S/12/2073, Jeddah Report, July 1934, p. 2; and Bullard, *Two Kings in Arabia*, letter of June 15, 1937, p. 161.

[249] Jarman (ed.), *The Jedda Diaries*, vol. 4, Jeddah Report, May 1938, p. 304.

[250] Ibid., April 1940, p. 526.

[251] *Umm al-Qurā*, 721, September 30, 1938; 722, October 8, 1938; 723, October 14, 1938; 726, November 4, 1938; 732, December 23, 1938; 733, December 30, 1938; 735, January 13, 1939; 736, January 20, 1939; 740, February 17, 1939; 741, February 24, 1939; 760, July 7, 1939; 761, July 14, 1939; and 762, July 12, 1939.

context of hospitality offered to visitors expressing their condolences, seems to have been an object of criticism.[252]

Overall, local society proved quite inventive in subverting activities of the *Hai'a*. Thus, Sufi recitations were held in backrooms or gramophones wrapped in towels to dampen their sound.[253] Popular dances like the *mizmār* or the female carnival *al-Qays*, discussed in Chapter 5, were practised in enclosed spaces or outside of town in order to avoid attention. However, this eventually deprived them of their social context and, by the end of the period under consideration, led to their gradual disappearance.[254] Many other practices and traditions, from Sufism and the celebration of the Prophet's birthday to social customs related to condolences, lingered on, although, once again, they no longer dominated social life in the same way as before. The disappearance of some of these customs must, however, also be contextualised within a dominant strand of modernisation, which converged with the discourse on religious reform.

A further issue of a more secular nature was the introduction of Saudi national dress.[255] It consisted of the Najdi attire of *ghuṭra* (headcloth) and *thawb* (long white garment) for men and was mandatory for all government employees. The Hijazi turban and male dress, still used by those not involved with the government, was thus relegated to second rank.[256] Indeed, the legality of wearing a turban incited a journalistic debate in the journal *Umm al-Qurā*.[257] A campaign advertising sartorial unity as a matter of moral harmony promoted standardisation in accordance with a hegemonic (Najdi) model.[258] This complemented the prohibition of silk in men's clothes and the shaving of the beards.

[252] *Umm al-Qurā*, 722, October 8, 1938.
[253] Interview, Sāmī Khumayyis, Jeddah, March 21, 2010.
[254] For the development of *al-Qays* in Saudi times; cf. Freitag, *Playing with Gender*, here pp. 75–6.
[255] Mai Yamani, 'Evading the Habits of a Life Time: The Adaptation of Hejazi Dress to the New Social Order' in N. Lindisfarne-Tapper (ed.), *Languages of Dress in the Middle East* (Richmond: Curzon Press, 1997), pp. 55–66.
[256] For a detailed description of traditional Hijazi dress with photographs of male dress and headgear, see Ṭrābulsī, *Jidda*, pp. 397–412.
[257] *Umm al-Qurā*, 401, August 19, 1932, with references to earlier contributions on the debate.
[258] *Ṣawṭ al-Ḥijāz*, 399, August 16, 1939; and Jarman (ed.), *The Jedda Diaries*, vol. 3, p. 169, Jeddah Report, December 1930. The exact dating is difficult to confirm, as neither al-Rasheed, *A History of Saudi Arabia*, p. 201, nor Steinberg, *Religion und Staat in Saudi-Arabien*, p. 550, provide exact dates.

Women were advised to wear loose external clothing rather than the specifically Hijazi dresses.[259] While the question of dress clearly had religious overtones, the attempt at standardisation was very much in line with similar moves to sartorially regulate elsewhere in the Middle East, which started during late Ottoman times. The major difference was that, while Atatürk banned the fez and attempted to prescribe bare faces and possibly heads for women, the Saudi government opted for a distinctly conservative and religiously connoted variant linked to one particular region, the Najd. Interestingly, when similar dress codes were introduced in the Arab Gulf emirates in the 1970s and 80s, this was done to distinguish the relatively few locals from the majority of foreign workers, as well as from the westerners with their strong cultural influence.[260] While serving as a tool to foster national cohesion in both cases, the distinction of locals from foreigners was not the prime Saudi motive in the 1930s. Rather, the idea was to mould different regional sartorial styles into one common (Saudi) nation along the Najdi model.

Irrespective of the strong religious policies and their influence on social life, both the Saudi archives and the newspapers reflect an endeavour to modernise the country administratively and to develop its infrastructure and economy. Obviously, the means were very limited until after World War II, in spite of the search for minerals and water, and foreign observers were sceptical of the ability of Ibn Saʿūd's advisors.[261] Thus, measures such as the unification of school uniforms at the very few government schools in Mecca, Medina, and Jeddah, announced in March 1938, probably mostly had a symbolic character and are indicative of the increasing desire to regulate as many aspects of life as possible.[262] However, projects such as hospitals, water provision, the attempt to found a national shipping company, to construct lighthouses, improve harbour facilities, or set up a school to train pilots and set up an airline, all recorded in *Umm al-Qurā* and *Ṣawṭ al-Ḥijāz*, the two major local newspapers of the 1930s and 1940s, testify to the strong desire to modernise the country in a way which foreshadowed post World War II developments.

259 Ochsenwald, *Islam and Loyalty*, pp. 29–30.
260 Onley, *Transnational Merchant Families*, here p. 78.
261 E.g. Jarman (ed.), *The Jedda Diaries*, vol. 2, Jeddah Report, July 1927, p. 466.
262 *Ṣawṭ al-Ḥijāz*, March 29, 1938.

8 The Disappearance and Return of Old Jeddah: On the Temporality of Translocal Relations

The slogan of 'Jeddah ghayr' – Jeddah is different – is nowadays celebrated in the context of the slogan 'Historic Jeddah, the Gate to Makkah', which made its way onto the World Heritage List in 2014. In the short description of the property, the city is described as a 'thriving multicultural centre' with a 'cosmopolitan population' consisting of 'Muslims from Asia, Africa and the Middle East'.[1] Touristic events make a point of highlighting a rich cultural heritage, comprising buildings, dress, and food. Besides the summer festival mentioned in the introduction, a winter fair with the fancy title 'How we were' (*Kunnā kidā*) was held between 2014 and 2017 in the small part of historic Jeddah which is being lovingly restored.[2] Tourists who visit such festivals or stroll along the beautiful Jeddah corniche and compare it to the dusty streets of the cities of the Saudi interior usually join the choir of appreciative voices.

The Transformation of Jiddawi Society since 1947

Images of supposed historical continuity do more to veil history than to illuminate it. This book has traced changes over a period of 100 years from the 1840s to just after World War II. During this period, the Ottoman Empire, which had re-established direct rule in Jeddah in 1840, transformed itself and then disappeared in the 'Arab Revolt'. In its stead, the abortive Arab Kingdom under Sharif Ḥusayn b. ʿAlī and his son ʿAlī was established. In December 1925 this, in turn, succumbed to the siege of the Sultan of the Najd, ʿAbd al-ʿAzīz b. ʿAbd

[1] UNESCO. 'Historic Jeddah, the Gate to Makkah'. *unesco.org*. whc.unesco.org/en/list/1361/ (accessed July 20, 2018).

[2] Images of the Kunnā kidā festivals are widely spread on the internet, e.g. Somaya Hussein (June 01, 2016). 'Mahrajān Jidda al-tārīkhiyya (Kunna Kidā) fī nuskhatihi al-thālitha li-ʿām 2016m'. Article on *almrsal.com*. www.almrsal.com/post/301239 (accessed July 20, 2018).

al-Raḥmān b. Saʿūd and led to the eventual establishment of the Kingdom of Saudi Arabia in 1932. The discovery of oil in commercial quantities in 1938, the large-scale extraction of which started after World War II when the story told in this book ends, has since transformed Saudi Arabia considerably.

Chapter 4 has shown the incremental changes in the urban space of Jeddah since the 1840s, notably the significant extension of the urban surface by creating land on the seaside, the increasing density of residential and commercial buildings and attempts to provide piped water and street lighting. This was accompanied by the development of an increasingly differentiated urban administration, as shown in Chapter 7, ranging from the formalisation of the quarter structure to a municipality supervised by an elected council. A newly created police-force controlled harbour and urban space, while sanitary services were developed mostly, but not exclusively, for the sake of the pilgrims. While urbanites considered residence outside of the city walls dangerous until 1926, some suburbs on the foothills of the mountain range to the east had become summer residences during late Ottoman times. After Ibn Saʿūd secured the countryside in 1926 and built a palace on the outskirts of al-Nuzla al-Yamaniyya, al-Kandara, and the area north of the old city, al-Baghdādiyya, began to slowly develop.

Since 1947, rapid urban development has transformed the small city, which then numbered some 50,000 inhabitants, into a multi-million metropolis. The new apartment buildings and villas built outside of the historic centre offered more modern amenities than the houses in *al-Balad*, the old city. The more affluent families left first, eventually followed by poorer ones. They were replaced by even poorer migrants from other parts of the Kingdom, often from the southern province of ʿAsīr, or Yemen. These groups left the old city by the early 1980s.[3] New migrants arrived, often without proper papers, from Somalia, Eritrea, and the Sudan, as well as from Yemen and Bangladesh, and moved into often crowded buildings. They often had only the most basic infrastructure with regard to water or electricity but were rented out at a high price. In spite of first attempts at conserving and slowly modernising the urban fabric of *al-Balad* in the1970s, the old city

[3] Tariq Sijeeni, 'Contemporary Arabian City: Muslim *Ummah* in Sociocultural and Urban Design Context', PhD Thesis, University of Michigan (1995), p. 81; and Bokhari, Jeddah, p. 278.

deteriorated due to lack of maintenance, lack of proper sewage, and destruction through rain and fire.[4]

Many couples set up matrimonial households and moved out of the patrilocal family residences. New building materials and styles barred, rather than encouraged, social interaction in the new quarters. Rather than living within a walled city, many people now resided in villas or, in the case of some of the old families who wanted to maintain their close interaction while gaining more space, in compounds surrounded by high walls. Large numbers of immigrants from other parts of the Kingdom, as well as labour migrants and technical experts from many parts of the world, arrived in Jeddah from the 1960s. They often, but not always, lived in secluded compounds and camps. All of these developments changed the ways in which residents of Jeddah, old and new, encountered and interacted with each other.

To this needs to be added that the nature of the pilgrimage, discussed in Chapters 6 and 7, has changed considerably. While the transport revolution of the nineteenth century had replaced sail by steam, from the 1930s onwards, and particularly after the 1950s, maritime transport was overwhelmingly replaced by air travel in combination with motorised transport to Mecca and Medina. Beginning in the 1950s, pilgrims, who now travelled in increasingly large national groups, were accommodated in the newly constructed pilgrims' cities. Increasing numbers, as well as the relative wealth of the pilgrims, prompted many to look for accommodation in the hotels that sprang up in and outside of the old city. Meanwhile, the pilgrims' cities became a temporary residence of poorer pilgrims. Pilgrims still stayed in private homes but, increasingly, this practice has become reserved for relatives or friends of Jeddah residents. The changing nature of the pilgrimage, widely reflected in the literature, not only affected practices by pilgrims and the interaction between them, but also significantly decreased contact between local residents and pilgrims.[5] In 1981 a large new Hajj Terminal opened at King Abdulaziz Airport in Jeddah. Since then, pilgrims are transported directly from the airport to Mecca by bus or taxi. A new high-speed rail link, which was inaugurated in September

4 Bagader, *The Evolution of Built Heritage Conservation Policies*, describes the development of the urban fabric and conservation attempts in much detail.

5 An interesting reflection on the modern hajj is, for example, Abdellah Hammoudi, *A Season in Mecca: Narrative of a Pilgrimage*, 1st American edn. (New York: Hill and Wang, 2006).

2018, reduces travel times between Jeddah and Mecca to less than half an hour. The notion of Jeddah as an entrance hall, *dihliz*, to Mecca has therefore become, at best, a symbol, with the Hajj Terminal serving as its architectural manifestation. The extension of the validity of visas issued for *'umra* allowing for travel within the Kingdom is meant to attract pilgrims for a holiday in Jeddah and other parts of the Kingdom of Saudi Arabia in the context of the new economic vision discussed in Chapter 1. Such touristic stays would, however, be quite different from the earlier accommodation of pilgrims.[6]

Schooling, first for boys and later for girls, became widespread from the 1950s onwards as the Kingdom obtained the means to invest in its educational infrastructure. Since religion occupied an important part in the curriculum it is not surprising that practices and beliefs considered to be objectionable by Wahhabi Islam were condemned in the textbooks and schools.[7] With economic development, diverse trajectories of training and further education emerged, including universities.

As a consequence of the emergence of the oil economy, the occupational landscape of Jeddah changed dramatically beyond the rather exclusive concerns of the Hijazi elite of *ashrāf*, businessmen, scholars, and pilgrims' guides whose disappearance or rather weakening was mourned by Yamani.[8] Merchants, discussed in Chapter 6, became entrepreneurs, mechanics were needed instead of camel-drivers and imported goods started to push aside local products. The development of the oil and later the chemical industry, the large building sector and the introduction of modern technologies all contributed to a great diversification of professional trajectories and consequently to a weakening of the guilds, in which the traditional trades and crafts were represented. They were never replaced by trade unions. In addition, the proliferation of new professions, with workplaces often situated in tower blocks rather than in the market or entrance halls of private homes, considerably changed the rhythm of life.

All of these factors further complicated social interactions within the apartment blocks, streets, and the new quarters, which often became mere administrative units rather than spaces of active social

[6] Bianchi, *Guests of God*, p. 11.

[7] Michaela Prokop, 'Saudi Arabia: The Politics of Education', *International Affairs*, 79 (2003), pp. 77–89, here pp. 77–82.

[8] Yamani, *Cradle of Islam*, pp. 39–40.

interaction.[9] This was exacerbated by a decidedly conservative turn in the late 1970s which, if anything, further strengthened tendencies of social exclusion and separation (including that of the sexes). In an interesting initiative, there have been recent attempts to foster renewed neighbourhood cohesion through social and cultural activities in the new quarters of Jeddah, where residents, who move in and out of their high-walled villas in cars with tinted windows, normally would not meet each other.[10] In contrast, it seems that in *al-Balad* and the 'informal areas' immediately surrounding it, i.e. the old villages, the system of mutual neighbourhood support still exists.[11]

Many of the processes discussed above would commonly be summed up under the heading of 'modernisation'. Together they led to the disappearance of many of the religious and social institutions discussed in Chapter 5. Some, like Sufism, survived and adapted to the changing circumstances. Others were practised privately until were once again tolerated, such as larger meetings to remember the Birthday of the Prophet.[12]

The process of bureaucratisation, which evolved slowly during the nineteenth and early twentieth century, has accelerated. Urban and district administration, as well as diverse national ministries, are involved in most planning processes while, in Ottoman times, only health and military matters required imperial intervention. The state has grown more powerful, so much so that, for a period lasting from the 1960s to 2005, even the limited elective element in the municipal councils was almost generally dismissed.[13] In general, one may argue that, with the expansion of state activity, as well as the coercive mechanisms and increasing state wealth, the formal consultative mechanisms of the Ottoman era have all but disappeared. Until recently it appeared that the more or less 'voluntary' contributions of rich merchants to urban development had been made superfluous by the

[9] These processes are well analysed in Maneval, *The Architecture of Everyday Life*.

[10] Oral information from a female resident of al-Muḥammadiyya, a quarter in the north of Jeddah which was built in the 1990s, Jeddah, March 2016, March 2017, December 2017.

[11] Difalla, *Jeddah's Slum Areas*, pp. 62–3.

[12] Yamani, *Cradle of Islam*, pp. 111–5.

[13] On this issue, as well as the organisation of local administration; cf. Jannis Hagmann, 'Die Flutkatastrophe von Jidda 2009: Eine Fallstudie anhand von Presse, Petitionen & Facebook', MA Thesis, Freie Universität Berlin (2011), pp. 35–8.

revenues derived from oil exports.[14] This does not mean that merchants and entrepreneurs no longer have avenues for making their wishes heard – even beyond the Chambers of Commerce and Industry which arguably replaced the Merchant Councils to some extent, though they do have somewhat different functions – but they are perhaps less formally embedded.

The legal ambiguity of who was a Jiddawi or a Hijazi, encountered in the mid-nineteenth century, has all but disappeared. In Chapter 7 the slow evolution of the Ottoman legislation on nationality and the related question of the permissibility to settle and own land in the Hijaz was discussed against the backdrop of different imperial powers attempting to control those subjects who were visiting or sojourning in Ottoman lands. During early Saudi times, Saudi nationality was extended to all Ottoman subjects who did not object in a bid to consolidate the population of the Hijaz. In 1955 a law on Saudi nationality was passed, which has since been modified a number of times. While the residents from Ottoman times continued to be technically entitled to Saudi nationality and (Muslim) residents can apply for nationalisation after ten years of residence, such requests are only rarely granted and the nationality law seems to be applied somewhat haphazardly.[15] The largescale integration of people who had settled in the Hijaz, initiated by the Ottoman nationality law, was confirmed, but only until 1926, i.e. when Saudi rule was established. Later arrivals were excluded, which means that, effectively, the permanent settlement and eventual naturalisation of people was ended. A number of Arabs of tribal origin, but also large numbers of Palestinians and Rohingya Muslims fleeing Burma in the 1960s, have thus become permanent

[14] The arrest of, and extraction of funds from a large number of leading businessmen and members of the royal family in the autumn of 2017 shows interesting structural similarities to the earlier extraction of contributions, even if it was dressed in the garb of the fight against corruption. This war reported widely, cf. Kevin Sullivan and Kareem Fahim (November 05, 2018). 'A year after the Ritz-Carton roundup, Saudi elites remain jailed by the crown prince'. Article on *washington.post.com*. www.washingtonpost.com/world/a-year-after-the-ritz-carlton-roundup-saudi-elites-remain-jailed-by-the-crown-prince/2018/11/05/32077a5c-e066-11e8-b759-3d88a5ce9e19_story.html?utm_term=.50ef345e440f.

[15] For the law and subsequent modifications and related statutory instruments, see Kingdom of Saudi Arabia Ministry of Interior Ministerial Agency of Civil Affairs. 'Saudi Arabian Citizenship System', www.refworld.org/pdfid/3fb9eb6d2.pdf (accessed October 7, 2019).

residents of the Kingdom without nationality and often insecure residency status.[16] Another large group are illegal immigrants, who have often been resident in the country for decades. After the pilgrimage season, large number of illegal migrants are regularly deported, though nowadays this is done less because they are begging in the streets and more because they have tried to circumvent immigration restrictions and find jobs in the Kingdom.[17]

These phenomena notwithstanding, labour migration to the Kingdom has soared until recently, in spite of recurrent attempts at limiting the numbers of foreign workers, and at making sure that they are only employed where no suitable national employees or workers could be found.[18] One particularly large area of employment is domestic work, the conditions of which have been occasionally likened to 'contract enslavement', although more recently, the Saudi government is attempting to enforce stricter adherence to domestic workers rights.[19] Although some of the abuses to which slaves were subjected, including sexual labour, are still on occasion inflicted on domestic servants, there are also a number of significant differences: Domestic labourers today usually enter their contracts voluntarily. No matter how long these contracts last for women who work in particular households, they are bound to end eventually, resulting in

[16] Aya Batrawy (September 21, 2017). 'Rohingya crisis: Saudi Arabia stays silent on growing humanitarian disaster despite oil interests and historic ties'. Article on *Independent.co.uk*. www.independent.co.uk/news/world/middle-east/rohingya-crisis-latest-saudi-arabia-burma-muslim-refugees-persecution-rakhine-oil-bangladesh-china-a7958716.html; and Institute on Statelessness and Inclusion, the Global Campaign for Equal Nationality Rights and the European Saudi Organization for Human Rights (March 29, 2018). 'Joint Submission to the Human Rights Council at the 31st Session of the Universal Periodic Review. Saudi Arabia', www.institutesi.org/UPR31_SaudiArabia.pdf.

[17] E.g. *arabnews.com* (November 14, 2017). 'Saudi Arabia to launch anti-illegal residency campaign Nov. 15'. www.arabnews.com/node/1193356/saudi-arabia; and BBC News (December 10, 2007). 'Indonesians deported from Mecca'. Article on *bbc.co.uk*, http://news.bbc.co.uk/2/hi/middle_east/7137096.stm.

[18] On the development of labour migration and its legal framework; cf. Gennaro Errichiello, 'Foreign Workforce in the Arab Gulf States (1930–1950): Migration Patterns and Nationality Clause', *The International Migration Review*, 46 (2012), pp. 389–413; Onn Winckler, 'The Immigration Policy of the Gulf Cooperation Council (GCC) States', *Middle Eastern Studies*, 33 (1997), pp. 480–93.

[19] Romina Halabi, 'Contract Enslavement of Female Migrant Domestic Workers in Saudi Arabia and the United Arab Emirates', *Research Digest: Human Rights and Contemporary Slavery* (2008), pp. 43–58.

the departure of the women. However, until the abolition of slavery, pregnancy and childbirth by female slaves could lead to the full-scale integration of these women as (usually inferior) de facto wives and of their offspring as legitimate children, domestic servants who find themselves in similar circumstances nowadays face imprisonment, deportation, and worse.[20] All contract labourers are barred from remaining permanently in the Kingdom. This means that, nowadays, careers similar to those explored in Chapter 3, such as those of Zaynal ʿAlī Riḍā or Sālim Bin Maḥfūẓ, are no longer realistic prospects even for those migrants who manage to obtain legal or illegal employment in the Kingdom.

Even without a detailed exploration it is clear that the Saudi Arabian nationality and residency legislation has restricted further the permeability of borders and particularly the choice of residence, which had been wide open in Ottoman times. In contrast to Ottoman times, real estate property in the Hijaz could now be acquired by foreigners, with the continued exception of Mecca and Medina (unless it was inherited). Contrary to late Ottoman times, foreigners could also endow land for charitable purposes, although only if the *waqf* was placed under the administration of the Higher Saudi Council of Endowments.[21]

The development of the legal conditions of being or becoming Hijazi, or even of residing in the Hijaz and Jeddah, has been discussed at some length in Chapter 7 to illustrate the degree to which changing political frameworks shape the possibilities, developments, and later explanations of translocal connections. They thus illustrate how, in an age of nation-states, the notion of belonging has become circumscribed in comparison to identity in the more fluid – albeit itself dynamic – earlier imperial period. This stands in contrast to the ideology of the unity of the Muslim *umma* ('nation'), which holds its annual meeting (the hajj) in the Mecca, the 'mother of (all) villages' under the explicit

[20] Human Rights Watch, 'As if I'm not Human: Abuses against Asian Domestic Workers in Saudi Arabia', 2008, pp. 91–3.

[21] Al-Mamlaka al-ʿArabiyya al-Saʿūdiyya, *Niẓām Tamalluk ghayr al-Saʿūdiyyīn li-l-ʿAqār wa-Istithmārihi*, Rabīʿ al-Thānī 17, 1421/July 20, 2000, Art. 5. This replaced an earlier law of September 1970 which I have been unable to trace. Most laws and their modifications (but not the one of 1970) can be found at the National Center for Document and Archives website, www.ncar.gov.sa/Home/Index (accessed July 25, 2018).

protection of the 'Guardian of the Two Holy Mosques', i.e. the Saudi King. It was in reaction to globalisation – both in the imperial variant of the nineteenth and the transnational one of the twentieth century – that not only regional (Arab) and national (Saudi), but also regional (Hijazi) and local (Jiddawi, Meccan, Medinese) identities returned to the fore. This is quite typical of translocal contexts more generally, where processes of widening spatial horizons often go hand in hand with the establishment of new frontiers, the introduction of new distinctions and limitations.[22]

In the case at hand, one might argue that the Muslim *umma*, historically divided between empires even at times when people were reasonably free to move and settle in other regions under Muslim rule, came under increased scrutiny and restrictive regulations in the imperial age, as witnessed by the different hajj regimes discussed in Chapters 6 and 7. The current arrangement of nation-states turns the different parts of the Muslim *umma* first and foremost into national subjects. Nowhere is this more evident than in Mecca and Medina, with their restrictions on land ownership and the limited length of lease agreements, but it does, of course, also affect the possible relations between different Muslims in Mecca's *dihlīz*, Jeddah. While contacts between locals and foreigners were never devoid of hierarchies, new regulations by nation states cement these in hitherto unknown ways.

These changes also illustrate another crucial dimension of translocality, namely its temporal aspect. This has been demonstrated on occasion, but the fairly long history of a city like Jeddah, intensely enmeshed in networks of commercial and spiritual exchange, brings this out in a particularly poignant way.[23] To what extent, one could ask provocatively, does the past which is nowadays remembered and enacted nostalgically still contain the cosmopolitan aspects which the hosting of the 'Guests of God' also implied, as this book has demonstrated? Are some of the old convivial practices still in place, or have new ones developed?

22 Freitag and Oppen, *Introduction: 'Translocality'*, here pp. 4, 8.

23 This perspective underlies, for example the contribution by Margrit Pernau, 'Shifting Globalities – Changing Headgear: The Indian Muslims Between Turban, Hat and Fez' in U. Freitag and A. v. Oppen (eds.), *Translocality: The Study of Globalising Processes from a Southern Perspective*, Studies in Global Social History (Leiden and Boston: Brill, 2010), 249–67.

Nostalgia for Which Past?

In an interview-based study on youth identities published in 2000, Yamani points out that regional and tribal affiliations still play a major role in the identities of Saudi youth in spite of an overarching Saudi-Muslim identity.[24] Altorki and Yamani, writing more or less about the same group of *ʿawāʾil,* Hijazi elite families resident in Jeddah, both note the continuity of social interaction among the members of the group. Yamani's study, published almost twenty years after Altorki, helps to historicise Altorki's finding by noting how the 1980s and 1990s marked a turning point. Until then, Hijazis had a stake in Saudi nation-building. The recession of the mid-1980s, together with a reaction against globalisation and an increased focus on (overall) Saudi identity in the 1990s increased the tendency to reassert a more regional identity founded in what was understood to have been a common past.[25]

Authors like Altorki and Yamani thus attest, from somewhat different angles and points in time but in a similar vein, the resilience of a notion of Jiddawi or, more generally, Hijazi identity among elite families. This found its expression, according to Altorki's account of the mid-1980s, in such practices as visiting and intermarriage, while Yamani includes a wide range of practices related to the life-cycle, as well as to religious occasions.[26] Many of these local customs form a core theme in the local histories and memoirs used for this book, notably in Chapter 5.[27] A distinct sense of local identity informed many of the Jiddawis who helped with the research for this book between 2006 and 2017 by providing materials, pointing out relevant literature or sharing stories from their own families' histories. A pictorial record of local identity is preserved by Ṣafiyya b. Zaqr, one of the pioneering female painters of Jeddah,[28] while historical images of the city and its people, primarily from the late nineteenth

[24] Yamani, *Changed Identities*, pp. 8–9, 22–5.

[25] Yamani, *Cradle of Islam*, pp. 18–19.

[26] Altorki, *Women in Saudi Arabia*; and Yamani, *Cradle of Islam*.

[27] Jörg Determann, *Historiography in Saudi Arabia: Globalization and the State in the Middle East*, Library of Middle East History (London: Tauris, 2014), vol. 42, pp. 65–76, on local Hijazi historiography notes a similar trend. On cities as a site for memory and nostalgia; cf. Anita Bakshi, *Topographies of Memories: A New Poetics of Commemoration* (Basingstoke: Palgrave Macmillan, 2017).

[28] For more information on Safiyya Bin Zaqr and her gallery see http://daratsb.com/ar/ (accessed July 23, 2018).

and the first half of the twentieth century, are circulated via social media messenger services. A recent encyclopaedia of Jeddah, aiming to 'tell about the history of the city, its society and deep-rooted civilization', is dedicated to 'the businessmen, writers, poets and men of letter who devoted their lives to giving and dedicated their successful path to the service of their country', contributing 'towards the building of the nation and its man'.[29] This is an explicit case of what Determann has called 'local contribution histories'.[30] While clearly written in the context of the World Heritage nomination, as evidenced, for example, by the subtitle 'Gate to the Two Holy Mosques', the work consists to about one third of the biographies of prominent merchants and businessmen and of people involved in media and the arts, in each case including a few women.

The nostalgia for old Jeddah (and the old Hijaz) glosses over a number of significant changes in local society. One significant example is marriage practices. Altorki observed in the 1980s that the old elite families she worked with preferred endogamy.[31] This tendency was possibly furthered by the fact that Najdi men have been and still are quite willing to marry Hijazi women, but rarely allow their daughters to marry Hijazi men due to their concern with the genealogy of the offspring, which is commonly only considered via the male line.[32] Obviously, an ideological reaction to such Najdi attitudes does not need to reflect general practice. Even in Ottoman and Sharifian times, first cousin marriages might have been preferable to that of local women to foreigners. However, the rather categorical position on this topic encountered a number of times in conversations with both Najdis and Hijazis seems to reflect a closure of Jiddawi society which stands in obvious contrast to the open image celebrated for the past, as well as to past practices.[33] Yamani considers this tendency to be a socially driven 'tribalisation' in two ways, first because it reflects and reacts to norms from the tribally dominated Najd region, and secondly because it constitutes a departure from earlier marriage practices. She also

[29] ʿĀyiḍ al-Turkī, *Mawsūʿat Jidda: Bawābat al-Ḥaramayn al-Sharīfayn* (Jeddah, 2012), Introduction, Dedication (no page numbers).

[30] Determann, *Historiography in Saudi Arabia*, p. 140.

[31] Altorki, *Women in Saudi Arabia*, p. 124.

[32] Cf. Chapter 1, Sawaf, *Encountering the State*, pp. 53–7 and pp. 172–94 for current attempts to develop an alternative vision of genealogy.

[33] This point was made repeatedly in interviews in Jeddah, March 2015 and 2017.

laments the 'nationalisation' of marriage, namely the legal prescription for women to marry Saudi nationals, thus all but ending the process by which foreign men could integrate into local society with relative ease through marriage.[34]

A clear distinction between Hijazis and Najdis was also made in many defiant comments on the state of the old city of Jeddah before its acceptance as a World Heritage site. Why, interlocutors asked repeatedly, was so much government money poured into the restoration of the old Saudi capital al-Dirʿiyya, consisting of mere mud-brick buildings, while old Jeddah, with its beautiful coral stone houses and intricately carved wooden *rawāshīn*, was left to rot and burn down? In 2010 al-Ṭurayf, the palace district of al-Dirʿiyya, was registered as the 'first capital of the Saudi Dynasty' from where 'the spread of the Wahhabi reform inside the Muslim religion' began.[35] Apart from the problematic comparison of the relative worth of different types of buildings, such views clearly reflect a sense of neglect and relative political marginalisation, irrespective of whether or not such a perspective reflects the political reality. Similarly, such a discourse glosses over local factors in the decay of the old city in which, after all, the majority of the buildings are privately owned.[36] Instead, this type of discourse stresses the unilateral responsibility of a Saudi government, seen at best as negligent and often suspected of deliberately destroying the architectural heritage of a culturally superior region of the Kingdom (Hijaz) in order to cement the rule of a dynasty from Najd.

While the Jiddawis who put forward such positions proudly assert their distinct identity, another trend is noticeable which points to a certain adaptation to the culturally hegemonic discourse of Arabness and tribalism. The 'ironic reversal of the transnationalism of the past' through Arabisation, noted by Onley for the Gulf, can be found in Jeddah not only in the endogamous marriage practices mentioned

[34] Yamani, *Cradle of Islam*, pp. 77–8, 81–4.

[35] UNESCO, *At-Turaif District in ad-Dir'iyah*, whc.unesco.org/en/list/1329 (accessed July 24, 2018). The comments were made in many formal and informal conversations about the state of the old city of Jeddah during research trips in 2009–13.

[36] Issues such as unclear ownership, large numbers of heirs who cannot agree on what to do with the property, questions of investment opportunities, and more recently restrictions imposed for reasons of conservation are often at the core of decay, together with fire and collapse due to water damage.

above, but also in the Arabisation of lineages.[37] Thus, the overwhelming majority of families with origins in the wider Arab and Muslim world nowadays claim that their families were among those who, once upon a time, migrated from the Hijaz to other Arab and Muslim regions. Given that the early Muslim conquests, as well as trade connections, were invariably linked to the Hijaz, this possibility of such a migratory trajectory does, of course, exist in every single case. Even if one of the forefathers of a particular family migrated a few hundred years ago, however, a reduction of the lineage to this individual (at the expense of other male forbearers hailing from other regions, and of all female ancestors) is a very selective account of genealogy. Furthermore, it is the recurrent existence of these genealogical claims which suggests that many families are keen on stressing their own Arabness to comply with the dominant ideology while, in a more abstract sense, they emphasise the multicultural heritage of 'Jeddah ghayr'. The 'marginalised cosmopolitan elite' does, then, display a distinctly regionalist outlook both in the narrative of its own history and in its social practices.[38]

Much more in line with the past is the agreement of urban authorities and planners and the old elite on the exclusive historical value of *al-Balad*. This means that the old suburbs are nowadays classified as *ʿashwāʾiyyāt* (informal settlements, also translated as 'slums') that should be gentrified. This coincides with the old idea that the inhabitants of these suburbs are potentially unruly and uncivilised Bedouin. That this does not match the way long-term residents of these suburbs see themselves is manifested in the history of *al-Nuzla al-Yamaniyya* which was discussed in Chapter 4, but also in an MA thesis by a young urban planner. He discussed how a suburb which had developed more or less organically 'perhaps before regulations' came to be regarded as an (irregular) slum.[39] Interestingly, when news of the intended gentrification spread, it actually united the inhabitants of *al-Nuzla* in their resistance to plans which saw no room for them in the projected quarter. In a rare show of strength, they actually defied a royal decree for their eviction.[40]

37 Onley, *Transnational Merchant Families*, here p. 79.

38 Yamani, *Cradle of Islam*, p. 21.

39 Difalla, *Jeddah's Slum Areas*, pp. 11–22, 34–46, 60, also a review of recent critical literature on 'slums' and 'informal areas'.

40 Ibid., pp. 41–6.

A quite different story is that of an art project. It provided female residents of the quarter of al-Ruways with cameras and photographic training and asked them to take pictures of their quarter. This project, published as an exhibition and a book, was interpreted by the quarter's *'umda* as support 'for the longevity and survival of our beloved district'.[41] In view of the intended demolition and rebuilding of this quarter, one sees, once again, the emergence of an interest in the quarter's history, people and lifestyle.

In both cases, the former suburbs and current 'informal settlements' are firmly depicted as forming an integral part of the city of Jeddah. Furthermore, the project on Ruways not only brought together students at a private female college and women from Ruways, some of them illegal immigrants, but also obtained the support of a very respected historian and member of an old Jeddah family, Dr. ʿAdnān al-Yāfī. This shows that, while the overwhelming nostalgia concentrates on *al-Balad*, questions of urban development can mobilise across the divide of the former city wall. More importantly in terms of societal development, they also transcend the usual divides of Saudi and foreigner, or Jiddawi/Hijazi and 'immigrant from other parts of the Kingdom' in a new way. This is all the more significant because the 'foreigners' are of the usually undesired type: They come from Nigeria, Somalia, Yemen, from Bangladesh, India, or Pakistan and are, like the Saudis with whom they share these quarters, members of a relatively poor segment of the urban society.

'Jeddah Ghayr' beyond Infotainment

Clearly, many of the official celebrations of Jeddah's multicultural heritage aim at attracting and entertaining fleeting visitors. However, the overall attention given to, and the controversies about, the old city of Jeddah have sparked a renewed interest in the urban heritage among the local population, both in terms of its architecture and its former inhabitants, their histories and customs. While in Mecca and Medina, only the holy sites, with their global appeal to Muslim identity, have survived the hype of ultramodern development, the old city of Jeddah has all the more become an emblem of a distinct Hijazi way of life.

41 *The Story of Ten – Ḥikāyat 10* (Jeddah, 2013), Talal al-Jahdali, 'A Word from the Mayor of Ruwais Dst.', p. 29.

Jeddah is advertised and remembered as a multicultural city, even if the elite of former inhabitants strives to Arabise their own heritage in line with the overall dominant genealogical. Thus, the changing power relationships since the mid-nineteenth century, which tended to enhance the distinction between Jiddawi and foreigner, and the more distinctly Arab discourse since 1926, have left their mark on the social construction of individual identities, although the overall historical imagery still emphasises an earlier openness.[42]

The historical memory, both by high government officials and local elites, usually glosses over social distinctions which used to exist between the wealthy merchants and their slaves, or between pilgrims' guides and porters. Thus, the literature on common customs and traditions, dress, and religious practices does not distinguish between the different social strata of Jeddah, but rather assumes the rituals and ceremonies by the elite 'representatives of Hijazi urban culture and traditions . . . filter down to the rest of Hijazi society'.[43]

For a number of decades many of the *ʿawʾāil*, the (elite) 'Jeddah families' would have stressed their openness towards other upper (and upper middle) class cosmopolites. Even if there was a preference for social intercourse with Muslims, they also developed strong ties with the West, notably the United States where, nowadays, many spend time studying.[44] On average, they had little interest in, or sympathies for, poor immigrants, especially for those from foreign countries and even more so if these did not have a regular legal status. This did not preclude that extensive charity networks still linked these socially very distinct groups, although governmental attempts at channelling and limiting the dispensation of charity to Saudis at the exclusion of foreigners (except for orphans or children of Saudi mothers) through institutional controls further reinforced the lines separating nationals from foreigners.[45]

42 On the social construction of collective identities in an urban context and the importance of place as a source of memory see William Neill, *Urban Planning and Cultural Identity* (Abingdon: Routledge, 2004), pp. 10–17.

43 Yamani, *Cradle of Islam*, p. 21.

44 Ibid., p. 18, who also notes a certain ambivalence towards the West. With respect to the orientation towards the United States, there is a clear analogy to the cultural orientation of the Gulf emirates discussed by Onley.

45 On the charities see Nora Derbal, 'Charity for the Poor in Jeddah, Saudi Arabia, 1961–2015', PhD Thesis, Freie Universität Berlin (2017), pp. 148–52.

However, this rather elitist perspective has started to change since the catastrophic floods in Jeddah in 2009 which killed several hundred people and damaged the poorer southern and eastern suburbs.[46] The severity of the events, which also highlighted years of bad urban planning and corruption, kickstarted a hitherto unprecedented campaign, which was led by youth activists. Their immediate aim was to assist the victims of the flood and to inform the public about what had happened. This activism, which was at best semi-legal, was a new form of mass solidarity by mostly middle-class urban youth with inhabitants of the poorer quarters. At the same time, it sparked a widespread critical debate and fostered at least temporary interest in issues related to urban planning.

While the groups which initiated the resistance of residents of *al-Nuzla* against their eviction from their quarter were mostly local residents, and thus from a background which differed considerably from that of the youth activists mobilised in the context of the floods, they also voiced their interpretation of the 'right to the city'. The Dār al-Ḥikma initiative, which paired middle class university students with women from the poor quarter of al-Ruways, aimed to give them a photographic voice, is yet a third example of an initiative which at once reclaimed a voice in urban affairs and, at the same time, coupled this with a decidedly local and inclusive approach.

With regard to Los Angeles, architect and urban historian Hayden has argued that the 'awareness that every citizen's history is important . . . . Seeing each and every urban neighbourhood as part of the vernacular landscape of the city, past and present, creates a stronger sense of public memory in a multicultural city.'[47] Eventually, she argues, this creates an important sense of civic engagement and action. In the context of Jeddah in the twenty-first century, with stricter limits on political public culture than in the United States, the initiatives mentioned above contributed to the creation of a new, and different, civic spirit and identity. Joint activities, the common struggle to defend one's home and engagement with the population of quarters hit by the floods encouraged interaction and the recognition that people of different social universes inhabited the same city. In particular, the

[46] This topic has been analysed in detail by Hagmann, *Die Flutkatastrophe von Jidda*, for the events, see pp. 39–51.

[47] Dolores Hayden, 'The Power of Place: Claiming Urban Landscapes as People's History', *Journal of Urban History*, 20 (1994), pp. 466–85, here p. 483.

photographic project in *al-Ruways* and the activities in *al-Nuzla* demonstrated that, for all the socio-economic problems of these quarters, they had also preserved a spirit of community and cohesion which had been all but lost in the lush northern suburbs. This renewed urban identity was, once again, open to a multicultural and cosmopolitan outlook. Although it was at least partly initiated by members of the urban elite, it did not have the exclusive elite bias often associated with the term cosmopolitan. Even if the *dihlīz* of the old Jeddah buildings may have served its term as an architectural space, and if Jeddah no longer receives and absorbs the same number of newcomers into its society due to the fundamentally changed local, national, and international context, the idealised memory of Jeddah as a *dihlīz* which was of a solidary and inclusive nature has helped to inspire new inclusive practices. They show the potential of a renewed sense of 'Jeddah ghayr' as an open and tolerant city whose population is ready to invest itself in society. Eventually, this might even be a vision which could serve as a model both in and beyond Saudi Arabia.

Bibliography

Hicaz vilâyeti salnâmesi, defa 1 (Mecca: Vilayet Matbaası, 1301/1883–4).
Hicaz vilâyeti salnâmesi, defa 2 (Mecca: al-Matbaa al-Miriye al-Kaine, 1303/1885–6).
Hicaz vilâyeti salnâmesi, defa 3 (Mecca: Vilayet Matbaası, 1305/1887–8).
Hicaz vilâyeti salnâmesi, defa 4 (Mecca: Vilayet Matbaası, 1306/1888–8).
Hicaz vilâyeti salnâmesi, defa 5 (Mecca: Vilayet Matbaası, 1309/1892–3).
Madāris al-Falāḥ: al-Ḥaḍāra wa-l-Turāth (hectographed copies of testimonials, newspaper articles and interviews, often without precise indication of source) (n.d.).
'The Jeddah Massacre' in A. B. Becher (ed.), *The Nautical Magazine* (London: Brown Son & Ferguson), vol. 27, pp. 426–8. babel.hathitrust.org/cgi/pt?id=nyp.33433066364872;view=1up;seq=446 (accessed December 23, 2017).
'The Red Sea' in A. B. Becher (ed.), *The Nautical Magazine* (London: Brown Son & Ferguson), vol. 27, pp. 421–5.
The Story of Ten – Ḥikāyat 10 (Jeddah, 2013).
ʿAbd al-Raḥīm, ʿAbd al-Raḥīm ʿAbd al-Raḥmān, *Muḥammad ʿAlī wa-Shibh al-Jazīra al-ʿArabiyya 1819–1840*, 2 vols. (Cairo: Dār al-Kitāb al-Jāmiʿī, 1981).
ʿAbd al-Muʿṭī, Ḥussām Muḥammad, *al-ʿĀʾila wa-l-tharwa: al-Buyūt al-tijāriyya al-maghrabīyya fī Miṣr al-ʿuthmāniyya* (Cairo: al-Haiʾa al-Miṣriyya al-ʿĀmma li-l-Kitāb, 2008).
al-ʿAlāqāt al-miṣriyya al-ḥijāziyya fī 'l-qarn al-thāmin ʿashar (Cairo: al-Haiʾa al-Miṣriyya al-ʿĀmma li-l-Kitāb, 1999).
Abdul Karim, Mohammed, *Voyage de l'Inde à la Mekke: Par A'bdoûl-Kérym, favori de Tahmâs-Qouly-Khân extrait et traduit de la version anglaise de ses mémoires avec des notes géographiques, littéraires, & C.* (Paris: L'Imprimerie de Crapelet, 1797).
Abir, Mordechai, 'The "Arab Rebellion" of Amir Ghalib of Mecca (1788–1813)', *Middle Eastern Studies*, 7 (1971), pp. 185–200.
Abkar, ʿAbdallāh Muḥammad, *Ṣuwar min turāth Makka al-Mukarrama fī 'l-qarn al-rābiʿ ʿashar al-hijrī* (Beirut: Muʾassasat ʿUlūm al-Qurʾān/Damascus: Manār li-l-Nashr wa-l-Tawzīʿ, 1425/2004).

Abū 'l-Jadā'il, Khālid Ṣalāḥ Sanūsī, *Rawā lī wālidī wa-ṣaḥibuh* (Jeddah: Dār Manṣūr al-Zāmil, 1438/2017).
Abū Zayd, ʿAbd al-ʿAzīz ʿUmar, *Ḥikāyāt al-ʿaṭṭārīn fī Jidda al-qadīma: Dirāsat tārīkhiyya wa-Ṣuwar ijtimāʿiyya li-l-muʿtaqidāt wa-l-waṣfāt al-shaʿbiyya*, 2nd edn. (al-ʿĀmāl al-Thaqāfiyya, 1433/2012).
al-Miʿmārīyūn fī Jidda al-qadīma (Jeddah: al-ʿĀmāl al-Thaqāfiyya, 1437/ 2012 or 2013).
al-Usṭūra fī madīnat Jidda (Jeddah: Maktabat Kunūz al-Maʿrifa, 2016).
Abu-Lughod, Janet L., *Before European Hegemony: The World System A.D. 1250–1350* (New York: Oxford University Press, 1989).
Abu-Manneh, Butrus, 'Sultan Abdulhamid II and the Sharifs of Mecca (1880–1900)', *Asian and African Studies*, 9 (1973), pp. 1–21.
Adams L. O., *Notes on Roudaki Hall in Tehran, Iran*. www.operanostalgia.be/html/ROUDAKIHALL2016.html (accessed February 15, 2018).
Addonia, Sulaiman S. M. Y., *Die Liebenden von Dschidda: Roman* (Hamburg: Atlantik, 2015).
Adloff, Frank and Leggewie, Claus, *Das konvivialistische Manifest: Für eine neue Kunst des Zusammenlebens* (Bielefeld: Transcript, 2014).
Agmon, Iris, 'Women, Class, and Gender: Muslim Jaffa and Haifa at the Turn of the 20th Century', *International Journal of Middle East Studies*, 30 (1998), pp. 477–500.
Aḥmad, Muḥammad b. Aḥmad Sayyid and al-ʿAlawī, Abdūh b. Aḥmad, *Muḥammad Naṣīf: Ḥayyātuhu wa-āthāruh* (Beirut, Damascus, and Amman: al-Maktab al-Islāmī, 1994).
Ahmed, Chanfi, *West African 'Ulamā' and Salafism in Mecca and Medina: Jawāb al-Ifrīqī-the Response of the African*, Islam in Africa (Leiden, Boston: Brill, 2015), vol. 17.
Akcasu, A. Ebru, 'Migrants to Citizens: An Evaluation of the Expansionist Features of Hamidian Ottomanism, 1876–1909', *Die Welt des Islams*, 56 (2016), pp. 388–414.
Āl al-Shaykh, ʿAbdallāh b. ʿAbd al-Laṭīf, *Mashāhīr ʿulamāʾ Najd wa-ghayri-him* (Riyadh: Dār al-Yamāma, 1392/1972).
Āl Sībīh, Aḥmad ʿĀshūr, *al-Muʿallim Muḥammad ʿAwaḍ bin Lādin* (Riyadh: Muʾassasat al-Turāth, 1341 h./2009).
Alavi, Seema, *Muslim Cosmopolitanism in the Age of Empire* (Cambridge, MA and London: Harvard University Press, 2015).
al-ʿAlawī al-Shanqīṭī, ʿAbduh Walad Aḥmad (ed.), *Dīwān al-majmūʿ al-laṭīf fī banī Naṣīf*, 2 vols. (Riyadh: Maktabat al-Tawba, 1423/2002).
Albrecht, Andrea, *Kosmopolitismus: Weltbürgerdiskurse in Literatur, Philosophie und Publizistik um 1800* (Berlin and New York: Walter de Gruyter, 2005).

Alireza, Marianne, *At the Drop of a Veil: The True Story of a California Girl's Years in an Arabian Harem* (Boston: Houghton Mifflin Company, 1971).

Aljunied, Khairudin, *Muslim Cosmopolitanism: Southeast Asian Islam in Comparative Perspective* (Edinburgh: Edinburgh University Press, 2017).

Alorabi, Abdulraḥmān S., 'The Ottoman Policy in the Hejaz in the Eighteenth Century: A Study of Political and Administrative Developments, 1143–1202 A.H./1731–1788 A.D.', PhD Thesis, University of Utah (1988).

Altorki, Soraya, 'Some Considerations on the Family in the Arabian Peninsula in the Late Ottoman and Early Post-Ottoman Period' in A. e.-A. Sonbol (ed.), *Gulf Women* (Syracuse, New York, and London: Syracuse University Press; Eurospan [Distributor], 2012), pp. 277–309.

Women in Saudi Arabia: Ideology and Behavior among the Elite (New York and Guildford, CT: Columbia University Press, 1986).

Amīn, Bakrī Shaykh, *al-Ḥaraka al-adabiyya fī 'l-Mamlaka al-ʿArabiyya al-Saʿūdiyya* (Beirut: Dār Ṣādir, 1392/1972).

al-Amīn, Muḥsin b. ʿAbd al-Karīm, *Riḥlāt al-Sayyid Muḥsin al-Amīn* (Beirut: Dār al-Turāth al-Islāmī li-l-Ṭibāʿa wa-l-Nashr wa-l-Tawzīʿ, 1974).

al-Amr, Saleh Muhammad, 'The Hijaz under Ottoman Rule 1869/1914: Ottoman Vali, the Sharif of Mecca, and the Growth of British Influence', PhD Thesis, University of Leeds (1974).

al-ʿAmūdī, Muḥammad Saʿīd, *Min tārīkhinā*, 2nd edn. (Beirut: al-Dār al-Saʿūdiyya li-l-Nashr, 1967).

Anastassiadou, Meropi, *Salonique, 1830–1912: Une ville ottomane à l'âge des réformes*, The Ottoman Empire and Its Heritage (Leiden: Brill, 1997), vol. 11.

al-Anṣārī, ʿ. a.-R. a.-Ṭ. (ed.), *Dirāsāt tārīkh al-Jazīra al-ʿArabiyya* (Riyadh: Maṭbuʿāt Jāmiʿat al-Riyādh, 1399/1979).

al-Anṣārī, ʿAbd al-Qaddūs, *History of Aziziah Water Supply Juddah* (Jeddah, 1392/1972).

Mawsūʿat tārīkh madīnat Jidda, 2 (enlarged) (Jeddah: Maṭābiʿ al-Rawḍa, 1980).

Tārīkh al-ʿAyn al-ʿAzīziyya bi-Jidda: Lamaḥāt ʿan maṣādir al-miyāh fī 'l-Mamlaka al-ʿArabiyya al-Saʿūdiyya (Jeddah, n.d.).

Anscombe, Frederick F., *The Ottoman Gulf: The Creation of Kuwait, Saudi Arabia, and Qatar* (New York and Chichester: Columbia University Press, 1997).

Arnaud, Thomas-Joseph, *Voyage au pays de la reine de Saba: Suivi de Thomas-Joseph Arnaud et Alexandre Vayssière en Égypte. Préface d'Alexandre Dumas, Présenté par Claude Schopp* (Paris: Pygmalion, 2011).

al-Asad, Mohammad, 'The Mosque of Muhammad ʿAli in Cairo', *Muqarnas*, 9 (1992), pp. 39–55.

al-Asmarrī, Muḥammad b. Nāṣir, 'Tārīkh al-ḥayyāt al-ijtimāʿiyya fī Jidda: 1300–1343 h./1882–1925 m.', MA Thesis, King ʿAbd al-ʿAzīz University (2008/1429).

ʿAssāf, Manṣūr, 'Aḥmad al-Sibāʿī … shaykh al-muʾarrikhīn', al-Riyāḍ, January 05, 2018.

al-ʿAssāf, Manṣūr, 'Muḥammad Maghribī. Adīb al-Ḥijāz' (al-Riyāḍ, December 01, 2017).

Aydin, Cemil, *The Idea of the Muslim World: A Global Intellectual History* (Cambridge, MA: Harvard University Press, 2017).

Bā Dhīb, Muḥammad b. Abī Bakr b. ʿAbdallāh, 'Ḥasab Allāh, usra' in A. Z. Yamānī and ʿ. Ṣ. Tashkandī (eds.), *Mawsūʿat Makka al-Mukarrama wa-l-Madīna al-Munawwara* (London: Mu'assasat al-Furqān li-l-Turāth al-Islāmī, 2014), vol. 7, pp. 446–8.

Bā Ghaffār, Hind, *al-Aghānī al-shaʿbiyya fī 'l-Mamlaka al-ʿArabiyya al-Saʿūdiyya* (Jeddah: Dār al-Qādisiyya li-l-Nashr wa-l-Tawzīʿ, 1994).

Bā Nāja, ʿAbdallāh b.ʿAbd al-ʿAzīz, *Tārīkh Jidda min aqdam al-ʿuṣūr ḥattā nihāyat al-ʿahd al-ʿuthmānī* (Mecca, 2015).

Bā Qādir al-ʿAmūdī, Nūr Muḥammad, *al-Hijra al-rīfiyya al-ḥaḍariyya: Dirāsa fī takayyuf al-muhājirīn ilā madīnat Judda* (Beirut: Dār al-Munthakhab al-ʿArabī, 1994).

Bā Ṭarfī, Khālid Muḥammad, *Ibrāhīm al-Muḥammad al-Ḥassūn … yatadhakkar* (Jeddah, 1435/2014).

Jidda: Umm al-rakhāʾ wa-l-shidda, 2nd edn. (Madīna: Muʾassasat al-Madīna li-l-Ṣaḥāfa wa-l-Ṭibāʿa wa-l-Nashr, 1435/2014).

Sālim bin Maḥfūẓ … yatadhakkar (Jeddah, 1435/2014).

Badia y Leblich, Domingo, *Travels of Ali Bey in Morocco, Tripoli, Cyprus, Egypt, Arabia, Syria, and Turkey, between the Years 1803 and 1807*, 2 vols. (London: Longman, Hurst, Rees, Orme, and Brown, 1816).

Baer, Gabriel, 'The Administrative, Economic and Social Functions of Turkish Guilds', *International Journal of Middle East Studies*, 1 (1970), pp. 28–50.

Bagader, Mohammed Abubaker A., 'The Evolution of Built Heritage Conservation Policies in Saudi Arabia between 1970 and 2015: The Case of Historic Jeddah', PhD Thesis, University of Manchester (2016).

Baker, Randall, *King Husain and the Kingdom of Hejaz, Arabia Past and Present* (Cambridge: Oleander Press, 1979), vol. 10.

el-Bakri, Alia, 'Memories of the Beloved: Oral Histories from the 1916–19 Siege of Medina', *International Journal of Middle East Studies*, 46 (2014), pp. 703–18.

Bakshi, Anita, *Topographies of Memories: A New Poetics of Commemoration* (Basingstoke: Palgrave Macmillan, 2017).

Bakur, Muḥammad ʿAbd al-Karīm, *ʿĀʾila jiddāwiyya* (Riyadh: Muʾassasat al-Turāth, 2013).

Baldry, John, 'Foreign Interventions and Occupations of Kamaran Island', *Arabian Studies*, 4 (1978), pp. 89–111.

'The Ottoman Quarantine Station on Kamaran Island 1882–1914', *Studies in the History of Medicine*, 2 (1978), pp. 3–137.

Bang, Anne K., *Sufis and Scholars of the Sea: Family Networks in East Africa, 1860–1925*, Indian Ocean Series (London: Routledge Curzon, 2003).

Bardin, Pierre, *Algériens et Tunisiens dans l'Empire Ottoman de 1948 à 1914* (Paris: Ed. du Centre National de la Recherche Scientifique, 1979).

Barendse, René, *Arabian Seas 1700–1763*, 4 vols. (Leiden [etc.]: Brill Academic Publishers, 2009).

Başaran, Betül, *Selim III, Social Control and Policing in Istanbul at the End of the Eighteenth Century: Between Crisis and Order* (Boston: Brill, 2014).

Basīyū, Salīm, 'Jidda: Bāb al-ḥajj ilā bayt Allāh al-ḥarām', *al-ʿArabī* (1964), pp. 83–114.

Bassām, ʿAbdallāh b. ʿAbd al-Raḥmān b. Ṣāliḥ, *ʿUlamāʾ Najd khilāla thamāniyat qurūn*, 2nd enlarged edn., 6 vols. (Riyadh: Dār al-ʿĀṣima, 1419/1998–9 [1397/1977]).

al-Batanūnī, Muḥammad Labīb, *al-Riḥla al-ḥijāziyya li-walī 'l-niʿm al-Ḥājj ʿAbbās Ḥilmī Bāshā al-Thānī Khidīw Miṣr sanat 1327*, 2nd edn. (Cairo: Maṭbaʿat al-Gamāliyya, 1329 h./1911).

Behar, Cem, *A Neighborhood in Ottoman Istanbul: Fruit Vendors and Civil Servants in the Kasap İlyas Mahalle*, SUNY Series in the Social and Economic History of the Middle East (Albany: State University of New York Press, 2003).

Bentley, Jerry H., 'Sea and Ocean Basins as Frameworks of Historical Analysis', *Geographical Review*, 89 (1999), pp. 215–24.

Bianchi, Robert, *Guests of God: Pilgrimage and Politics in the Islamic World* (Oxford: Oxford University Press, 2004).

Bin ʿAfīf, Suʿād ʿAbūd, 'Mujtamaʿ al-ribāṭ: Dirāsa waṣfiyya li-asālīb al-riʿāya al-ijtimāʿiyya fī buyūt al-fuqarāʾ bi-madīnat Jidda, al-Mamlaka al-ʿArabiyya al-Saʿūdiyya', MA Thesis, King ʿAbd al-ʿAzīz University (1993).

bin Zaqr, Saʿīd b. Muḥammad b. ʿUbayd, *[unpublished memoirs]* (1984).

Birken, Andreas, *Die Provinzen des Osmanischen Reichs* (Unpubl., 1976).

Blake, George, *Gellatly's 1862–1962: A Short History of the Firm* (London: Blackie & Son Ltd, 1962).

Boberg, Dirk, *Ägypten, Naǧd und der Ḥiǧāz: Eine Untersuchung zum religiös-politischen Verhältnis zwischen Ägypten und den Wahhabiten, 1923–1936, anhand von in Kairo veröffentlichten pro- und antiwahhabitischen Streitschriften und Presseberichten, Europäische Hochschulschriften. Reihe XXVII, Asiatische und Afrikanische Studien* (Bern and New York: P. Lang, 1991), vol. 28.

Bokhari, Abdulla Y., 'Jeddah: A Study in Urban Formation', PhD Thesis, University of Pennslyvania (1978).

Bonnenfant, Paul and Gentilleau, Jeanne-Marie, 'Une Maison de Commerçant-armateur sur le mer Rouge: Bayt ʿAbd al-Udūd à al-Luḥayya (Yemen)' in D. Panzac (ed.), *Les Villes dans l'Empire Ottoman: Activités et Sociétés 2, Société Arabes et Musulmanes* (Paris: Ed. du CNRS, 1994), pp. 125–88.

Bové, M., 'Voyage aux Côtes de l'Arabie Heureuse', *Bulletin de la Société de Géographie*, 2e série (1834), pp. 145–65.

Boxberger, Linda, *On the Edge of Empire: Hadhramawt, Emigration, and the Indian Ocean, 1880s–1930s*, SUNY Series in Near Eastern Studies (Albany: State University of New York Press, 2002).

Bruce, James, *Travels to Discover the Source of the Nile in the Years 1768, 1769, 1770, 1771, 1772, and 1773: vol. 1*, 5 vols. (Edinburgh and London: J. Ruthven G. G. J. and J. Robinson, 1790).

Brunschvig, R., 'ʿAbd' in P. J. Bearman, T. Bianquis, C. E. Bosworth, E. J. van Donzel and W. P. Heinrichs (eds.), *Encyclopaedia of Islam*, 2nd edn., 12 vols. (Leiden: Brill, 1960–2005). dx.doi.org/10.1163/1573-3912_islam_COM_0003 (accessed February 22, 2018).

Buhl, Fr. and Jomier, J., 'Maḥmal' in P. J. Bearman, T. Bianquis, C. E. Bosworth, E. J. van Donzel and W. P. Heinrichs (eds.), *Encyclopaedia of Islam*, 2nd edn., 12 vols. (Leiden: Brill, 1960–2005). dx.doi.org/10.1163/1573-3912_islam_SIM_4789 (accessed October 5, 2018).

Bullard, Reader, *Two Kings in Arabia: Letters from Jeddah 1923–5 and 1936–9* (Reading: Ithaca Press, 1993).

Bulmuş, Birsen, *Plague, Quarantines and Geopolitics in the Ottoman Empire* (Edinburgh: Edinburgh University Press, 2012).

Burckhardt, John Lewis, 'Observations sur les habitants de la Mecque et de Djidda', *Nouvelles Annales des Voyages*, 50 2e série, 20 (1831), pp. 5–37, 129–63.

Burckhardt, John, *Travels in Arabia: Comprehending an Account of Those Territories in Hedjaz Which the Mohammedans Regard as Sacred*, vol. 1 (London: Colburn, 1829).

Burdett, Anita L. P., *The Slave Trade into Arabia 1820–1973*, 5 vols. (Slough: Archive Editions, 2006).

Burke, Peter, 'History of Events and the Revival of Narrative' in P. Burke (ed.), *New Perspectives on Historical Writing* (Cambridge: Polity Press, 1991), pp. 233–48.

Burton, Richard Francis, *Personal Narrative of a Pilgrimage to el Medinah and Meccah* (ed. Isabel Burton), 2nd edn. (London: Longman Brown Green Longmans and Roberts, 1857).

Büssow, Johann, *Hamidian Palestine: Politics and Society in the District of Jerusalem, the Ottoman Empire and Its Heritage* (Leiden: Brill, 2011), vol. 46.

Buzpınar, Tufan, 'Opposition to the Ottoman Caliphate in the Early Years of Abdülhamīd II: 1877–1882', *Die Welt des Islams*, 36 (1996), pp. 59–89.

Can, Lâle, 'The Protection Question: Central Asians and Extraterritoriality in the Late Ottoman Empire', *International Journal of Middle East Studies*, 48 (2016), pp. 679–99.

Carter, J. R. L, *Leading Merchant Families of Saudi Arabia* (London: Scorpion Publications; D.R. Llewellyn Group, 1979).

Casale, Giancarlo, 'The Ottoman Administration of the Spice Trade in the Sixteenth-Century Red Sea and Persian Gulf', *Journal of the Economic and Social History of the Orient*, 49 (2006), pp. 170–98.

The Ottoman Age of Exploration (New York and Oxford: Oxford University Press, 2010).

Caudill, Mark A., *Twilight in the Kingdom: Understanding the Saudis*, foreword by Steve Coll (Westport, CN and London: Praeger Security International, 2006).

Çelik, Zeynep, *Empire, Architecture, and the City: French-Ottoman Encounters, 1830–1914*, Studies in Modernity and National Identity (Seattle and London: University of Washington Press, 2008).

Certeau, Michel de, *The Practice of Everyday Life*, Paperback (University of California Press, 1988).

Chantre, Luc, 'Le Pèlerinage à La Mecque à l'époque coloniale (v. 1866–1940): France – Grande-Bretagne – Italie', PhD Thesis, Université de Poitiers (2012).

Pèlerinages d'Empire: Une histoire européenne de pèlerinage à la Mecque (Paris: Éditions de la Sorbonne, 2018).

Chaudhry, Kiren Aziz, *The Price of Wealth: Economies and Institutions in the Middle East* (Ithaca: Cornell University Press, 1997).

Cheta, Omar Youssef, 'Rule of Merchants: The Practice of Commerce and Law in Late Ottoman Egypt, 1841–1876', PhD Thesis, New York University (2014).

Chiffoleau, Sylvia, 'Le pèlerinage à la Mecque à l'époque coloniale: Matrice d'une opinion publique musulmane?' in S. Chiffoleau and A. Madoeuf (eds.), *Les Pèlerinages au Maghreb et au Moyen-Orient: Espaces Publics, Espaces du Public* (Beyrouth: Institut Français du Proche-Orient, 2005), pp. 131–63.

Le voyage à la Mecque: Un pèlerinage mondial en terre d'Islam, Collection Histoire (Paris: Berlin, 2015).

Çiçek, M. Talha, 'Negotiating Power and Authority in the Desert: The Arab Bedouin and the Limits of the Ottoman State in Hijaz, 1840–1908', *Middle Eastern Studies*, 52 (2016), pp. 260–79.

Clarence-Smith, William G., 'Hadhrami Entrepreneurs in the Malay World, c. 1750 to c. 1940' in U. Freitag and W. G. Clarence-Smith (eds.), *Hadhrami Traders, Scholars, and Statesmen in the Indian Ocean, 1750s–1960s* (Leiden, New York, and Köln: Brill Academic Publishers, 1997), pp. 297–314.

Clemow, F. G., *Les eaux de Djeddah: Communication faite au Conseil Supérieur de Santé le 11 Septembre 1906* (Constantinople, Imprimérie Loeffler, 1906).

Cohen, Erik, 'Pilgrimage and Tourism: Convergence and Divergence' in A. Morinis (ed.), *Sacred Journeys: The Anthropology of Pilgrimage* (Westport, CA: Greenwood Press, 1992), pp. 47–61.

Cole, Juan, 'Of Crowds and Empires: Afro-Asian Riots and European Expansion, 1857–1882', *Comparative Studies in Society and History*, 31 (1989), pp. 106–33.

Collins-Kreiner, N., 'The Geography of Pilgrimage and Tourism: Transformations and Implications for Applied Geography', *Applied Geography*, 30 (2010), pp. 153–64.

Commins, David Dean, *The Wahhabi Mission and Saudi Arabia,* Library of Modern Middle East Studies (London and New York: I.B. Tauris, 2006).

Constable, Olivia Remie, *Housing the Stranger in the Mediterranean World: Lodging, Trade, and Travel in Late Antiquity and the Middle Ages* (Cambridge: Cambridge University Press, 2003).

Cook, Michael, *Commanding Right and Forbidding Wrong in Islamic Thought* (Cambridge: Cambridge University Press, 2000).

Cooper, Frederick, *Colonialism in Question: Theory, Knowledge, History* (Berkeley: University of California Press, 2005).

Crecelius, Daniel, 'A Late Eighteenth-Century Austrian Attempt to Develop the Red Sea Trade Route', *Middle Eastern Studies*, 30 (1994), pp. 262–80.

Daḥlān, Aḥmad b. *Zaynī, Khulāṣat al-kalām fī bayān umarāʾ al-Ḥarām* (Cairo: al-Maṭbaʿa al-Khayriyya, 1305/1887–8).

al-Dailami, Ahmed, 'Purity and Confusion: The Hawala between Persians and Arabs in the Contemporary Gulf' in L. G. Potter (ed.), *The Persian*

Gulf in Modern Times: People, Ports, and History (New York: Palgrave Macmillan, 2014), pp. 299–326.

Dallal, Ahmad, 'The Origins and Objectives of Islamic Revivalist Thought, 1750–1850', *The Journal of the American Oriental Society*, 113 (1993), pp. 341–59.

d'Alòs-Moner, Andreu Martinez, 'Conquistadores, Mercenaries, and Missionaries: The Failed Portuguese Dominion of the Red Sea', *Northeast African Studies*, 12 (2012), pp. 1–28.

Dassy, G. F., *Notes on Sueis and Its Trade with the Ports of the Red Sea: With Tables of Exports and Imports, etc. for the First 6 Months of 1859* (London: Foreign and Commonwealth Office Collection, 1859).

Dawn, Ernest, 'The Amir of Mecca Al-Ḥusayn Ibn-ʿAli and the Origin of the Arab Revolt', *Proceedings of the American Philosophical Society*, 104 (1960), pp. 11–34.

de Corancez, Louis Alexandre Olivier, *The Founders of Saudi Arabia: The History of the Wahabis from Their Origin until the End of 1809* (Garnet: Reading, 1995).

de Gobineau, Arthur, *Trois ans en Asie* (Paris: Ernest Leroux, 1905).

Derbal, Nora, 'Charity for the Poor in Jeddah, Saudi Arabia, 1961–2015', PhD Thesis (Freie Universität Berlin) (2017).

Determann, Jörg Matthias, *Historiography in Saudi Arabia: Globalization and the State in the Middle East, Library of Middle East History* (London: Tauris, 2014), vol. 42.

d'Héricourt, Charles E. Xavier Rochet, 'Lettre de M. Rochet d'Héricourt à M. d'Avezac Moka, le 26 mai 1842', *Bulletin de la Société de Géographie*, 19 (2ième série), pp. 118–27.

Voyage sur la Côte Orientale de la Mer Rouge, dans le Pays d'Adel et le Royaume de Choa (Paris: Arthus Bertrand, 1841).

Didier, Charles, *Séjour chez le Grand-Chérif de la Mekke* (Paris: Librairie. Hachette et C.ie, 1857).

Difalla, Abdulla, 'Jeddah's Slum Areas: The Attempt to Redevelop al-Nuzla al-Yamania', MA Thesis, Ball State University (2015).

Diyāb, Muḥammad Ṣādiq, *al-Mufradāt al-ʿāmmiyya fī madīnat Jidda* (n.p.: al-Maṭbaʿa al-Maḥmūdiyya, 1429/2008).

Jidda: al-Tārīkh wa-l-ḥayyāt al-ijtimāʿiyya, 2nd edn. (Jeddah: Maṭābiʿ Muʾassasat al-Madīna li-l-Ṣaḥāfa, 2003).

Khawāja Yannī: Riwāya, 2nd edn. (Dubai: Madārik, 2016).

Dobbin, Christine, *Asian Entrepreneurial Minorities: Conjoint Communities in the Making of the World-Economy 1570–1940*, Monograph series/ Nordisk Institut for Asienstudier, Digital print (London: Routledge Curzon, 2005), vol. 71.

Doughty, Charles Montagu, *Travels in Arabia Deserta*, 2 vols. (London and Boston: Philip Lee Warner, new edn. 1888/1901).

Doumani, Beshara, 'Endowing Family: *Waqf*, Property Devolution, and Gender in Greater Syria, 1800 to 1860', *Comparative Studies in Society and History*, 40 (1998), pp. 3–41.

Family Life in the Ottoman Mediterranean: A Social History (Cambridge, New York, Melbourne, Delhi, and Singapore: Cambridge University Press, 2017).

Dubois, Colette, 'The Red Sea Ports during the Revolution in Transportation, 1800–1914' in L. Fawaz and C. Bayly (eds.), *Modernity and Culture: From the Mediterranean to the Indian Ocean* (New York: Columbia University Press, 2002), pp. 58–74.

Ed., 'Maḥalle' in P. J. Bearman, T. Bianquis, C. E. Bosworth, E. J. van Donzel and W. P. Heinrichs (eds.), *Encyclopaedia of Islam*, 2nd edn., 12 vols. (Leiden: Brill, 1960–2005). doi.org/10.1163/1573-3912_islam_SIM_4775 (accessed March 28, 2018).

Eldem, Edhem, 'The Undesirables of Smyrna, 1926', *Mediterranean Historical Review*, 24 (2009), pp. 223–7.

Elfateh, Muhammad Ahmed, 'Suakin (Sudan) and the Colonial Architecture of the Ottoman Empire in the Red Sea Region', PhD Thesis, Brandenburgische Technische Universität Cottbus-Senftenberg (2015).

Ener, Mine, 'Religious Prerogatives and Policing the Poor in Two Ottoman Contexts', *The Journal of Interdisciplinary History*, 35 (2005), pp. 501–11.

Erdem, Y. Hakan, *Slavery in the Ottoman Empire and Its Demise, 1800–1909*, St. Antony's Series (New York: St. Martin's Press, 1996).

Ergut, Ferdan, 'Policing the Poor in the Late Ottoman Empire', *Middle Eastern Studies*, 38 (2002), pp. 149–64.

'The State and Social Control: The Police in the Late Ottoman Empire and the Early Republican Turkey, 1839–1939', PhD Thesis, New School for Social Research (1999).

Errichiello, Gennaro, 'Foreign Workforce in the Arab Gulf States (1930–1950): Migration Patterns and Nationality Clause', *The International Migration Review*, 46 (2012), pp. 389–413.

Essner, Cornelia, 'Cholera der Mekkapilger und internationale Sanitätspolitik in Ägypten (1866–1938)', *Die Welt des Islams*, 32 (1992).

Evliyâ Çelebi, *Seyahatnâmesi*, 2 vols. (Istanbul: Yapı Kredi Yayınları, 2011).

Ewald, Janet and Clarence-Smith, William G., 'The Economic Role of the Hadhrami Diaspora in the Red Sea and Gulf of Aden, 1820s to 1930s' in U. Freitag and W. G. Clarence-Smith (eds.), *Hadhrami Traders, Scholars, and Statesmen in the Indian Ocean, 1750s–1960s* (Leiden, New York, and Köln: Brill Academic Publishers, 1997), pp. 281–96.

Facey, William, 'Jiddah: Port of Makkah, Gateway of the Indian Trade' in L. Blue, J. Cooper, T. Ross and J. Whitewright (eds.), *Connected Hinterlands: Proceedings of Red Sea Project IV; Held at the University of Southampton, September 2008, Society for Arabian Studies Monographs* (London: Archaeopress, 2009), pp. 165–76.

'Trade and Travel in the Red Sea Region' in P. Lunde and A. Porter (eds.), *Trade and Travel in the Red Sea Region: Proceedings of Red Sea Project I Held in the British Museum, October 2002*, Society for Arabian Studies Monographs (London, 2004), pp. 7–17.

al-Faḍlī, ʿAbbās b. Muḥammad Saʿīd, *al-Nuzla al-Yamāniyya: Ḥayy fī dhākirat Jidda* (Jeddah: Maktabat Dār Zahrān, 2010).

Farāhānī, M. Ḥ. and Farmayan, H. (eds.), *A Shi'ite Pilgrimage to Mecca 1885–1886: The Safarnâmeh of Mirzâ Moḥammad Ḥosayn Farâhâni*, 1st. edn. (Austin: University of Texas Press, 1990).

Faroqhi, Suraiya, *Artisans of Empire: Crafts and Craftspeople under the Ottomans,* Library of Ottoman Studies (London: Tauris, 2009), vol. 17.

'Red Sea Trade and Communications as Observed by Evliya Çelebi (1671–72)', *New Perspectives on Turkey*, 5–6 (1991), pp. 87–105.

Fawaz, Layla, *Merchants and Migrants in Nineteenth-Century Beirut,* Harvard Middle Eastern Studies (Cambridge, MA: Harvard University Press, 1983), vol. 18.

Fawaz, L. and Bayly, C. (eds.), *Modernity and Culture: From the Mediterranean to the Indian Ocean* (New York: Columbia University Press, 2002).

Ferret, M. M. and Galinier, *Voyage en Abyssinie dans les provinces du Tigré, du Samen et de l'Ahmara* (Paris: Paulin, 1847).

Field, Michael, *The Merchants: The Big Business Families of Saudi Arabia and the Gulf States*, 2nd edn. (Woodstock, NY: Overlook Press, 1985).

Finati, Giovanni, *Narrative of the Life and Adventures of Giovanni Finati,* W. J. Bankes (ed.), 2 vols. (London: John Murray, 1830).

Findley, C. V., 'Mukhtār' in P. J. Bearman, T. Bianquis, C. E. Bosworth, E. J. van Donzel and W. P. Heinrichs (eds.), *Encyclopaedia of Islam,* 2nd edn., 12 vols. (Leiden: Brill, 1960–2005). dx.doi.org/10.1163/1573-3912_islam_SIM_5472 (accessed January 12, 2019).

Fischer-Nebmaier, Wladimir, 'Introduction: Space, Narration, and the Everyday' in W. Fischer-Nebmaier, M. Berg and A. Christou (eds.), *Narrating the City: History, Space, and the Everyday* (New York and Oxford: Berghahn Books, 2015), pp. 1–55.

Foreign Office, *Foreign Office 1894. Annual Series. No. 1451 Diplomatic and Consular Reports on Trade and Finance. Turkey. Report for the*

Year 1893 on the Trade, & c., of the Consular District of Jeddah (1894).
Foster, W., *The Red Sea and Adjacent Countries at the Close of the Seventeenth Century as Described by Joseph Pitts, William Daniel and Charles Jacques Poncet*, Works Issued by the Hakluyt Society (Nendeln: Kraus Reprint, 1967), 2nd ser., no. 100.
Foster Sadlier, George., *Diary of a Journey across Arabia* (Bombay, 1866).
Freitag, Ulrike, 'A Twentieth-Century Merchant Network Centered on Jeddah: The Correspondence of Muḥammad b. Aḥmad Bin Ḥimd', *Journal of Northeast African Studies*, 17 (2017), pp. 101–29.
'Arab Merchants in Singapore: Attempt of a Collective Biography' in H. de Jonge and N. Kaptein (eds.), *Transcending Borders: Arabs, Politics, Trade and Islam in Southeast Asia* (Leiden: Brill Academic Publishers, 2002), pp. 109–142.
'"Cosmopolitanism" and "Conviviality"?: Some Conceptual Considerations Concerning the Late Ottoman Empire', *European Journal of Cultural Studies*, 17 (2014), pp. 375–91.
'Der Orientalist und der Mufti: Kulturkontakt im Mekka des 19. Jahrhunderts', *Die Welt des Islams*, 43 (2003), pp. 37–60.
'Helpless Representatives of the Great Powers?: Western Consuls in Jeddah, 1830s to 1914', *The Journal of Imperial and Commonwealth History*, 40 (2012), pp. 357–81.
Indian Ocean Migrants and State Formation in Hadhramaut: Reforming the Homeland, Social, Economic, and Political Studies of the Middle East and Asia (Leiden and Boston: Brill Academic Publishers, 2003), vol. 87.
'Jidda' in K. Fleet, G. Krämer, D. Matringe, J. Nawas and E. K. Rowson (eds.), *Encyclopaedia of Islam*, 3rd edn. (Leiden: Brill, 2007). dx.doi.org/10.1163/1573-3912_ei3_COM_32823 (accessed May 07, 2019).
'Playing with Gender: The Carnival of *al-Qays in Jeddah*' in N. Maksudyan (ed.), *Women and the City, Women in the City: A Gendered Perspective on Ottoman Urban History* (New York: Berghahn Books, 2014), pp. 71–85.
'Scholarly Exchange and Trade: Muḥammad Ḥusayn Naṣīf and His Letters to Christiaan Snouck Hurgronje' in M. Kemper and R. Elger (eds.), *The Piety of Learning: Islamic Studies in Honor of Stefan Reichmuth, Islamic History and Civilization* (Leiden and Boston: Brill, 2017), pp. 292–308.
'State-Society Relations through the Lens of Urban Development' in K. Fleet and E. Boyar (eds.), *Middle Eastern and North African Societies in the Interwar Period* (Leiden [etc.]: Brill, 2018), pp. 27–53.

'Symbolic Politics and Urban Violence in Late Ottoman Jeddah' in U. Freitag, N. Fuccaro, N. Lafi and C. Ghrawi (eds.), *Urban Violence in the Middle East: Changing Cityscapes in the Transition from Empire to Nation State, Space and Place* (New York: Berghahn Books, 2015), pp. 111–38.

(May 6, 2015). 'The Falah School in Jeddah: Civic Engagement for Future Generations? '. Article on *jadaliyya.com*. www.jadaliyya.com/pages/index/21430/the-falah-school-in-jeddah_civic-engagement-for-fu.

(2016). 'Urban Life in Late Ottoman, Hashemite and Early Saudi Jeddah, as Documented in the Photographs in the Snouck Hurgronje Collection in Leiden'. www.zmo.de/publikationen/WorkingPapers/freitag_2016.pdf.

'When Festivals Turned Violent in Jeddah, 1880s–1960s' in N. Fuccaro (ed.), *Violence and the City in the Modern Middle East* (Stanford: Stanford University Press, 2016), pp. 63–74, 250–55.

Freitag, Ulrike and Clarence-Smith, W. G. (eds.), *Hadhrami Traders, Scholars, and Statesmen in the Indian Ocean, 1750s–1960s* (Leiden, New York, and Köln: Brill Academic Publishers, 1997).

Freitag, Ulrike and Lafi, Nora (eds.), *Urban Governance under the Ottomans: Between Cosmopolitanism and Conflict* (Milton Park, Abingdon, Oxon: Routledge, 2014).

Freitag, Ulrike and Oppen, Achim von, 'Introduction: 'Translocality': An Approach to Connection and Transfer in Regional Studies' in U. Freitag and A. v. Oppen (eds.), *Translocality: The Study of Globalising Processes from a Southern Perspective, Studies in Global Social History* (Leiden and Boston: Brill, 2010), pp. 1–21.

Freitag, Ulrike, Pétriat, Philippe and Strohmeier, Martin, 'La Première Guerre Mondiale dans la Péninsule Arabique . . . enquête de ses sources', *Arabian Humanities*, 6 (2016), https://journals.openedition.org/cy/3029.

Fresnel, Fulgence, 'L'Arabie: Première partie', *Revue des Deux Mondes*, xvii (1839) pp. 241–57.

Fuccaro, Nelida, *Histories of City and State in the Persian Gulf: Manama since 1800*, Cambridge Middle East Studies (Cambridge and New York: Cambridge University Press, 2009), vol. 30.

'Introduction: Histories of Oil and Urban Modernity in the Middle East', *Comparative Studies of South Asia, Africa and the Middle East*, 33 (2013), pp. 1–6.

Füssel, Marian, *Zur Aktualität von Michel de Certeau: Einführung in sein Werk, Aktuelle und klassische Sozial- und Kulturwissenschaftler-innen* (Wiesbaden: Springer VS, 2018).

Gaenszle, Martin, '"Religiöser Kosmopolitismus": Der Nepali-Stadtteil in Benares, Indien', *Zeitschrift für Ethnologie*, 129 (2004), pp. 165–82.

Gelvin, James L., 'The "Politics of Notables" Forty Years After', *Middle East Studies Association Bulletin*, 40 (2006), pp. 19–29.

al-Ghamdi, Hassna, 'al-Khawaja Yanni (Yanni the Westerner): An Example of Muslim-Christian Tolerance in Jeddah during the 20th Century', *Academic Journal of Interdisciplinary Studies*, 6 (2017), pp. 61–6.

Ghazaleh, Pascale, 'Trading in Power: Merchants and the State in 19th Century Egypt', *International Journal of Middle East Studies*, 45 (2013), pp. 71–91.

Ghrawi, Claudia, 'Saudi Arabia's Urban Revolution: Oil Urbanization and Popular Politics in al-Aḥsāʾ (the Eastern Province), 1938–1970', PhD Thesis, Freie Universität (2017).

Gourisse, Benjamin, 'Order and Compromise: The Concrete Realities of Public Action in Turkey and the Ottoman Empire' in M. Aymes, B. Gourisse and É. Massicard (eds.), *Order and Compromise: Government Practices in Turkey from the Late Ottoman Empire to the Early 21st Century* (Leiden and Boston: Brill, 2015), pp. 1–24.

Grallert, Till, *To Whom Belong the Streets?: Property, Propriety, and Appropriation: The Production of Public Space in Late Ottoman Damascus, 1875–1914* (Berlin: FU Berlin (Microfiche), 2014).

Great Britain, *Parliamentary Papers: Reports from Committees*, 18 vols. (London: Her Majesty's Stationery Office, 1831), vol. 10.

Güler, M., Yılmaz, Ö. F. and Ovalıoğlu, İ. (eds.), *Belgelerle Osmanlı Devrinde Hicaz*, 2 vols. (Istanbul: Çamlıca, 2008).

al-Ḥaḍrāwī al-Makkī al-Shāfiʿī, Aḥmad b. Muḥammad b. Aḥmad, *al-Jawāhir al-muʿadda fī faḍāʾil Jidda*, ʿAlī Muḥammad ʿUmar (ed.) (Cairo: Maktabat al-Thaqāfa al-Dīniyya, 2002).

Hagmann, Jannis, 'Die Flutkatastrophe von Jidda 2009: Eine Fallstudie anhand von Presse, Petitionen & Facebook', MA Thesis, Freie Universität Berlin (2011).

Haines, Stafford Bettesworth, 'A Description of the Arabian Coast, Commencing from the Entrance of the Red Sea, and Continuing as Far as Messenaat: ... with Some Observations Relative to Its Population, Government, Commerce and Culture', *Transactions of the Bombay Geographical Society*, 11 (1852/53).

Halabi, Romina, 'Contract Enslavement of Female Migrant Domestic Workers in Saudi Arabia and the United Arab Emirates', *Research Digest: Human Rights and Contemporary Slavery* (2008), pp. 43–58.

al-Ḥamdī, Ṣabrī Fāliḥ, *Ḥarakat al-taḥdīth fī 'l-Mamlaka al-ʿArabiyya al-Saʿūdiyya 1926–1953* (Beirut: Arab Scientific Publishers, 1435/2014).

Hamilton, James, *Sinai, The Hedjaz, and Soudan: Wanderings around the Birth-Place of the Prophet and across the Aethiopian Desert, from Sawakin to Chartum* (Reading: Garnet Publishing, 1856/1993).

Hammoudi, Abdellah, *A Season in Mecca: Narrative of a Pilgrimage*, 1st American edn. (New York: Hill and Wang, 2006).
Ḥamza, Fuā'd, *Qalb Jazīrat al-'Arab*, 2nd edn. (Riyadh: al-Dāra, 1968).
Hanley, Will, 'Grieving Cosmopolitanism in Middle East Studies', *History Compass*, 6 (2008), pp. 1346–67.
Identifying with Nationality: Europeans, Ottomans, and Egyptians in Alexandria (New York: Columbia University Press, 2017).
Hanna, Nelly, *Making Big Money in 1600: The Life and Times of Isma'il Abu Taqiyya, Egyptian Merchant*, 1st edn. (Syracuse, NY: Syracuse University Press, 1998).
Hansen, Thomas Blom and Verkaaik, Oskar, 'Introduction: Urban Charisma: On Everyday Mythologies in the City', *Critique of Anthropology*, 29 (2009), pp. 5–26.
Hanssen, Jens, *Fin de Siècle Beirut: The Making of an Ottoman Provincial Capital*, Oxford Historical Monographs (Oxford: Clarendon Press, 2005).
al-Ḥarbī, Dalāl bte Mukhlid, 'al-Awḍā' al-dākhiliyya fī Jidda fī fatrat al-ḥiṣār 1343–144 h./1925 m. min khilāli ṣaḥīfat "Barīd al-Ḥijāz"', *al-Dar'iyya*, 47–8 (2010), 123–84.
Harre, Dominique, 'Exchanges and Mobility in the Western Indian Ocean: Indians between Yemen and Ethiopia, 19th–20th Centuries', *Les Chroniques du manuscrit au Yémen*, Special Issue 1 (2017), pp. 42–69.
Harrison, Mark, 'Disease, Diplomacy and International Commerce: The Origins of International Sanitary Regulation in the Nineteenth Century', *Journal of Global History*, 1 (2006), pp. 197–217.
'Quarantine, Pilgrimage, and Colonial Trade: India 1866–1900', *The Indian Economic and Social History Review*, 29 (1992), pp. 117–44.
Hashmi, Sohail, 'Political Boundaries and Moral Communities: Islamic Perspectives' in A. Buchanan and M. Moore (eds.), *States, Nations, and Borders: The Ethics of Making Boundaries* (Cambridge and New York: Cambridge University Press, 2003), pp. 181–227.
Hathaway, Jane, 'The Wealth and Influence of an Exiled Ottoman Eunuch in Egypt: The Waqf Inventory of 'Abbās Agha', *Journal of the Economic and Social History of the Orient*, 37 (1994), pp. 293–317.
Hawting, G. R., 'The Origin of Jedda and the Problem of al-Shu'ayba', *Arabica*, 31 (1984), pp. 318–26.
Hayden, Dolores, 'The Power of Place: Claiming Urban Landscapes as People's History', *Journal of Urban History*, 20 (1994), pp. 466–85.
Herzog, Christoph, 'Migration and the State: On Ottoman Regulations Concerning Migration since the Age of Mahmud II' in U. Freitag, M. Fuhrmann, N. Lafi and F. Riedler (eds.), *The City in the Ottoman Empire: Migration and the Making of Urban Modernity*, SOAS/

Routledge Studies on the Middle East (London and New York: Routledge, 2011), pp. 117–34.

Osmanische Herrschaft und Modernisierung im Irak: Die Provinz Bagdad, 1817–1917, Bamberger Orientstudien (Bamberg: University of Bamberg Press, 2012), vol. 4.

Hirschfeld, Christian Cay Lorenz, *Von der Gastfreundschaft: Eine Apologie für die Menschheit* (Leipzig: Weidmanns Erben und Reich, 1777).

Ho, Engseng, 'Names beyond Nations: The Making of Local Cosmopolitans', Études Rurales, *Comparative Studies in Society and History*, 163/164 (2002), pp. 215–31.

Hogarth, David George, *Hejaz before World War I*, reprint of 2nd edn., 1917, with a new Introduction by R. L. Bidwell (Cambridge: The Oleander Press, 1978).

Holt, Peter, 'Fallāta' in P. J. Bearman, T. Bianquis, C. E. Bosworth, E. J. van Donzel and W. P. Heinrichs (eds.), *Encyclopaedia of Islam*, 2nd edn., 12 vols. (Leiden: Brill, 1960–2005). http://dx.doi.org/10.1163/1573-3912_islam_SIM_2261 (accessed February 19, 2018).

Hopper, Matthew S., *Slaves of One Master: Globalization and Slavery in Arabia in the Age of Empire* (New Haven, CT: Yale University Press, 2015).

Horvath, Christina, 'The Cosmopolitan City' in M. Rovisco and M. Nowicka (eds.), *The Ashgate Research Companion for Cosmopolitism* (2011), p. 87.

Hourani, Albert, 'Ottoman Reform and the Politics of Notables' in Polk and Chambers (eds.), *Beginnings of Modernization in the Middle East: The Nineteenth Century*, Conference Proceedings (Chicago: University of Chicago Press, 1968), pp. 41–68.

Huber, Valeska, *Channelling Mobilities: Migration and Globalisation in the Suez Canal Region and Beyond, 1869–1914* (Cambridge and New York: Cambridge University Press, 2013).

'The Unification of the Globe by Disease?: The International Sanitary Conferences on Cholera, 1851–1894', *The Historical Journal*, 49 (2006), pp. 453–76.

al-Ḥujaylī, Sulṭān, 'al-Ṭawwāfa' mihna ḥufiẓat li-ahl Makka … wa-400 malyūn', al-Ḥayyāt, August 31, 2017.

Hūlākū, Matīn, *al-Khaṭṭ al-ḥadīdī al-ḥijāzī: al-Mashrū ʿ al-ʿimlāq li-l-Sulṭān ʿAbd al-Ḥamīd al-Thānī* (Cairo: Dār al-Nīl, 2011).

Hülgū, Matīn, 'Topal Osman Nuri Paşa Hayatı ve Faaliyetleri (1840–1898)', *Osmanlı Tarihi Araştırma ve Uygulama Merkezi Dergisi*, 5 (2005), pp. 145–53.

Human Rights Watch, 'As if I'm not Human: Abuses against Asian Domestic Workers in Saudi Arabia' 2008, pp. 91–3.

Hunwick, John O., 'The Same but Different: Africans in Slavery in the Mediterranean Muslim World' in J. O. Hunwick and E. T. Powell (eds.), *The African Diaspora in the Mediterranean Lands of Islam, Princeton Series on the Middle East* (Princeton, NJ: Markus Wiener Publishers, 2002), pp. ix–xxxvii.

Hurewitz, Jacob C., *Diplomacy in the Near and Middle East: A Documentary Record: 1914–1956*, vol. 2 (Princeton, NJ: Nostrand, 1956).

Hutson, Alaine S., 'Enslavement and Manumission in Saudi Arabia, 1926–38', *Critique: Critical Middle Eastern Studies*, 11 (2002), pp. 49–70.

Ībish, Y. (ed.), *Riḥalat al-Imām Muḥammad Rashīd Riḍā*, Jamaʿahā wa-ḥaqqaqahā Yūsuf Ībish (Beirut: al-Muʾassasa al-ʿArabiyya li-l-Dirāsāt wa-l-Nashr, 1971).

Ibn Jubayr, Muḥammad ibn Aḥmad and de Goeje, M. J., *The Travels of Ibn Jubayr* (Leyden: Brill, 1907).

Ilbert, Robert, *Alexandrie, 1830–1930: Histoire d'une communauté citadine*, Bibliothèque d'Étude (Cairo: Institut Français d'Archéologie Orientale, 1996), vol. 112.

Illich, Ivan, *Tools for Conviviality, Open Forum* (London: Calder and Boyars, 1973).

İnal, Onur, 'A Port and Its Hinterland: An Environmental History of Izmir in the Late Ottoman Period', PhD Thesis, University of Arizona (2015).

al-ʿĪsā, ʿAbd al-ʿAzīz b. Muḥammad Fahd, *Arshīf Mamlakat al-Ḥijāz wa-Salṭanat Najd wa-Mulḥaqātihā, 1343h–1346h* (Beirut: Dār al-Jadāwil, 2013).

Isin, Engin F., 'Ottoman Waqfs as Acts of Citizenship' in P. Ghazaleh (ed.), *Held in Trust: Waqf in the Islamic World* (Cairo and New York: American University of Cairo Press, 2011), pp. 209–26.

'Who Is the New citizen? Towards a Genalogy', *Citizenship Studies*, 1 (1997), pp. 115–32.

Ismāʿīl, Ṣābira Muʾmin, *Jidda khilāla 'l-fatra 1286–1327 H./1869–1908 M.: Dirāsa tārīkhiyya wa-ḥaḍāriyya fī 'l-maṣādir al-muʿāṣira* (Riyadh: Dārat al-Malik ʿAbd al-ʿAziz, 1418/1997–98).

Issawi, Charles, *The Fertile Crescent 1800–1914: A Documentary Economic History*, Studies in Middle Eastern History (New York: Oxford University Press, 1988).

al-Jabartī, ʿAbd al-Raḥmān, *ʿAbd al-Raḥmān al-Jabartī's History of Egypt* (Stuttgart: Franz Steiner, 1994).

Jacobs, Wouter et. Al., 'Rotterdam as a World Port City', *Port Planning, Design and construction*, 65 (2015), pp. 78–80.

al-Jamal, Shawqī, 'Wilāyat al-Ḥabash al-ʿuthmāniyya bayn Iyālat Jidda, wa-l-idāra al-miṣriyya (1881–1885)', *al-Dāra*, 22 (1417/1996), pp. 178–202.

Jarman, R. L. (ed.), *The Jedda Diaries 1919–1940:1928–1934*, Political Diaries of the Arab World: Saudi Arabia (Slough: Archive Editions, 1990), vols. 1–4.

al-Jifrī, Muḥammad Alī Ḥasan, *'Umar 'Abd Rabbuh: Ḥayyāt ... wa-sīra* (Jeddah: Maṭābi' Saḥar, 1438/2017).

Jomier, Jacques, *Le Maḥmal et la caravane égyptienne des pèlerins de la Mecque XIII.–XX. siècles*, Publications de l'Institut Français d'Archéologie Orientale Recherches d'Archéologie de Philologie et d'Histoire (Cairo: Imprimerie de l'Institut Français d'Archéologie Orientale, 1953).

Kābilī, Wahīb Aḥmad Fāḍil, *al-Ḥirafiyyūn fī madīnat Jidda: Fī 'l-qarn al-rābi' 'ashar al-hijrī*, 3rd edn. (s.n.: s.n., 1425/2004).

Kane, Eileen, *Russian Hajj: Empire and the Pilgrimage to Mecca* (Ithaca, NY: Cornell University Press, 2015).

Kant, Immanuel, *Zum ewigen Frieden: Ein philosophischer Entwurf* (Königsberg: Friedrich Nicolovius, 1795).

Kasım İzzeddin, *Hicaz'da Teşkilât ve Islahât-ı Sıhhiye ve 1330 Senesi Hacc-ı Şerifi: Hicaz Sıhhiye İdâresi, Senevi Rapor* (Istanbul: Matbaa-yi Amire, 1330/ 1911).

Kayali, Hasan, *Arabs and Young Turks: Turkish-Arab Relations in the Second Constitutional Period of the Ottoman Empire; 1908–1918* (Berkeley and London: University of California Press, 1988).

Kazimirski, Albert de Biberstein, *Dictionnaire Arabe-Français: Contenant toutes les racines de la langue Arabe, leurs dérivés ...* (Cairo: Imprimérie Khédivale, 1875).

Keane, T. F., *Six Months in the Hejaz: An Account of the Mohammedan Pilgrimage to Meccah and Medinah*, 2nd. edn. of Six Months in Mecca: An Account of the Mohammedan Pilgrimage to Meccah, London: Tinsley Brothers 1881. (London: Ward and Downey, 1887).

al-Khālid, Īnās bte Khalaf and al-Raḥḥāla, Muḥammad b. Sa'd, '*Qirā'at fī tārīkh anẓimat al-ḥajj wa-l-'umra fī ṣaḥīfat Umm al-Qurā*', Kursī al-Malik Salmān b. 'Abd al-'Azīz (1436/2010).

al-Kholaif, Ali Ibrahim, 'The Hijaz Vilayet 1869–1908: The Sharifate, the Hajj, and the Bedouins of the Hijaz', PhD Thesis, University of Wisconsin (1986).

Khoury, Philip S., 'The Urban Notables Paradigm Revisited', *Revue des mondes musulmans et de la Méditerranée*, 55–6 (1990), pp. 215–30.

Urban Notables and Arab Nationalism: The Politics of Damascus 1860–1920 (Cambridge: Cambridge University Press, 1983).

Kirli, Cengiz, 'A Profile of the Labor Force in Early Nineteenth-Century Istanbul', *International Labor and Working-Class History*, 60 (2001), pp. 125–40.

'Coffeehouses: Public Opinion in the Nineteenth-Century Ottoman Empire' in A. Salvatore and D. F. Eickelman (eds.), *Public Islam and the Common Good,* Social, Economic, and Political Studies of the Middle East and Asia, vol. 95, (Leiden and Boston: Brill, 2004), pp. 75–97.

Kostiner, Joseph, *The Making of Saudi Arabia, 1916–1936: From Chieftaincy to Monarchical State*, Studies in Middle Eastern History (New York: Oxford University Press, 1993).

Krause, Rolf Friedrich, *Stadtgeographische Untersuchungen in der Altstadt von Djidda/Saudi-Arabien: Eine Dokumentation* (Bonn: Ferd. Dümmlers Verlag, 1991).

Kresse, Kai, 'Interrogating "Cosmopolitanism" in an Indian Ocean Setting: Thinking Through Mombasa on the Swahili Coast' in D. N. Maclean and S. K. Ahmed (eds.), *Cosmopolitanisms in Muslim Contexts: Perspectives from the Past, Exploring Muslim Contexts* (Edinburgh: Edinburgh University Press, 2012), pp. 31–50.

Kuneralp, Sinan, *Son Dönem Osmanlı Erkân ve Ricali: (1839–1922): Prosopografik Rehber* (Istanbul: İsis, 1999).

Kürchhoff, D., 'Alte und neue Handelslstraßen und Handelsmittelpunkte an den afrikanischen Küsten des Roten Meeres und des Golfes von Aden, sowie in deren Hinterländern', *Geographische Zeitschrift*, 14 (1908), pp. 251–67.

La Rue, George Michael, 'Seeking Freedom in Multiple Contexts: An Enslaved Sudanese Woman's Life Trajectory, ca. 1800–1834', *Journal of Global Slavery*, 2 (2017), pp. 11–43.

Labib, Subhi Y., *Handelsgeschichte Ägyptens im Spätmittelalter (1171–1517)* (Wiesbaden: Franz Steiner, 1965).

Lafi, Nora, *Esprit civique et organisation citadine dans l'Empire ottoman (XVe–XXe siècles)*, The Ottoman Empire and its Heritage (Leiden and Boston: Brill, 2018), vol. 64.

Une ville du Maghreb entre ancien régime et réformes ottomanes: Genèse des institutions municipales à Tripoli de Barbarie (1795–1911), Villes, histoire, culture, société Nouvelle série (Paris: L'Harmattan, 2002).

Lange, Katharina, 'Histories of the Wulda: An Ethnographic-Historical Approach to Tribal Identity and Belonging in Syria, 19th–21st century', Habilitation, University of Leipzig (2017).

Lawson, Fred Haley, *The Social Origins of Egyptian Expansionism during the Muhammad Ali Period* (New York: Columbia University Press, 1992).

Le Chatelier, Alfred, *Les confréries musulmanes du Hedjaz* (Paris: Ernest Leroux, 1887).

Lefebvre, Henri, *The Production of Space* (Malden, MA, Oxford, and Carlton-Melbourn: Blackwell Publishing, 1991).

Leichtman, Mara and Schulz, Dorothea, 'Introduction to Special Issue: Muslim Cosmopolitanism: Movement, Identity, and Contemporary Reconfigurations', *City & Society*, 24 (2012), pp. 1–6.

Levi, Giovanni, 'On Microhistory' in P. Burke (ed.), *New Perspectives on Historical Writing* (Cambridge: Polity Press, 1991), pp. 93–113.

Lévy, Noémi, 'Une institution en formation: La police ottomane à l'époque d'Abdülhamid II', *European Journal of Turkish Studies. Social Sciences on Contemporary Turkey*, 8 (2008).

Lewis, Bernard, 'Baladiyya' in P. J. Bearman, T. Bianquis, C. E. Bosworth, E. J. van Donzel and W. P. Heinrichs (eds.), *Encyclopaedia of Islam*, 2nd edn., 12 vols. (Leiden: Brill, 1960–2005). dx.doi.org/10.1163/1573-3912_islam_COM_0095 (accessed October 7, 2019).

Limbert, Mandana, 'Marriage, Status and the Politics of Nationality in Oman' in A. Alsharekh (ed.), *The Gulf Family: Kinship Policies and Modernity* (London: Saqi Books, 2007), pp. 167–79.

Long, David Edwin, *The Hajj Today: A Survey of the Contemporary Pilgrimage to Makkah* (Albany: State University of New York Press, 1979).

Low, Michael Christopher, 'Empire and the Hajj: Pilgrims, Plagues, and Pan-Islam under British Surveillance, 1865–1908', *International Journal of Middle East Studies*, 40 (2008), pp. 269–90.

'Ottoman Infrastructures of the Saudi Hydro-State: The Technopolitics of Pilgrimage and Potable Water in the Hijaz', *Comparative Studies in Society and History*, 57 (2015), pp. 942–74.

'The Mechanics of Mecca: The Technopolitics of the Late Ottoman Hijaz and the Colonial Hajj', PhD Thesis, Columbia University (2015).

'The "Twin Infection": Pilgrims, Plagues, and Pan-Islam under British Surveillance, 1865–1924', Paper at Graduate Conference: Crossing Boundaries, Spanning Regions: Movements of People, Goods and Ideas, 10 March, 2006.

Maclean, D. N. and Ahmed, S. K. (eds.), *Cosmopolitanisms in Muslim Contexts: Perspectives from the Past*, Exploring Muslim Contexts (Edinburgh: Edinburgh University Press, 2012).

Maghribī, Muḥammad ʿAlī, *Aʿlām al-Ḥijāz*, 2nd edn., 4 vol. (1st edn. of vol. 4) (Jeddah: Maṭābiʿ Dār al-Bilād, 1405/1985).

Maḥmūd, Aḥmad Muḥammad, *Riḥalāt al-ḥajj*, Jamharat al-Riḥalāt, 3 vols. (Jeddah: al-Maṭbaʿa al-Maḥmūdiyya, 1430/2009).

Maḥmūd Y., *Sīrat al-muʾarrikh ʿAbd al-Quddūs al-Anṣārī wa-ahamm injāzātuh*. www.almrsal.com/post/288338 (January 04, 2019).

Manāʿ, ʿAbdallāh, *Baʿḍ al-ayyām baʿḍ al-layālī: Aṭrāf min qiṣṣat ḥayyātī*, 2nd edn. (Jeddah: Dār al-Funūn, 2009).

Tārīkh mā lam yu'arrakh: Jidda, al-insān wa-l-makān (Jeddah: Dār al-Marsā, 2011/1432).

Maneval, Stefan, 'The Architecture of Everyday Life in Twentieth Century Jiddah', PhD Thesis, Freie Universität Berlin (2015).

al-Manqarī, Muḥammad, *'Abd al-Majīd 'Alī al-Shubukshī: Rajul al-amn wa-l-ṣaḥāfa wa-l-adab* (Jeddah: Maktab al-A'māl al-Thaqāfiyya, 1432 h./2010).

Mansī, 'Abdallāh Sarrāj 'Umar, *Jidda fī 'l-tārikh al-ḥadīth min 923 H. ilā 1344 H./1517 M. ilā 1926 M.* (n.p., 2015).

Mantran, Robert, 'Ḥisba – Ottoman Empire' in P. J. Bearman, T. Bianquis, C. E. Bosworth, E. J. van Donzel and W. P. Heinrichs (eds.), *Encyclopaedia of Islam*, 2nd edn., 12 vols. (Leiden: Brill, 1960–2005). dx.doi.org/10.1163/1573-3912_islam_COM_0293 (accessed October 7, 2919).

Ma'rūfughlū, Sinān, *Najd wa-l-Ḥijāz fī 'l-wathā'iq al-'uthmāniyya* (London: Dār al-Sāqī, 2002).

Massicard, Élise, 'The Incomplete Civil Servant?: The Figure of the Neighbourhood Headman (Muhtar)' in M. Aymes, B. Gourisse and Élise Massicard (eds.), *Order and Compromise: Government Practices in Turkey from the Late Ottoman Empire to the Early 21st Century*, Social, Economic, and Political Studies of the Middle East and Asia (Leiden: Brill, 2015), pp. 256–90.

Matthiesen, Toby, 'Centre–Periphery Relations and the Emergence of a Public Sphere in Saudi Arabia: The Municipal Elections in the Eastern Province, 1954–1960', *British Journal of Middle Eastern Studies*, 42 (2014), pp. 1–19.

Mauss, Marcel, *Die Gabe: Form und Funktion des Austauschs in archaischen Gesellschaften,* Suhrkamp-Taschenbuch Wissenschaft, 1st edn. (Frankfurt am Main: Suhrkamp, 1968), vol. 743.

McGregor, Richard J., 'Grave Visitation/ Worship' in K. Fleet, G. Krämer, D. Matringe, J. Nawas and E. K. Rowson (eds.), *Encyclopaedia of Islam*, 3rd edn. (Leiden: Brill, 2007). dx.doi.org/10.1163/1573-3912_ei3_COM_27519 (accessed April 19, 2018).

Medick, Hans, 'Turning Global?: Microhistory in Extension', *Historische Anthropologie*, 24 (2016), pp. 241–52.

Mehmed Şakir, *Hicaz'ın ahvâl-i umûmiye-i sıhhiye ve ıslahât-ı hazırasına dair bazı müşahedat ve mülahazât-ı bendeğami hâvi bir layiha-i tıbbiye* (Constantinople, 1303/1890).

Meneley, Anne, *Tournaments of Value: Sociability and Hierarchy in a Yemeni Town*, Anthropological Horizons (Toronto and London: University of Toronto Press, 1996), vol. 9.

Mermier, Franck, *Le cheikh de la nuit: Sanaa; Organisation des souks et société citadine*, Bibliothèque Arabe Collection Hommes et Sociétés (Arles and Paris: Actes Sud; Sindbad, 1997).

Miers, Suzanne, 'Diplomacy versus Humanitarianism: Britain and Consular Manumission in Hijaz 1921–1936', *Slavery & Abolition*, 10 (1989), pp. 102–28.

'Slavery and the Slave Trade in Saudi Arabia and the Arab States on the Persian Gulf, 1925–63' in G. Campbell (ed.), *Abolition and Its Aftermath in Indian Ocean Africa and Asia*, Studies in Slave and Post-Slave Societies and Cultures (London and New York: Routledge, 2005), pp. 120–36.

Miller, Michael B., 'Pilgrims' Progress: The Business of the Hajj', *Past and Present*, 191 (2006), pp. 189–228.

Minawi, Mostafa, *The Ottoman Scramble for Africa: Empire and Diplomacy in the Sahara and the Hijaz* (Stanford, CA: Stanford University Press, 2016).

Miran, Jonathan, 'Endowing Property and Edifying Power in a Red Sea Port: Waqf, Arab Migrant Entrepreneurs, and Urban Authority in Massawa, 1860s–1880s', *The International Journal of African Historical Studies*, 42 (2009), pp. 151–78.

'From Bondage to Freedom on the Red Sea Coast: Manumitted Slaves in Egyptian Massawa, 1873.1885', *Slavery & Abolition*, 34 (2013), pp. 135–57.

Red Sea Citizens: Cosmopolitan Society and Cultural Change in Massawa (Bloomington: Indiana University Press, 2009).

'Red Sea Translocals: Hadrami Migration, Entrepreneurship, and Strategies of Integration in Eritrea, 1840s–1970s', *Northeast African Studies*, 12 (2012), pp. 129–67.

'The Red Sea' in D. Armitage, A. Bashford and S. Sivasundaram (eds.), *Oceanic Histories*, Cambridge Oceanic Histories (Cambridge, New York, Melbourne, Delhi, and Singapore: Cambridge University Press, 2018), pp. 156–81.

Miran, Jonathan and Layish, Aharon, 'The Testamentary *Waqf* as an Instrument of Elite Consolidation in Early Twentieth-Century Massawa (Eritrea)', *Islamic Law and Society*, 25 (2018), pp. 78–120.

Mishra, Saurabh, *Pilgrimage, Politics, and Pestilence: The Haj from the Indian Subcontinent, 1860–1920* (Oxford: Oxford University Press, 2011).

al-Muʿabbadī, Mubārak Muḥammad, *al-Nashāṭ al-tijārī li-mināʾ Jidda khilāla 'l-ḥukm al-ʿuthmānī al-thānī 1256 h./ 1840 m.–1335 h./1916 m.* (Jeddah: al-Nādī al-Adabī al-Thaqāfī bi-Jidda, 1993).

al-Muhaimid, Yusuf, *Wolves of the Crescent Moon: A Novel* (New York: Penguin Books, 2007).

Muḥammad, Wahīṃ Ṭālib, *Tārīkh al-Ḥijāz al-siyāsī 1916–1925* (Beirut: al-Dār al-ʿArabiyya li-l-Mawsūʿāt, 1427/2007).
Munt, T. H. R., *The Holy City of Medina: Sacred Space in Early Islamic Arabia*, Cambridge Studies in Islamic Civilization (New York: Cambridge University Press, 2014).
Musil, Alois, *Zur Zeitgeschichte von Arabien* (Wien and Leipzig: Manz Verlag, Verlag S. Hirzel, 1918).
Nallino, Carlo Alfonso, *Raccolta di Scritti Editi e Inediti, Pubblicazioni dell'Istituto per l'Oriente* (Rome: Istituto per l'Oriente, 1939).
al-Naqar, ʿUmar, 'Takrūr: The History of a Name', *Journal of African History*, 10 (1969), pp. 365–74.
Naṣīf, Ḥusayn Muḥammad, *Māḍī 'l-Ḥijāz wa-ḥāḍiruhu* ([s.n.], 1349/1930).
Naṣīf, Muḥammad Ḥusayn, 'Min azamāt al-māʾ fī Jidda', *al-Manhal*, 28 (1967), pp. 484–5.
Nasr, Ahmad A. and Bagader, Abu Bakar A., 'Al-Gēs: Women's Festival and Drama in Mecca', *Journal of Folklore Research*, 38 (2001), pp. 243–62.
Neill, William J.V., *Urban Planning and Cultural Identity* (Abingdon: Routledge, 2004).
Niebuhr, Carsten, *Reisebeschreibung nach Arabien und andern umliegenden Ländern* (Zürich: Manesse, 1992/1774).
Travels through Arabia and Other Countries in the East (Edinburgh: R. Morison and Son, 1792).
al-Nimr, Muḥammad b. ʿAbdallāh b. Hāshim, *Ḥārat al-Baḥr: Mawṭin al-ābāʾ wa-l-ajdād* (Jeddah: Dār Manṣūr al-Zāmil, 1438/2016–17).
Nippa, Annegret, Herbstreuth, Peter and Burchardt, Hermann, *Unterwegs am Golf: Von Basra nach Maskat, Photographien von Hermann Burchardt* (Berlin: Schiler, 2006).
Norris, J. A., 'Second Anglo-Afghan War (1878–80)' in E. Yar-Shater (ed.), *Encyclopædia Iranica* (New York: Columbia University Center for Iranian Studies, 1996). www.iranicaonline.org/articles/anglo-afghan-wars (accessed December 29, 2017).
Nowicka, Magdalena and Vertovec, Steven, 'Comparing Convivialities: Dreams and Realities of Living-with-Difference', *European Journal of Cultural Studies*, 17 (2014), pp. 341–56.
Numan, Nurtāç, 'The Emirs of Mecca and the Ottoman Government of Hijaz, 1840–1908', License Thesis, Boğaziçi Üniversitesi (2006).
Nūrwalī, Muḥammad Ṭāhir ʿAbd al-Raḥmānʿ Abd al-Qādir, *Ṣafaḥāt mūjaza min al-sīra al-mushriqa li-jaddinā ʿAbd al-Qādir Nūrwalī* (Jidda, 1431/2009).
Ochsenwald, William L., 'Islam and Loyalty in the Saudi Hijaz, 1926–1939', *Die Welt des Islams*, 47 (2007), pp. 7–32.
Religion, Society, and the State in Arabia: The Hijaz under Ottoman Control, 1840–1908 (Columbus: Ohio State University Press, 1984).

'The Commercial History of the Hijaz Vilayet, 1840–1908', *Arabian Studies*, 6 (1982), pp. 57–76.

'The Financial Basis of Ottoman Rule in the Hijaz, 1840–1877' in W. W. Haddad and W. L. Ochsenwald (eds.), *Nationalism in a Non-National State: The Dissolution of the Ottoman Empire* (Columbus: Ohio State University Press, 1977), pp. 129–49.

'The Jidda Massacre', *Middle Eastern Studies*, 13 (1977), pp. 314–26.

O'Fahey, Rex S., *Enigmatic Saint: Ahmad Ibn Idris and the Idrisi Tradition* (London: Hurst, 1990).

O'Fahey, Rex S. and Radtke, Bernd, 'Neo-Sufism Reconsidered', *Der Islam*, 70 (1993), pp. 52–87.

Onley, James, *The Arabian Frontier of the British Raj: Merchants, Rulers, and the British in the Nineteenth-Century Gulf* (New York: Oxford University Press, 2007).

'Transnational Merchant Families in the Nineteenth- and Twentieth-Century Gulf' in M. al-Rasheed (ed.), *Transnational Connections and the Arab Gulf* (London: Routledge, 2005), pp. 59–89.

Örs, İlay Romain, *Diaspora of the City: Stories of Cosmopolitanism from Istanbul and Athens*, Palgrave Studies in Urban Anthropology (New York: Palgrave Macmillan, 2016).

Ortaylı, İlber, *Studies on Ottoman Transformation, Analecta Isisiana* (Istanbul: Isis Press, 1994), vol. 10.

Osmanoğlu, Ahmed Emin, 'Hicaz Eyaletinin Teşekkülü (1841–1864)', MA Thesis, Marmara University (2004).

Özbek, Nadir, '"Beggars' and 'Vagrants" in Ottoman State Policy and Public Discourse, 1875–1914', *Middle Eastern Studies*, 45 (2009), pp. 783–801.

Özcan, Azmi, *Pan-Islamism: Indian Muslims, the Ottomans and Britain 1877–1924*, The Ottoman Empire and Its Heritage (Leiden: Brill, 1997), vol. 12.

Panzac, D. (ed.), *Les Villes dans l'Empire Ottoman: Activités et Sociétés 1*, Société Arabes et Musulmanes (Paris: Ed. du CNRS, 1991), vol. 5.

Les Villes dans l'Empire Ottoman: Activités et Sociétés 2, Société Arabes et Musulmanes (Paris: Ed. du CNRS, 1994), vol. 9.

Parolin, Gianluca Paolo, *Citizenship in the Arab World: Kin, Religion and Nation-State*, IMISCOE Research (Amsterdam: Amsterdam University Press, 2009).

Peacock, Andrew, 'Jeddah and the India Trade in the Sixteenth Century: Arabian Context and Imperial Policy' in D. Agius, E. Khalil, E. Scerri and A. Williams (eds.), *Human Interactions with the Environment in the Red Sea: Selected Papers of Red Sea Project VI* (Leiden: Brill, 2017), pp. 290–322.

'Suakin: A Northeast African Port in the Ottoman Empire', *Northeast African Studies*, 12 (2012), pp. 29–50.

Pearson, Michael Naylor, *The Indian Ocean,* Seas in History (London and New York: Routledge, 2003).

Pernau, Margrit, 'Shifting Globalities – Changing Headgear: The Indian Muslims Between Turban, Hat and Fez' in U. Freitag and A. v. Oppen (eds.), *Translocality: The Study of Globalising Processes from a Southern Perspective, Studies in Global Social History* (Leiden and Boston: Brill, 2010), pp. 249–67.

Pesce, Angelo, *Jiddah: Portrait of an Arabian City*, rev. edn. (London: Falcon Press, 1977).

Peskes, Esther, *Muḥammad B. ʿAbdalwahhāb (1703–92) im Widerstreit: Untersuchungen zur Rekonstruktion der Frühgeschichte der Wahhābīya*, Beiruter Texte und Studien (Stuttgart: Steiner, 1993), vol. 56.

Peters, F. E., *Jerusalem and Mecca: The Typology of the Holy City in the Near East*, New York University Studies in Near Eastern Civilization (New York: New York University Press, 1986), vol. 11.

Peters, R. et al., 'Waḳf' in P. J. Bearman, T. Bianquis, C. E. Bosworth, E. J. van Donzel and W. P. Heinrichs (eds.), *Encyclopaedia of Islam*, 2nd edn., 12 vols. (Leiden: Brill, 1960–2005). dx.doi.org/10.1163/1573-3912_islam_COM_1333 (accessed January 02, 2019).

Pétriat, Philippe, 'For Pilgrims and for Trade: Merchants and Public Works in Ottoman Jeddah', *Turkish Historical Review*, 5 (2014), pp. 200–20.

Le Négoce des Lieux Saints: Négociants Hadramis de Djedda, 1850–1950, Bibliothèqe Historique des Pays d'Islam (Paris: Publications de la Sorbonne, 2016), vol. 9.

'Les Grandes Familles Marchandes Hadramies de Djedda, 1850–1950', PhD Thesis, Université Paris 1 (2013).

Pétriat, Philippe (ed.), *Une Histoire Partagée. Sources Françaises sur l'Histoire de l'Arabie: Hedjaz et Najd 1839–1943* (2014).

Pollock, Sheldon, 'Cosmopolitan and Vernacular in History', *Public Culture*, 12 (2000), pp. 591–625.

Pollock, Sheldon, Bhaba, Homi K., Breckenridge, Carol A. and Chakrabarty, Dipesh, 'Cosmopolitanisms', *Public Culture*, 12 (2000), pp. 577–89.

Power, Timothy, 'The Red Sea under Caliphal Dynasties, c. 639–1171', *History Compass*, 16 (2018).

Prange, Sebastian R., *Monsoon Islam: Trade and Faith on the Medieval Malabar Coast*, Cambridge Oceanic Histories (Cambridge: Cambridge University Press, 2018).

Prätor, Sabine, *Der arabische Faktor in der jungtürkischen Politik: Eine Studie zum osmanischen Parlament der II. Konstitution (1908 – 1918)*, Islamkundliche Untersuchungen (Berlin: Schwarz, 1993), vol. 170.

Pritzkat, Thomas, *Stadtentwicklung und Migration im Südjemen: Mukalla und die hadhramitische Auslandsgemeinschaft*, Jemen-Studien (Wiesbaden: Reichert, 2001), vol. 16.

Prokop, Michaela, 'Saudi Arabia: The Politics of Education', *International Affairs*, 79 (2003), pp. 77–89.

Provence, Michael, *The Last Ottoman Generation and the Making of the Modern Middle East* (Cambridge: Cambridge University Press, 2017).

al-Qashʿamī, Muḥammad ʿAbd al-Razzāz, *Muḥammad Ṣāliḥ Naṣīf: al-rāʾid al-ṣahafī* (Jeddah: al-Nādī al-Adabī al-Thaqāfī bi-Jidda, 2010).

Qazzāz, Ḥasan ʿAbd al-Ḥayy, *Ahl al-Ḥijāz bi-ʿabqihim al-tārīkhī* (Medina: Maṭābiʿal-Madīna li-l-Ṣaḥāfa, 1415/1995–6).

Quataert, Donald, 'Labor History and the Ottoman Empire, c. 1700–1922', *International Labor and Working-Class History*, 60 (2001), pp. 93–109.

al-Qurashī al-Hāshimī, Jārallāh Muḥammad b. Fahd, *Faḍl Jidda wa-aḥwāluhā wa-qurbuhā min Makka: Li-l-ʿallāma al-Shaykh Jārallāh Muḥammad b. Fahd al-Qurashī al-Hāshimī al-mutawaffī sanat 554 H.* (Jeddah, 1433/2012–13).

Rafeq, Abdul-Karim, 'Ownership of Real Property by Foreigners in Syria, 1869–1873' in R. Owen and M. P. Bunton (eds.), *New Perspectives on Property and Land in the Middle East, Harvard Middle Eastern Monographs* (Cambridge, MA: Harvard University Press, 2000), pp. 175–239.

Raqqām, Muḥammad Darwīsh, *Jidda: Ḥikāyāt min al-zaman al-jamīl* (Jeddah: al-ʿĀmāl al-Thaqāfiyya, 1436/2014–15).

al-Rasheed, Madawi, *A History of Saudi Arabia* (New York: Cambridge University Press, 2002).

Rathjens, Carl and Wissmann, Hermann von, 'Landschaftskundliche Beobachtungen im südlichen Hedjaz', *Erdkunde: Archiv für wissenschaftliche Geographie*, 1 (1947), pp. 61–89, 200–5.

Raymond, André, 'A Divided Sea: The Cairo Coffee Trade in the Red Sea Area during the Seventeenth and Eighteenth Centuries' in L. Fawaz and C. Bayly (eds.), *Modernity and Culture: From the Mediterranean to the Indian Ocean* (New York: Columbia University Press, 2002), pp. 46–57.

Artisans et commerçants au Caire au XVIIIe siècle (Damas: Institut Français de Damas, 1973–4).

'The Spatial Organization of the City' in S. K. Jayyusi, R. Holod, A. Petruccioli and A. Raymond (eds.), *The City in the Islamic World* (Leiden and Boston: Brill, 2008), vol. 1, pp. 47–70.

'Une liste des corporations de métiers au Caire en 1801', *Arabica*, 4 (1957), pp. 150–63.

Reese, Scott, *Imperial Muslims: Islam, Community and Authority in the Indian Ocean, 1839–1937* (Edinburgh: Edinburgh University Press, 2018).

Reid, Anthony, 'Habib Abdur-Rahman Az-Zahir (1833-1896)', *Indonesia*, 13 (1972), pp. 37–60.

Riḍwān, Maḥmūd, *Qālū ʿan Muḥammad ʿAlī Zaynal* (hectographed collection of articles and interviews, often without precise indication of sources) (n.d.).

Rifʿat, Ibrāhīm, *Mirʾāt al-Ḥaramayn: al-Riḥlāt al-ḥijāziyya wa-l-ḥajj wa-mashāʾiruhu al-dīniyya muḥallātan bi-miʾat al-ṣuwar al-shamsiyya*, 2 vols. (Cairo: Maṭbaʿat Dār al-Kutub, 1344/1925).

al-Rīḥānī, Amīn, *Mulūk al-ʿarab*, vol. 1 (Beirut: Maṭābiʿ Ṣādir Rīḥānī, 1951).

Roff, William, 'Sanitation and Security: The Imperial Powers and the Nineteenth Century Hajj', *Arabian Studies*, 6 (1982), pp. 143–60.

Rossi, Benedetta, 'Migration and Emancipation in West Africa's Labour History: The Missing Links', *Slavery & Abolition*, 35 (2014), pp. 23–46.

Rossi, Ettore, 'Arabia', *Oriente Moderno*, 11 (1931), pp. 189–92.

Oriente Moderno, 15 (1935), pp. 95–7.

Rossi, Ettore and U.F., 'Arabia', *Oriente Moderno* 11 (1931), pp. 156–7.

Rüppell, Eduard, *Reise in Abyssinien*, 2 vols + Atlas, vol. 1 (Frankfurt: Schmerber, 1838–40).

Reise in Nubien, Kordofan und dem peträischen Arabien vorzüglich in geographisch-statistischer Hinsicht (Frankfurt am Main: Friedrich Wilmans, 1829).

Ryad, Umar, 'Anti-Imperialism and the Pan-Islamic Movement' in D. Motadel (ed.), *Islam and the European Empires*, The Past & Present Book Series, 1st edn. (Oxford: Oxford University Press, 2014), pp. 131–49.

Ṣabbān, Suhayl, *Jidda fī wathāʾiq al-arshīf al-ʿuthmānī* (typescript, prepared as part of project of Encyclopedia of Jeddah) (n.d., 2005?).

Murāsalāt al-Bāb al-ʿĀlī ilā wilāyat al-Ḥijāz (Makka al-Mukarrama, al-Madīna al-Munawwara) fī 'l-fatra min 1283h ilā 1291h (Mecca: Mu'assasat al-Furqān li-l-Turāth al-Islāmī, 2004).

Ṣabbān, Suhayl (ed.), *Nuṣūṣ ʿuthmāniyya ʿan al-ʿawḍāʿ al-thaqāfiyya fī 'l-Ḥijāz: al-Awqāf, al-madāris, al-maktabāt* (Riyadh: Maktabat al-Malik ʿAbd al-ʿAziz al-ʿĀmma, 1422/2001).

Ṣabrī, Ayyūb, *Mirʾāt al-Ḥaramayn: A History of Mecca and Medina*, vol. 3 (s.l., 1886).

Ṣādiq Bāshā, Muḥammad, *al-Riḥlāt al-ḥijāziyya*, ed. Muḥammad Hammām Fikrī (Beirut: Badr li-l-Nashr wa-l-Tawzīʿ, 1999).

Sajdi, D. (ed.), *Ottoman Tulips, Ottoman Coffee: Leisure and Lifestyle in the Eighteenth Century* (London and New York: Tauris, 2007).

Salīm, Ḥasan ʿAbd al-Wahhāb Ḥusayn, 'al-Ṭawwāfa wa-l-muṭawwifūn fī 'l-ʿaṣr al-mamlūkī' in Kursī al-Malik Salmān (ed.), *al-Ṭawwāfa wa-l-muṭawwifūn: Iṣdār nadwat al-ṭawwāfa wa-l-muṭawwifīn*, 3 vols. (Riyadh, 2017), vol. 1, pp. 245–70.

Samin, Nadav, *Of Sand or Soil*, Princeton Studies in Muslim Politics (Princeton: Princeton University Press, 2015).

'Our Ancestors, Our Heroes: Saudi Tribal Campaigns to Suppress Historical Docudramas', *British Journal of Middle Eastern Studies*, 41 (2014), pp. 266–86.

Saraçoğlu, M. Safa, 'Economic Interventionism, Islamic Law and Provincial Government in the Ottoman Enmpire', *Journal of the Ottoman and Turkish Studies Association*, 2 (2015), pp. 59–84.

Sarıyıldız, Gülden, *Hicaz karantina teşkilâtı (1865–1914)* (Ankara: Türk Tarih Kurumu Basımevi, 1996).

Saßmannshausen, Christian, 'Reform in Translation: Family, Distinction, and Social Mediation in Late Ottoman Tripoli', PhD Thesis, Freie Universität Berlin (2012).

Savignac, Raphaël, 'Carnet de guerre de 1914–1918: Épisode de son voyage au Hedjaz, comme officier de renseingement dans la marine' (1917). Unpubl. manuscript, transcribed by Jean-Michel de Tarragon, École biblique et archéologique française de Jérusalem.

Sawaf, Zina, 'Encountering the State: Women and Intimate Lives in Riyadh, Saudi Arabia', PhD Thesis, Graduate Institute of International and Development Studies (2017).

Sayyid, Yūsuf al- Saʿātī and Amīn, Bā ʿĪsā Ṣāliḥ, *Nādī al-Ittiḥād: Iṣdār khāṣṣ bi-munāsabat murūr tisʿīna ʿāman ʿalā al-taʾsīs* (Jeddah: Mansour Al Zamil, 1438/2017).

Schatkowski-Schilcher, Linda, *Families in Politics: Damascene Factions and Estates of the 18th and 19th Centuries* (Stuttgart: Franz Steiner, 1985).

Schienerl, Jutta, *Der Weg in den Orient: Der Forscher Ulrich Jasper Seetzen: Von Jever in den Jemen (1802–1811)*, Schriftenreihe des Staatlichen Museums für Naturkunde und Vorgeschichte (Oldenburg: Isensee Florian GmbH, 2000).

Schull, Kent F., *Prisons in the Late Ottoman Empire: Microcosms of Modernity* (Edinburgh: Edinburgh University Press, 2014).

Sedgwick, Mark J. R., 'Saudi Sufis: Compromise in the Hijaz, 1925–40', *Die Welt des Islams*, 37 (1997),pp. 349–68.

Seetzen, Ulrich Jasper, 'Auszug aus einem Briefe des Kaiserl. Russ. Collegienassessors Herrn Dr. Seetzen an Herrn von Hammer aus Mocha den 14. November 1810', *Fundgruben des Orients*, 2 (1811), pp. 275–84.

'Auszug aus einem Schreiben dess Russ. Kais. Kammer-Assessors Dr. U. J. Seetzen', *Monatliche Correspondence zur Beförderung der Erd- und Himmelkunde*, 27 (1813).

Serjeant, Robert B., 'Ḥaram and Ḥawṭah, the Sacred Enclave in Arabia' in R. B. Serjeant (ed.), *Arabian History and Civilisation* (Aldershot, Burlington USA, Singapore, and Sydney: Ashgate Variorum Reprints, 1981).

al-Shāfiʿī, ʿAbd al-Qādir b. Aḥmad b. Muḥammad b. Faraj, *Bride of the Red Sea: A 10th/16th Century Account of Jeddah*, Translation of: al-Silāḥ wa-l-ʿuddah fī tārīkh bandar Judda, Occasional Papers Series (University of Durham, 1984), vol. 22.

al-Shaʿfī, Muḥammad b. Saʿīd, *al-Tijāra al-khārijiyya li-madīnat Jidda fī 'l-ʿahd al-ʿuthmānī 1840/ 1916* (Riyadh, 1428/2007).

al-Shāmikh, Muḥammad ʿAbd al-Raḥmān, *Nashʾat al-ṣiḥāfa fī 'l-Mamlaka al-ʿArabiyya al-Saʿūdiyya* (n.p.: Dār al-ʿUlūm li-l-Tibāʿa wa-l-Nashr, 1982).

Sharif, Malik, *Imperial Norms and Local Realities: The Ottoman Municipal Laws and the Municipality of Beirut (1860–1908)*, Beiruter Texte und Studien (Beirut and Würzburg: in Commission at Ergon Verlag, 2014), vol. 105.

al-Sharīf, ʿAbdallāh Farrāj, *Dhikrayāt Muḥammad Darwīsh Raqqām: Jidda dākhil al-sūr* (Jeddah: al-Maṭbaʿa al-Maḥmūdiyya, 2013).

al-Sharif, Manal, *Losfahren* (Zürich: Secession Verlag, 2017).

al-Shāṭirī, Sālim b. ʿAbdallāh b. ʿUmar, *Risāla mukhtaṣira fī tārīkh qabīlat Āl Bin Lādin* (Tarīm, 2011).

Shaw, Stanford Jay and Shaw, Ezel Kural, *History of the Ottoman Empire and Modern Turkey: Volume 2: Reform, Revolution, and Republic: the Rise of Modern Turkey, 1808–1975* (Cambridge: Cambridge University Press, 1977).

al-Shibīlī, ʿAbd al-Raḥmān, 'Min usra rāʾida fī 'l-tijāra wa-l-shūrā wa-l-siyāsa wa-l-tarḥāl', al-Sharq, Dhū 'l-Qaʿida 1425/December 2004.

Shinde, Kiran A., 'Entrepreneurship and Indigenous Enterpreneurs in Religious Tourism in India', *International Journal of Tourism Research*, 12 (2010), pp. 523–35.

Shryock, Andrew, 'The New Jordanian Hospitality: House, Host, and Guest in the Culture of Public Display', *Comparative Studies in Society and History*, 46 (2004), pp. 35–62.

al-Sibāʿī, Aḥmad, *Tārīkh Makka*, 2 vols. (Mecca: Maktabat Iḥyāʾ al-Turāth al-Islāmī, 1999).

Siddiqui, Mona, *Hospitality and Islam: Welcoming in God's Name* (New Haven, CT and London: Yale University Press, 2015).

Sijeeni, Tariq A., 'Contemporary Arabian City: Muslim *Ummah* in Sociocultural and Urban Design Context', PhD Thesis, University of Michigan (1995).

Sikandar Begum (Nawab of Bhopal), *A Princess's Pilgrimage*, Siobhan Lambert-Hurley (ed.) (Bloomington: Indiana University Press, 2008).

Singha, Radhika, 'Passport, Ticket, and India-Rubber Stamp: "The Problem of the Pauper Pilgrim" in Colonial India c. 1882–1925' in A. Tambe and H. Fischer-Tiné (eds.), *The Limits of British Colonial Control in South*

Asia: Spaces of Discorder in the Indian Ocean Region, Routledge Studies in the Modern History of Asia (London: Routledge, 2009), pp. 49–83.

Sivasundaram, Sujit, Bashford, Alison and Armitage, David, 'Introduction' in D. Armitage, A. Bashford and S. Sivasundaram (eds.), *Oceanic Histories,* Cambridge Oceanic Histories (Cambridge: Cambridge University Press, 2018), pp. 1–28.

Slight, John, 'British Colonial Knowledge and the Hajj in the Age of Empire' in U. Ryad (ed.), *The Hajj and Europe in the Age of Empire*, Leiden Studies in Islam & Society (Leiden and Boston: Brill, 2017), pp. 80–111.

The British Empire and the Hajj: 1865–1956 (Cambridge: Harvard University Press, 2015).

Snouck Hurgronje, Christiaan, *Mekka: Aus dem Heutigen Leben*, 2 vols. (The Hague: Martinus Nijhoff, 1888–9), vol. 2.

Mekka: Die Stadt und Ihre Herren, 2 vols. (The Hague: Martinus Nijhoff, 1888–9), vol. 1.

'Some of My Experiences with the Muftis of Mecca', *Jaarsverslagen, Oostersch Instituut Leiden*, 4 (1941), pp. 2–16.

Verspreide Geschriften vol. 3, (Bonn and Leipzig: Schroeder, 1924).

Sobe, Noah W., 'Rethinking 'Cosmopolitanism' as an Analytic for the Comparative Study of Globalization & Education', *Current Issues in Comparative Education*, 12 (2009), pp. I–XX.

Sobh, Rana, Belk, Russel W. and Wilson, Jonathan A. J., 'Islamic Arab Hospitality and Multiculturalism', *Marketing Theory*, 13 (2013), pp. 443–63.

Somel, Selçuk Akşin, 'Osman Nuri Paşa'nın 17 temmuz 1885 tarihli Hicaz raporu', *Ankara Üniversitesi Dil ve Tarih-Coğrafya Fakültesi Tarih Bölümü Tarih Araştırmaları Dergisi*, 18/29 (1996), pp. 1–38.

Soubhy, Saleh, *Pèlerinage à la Mecque* (Le Caire: Imprimerie Nationale, 1894).

Stausberg, Michael, 'Religion and Spirituality in Tourism' in A. A. Lew, C. M. Hall and A. M. Williams (eds.), *The Wiley Blackwell Companion to Tourism* (Hoboken: Wiley-Blackwell, 2014), pp. 349–60. onlinelibrary.wiley.com/doi/full/10.1002/9781118474648.ch28.

Steinberg, Guido, *Religion und Staat in Saudi-Arabien: Die Wahhabitischen Gelehrten 1902–1953* (Würzburg: Ergon, 2002).

Steppat, Fritz, 'Eine Bewegung unter den Notabeln Syriens 1877–78: Neues Licht auf die Entstehung des arabischen Nationalismus', *Zeitschrift der Deutschen Morgenländischen Gesellschaft* Supp. 1, XVII. (Deutscher Orientalistentag Würzburg, 1968 [part 2:1969]), pp. 631–49.

Stratkötter, Rita, *Von Kairo nach Mekka: Sozial- und Wirtschaftsgeschichte der Pilgerfahrt nach den Berichten des Ibrāhīm Rif'at Bāšā: Mir'āt al-Ḥaramain*, Islamkundliche Untersuchungen (Berlin: Klaus Schwarz, 1991), vol. 145.

al-Surayḥī, Sa'īd, *al-Ruways* (Beirut: Jadāwil, 2013).

Tamisier, Maurice, *Voyage en Arabie*, Reproduction of the Paris Edition of 1840 (Graz: Akademische Druck- und Verlagsanstalt, 1840/1976).

Tauber, Eliezer, *The Arab Movements in World War I* (London and Portland, OR: Frank Cass, 1993).

Teitelbaum, Joshua, *The Rise and Fall of the Hashimite Kingdom of Arabia*, (London: Hurst & Company, 2001).

al-Thaqafī, 'Abdallāh b. Zāhid, *al-'Imāra bi-madīnat Jidda fī 'l-'aṣr al-'uthmānī 923–1334 h./1517–1916*, 2 vols. (Riyadh: Dārat al-Malik 'Abd al-'Aziz, 1436/2010).

Thielmann, Jörn, 'Ḥisba (Modern Times)' in K. Fleet, G. Krämer, D. Matringe, J. Nawas and E. K. Rowson (eds.), *Encyclopaedia of Islam*, 3rd edn. (Leiden: Brill, 2007). dx.doi.org/10.1163/1573-3912_ei3_COM_30485 (accessed July 03, 2018).

Thompson, Mark, 'Assessing the Impact of Saudi Arabia's National Dialogue: The Controversial Case of the Cultural Discourse', *Journal of Arabian Studies*, 1 (2011), pp. 163–81.

Thos. Cook & Son, *The Mecca Pilgrimage: Appointment by the Government of India of Thos. Cook & Son* (London: n.d., 1893).

al-Thubaytī, 'Abdallāh b. 'Alī al-Raqīb, *Ḥiṣār Jidda min khilāl jarīdatay Umm al-Qurā wa-Barīd al-Ḥijāz* (Beirut: Jadāwil, 2015).

Tilly, Charles, 'Citizenship, Identity and Social History', *International Review of Social History*, 40 (1995), pp. 223–36.

Toksöz, Meltem, *Nomads, Migrants and Cotton in the Eastern Mediterranean: The Making of the Adana-Mersin Region 1850–1908* (Leiden: Brill, 2010).

Toledano, Ehud R., *As If Silent and Absent: Bonds of Enslavement in the Islamic Middle East* (New Haven, CT: Yale University Press, 2007).

Slavery and Abolition in the Ottoman Middle East (Seattle and London: Washington University Press, 1998).

The Ottoman Slave Trade and its Suppression: 1840–1890 (Princeton: Princeton University Press, 1982).

Ṭrābulsī, Muḥammad Yūsuf Muḥammad Ḥasan, *Jidda: Ḥikāyat madīna*, 2nd rev. edn. (1st edn. 2006) (Riyadh: Distributed by Maktabat Kunuz al-Marifa, 1429/2008).

Rā'idāt min ahālī Jidda (Al Madinah Printing & Publishing Co., 1439/2018).

Tresse, René, *Le pèlerinage syrien aux villes saintes de l'Islam* (Paris: Chaumette, 1937).
Tuchscherer, Michel, 'Activités des Turcs dans le commerce de la Mer Rouge au XVIIIe ^{s}Siècle' in D. Panzac (ed.), *Les Villes dans l'Empire Ottoman: Activités et sociétés 1, Société Arabes et Musulmanes* (Paris: Ed. du CNRS, 1991), pp. 321–64.
'Trade and Port Cities in the Red Sea: Gulf of Aden Region in the Sixteenth and Seventeenth Century' in L. Fawaz and C. Bayly (eds.), *Modernity and Culture: From the Mediterranean to the Indian Ocean* (New York: Columbia University Press, 2002), pp. 28–45.
al-Turkī, ʿĀyiḍ, *Mawsūʿat Jidda: Bawābat al-Ḥaramayn al-Sharīfayn* (Jeddah, 2012).
Turner, Victor, 'The Center out There: Pilgrim's Goal', *History of Religions*, 12 (1973), pp. 191–230.
Um, Nancy, 'Reflections on the Red Sea Style: Beyond the Surface of Coastal Architecture', *Northeast African Studies*, 12 (2012), pp. 243–72.
'Spatial Negotiations in a Commercial City: The Red Sea Port of Mocha, Yemen, during the First Half of the Eighteenth Century', *Journal of the Society of Architectural Historians*, 62 (2003), pp. 178–93.
The Merchant Houses of Mocha: Trade and Architecture in an Indian Ocean Port, Publications on the Near East (Seattle: University of Washington Press, 2009).
UNESCO, *At-Turaif District in ad-Dir'iyah.* whc.unesco.org/en/list/1329 (accessed July 24, 2018).
Historic Jeddah, the Gate to Makkah. whc.unesco.org/en/list/1361/ (accessed July 20, 2018).
van den Boogert, Maurits, *The Capitulations and the Ottoman Legal System: Qadis, Consuls, and Beratlıs in the 18th Century* (Leiden: Brill, 2005).
van der Meulen, Daniël, *The Wells of Ibn Sa'ud* (London: Murray, 1957).
van Leeuwen, Marco H.D., 'Guilds and Middle-Class Welfare, 1550–1800: Provisions for Burial, Sickness, Old Age, and Widowhood', *The Economic History Review*, 65 (2012), pp. 61–90.
Vassiliev, Alexei, *The History of Saudi Arabia* (London: Saqi Books, 2000).
Viscount Valentia, Earl of Mountnorris (Annesley, George), *Voyages and Travels to India, Ceylon, the Red Sea, Abyssinia, and Egypt in the Years 1802,1803,1804,1805, and 1806*, vol. 3 (London, 1809).
Wall, R., Hareven, T. K. and Ehmer, J. (eds.), *Family History Revisited: Comparative Perspectives*, The Family in Interdisciplinary Perspective (Newark, NJ: University of Delaware Press; Associated University Presses, 2001).

Walz, Terence, 'Sudanese, Habasha, Takarna, and Barabira: Trans-Saharan Africans in Cairo as Shown in the 1848 Census' in T. Walz and K. M. Cuno (eds.), *Race and Slavery in the Middle East: Histories of Trans-Saharan Africans in Nineteenth-Century Egypt, Sudan, and the Ottoman Mediterranean* (Cairo: The American University of Cairo Press, 2010), pp. 43–76.

al-Wardī, ʿAlī, *Qiṣṣat al-ashrāf wa-Ibn Saʿūd*, 3rd edn. (London: Alwarrak Publishing Ltd., 2007).

Weber, Stefan, *Damascus: Ottoman Modernity and Urban Transformation 1808–1918*, 2 vols. (Aarhus: Aarhus University Press, 2009).

Wellsted, J.R., 'Observations on the Coast of Arabia between Rás Mohammed and Jiddah', *Journal of the Royal Geographic Society*, 6 (1836), pp. 51–96.

Wensinck, A. J. and Marçais, Ph., "ʿĀshūrāʾ" in P. J. Bearman, T. Bianquis, C. E. Bosworth, E. J. van Donzel and W. P. Heinrichs (eds.), *Encyclopaedia of Islam*, 2nd edn., 12 vols. (Leiden: Brill, 1960–2005). dx.doi.org/10.1163/1573-3912_islam_COM_0068 (accessed March 29, 2018).

Werbner, Pnina, 'Vernacular Cosmopolitanism as an Ethical Disposition' in L. Baskins (ed.), *Islamic Studies in the Twenty-First Century: Transformations and Continuities* (Amsterdam: Amsterdam University Press, 2016), pp. 223–40.

Wick, Alexis, *The Red Sea: In Search of Lost Space* (Oakland, CA: University of California Press, 2016).

Wietschorke, Jens, 'So Tickt Berlin?: Städtische Eigenlogiken in der Diskussion', *Aus Politik und Zeitgeschichte*, 48 (2017), http://www.bpb.de/apuz/260056/so-tickt-berlin-staedtische-eigenlogiken-in-der-diskussion?p=all <8svvrddrf Frvrmnrt 11, 2019).

Willis, John M., 'Azad's Mecca: On the Limits of Indian Ocean Cosmopolitanism', *Comparative Studies of South Asia, Africa and the Middle East*, 34 (2014), pp. 574–81.

'Governing the Living and the Dead: Mecca and the Emergence of the Saudi Biopolitical State', *American Historical Review*, 122 (2017), pp. 346–70.

Winckler, Onn, 'The Immigration Policy of the Gulf Cooperation Council (GCC) States', *Middle Eastern Studies*, 33 (1997), pp. 480–93.

Wise, Henry, 'Acceleration of the Overland Mails', *The Nautical Magazine and Naval Chronicle*, 13 (1844), pp. 104–5.

Wishnitzer, Avner, *Reading Clocks, Alla Turca: Time and Society in the Late Ottoman Empire* (Chicago: University of Chicago Press, 2015).

al-Yāfī, ʿAdnān ʿAbd al-Badīʿ, *Jidda fī shadhrāt al-Ghazzāwī* (Jeddah, 1431/2010).

al-Nashʾa wa-l-takwīn: Dirāsa taṭbīqiyya min khilāl Āl al-Yāfi. (Cairo: Dār al-Qāhira, 2005).
'al-Ruwais: A District in the Heart of Jeddah' in *The Story of Ten – Ḥikāyat 10* (Jeddah, 2013), pp. 10–6.
The Arab Family: Origin and Formation. An Applied Study through the Al-Yafi Family (Jeddah, 1437/2016).
Yamani, Mai, *Changed Identities: The Challenge of the New Generation in Saudi Arabia* (London: The Royal Institute of International Affairs, Middle East Programme, 2000).
Cradle of Islam: The Hijaz and the Quest for an Arabian Identity (London and New York: I.B. Tauris, 2004).
'Evading the Habits of a Life Time: The Adaptation of Hejazi Dress to the New Social Order' in N. Lindisfarne-Tapper (ed.), *Languages of Dress in the Middle East* (Richmond: Curzon Press, 1997), pp. 55–66.
Yazbak, Mahmoud, *Haifa in the Late Ottoman Period, 1864–1914: A Muslim Town in Transition* (Leiden, Boston, and Köln: Brill, 1990).
Young, George, *Corps de Droit Ottoman: Recueil des Codes, Lois, Règlements, Ordonnances et Actes les Plus Importants du Droit Intérieur, et d'Études sur le Droit Coutumier de l'Empire Ottoman*, 6 vols. (Oxford: Clarendon Press, 1905), vol. 1.
Yūsuf, ʿImād ʿAbd al-ʿAzīz, *Al-Ḥijāz fī 'l-ʿahd al-ʿuthmānī 1876–1918* (London: Alwarrak Publishing Ltd., 2011).
Zandi-Sayek, Sibel, *Ottoman Izmir: The Rise of a Cosmopolitan Port, 1840–1880* (Minneapolis: University of Minnesota Press, 2012).
Zilfi, Maldine, 'Servants, Slaves, and the Domestic Order in the Ottoman Middle East', *Hawwa*, 2 (2004), pp. 1–33.
al-Ziriklī, Khayr al-Dīn, *al-Aʿlām: Qāmūs tarājim li-ashhar al-rijāl wa-l-nisāʾ min al-ʿarab wa-l-mustaʿribīn wa-l-mustashriqīn*, 15th edn. (Beirut: Dār al-ʿIlm li-l-Malāyīn, 2002).
Shibh al-Jazīra fī ʿahd al-Malik ʿAbd al-ʿAziz (Beirut: Maṭābiʿ Dār al-Qalam, 1970).
Zubaida, Sami, 'Middle Eastern Experiences of Cosmopolitanism' in S. Vertovec and R. Cohen (eds.), *Conceiving Cosmopolitanism: Theory, Context and Practice* (Oxford: Oxford University Press, 2002), pp. 32–41.

Index

Abdülhamid II 68, 75, 305
Abdur Razzack 72
Abū Dā'ūd, Sulaymān 160, 171, 186
Abyssinia and Abyssians *See also* Ethiopia and Ethiopians, Habeş
Abyssinia and Abyssinians 3, 52
Aden 20, 35, 44, 50, 52, 56, 68, 85, 88, 95, 219–20, 222, 234
  occupation of 49, 52, 58
Afghanistan and Afghans 69–71, 179, 259, 298
Africa and Africans 68, 100–2, 104–11, 146, 148–50, 245, 303, *See also* Hajj and 'Umra, migration, trade, slavery
  association 179
  East 220
  labour 182
  North 42, 71, 317
  West 78, 101, *See also* Takrūnīs
Agha Khan 298
Agha, 'Abdallāh 59, 61–2, 241, 274
agriculture 104, 151
Aḥmad Ibn 'Īsā 198
Ahmet Ratip Pasha 91
al-Aḥsā' 248, 292
al-'Alawī b. Sahl, Faḍl *See* Sayyid Faḍl
al-Ālūsī, Nu'mān Effendi 237
Albanians 61
alcohol 16, 174, 187, 300–3, 322, *See also* bar, women
  Boosa 114
  whisky 322
  wine 63, 103, 301
Aleppo 46, 133
Alexandria 44, 52, 125, 234, 236, 308, 318
Algeria and Algerians 68–9, 71, 250, 259, 299, 306, 308, 314–15, 317
'Alī b. Ḥusayn 79, 126, 211, 287–90, 328
'Alī Pasha, Muḥammad 104, 274
'Alī Riḍā, *family* 16, 85, 91–8, 144, 162, 166, 209, 216, 249, 281
  'Abdallāh 78, 93–4, 209, 249, 287, 289, 293
  'Alī Akbar 93
  Ḥusayn 93
  Muḥammad 152
  Muḥammad 'Alī Zaynal 94, 144, 167, 206, 214
  Qāsim Zaynal 75, 94, 144, 281, 288–91, 293
  Yūsuf Zaynal 144
  Zaynal 91–4, 209, 225, 315, 335
almsgiving 137, 159, 168, 189, 248, 310, 323
America 67
Arab nationalism 76
'Arab, Muḥammad Fāḍil 224
architecture 2, 13–18, 34, 114, 116, 134–44, 162, 205, 329
  Red Sea 14, 140
Armenians 53, 63, 87, 105, 299, 318
Arnaud, Thomas-Joseph 57
'Ashmāwī, *family* 164
'Āshūr, *family* 165, 280
'āshūrā' 159, 189, 258
Asia and Asians 66, *See also* Hajj and 'Umra, migration, trade
  Central 179, 258, 317
  East 52
  South 189
  Southeast 67, 158, 179, 214, 216–17, 219, 225, 254, 258, 306, 314
  West 42
'Asīr 50, 76, 81, 294, 329
Austria and Austrians 157, 302

Bā Dīb, *family* 167
'Abd al-Qādir 285
Bā Ghaffār, *family* 281
'Abd al-Ghaffār 280
Muḥammad Ṣāliḥ 280
Ṣāliḥ 285
Bā Hārūn, Ḥasan 280
Bā 'Ishn, *family* 164–7, 224, 280–1
Aḥmad 232, 281
Bā Junayd, *family* 167
Bā Khashwayn, *family* 3
Bā Nāja, *family* 109, 116, 163–6, 233–4, 237, 240, 281
'Abd al-Raḥmān 287
'Abdallāh 240, 242, 282, 317
'Abdallāh b. Yūsuf 109
'Alī b. Muḥammad 316
Muḥammad Ṣāliḥ 291
'Uthmān 216
Yūsuf 135
Badia y Leblich, Domingo Francisco Jorge 47–9
Baghdad 41, 220, 243, 272, 284
al-Baghdādī, *family*
Mūsā 239, 243, 285
al-Baghdādī, Yūsuf Ya'qūb *See* Yusef, Alim
Bahrain 36, 93–4, 205, 237, 246, 248
Bakhsh, *family* 98
Karīm Raḥim 99
al-Balad 2, 5, 32, 116, 132–4, 138, 140, 155, 160, 164, 188, 329, 332, 340–1
Banyans 57
bar 63, 318
barḥa 142
Barqāwī, *family* 101
Basra 44, 220, 223
al-Bassām, *family* 236, 238, 245, 280–1
'Abdallāh 235
Aḥmad 236
Sulaymān b. 'Abdallāh 236
baṣṣāṣ 278, 297
bazaar *See* market
Bedouins 16, 41, 50, 64–5, 72–6, 81, 114, 147, 151, 154, 261, 267–70, 297, 309, 340, *See also* Ikhwān, emir, Hajj and 'Umra, revolt, sharifs, transport, tribe and tribalism
attacks 68, 72, 158, 226, 240, 282, 286, 295
culture 7, 81
Hajj 250, 270
plundering 147
security 80, 250
settlements 89, 146, 151
slavery 108, 285
Sufism 201
transport 91, 225–6, 269
urbanisation 86
water 128
Beirut 33–4, 113, 121, 125, 210, 280, 284, 301
Bethlehem 220
Bin 'Abd al-Wahhāb, *family*
'Abd al-Laṭīf 237
'Abd al-Raḥmān 237
Bin Ḥimd, *family* 234
Muḥammad 232, 234–6
Bin Lādin, *family* 98, 246, 294
Muḥammad 'Awaḍ 97–8, 153
Bin Maḥfūẓ, *family* 246, 294
Sālim 98–100, 167, 335
Bin Mu'ammar, 'Abd al-'Azīz 293
Bin Muḥammad, *family*
'Abdallāh 239
Ḥusayn 69, 71, 259, 298
Bin Zaqr, *family* 281
Ṣafiyya 337
boatmen 102, 108, 116, 133, 159–60, 173, 180, 183–6, 322
Bohras 138
Bombay 51, 93–4, 205, 219, 222, 225, 234, 246–8, 264
Bornu 101
British Empire and Britons 20, 44–83, 87, 92, 111, 126–8, 131, 156, 187, 216, 222, 241–6, 250, 253, 260, 263–4, 281–2, 298, 304, 306–21, *See also* Christianity and Christians, consulates, dress, East India Company, Europe, Europeans, Hajj and 'Umra, imperialism, merchants, nationality, trade, West and Westerners
bombardment of Jeddah 62
Pax Britannica 94
builders 180, 183

Bukhara 179
Burckhardt, John Lewis 56–7, 114, 136, 146
Burma 95
Burton, James 136

Cairo 5, 12, 41, 44–5, 51, 54, 62, 75–6, 85–6, 109, 129, 180, 210, 220, 223, 229, 233, 294
Calcutta 94, 164, 219–20, 234
caliph and caliphate 69, 71, 78
caravanserai 136
carpenters 185
Caucasians 105
Çelebi, Evliya 44
celebrations 125, 129, 160, 168, 175, 178, 189–96, 200, 258, 324, 326, 341
  ʿĪd 175, 187
cemetery 139–40, 143, 155–8, 191–203, 300
Chad 101
charity 93, 166, 310, 342
China 152
Christianity and Christians 13, 20, 45, 60, 62–3, 67–9, 103–4, 106, 156–8, 174, 220, 298–9, 318
  alcohol 301–3
  massacre of 65
  migration to Jeddah 50
  privileges 312
  tradition 8
Circassians 105
city wall 2–3, 5, 16, 32, 41, 44, 49, 82, 88, 91, 102, 114–19, 123, 131, 133, 146–56, 214, 256, 263, 268, 329, 341
clubs 207–9, 288
coal 51–3, 56, 94, 146, 188, 225, 242, 247
coffeehouse 12, 108, 123, 134, 142, 146, 173–5, 183–4, 256, 278, 324
Constantinople *See* Istanbul
consulates 53, 61, 72, 82, 116, 123, 279, 286, 298, 320
  Algerian consulate 314
  Austrian consulate 258
  British (vice-)consul 53, 59, 61–2, 69–70, 72, 250, 259, 285–6, 288, 298, 301, 306, 309
  British consulate 27, 53, 62, 87, 111, 241–2, 257, 263, 281, 307–8, 310–21
  Dutch consulate 27, 173, 190, 242, 258, 286
  European consulates 52, 58, 60–2, 64–6, 69, 79, 134, 157, 179, 299, 301
  French consulate 27, 53–4, 59, 62–3, 108, 241, 257, 263, 267–8, 298–9, 301–2, 313
  Greek consulate 258
  Iranian consulate 27, 92, 258
  Persian consulate 190
  Russian consulate 27, 72, 258
  Swedish consulate 258
conviviality 6, 25–7, 36
cosmopolitanism 6, 8, 20–7, 34
council 120, 274–87, 291–2, 329
  Administrative Council 91, 236, 276, 284–7, 291–2
  Advisory Council 293
  Chamber of Commerce 281, 287, 333
  Chamber of Industry 333
  Commercial Council 90, 233, 244, 284–5
  Consultative Assembly 291
  Consultative Council 248
  Council of Elders 287
  District Administrative Council 296
  Health Council 262
  Judicial Council 276
  Local Council 81
  Merchant Council 61, 230–2, 275–6, 333
  Municipal Council 123–4, 267, 276–80, 291–2, 332
  Ottoman reform 294
  Provincial Council 123, 274–5
  quarters 171
  Sanitary Council 278
  Supervisory Council 296
court 132, 230–2, 276
criminality 223, 250, 258, 268–9, 271, 277, 294–311, 322–7, *See also* judiciary

crisis 67–8, 71, 86, 222
  economic 232
  trade 222
custom 188–9, 337
  local 24
customs 8, 24, 41, 45–6, 49, 51, 56, 86, 161, 185, 219, 222, 231, 241, 306
  customs house 123, 255, 277, 282, 300
  monopoly 219
  superintendent 283, 288

d'Héricourt, Rochet 57, 157
al-Dabbāgh, Muḥammad Ṭāhir 289, 294
Daḥlān, Aḥmad Zaynī 70, 210, 237
Damascus 33, 41, 113, 125, 284
dance 102, 175, 195–6, 202, 322, 326, *See also mizmār*
de Fresnel, Fulgence 59
de Gobineau, Arthur 58
Dhū ʿAwn, *group of Sharifian descent* 90
  Muḥammad b. ʿAwn 239
Dhū Zayd, *group of Sharifian descent* 90
dihlīz 13–17, 22, 140
al-Dirʿiyya 339
disease 37, 66, 120, 195, 263–5, 304, 310, 315, *See also* health, hygiene, quarantine, sanitation
  bubonic plague 265
  cholera 66, 72, 148, 261, 264–5, 305
  plague 250, 264
  sanitation 72
dress 3, 9, 12, 53, 57, 102, 188, 326–7
drought 309
Dubai 94, 205
Dutch *See* Netherlands, The and Dutchmen

East India Company 48–9, 51, 53, 241
education 23, 102, 204–7, 277
Egypt 37, 41–61, 65–70, 105, 144, 224, 227, 230, 233, 306, *See also* merchants, migration, nationality
  rule over the Hijaz 5, 50, 89, 117, 275
Egyptians 28, 81, 86, 96, 204, 211, 274, 295, 303, 324
elections 74, 289
elites 35, 80, 86, 98–100, 163–8, 209, 212, 244–9, 289, 331, 338, 342, *See also* notables
  merchant 86, 88, 294
el-Tūr 262
emir 5, 11, 34, 41, 44–9, 54–5, 58–60, 69, 72, 75, 86–8, 91, 119, 129, 175, 231, 239, 243–4, 272, *See also* sharifs
  agent of 62, 86, 90, 239, 242–3, 272, 282
  assassination of 70
  Bedouins 268
  cooperation with British Empire 69
  Hadhramis, and 88
  Ottomans, and 55, 64, 67, 69, 71, 75, 268, 271, 275, 306
  pilgrimage, and 182, 241, 251
  Young Turks, and 75
endowment 86, 89, 101, 132, 135, 164–7, 171, 285, 317, 335
Eritrea and Eritreans 158, 234
Ethiopia and Ethiopians 105, 151, 156, *See also* Abyssinia and Abyssinians, Habeş
Europe 37, 42, 56, 62–3, 65, 219, 224, *See also* consulates, dress, Hajj and ʿUmra, imperialism, migration, trade
  Red Sea 37, 46, 48, 51, 58
  trade 51, 144
Europeans 12, 52, 103, 301–2

factory 45, 153
al-Faḍl, *family* 235–6, 245–9, 293
  ʿAbd al-Raḥmān 246
  ʿAbdallāh b. Muḥammad 247–9, 291
  ʿAbdallāh b. Ṣāliḥ 247
  ʿAbdallāh Ibrāhīm 232
  Ibrāhīm b. ʿAbd al-Raḥmān 249
  Muḥammad b. ʿAbd al-Raḥmān 247–8
    Ṣāliḥ b. ʿAbdallāh 246–7
Fallāta 101

family 37, 85–6, 95, 100, 110, 161–9, 233, 330, 338–9, *See marriage*, tribe and tribalism, specific family names
elite 98
endowment 109, 132
families, old 3, 5, 88, 236
history 89, 96
polygamy 162
famine 76, 223
Fayṣal b. Ḥusayn 75, 207, 246, 248
fishermen 86, 101
foodstuffs 94, 137, 148, 189, 234, 246, 248
bread 134
butter 219
chickpeas 234
coffee 13, 44, 76, 182, 219, 231, 234, *See also* coffeehouse
dates 219, 244
fish 150
flour 76
fruits 134, 146
grain 134, 137, 141, 146, 148, 219, 233–4, 242, 244, 246, 309
herbs 147
nuts 189
oil 134
rice 76, 95, 189, 219, 234, 309
spices 37, 42, 44, 219, 234
sugar 76, 219, 231, 269
tea 13, 231, 234
vegetables 146
football 175, 178, 213–17, 322
France and Frenchmen 46–9, 51, 54, 156, 231, 260, 262, 264, 269, 308, 313, 315, 317, *See also* Christians and Christianity, consulates, Europe, Europeans, Hajj and ʿUmra, imperialism, merchants, nationality, trade, West and Westerners
Fresnel, Fulgence 52, 274

gas 131
gendarmerie 295–6, *See also* police
gentrification 116, 152, 340, 343
Georgians 105
Ghālib, *family* 166
ʿAbd al-Muṭṭalib 239, 274
al-Ghāzī, *family* 87
gold 13, 82, 322
governorate 276
Greece and Greeks 13, 51, 57–8, 63–4, 87–8, 174, 220, 222, 300, 302, 318
guilds 137, 178, 180–8, 229, 231, 244, 251, 279, 281–7
boatmen 159, 173, 180, 184–7
merchants 232
shaykh 62, 96, 127, 159–60, 173, 182–5, 229, 232, 253, 283–4

al-Ḥabashī, Ṣufyān b. ʿAbdallāh 109, 240
Habeş 44, 46, 54, *See also* Abyssinia and Abyssinians, Ethiopia and Ethiopians
Hadhramaut and Hadhramis 64, 74, 85, 88, 97–100, 138, 143, 153, 166–7, 188, 197, 202, 232, 246, 259, 282, 311, 316, *See also* migration, trade, Yemen and Yemenis
association 88, 179–80
Haifa 284
Ḥāʾil 239
Hajj and ʿUmra 2–12, 20–4, 40–7, 50, 65–8, 77, 106, 117, 127, 190, 195, 203, 223, 243, 248–70, 297–300, 303–11, 330–1, *See also* Bedouins, *maḥmal*, women, Wahhabiyya
accommodation 4, 6, 8, 14, 124, 140, 144, 152, 249, 251, 254–7, 262, 267
Africa, from 100–2, 107, 146, 306
Arabian Peninsula, from 243, 248, 309
Asia (Central), from 251
Asia (South), from 4, 243, 251–3, 304, 307, 309, 317–18
Asia (Southeast), from 4, 225, 243, 254, 306, 308
Egypt, from 203, 236, 251–4
European influence on 250, 253, 260, 263–4, 304, 308, 311, 315
infrastructure 151, 192, 225–8, 241–3, 249, 252–4, 274

Hajj and ʿUmra (cont.)
Ottoman Empire, from 49
pilgrimage season 2, 10, 94, 106, 137–8, 144, 256–7, 284, 322, 334
Saudi changes to 80–1, 254–5, 261, 264–5, 270
Shiites 138
slavery, and 249
transport 4–5, 35, 41–2, 52, 56, 90, 94, 100–1, 106, 120, 151, 188–91, 225–8, 241–3, 250, 254, 257, 262, 268–9
transport monopoly 66, 242–3, 250, 252, 292
Hamilton, James 63, 146
Hammed Nasser 48
Ḥanbalī legal school 80
ḥaram 7
Ḥarb, *tribe* 91, 240, 297
harbour *See* port
Ḥasab Allāh, Muḥammad 237
Haussa 101
ḥawsh 134–41, 193
ḥawṭa 7
al-Hazzāzī, *family* 164, 249
Aḥmad 291
health 66–7, 71–2, 81, 117, 119, 123–4, 128, 253–4, 260–7, 278, *See also* disease, hospital, hygiene, quarantine, sanitation
hijra 7
Hodeida 41, 43, 56, 68, 114, 219–20, 262, 309
holiday 190, 200
ʿĪd 155, 175, 191–2
hospital 72, 117, 127, 140, 262, 264–7
hospitality 6–9, 12–13, 20
hostel 132, 135, 138–40, 256, *See also* *ḥawsh*
hotel 256
Ḥusayn b. ʿAlī 74–80, 126, 160, 182, 209, 211, 238, 244–7, 253, 281, 287–8, 310, 322, 328
Bedouins 75, 269
hygiene 66–7, 72, 81, 171, *See also* disease, health, hospital, quarantine, sanitation
Ibn Rashīd 239, 247
Ibn Saʿūd *See* Saʿūd, *family*
Ibrāhīm Pasha 57
ice factory 129
al-Idrīsī, Muḥammad 76
Idrisiyya 202
Ikhwān 78–9, 81, 270, 323, *See also* Bedouins
imperialism 63, 257–60, 298, 304, 311
anti- 37, 60, 66, 69–70, 258–60
British Empire 101, 259, 306, 319
Europe 21, 58
France 101, 259, 319
India and Indians 20, 34, 56–8, 61–5, 69–70, 80, 85–7, 92–6, 98–102, 128, 140, 152, 188, 233, 235, 241, 245, 314, 321, *See also* Banyans, Asia and Asians, Hajj and ʿUmra, merchants, trade
association 179
Great Indian Revolt 62, 259
schools 204
Indian Ocean 4, 17–20, 33–4, 36, 40–2, 52, 58, 179
Iran and Iranians 94, 189, 281, *See also* Hajj and ʿUmra, migration, Persia and Persians
Iraq and Iraqis 79, 81, 215, 245, *See also* Hajj and ʿUmra, maḥmal, migration, trade
Ismāʿīl, Muḥammad 232
Ismāʿīliyya 138
Istanbul 33, 41–2, 66, 90, 113, 125, 129, 220
Italy and Italians 42, 48, 64, 318
Izmir 33–4, 73, 113, 280

Jamjūm, *family* 249
Muḥammad Ṣalāḥ 207
Muḥammad Ṣāliḥ 281
janissaries 295
Jawhar, Ṣāliḥ 61, 230, 232, 281, 312, 314
al-Jazāʾirī, ʿAbd al-Qādir 69, 71
Jeddah massacre 55, 63–4, 87, 164, 230, 232, 241, 243, 259, 296, 298, 312
jihad 47, 59, 70, 76
al-Jīlānī, *family* 46, 48, 86
Ibrāhīm 48
Muḥammad Ṣāliḥ 313

Judaism and Jews 8, 13, 157
judiciary 184, 192, 277, 283, 298–9, 308, 324–5
al-Juffālī, *family* 245

Kaʿba 6, 47, 56, 192
Kaʿkī, *family* 99–100
ʿAbd al-ʿAzīz 99
Kamaran Island 67, 262–4
Kâmil Pasha 61
Kandarah 155
Karachi 246–8
kaymakam 55, 62, 78, 91, 94, 104, 117, 120–1, 126, 190, 209, 239–40, 243, 267, 272–3, 276–7, 281–7, 293, 302, 313
emir 272
Young Turk revolution 74
khān 44, *See* hostel
Khartum 220
al-Khaṭīb, Muḥibb al-Dīn 211
Khilāfa-movement 247
Khunjī, *family* 165, 167, 280
ʿAbd al-Raʿūf 281
al-Khurayjī, *family* 245
al-Khurma 77
Kingdom of the Hijaz 7, 37, 77–9, 90, 94, 101, 107, 129, 194, 222–3, 227, 244, 264–6, 269, 287, 296, 310, 320, 328
Kuwait 93

lagoon 40, 121, 133
Lebanon 63
Libya 101
Lingah 92
al-Līth 276
Liverpool 220
London 94
looting 62
al-Luḥayya 43, 57

Mahdist movement 68, 70
maḥmal 56, 192–3, 196, 270, 322
Malaysians 210, 213–14, 242
Maltese 314, 318
Mamluks 42
Manāʿ, *family* 159–62, 166, 187
ʿAbdallāh 159
marginalization 23, 339–40
market 2, 41, 49, 86, 96, 116, 120, 125, 134–7, 140–8, 232, 277, 298
inspector 59–61, 169, 184, 240–1, 273–4, 278, 295
marriage 9, 100, 109, 176–7, 190–1, 319, 325, 337–9
marital alliances 93, 162, 243
slavery 109–11
Marseilles 220
Mashāṭ, *family* 280
Massawa 41, 60, 85, 87–8, 105, 114, 167
Mauretania 100, *See also* Shanāqiṭa
mawlid 323, 326, 332
mayor 126
Mecca 2–19, 34, 79, 90, 130, 179, 202–5, 220, 262, 269, 272, 286–8, 320–2
administration 291
book trade 209
Mecca uprising 55
Ḥanafī mufti of 289
sanctity of 36, 41, 335, 341
Sufism 201
Mecca Gate 12–13, 118, 126, 131, 133, 146–8, 155–6, 264
Medina 4, 9, 15–16, 19, 21–2, 65, 104, 168, 191, 196, 202, 223–8, 246–8, 262, 268, 320–2
administration 276, 291
sanctitiy of 12, 36
sanctity of 317, 335, 341
Sufism 201
Medina Gate 114, 117–19, 131, 151
Mediterranean Sea 17–20, 113, 234
Mehmed Ali 5, 48–50, 52, 57, 89, 117, 156
merchants 3, 14, 42–9, 59–62, 65–8, 75, 77–8, 81, 85–7, 90, 93–6, 99, 120–7, 131, 141, 163, 185, 222–49, 258, 263, 270, 279, 281–7, 294, 301, 331, *See also* guilds; trade
British 45, 62, 281
Christian 12, 34, 64, 88
Egyptian 45, 50
European 12–13, 42, 44–6, 50, 87, 220, 223, 281
flow of ideas 198, 208, 237–9
French 51

merchants (cont.)
Greek 57, 63, 220, 228
Hadhrami 57, 61, 74, 109, 220, 225, 229, 282
Hijazi 294
Indian 43, 45, 49–50, 56–7, 59, 87, 127, 140, 222, 228–9, 232, 281–2
Jewish 34, 42
Lebanese 232
Meccan 90, 235, 282
Medinese 235, 282
Moroccan 86, 228
Najdi 232, 235–6, 245, 281, 290
organisation of 62, 90–1, 127, 179, 181, 183, 229–33, 253, 282–3
Ottoman 62, 253
Persian 43, 92, 190, 281
Mersin 34, 113
Midhat Pasha 73
midwifing 187, 278
migration 2–5, 9, 22–4, 34, 82, 86, 89–104, 109, 135, 167, 178–9, 186, 311, 330, 333–5, *See also* Hajj and ʿUmra, refugees
Afghanistan, from 88, 315
Africa (East), from 33, 82–3, 100–2, 259, 303, 328–9, 341
Africa (North), from 3, 88, 96, 101, 314, 328
Africa (West), from 3, 34, 88, 100–2, 259, 328, 341
Asia (Central), from 3, 88, 328
Asia (South), from 33, 35, 83, 88, 328–9, 341
Asia (Southeast), from 3, 33, 88, 328, 333
Egypt, from 3, 88, 91, 96, 303
Europe, from 3, 88
Hadhramaut, from 2–3, 33, 88, 98, 316
Iran, from 3
Iraq, from 3, 88
Najd, from 88, 245–6, 294
Ottoman Empire, from 3, 89–104
Palestine, from 333
Persia, from 88, 91
Russia, from 314
slavery, and 109–11
Syria, from 3, 88, 96
Turkey, from 88
Yemen, from 3, 33, 82–3, 88, 329, 341
mill 51, 108, 117
millet 179
Mirdād, Muḥammad 285
mirkāz 142, 173
mizmār 175–7, 194, 214, 323, 326, *See also* dance
Mocha 41–2, 45, 57, 114, 141, 262
money-changers 185
monsoon 4, 18, 34, 40, 56–7
morality 184, 294, 300–3, 321–7
Morocco and Moroccans 86
Moscoudi, Sava 220, 222
Moses Wells 67, 262
mosque 44, 116, 132, 137–8, 144, 197, 273, 324
endowment 167
Mosque, Ḥanafī 116, 137, 164, 190
muezzin 184, 200
mufti 28, 70, 128, 210, 237, 277, 287, 307
muḥarram 3, 189–90
muḥtasib See market
al-Mukallā 94, 262
mukharrij 151, 183, 227, 254, 267, 269
municipality 119, 123, 183–4, 209, 277–80, 284, 292, 329
Municipal Council *See* councils
music 102, 175, 178, 190–1, 193, 195, 201–2, 208, 303, 321–6
muṭawwif See pilgrims' guides

nāʾib See pilgrims' guides
Najd 47, 227
Najd and Najdīs 23–4, 35–6, 54, 81, 195, 208, 236–9, 244–7, 271, 292–3, 319, 323–7, 338–9, *See also* migration, merchants, trade
conservatism 82, 321
Namık Pasha 301
al-Nāniyya, *family* 245
Napoleon Bonaparte 46, 229
Nāshid Pasha 121
Naṣīf, family 90–6, 98, 100, 141, 164–6, 204, 216
(Ḥājj) ʿAbdallāh 62, 90, 290
Abū Bakr 90
Ḥusayn 91, 239
Ḥusayn b. Muḥammad 288

Muḥammad (d. 1689–70) 90
Muḥammad Ḥusayn 91, 99, 200, 208–9, 211–12, 237–40, 255, 287–90, 293, 321
Muḥammad Ṣāliḥ 212, 289
'Umar 90, 99, 204, 207–8, 239–44, 255, 280, 282
Nasser, Hammed 48
nationality 311–21, 333–4, *See also* passport
British 312, 316
Egyptian 321
French 313
Hijazi 319–20
inheritance 315–16
Ottoman 62, 180, 281, 311–18
Saudi 318–21, 333–6
Nāẓir, Ibrāhīm 285
Netherlands, The and Dutchmen 45, 189, 232, 241, 258–9, 264, 281, 308, *See also* Christians and Chrisianity, Europe and Europeans, Hajj and 'Umra, nationality
newspapers 195, 209–13, 292
al-Bilād al-Sa'ūdiyya 213
al-Ḥijāz 210–11
al-Iṣlāḥ al-Ḥijāzī 210
al-Manhal 213
al-Nidā' al-Islāmī 213
al-Qibla 211–12
Barīd al-Ḥijāz 211
Egyptian 290
Ṣafā' al-Ḥijāz 211
Ṣawt al-Ḥijāz 212–15
Ṣawṭ al-Ḥijāz 327
Shams al-Ḥaqīqa 210
Umm al-Qurā 195, 199, 212, 214–15, 267, 323, 326–7
Niebuhr, Carsten 12–13, 120, 156
Nigeria and Nigerians 42, 101, 107, 341
al-Nimr, *family* 167
notables 77–9, 109, 119–24, 129–31, 163, 177, 204, 244, 255, 271–94
Nūrī Pasha, Osman 71, 120–1, 126, 210, 267
Nūrwalī, *family* 93–6
'Abd al-Qādir 95
Ogilvie, Alexander 59
oil 5, 11, 22, 36, 81–2, 181, 244, 329, 331, 333
Oromo 106
Ottman Empire and Ottomans *See also* Bedouins, emir, Hajj and 'Umra, migration, nationality, Provincial Law, sharifs, Tanzimat, trade, Young Turks
Ottoman Empire and Ottomans 5, 13, 23, 34–7, 46, 50, 54–64, 67–77, 85, 102–4, 108, 117–19, 129, 169–70, 204, 222, 226–31, 252, 265–8, 271, 277–82, 305, 310, 315, 327
governor 44–5, 49, 54–5, 59–64, 71–2, 74, 89–91, 113, 117, 175, 230–1, 240, 243, 265, 271–4, 279, 282, 306
military 3, 42–7, 49, 60, 65, 68, 71–5, 102, 117–19, 234, 246, 260–1, 271–5, 286, 297–300, 319, 332
modernisation 33, 71, 119–26
parliament 74–5, 94, 289
quarantine 72
Suez Canal 65
sultan 7, 11, 47, 68–9, 71, 73–4, 76, 120, 176
Ottoman Empire, Ottoman 43

pan-Islamism 55, 69–71, 259–60
Paris 94
passport 124, 277, 304–9, 315–16, *See also* nationality
pearl 248
Persia and Persians 91–3, 96, 174, 179, 225, 298, 313, 315, *See also* Hajj and 'Umra, merchants, migration, Iran and Iranians
Persian Gulf 58, 105, 220, 227, 245
Philby, Harry St. John 79, 91, 102, 151, 226, 245–6, 289
pilgrims' guides 11, 38, 101, 106, 133, 144–6, 152, 163, 180–2, 192, 218, 223, 227, 243, 251–7, 279, 307, 317–18, 331, 342
school for 255, *See also* transport

police 140, 171, 177, 262, 273, 294–7, 303–4, 306, 329, *See also* gendarmerie
religious police 81, 170, 174, 323–5
political parties 288–94
Committee of Union and Progress 73, 76
National Party 209, 211, 289
Party of Free Hijazis 294
poor 10, 78, 83, 93, 101, 114–17, 132, 138, 146, 151, 160, 166, 171, 189–90, 197, 250–3, 262, 277, 283, 303, 317, 329
vagrancy 303–11
Port Said 113, 222
porters 102, 108, 187, 282–4
Portuguese Empire and Portuguese 37, 42
postal service 121, 130, 137, 277
prayer 155, 189, 201, 203–4, 209, 322, 325, *See also* religion
Friday 47
printing 208–13
prison 62, 74, 174, 290, 299, 335
prostitution 16, 116, 149, 187, 301, 303, 322
Provincial Law 33, 55, 64, 170, 273, 275–7, 295, 313

Qābil, *family* 89
ʿAbd al-Qādir 209
Muḥammad ʿAlī 290
Sulaymān 90, 126, 209, 232, 249, 281, 289–91
quarantine 67, 72, 123–4, 255, 261–5, 278, *See also* disease, health, hospital, hygiene, sanitation
quarters 75, 121, 133–4, 140–4, 149, 169–80, 191, 286, 331–2
administration 277, 279, 286, 329
al-Baghdādiyya 329
al-Baḥr 133, 159, 162, 165, 175–6, 184, 193
Bīsha 106, 148–50
guards 171, 176, 294
al-Hindāwiyya 148
al-Kandara 329
al-Maẓlūm 133, 144, 164, 192
Nakutu 101, 131, 140, 148–50, 303
al-Nuzla al-Yamāniyya 268, 329, 340, 343–4
al-Ruways 101, 150, 154, 341, 343–4
al-Shām 102, 116, 133, 141, 164, 175, 177, 192, 234
suburbs 5, 82, 88, 101, 108, 117, 131, 191, 268, 329, 340–1, 343
al-Suwākinī 114, 302
al-Takārna 148–50
violence 176–8
al-Yaman 96, 133, 139, 143–4, 175, 177, 184, 192, 198
Qunfudhah 262
Quṣaybī, *family* 236

Rābigh 199, 254, 276
al-Rafīq, ʿAwn 71–2, 75, 198–9, 201, 208, 239, 252, 317
Ramaḍān 175, 191–2
al-Rashid, Harun 186
Ratip Pasha, Ahmed 240
real estate 95, 163, 278, 312, 317, 320, 335–6
Red Sea 17–20, 33–4, 40–54, 56–8, 63, 66–7, 86, 88, 107, 261–5, *See also* trade, transport
imperialism 48–9, 76
pearling 104, 108
ports 42, 46, 50, 64, 85, 114
shipping 5, 34, 37, 40, 52
refugees 66, 68, 288, 305
religion 6–12, 20, 60, 106, 110, 155–8, 161, 166, 178, 188–204, 246, 277, 313, 324, 331, 337, *See* also celebrations, Christianity and Christians, custom, endowment, Hajj and ʿUmra, holiday, Jews and Judaism, morality, mosque, muezzin, mufti, police, saints, scholars, tombs, Sufism, Wahhabiyya, *zāwiya*
calendar 188–96
revolt 59–60, 63, 69–70, 81, 87–8, 226, 263, 273–4, 286
Arab Revolt 37, 76–7, 107, 126, 328
ribāṭ 164–5, 167, 171, 281, 309–10, *See* hostel
Riḍā, Muḥammad Rashīd 208

Rif'at Pasha, Ibrāhīm 128, 193, 236
al-Rīḥānī, Amīn 79
Riyadh 23, 79, 237, 291
Rüppell, Eduard 53, 116
Russia and Russians 68–9, 305, 314–15, *See also* migration
  Muslims 12

Ṣabbān, 'Abd al-Ra'ūf 294
saint 156
saints 139, 197–200
Salāma, 'Alī 289–90
Salonica 33–4, 113
Sana'a 133
sancak 170, 276, 286
sanitation 66–7, 72, 104, 127, 253–5, 257, 260–7, 277, 280, 309–11, 329, *See also* council, disease, health, hospital, hygiene, sanitation
  al-Saqāṭ, *family* 86
al-Saqqāf, *family*
  'Abd al-Raḥmān 225, 259
Sarkiz, George 53
Sarrāj, 'Abdallāh 287
Sa'ūd, *family* 50, 89, 195, 202, 248
  'Abd al-'Azīz b. 'Abd al-Raḥmān (Ibn Sa'ūd) 7, 37, 77–82, 111, 152, 202, 222–7, 236, 239, 245–8, 251–5, 270, 289–93, 311, 318–20, 324, 328–9
  Fayṣal b. 'Abd al-'Azīz 81
  Fayṣal b. Turkī 239
  Salmān b. 'Abd al-'Azīz 24
Saudi Arabia 2, 5, 10, 17, 23, 28, 35, 80–1, 90, 94, 129, 185, 199–200, 223–4, 270
  administration 35, 236, 245, 291–2, 327, 332–3
  education 205, 207
  first Saudi state 37
Savignac, Raphaël 148, 299
Sayyid Faḍl 59, 258
sayyids 97, 199
scholars 12, 28, 59, 95, 101, 117, 120, 192, 199, 207–9, 237–9, 287, 307, 323, 331
schools 134, 167, 204, 235–6, 255, 327, 331
  al-Falāḥ 94, 167, 205–6, 235–6
  al-Najāḥ 204, 247
  Koranic schools 204, 207, 235
  Madrasa Naṣīfiyya 99
  rüşdiye 204, 206–7, 235
Scottland 45
servants 13–15, 17, 86, 104, 107–8, 140–1, 159, 162, 299–300, 334–5
şevne See warehouse
Shāfi'iyya 28, 70, 209, 237
shahbandar 34
Shaḥḥāta, *family* 164, 166
Shanāqiṭa 100, 102, *See also* Mauretania
Sharaf al-Dīn, Ṣadīqa 99, 207
sharifs 11, 41, 46–7, 50, 56, 58–9, 64–72, 75, 86, 90, 96, 143, 279, 287, 331, *See also* emir, Kingdom of the Hijaz, emir
  agent of 93
  merchants, and 81
  trade 239
    al-Shaykh, 'Abd al-Malik b. Ibrāhīm 324
shī'a 159, 189–90
al-Shīrāzī, Mullā Ḥusayn 209
shop 44
shops 63, 108, 126, 132, 135, 147, *See also ḥawsh*
Singapore 225
slavery 30, 68, 74, 86, 94, 104–11, 140, 148–51, 162–3, 190, 282, 298–300, *See also* Africa and Africans
  abolition 111
  Circassians 105
  conversion 106
  Georgians 105
  manumission 108–11, 300
  religion 106
  trade 59–60, 88, 107, 111, 219, 285, 297, 303
  women 99, 104–7, 109–11, 159, 162, 188, 303, 335
Soviet Union 80
sports 142, 175, 178, 187, 190, 204, 209, 213–17, 322
Suakin 41, 43, 46, 100, 114, 129, 219, 241
Sudan and Sudanese 68, 70, 85, 101–2, 201, 220, 234, 306, 321

al-Sudayrī, Aḥmad 239, 246
Suez 43, 51, 130, 219–20, 222, 308
Suez Canal 37, 52, 56, 65, 67, 222, 257
Sufism 75, 138–40, 178, 190, 199, 201–3, 209, 322–3, 326, *See also* Bedouins, saints, tombs, *zāwiya*
'Alawiyya order 139, 143, 202
Naqshbandiyya order 201
Qādiriyya order 68
Sanūsiyya order 139, 144, 201–3
Sulaymān, *family* 245
'Abdallāh 249, 293
Sunbul, *family* 165
sūq See market
Surat 95
Syria and Syrians 65, 69, 73, 76, 81, 105, 233, 245, *See also* maḥmal, migration

Ṭaha, *family* 164
Ṭā'if 73, 79, 95, 130, 144, 152, 199, 225, 246, 255, 272, 324
massacre 288
Takrūnīs 78, 88, 100–1, 106, 108, 111
Tangiers 315
Tanzimat 5, 33–4, 54–64, 73, 89, 113, 230, 260, 274–6, 278
Ṭawīl, Muḥammad 177, 209, 289, 293
taxes 49, 78, 168–9, 182, 185, 222, 231, 241, 244, 248, 273, 278, 285, 309
pilgrimage 80, 223
telegraph 65, 73, 129, 137, 198, 225, 277
Thomas Cook 240–3, 250
al-Tilmisānī, 'Abd al-Qādir 208, 238, 268–9
tombs 139, 155–6, 196–203, 208, 322–3
tomb of Eve 155–6, 197, 199–200
tomb of the Prophet 191
visits 191–203, 322
tourism 1, 9–12, 328, 331
trade 3, 12–15, 17–19, 31, 33, 37, 56, 61, 65, 67, 94–5, 99, 144, 209, 218–50, 268–9, 282, 285–6, 303, *See also* customs, foodstuffs, transport
caravan 41–2, 44, 80, 227, 268
import 219–20, 222, 231, 233–4, 246, 301, 322
India 44, 50–1, 59, 62, 219–20, 222, 233–4, 236, 241, 245, 248
Indian Ocean 3, 35, 37, 41, 56, 257
international 23, 31, 42, 82, 86, 89, 219, 233
Mediterranean 3, 35, 37, 41, 219
Red Sea 40–54, 56–8, 62, 219–20, 224, 234
wholesale 2, 137, 146, 232–3, 285–6
translocality 17, 26–7, 167, 297
transport 45, 65, 68, 81, 91, 146, 181, 223–8, 268, 330–1
air 5
caravan 4, 19, 50, 56, 92, 151, 226, 228, 250, 257, 269, 299, 323
land 146, 183, 191, 257
monopoly 45, 241
motor 5, 82, 130, 148, 225–7, 246, 248–9, 257
rail 73, 130, 193, 225
sail 4, 37, 65, 68, 86, 90, 185, 224, 249–50
steamshipping 4, 34, 37, 51–2, 56, 58, 65–6, 90, 224–5, 230–1, 250, 257
treaties 61, 80, 111, 313, 316
treaty of Balta Limanı 56
Treaty of Jeddah 80, 111, 319
tribe and tribalism 16, 36, 49, 58, 77, 86, 96, 153, 201, 223, 227, 245, 268–70, 287, 338–40, *See also* Bedouins
conflict 268
genealogy 96–8, 100, 154
lineages 9, 16, 92, 154, 245, 337–8
Tripoli (Lebanon) 33, 113
Tunis 308, 315
Tunisians 250, 308
al-Tūr 67, 262
Turaba 77
Turkey and Turks 78, 102–3, 107, 174, 185, 283, *See also* migration
al-Turkī, *family* 245
'Alī 290
Nāṣir 290

ʿumda 133, 169–71, 179, 183–4, 294, 296, 341
umma 6, 288, 293, 335–6
ʿUnayza 236, 246, 248
ʿUrābī Revolt 68, 70, 306
USA 82
ʿUthmān b. ʿAffān 40–1

Valentia, Viscount 48
van de Pol, Arthur Neervort 281
Vision 2030 10

Wahhabiyya and Wahhabis 46–50, 80, 85, 195, 198, 202, 236–9, 269, 271, 321–7, 331, 339
  religious policies 195, 198–200, 216, 331
  al-Wajh 67, 262
wakīl *See* pilgrims' guides
war 49, 58, 68–9, 85, 123, 231, 254, 266, 288–9, 291
  Anglo-Afghan 68–70
  Crimean War 59
  Italian-Ottoman 76
  Ottoman-Russian 68
  Russo-Turkish 305–6
  World War I 73–8, 107, 193, 206, 222–3, 225, 233, 246, 318
  World War II 5, 82, 85, 213, 224, 294
warehouse 44, 137, 234, 277, 282, *See also ḥawsh*
water 67, 72, 81, 83, 266, 287
  ʿAzīziyya waterworks 83, 144
  carriers 180, 187, 257, 287
  cisterns 72, 86, 90, 119, 126, 128, 151, 203, 287
  desalination 94, 128–9, 260–1
  provision 62, 78, 117, 126–9, 132, 167, 257, 260–1, 329
  shortage 106, 124
  Zamzam 195, 254
welfare 248
West and Westerners 29, 37, 51–4, 58, 63, 65, 69, 131, 157, 208, 253, 257–9, 342, *See also* Europe and Europeans
  anti-Western sentiment 58, 63
  imperialism 27, 37, 305
wikāla 44, 135–7, 140, 256, *See also ḥawsh,* warehouse
women 9, 14, 84, 99, 106, 108, 135–8, 140, 168, 175, 186, 190–2, 197–9, 256, 299, 303, 316, 319, 323, 327, 334–9, 343, *See also* familiy, marriage, servants, slavery
  al-Qays 196, 326
  ceremonies 168
  education 99, 204, 207
  Hajj 254, 256, 278
  household 163
  inheritance 300
  labour 104, 149, 187–8, 207
  property 166
  segregation 160
  slavery *See* slavery

Yamanī, ʿAlī 240, 282
Yanbuʿ 12, 65, 67, 114, 260, 262
Yanni, Khawaja 63
Yemen and Yemenis 44, 50–4, 58, 64, 67, 76, 85–7, 101, 106, 137, 200, 203, 214, 234, 262, 285, 311, *See also* migration, trade
  association 179
  Imam of 57
Young Turks 73–6, 94, 210–11, 296
youth 142, 175–7, 207, 212–16, 337, 343
Yusef, Alim 53
Yusr, Faraj 57, 62, 127–8, 164, 167, 280–1

Zāhid, *family* 91, 93, 162
Ẓāhir, Aḥmad 153
Zanzibar 106, 316
zāwiya 138–40, 143, 201, 256
  al-Zughaybī, *family* 245

Printed in the USA
CPSIA information can be obtained
at www.ICGtesting.com
CBHW061814140224
4348CB00009B/464

9 781108 746205